# International Law

*International Law: Our Common Future* offers a dynamic approach to the study of international law that actively engages students in ways that more traditional textbooks do not. One way this is achieved is by focusing on recent events, including international terrorism, extraordinary rendition, the legality of drone strikes, environmental devastation, and human rights. Another is by having students wrestle with actual court rulings rather than being given short summaries of these decisions. These cases, which are from a wide array of international, regional, and domestic tribunals, are followed by a series of provocative and challenging questions and prompts that will naturally lead to classroom discussion and debate.

The book recognizes the importance of visual media in terms of student learning. In addition to photographs of individuals and events that feature prominently in the development of international law, each chapter has sections entitled "International Law at the Movies" which highlight feature films and documentaries that explore the topic at hand.

What students will quickly come to realize is that international law is not a distant and abstract entity, but rather, is intimately connected to various aspects of their daily lives. The book shows some of the remarkable changes in international law, most notably the declining importance of the role of the state. As a final point, the book is written in an engaging, almost conversational, style that is accessible to students in a wide array of academic disciplines.

**Mark Gibney** is the Belk Distinguished Professor at the University of North Carolina–Asheville and an affiliated scholar at the Raoul Wallenberg Institute in Lund, Sweden. From 2014–2016 he served as the inaugural Raoul Wallenberg Visiting Professor of Human Rights and Humanitarian Law at the Faculty of Law, Lund University and the Raoul Wallenberg Institute. Gibney is one of the founding members of the Extraterritorial Obligations (ETO) Consortium, and he serves on the Board of Editors of *Human Rights Quarterly*, the *Journal of Human Rights*, and the *International Studies Journal* (Iran). Since 1984, Gibney has directed the Political Terror Scale (PTS) (PoliticalTerrorScale.org), which measures levels of physical integrity violations in more than 190 states, and this work has recently been expanded to include the Societal Violence Scale (SVS), which provides a comparative analysis of human rights violations by non–state actors. His recent book publications include: *International Human Rights Law: Returning to Universal Principles* (2015, 2d ed.); *Litigating Transnational Human Rights Obligations: Alternative Judgments* (2014); *Handbook of Human Rights* (2014); and *Watching Human Rights: The 101 Best Films* (2013).

**Praise for *International Law: Our Common Future***

"This textbook on international law is innovative in its pedagogical approach. Rather than seeing international law as something alien and non-relevant for us as individual citizens, Gibney very convincingly brings international law home. He demonstrates how these sets of rules are relevant in our daily lives, how we are all affected, and largely protected by international law, and ultimately how we all depend on strong and functioning international law for a common future. This is an exciting book for anyone teaching or learning international law."

**Sigrun Skogly**, *Lancaster University, UK*

"In this much-needed and refreshing volume, Mark Gibney breaks with the century-old idiosyncrasies of what an international law text book should look like. His problem-centered approach is likely to find favor with both students and teachers."

**Thomas Gammeltoft-Hansen**, *University of Copenhagen, Denmark*

"At last – an innovative and highly accessible case-driven international law textbook for undergraduates! Gibney's plain-language approach demystifies the often-esoteric complexity of the subject by examining the intersectionalites between international and domestic law in key areas of concern – international terrorism, warfare, and human rights. Engagingly written and often including concurring and dissenting opinions, *International Law: Our Common Future* is an excellent active-learning text for the student-centered classroom."

**Daniel J. Whelan**, *Hendrix College, USA*

"Instructors of undergraduate international law courses have long been looking for a book like Mark Gibney's *International Law: Our Common Future*. He has effectively created a very accessible, interesting, and engaging text that at the same time gives students a solid introduction to the nature and functioning of international law within international politics, including analysis of several key areas, such as terrorism, war, and human rights. Most innovative compared to other texts is the illustrative use of multiple cases and court decisions, a clear writing style revealing the practical nature of the politics and daily life of international law, and sections on learning about international law through film. This book will be a great teaching tool and text in my political science course in international law."

**Safia Swimelar**, *Elon University, USA*

"Mark Gibney's new text covers a full range of topics in international law, but it will be particularly useful to those interested in national and international security. The selection of judicial rulings provides a splendid introduction to contentious legal (and moral) debates as they have actually played out in national and international courts and tribunals."

**David Kinsella**, *Portland State University, USA*

# International Law
## Our Common Future

**Mark Gibney**

Routledge
Taylor & Francis Group

NEW YORK AND LONDON

First published 2020
by Routledge
52 Vanderbilt Avenue, New York, NY 10017

and by Routledge
2 Park Square, Milton Park, Abingdon, Oxon OX14 4RN

*Routledge is an imprint of the Taylor & Francis Group, an informa business*

*British Library Cataloguing-in-Publication Data*
A catalogue record for this book is available from the British Library

*Library of Congress Cataloging-in-Publication Data*
A catalog record has been requested for this book

ISBN: 978-1-138-10445-7 (hbk)
ISBN: 978-1-138-10446-4 (pbk)
ISBN: 978-1-315-10223-8 (ebk)

Typeset in Minion Pro
by Apex CoVantage, LLC

Visit the eResources: www.routledge.com/9781138104464

Cover art credit:
"María, inside since April 14, 2014"
Charcoal and acrylic on canvas (2015)
Artist: Ben Betsalel (BenBetsalel.com)
The cover image is from a prison project in Colombia, "Human Beings Inside and Outside," done in collaboration with the International Committee of the Red Cross (ICRC).

# Contents

# Detailed Contents

# Acknowledgments

Paulina Kordys and Grace Van Dyke were tireless research assistants for this project, especially in helping me edit down judicial opinions that oftentimes ran for hundreds of pages. I am deeply grateful for their work and the good cheer they maintained throughout. I would also like to thank the anonymous reviewers, whose comments and insights were invaluable. Finally, I am indebted to Ben Betsalel for allowing me to use one of his images for the cover of this book. Ben is a treasured friend and old tennis partner whose visually stunning portraits from conflict areas all over the globe serve to remind us of the humanity behind international law.

## A Note on Editing Cases

In terms of the editing of the cases, my goal is to make these judicial rulings as readable as possible. To do this, whenever possible I have avoided using ellipses to signify that words, sentences, paragraphs, and even pages have been removed. I do this for two reasons. One is that, given the amount of material that has been taken out, there would be ellipses dotting the entire page. The other reason is that as a reader I find ellipses quite distracting, and I assume others do as well. With this as a caveat, let me assure the reader that I have not rearranged or changed any of the language in the opinions and have sought to preserve the meaning but also the flow of these rulings.

The cases used in this book come from a variety of sources. For those interested, the full opinions can be found on the links to these cases at the end of the book.

# Preface

When asked what I do for a living, I readily reply that I am an international human rights lawyer. This is true – but only in part. For the past three and a half decades, in addition to teaching undergraduate courses in international law, I regularly teach domestic (U.S.) law classes as well. I bring this up because what has long bothered me is that the domestic law classes are much better received by students (or at least I think they are) than courses in my own area of expertise. This book is my attempt to rectify this situation.

In my experience, there are several problems with the manner in which international law is commonly taught. For one thing, there almost seems to be a concerted effort to avoid controversy or even political relevance. As a reaction to this, one of the things I have done in this book is to place a premium on issues that are both topical and exciting to students.

What I am quite interested in promoting is active learning, and one of the best ways of achieving this is by having students read and wrestle with judicial opinions, as opposed to simply being instructed that case X stands for proposition Y. In that way, this book is centered around a number of judicial rulings from a variety of sources – international tribunals, regional institutions, supreme courts, constitutional courts, and even trial proceedings at the domestic level – that deal with various aspects of international law. In addition, I often include concurring and dissenting opinions as a way of helping to achieve this goal of engaged learning. The question repeatedly posed in the Notes and Comments section following the end of a case is this: which opinion is better reasoned – and why?

The **Introduction** provides an overview of the subject, mainly told through a story of an American college student going abroad for a semester and (unknowingly) encountering international law in various settings. What is international law, how does it affect our daily lives, where do you find international law, and how do you interpret it? It is commonplace to think of domestic law and international law as being separate and distinct from one another. I take a different approach and see the two as oftentimes blending together – to the point where it is difficult to determine where one begins and the other one ends.

The "state" serves as the foundational principle in international law and to a large extent this is reflected in the pages of this book. However, what also has to be recognized is the manner in which the "state" itself has started to change – and along with that, international law as well.

**Plan of the Book**

*Part I: International Terrorism*

International terrorism presents one of the greatest security threats of our age. But terrorism also tests the limits of a state–centric approach to international law, and it is the subject matter of Part I. **Fighting Terrorism Through Law** (Chapter 1) examines the role that law might play in combating international terrorism – whether it is bringing suit against states that provide "material support" to terrorist organizations – but also the manner in which the fight against international terrorism has begun to challenge the principle of state sovereignty.

Without question, the most (in)famous prison facility in the world is in Guantanamo Bay, Cuba. **Detaining "Enemy Combatants" and Suspected Terrorists** (Chapter 2) analyzes the rights under international/domestic law that suspected terrorists housed in this facility and in other foreign locations have been granted. The focus of this chapter is the remarkable involvement of the U.S. Supreme Court, which repeatedly ignored entreaties from both the George W. Bush administration but also the U.S. Congress to remove itself from the conduct of the "war on terrorism." Still, it is by no means clear whether law has triumphed over politics. And what also remains unclear is whether the Trump administration will keep the Guantanamo prison open or perhaps even increase the number of "enemy combatants" held there.

The "war on terrorism" has brought a new term into the popular lexicon: **Extraordinary Rendition** (Chapter 3). Under this practice, suspected terrorists are kidnapped and shipped off to other states where they face "enhanced interrogation" (i.e., torture) – or worse. It is estimated that nearly a quarter of all countries participated in these practices in one form or another, and yet restitution and accountability efforts have been few and far between.

## Part II: Warfare

While the "war on terrorism" represents a new kind of warfare, the old form is still very much in evidence. **Jus ad Bellum** (Chapter 4) provides an overview of the laws and norms regulating when a state can resort to warfare. However, what the chapter also deals with are some of the newer forms of "warfare," particularly the increased use of drones but also cyberattacks from governmental and nongovernmental sources that target their counterparts in other lands.

**Jus in Bello** (Chapter 5) provides an overview of international humanitarian law – or what is more commonly referred to as the "laws of war." The chapter focuses on two different extremes. One is the legality of using nuclear weapons, which would result in the deaths of hundreds of thousands if not millions of civilians. At the other extreme is targeted assassination, oftentimes through the use of drone strikes. The chapter closes by using the Israeli-Palestinian conflict as a case study on the laws of war.

## Part III: Accountabilty, Responsibility, and Immunity

The next three chapters focus on establishing and enforcing accountability under international law. **Individual Accountability** (Chapter 6) traces the slow and uneven but growing expectation that individuals should be held accountable for violating international humanitarian and human rights standards whenever this is possible.

In recent years there has been an explosion of **International Crimes** (Chapter 7), as evidenced by the fact that in 2017 alone an estimated $485 billion was lost worldwide through cybercrime operations, a 30% increase in just three years. This chapter focuses on various kinds of transnational criminal behavior, including drug trafficking, corruption, extradition practices, and piracy.

**Corporate Accountability** (Chapter 8) shows the uneven development of holding multinational corporations (MNCs) accountable under international law. On the one hand, the recent U.S. Supreme Court ruling in *Jesner v. Arab Bank* (2018) provides a strong indication that corporations will no longer be subject to suit in the United States under the Alien Tort Statute. Yet, on the other hand, corporations are increasingly being viewed as having human rights obligations, and along with this, there has been an increased effort to ensure that "home" states regulate the extraterritorial practices of their own MNCs.

**State Responsibility and Jurisdictional Limitations** (Chapter 9) deals with situations where states have violated international law by committing an "internationally wrongful act." The routine cases invariably involve instances where a state acts directly. However, much of the chapter focuses on the more nuanced cases when states act indirectly, usually by providing massive amounts of aid and assistance to entities (state and non-state actors alike) in other lands, which is then used in the commission of gross and systematic human rights violations. A separate issue involves jurisdictional limitations, and the question is not so much whether a state has violated international law standards but rather whether individuals negatively affected by these actions were within the "jurisdiction" of the offending state.

Another way states continue to be protected are by a phalanx of **Foreign and Domestic Immunities** (Chapter 10). Thus, one of the quandaries international law continues to struggle with is how to restrict unlawful state behavior while at the same time respecting the principle of state sovereignty.

### Part IV: Human Rights

Although many of the topics covered in this book involve human rights – the right to be free from torture; the right to life; the right to an effective remedy, and so on – this last section is devoted exclusively to this topic, especially economic, social, and cultural rights. **Poverty and Disease** (Chapter 11) examines the manner in which the "necessities of life" are (or are not) protected by international law. Most of the cases in this chapter are from the Constitutional Court of South Africa, a country whose constitution is based squarely on international law principles but where implementation of those rights has been severely hampered by the state's abject poverty.

Human rights has been a central feature of this book, whether it involves those who have been subjected to extraordinary rendition, torture victims, civilians killed in civil conflict, and so on. **Vulnerable Populations** (Chapter 12) continues with this by focusing on the protection needs of vulnerable populations: refugees, women, children, indigenous populations, LGBTQ populations, and disabled persons. To what extent has international law been successful in protecting individuals who have been cast to the fringes of society?

### Conclusion: The Way Forward

### Features of This Innovative Text

This book is specifically designed to appeal to student interest, to promote active learning, and to integrate carefully edited court cases with explanatory text. Here are just a few of the features devoted to achieving these goals:

- Boxed text highlighting current events
- "International Law at the Movies" boxes
- Photos illustrating key moments and figures in international law
- Cases carefully edited and set off from the main text

- Notes and Comments following court case excerpts
- References for each chapter divided into key types of sources including Books and Articles, Reports, Agreements, and Cases (international, regional, and domestic tribunals)
- Glossary of key terms putting terms in context with events
- Filmography
- Table of Cases

# Introduction

## International Law in Our Lives

Let's suppose you are an undergraduate at an American university about to spend a semester abroad studying at the University of Copenhagen. You are a U.S. citizen, and months before your departure date you apply for and receive your first passport, something you will treasure the rest of your life. You have a direct flight to Kastrup airport in Copenhagen, Denmark but you also notice from the trip guide on the airplane that you will be passing over the airspace of several other countries on your travels. After you land and collect your luggage, you proceed to immigration control, going to the line for non–EU citizens. When your turn comes, you present your small, shiny, virgin blue book to the immigration official behind the plexiglass window. She merely glances at you, opens the book, and proceeds to place the first stamp in your passport.

When you get to your new student accommodations you get unpacked, call your family to tell them that you have arrived, and then send emails to friends with this same news. Soon enough, you meet some of the other study abroad students who come from countries all over the globe. Later on, you also get to do a little sightseeing, and during your visit to the charming Nyhavn harbor you pick up a postcard, find a post office, and send it to one of your professors at your home university who collects such things.

That first evening, you go out with some of the other study abroad students to check out the nightlife of Copenhagen. One thing you notice immediately is that the drinking age in Denmark is 15 (that is not a misprint) and not 21 as it is in the United States, and you take full advantage of this newfound freedom.

Unfortunately, a fight breaks out in the bar and a number of people get arrested – including you and some of the other study abroad students. As a result, you are forced to make a call to the U.S. Embassy in Denmark, and due to the intervention of that office you are released after spending a few hours in detention.

---

### Box I.1: Travel Bans

Much has been made of President Trump's various travel bans announced at the onset of his administration, which severely limited immigration from a number of countries with large Muslim populations. Under the Immigration and Nationality Act, the president has the authority to restrict the entry of aliens whenever he finds that their entry "would be detrimental to the interests of the United States." Relying on that authority, in *Trump v. Hawaii* (2018), the U.S. Supreme Court ruled that the president was acting within his statutory authority based on valid national security concerns.

What about the flip side to this? Can a government prohibit its citizens from traveling to particular countries? In *Regan v. Wald* (1984), the U.S. Supreme Court upheld a travel restriction that prevented American citizens from traveling to Cuba.

Finally, in *Haig v. Agee* (1981), the U.S. Supreme Court upheld the revocation of the passport of Philip Agee, who had worked in covert operations for the CIA from 1957 to 1968. After leaving the CIA, Agee called a press conference and declared his intent to expose state secrets as well as the identities of American agents working in the field. In response, President Jimmy Carter instructed his secretary of state to revoke Agee's U.S. passport. Agee brought suit, but the Supreme Court ruled that the executive branch could use its power to issue passports – or not issue them – as a way of carrying out the country's foreign policy.

Aside from whether you agree or disagree with these rulings, a larger question is whether these issues would be better addressed by means of international law rather than though domestic law.

---

What does any of this have to do with international law? Actually, many of these events involve international law although this might not be readily apparent. Let's start with the passport. We live in a world of nation-states where nationality still matters enormously and your American passport serves as proof that you are a citizen of the United States. Among other things, what this also means is that you can never be denied entry to your home country, although this principle has been tested with respect to individuals who went off to fight for the Islamic State (ISIS).

But what about Denmark? One of the hallmarks of state sovereignty is the ability to control the entry of noncitizens. This is usually done by requiring that a would-be visitor first obtain a visa, which grants the holder permission to enter, invariably for a limited period of time and for a specified purpose. Yet, because of a treaty between Denmark and the United States, you are exempt from the visa requirement, although some of the other study abroad students, especially those from Asia and Africa, are not so lucky.

---

### Box I.2: Citizenship

Although citizenship is one of the most important principles in international law – bestowing the right to have rights, in the words of Hannah Arendt (1951) – it is left up to each state to determine who is a citizen of that country, although a state cannot demand international recognition of the rules it establishes (*Nottebohm Case (Liechtenstein v. Guatemala)* 1955).

There are two basic principles that guide the acquisition of nationality, although these two are not mutually exclusive. One is birth on the soil of that state (*jus soli*). The other is the conferral of nationality based on blood (*jus sanguinis*).

In addition to acquiring citizenship at birth, most countries will also grant citizenship to those who have been lawful residents for a specified period of time. In the United States, for example, a permanent resident alien is eligible for U.S. citizenship after residing for five years (three years if married to an American citizen). However, an enduring problem in some countries is when lawfully admitted individuals are unable to obtain citizenship no matter how many years they or their families have lived there.

The flip side to this is the loss of citizenship. You might be shocked to learn that under the 1907 Expatriation Act, women would lose their U.S. citizenship when they married a foreign national. This law was changed a short time later and losing one's U.S. citizenship now involves a purposeful act by the individual. In an important decision, a unanimous U.S. Supreme Court ruled in *Maslenjak v. United States* (2017) that the government could not denaturalize someone who had lied in both her application for refugee status and subsequently in seeking American citizenship unless it could establish that these false statements were material in being granted citizenship.

Still, the "war on terror" has brought this issue to the fore in that some states have denaturalized individuals who have joined ISIS. The United Kingdom has already applied this sanction against some naturalized citizens, not native-born citizens, although the law would allow the loss of citizenship for this latter group as well. Furthermore, there has been some discussion about the government removing the British citizenship of Asma al-Assad, the British wife of the brutal Syrian dictator Bashar al-Assad.

Finally, some 10 million people are stateless. As its name indicates, these are individuals who are not nationals of any country.

One of the questions to consider is whether there should be international law standards governing issues relating to citizenship – or should this continue to be left to individual states? Finally, should states be able to remove citizenship, thereby creating an enormous burden of protection for the rest of the international community?

What you also come to notice in the weeks and months ahead is that the European students do not carry their passports when they travel to other countries in Europe. This is due to the *Schengen Agreement,* an international agreement between 26 states that allows European citizens unfettered (and unchecked) entrance into these other European states. You do not have this same right as an American, although you find in your travels by train throughout Europe that you have not been asked to produce your passport, at least not yet.

---

### Box I.3: Foreign Arrests

In the scenario posited, the American college student studying abroad who was arrested after a bar fight in Copenhagen immediately contacted the U.S. Embassy. Note, however, that under Article 36 of the *Vienna Convention on Consular Relations* (1963), the arresting state has a legal obligation to notify the embassy staff of the criminal defendant's country when one of its nationals has been arrested.

What brought this issue out into the international spotlight were a series of cases handed down by the International Court of Justice and the U.S. Supreme Court. The first case involved the LaGrand brothers, two German nationals who had lived in the United States since they were children. Their attempt to rob a bank in Arizona went badly, resulting in a death. Arizona officials made no attempt to contact the German consulate office even after state officials became aware that the LaGrand brothers were not U.S. citizens. Germany then obtained a provisional stay from the International Court of Justice just hours before Walter LaGrand was to be executed. However, the U.S. Solicitor General took the position that such rulings by the ICJ have no domestic (U.S.) effect and the U.S. Supreme Court refused to stay the execution. Germany proceeded with its action against the United States, while the U.S. government took the position that the *Vienna Convention on Consular Relations* does not grant rights to individuals. In its decision in *Germany v. United States* (2001) the ICJ ruled in favor of Germany. In 1999, Walter LaGrand was put to death by use of cyanide gas and a week later Karl died by means of lethal injection.

*Medellín v. Texas* (2008) is based on a similar scenario. In this case, Mexican officials were not notified when a group of Mexican nationals were arrested in the United States for allegedly carrying out a gang rape. Mexico brought a case against the United States before the International Court of Justice where the Court ruled, as it had previously, that the failure to notify Mexican officials was in violation of the *Vienna Convention on Consular Relations*. Still, the U.S. Supreme Court held that the treaty was not self-executing – which is to say, it would not bestow any rights on individuals in the absence of congressional action – and thus neither the Convention itself nor the ICJ ruling in *Mexico v. United States* (2004) had any domestic effect.

---

Let us return to the flight that you took to Denmark. Under international law, countries not only control their own territory but they also control the airspace above this as well. What this means is that all of the countries you flew over could have denied the use of "their" airspace, thereby causing the flight to take an alternative route. Fortunately, a large majority of countries are a state party to the 1944 *Chicago Convention on International Civil Aviation*, an international treaty that regulates various aspects of air travel, including airspace, so that flights such as yours proceed without a problem. On the other hand, it would not be wise to take a flight over North Korea, which guards its airspace zealously.

---

**Box I.4: Defending Airspace and the Lockerbie Case**

There have been several high visibility incidents where commercial aircraft were shot down for flying over the airspace of another country, which led to greatly increased political tensions. The downing of KAL-007 occurred in 1983 during the height of the Cold War, bringing the United States and the (former) Soviet Union quite close to a real war. The flight of Korean Airlines 007 from Anchorage, Alaska to Seoul, South Korea drifted (accidently or not) into the airspace of the Soviet Union. According to the Soviet leadership, this was a direct provocation by the United States to test Soviet military preparedness. However, the U.S. government took the position that the Soviet Union was well aware that KAL-007 was not a spy plane and that the shooting down of the aircraft was nothing less than a cold blooded killing of all those aboard.

A more recent event occurred in 2014 and it involved Malaysian Airlines flight MH-17 en route from Amsterdam to Kuala Lumpur. The plane was downed in the airspace over an area of the Ukraine that had recently come under the control of pro-Russian forces. What followed was international condemnation of the Putin government in Russia, which was viewed as the instigator of this action, although it is not clear if Russia had any legal responsibility, a topic we return to in Chapter 9 dealing with the law on state responsibility (Gibney 2015).

A different twist to this was the Lockerbie bombing case in which two Libyan nationals were accused of masterminding an operation that resulted in a commercial aircraft being blown up over the airspace above Lockerbie, Scotland in 1988. Eventually, an agreement was reached to allow criminal proceedings before Scottish judges sitting at Camp Zeist in the Netherlands.

---

What about your communication with people back home? International phone calls are regulated by the *International Telecommunications Union* (originally the International Telegraph Union), which is a specialized U.N. agency first established in 1865 – decades before there were any telephones. And that postcard? Your professor back home received it a few days after it was sent, thanks to the *Universal Postal Union*, another specialized U.N. agency, which was created in 1875.

## Box I.5: Territory

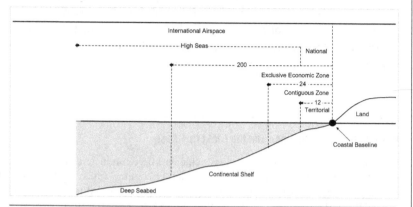

**Figure 0.1** Sea Zones

Territory is a foundational principle under international law. A state is presumed to be acting lawfully when it operates within its own territorial borders. However, the opposite presumption is at play when a country acts in the territory of some other state.

As shown by this figure, a state's "territory" does not coincide exactly with what appears on a world map. If a state has a coastline, it also "owns" the *airspace* 12 nautical miles out from the point of contact between land and sea (baseline). In addition, a state "owns" the *territorial sea* as well – which was set at 12 nautical miles under the *United Nations Convention on the Law of the Sea* (UNCLOS). However, at the same time that the territorial sea was extended to 12 miles (it previously had generally been recognized as being 3 miles), UNCLOS also extended the right of "innocent passage," allowing commercial ships to navigate through another state's territorial waters.

Moving further outward is the *contiguous zone*, which is 24 nautical miles from the baseline, where a state is able to exercise limited sovereign jurisdiction to pursue certain national policies, such as those involving environmental protection.

Moving out further, the *exclusive economic zone* (EEZ) is the area from 24 to 200 nautical miles. Under Article 56 of UNCLOS, a coastal state enjoys sovereign rights for "exploring and exploiting, conserving and managing the natural resources" in these waters and the seabed below. Beyond this are the *high seas*, which, it should be pointed out, cover nearly ¾ of the earth's surface and host ⁵/₄ of the planet's life forms.

You will also notice in Figure 0.1 the *continental shelf*, which is a gradual slope away from the coastal baseline. The coastal state has full sovereign rights over all of the natural resources and it can exclude all other states from exploiting these resources (Murphy 2006: 347). If a state's continental shelf falls short of 200 miles the legal continental shelf will still be extended to 200 nautical miles; if it extends beyond 200 miles, the legal continental shelf will be extended until the natural prolongation ends – but no further than 350 nautical miles.

There are entire classes devoted exclusively to the "law of the sea" and thus it is only possible to touch on this subject. However, let me mention two issues of contention. One involves the "baseline," from which 200 nautical miles are measured. Can a state (such as China) extend its baseline outwards by building "artificial" islands? A second issue is how "exclusive" a state can be in its EEZ.

## Box I.6: Terra Nullius, the Polar Caps, and Outer Space

*Terra Nullius* is an old concept in international law that allows states to occupy and own land that, according to the literal translation of the term, "nobody owns." Among other things, this doctrine was used by Great Britain to make the entire continent of what became Australia part of the British Crown on the basis that the continent was unoccupied. What this conveniently ignored, of course, was the aboriginal population already living there. The term "terra nullius" has fallen into disuse for two reasons. One is its racist past. The second is that with the exception of the polar regions, no area of the globe is considered to be unoccupied.

Most of the Arctic is not land as such but a solid mass of ice, so it is not clear whether this area of the globe would even qualify as "territory" as such. Still, a number of surrounding states, most notably Canada, Finland, Denmark, Iceland, Norway, Russia, Sweden, and the United States, have laid claim to the Arctic. With climate change proceeding at a rapid pace and with the expectation that there are valuable minerals under the surface and with sea lanes opening up, territorial disputes will most assuredly increase (Epps 2009: 51).

In terms of the other end of the globe, the main treaty is the 1959 *Antarctic Treaty*, which entered into force in 1961. What is notable is that all of the states claiming territory in the Antarctic are party to this. This treaty states that the Antarctic shall be "used for peaceful purposes only," and it also prohibits "any measures of a military nature." In addition, the treaty promotes freedom of scientific investigation. At the present time at least, states seem willing to allow Antarctica to remain unclaimed.

Finally, there is the matter of outer space. In a different era, international law might have allowed the United States (which has been the only country to place a man on the moon) or the (former) Soviet Union (which was the first to put a man in outer space) to claim the heavens on the basis of *terra nullius*. Fortunately, this era has passed. The major international treaty regulating the heavens is the *Treaty on Principles Governing the Activities in the Exploration and Uses of Outer Space, Including the Moon and Other Celestial Bodies* (Outer Space Treaty). The treaty entered into force in 1967 and it has been ratified by more than 90 states. The treaty specifies that any exploration of space is to be carried out "for the benefit and in the interests of all countries." In addition, the Outer Space Treaty specifies that outer space is only to be used for "peaceful purposes," and it specifically prohibits nuclear weapons. A subsequent treaty, *Agreement Governing the Activities of States on the Moon and Other Celestial Bodies* (Moon Treaty), which entered into force in 1984, specifies that natural resources are the "common heritage of mankind." However, less than 20 countries are a state party to the Moon Treaty – and conspicuously absent is the United States.

There is also the matter of Danish drinking laws. As a general rule, the law of the territorial state governs. Or to phrase this another way, when in Denmark do as Danish law tells you to do, and in this instance Danish law says that you can drink alcohol at 15. Yet, states maintain an "interest" in the activities of their own citizens even when they are outside the country's national borders. This is termed the nationality principle. What this means is that, at least in theory, it would not be against international law for a country to apply its laws extraterritorially to its nationals. In that way, the U.S. government could mandate the drinking age for American citizens even when they are outside the United States. This certainly sounds strange, and in any event there is no indication that the U.S. has any interest in regulating the drinking practices of its citizens when they are overseas.

---

### Box I.7: The Scope of International Law: The *Lotus* Case (France v. Turkey)

The *Lotus* case involved a collision between a French vessel (*Lotus*) and a Turkish ship (*Boz-Kourt*), which resulted in the sinking of the latter and the death of eight Turkish crewmen. The ten survivors of the *Boz-Kourt* were taken to Turkey by the *Lotus*, where legal proceedings began against some of the Turkish crew but also against Demons, the officer on watch on the *Lotus*. France then brought this action against Turkey before the Permanent Court of International Justice (the predecessor of today's International Court of Justice) on the grounds that, as a French sailor, it was France's responsibility to try Demons and that Turkey was acting in violation of international law.

After affirming the general principle that a state is prohibited from acting within the territory of some other state, the PCIJ gave an expansive interpretation of what a state can do within its own territory, but more than that, the freedom states have to act in the absence of a specific international law prohibition:

> It does not, however, follow that international law prohibits a State from exercising jurisdiction in its own territory, in respect of any case which relates to acts which have taken place abroad, and in which it cannot rely on some permissive rule of international law. Such a view would only be tenable if international law contained a general prohibition to States to extend the application of their laws and the jurisdiction of their courts to persons, property and acts outside their territory, and if, as an exception to this general prohibition, it allowed States to do so in certain specific cases. *But this is certainly not the case under international law as it stands at present. Far from laying down a general prohibition to the effect that States may not extend the application of their laws and the jurisdiction of their courts to persons, property and acts outside their territory, it leaves them in this respect a wide measure of discretion,* which is only limited in certain cases by prohibitive rules; as regards other cases, every State remains free to adopt the principles which it regards as best and most suitable (emphasis supplied).

Still, there might be instances where a country might do this. For example, when Canada legalized the recreational use of marijuana in early 2019, the government of South Korea made it known that it will remain illegal for Korean citizens visiting Canada to "consume" marijuana back home, although it is not clear whether any returning citizens will be subject to drug testing. Another example of the use of the nationality principle can be found under Danish law where it is a criminal offense for Danish nationals and persons residing within Danish territory to have sexual relations with a minor – not just in Denmark, but any other place in the world – so long as it is also prohibited by the state where these events took place (Svensson 2006).

---

**Box I.8: Sources of Criminal Jurisdiction**

Under international law, there are five different sources that enable a state to exercise criminal jurisdiction. The first, and most common, is the *territorial principle*, namely, that the criminal act occurs within the territorial borders of that state. The second is the *nationality principle* referenced in the text. The third is the *passive personality principle*, which allows states to punish acts abroad that are harmful to its own nationals. The fourth is the *protective principle* through which a state assumes jurisdiction over aliens outside its territorial borders whose actions affect the security of that state. Finally, the *universality principle* allows states to try individuals who, it is alleged, have committed certain "universal" crimes such as piracy or torture.

---

The final issue from your adventuresome first day in Denmark involves your call to the U.S. Embassy to get you out of jail. You will notice that many of the other study abroad students also sought help from their own governments. What this shows is that citizenship has its privileges and one of the most important of these is that governments have a responsibility – or at least seem to act as if they have a responsibility – to provide assistance to their own nationals when they are in a situation of distress in some other land. The most visible manifestation of this principle occurs when there is a natural disaster in another country or where a military coup prompts evacuation. However, as indicated by the *Barcelona Traction* case (Box I.9), the decision to act (or not act) seems to be one decided solely by the government itself.

---

**Box I.9: Diplomatic Protection: The Barcelona Traction Case (Belgium v. Spain)**

Barcelona Traction, Light and Power Company Limited was incorporated in Canada, although a majority of its shareholders were Belgian nationals. After the company had been negatively affected by acts of the Spanish government, Belgium brought a

*(Continued)*

## Box I.9: Continued

claim against Spain. The ICJ sided with Spain's objection regarding Belgium's ability to bring this claim.

> The Court would here observe that, within the limits prescribed by international law, a State may exercise diplomatic protection by whatever means and to whatever extent it thinks fit, for it is its own right that the State is asserting. Should the natural or legal persons on whose behalf it is acting consider that their rights are not adequately protected, they have no remedy in international law. All they can do is to resort to municipal law, if means are available, with a view to furthering their cause or obtaining redress. The municipal legislator may lay upon the State an obligation to protect its citizens abroad, and may also confer upon the national a right to demand the performance of that obligation, and clothe the right with corresponding sanctions. However, all these questions remain within the province of municipal law and do not affect the position internationally.

Continuing:

> The State must be viewed as the sole judge to decide whether its protection will be granted, to what extent it is granted, and when it will cease.

## Box I.10: Are Embassies Foreign Territory?

There is a common (mis)perception that embassies are foreign territory – that the embassy of Saudi Arabia in the United States, for example, is actually Saudi territory. This is incorrect. This embassy in Washington D.C. is on American soil. However, foreign embassies are inviolate, which is the reason why Julian Assange, the founder of Wikileaks, was until April 2019 safely housed in the Ecuadorian embassy in London without any fear that British agents will barge in and arrest him.

There are, however, instances where this principle has been breached. No doubt, the most politically charged example of this was the Iranian hostage situation. On November 4, 1979, a group of Iranian "students" stormed into the American Embassy in Tehran and for the next 444 days held hostage a group of U.S. diplomats and citizens (some of whom were CIA agents). In response, the United States brought a case against Iran before the International Court of Justice. In *United States v. Iran* (1989), the ICJ ruled that Iran had violated international law through its failure to protect the diplomatic staff.

Related to this is the issue of the personal inviolability of all diplomatic agents. Article 29 of the *Vienna Convention on Diplomatic Relations* states:

> The person of a diplomatic agent shall be inviolable. He shall not be liable to any form of arrest or detention. The receiving State shall treat him with due

respect and shall take all appropriate steps to prevent any attack on his person, freedom or dignity.

If this sounds as if diplomatic staff are "above the law" you would be correct. The premise is that the host state is not to interfere with the diplomatic work of this other sovereign state. On the other hand, host states are not defenseless. For particularly serious offenses, they might expel a diplomat as *persona non grata*. What could also happen is that (diplomatic) pressure might be applied against the home state to waive diplomatic immunity to allow prosecution by the host state to proceed.

One of the most telling and gruesome episodes of this principle involved the murder of Jamal Khashoggi, a dissident Saudi journalist who was tortured and killed while visiting the Saudi consulate in Istanbul on October 2, 2018. As of this writing, Khashoggi's body has never been found. It is assumed that Saudi security agents who had flown into Turkey earlier in anticipation of Khashoggi's appointment departed with his dismembered body. The reason we know of Khashoggi's fate is that Turkey had wired the Saudi consulate – which is itself a violation of international law (Milanovic 2019).

**Photo 0.1** Murdered Saudi Journalist Jamal Khashoggi
*Source:* © Associated Press

In any case, your own messy situation is nothing like this, although I suppose one might make the claim that by acting on your behalf the U.S. government is "interfering" in the domestic affairs of Denmark. Still, you are quite pleased that the U.S. Embassy was able to effectuate your release – and has done so without any mention of this to your parents or to your home university.

---

### Box I.11: State Responsibility for Harm to Another State's Citizen

One of the rationales for why individuals have few, if any, rights under traditional international law is citizens would be protected by their state – at home but also abroad. Reflective of this were a series of cases brought by the United States in the 1920s either before a special claims tribunal or else before the Permanent Court of International Justice (PCIJ). In the *Mavrommatis Palestine Concessions (Jurisdiction)* decision in 1924, the PCIJ explained that when a state took up the cause of one of its own nationals against another state, this dispute then:

> entered upon a new phase; it entered the domain of international law, and became a dispute between two States. . . . It is an elementary principle of international law that a State is entitled to protect its subjects, when injured by acts contrary to international law committed by another State, from whom they have been unable to obtain satisfaction through the ordinary channels. By taking up the case of one of its subjects and by resorting to diplomatic action or international judicial proceedings on his behalf, a State is in reality asserting its own rights – its right to ensure, in the person of its subjects, respect for the rules of international law.

However, what if a state does not protect its citizens – either within its own domestic realm or when these individuals are in other states?

---

### The Nature of International Law

This small vignette is intended to show a number of things. One is that international law happens to be all around us, and yet we are seldom aware of this. Another thing this is intended to show is that international law generally "works." I raise this issue because I find that the most common charge against international law is that it is not really "law" – and the rationale for this is that there is no means of enforcement.

My (pithy) response is to ask whether people ever speed on highways. Without fail, this always elicits a chuckle from the audience, for obvious reasons. But my point is a serious one. No one would ever conclude that domestic law is not "law" because most people drive over the speed limit and they can do so with near impunity. Why, then, should international law be dismissed for this same reason? Of course, another way of looking at this is to return to our example and think about what the world would look like without international law: a world where flights and mail and telephone calls and all manner of things were carried out on a completely ad hoc basis. Any chance the postcard you sent will ever arrive?

Yet, this is not to suggest that enforcement is not a problem in international law. It certainly is a problem, especially in the area of human rights. However, what this ignores is the manner in which international law is, much more often than not, adhered to by states. In this example, transatlantic mail is delivered, telephone calls to people in other countries go through, commercial airliners routinely fly over the territory of other countries, and so on. As this shows, one important reason why international law "works" is that it is in the interest of states – individually as well as collectively – to do so. What also needs to be pointed out is that there are now a multitude of judicial institutions – international, regional, and domestic – that routinely address international law issues. In the words of Louis Henkin: "almost all nations observe almost all principles of international law and almost all of their obligations almost all of the time" (Henkin 1979: 47).

---

### Box I.12: International Adjudicatory Bodies

There are literally hundreds of international courts and other adjudicatory bodies, so no attempt will be made to list all of these (Martinez 2003). On the international level, I will make mention of a few. One is the *International Court of Justice* (ICJ) located in the Hague, which is limited to state-state claims. The *International Criminal Court* (ICC) is also located in the Hague and it prosecutes individuals accused of directing or carrying out one of the four international crimes specified in the 1998 Rome Treaty, which led to the establishment of the ICC in 2002. As the World Trade Organization (WTO) has grown in importance, its *Dispute Settlement Body* (DSB) has as well. Finally, the *International Body for the Law of the Sea* (ITLOS) in Hamburg, Germany is an independent judicial body established by the 1983 Law of the Sea (See Box 1.5).

At the United Nations, each of the international human rights conventions has an accompanying treaty body. For example, the *Torture Convention* is administered by the *Committee Against Torture (CAT)*, which also hears complaints by individuals against states that have also become parties to the Optional Protocol. The name of the treaty body corresponds with the name of the treaty – with the exception of the *International Covenant on Civil and Political Rights*, which is administered by the *Human Rights Committee*.

On the regional level, the *European Court of Human Rights* (ECtHR) in Strasbourg, France is widely recognized as the leading human rights adjudicatory body in the world and it is not to be confused (although it often is) with the *European Court of Justice* (ECJ), located in Luxembourg. In the Americas, there is the *Inter-American Commission of Human Rights* (Washington D.C.) as well as the *Inter-American Court of Human Rights* (IACHR) in San Jose, Costa Rica. In Africa, there is the *African Commission on Human Rights and Peoples' Rights* (Banjul, the Gambia) and the *African Court of Human Rights and Peoples' Rights* in Arusha, Tanzania.

Finally, domestic courts are increasingly being asked to rule on issues involving international law, as evidenced by many of the cases in this book (Nollkaemper 2007).

---

## Where Do You Find International Law?

Yet, it is not only the apparent lack of an international constabulary force (or something like this) that makes international law suspect in the eyes of many.

What also seems troublesome is that it is not always clear what international law is or where it comes from. For example, is there really a "law" as such that mandates that states intervene diplomatically on behalf of their citizens who are experiencing difficulties in another country, as was the case with the U.S. Embassy in the situation posited?

Although there are several sources of international law, the two most common are *custom* and *treaty*. As its name suggests, customary international law focuses on state practice. More than this, customary international law is based not only on how states act (or say they act) but on whether they also feel obligated to do so, which in international law is called *opinio juris*.

---

**Box I.13: Sources of International Law**

The most authoritative enumeration of the sources of international law is set forth in Article 38 (1) of the *Statute of the International Court of Justice*:

The Court, whose function is to decide in accordance with international law such disputes as are submitted to it, shall apply:

   a. International conventions, whether general or particular, establishing rules expressly recognized by the contesting states;
   b. International custom, as evidence of a general practice accepted as law;
   c. The general principles of law recognized by civilized nations;
   d. ... judicial decisions and the teachings of the most highly qualified publicists of the various nations, as subsidiary means for the determinations of rules of law.

---

In some cases, customary international law is not formalized. Much like the "unwritten" rules in baseball and other sports, one of the problems with this is that there is oftentimes no agreement on whether a particular "custom" happens to exist or not. Furthermore, even when a customary practice can be established, it is oftentimes difficult to determine whether states are following this custom because they believe they have a legal obligation to do so – which is a prerequisite for the creation of customary international law – or whether they are doing so for some other reason.

---

**Box I.14: Customary Law: The *Paquete Habana***

The *Paquete Habana* (1900) is perhaps the most famous ruling involving customary international law. The backdrop for this was the Spanish-American War and the U.S.

naval blockade of Cuba. Two fishing vessels leaving Cuba – the *Paquete Habana* and the *Lola* – were captured by U.S. merchant vessels and held as prizes of war. However, after an exhaustive analysis of state practices spanning centuries, the U.S. Supreme Court ruled that under customary international law fishing ships of this particular nature are exempt from capture.

Other times, customary international law is quite formalized. An excellent example of this is the Universal Declaration of Human Rights. The key term here is "declaration," as opposed to a "covenant" or "convention." Still, most international lawyers would agree that the UDHR is now an essential part of international law – customary international law, to be more specific – and the reason for this is that states feel bound by its provisions. This, of course, does not mean that states necessarily always act in accordance with the UDHR. However, what it does mean is that these provisions are viewed as applicable legal standards.

---

### Box I.15: Opinio Juris? State Apologies

In the mid-1990s, governmental leaders started to apologize for various policies they had enacted in the past. Many of these apologies were to domestic groups, but a number were directed at foreign governments and the people in those states. One such apology was President Bill Clinton's apology for supporting various genocidal regimes in Guatemala in the 1980s:

> For the United States it is important that I state clearly that support for military forces and intelligence units which engaged in violence and widespread repression was wrong, and the United States must not repeat that mistake.
>
> (Clinton 1999)

Does Clinton's apology have any legal effect? Is the statement evidence of a customary international law principle that a state has committed an internationally wrongful act in providing material and political support to a genocidal regime (Gibney and Roxström 2001)?

---

The other main source of international law consists of treaties, which includes both bilateral and multilateral agreements. Much more international law is now made through international and regional agreements and for this reason there will be a much greater emphasis on this. One important reason for the ascendancy of treaty law is that one of the prerogatives of state sovereignty is that states should only be bound by the law they agree to be bound by. Customary law does not work this way in the sense that it binds all states. Treaties are different. States decide for themselves whether to become a party to a particular treaty or not.

## How International Treaty Law Is Made

There is no special formula for how international treaty law is made. In terms of bilateral treaties, the governments of two countries decide to pursue a certain policy end that both feel can best be achieved by means of legal cooperation. The two countries then negotiate an agreement that is palatable to both sides. Extradition treaties are a good example of a bilateral treaty. The end goal here is the pursuit of criminal justice. The means for this consist of a bilateral treaty that sets forth the conditions under which there will be prisoner exchanges between these two countries.

---

### Box I.16: Unfair or Void Treaties

Guantanamo Bay, Cuba is in the news constantly due to the "enemy combatants" being held there. However, it has long been a bone of contention between the United States and Cuba. The U.S. first seized this part of the southeastern part of Cuba in 1898 during the Spanish-American War. In 1903, the United States and the newly created Cuban government signed the Platt Amendment, which led to the establishment of a naval base for the specific reason of allowing the United States to maintain Cuban independence. In 1934, the two countries signed a treaty allowing the United States a perpetual lease but specifying that this area continued to be Cuban "sovereign" territory. However, since the 1959 Revolution which brought Fidel Castro to power, the Cuban government has unsuccessfully sought to reclaim Guantanamo Bay. Instead, the United States has rebuffed such efforts. In response, for decades the Cuban government has refused to accept any money from the United States for "renting" this part of Cuba.

The treaty involving the Panama Canal had a different ending. In 1903, shortly after obtaining its independence from Colombia, Panama signed a treaty with the United States granting the U.S. the right to defend the Panama Canal as a means of maintaining its neutral operation. In the 1960s, students demonstrated in favor of reestablishing Panamanian sovereignty, but were met by force from the American military. Diplomatic efforts proved to be unsuccessful until President Jimmy Carter took up this issue and the result was the Panama Canal Treaty of 1977, which granted Panama full sovereign control as of January 1, 2000.

The final example is the Treaty of Guadalupe Hidalgo, a treaty between the United States and Mexico that was signed February 2, 1848 – at a time when invading American soldiers were occupying the capital and had seized various ports and custom stations – which resulted in the annexation of Texas as well as ceding to the United States what are now parts of Arizona, New Mexico, and California.

Were these treaties "fair"? Article 52 of the *Vienna Convention on the Law of Treaties* states that a "coerced" treaty is void. Would this principle apply to any of these treaties? Is it a sovereign right of a country to give up its sovereign rights? Or is this, by definition, contrary to international law principles?

The biggest difference with multilateral treaties is the number of states involved. Once again, there is a certain policy end – i.e., eliminating discrimination against women, or prohibiting torture, or establishing safety standards for international air travel – and states conclude that the best means of achieving this is to work in cooperation with other states. To do this, a treaty is drafted, and then this document is open for signature, which means that the signing state intends to ratify this instrument, but also that until then it will act in accordance with the provisions of the treaty.

### Box I.17: Terminating or Withdrawing From International Treaties

It is assumed that a treaty remains in force and its provisions carried out in good faith by state parties. However, treaties can be terminated, or else states can unilaterally withdraw from treaties they have entered into. In many instances, the treaty will specify the conditions of termination. A "material breach" by a party enables the other party (or parties) to terminate or suspend the treaty. In addition, treaties can be terminated on the basis of an impossibility of performance, or else on the ground that there has been a fundamental change of circumstances.

The *Rome Statute* – creating the International Criminal Court – and the *Paris Climate Agreement* provide two examples where the United States had initially committed itself to following international practice, but then later, due to domestic political pressures, reversed itself. In terms of the ICC, in the waning hours of his presidency President Bill Clinton signed the Rome Statute, and in doing so committed the United States to be bound by its provisions – even if the U.S. Senate never formally ratified the treaty. However, in May 2002, President George W. Bush acted to "unsign" the ICC treaty, although the legal implications of this remain unclear.

More recently, in 2015 the United States was one of 195 countries that agreed to be bound by the Paris Climate Agreement, whose goal is to severely reduce the emission of greenhouse gases. Two things are important to note. The first is that the Paris Climate Agreement is technically not a treaty as such because all of the greenhouse gas reductions were voluntary in nature and therefore not legally binding on states. The second is that the United States entered into the agreement by means of an executive order and not through the treaty making process. In 2017, President Donald Trump removed the United States from the Paris Climate Agreement, also by means of an executive agreement.

Different states have different means of ratification. For example, in the United States the U.S. Constitution (Article 2, Section 2) specifies a process whereby the president is given the power, by and with the consent of the Senate, to make treaties – so long as $^2/_3$ of the members present concur. If this occurs, the U.S. government has become a state party to this particular international agreement.

---

### Box I.18: The Rise of Executive Agreements . . . and the Decline of Treaties

The U.S. Constitution makes no mention of Executive Agreements – only treaties – but there is no question that Executive Agreements now dwarf the number of treaties entered into, and the disparity between the two has only continued to grow. For the period 1990 to 2012, the United States entered into 366 treaties, while the president issued 5,491 Executive Agreements. What this means is that only 6.2% of the international agreements entered into by the United States during this time followed the route set forth in the Constitution. In some cases, the president will be acting in accordance with the already expressed wishes of the Congress, but in the vast majority of cases he will be acting unilaterally, and perhaps even against congressional sentiment (Bradley and Goldsmith 2018).

---

Note, however, that the would-be ratifying state might have certain qualms about various provisions and it wants to specify its position. What are increasingly common in the treaty ratification process are RUDs: Reservations, Understandings, and Declarations. For example, in its ratification of the *Convention Against Torture*, the U.S. government specified that the term "cruel, inhuman or degrading treatment" was to be interpreted in a manner that was consistent with the 5th, 8th, and 14th Amendments of the U.S. Constitution. Or to explain this another way, according to this "understanding" of the U.S. government, capital punishment is not prohibited by CAT. However, what is less clear is the legal effect of RUDs. Based on the principle that states are only bound by international law that they agree to, one could make the argument that in any dispute regarding the provisions of a treaty, this state's interpretation reigns supreme. On the other hand, is an international treaty really a binding treaty when each state is able to interpret it in the fashion that it wants?

The issue of when an international treaty becomes binding is generally specified in the treaty itself. For example, the last major U.N. human rights treaty, the *Convention on the Rights of Persons with Disabilities*, specifies that the instrument will go into effect on the 30th day after the 20th state has ratified the treaty. What is important to note is that even when an international treaty obtains the requisite number of ratifying states, the "law" is only binding on those states that have ratified the treaty.

When a country becomes a state party to a treaty it thereby assumes certain international legal obligations. A different question altogether involves the domestic effect of this action. A self-executing treaty, as its name indicates, immediately becomes part of the "law of the land" so that individuals can use the treaty as a means of protection; while a non–self-executing treaty requires a further act of the legislative body in order to be applied domestically. Of course, determining which of these two categories a particular treaty falls into is sometimes not self-evident.

This, then, leads us to the question of the relationship between domestic and international law. There are essentially two schools of thought on this matter. The monist approach sees the two as being elements of the same system. The dualist approach, on the other hand, sees international law and domestic law as being separate and distinct from one another. How one approaches the question of a treaty being self-executing or not might depend largely on whether they are monists or dualists.

## What Constitutes International Law?

It used to be common to make a sharp distinction between domestic and international law, as if the two operate in completely separate and distinct spheres. This book takes a different approach, seeing the two as oftentimes blending into one another. In that way, when a country becomes a state party to an international treaty, what it is thereby doing is making international law a part of its own domestic law. Consider the prohibition against torture, which we will turn to in a moment. The *Convention Against Torture* mandates that by means of their domestic law, states parties will make torture a crime. Thus, are we speaking about international law, domestic law – or both? I say both.

Related to this is the question of what constitutes "international law." Once again, I tend to take a liberal approach and include law that transcends national boundaries, whether this law is interpreted by an international body (i.e., International Court of Justice), a regional institution (i.e., European Court of Human Rights), or a domestic court, such as the U.S. Supreme Court.

## The Interpretation of Treaties

Treaties, like all other agreements, need to be interpreted and quite often the instrument itself will provide insight in terms of how this is to be done. Still, there will be times when the state parties cannot find the necessary agreement. As a way of providing guidance to states, there is an international treaty on treaty interpretation: the *Vienna Convention on the Law of Treaties*. Of particular importance is Article 31 (1): "A treaty shall be interpreted in good faith in accordance with the ordinary meaning to be given to the terms of the treaty in their context and in the light of its object and purpose."

---

### Box I.19: The "Ticking Time Bomb" Case

In its 1999 decision in *Judgment on the Interrogation Methods Applied by the General Security Services (Shin Bet),* the Israeli Supreme Court ruled that the use of torture as an interrogation method was illegal under international law. However, at the same time, the Court left open the possibility of the use of "moderate physical pressure" in order to stop an imminent attack, or what has more commonly been referred to as the "ticking time bomb."

In the period since 1999, more than a thousand complaints of torture have been filed, yet not a single Shin Bet agent has been indicted. Has the Court's ruling simply been ignored – or has the "ticking time bomb" exception swallowed up the general prohibition against torture?

---

Let's now turn to an example of treaty interpretation. One of the questions prompted by the "war on terror" involves waterboarding. Article 1 (1) of the *Convention Against Torture* defines "torture" as:

> any act by which severe pain or suffering, whether physical or mental, is intentionally inflicted on a person for such purposes as obtaining from him or a third person information or a confession, punishing him for an act he or a third person has committed or is suspected of having committed, or intimidating or coercing him or a third person, or for any reason based on discrimination of any kind, when such pain or suffering is inflicted by or at the instigation of or with the consent or acquiescence of a public official or other person acting in an official capacity. It does not include pain or suffering arising only from, inherent in or incidental to lawful sanctions.

Although nearly all international lawyers view waterboarding as "torture," attorneys for the George W. Bush administration took a much different position (Working Group Report 2003). One difference related to the "intent" requirement. The view expressed by the Bush administration was that in order to constitute "torture," the infliction of severe pain or suffering must be the *primary intent* of the perpetrator so that even if the government agent knows that severe pain will result from his actions, if causing such harm is not his objective, he lacks the requisite specific intent. In that way, at least according to attorneys for the Bush White House, a defendant is guilty of torture only if he acts with the express purpose of inflicting severe pain or suffering.

---

**Box I.20: *Pacta Sunt Servanda* and the Trump Administration**

One of the founding principles of international law is *pacta sunt servanda*: treaties must be observed. Compare that principle with the first year of the Trump presidency, which resulted in the removal of the United States from both the *Paris Climate Agreement* and the nuclear treaty with Iran, as well as the threat to take the U.S. out of the *North Atlantic Free Trade Agreement* (NAFTA).

---

Another controversial position involved the meaning of the term "severe pain or suffering." Contrary to what had been (and still is) the dominant interpretation, Bush administration lawyers maintained that the pain that was inflicted had to rise to the level of "death, organ failure, or the permanent impairment of a significant bodily function."

---

**Box I.21: Is the Commander in Chief Above International Law?**

In addition to (re)interpreting the definition of "torture," officials of the Bush administration also claimed that when the president is acting in his capacity as commander in chief his powers supersede international law. According to a White House memo:

> Even if an interrogation method [might arguably constitute torture], and application of the statute was not held to be an unconstitutional infringement of the President's Commander-in-Chief authority, we believe that under current circumstances certain justifications [including military necessity and/or self defense] might be available that would potentially eliminate criminal liability
> (Bybee 2002)

Note, however, Article 6 (par. 2) of the U.S. Constitution, which reads:

> This Constitution, and the Laws of the United States which shall be made in Pursuance thereof; and all Treaties made, or which shall be made, under the Authority of the United States, shall be the supreme Law of the Land; and the Judges in every State shall be bound thereby, any Thing in the Constitution or Laws of any State to the Contrary notwithstanding.

What is your view: can the President of the United States – or any head of state, for that matter – simply ignore international law?

---

**Box I.22: The *Charming Betsey* Principle**

This principle from the U.S. Supreme Court ruling in *Murray v. Charming Betsey* (1804) states that when interpreting a federal (U.S.) statute, a domestic court should

*(Continued)*

**Box I.22: Continued**

presume "that the congressional act did not deliberately intend to infringe" principles of international law. The importance of the *Charming Betsy* principle is that, whenever possible, domestic and international law should be interpreted as being consonant with one another.

### Box I.23: Is Torture the Same as Cruel, Inhuman or Degrading Treatment?

Although commonly referred to as the *Convention Against Torture*, the full name of this international treaty is the *Convention Against Torture and Other Cruel, Inhuman or Degrading Treatment*. Is "torture" the same as "cruel, inhuman or degrading treatment"? It was commonly assumed that these two terms were interchangeable. However, in the case of *Ireland v. United Kingdom* (1978), the European Court of Human Rights drew a distinction between these two. Note, however, that states must abide by both prohibitions. That is, they must not torture – but they are also prohibited from engaging in "cruel, inhuman or degrading treatment."

The question, then, is whether in defending the practice of waterboarding, the Bush administration misread the *Torture Convention*. In my view, they have. The "object and purpose" of the *Torture Convention* is to protect every human being from serious physical and mental harm. However, an interpretation of the treaty that would allow extraordinarily harsh treatment – just up to the point of inflicting death, organ failure, or the permanent impairment of a significant bodily function – would most decidedly fail to meet the requirement that a treaty be interpreted in "good faith."

### Box I.24: Is International Law All Created Equal?

The short answer is no – international law is not all created equal. Rather, there is a hierarchy of norms with *jus cogens* or peremptory norms at the apex. The prohibition against torture is an example of a *jus cogens* norm. What this means is that no exceptions (derogations) are permissible. For example, the *International Covenant on Civil and Political Rights* (ICCPR) has a clause that allows for the suspension of certain rights in a time of a "public emergency which threatens the life of the nation and the existence of which is officially proclaimed." However, no derogation/suspension is allowed for *jus cogens* norms, which include the right not to be tortured.

## The Changing Nature of the State

Traditionally, public international law focused solely on states and states certainly retain their central position. However, there is now at least as much emphasis on individuals and corporations, and increasingly the role of states involves regulating these entities. Consider the issue of climate change. The problem to be addressed has little to do with pollution caused by states and state entities themselves, which would be quite negligible. Rather, the more pertinent issue is what states can (and cannot) do to limit greenhouse gas emissions brought about by a populace that increasingly relies on automobiles and appliances such air conditioners, but also private corporations that pollute airways and the waterways. In addition, international law has increasingly placed responsibilities on private entities (Knox 2008).

Beyond this, what also has changed is the "state" itself. When this book project began, ISIS controlled a large swath of territory in parts of Syria and Iraq. How does international law deal with an entity like this? Or with the relatively recent phenomenon of international terrorist networks?

---

### Box I.25: The Recognition of States – and Governments

Article 1 of the *Montevideo Convention on Rights and Duties of States* provides, "The State as a person of international law should possess the following qualifications: a) a permanent population; b) a defined territory; c) government; and d) capacity to enter into relations with the other States."

As you can see, these standards are rather nebulous, which helps explain why China and Liechtenstein are both "states," notwithstanding the enormous differences in geographic size and population – not to mention political power.

But perhaps the more interesting question is why certain "people" do not have their own state. For the Kurdish people, who are located in several countries including Turkey, Iraq, and Syria, the answer might be that there is no "defined territory." However, perhaps the better explanation is that, for whatever reason, other states are hesitant to recognize a Kurdish state. And when the Iraqi Kurds voted in favor of an independent state in 2017, the response of the Iraqi army was both harsh and decisive – and the international community hardly weighed in on this matter.

The issue of Palestinian statehood has certainly been a divisive political issue. As of September 2015, fully 136 of the 193 member states of the United Nations had recognized the State of Palestine based on pre-1967 borders. Yet, virtually all of the Western democracies have not recognized a Palestinian state (Sweden being the exception). However, on December 17, 2014 the European Parliament voted 498–88 to recognize Palestinian statehood – at least in principle (whatever that means). So is Palestine a state? Is the number of states that offer recognition key – or is it more important which states do (or do not) offer recognition?

The recognition (or non-recognition) of new governments is a separate and distinct matter than whether states are recognized. For example, for years after the communist government came to power in China in 1949, the United States continued to recognize the ousted government, residing on the island of Taiwan, as "China." It was not until 1979 that the U.S. recognized Beijing rule.

Even warfare itself – the quintessential of all state practices – has been trans-formed. An excellent example of this is that during the war in Iraq, there were as many private contractors working on behalf of the United States and its allies as there were enlisted personnel. Do the rules of war apply to these entities?

Yet, the change to the international order goes well beyond issues relating to human security. Multinational corporations with assets much greater than only a handful of states now buy and sell in all four corners of the globe. What country should regulate these financial behemoths? Or perhaps a better question to ask is this: what country could? Mark Zuckerberg, the CEO and founder of Facebook, was quite frank about the power and influence of his company when he pointed out that "in a lot of ways Facebook is more like a government than a traditional company."

International law has been based on a conceptualization of the state that coin-cides exactly with the geographical land mass laid out in world maps. However, states now operate outside their own territorial borders almost as a matter of course. According to a December 2017 *New York Times* report (Nixon 2017), the United States has security agents in some 70 different countries.

Immigration control measures are now being pushed further and further away from the would-be receiving state (Gammeltoft-Hansen 2011). What law, if any, applies in these kinds of situations? Another phenomenon that challenges our conception of the "state" is land grabbing. Under this scenario, a private entity from one state owns large tracts of land in some other country, invariably to grow certain kinds of crops and ship these goods back home or to the international market. But the issue this raises is what constitutes a "state" when foreign concerns own large tracts of land in another country?

Yet, even where states act directly and territorial borders remain intact, the world has fundamentally changed. One of the more obvious indications of this is that more people (60 million) are outside their country of origin and/or national-ity than at any time in history.

Still, this blurring of distinctions goes well beyond the issue of citizenship. For example, ships now change the flag they fly under – seemingly, almost as a mat-ter of course. There is also the law governing outer space, but nearly all of us now spend a considerable period of time each day in a place (if we could call it that) called cyberspace that seemingly transcends any (and all) national borders, but what this also means is that it transcends any (and all) purely domestic regulation as well.

The more important point is that the state-centric focus that has long been dominant in international law not only does not tell us much, it actually provides a simplistic and even misleading view of the way the way the world actually works. Although this book will focus on what is traditionally thought of as "public" international law, as opposed to "private" international law, one of the claims I will be making is that this nice, clear distinction oftentimes does not hold up in practice. Rather, much of "public" international law involves private entities, while much of "private" international law involves the practices of states (Koh 1991).

---

### Box I.26: The Dissolution of States – and the Formation of New Ones

Although states – and the territorial boundaries of those states – might appear to be static when seen on a world map, this can be quite misleading. Certainly, one of the most dramatic changes was the breakup of the Soviet Union on December 26, 1991 and the recognition of the independence of the former Soviet Republics along with the creation of what was then known as the Commonwealth of Independent States (CIS). Rivaling this in terms of political importance was the breakup of Yugoslavia in the early 1990s, which resulted in years of war.

If you look at a map of Europe before 1990 you will also see two countries that no longer exist. The first is East Germany, which was reunited with West Germany to form what is now (and had been) the Federal Republic of Germany. The other is Czechoslovakia, which as the result of the "velvet divorce" on January 1, 1993 split into two separate states: the Czech Republic and Slovakia.

Finally, the year 2017 marked the 70th anniversary of the partition of India into two separate states: India and Pakistan. This was anything but an amicable separation, as Hindus and Sikhs fled what became Pakistan, and millions of Muslims left India for Pakistan. It is estimated that between 200,000 and 2 million people were killed as a result of ensuing riots. And what should also be pointed out is the continual political tension between these two countries, both of which possess nuclear weapons.

---

## A Brief Look at the Past . . . With an Eye Toward International Law in the Future

I will close this chapter by giving a brief history of international law. However, rather than simply looking at the past, I will also say a few things about the direction that international law needs to go in in the future, a theme that will be developed throughout the book and taken up more directly in the conclusion.

Although there were some rudiments of international law in earlier periods of history, perhaps the most natural place to start is the Treaty of Westphalia (1648), which ended the Thirty Years' War, but more importantly for our purposes, established a system of sovereign states that controlled well-defined (although at times contested) territories in which each state was recognized as having absolute rule.

One of the tensions in international law, at least at the outset, was the extent to which this law was to be based on natural law principles, as opposed to those who took a more secular approach. Those falling on the natural law side would include

Francisco de Vitoria (1486–1546), whose writings on the inhumane treatment of indigenous populations in the New World are still referenced today, and Francisco Suarez (1548–1617). However, by the time of Hugo Grotius (1583–1645) – generally regarded as the "father of international law" – the natural law elements grew more muted. This secular trend continued, as reflected in the works of such writers as Emmerich de Vattel (1714–1767). Today, it is common to think of international law as devoid of any natural law underpinnings, although some remain, most notably the whole notion of "just war" theory.

In the 19th century as the intercourse between states increased, international law expanded as well. One noteworthy change was the enormous increase in the number of international and bilateral treaties, which served to bind the interests and policies of states – although the advent of World War I shows the possible negative side of entangling alliances as well. After the experience of World War I, international law achieved an unprecedented prominence, most notably in the creation of the League of Nations, which was established to ensure that this was the "war to end all wars."

Unfortunately, what soon ensued was the single greatest tragedy in human history. However, rather than rejecting international law, in the post-World War II period international law gained even more strength and visibility. The United Nations that was established was similar to the League of Nations, but it was hardly its mirror. For one thing, international peace and security was placed squarely with the U.N. Security Council, and thus, in the hands of the world's great powers. In addition, the Nuremberg/Tokyo trials showed that the enforcement of international law was not only possible, it was essential. And within a remarkable two-day period in December 1948, the U.N. General Assembly adopted the *Genocide Convention* and the *Universal Declaration of Human Rights (UDHR)*.

If a group of Martians were to travel to Earth and were shown the panoply of international law that now exists, particularly human rights law, they would be convinced that they had landed on the perfect planet: war was a relic of the past; torture did not exist; all people had sufficient food, water, medicine, and shelter; all children received an education; women were treated equal to men; disabled persons are essential contributors to every society, and so on. What the Martians would also be led to believe – quite falsely, it turns out – is that the seas are clean and teeming with life and the skies free of pollutants that could bring us all harm.

The problem is that international law has never fully come to terms with its inherent inconsistencies. On the one hand, there is the codification and institutionalization of international law itself. This, however, has been countered time and time again by the continued dominance of the principle of state sovereignty. Return to the issue of torture. States have shown no hesitancy in becoming a state party to the *Torture Convention*. Yet, there is simply no evidence that this has brought about any meaningful change in state practice (Hathaway 2002). The primary reason for this is that states can be certain that they will not be held to account if they do continue to torture. More than this, as we will see in some of the ensuing chapters, even states where the prohibition against torture had seemingly taken root now found it expedient in the "war on terrorism" to engage in torture themselves or, more accurately and certainly more conveniently, to have other states carry out these barbaric practices for them.

To be clear, as indicated earlier in this Introduction and to paraphrase Lou Henkin, most states almost always follow international law almost all the time. But the truth is that when states do ignore international law they can often do so with impunity and as we will see, there are any number of "doctrines" for states to hide behind in doing so. The larger point is that what is needed now, arguably more than ever, is a different kind of international law.

How this will take place is not clear. Yet, if the "how" question remains murky, the "why" question is crystal clear. The most intractable problems afflicting this planet – global warming, corruption, sex and drug trafficking, the denial of basic human rights, terrorism, and so on – cannot be solved by any one state. The growth of international law reflects this reality. However, what is needed is something more. What has to be established is a system where international law becomes more, well, law. An approach that, in the name of protecting state sovereignty, has allowed states to simply police themselves has had all-too-obvious limitations. What is needed is a system where states are held responsible for violating international law standards. I will close this Introduction on a positive note by taking the position that, with some prodding from below, international law is more than capable of making this transformation.

## References

### Books and Articles

Hannah Arendt, *The Origins of Totalitarianism*, New York, NY: Schocken (1951)

Curtis A. Bradley and Jack L. Goldsmith, "Presidential Control Over International Law," *Harvard Law Review* 131: 1201–97 (2018)

Valerie Epps, *International Law*, 4th ed., Durham, NC: Carolina Academic Press (2009)

Thomas Gammeltoft-Hansen, *Access to Asylum: International Refugee Law and the Globalisation of Migration Control*, Cambridge: Cambridge University Press (2011)

Mark Gibney, "The Downing of MH17: Russian Responsibility?" *Human Rights Law Review* 15: 169–78 (2015)

Mark Gibney and Erik Roxström, "The Status of State Apologies," *Human Rights Quarterly* 23: 911–39 (2001)

Oona Hathaway, "Do Human Rights Treaties Make a Difference?" *Yale Law Journal* 111: 1935–2042 (2002)

Louis Henkin, *How Nations Behave: Law and Foreign Policy*, 2nd ed., New York, NY: Columbia University Press (1979)

John Knox, "Horizontal Human Rights Law," *American Journal of International Law* 102: 1–47 (2008)

Harold Hongju Koh, "Transnational Public Law Litigation," *Yale Law Journal* 100: 2347–402 (1991)

Jenny Martinez, "Towards an International Judicial System," *Stanford Law Review* 56: 429–529 (2003)

Marko Milanovic, "The Murder of Jamal Khashoggi: Immunities, Inviolability and the Human Right to Life," *Human Rights Law Review* (forthcoming)

Sean Murphy, *Principles of International Law*, St. Paul, MN: Thomson/West (2006)

Ron Nixon, "Averting Terror in U.S., at Posts in 70 Countries," *New York Times*, (December 27, 2017), p. 1

Andre Nollkaemper, "Internationally Wrongful Acts in Domestic Courts," *American Journal of International Law* 101: 760–99 (2007)

Naomi Svensson, "Extraterritorial Accountability: An Assessment of the Effectiveness of Child Sex Tourism Laws," *Loyola of Los Angeles International and Comparative Law Review* 28: 641–64 (2006)

### U.S. Government Reports

Jay S. Bybee, "Memorandum for Alberto R. Gonzales, Re: Standards of Conduct and Interrogation Under 18 U.S.C. Secs. 2340–2340A," 1 August 2002 (U.S.)

President Bill Clinton, *Remarks by the President in Roundtable Discussion on Peace Efforts*, National Palace of Culture, Guatemala City, Guatemala, 10 March 1999, available at: www.gpo.nara/pubpaps/srchpaps.html

Department of Defense, "Working Group Report on Detainee Interrogation in the Global War on Terrorism: Assessment of Legal, Historical, Policy and Operational Considerations," 6 March 2003 (U.S.)

### Cases

*Barcelona Traction, Light and Power Company Limited (Belgium v. Spain)*, ICJ (1970)

*Case Concerning Avena and Other Mexican Nationals (Mexico v. United States)*, ICJ (2004)

*Case Concerning United States Diplomatic and Consular Staff in Tehran (United States v. Iran)*, ICJ (1980)

*Haig v. Agee*, 453 U.S. 280 (1981)

*Ireland v. United Kingdom*, ECtHR (1978)

*Judgment on the Interrogation Methods Applied by the General Security Services (Shin Bet)*, Israeli H.C. (1999)

*LaGrand (Germany v. United States)*, ICJ (2001)

*Lotus Case (France v. Turkey)*, PICJ (1927)

*Maslenjak v. United States*, 582 U.S. ____ (2017)

*Mavrommatis Palestine Concessions (Jurisdiction)*, PICJ (1924)

*Medellin v. Texas*, 552 U.S. 491 (2008)

*Murray v. The Charming Betsey*, 6 U.S. 64 (1804)

*Nottebohm Case, Liechtenstein v. Guatemala*, ICJ (1955)

*Paquete Habana*, 175 U.S. 677 (1900)

*Regan v. Wald*, 468 U.S. 222 (1984)

*Trump, et al. v. Hawaii, et al.*, 585 U.S. ____ (2018)

### International Agreements

Agreement Concerning a Scottish Trial in the Netherlands, 18 September 1998, UKTS No. 43 (1999); 117 ILR 664, 666

Agreement Governing the Activities of States on the Moon and Other Celestial Bodies (Moon Treaty), 5 December 1979, entry into force 11 July 1984

Antarctic Treaty, signed 1 December 1959, entry into force 1961

Chicago Convention on International Civil Aviation, T.I.A.S. 1591, 15 U.N.T.S. 295 (1944)

Convention Against Torture and Other Cruel, Inhuman or Degrading Treatment or Punishment, adopted and opened for signature 10 December 1984, entry into force 26 June 1987

Convention on the Law of the Sea, opened for signature on 10 December 1982, entry into force November 1994

Convention on the Prevention and Punishment of the Crime of Genocide, approved and proposed for signature 9 December 1948, entry into force 12 January 1951

Convention on the Rights of Persons with Disabilities, adopted 13 December 2006, entry into force 3 May 2008

International Covenant on Civil and Political Rights, adopted 16 December 1966, entry into force 23 March 1976

International Telecommunications Union, founded 17 May 1865

Montevideo Convention on the Rights and Duties of States, enacted 26 December 1933, entry into force 26 December 1934

North Atlantic Free Trade Agreement (NAFTA) (Canada, Mexico and the United States), signed 17 December 1992, entry into force 1 January 1994

Paris Agreement, adopted 12 December 2015, entry into force 4 November 2016

Rome Statute of the International Criminal Court, adopted on 17 July 1998, entry into force 1 July 2002

Schengen Agreement, International Convention initially approved by Belgium, France, West Germany (later Germany), Luxembourg, and the Netherlands in Schengen, Luxembourg, on 14 June 1985

Statute of the International Court of Justice, San Francisco, 24 October 1945

Treaty on Principles Governing the Activities in the Exploration and Uses of Outer Space, Including the Moon and Other Celestial Bodies (Outer Space Treaty), opened for signature 27 January 1967, entry into force 10 October 1967

Universal Declaration of Human Rights, adopted by the United Nations General Assembly, 10 December 1948

Universal Postal Union, established by the Berne Treaty of 1874, became a specialised agency of the UN in 1948

Vienna Convention on Consular Relations, signed in Vienna on 24 April 1963, entered into force 19 March 1967

Vienna Convention on Diplomatic Relations, signed in Vienna on 18 April 1961, entered into force on 24 April 1964

Vienna Convention on the Law of Treaties, done at Vienna on 23 May 1969, entry into force on 27 January 1980

# Part I
## International Terrorism

# 1
## Fighting Terrorism Through Law

### The Events of September 11, 2001

On September 11, 2001, a group of al-Qaeda hijackers commandeered four commercial airplanes departing from various cities on the East Coast of the United States. Two of these planes were flown into the World Trade Center buildings in New York City, causing these two structures to collapse and bringing about the deaths of more than 3,000 people. Another plane was flown into the Pentagon building outside of Washington D.C., resulting in massive damage to the structure and the additional loss of life, while the fourth plane, which was believed to be heading toward the White House, crashed in a field in western Pennsylvania after passengers fought against the hijackers, causing it to crash.

Domestically, the U.S. Congress gave the president an enormous amount of authority to fight the "war on terrorism," as the Bush administration termed it, by passing the *Authorization for the Use of Military Force*, which the administration interpreted as authority to combat terrorism whenever and wherever the threat arose. The administration moved equally aggressively in the international arena. On September 21, 2001, in a nationally televised address before Congress, Bush demanded that the Taliban government in Afghanistan immediately and unconditionally surrender any and all al-Qaeda members on its soil, dismantle al-Qaeda training camps, and give the United States unfettered access to suspected al-Qaeda facilities. When this request was rebuffed, on October 7 the United States initiated a military campaign against Afghanistan, aided by Afghan forces of the Northern Alliance, to depose the Taliban-led government and root out al-Qaeda. On March 19, 2003, the Bush administration greatly expanded the war on terrorism

33

**Photo 1.1** The Falling of the Twin Towers on 9/11
*Source*: © Associated Press

by leading an invasion of Iraq based on the claim that the Saddam Hussein regime possessed weapons of mass destruction and was in league with al-Qaeda forces.

The events of 9/11 were certainly not the first acts of "international terrorism." However, that day the world entered into a new age – the age of terrorism – and as you well know, since then there have been repeated terrorist attacks in locales all over the globe. In 2017 alone, and merely cataloging terrorist attacks in major Western cities, this included attacks in: New York City (December 11 and October 31), Barcelona (August 17), London (June 3), and Stockholm (April 7), as well as the suicide bomber who killed 22 people at an Ariana Grande concert in Manchester (May 22).

As noted in the Introduction, international law has traditionally only governed relations among and between states. Yet, the most visible and arguably one of the most pressing security issues of our age involves a myriad of non-state actors residing in a number of countries that share a goal of disrupting and perhaps even dismantling the international order.

### Box 1.1: Terrorism Under International Law

Although the term "terrorism" is used all the time, it might be surprising to learn that there is no official definition of terrorism under international law. One reason for this relates to the old adage that "one person's terrorist is another person's free-dom fighter." One such example of this is the African National Congress in South Africa, which was considered by many as a "terrorist" organization after the ANC decided to take up arms against the apartheid regime. Similarly, while the Israeli government has long considered Hamas to be a terrorist organization, in their effort to remove the British from Palestine, Israeli "freedom fighters" carried out a number of attacks that by today's standards would be considered as "terrorism."

## Terrorism Before 9/11

In this chapter our focus is on efforts to address international terrorism through the law, either by holding "terrorists" themselves responsible, or more likely, states that provide "aid and assistance" to terrorists or terrorist organizations. Our first case, *Tel-Oren v. Libyan Arab Republic* (1984), was handed down a few years after the Second Circuit Court of Appeal's landmark ruling in *Filartiga v. Pena-Irala* (1980). In *Filartiga*, the son of a political dissident in Paraguay was tortured and killed by police forces working under the direction of police captain Pena-Irala. After the Filartiga family learned of Pena-Irala's whereabouts in the United States, they filed a civil action against him on the basis of the Alien Tort Statute (ATS)

**Photo 1.2** Dolly Filartiga With a Picture of Her Brother Joelito

*Source:* © Associated Press

from the Judiciary Act of 1789, which reads in its entirety: "The district courts shall have original jurisdiction of any civil action by an alien for a tort only, committed in violation of the law of nations or a treaty of the United States." In a landmark ruling, the Second Circuit held that the Filartiga family could proceed with its suit. Pena-Irala then returned to Paraguay, while the Filartiga family was awarded a default judgment of $10 million.

In *Tel-Oren*, victims of a terrorist attack carried out in Israel sought to invoke the ATS against a group of non-state actors, including the Palestinian Liberation Organization. As you will see, all three circuit judges concur with the ruling of the district court that the suit should be dismissed. However, their reasoning differs sharply. What should also be of great interest are the diverging views regarding international law itself.

---

## Tel-Oren v. Libyan Arab Republic, 726 F.2d 774 (D.C. Cir. 1984)

BEFORE EDWARDS AND BORK, CIRCUIT JUDGES, AND ROBB, SENIOR CIRCUIT JUDGE

### PER CURIAM

Plaintiffs in this action, mostly Israeli citizens, are survivors and representatives of persons murdered in an armed attack on a civilian bus in Israel in March 1978. They filed suit for compensatory and punitive damages in the District Court, naming as defendants the Libyan Arab Republic, the Palestine Liberation Organization, the Palestine Information Office, the National Association of Arab Americans, and the Palestine Congress of North America.

In their complaint, plaintiffs alleged that defendants were responsible for multiple tortious acts in violation of the law of nations, treaties of the United States, and criminal laws of the United States, as well as the common law. For purposes of our jurisdictional analysis, we assume plaintiffs' allegations to be true. The District Court dismissed the action both for lack of subject matter jurisdiction and as barred by the applicable statute of limitations. We affirm the dismissal of this action. Set out below are separate concurring statements of Judge Edwards, Judge Bork, and Senior Judge Robb, indicating different reasons for affirming the result reached by the District Court.

### HARRY T. EDWARDS, CIRCUIT JUDGE, CONCURRING

This case deals with an area of the law that cries out for clarification by the Supreme Court. We confront at every turn broad and novel questions about the definition and application of the "law of nations." As is obvious from the laborious efforts of opinion writing, the questions posed defy easy answers.

At issue in this case is an aged but little-noticed provision of the First Judiciary Act of 1789, which gives federal courts jurisdiction over a minute class of cases implicating the law of nations. Thus, it is not startling that the central controversy of this action has now produced divided opinions between and within the circuits. The opinions of Judge

Bork and Judge Robb are fundamentally at odds with the decision of the Second Circuit in *Filartiga v. Pena-Irala*, which, to my mind, is more faithful to the pertinent statutory language and to existing precedent. Although I cannot concur in the opinions of my colleagues, I do agree with them that the decision of the District Court should be affirmed. I write separately to underscore the rationale for my decision; I do this because, as will be apparent, there are sharp differences of viewpoint among the judges who have grappled with these cases over the meaning and application of 28 U.S.C. § 1350 (1976).

On March 11, 1978, thirteen heavily armed members of the Palestine Liberation Organization (hereinafter "the PLO") turned a day trip into a nightmare for 121 civilian men, women and children. The PLO terrorists landed by boat in Israel and set out on a barbaric rampage along the main highway between Haifa and Tel Aviv. They seized a civilian bus, a taxi, a passing car, and later a second civilian bus. They took the passengers hostage. They tortured them, shot them, wounded them and murdered them. Before the Israeli police could stop the massacre, 22 adults and 12 children were killed, and 73 adults and 14 children were seriously wounded. Most of the victims were Israeli citizens; a few were American and Dutch citizens. They turned to our courts for legal redress and brought this action. The District Court dismissed the action for lack of subject matter jurisdiction. The critical issue on appeal is whether plaintiffs alleged sufficient facts to meet the jurisdictional elements of those sections.

My inquiry into the sufficiency of plaintiffs' allegations is guided by the Second Circuit's decision in *Filartiga*. For reasons set out below, I adhere to the legal principles established in *Filartiga* but find that factual distinctions preclude reliance on that case to find subject matter jurisdiction in the matter now before us. Specifically, I do not believe the law of nations imposes the same responsibility or liability on non-state actors, such as the PLO, as it does on states and persons acting under color of state law. Absent direction from the Supreme Court on the proper scope of the obscure section 1350, I am therefore not prepared to extend *Filartiga*'s construction of section 1350 to encompass this case.

Section 1350 provides that a district court shall have original jurisdiction over civil actions "*by an alien for a tort only, committed in violation of the law of nations or a treaty of the United States.*" In the absence of an allegation of a treaty violation, the critical issue in *Filartiga* was whether torture constitutes a violation of the law of nations. In determining that it does, Judge Kaufman reviewed the accepted sources of international law – the usage of nations, judicial opinions and the works of jurists – and concluded that *official torture* of both aliens and citizens is prohibited by the law of nations. That section 1350 was enacted in the Judiciary Act of 1789, when world perceptions both of the role of international law and its substantive provisions differed considerably from perceptions of today, did not preclude this result. Judge Kaufman took guidance from *The Paquete Habana*, (holding that the traditional prohibition against seizure of an enemy's coastal fishing vessels had ripened from a standard of comity into a settled rule of international law), and observed that "courts must interpret international law not as it was in 1789, but as it has evolved and exists among the nations of the world today."

The opinion thus established several propositions. First, the "law of nations" is not stagnant and should be construed as it exists today among the nations of the world. Second, one source of that law is the customs and usages of civilized nations, as articulated by jurists and commentators. Third, international law today places limits on a state's power to torture persons held in custody, and confers "fundamental rights upon all people" to be free from torture. Fourth, section 1350 opens the federal courts for adjudication of the rights already recognized by international law.

Because I am substantially in accord with these four propositions, and Judge Bork and Judge Robb apparently are not, I am unable to join in their opinions. First, and most fundamentally, I diverge from the views of my colleague Judge Bork regarding the necessary elements of this court's jurisdiction. The Second Circuit did not require plaintiffs to point to a specific right to sue under the law of nations in order to establish jurisdiction under section 1350; rather, the Second Circuit required only a showing that the defendant's actions violated the substantive law of nations. In contrast, Judge Bork would deny jurisdiction to any plaintiff – presumably including those in *Filartiga* – who could not allege a specific right to sue apart from the language of section 1350 itself.

Judge Bork's suggestion that section 1350 requires plaintiffs to allege a right to sue granted by the law of nations is seriously flawed. Initially, it assumes that the "law of nations" could provide a specific, articulated right to sue in a form other than a treaty or executive agreement. Yet no evidence is offered to indicate that jurists or commentators have ever looked to the law of nations to determine when a wrongful deed is *actionable*. This absence of evidence is not surprising, because it is clear that "international law itself, finally, does not require any particular reaction to violations of law. . . . Whether and how the United States wished to react to such violations are domestic questions. . . . "

In consequence, to require international accord on a right to sue, when in fact the law of nations relegates decisions on such questions to the states themselves, would be to effectively nullify the "law of nations" portion of section 1350. There is a fundamental principle of statutory construction that a statute should not be construed so as to render any part of it "inoperative or superfluous, void or insignificant," and there exists a presumption against a construction yielding that result. Yet, the construction offered by Judge Bork would have the effect of voiding a significant segment of section 1350.

Judge Bork argues that the statute retains meaning under his interpretation because he recognizes that the drafters of section 1350 perceived of certain offenses against the law of nations. He enumerates three offenses recognized by Blackstone – violation of safe-conducts, infringement of the rights of ambassadors, and piracy – and insists that these were the offenses that the drafters of section 1350 had in mind. This explanation is specious, not responsive. Judge Bork does nothing more than concede that, in 1789, the law of nations clause covered three substantive offenses. However, under his construction of section 1350, this concession is meaningless unless it is also shown that the law of nations created a private right of action to avenge the three law of nations violations to which Blackstone averted – a showing that would require considerable skill since the law of nations simply does not create rights to sue. Indeed, in the very passage quoted by Judge Bork, Blackstone makes clear that it was the municipal laws of England, not the law of nations, that made the cited crimes offenses.

While I endorse the legal principles set forth in *Filartiga*, I also believe the factual distinctions between this case and the one faced by the Second Circuit mitigate its precedential value in this case. To be sure, the parallels between the two cases are compelling. Here, as in *Filartiga*, plaintiffs and defendants are both aliens. Plaintiffs here allege torture in their complaint, as did plaintiffs in *Filartiga*. Here, as in *Filartiga*, the action at issue undoubtedly violated the law of the nation in which it occurred (in this case, the law of Israel).

The two fact patterns diverge, however, on the issue of *official torture*. The Palestine Liberation Organization is not a recognized state, and it does not act under color of any recognized state's law. In contrast, the Paraguayan official in *Filartiga* acted under color of state law, although in violation of it. The Second Circuit surveyed the law of nations and concluded that *official torture* constituted a violation. Plaintiffs in the case before us do not allege facts to show that official or state-initiated torture is implicated in this action. Nor do I think they could, so long as the PLO is not a recognized member of the community of nations.

The question therefore arises whether to stretch *Filartiga*'s reasoning to incorporate torture perpetrated by a party other than a recognized state or one of its officials acting under color of state law. The extension would require this court to venture out of the comfortable realm of established international law – within which *Filartiga* firmly sat – in which states are the actors. It would require an assessment of the extent to which international law imposes not only rights but also obligations on individuals. It would require a determination of where to draw a line between persons or groups who are or are not bound by dictates of international law, and what the groups look like. Would terrorists be liable, because numerous international documents recognize their existence and proscribe their acts? Would all organized political entities be obliged to abide by the law of nations? Would *everybody* be liable? As firmly established as is the core principle binding states to customary international obligations, these fringe areas are only gradually emerging and offer, as of now, no obvious stopping point. I am not prepared to extend the definition of the "law of nations" absent direction from the Supreme Court.

I turn next to consider whether terrorism is itself a law of nations violation. While this nation unequivocally condemns all terrorist attacks, that sentiment is not universal. Indeed, the nations of the world are so divisively split on the legitimacy of such aggression as to make it impossible to pinpoint an area of harmony or consensus. Unlike the issue of individual responsibility, which much of the world has never even reached, terrorism has evoked strident reactions and sparked strong alliances among numerous states.

I do not believe that under current law terrorist attacks amount to law of nations violations.

To witness the split one need only look at documents of the United Nations. They demonstrate that to some states acts of terrorism, in particular those with political motives, are legitimate acts of aggression and therefore immune from condemnation.

The divergence as to basic norms of course reflects a basic disagreement as to legitimate political goals and the proper method of attainment. Given such disharmony, I cannot conclude that the law of nations – which, we must recall, is defined as the principles and rules that states feel themselves bound to observe, and do commonly observe – outlaws politically motivated terrorism, no matter how repugnant it might be to our own legal system.

In light of the foregoing, I conclude that the appellants have not, and could not, allege facts sufficient to remain in court under existing precedent. I therefore vote to affirm the District Court's dismissal for lack of subject matter jurisdiction.

### BORK, CIRCUIT JUDGE, CONCURRING

Historical research has not as yet disclosed what section 1350 was intended to accomplish. The fact poses a special problem for courts. A statute whose original meaning is hidden from us and yet which, if its words are read incautiously with modern assumptions in mind, is capable of plunging our nation into foreign conflicts, ought to be approached by the judiciary with great circumspection. It will not do simply to assert that the statutory phrase, the "law of nations," whatever it may have meant in 1789, must be read today as incorporating all the modern rules of international law and giving aliens private causes of action for violations of those rules. It will not do because the result is contrary not only to what we know of the framers' general purposes in this area but contrary as well to the appropriate, indeed the constitutional, role of courts with respect to foreign affairs.

What little relevant historical background is now available to us indicates that those who drafted the Constitution and the Judiciary Act of 1789 wanted to open federal courts to aliens for the purpose of avoiding, not provoking, conflicts with other nations. *The Federalist* No. 80 (A. Hamilton). A broad reading of section 1350 runs directly contrary to that desire. It is also relevant to a construction of this provision that until quite recently nobody understood it to empower courts to entertain cases like this one or like *Filartiga*.

What kinds of alien tort actions, then, might the Congress of 1789 have meant to bring into federal courts? According to Blackstone, a writer certainly familiar to colonial lawyers, "the principal offences against the law of nations, animadverted on as such by the municipal laws of England, [were] of three kinds; 1. Violation of safe-conducts; 2. Infringement of the rights of ambassadors; and 3. Piracy." One might suppose that these were the kinds of offenses for which Congress wished to provide tort jurisdiction for suits by aliens in order to avoid conflicts with other nations.

If it is in large part because "the Law of Nations is primarily a law between States," that international law generally relies on an enforcement scheme in which individuals have no direct role, that reliance also reflects recognition of some other important characteristics of international law that distinguish it from municipal law. Chief among these is the limited role of law in the international realm. International law plays a much less pervasive role in the ordering of states' conduct within the international community than does municipal law in the ordering of individuals' conduct within nations. Unlike our nation, for example, the international community could not plausibly be described as governed by laws rather than men. "[I]nternational legal disputes are not as separable from politics as are domestic legal disputes. . . . "

International law, unlike municipal law (at least in the United States), is not widely regarded as a tool of first or frequent resort and as the last word in the legitimate resolution of conflicts. Nations rely chiefly on diplomacy and other political tools in their dealings with each other, and these means are frequently incompatible with declarations of legal rights. Diplomacy demands great flexibility and focuses primarily on the future rather than on the past, often requiring states to refrain, for the sake of their future relations, from pronouncing judgment on past conduct. Since states adopt international law to improve their relations with each other, it is hardly surprising in the current world that they should generally retain for themselves control over the ability to invoke it. Nor is it surprising that international law is invoked less often to secure authoritative adjudications than it is to bolster negotiating positions or to acquire public support for foreign-relations policies.

This remains true even as international law has become increasingly concerned with individual rights. Some of the rights specified in the documents relied upon by appellants as stating principles of international law recognizing individual rights are clearly not expected to be judicially enforced throughout the world.

The meaning and application of section 1350 will have to await clarification elsewhere. Since section 1350 appears to be generating an increasing amount of litigation, it is to be hoped that clarification will not be long delayed. In the meantime, it is impossible to say even what the law of this circuit is. Though we agree on nothing else, I am sure my colleagues join me in finding that regrettable.

### Robb, Senior Circuit Judge, Concurring

I concur in the result, but must withhold approval of the reasoning of my colleagues. Both have written well-researched and scholarly opinions that stand as testaments to the difficulty which this case presents. Both agree that this case must be dismissed though their reasons vary greatly. Both look backward to *Filartiga v. Pena-Irala*, and forward to the future efforts of others maimed or murdered at the hands of thugs clothed with power who are unfortunately present in great numbers in the international order. But both Judges Bork and Edwards fail to reflect on the inherent inability of federal courts to deal with cases such as this one. It seems to me that the political question doctrine controls. This case is nonjusticiable.

Tort law requires both agreement on the action which constitutes the tort and the means by which it can be determined who bears responsibility for the unlawful injury. Federal courts are not in a position to determine the international status of terrorist acts. Judge Edwards, for example, notes that "the nations of the world are so divisively split on the legitimacy of such aggression as to make it impossible to pinpoint an area of harmony or consensus." This nation has no difficulty with the question in the context of this case, of course, nor do I doubt for a moment that the attack on the Haifa highway amounts to barbarity in naked and unforgivable form. No diplomatic posturing as represented in sheaves of United Nations documents – no matter how high the pile might reach – could convince me otherwise. But international "law", or the absence thereof, renders even the search for the least common denominators of civilized conduct in this area an impossible-to-accomplish judicial task. Courts ought not to engage in it when that search takes us towards a consideration of terrorism's place in the international order. Indeed, when such a review forces us to dignify by judicial notice the most outrageous of the diplomatic charades that attempt to dignify the violence of terrorist atrocities, we corrupt our own understanding of evil.

Even more problematic would be the single court's search for individual responsibility for any given terrorist outrage. International terrorism consists of a web that the courts are not positioned to unweave. To attempt to discover the reach of its network and the origins of its design may result in unintended disclosures imperiling sensitive diplomacy. This case attempts to focus on the so-called P.L.O. But which P.L.O.? Arafat's, Habash's, or Syria's? And can we conceive of a successful attempt to sort out ultimate responsibility for these crimes? Many believe that most roads run East in this area. Are courts prepared to travel these highways? Are they equipped to do so? It is one thing for a student note-writer to urge that courts accept the challenges involved. It is an entirely different matter for a court to be asked to conduct such a hearing successfully. The dangers are obvious. To grant the initial access in the face of an overwhelming probability of frustration of the trial process as we know it is an unwise step. As courts could never compel the allegedly responsible parties to attend proceedings much less to engage in a meaningful judicial process, they ought to avoid such imbroglios from the beginning.

---

## Notes and Comments:

1. Which opinion – if any – do you agree with the most? Or are you of the view that the Alien Tort Statute (or something like this) might be quite useful as a tool against international terrorism?
2. Do some countries have a stronger interest in fighting terrorism – and if so, which ones (and why) (Colangelo 2007)?
3. *Tel-Oren* is certainly not the last word on whether "terrorist organizations" can be sued. In 1985, the brutal Klinghoffer murder drew worldwide attention. Leon Klinghoffer was a U.S. citizen of Jewish heritage who was aboard the *Achille Lauro* cruise ship with his wife to celebrate their 36th wedding anniversary. A group of PLO operatives hijacked the boat on the Mediterranean Sea demanding that Israel free PLO members in detention. Nothing ensued from this and the hijackers responded by killing the

wheelchair-bound Klinghoffer and tossing his body into the sea. The family brought a suit in federal district court against the PLO under the Alien Tort Statute, but the case was dismissed. However, the Court of Appeals reversed and re-instituted the suit on the basis that federal admiralty law might be implicated. *Klinghoffer v. S.N.C. Achille Lauro* (1991). In 1997, the PLO and the Klinghoffer family reached an out of court settlement, with both sides claiming victory. Klinghoffer's name lives on in popular culture, most notably the opera *The Death of Klinghoffer* written and initially directed by the renowned Peter Sellars.

4. Partly in response to *Tel-Oren* and *Klinghoffer*, Congress passed the Antiterrorism Act of 1990 (ATA), which explicitly authorizes a private cause of action for American citizens who suffer death or injury "by reason of any act of international terrorism." However, the ATA gained much more prominence following 9/11.

5. We return to a discussion of the Alien Tort Statute in Chapter 8 **Corporate Accountability**. In *Jesner v. Arab Bank* (2018) the U.S. Supreme Court held that the ATS could not be used as a jurisdictional vehicle to hold multinational corporations liable. However, what is now unclear is whether this would affect *Filartiga*-type situations as well.

---

### Box 1.2: International Law at the Movies: Terrorism

Terrorism has been no stranger to the cinema – documentary and feature film alike – and thus we will begin with *The Battle of Algiers* (1966), a feature film that gives every appearance of being a documentary on the fight for Algerian independence in the 1950s and 1960s. Ironically enough, those who would now be thought of as "terrorists" – the Algerian resistance that goes so far as targeting civilians – come off as the "good guys," while the French army fighting against the "terrorists," albeit by means of torture or worse, are the "bad guys."

The event that truly propelled "terrorism" onto the international stage was the massacre of a group of Israeli athletes at the 1972 Summer Olympic Games in Munich. It would not be hyperbole to say that there was a worldwide audience witnessing how the "Peace Games" were instantly transformed into something quite different. The documentary *One Day in September* (1999) does a superb job of presenting the unfolding drama carried live on ABC Sports, which had been covering the Games. Much less successful was the feature film *Munich* (2005), directed by Steven Spielberg, which told the story of Israel's vengeful response to the Olympic massacre.

It is common to think of European terrorist attacks as something new. The Irish Republican Army was considered to be a "terrorist" organization by the United Kingdom and there are several superb feature films relating to "the Troubles." In

*Hunger* (2008) Michael Fassbender provides a stunning portrait of IRA operative Bobby Sands, who led a hunger strike against prison regulations. *In the Name of the Father* (1993) stars Daniel-Day Lewis as Gerry Conlon, one of the "Guildford Four" convicted – wrongfully, as it turns out – for carrying out an IRA bombing attack. *Bloody Sunday* (2002) is a faux documentary recounting the massacre of a group of Catholics following Sunday mass, demonstrating for civil rights in Derry, Northern Ireland. *Omagh* (2004) provides the wrenching story of a family's attempt to overcome the death of their teenage son killed in an IRA car bomb attack.

Of course, the United Kingdom was not alone in being targeted for terrorist attacks. In Italy, the Red Brigades succeeding in abducting and killing a former Prime Minister. Their counterpart in Germany was the Baader-Meinhof group, depicted in the feature film *The Baader-Meinhof Complex* (2008).

One of the most intelligent and moving documentaries on the aftermath of the September 11 attacks on the United States is *USA v. Al-Arian* (2007). Sami Al-Arian, previously feted by the George W. Bush administration, is a University of South Florida professor who was charged with aiding and abetting terrorist acts in the Middle East.

**Photo 1.3**  The 1972 Olympics: Terrorism Enters the World Stage
*Source:* © Associated Press

## Box 1.3: Criminal Trials Against Suspected Terrorists in U.S. Courts

Although the focus here is on civil proceedings against states and private entities that engage in or act in support of terrorist activities, what should not be ignored are criminal prosecutions brought against alleged terrorist masterminds and operatives. According to the NGO Human Rights First (2018), as of February 2018, federal

*(Continued)*

**Box 1.3: Continued**

> criminal courts in the United States have convicted more than 660 individuals on terrorism-related charges since September 11, 2001 – compared with the eight convictions through military commissions, which will be more fully discussed in the next chapter. These convictions were the result of trials in 63 different U.S. federal courts. Moreover, federal prisons hold more than 400 individuals convicted of terrorism-related offenses, while only three of the eight Guantanamo convicted detainees remain in prison.

Although there has been relative peace in Northern Ireland since the Good Friday Agreement in April 1998, the Irish Republican Army (IRA) had long been considered a "terrorist" organization – at least by the United Kingdom. In the *McCann* case we examine what the European Court of Human Rights (ECtHR) views as a "lawful" response to terrorism.

---

## *McCann and Others v. United Kingdom,* ECtHR, App. No. 18984/91 (1995)

*[The facts of this case have all the elements of a spy thriller – except, perhaps, for the ending. British authorities had obtained intelligence information that operatives of the Irish Republican Army were planning a car bombing attack in Gibraltar. Three suspected IRA members – McCann, Farrell, and Savage – entered Gibraltar unimpeded by security authorities, but were monitored by British officials. After parking their car, McCann and Farrell went off together, but were soon gunned down when they made what British soldiers interpreted as a dangerous gesture. Almost instantaneously, Savage was also killed at close range when he appeared to be reaching for what was thought to be a detonation device. No weapons were found on any of the deceased and no bomb was found in the car driven by this threesome.*

*Following an inquest in Gibraltar, the jury determined that the killings were lawful. The applicants were dissatisfied with the verdicts and commenced an action in the High Court of Justice in Northern Ireland and eventually pursued a claim before the European Court of Human Rights (ECtHR), which ruled that there was no evidence of intentional killings. However, as set forth in the following, the Court ruled that there had been a violation of Article 2 of the European Convention. Most pertinent to this case is Article 2(2), which provides:*

> *Deprivation of life shall not be regarded as inflicted in contravention of this Article when it results from the use of force which is no more than absolutely necessary:*
>
> *a) in defence of any person from unlawful violence;*
> *b) in order to effect a lawful arrest or to prevent the escape of a person lawfully detained;*
> *c) in action lawfully taken for the purpose of quelling a riot or insurrection*

*McCann was a 10–9 ruling and also included below are segments of a powerful nine-judge dissent that essentially accuses the majority of practicing 20/20 hindsight vision.]*

In carrying out its examination under Article 2 of the Convention, the Court must bear in mind that the information that the United Kingdom authorities received that there would be a terrorist attack in Gibraltar presented them with a fundamental dilemma. On the one hand, they were required to have regard to their duty to protect the lives of the people in Gibraltar including their own military personnel and, on the other, to have minimum resort to the use of lethal force against those suspected of posing this threat in the light of the obligations flowing from both domestic and international law. Several other factors must also be taken into consideration.

In the first place, the authorities were confronted by an active service unit of the IRA composed of persons who had been convicted of bombing offences and a known explosives expert. The IRA, judged by its actions in the past, had demonstrated a disregard for human life, including that of its own members.

Secondly, the authorities had had prior warning of the impending terrorist action and thus had ample opportunity to plan their reaction and, in co-ordination with the local Gibraltar authorities, to take measures to foil the attack and arrest the suspects. Inevitably, however, the security authorities could not have been in possession of the full facts and were obliged to formulate their policies on the basis of incomplete hypotheses.

Against this background, in determining whether the force used was compatible with Article 2, the Court must carefully scrutinise not only whether the force used by the soldiers was strictly proportionate to the aim of protecting persons against unlawful violence but also whether the anti-terrorist operation was planned and controlled by the authorities so as to minimise, to the greatest extent possible, recourse to lethal force. The Court will consider each of these points in turn.

It is recalled that the soldiers who carried out the shooting were informed by their superiors, in essence, that there was a car bomb in place which could be detonated by any of the three suspects by means of a radio-control device which might have been concealed on their persons; that the device could be activated by pressing a button; that they would be likely to detonate the bomb if challenged, thereby causing heavy loss of life and serious injuries, and were also likely to be armed and to resist arrest.

As regards the shooting of Mr McCann and Ms Farrell, the Court recalls the Commission's finding that they were shot at close range after making what appeared to Soldiers A and B to be threatening movements with their hands as if they were going to detonate the bomb.

As regards the shooting of Mr Savage, the evidence revealed that there was only a matter of seconds between the shooting at the Shell garage (McCann and Farrell) and the shooting at Landport tunnel (Savage). The Commission found that it was unlikely that Soldiers C and D witnessed the first shooting before pursuing Mr Savage who had turned around after being alerted by either the police siren or the shooting.

Soldier C opened fire because Mr Savage moved his right arm to the area of his jacket pocket, thereby giving rise to the fear that he was about to detonate the bomb. In addition, Soldier C had seen something bulky in his pocket which he believed to be a detonating transmitter. Soldier D also opened fire believing that the suspect was trying to detonate the supposed bomb.

It was subsequently discovered that the suspects were unarmed, that they did not have a detonator device on their persons and that there was no bomb in the car.

The Court accepts that the soldiers honestly believed, in the light of the information that they had been given, that it was necessary to shoot the suspects in order to prevent them from detonating a bomb and causing serious loss of life. The actions which they took, in obedience to superior orders, were thus perceived by them as absolutely necessary in order to safeguard innocent lives.

The question arises, however, whether the anti-terrorist operation as a whole was controlled and organised in a manner which respected the requirements of Article 2 and whether the information and instructions given to the soldiers which, in effect, rendered inevitable the use of lethal force, took adequately into consideration the right to life of the three suspects.

The Court first observes that, as appears from the operational order of the Commissioner, it had been the intention of the authorities to arrest the suspects at an appropriate stage. Indeed, evidence was given at the inquest that arrest procedures had been practised by the soldiers before 6 March and that efforts had been made to find a suitable place in Gibraltar to detain the suspects after their arrest.

It may be questioned why the three suspects were not arrested at the border immediately on their arrival in Gibraltar and why, as emerged from the evidence given by Inspector Ullger, the decision was taken not to prevent them from entering Gibraltar if they were believed to be on a bombing mission. Having had advance warning of the terrorists' intentions it would certainly have been possible for the authorities to have mounted an arrest operation. Although surprised at the early arrival of the three suspects, they had a surveillance team at the border and an arrest group nearby. In addition, the Security Services and the Spanish authorities had photographs of the three suspects, knew their names as well as their aliases and would have known what passports to look for.

On this issue, the Government submitted that at that moment there might not have been sufficient evidence to warrant the detention and trial of the suspects. Moreover, to release them, having alerted them to the authorities' state of awareness but leaving them or others free to try again, would obviously increase the risks. Nor could the authorities be sure that those three were the only terrorists they had to deal with or of the manner in which it was proposed to carry out the bombing.

The Court confines itself to observing in this respect that the danger to the population of Gibraltar – which is at the heart of the Government's submissions in this case – in not preventing their entry must be considered to outweigh the possible consequences of having insufficient evidence to warrant their detention and trial. In its view, either the authorities knew that there was no bomb in the car – which the Court has already discounted – or there was a serious miscalculation by those responsible for controlling the operation. As a result, the scene was set in which the fatal shooting, given the intelligence assessments which had been made, was a foreseeable possibility if not a likelihood.

The decision not to stop the three terrorists from entering Gibraltar is thus a relevant factor to take into account under this head.

The Court notes that at the briefing on 5 March attended by Soldiers A, B, C, and D it was considered likely that the attack would be by way of a large car bomb. A number of key assessments were made. In particular, it was thought that the terrorists would not use a blocking car; that the bomb would be detonated by a radio-control device; that the detonation could be effected by the pressing of a button; that it was likely that the suspects would detonate the bomb if challenged; that they would be armed and would be likely to use their arms if confronted.

In the event, all of these crucial assumptions, apart from the terrorists' intentions to carry out an attack, turned out to be erroneous. Nevertheless, as has been demonstrated by the Government, on the basis of their experience in dealing with the IRA, they were all possible hypotheses in a situation where the true facts were unknown and where the authorities operated on the basis of limited intelligence information.

In fact, insufficient allowances appear to have been made for other assumptions. For example, since the bombing was not expected until 8 March when the changing of the guard ceremony was to take place, there was equally the possibility that the three terrorists were on a reconnaissance mission. While this was a factor which was briefly considered, it does not appear to have been regarded as a serious possibility.

In addition, at the briefings or after the suspects had been spotted, it might have been thought unlikely that they would have been prepared to explode the bomb, thereby killing many civilians, as Mr McCann and Ms Farrell strolled towards the border area since this would have increased the risk of detection and capture. It might also have been thought improbable that at that point they would have set up the transmitter in anticipation to enable them to detonate the supposed bomb immediately if confronted.

Moreover, even if allowances are made for the technological skills of the IRA, the description of the detonation device as a "button job" without the qualifications subsequently described by the experts at the inquest, of which the competent authorities must have been aware, over-simplifies the true nature of these devices.

It is further disquieting in this context that the assessment made by Soldier G, after a cursory external examination of the car, that there was a "suspect car bomb" was conveyed to the soldiers, according to their own testimony, as a definite identification that there was such a bomb. It is recalled that while Soldier G had experience in car bombs, it transpired that he was not an expert in radio communications or explosives; and that his assessment that there was a suspect car bomb, based on his observation that the car aerial was out of place, was more in the nature of a report that a bomb could not be ruled out.

In the absence of sufficient allowances being made for alternative possibilities, and the definite reporting of the existence of a car bomb which, according to the assessments that had been made, could be detonated at the press of a button, a series of working hypotheses were conveyed to Soldiers A, B, C and D as certainties, thereby making the use of lethal force almost unavoidable.

However, the failure to make provision for a margin of error must also be considered in combination with the training of the soldiers to continue shooting once they opened fire until the suspect was dead. As noted by the Coroner in his summing-up to the jury at the inquest, all four soldiers shot to kill the suspects. Soldier E testified that it had been discussed with the soldiers that there was an increased chance that they would have to shoot to kill since there would be less time where there was a "button" device. Against this background, the authorities were bound by their obligation to respect the right to life of the suspects to exercise the greatest of care in evaluating the information at their disposal before transmitting it to soldiers whose use of firearms automatically involved shooting to kill.

Although detailed investigation at the inquest into the training received by the soldiers was prevented by the public interest certificates which had been issued, it is not clear whether they had been trained or instructed to assess whether the use of firearms to wound their targets may have been warranted by the specific circumstances that confronted them at the moment of arrest.

Their reflex action in this vital respect lacks the degree of caution in the use of firearms to be expected from law enforcement personnel in a democratic society, even when dealing with dangerous terrorist suspects, and stands in marked contrast to the standard of care reflected in the instructions in the use of firearms by the police which had been drawn to their attention and which emphasised the legal responsibilities of the individual officer in the light of conditions prevailing at the moment of engagement.

This failure by the authorities also suggests a lack of appropriate care in the control and organisation of the arrest operation.

In sum, having regard to the decision not to prevent the suspects from travelling into Gibraltar, to the failure of the authorities to make sufficient allowances for the possibility that their intelligence assessments might, in some respects at least, be erroneous and to the automatic recourse to lethal force when the soldiers opened fire, the Court is not persuaded that the killing of the three terrorists constituted the use of force which was no more than absolutely necessary in defence of persons from unlawful violence within the meaning of Article 2 para. 2 (a) of the Convention.

### Joint Dissenting Opinion

Before turning to the various aspects of the operation which are criticised in the judgment, we would underline three points of a general nature.

First, in undertaking any evaluation of the way in which the operation was organised and controlled, the Court should studiously resist the temptations offered by the benefit of hindsight. The authorities had at the time to plan and make decisions on the basis of incomplete information. Only the suspects knew at all precisely what they intended; and it was part of their purpose, as it had no doubt been part of their training, to ensure that as little as possible of their intentions was revealed. It would be wrong to conclude in retrospect that a particular course would, as things later transpired, have been better than one adopted at the time under the pressures of an ongoing anti-terrorist operation and that the latter course must therefore be regarded as culpably mistaken. It should not be so regarded unless it is established that in the circumstances as they were known at the time another course should have been preferred.

Secondly, the need for the authorities to act within the constraints of the law, while the suspects were operating in a state of mind in which members of the security forces were regarded as legitimate targets and incidental death or injury to civilians as of little consequence, would inevitably give the suspects a tactical advantage which should not be allowed to prevail. The consequences of the explosion of a large bomb in the centre of Gibraltar might well be so devastating that the authorities could not responsibly risk giving the suspects the opportunity to set in train the detonation of such a bomb. Of course the obligation of the United Kingdom under Article 2 para. 1 of the Convention extended to the lives of the suspects as well as to the lives of all the many others, civilian and military, who were present in Gibraltar at the time. But, quite unlike those others, the purpose of the presence of the suspects in Gibraltar was the furtherance of a criminal enterprise which could be expected to have resulted in the loss of many innocent lives if it had been successful. They had chosen to place themselves in a situation where there was a grave danger that an irreconcilable conflict between the two duties might arise.

Thirdly, the Court's evaluation of the conduct of the authorities should throughout take full account of (a) the information which had been received earlier about IRA intentions to mount a major terrorist attack in Gibraltar by an active service unit of three individuals; and (b) the discovery which had been made in Brussels on 21 January 1988 of a car containing a large amount of Semtex explosive and four detonators, with a radio-controlled system – equipment which, taken together, constituted a device familiar in Northern Ireland.

In the light of (a), the decision that members of the SAS should be sent to take part in the operation in response to the request of the Gibraltar Commissioner of Police for military assistance was wholly justifiable. Troops trained in a counter-terrorist role and to operate successfully in small groups would clearly be a suitable choice to meet the threat of an IRA active service unit at large in a densely populated area such as Gibraltar, where there would be an imperative need to limit as far as possible the risk of accidental harm to passers-by.

The detailed operational briefing on 5 March 1988 shows the reasonableness, in the circumstances as known at the time, of the assessments then made. The operational order of the Gibraltar Commissioner of Police, which was drawn up on the same day, expressly proscribed the use of more force than necessary and required any recourse to firearms to be had with care for the safety of persons in the vicinity. It described the intention of the operation as being to protect life; to foil the attempt; to arrest the offenders; and the securing and safe custody of the prisoners.

As regards the particular criticisms of the conduct of the operation which are made in the judgment, foremost among them is the questioning of the decision not to prevent the three suspects from entering Gibraltar. It is pointed out in paragraph 203 that, with the advance information which the authorities possessed and with the resources of personnel at their disposal, it would have been possible for them "to have mounted an arrest operation" at the border.

The judgment does not, however, go on to say that it would have been practicable for the authorities to have arrested and detained the suspects at that stage. Rightly so, in our view, because at that stage there might not be sufficient evidence to warrant their detention and trial. To release them, after having alerted them to the state of readiness of the authorities, would be to increase the risk that they or other IRA members could successfully mount a renewed terrorist attack on Gibraltar. In the circumstances as then known, it was accordingly not "a serious miscalculation" for the authorities to defer the arrest rather than merely stop the suspects at the border and turn them back into Spain.

We further question the conclusion that the use of lethal force was made "almost unavoidable" by failings of the authorities in these respects. Quite apart from any other consideration, this conclusion takes insufficient account of the part played by chance in the eventual outcome. Had it not been for the movements which were made by McCann and Farrell as Soldiers A and B closed on them and which may have been prompted by the completely coincidental sounding of a police car siren, there is every possibility that they would have been seized and arrested without a shot being fired; and had it not been for Savage's actions as Soldiers C and D closed on him, which may have been prompted by the sound of gunfire from the McCann and Farrell incident, there is every possibility that he, too, would have been seized and arrested without resort to shooting.

The implication that the authorities did not exercise sufficient care in evaluating the information at their disposal before transmitting it to soldiers "whose use of firearms automatically involved shooting to kill" appears to be based on no more than "the failure to make provision for a margin of error" to which the beginning of the paragraph refers.

As regards any suggestion that, if an assessment on the issue had been required by their training or instruction to be carried out by the soldiers, shooting to wound might have been considered by them to have been warranted by the circumstances at the time, it must be recalled that those circumstances included a genuine belief on their part that the suspects might be about to detonate a bomb by pressing a button. In that situation, to shoot merely to wound would have been a highly dangerous course: wounding alone might well not have immobilised a suspect and might have left him or her capable of pressing a button if determined to do so.

More generally as regards the training given, there was in fact ample evidence at the inquest to the effect that soldiers (and not only these soldiers) would be trained to respond to a threat such as that which was thought to be posed by the suspects in this case – all of them dangerous terrorists who were believed to be putting many lives at immediate risk – by opening fire once it was clear that the suspect was not desisting; that the intent of the firing would be to immobilise; and that the way to achieve that was to shoot to kill. There was also evidence at the inquest that soldiers would not be accepted for the SAS unless they displayed discretion and thoughtfulness; that they would not go ahead and shoot without thought, nor did they; but they did have to react very fast. In addition, evidence was given that SAS members had in fact been successful in the past in arresting terrorists in the great majority of cases.

We are far from persuaded that the Court has any sufficient basis for concluding, in the face of the evidence at the inquest and the extent of experience in dealing with terrorist activities which the relevant training reflects, that some different and preferable form of training should have been given and that the action of the soldiers in this case "lacks the degree of caution in the use of firearms to be expected of law-enforcement personnel in a democratic society".

Accordingly, we consider the concluding stricture, that there was some failure by the authorities in this regard suggesting a lack of appropriate care in the control and organisation of the arrest operation, to be unjustified.

We would ourselves follow the reasoning and conclusion of the Commission in its comprehensive, painstaking and notably realistic report. Like the Commission, we are satisfied that no failings have been shown in the organisation and control of the operation by the authorities which could justify a conclusion that force was used against the suspects disproportionately to the purpose of defending innocent persons from unlawful violence. We consider that the use of lethal force in this case, however regrettable the need to resort to such force may be, did not exceed what was, in the circumstances as known at the time, "absolutely necessary" for that purpose and did not amount to a breach by the United Kingdom of its obligations under the Convention.

---

## Notes and Comments:

1. Which opinion do you agree with? How should security officials respond to situations where they might have some, but not overwhelming, evidence of an impending terrorist attack?
2. In light of the terrorist attacks that have been carried out since *McCann*, do you think the ECtHR would render the same decision today?

## Providing "Material Support" to Terrorists

One of the vehicles for fighting terrorism is to choke off funding sources. The next two cases focus on the possible legal consequences of providing "material support" to "terrorist organizations." In *Humanitarian Law Project*, a group that seeks to provide training in human rights law and international diplomacy to designated "terrorist organizations" challenges whether this constitutes "material support" under U.S. law. This case is followed by *Flatow v. Islamic Republic of Iran*, which worked a fundamental change in sovereign immunity law in the United States.

## *Humanitarian Law Project et al. v. Holder,*
## 561 U.S. 1 (2010)

CHIEF JUSTICE ROBERTS DELIVERED THE OPINION OF THE COURT

Congress has prohibited the provision of "material support or resources" to certain foreign organizations that engage in terrorist activity. That prohibition is based on a finding that the specified organizations are so tainted by their criminal conduct that any contribution to such an organization facilitates that conduct, from the Antiterrorism and Effective Death Penalty Act of 1996 (AEDPA). The plaintiffs in this litigation seek to provide support to two such organizations. Plaintiffs claim that they seek to facilitate only the lawful, nonviolent purposes of those groups, and that applying the material-support law to prevent them from doing so violates the Constitution.

This litigation concerns 18 U. S. C. §2339B, which makes it a federal crime to knowingly provide material support or resources to a foreign terrorist organization. Congress has amended the definition of "material support or resources" periodically, but at present it is defined as follows:

"The term 'material support or resources' means any property, tangible or intangible, or service, including currency or monetary instruments or financial securities, financial services, lodging, training, expert advice or assistance, safehouses, false documentation or identification, communications equipment, facilities, weapons, lethal substances, explosives, personnel (1 or more individuals who may be or include oneself), and transportation, except medicine or religious materials."

In 1997, the Secretary of State designated 30 groups as foreign terrorist organizations. Two of those groups are the Kurdistan Workers' Party (also known as the Partiya Karkeran Kurdistan (PKK) and the Liberation Tigers of Tamil Eelam (LTTE)). The PKK is an organization founded in 1974 with the aim of establishing an independent Kurdish state in southeastern Turkey. The LTTE is an organization founded in 1976 for the purpose of creating an independent Tamil state in Sri Lanka. The District Court in this action found that the PKK and the LTTE engage in political and humanitarian activities. The Government has presented evidence that both groups have also committed numerous terrorist attacks, some of which have harmed American citizens. The LTTE sought judicial review of its designation as a foreign terrorist organization and the D. C. Circuit upheld that designation. The PKK did not challenge its designation.

Plaintiffs in this litigation are two U. S. citizens and six domestic organizations: the Humanitarian Law Project (HLP) (a human rights organization with consultative status to the United Nations); Ralph Fertig (the HLP's president, and a retired administrative law judge); Nagalingam Jeyalingam (a Tamil physician, born in Sri Lanka and a naturalized U. S. citizen); and five nonprofit groups dedicated to the interests of persons of Tamil descent. In 1998, plaintiffs filed suit in federal court challenging the constitutionality of the material-support statute. Plaintiffs claimed that they wished to provide support for the humanitarian and political activities of the PKK and the LTTE in the form of monetary contributions, other tangible aid, legal training, and political advocacy, but that they could not do so for fear of prosecution under §2339B.

Everyone agrees that the Government's interest in combating terrorism is an urgent objective of the highest order. Plaintiffs' complaint is that the ban on material support, applied to what they wish to do, is not "necessary to further that interest." The objective of combating terrorism does not justify prohibiting their speech, plaintiffs argue, because their support will advance only the legitimate activities of the designated terrorist organizations, not their terrorism.

Whether foreign terrorist organizations meaningfully segregate support of their legitimate activities from support of terrorism is an empirical question. When it enacted §2339B in 1996, Congress made specific findings regarding the serious threat posed by international terrorism. One of those findings explicitly rejects plaintiffs' contention that their support would not further the terrorist activities of the PKK and LTTE: "Foreign organizations that engage in terrorist activity are so tainted by their criminal conduct that *any contribution to such an organization* facilitates that conduct."

Plaintiffs argue that the reference to "any contribution" in this finding meant only monetary support. There is no reason to read the finding to be so limited, particularly because Congress expressly prohibited so much more than monetary support in §2339B. Congress's use of the term "contribution" is best read to reflect a determination that any form of material support furnished to a foreign terrorist organization should be barred, which is precisely what the material-support statute does. Indeed, when Congress enacted §2339B, Congress simultaneously removed an exception that had existed in the previous statute, §2339A, for the provision of material support in the form of humanitarian assistance to persons not directly involved in terrorist activity. That repeal demonstrates that Congress considered and rejected the view that ostensibly peaceful aid would have no harmful effects.

Material support meant to "promote peaceable, lawful conduct," can further terrorism by foreign groups in multiple ways. Material support is a valuable resource by definition. Such support frees up other resources within the organization that may be put to violent ends. It also importantly helps lend legitimacy to foreign terrorist groups – legitimacy that makes it easier for those groups to persist, to recruit members, and to raise funds – all of which facilitate more terrorist attacks. Terrorist organizations do not maintain *organizational* 'firewalls' that would prevent or deter sharing and commingling of support and benefits. Investigators have revealed how terrorist groups systematically conceal their activities behind charitable, social, and political fronts. Indeed, some designated foreign terrorist organizations use social and political components to recruit personnel to carry out terrorist operations, and to provide support to criminal terrorists and their families in aid of such operations.

Money is fungible, and when foreign terrorist organizations that have a dual structure raise funds, they highlight the civilian and humanitarian ends to which such moneys could be put. But there is reason to believe that foreign terrorist organizations do not maintain legitimate *financial* firewalls between those funds raised for civil, nonviolent activities, and those ultimately used to support violent, terrorist operations. Thus, funds raised ostensibly for charitable purposes have in the past been redirected by some terrorist groups to fund the purchase of arms and explosives. There is evidence that the PKK and the LTTE, in particular, have not respected the line between humanitarian and violent activities.

The dissent argues that there is "no natural stopping place" for the proposition that aiding a foreign terrorist organization's lawful activity promotes the terrorist organization as a whole. But Congress has settled on just such a natural stopping place: The statute reaches only material support coordinated with or under the direction of a designated foreign terrorist organization. Independent advocacy that might be viewed as promoting the group's legitimacy is not covered.

Providing foreign terrorist groups with material support in any form also furthers terrorism by straining the United States' relationships with its allies and undermining cooperative efforts between nations to prevent terrorist attacks. We see no reason to question Congress's finding that international cooperation is required for an effective response to terrorism, as demonstrated by the numerous multilateral conventions in force providing universal prosecutive jurisdiction over persons involved in a variety of terrorist acts, including hostage taking, murder of an internationally protected person, and aircraft piracy and sabotage. The material-support statute furthers this international effort by prohibiting aid for foreign terrorist groups that harm the United States' partners abroad. A number of designated foreign terrorist organizations have attacked moderate governments with which the United States has vigorously endeavored to maintain close and friendly relations, and those attacks threaten the social, economic and political stability of such governments. Other foreign terrorist organizations attack our NATO allies, thereby implicating important and sensitive multilateral security arrangements.

In analyzing whether it is possible in practice to distinguish material support for a foreign terrorist group's violent activities and its nonviolent activities, we do not rely exclusively on our own inferences drawn from the record evidence. We have before us an affidavit stating the Executive Branch's conclusion on that question. The State Department informs us that the experience and analysis of the U. S. government agencies charged with combating terrorism strongly support Congress's finding that all contributions to foreign terrorist organizations further their terrorism (looking to similar affidavits to support according weight to national security claims). In the Executive's view, given the purposes, organizational structure, and clandestine nature of foreign terrorist organizations, it is highly likely that any material support to these organizations will ultimately inure to the benefit of their criminal, terrorist functions – regardless of whether such support was ostensibly intended to support non-violent, non-terrorist activities.

Our precedents, old and new, make clear that concerns of national security and foreign relations do not warrant abdication of the judicial role. We do not defer to the Government's reading of the First Amendment, even when such interests are at stake. We are one with the dissent that the Government's "authority and expertise in these matters do not automatically trump the Court's own obligation to secure the protection that the Constitution grants to individuals." But when it comes to collecting evidence and drawing factual inferences in this area, the lack of competence on the part of the courts is marked and respect for the Government's conclusions is appropriate.

One reason for that respect is that national security and foreign policy concerns arise in connection with efforts to confront evolving threats in an area where information can be difficult to obtain and the impact of certain conduct difficult to assess. The dissent slights these real constraints in demanding hard proof – with detail, specific facts, and specific evidence – that plaintiffs' proposed activities will support terrorist attacks. That would be a dangerous requirement. In this context, conclusions must often be based on informed judgment rather than concrete evidence, and that reality affects what we may reasonably insist on from the Government. The material-support statute is, on its face, a preventive measure – it criminalizes not terrorist attacks themselves, but aid that makes the attacks more likely to occur. The Government, when seeking to prevent imminent harms in the context of international affairs and national security, is not required to conclusively link all the pieces in the puzzle before we grant weight to its empirical conclusions.

At bottom, plaintiffs simply disagree with the considered judgment of Congress and the Executive that providing material support to a designated foreign terrorist organization – even seemingly benign support – bolsters the terrorist activities of that organization. That judgment, however, is entitled to significant weight, and we have persuasive evidence before us to sustain it. Given the sensitive interests in national security and foreign affairs at stake, the political branches have adequately substantiated their determination that, to serve the Government's interest in preventing terrorism, it was necessary to prohibit providing material support in the form of training, expert advice, personnel, and services to foreign terrorist groups, even if the supporters meant to promote only the groups' nonviolent ends.

### Justice Breyer, with Whom Justices Ginsburg and Sotomayor Join, Dissenting

Like the Court, and substantially for the reasons it gives, I do not think this statute is unconstitutionally vague. But I cannot agree with the Court's conclusion that the Constitution permits the Government to prosecute the plaintiffs criminally for engaging in coordinated teaching and advocacy furthering the designated organizations' lawful political objectives. In my view, the Government has not met its burden of showing that an interpretation of the statute that would prohibit this speech and association related activity serves the Government's compelling interest in combating terrorism.

Throughout, the majority emphasizes that it would defer strongly to Congress' informed judgment. But here, there is no evidence that Congress has made such a judgment regarding the specific activities at issue in these cases. In any event, whenever the fundamental rights of free speech and assembly are alleged to have been invaded, it must remain open for judicial determination whether there actually did exist at the time a clear danger; whether the danger, if any, was imminent; and whether the evil apprehended was one so substantial as to justify the stringent restriction interposed by the legislature. In such circumstances, the judicial function commands analysis of whether the specific conduct charged falls within the reach of the statute and if so whether the legislation is consonant with the Constitution. Hence, a legislative declaration does not preclude enquiry into the question whether, at the time and under the circumstances, the conditions existed which are essential to validity under the Federal Constitution.

I concede that the Government's expertise in foreign affairs may warrant deference in respect to many matters, e.g., our relations with Turkey. But it remains for this Court to decide whether the Government has shown that such an interest justifies criminalizing speech activity otherwise protected by the First Amendment. And the fact that other nations may like us less for granting that protection cannot in and of itself carry the day.

In sum, these cases require us to consider how to apply the First Amendment where national security interests are at stake. When deciding such cases, courts are aware and must respect the fact that the Constitution entrusts to the Executive and Legislative Branches the power to provide for the national defense, and that it grants particular authority to the President in matters of foreign affairs. Nonetheless, this Court has also made clear that authority and expertise in these matters do not automatically trump the Court's own obligation to secure the protection that the Constitution grants to individuals. "We have long since made clear that a state of war is not a blank check . . . when it comes to the rights of this Nation's citizens." In these cases, for the reasons I have stated, I believe the Court has failed to examine the Government's justifications with sufficient care. It has failed to insist upon specific evidence, rather than general assertion. It has failed to require tailoring of means to fit compelling ends. And ultimately it deprives the individuals before us of the protection that the First Amendment demands.

---

## Note and Comments:

1. Do you agree with the majority opinion that aid to "terrorist" organizations of virtually any kind would (or could) further the nefarious activities of this organization? Or do you think that the Court has gone too far in its ruling that even such things as providing training in international human rights law constitutes "material support"?

### The "Terrorism" Exception to Sovereign Immunity

Sovereign immunity is based on the principle of the sovereign equality of all states and it has been one of the foundational principles in all international law (Chapter 10). On the other hand, there is no international legal standard as such. Rather, each state determines under its own (domestic) law the extent to which it will grant immunity to other states. Historically, states enjoyed absolute immunity. However, beginning in the 20th century, sovereign immunity has become more restrictive. One reason for this is that states are increasingly engaged in commercial activities and the thought is that they should not receive protection that is not afforded private concerns carrying out the same functions. Or to put this in concrete terms, why should a state-run airline such as Alitalia receive sovereign immunity protection but Delta airlines does not?

But the post-World War II human rights revolution is another reason why sovereign immunity has become (somewhat) more limited. The principle behind this approach is that declaring that all individuals have certain specified rights – but then allowing offending states to avoid being held to account for violating those rights – was inconsistent at best and hypocritical at worst.

Consider sovereign immunity under U.S. law. Until 1952 the United States followed the "absolute immunity" standard. The leading case was the *Schooner Exchange v. M'Faddon* (1812) where U.S. citizens who had had their ship confiscated by the French navy were trying to reclaim it when it was docked in an American port. However, their suit against France was dismissed on the basis of sovereign immunity. In oft-quoted language, Chief Justice Marshall ruled that no foreign state could be forced to stand before a tribunal in another state.

> One sovereign being in no respect amenable to another; and being bound by obligations of the highest character not to degrade the dignity of his nation, by placing himself or its sovereign rights within the jurisdiction of another, can be supposed to enter a foreign territory only under an express license, or in the confidence that the immunities belonging to his independent sovereign station, though not expressly stipulated, are reserved by implication, and will be extended to him.

The first seeds of change in U.S. law took place in 1952 by means of the so-called Tate Letter, from the State Department's Acting Legal Adviser Jack B. Tate, whereby the United States adopted the restrictive approach to sovereign immunity: "[T]he immunity of the sovereign is recognized with regard to sovereign or public acts (*jure imperii*) of a state, but not with respect to private acts (*jure gestionis*)." However, without statutory guidance, the executive branch was in a position to dictate to the judicial branch when and if sovereign immunity was to be granted.

Because of the constitutional infirmities inherent in this arrangement, in 1976 Congress passed the *Foreign Sovereign Immunity Act* (FSIA), which remains the governing law to this date.

Under the FSIA, foreign states receive sovereign immunity in U.S. courts subject to the following exceptions: 1) waiver of immunity, 2) the foreign state was engaged in a commercial activity in the United States, 3) property taken in violation of international law, 4) rights to property in the U.S. are acquired by succession or gift, 5) tortious acts committed in the United States, and 6) enforcement of an arbitration agreement with or for a private party.

In 1996, a seventh exception was added, commonly referred to as the "terrorism" exception. However, this is a bit misleading. For one thing, only U.S. citizens can bring a cause of action on the basis of this exception. This stands in contrast to the *Alien Tort Statute*, under which foreign nationals could bring suit against individuals who had violated the "law of nations" and who were found within the territorial boundaries of the United States. A second thing to note is which states fall under the "state sponsors of terrorism" exception. One might think that Saudi Arabia – the home country of most of the 9/11 hijackers – would be on this list, but that is incorrect. Instead, the legislation specifies that only those countries listed by the U.S. State Department as "state sponsors of terrorism" will be denied sovereign immunity protection. The countries listed have changed over time and at present there are only three states: Iran, Sudan, and Syria. At no time was Saudi Arabia ever included as a "state sponsor of terror."

The *Flatow* case was not only the first case to be decided under the "state sponsors of terrorism" legislation, but arguably it was the driving force behind the amendment, as indicated by the retroactive application of the act to include the sad killing of an American exchange student, Alisa Flatow, while riding a bus in Israel. The Shaqiqi faction of the Palestine Islamic Jihad, a group that Iran had provided approximately $2 million to each year, claimed responsibility for the attack. The present suit is being brought against the state of Iran based on its sponsorship of the group that carried out the bombing.

---

## *Flatow v. Islamic Republic of Iran*, 999 F.Supp. 1 (D.D.C. 1999)

As this action is brought against a foreign state, its intelligence service acting as its agent, and three of its officials, acting in their official capacity, the Foreign Sovereign Immunities Act of 1976, 28 U.S.C. §§ 1602–1611 *et seq.* ["FSIA"], as amended, controls this action.

Although the events complained of herein occurred more than a year prior to the enactment of the Antiterrorism and Effective Death Penalty Act of 1996, 28 U.S.C. § 1605(a)(7) provides a basis for subject matter jurisdiction. Congress has expressly directed the retroactive application of 28 U.S.C. § 1605(a)(7) in order to further a comprehensive counterterrorism initiative by the legislative branch of government:

> The amendments made by this subtitle shall apply to any cause of action arising before, on or after the date of the enactment of this Act [April 24, 1996].

This action is brought pursuant to a new exception to the FSIA which was created as part of a federal initiative to combat international terrorism, the Antiterrorism and Effective Death Penalty Act of 1996. The state sponsored terrorism provisions represent a sea change in the United States' approach to foreign sovereign immunity. For the first time, Congress has expressly created an exception to immunity designed to influence the sovereign conduct of foreign states and affect the substantive law of liability for non-immune acts.

The state-sponsored terrorism provision adopts the definition of "provid[ing] material support or resources" set forth in the federal criminal code. 28 U.S.C. § 1605(a)(7) incorporates 18 U.S.C. § 2339A(a) by reference, which provides that:

> material support or resources means currency or other financial securities, financial services, lodging, training, safehouses, false documentation or identification, communications equipment, facilities, weapons, lethal substances, explosives, personnel, transportation, and other physical assets, but does not include humanitarian assistance to persons not directly involved in such violations.

This Court concludes that the routine provision of financial assistance to a terrorist group in support of its terrorist activities constitutes "providing material support or resources" for a terrorist act within the meaning of 28 U.S.C. § 1605(a)(7). Furthermore, as nothing in 18 U.S.C. § 2339A or 28 U.S.C. § 1605(a)(7) indicates otherwise, this Court also concludes that a plaintiff need not establish that the material support or resources provided by a foreign state for a terrorist act contributed directly to the act from which his claim arises in order to satisfy 28 U.S.C. § 1605(a)(7)'s statutory requirements for subject matter jurisdiction. Sponsorship of a terrorist group which causes the personal injury or death of a United States national alone is sufficient to invoke jurisdiction.

---

**Notes and Comments:**

1. What do you make of the doctrine of foreign sovereign immunity? In your view, when should states enjoy sovereign immunity protection – if ever – and when should this be denied?
2. Is there any indication that the Iranian government exercised any form of "effective control" over the recipients of the funding?
3. The "Flatow Amendment" allows for a cause of action against "an official, employee, or agent of a foreign state" and not against the foreign state itself and in at least one case, *Cicippio-Puleo v. Iran*, the D.C. Circuit Court of Appeals limited the claims in such manner.

---

The Flatow family won a default judgment against Iran, but then faced the problem of executing on this. In 2000, the Clinton administration agreed to pay off the claims of the Flatow family and other U.S. nationals who also had judgment claims against Iran, but with the expressed view that the U.S. Treasury would be reimbursed from Iranian assets that were located in the United States. However, the U.S. Treasury was never reimbursed, something which only came to light after the Obama administration entered into an agreement with Iran on halting that country's nuclear weapons program.

### Suing for September 11

Victims (and their decedents) of the 9/11 attacks have sought to hold states such as Saudi Arabia responsible for their financial support of the hijackers as well as for the training they received. One of the exceptions for sovereign immunity under the *Foreign Sovereign Immunity Act* (FSIA) is for "tortious" acts by a foreign state that are committed in the United States. It was this exception to foreign sovereign immunity that was relied upon in *Letelier v. Chile* (1980) involving a car bombing at Sheridan Circle in Washington D.C. that killed Orlando Letelier, a former Chilean diplomat in the Allende government who was in exile in the United States following the 1973 coup that brought Augusto Pinochet to power.

---

## *In re Terrorists Attacks IV,* 134 F. Supp. 3d 774 (S.D.N.Y. 2015)

This case involves claims by families and estates of the victims of the September 11, 2001 terrorist attacks, individuals injured by the attacks, and various commercial entities that incurred damages and losses as a result of the attacks. The moving defendants are the Kingdom of Saudi Arabia ("Saudi Arabia") and the Saudi High Commission for Relief of Bosnia & Herzegovina ("SHC") (collectively, "Defendants"). Plaintiffs allege that agents and employees of the Saudi government bear responsibility for the September 11, 2001 attacks because they directly and knowingly assisted the hijackers and plotters who carried out the attacks. They allege further that al Qaeda's development into a terrorist organization was fueled principally by financial and operational support from Saudi government "da'awa organizations" (described by Defendants as "charities"), including the SHC.

Defendants move this Court to dismiss Plaintiffs' Complaint for lack of subject matter jurisdiction on the basis that Defendants are immune from suit under the Foreign Sovereign Immunities Act ("FSIA").

With respect to the claims against Saudi Arabia and the SHC, the parties agree that the only potentially applicable exception to immunity is the noncommercial tort exception. See 28 U.S.C. § 1605(a)(5). The FSIA's noncommercial tort exception reads in pertinent part:

(a) A foreign state shall not be immune from the jurisdiction of courts of the United States or of the States in any case- (5) . . . in which money damages are sought against a foreign state for personal injury or death, or damage to or loss of property, occurring in the United States and caused by the tortious act or omission of that foreign state or of any official or employee of that foreign state while acting within the scope of his office or employment; except this paragraph shall not apply to (A) any claim based upon the exercise or performance or the failure to exercise or perform a discretionary function regardless of whether the discretion be abused. . . .

For the noncommercial tort exception to apply, inter alia, (1) "the 'entire tort' must be committed in the United States," *In re Terrorist Attacks (SJRC)*, and (2) the tortious act or omission cannot be a "discretionary function."

### THE ENTIRE TORT RULE

The noncommercial tort exception "covers only torts occurring within the territorial jurisdiction of the United States." *Amerada Hess Shipping Corp.*, 488 U.S. at 441. In April 2013, the Second Circuit dismissed two Saudi instrumentalities, the Saudi Joint Relief Committee ("SJRC") and the Saudi Red Crescent Society ("SRC"), from this multidistrict litigation based on Plaintiffs' failure to allege facts that satisfy the entire tort rule. The Second Circuit held:

Although the September 11, 2001 attacks constitute a 'tort,' the SJRC and the SRC are not alleged to have participated in that 'tort.' Instead, the 'torts' allegedly committed by the SJRC and the SRC only involve giving money and aid to purported charities that supported al Qaeda. The September 11, 2001 attacks thus are distinct and separate from the 'torts' allegedly committed by the SJRC and the SRC.

Plaintiffs did not allege that "any employees of the SJRC or SRC – or anyone controlled by these entities – committed a tortious act in the United States." The Second Circuit held that the SJRC's and SRC's tortious activities – donating money to purported al Qaeda supporters – occurred abroad and, therefore, did not satisfy the entire tort rule.

### THE DISCRETIONARY FUNCTION EXCLUSION

The discretionary function exclusion to the FSIA's noncommercial tort exception "provides that a foreign sovereign retains immunity under the FSIA even if its act or omission is deemed to be tortious if the act is 'based upon the exercise or performance or the failure to exercise or perform a discretionary function regardless of whether the discretion [is] abused.'" This "'exception to the exception' . . . preserves the immunity of a sovereign nation when it would otherwise be abrogated by the tortious activity exception 'if two conditions are met: (1) the acts alleged to be negligent must be discretionary, in that they involve an element of judgment or choice and are not compelled by statute or regulation, and (2) the judgment or choice in question must be grounded in considerations of public policy or susceptible to policy analysis.'" "The discretionary function rule is designed to prevent judicial second-guessing of decisions grounded in social, economic, and political policy of a foreign state through the medium of an action in tort."

Judge Casey ruled in 2005 that the FSIA's tort exception does not provide jurisdiction over Plaintiffs' claims against Saudi Arabia and the SHC because Defendants' alleged actions involved the exercise of policy discretion. He held that "Saudi Arabia's treatment of and decisions to support Islamic charities are purely planning level 'decisions grounded in social, economic, and political policy.'" With respect to the SHC, Judge Casey held:

SHC offers undisputed evidence that all decisions regarding the distribution of humanitarian relief funds were within the sole discretion of its Chairman Prince Salman and the advisors he selected. Further, SHC was guided by the Kingdom's policies regarding Bosnia-Herzegovina in making its funding determinations. Accordingly, SHC's alleged misuse of funds and/or inadequate record-keeping – even if it resulted in the funds going to terrorists – was the result of a discretionary function and cannot be the basis for overcoming SHC's immunity.

Thus, both defendants were dismissed on the ground that the discretionary function exclusion barred application of the noncommercial tort exception.

---

**Notes and Comments:**

1. Where does the notion of the "entire tort" come from? Would you read the statute the same way as the court does?

2. Is this case consistent with the "material support" cases – *Holder* and *Flatow* in particular? Could one make the argument that both the Saudi state and various charitable organizations associated with the state provided "material support" to the September 11 hijackers?

3. Another example of the "entire tort" rule being applied was in *John Doe (Also Known as Kidane) v. Ethiopia* (D.C. Cir. 2017) where the plaintiff charged that the Ethiopian government had sent him an email attachment that he opened that contained FinSpy, which the government then used to spy on him. The Court of Appeals for the District of Columbia dismissed the case on the basis that the spying operation originated in Ethiopia and thus the "entire tort" did not occur in the United States. Do you agree with this holding?

4. In *Jesner v. Arab Bank* (2018) (Chapter 8), the U.S. Supreme Court ruled that without congressional authority, the *Alien Tort Statute* could not serve as a basis of a suit against a corporation. In this case, it was alleged that the Arab Bank, a Jordanian institution, was funneling money to terrorist organizations. Has the executive branch now lost an important tool in the fight against international terrorism?

---

**Box 1.4: Justice Against Sponsors of Terrorism Act (JASTA)**

A few months after *In re Terrorist Attacks on September 11, 2001* was handed down, Congress passed the *Justice Against Sponsors of Terrorism Act (JASTA)*, overriding President Obama's veto. JASTA makes several major changes to U.S. sovereign immunity law. The first is that it broadens the existing "terrorism" exception beyond countries that are listed as "state sponsors of terrorism." In addition, it eliminates the "entire tort" rule. After JASTA, U.S. citizens can sue foreign countries and their officials in U.S. courts under the Anti-Terrorism Act for an "act of international terrorism . . . regardless [of] where the tortious act or acts of the foreign state occurred." Note, however, that the state cannot be sued on the basis of omissions or where the state was simply negligent in its actions.

The second change effectuated by JASTA was to expand civil liability for organizations. Prior to JASTA, most U.S. courts held that the ATA did not permit aiding and abetting or civil conspiracy liability, or what was often called "secondary liability." JASTA specifically authorizes suits against any person who: "aids and abets, by knowingly providing substantial assistance, or who conspires with the person who committed such an act of international terrorism." Note that the definition of "person" subject to liability includes "corporations, companies, associations, firms, partnerships, societies, and joint stock companies, as well as individuals."

Although JASTA did not single out any particular state, it was commonly accepted that the legislation was aimed squarely at Saudi Arabia, which responded in kind with threats of economic retaliation if the bill became law. What will ensue from this is not evident at this time. In October 2016, U.S. Secretary of State John Kerry and Saudi Foreign Minister Adel al-Jubeir discussed ways in which to fix problems associated with JASTA. The position of the Trump administration is also unclear. As a candidate, Trump sharply criticized President Obama's veto of JASTA. However, Saudi Arabia has been pressing the Trump administration to modify, if not abandon, the legislation (Schnably 2017).

In the first judicial ruling on this matter on March 28, 2018, the U.S. District Court for the Southern District of New York denied Saudi Arabia's motion to dismiss a lawsuit for alleged involvement in the September 11 attacks (*In Re Terrorist Attacks on September 11, 2001* (03-MDL-1570 (GBD). One question to consider is whether JASTA is consistent with international law. For one thing, only the United States and Canada have enacted legislation such as this. On the other hand, neither exception has provoked the kind of widespread protests from other states that one might expect in the case of a clear violation of customary international law.

---

### Box 1.5: International Law at the Movies: Mass Surveillance

Edward Snowden is certainly the name most associated with international surveillance. It was Snowden who in 2013 flew to Hong Kong and met with journalists Glenn Greenwald, Ewen MacAskill, and Laura Poitras, the latter who went on to direct the documentary *Citizenfour* (2014). Oliver Stone made his own attempt to tell this story in the feature film *Snowden* (2016).

Hollywood has also depicted a world with virtually no privacy. One of the earliest efforts was the spy thriller *Enemy of the State* (1998) starring Will Smith. *Minority Report* (2002) with Tom Cruise depicts a world where individuals who have nothing more than a "criminal mind" can be arrested and convicted. And *Spectre* (2015) is a James Bond flick involving a criminal syndicate attempting to hijack an international surveillance system.

*(Continued)*

## Box 1.5: Continued

> Finally, mention should be made of two art-house films that deal with issues of surveillance and privacy. The first is the outstanding German film *The Lives of Others* (2006), which depicts the spying of the East German secret police (Stasi) before the fall of Berlin Wall. The other is *V for Vendetta* (2005), a film that already enjoys cult status about a future where we are all being watched – and the rebellion to set mankind free!

## Surveillance and Internet Censorship

The "global war on terrorism" has brought forward unprecedented levels of governmental secrecy and surveillance. Consider the actions of two individuals – traitors to some; heroes to others. Julian Assange is the founder Wikileaks who publicly disseminated foreign intelligence unfavorable to the United States. Until his arrest in April 2019, Assange had been living in the Ecuadorian embassy in London for seven years.

### Box 1.6: The Right to Privacy Under International Law

Privacy is a human right set forth in both the Universal Declaration of Human Rights (Art. 12) and the International Covenant on Civil and Political Rights (Art. 17). The right to privacy is not only vital in its own right, but also because of the way it serves to protect other human rights. As expressed by the U.N. High Commissioner for Human Rights in the report *The Right to Privacy in the Digital Age*:

> While the mandate for the present report focused on the right to privacy, it should be understood that other rights also may be affected by mass surveillance, the interception of digital communications and the collection of personal data. These include the rights to freedom of opinion and expression, and to seek, receive and impart information; to freedom of peaceable assembly and association; and to family life – rights all linked closely with the right to privacy and, increasingly, exercised through digital media.

(par 14)

Edward Snowden's revelations of the extent of National Security Agency (NSA) spying sent shock waves throughout the world. Among the things that have been established thus far are the following: the NSA has conducted a massive metadata surveillance program that catalogs every single phone call and email sent or received by United States citizens; and it has wiretapped the offices of dozens of foreign leaders (including some of those "friendly" to the United States, most notably Chancellor Angela Merkel of Germany), as well as ordinary citizens of other countries.

---

### Box 1.7: NSA Surveillance: Where Is International Law?

The National Security Agency (NSA) engages in two different types (at least) of surveillance. One is traditional wiretapping. After revelations of abuses by U.S. spy agencies, in 1978 Congress passed the *Foreign Intelligence Surveillance Act* (FISA), which mandated that a warrant be obtained by the executive prior to all wiretapping, domestic and foreign alike. To accomplish this, the Act created the Foreign Intelligence Surveillance Court (FISC), made up of 11 sitting federal judges selected by the Chief Justice of the U.S. Supreme Court. Is the FSIC a rubber stamp? To use 2012 as an example, of the 1,856 warrant requests that year, all but one was granted!

Following the events of September 11, the Bush administration issued a private executive order instituting the Terrorist Surveillance Program (TSP), which limited the warrant requirement to communications that were solely domestic or those involving U.S. nationals in foreign lands. The TSP program was unveiled to public scrutiny by *The New York Times* in December 2005, and despite heavy criticism, Congress has continued to reauthorize the program.

**Photo 1.4** Former U.S. Government Analyst Edward Snowden

*Source:* © Kyodo

To an American audience at least, Edward Snowden's most stunning revelation was that security officials were gathering information on every phone call and every email sent by U.S. nationals in what is commonly referred to as the "metadata" program. Although President Obama defended the program on the grounds that "no one is listening to your calls," Snowden has said that he and other analysts did so whenever they would want to do so.

In short, the U.S. government has been able to wiretap the phone conversations (and perhaps more than that) of foreign nationals (and U.S. nationals so long as they

*(Continued)*

**Box 1.7: Continued**

are not the primary target) and to collect and store information on all phone calls and all emails sent by U.S. nationals – all in the name of engaging in the "war on terrorism." Where is international law in all this? Or perhaps the better question is to ask where international law should be in all this?

In the case that follows, a challenge is made as to whether Facebook in Ireland can lawfully transfer information to Facebook in the United States in light of the U.S. surveillance practices disclosed by Snowden.

---

## Maximillian Schrems v. Data Protection Commissioner, European Union Court of Justice, 2015

This request for a preliminary ruling relates to the protection of individuals with regard to the processing of personal data and the free movement of such data. The request has been made in proceedings between Mr Schrems and the Data Protection Commissioner ('the Commissioner') concerning the latter's refusal to investigate a complaint made by Mr Schrems regarding the fact that Facebook Ireland Ltd ('Facebook Ireland') transfers the personal data of its users to the United States of America and keeps it on servers located in that country.

DATA PROTECTION DIRECTIVE 95/46

Article 1

### Object of the Directive

1. In accordance with this Directive, Member States shall protect the fundamental rights and freedoms of natural persons, and in particular their right to privacy with respect to the processing of personal data.

Article 25

### Principles

1. The Member States shall provide that the transfer to a third country of personal data which are undergoing processing or are intended for processing after transfer may take place only if, without prejudice to compliance with the national provisions adopted pursuant to the other provisions of this Directive, the third country in question ensures an adequate level of protection.
2. The adequacy of the level of protection afforded by a third country shall be assessed in the light of all the circumstances surrounding a data transfer operation or set of data transfer operations; particular consideration shall be given to the nature of the data, the purpose and duration of the proposed processing operation or operations, the country of origin and country of final destination, the rules of law, both general and sectoral, in force in the third country in ques-

tion and the professional rules and security measures which are complied with in that country.

### The Dispute in the Main Proceedings and the Questions Referred for a Preliminary Ruling

Mr Schrems, an Austrian national residing in Austria, has been a user of the Facebook social network ('Facebook') since 2008.

Any person residing in the European Union who wishes to use Facebook is required to conclude, at the time of his registration, a contract with Facebook Ireland, a subsidiary of Facebook Inc. which is itself established in the United States. Some or all of the personal data of Facebook Ireland's users who reside in the European Union is transferred to servers belonging to Facebook Inc. that are located in the United States, where it undergoes processing.

On 25 June 2013 Mr Schrems made a complaint to the Commissioner by which he in essence asked the latter to exercise his statutory powers by prohibiting Facebook Ireland from transferring his personal data to the United States. He contended in his complaint that the law and practice in force in that country did not ensure adequate protection of the personal data held in its territory against the surveillance activities that were engaged in there by the public authorities. Mr Schrems referred in this regard to the revelations made by Edward Snowden concerning the activities of the United States intelligence services, in particular those of the National Security Agency ('the NSA').

Since the Commissioner took the view that he was not required to investigate the matters raised by Mr Schrems in the complaint, he rejected it as unfounded. The Commissioner considered that there was no evidence that Mr Schrems' personal data had been accessed by the NSA.

Mr Schrems brought an action before the [Irish] High Court challenging the decision at issue in the main proceedings. After considering the evidence adduced by the parties to the main proceedings, the High Court found that the electronic surveillance and interception of personal data transferred from the European Union to the United States serve necessary and indispensable objectives in the public interest. However, it added that the revelations made by Edward Snowden had demonstrated a 'significant over-reach' on the part of the NSA and other federal agencies.

According to the High Court, Union citizens have no effective right to be heard. Oversight of the intelligence services' actions is carried out within the framework of an *ex parte* and secret procedure. Once the personal data has been transferred to the United States, it is capable of being accessed by the NSA and other federal agencies, such as the Federal Bureau of Investigation (FBI), in the course of the indiscriminate surveillance and interception carried out by them on a large scale.

The High Court stated that Irish law precludes the transfer of personal data outside national territory save where the third country ensures an adequate level of protection for privacy and fundamental rights and freedoms. The importance of the rights to privacy and to inviolability of the dwelling, which are guaranteed by the Irish Constitution, requires that any interference with those rights be proportionate and in accordance with the law.

The High Court held that the mass and undifferentiated accessing of personal data is clearly contrary to the principle of proportionality and the fundamental values protected by the Irish Constitution. In order for interception of electronic communications to be regarded as consistent with the Irish Constitution, it would be necessary to demonstrate that the interception is targeted, that the surveillance of certain persons or groups of persons is objectively justified in the interests of national security or the suppression of crime and that there are appropriate and verifiable safeguards. Thus, according to the High Court, if the main proceedings were to be disposed of on the basis of Irish law alone, it would then have to be found that, given the existence of a serious doubt as to whether the United States ensures an adequate level of protection of personal data, the Commissioner should have proceeded to investigate the matters raised by Mr Schrems in his complaint and that the Commissioner was wrong in rejecting the complaint.

It is clear from the express wording of Article 25(6) of Directive 95/46 that it is the legal order of the third country covered by the Commission decision that must ensure an adequate level of protection.

Accordingly, when examining the level of protection afforded by a third country, the Commission is obliged to assess the content of the applicable rules in that country resulting from its domestic law or international commitments and the practice designed to ensure compliance with those rules.

Also, in the light of the fact that the level of protection ensured by a third country is liable to change, it is incumbent upon the Commission to check periodically whether the finding relating to the adequacy of the level of protection ensured by the third country in question is still factually and legally justified. Such a check is required, in any event, when evidence gives rise to a doubt in that regard.

As has been found in the present judgment, in order for the Commission to adopt a decision pursuant to Article 25(6) of Directive 95/46, it must find, duly stating reasons, that the third country concerned in fact ensures, by reason of its domestic law or its international commitments, a level of protection of fundamental rights essentially equivalent to that guaranteed in the EU legal order, a level that is apparent in particular from the preceding paragraphs of the present judgment.

However, the Commission did not state that the United States in fact 'ensures' an adequate level of protection by reason of its domestic law or its international commitments.

It is apparent the national supervisory authorities must be able to examine, with complete independence, any claim concerning the protection of a person's rights and freedoms in regard to the processing of personal data relating to him. That is in particular the case where, in bringing such a claim, that person raises questions regarding the compatibility of a Commission decision with the protection of the privacy and of the fundamental rights and freedoms of individuals.

---

## Notes and Comments:

1. International surveillance operations challenge three foundational principles of international law. One is *state sovereignty* on the basis that surveillance conducted by one state in another state is, by definition, an interference in the affairs of this other state. The second is *territory*. What does territory mean in an age when an email sent to a colleague who is literally across the hall appears on this person's computer almost instantly – but has been routed through the "territory" of one or more other countries? The third is *jurisdiction*. If the National Security Agency (NSA) has monitored the phone conversations of 60 million Spanish citizens, as Edward Snowden has claimed, does this then mean that every

one of these Spanish nationals was thereby within the "jurisdiction" of the United States (Gibney 2017)?

2. In *Google v. Spain* – better known as the "right to be forgotten" case – the European Court of Justice ruled that European citizens have a right to demand that internet search engines, such as Google, remove private information when this information is no longer relevant.

3. On May 25, 2018, the General Data Protection Regulation (GDPR) went into effect, which seeks to protect European Union citizens from privacy and data breaches. Arguably, the biggest change is the move away from a strictly territorial approach, as the GDPR applies to all companies that process the personal data of those within the EU regardless of the company's physical location.

4. As a segue to the topic of "state terror," Google shut down its Chinese operations in 2010 after it discovered it was the target of a cyberattack from within the country, and it also found that the Gmail accounts of a number of Chinese human rights activists had been hacked. When it first established its services in that country, Google abided by the Chinese government's censorship policies. However, following the 2010 cyberattack, the company refused to further comply with the government's requests to filter its search results and instead directed all Chinese traffic to its uncensored Hong Kong version of its search engine. The problem is that Google then became inaccessible to most Chinese users.

Given that twice as many people use the internet in China as there are residents in the United States, Google is losing out on a lucrative market, and it now has plans to begin operations there again in the near future. Note that it is not uncommon for the major internet companies to abide by local practices – practices that amount to censorship, at least according to Western (and particularly U.S.) standards. As a way of providing some transparency, Google, Facebook, and Twitter all publish annual reports detailing the number and type of content-takedowns or user-information requests from each country they operate in.

Is internet censorship something that should be handled by international law? Or perhaps the better question is this: is internet censorship something that could be handled by international law?

## State Terror

We will close this chapter by briefly examining a different kind of "terror," namely, terror carried out by the state against its own population in the form of disappearances, summary executions, and torture. Somehow, these forms of terror receive much less media attention than what is now more commonly referred to as "terrorism," although vastly more people are killed or injured by the harmful practices of their own governments than they are by those who are designated as "terrorists."

One of the landmark rulings in this realm is the *Velasquez Rodriguez* case handed down by the Inter-American Court of Human Rights. The basis of the case is the claim that Angel Manfredo Velasquez Rodriguez had been disappeared by Honduran authorities or those associated with the Honduran government. Velasquez Rodriguez was the first contentious case decided by the IACHR by an individual alleging systematic state terror.

---

## *Velasquez Rodriguez v. Honduras*, IACtHR (1988)

Before weighing the evidence, the Court must address some questions regarding the burden of proof and the general criteria considered in its evaluation and finding of the facts in the instant proceeding.

Because the Commission is accusing the Government of the disappearance of Manfredo Velásquez, it, in principle, should bear the burden of proving the facts underlying its petition.

The Commission's argument relies upon the proposition that the policy of disappearances, supported or tolerated by the Government, is designed to conceal and destroy evidence of disappearances. When the existence of such a policy or practice has been shown, the disappearance of a particular individual may be proved through circumstantial or indirect evidence or by logical inference. Otherwise, it would be impossible to prove that an individual has been disappeared.

The Government did not object to the Commission's approach. Nevertheless, it argued that neither the existence of a practice of disappearances in Honduras nor the participation of Honduran officials in the alleged disappearance of Manfredo Velásquez had been proven.

The Court finds no reason to consider the Commission's argument inadmissible. If it can be shown that there was an official practice of disappearances in Honduras, carried out by the Government or at least tolerated by it, and if the disappearance of Manfredo Velásquez can be linked to that practice, the Commission's allegations will have been proven to the Court's satisfaction, so long as the evidence presented on both points meets the standard of proof required in cases such as this.

The Court cannot ignore the special seriousness of finding that a State Party to the Convention has carried out or has tolerated a practice of disappearances in its territory. This requires the Court to apply a standard of proof which considers the seriousness of the charge and which, notwithstanding what has already been said, is capable of establishing the truth of the allegations in a convincing manner.

The practice of international and domestic courts shows that direct evidence, whether testimonial or documentary, is not the only type of evidence that may be legitimately considered in reaching a decision. Circumstantial evidence, indicia, and presumptions may be considered, so long as they lead to conclusions consistent with the facts.

Circumstantial or presumptive evidence is especially important in allegations of disappearances, because this type of repression is characterized by an attempt to suppress all information about the kidnapping or the whereabouts and fate of the victim.

The international protection of human rights should not be confused with criminal justice. States do not appear before the Court as defendants in a criminal action. The objective of international human rights law is not to punish those individuals who are guilty of violations, but rather to protect the victims and to provide for the reparation of damages resulting from the acts of the States responsible.

The State controls the means to verify acts occurring within its territory. Although the Commission has investigatory powers, it cannot exercise them within a State's jurisdiction unless it has the cooperation of that State.

The Court now turns to the relevant facts that it finds to have been proven. They are as follows:

a. During the period 1981 to 1984, 100 to 150 persons disappeared in the Republic of Honduras, and many were never heard from again.

b. Those disappearances followed a similar pattern, beginning with the kidnapping of the victims by force, often in broad daylight and in public places, by armed men in civilian clothes and disguises, who acted with apparent impunity and who used vehicles without any official identification, with tinted windows and with false license plates or no plates.

c. It was public and notorious knowledge in Honduras that the kidnappings were carried out by military personnel or the police, or persons acting under their orders.

d. The disappearances were carried out in a systematic manner, regarding which the Court considers the following circumstances particularly relevant:

i. The victims were usually persons whom Honduran officials considered dangerous to State security. In addition, the victims had usually been under surveillance for long periods of time.

ii. The arms employed were reserved for the official use of the military and police, and the vehicles used had tinted glass, which requires special official authorization. In some cases, Government agents carried out the detentions openly and without any pretense or disguise; in others, government agents had cleared the areas where the kidnappings were to take place and, on at least one occasion, when government agents stopped the kidnappers they were allowed to continue freely on their way after showing their identification.

iii. The kidnappers blindfolded the victims, took them to secret, unofficial detention centers and moved them from one center to another. They interrogated the victims and subjected them to cruel and humiliating treatment and torture. Some were ultimately murdered and their bodies were buried in clandestine cemeteries.

iv. When queried by relatives, lawyers and persons or entities interested in the protection of human rights, or by judges charged with executing writs of HABEAS corpus, the authorities systematically denied any knowledge of the detentions or the whereabouts or fate of the victims. That attitude was seen even in the cases of persons who later reappeared in the hands of the same authorities who had systematically denied holding them or knowing their fate.

v. Military and police officials as well as those from the Executive and Judicial Branches either denied the disappearances or were incapable of preventing or investigating them, punishing those responsible, or helping those interested discover the whereabouts and fate of the victims or the location of their remains. The investigative committees created by the Government and the Armed Forces did not produce any results. The judicial proceedings brought were processed slowly with a clear lack of interest and some were ultimately dismissed

Disappearances are not new in the history of human rights violations. However, their systematic and repeated nature and their use not only for causing certain individuals to disappear, either briefly or permanently, but also as a means of creating a general state of anguish, insecurity and fear, is a recent phenomenon. Although this practice exists virtually worldwide, it has occurred with exceptional intensity in Latin America in the last few years.

Without question, the State has the right and duty to guarantee its security. It is also indisputable that all societies suffer some deficiencies in their legal orders. However, regardless of the seriousness of certain actions and the culpability of the perpetrators of certain crimes, the power of the State is not unlimited, nor may the State resort to any means to attain its ends. The State is subject to law and morality. Disrespect for human dignity cannot serve as the basis for any State action.

The forced disappearance of human beings is a multiple and continuous violation of many rights under the Convention that the States Parties are obligated to respect and guarantee.

---

## Note and Comments:

1. Naomi Roht-Arriaza (1990) has done some of the best work on the meaning of *Velasquez*, and she describes the importance of the investigatory aspects of this case:

> The opinion posits a state's duty to prevent, investigate, and punish any violation of the rights recognized by the Convention. In addition, the state must attempt to restore the right violated, actually restore it if possible. The court asserted that article I's duty to "respect" rights implies a limitation on government power: a "negative" obligation not to interfere with the exercise of a right. But its obligation to "ensure" rights places an affirmative duty on the states parties. This obligation implies the duty of the States Parties to organize the governmental apparatus and, in general, all the structures through which public power is exercised, so that they are capable of juridically ensuring the free and full enjoyment of human rights.
>
> (1990: 470–71)

---

### Box 1.8: Where Is "State Terror" the Worst?

The Political Terror Scale (PTS) (www.politicalterrorscale.org) provides an ordinal measure of physical integrity rights violations – torture, political imprisonment, disappearances, and summary executions – for more than 190 countries going back to 1976. Each country is coded on a scale of 1–5 based on "data" from the U.S. State Department, Amnesty International, and Human Rights Watch, with a high score representing worse human rights conditions and a lower score indicating more respect for human rights.

Which countries do you think had the "worst" human rights record over the past 40 years? Looking at the number of years that a country was coded as a 5 (State

Department), representing the "worst" levels of physical integrity violations, in descending order the "dirty dozen" consists of 1) Afghanistan, 2) The Sudan, 3) Iraq, 4) Democratic Republic of the Congo, 5) Colombia, 6) North Korea, 7) Angola, 8) Burundi, 9) Somalia, 10) Myanmar, 11) Iran, and 12) Sri Lanka.

---

### Box 1.9: International Law at the Movies: State Terror

Needless to say, there have been a lot of great films dealing with various aspects of "state terror." One place to start is South Africa, which was under apartheid rule – the legal separation of blacks and whites – until the early 1990s and the target of countless United Nations resolutions condemning such practices. Two feature films in particular stand out. One is *A Dry White Season* (1989) with Hollywood stars Donald Sutherland and Marlon Brando. A second is *Cry Freedom* (1987), with Denzel Washington playing the remarkable anti-apartheid activist Steven Biko. In terms of documentaries, *Long Night's Journey Into Day* (2000) provides an intelligent and passionate analysis of the country's Truth and Reconciliation Commission, which was premised on the principle that establishing the country's truth represented the highest form of justice. Finally, *Amandla! A Revolution in Four Part Harmony* (2002) allows anti-apartheid activists – terrorists in the eyes of some – to tell their own story, oftentimes in song.

Few parts of Latin America escaped war or oppression in the 1980s. The director Pamela Yates has made a series of documentaries that not only provide great insight into the genocide carried out against the indigenous population in Guatemala at that time, but outtakes from these films have even been used to establish the genocide itself. Her first film on this subject was *When the Mountains Tremble* (1983), which helped bring to the world's attention the massive atrocities in that country. Decades later, she returned to this topic, initially with *Granito: How to Nail a Dictator* (2011) and then *500 Years* (2017) about the efforts to bring the architects of this state terror to justice. In addition to her work on Guatemala, her film *State of Fear: The Truth About Terrorism* (2015) tells the story of the horrors under the Fujimori dictatorship in Peru. *Missing* (1982) stars two Hollywood giants – Jack Lemmon and Sissy Spacek – and the backdrop of this deeply moving film is the September 11, 1973, military coup of the Allende regime in Chile. Finally, *The Official Story* (1985) is a feature film that revolves around the human consequences of the "Dirty War" in Argentina.

Different aspects of Iran's "state terror" have been told in various ways. In *The Circle* (2000), women are constantly being harassed by the self-appointed guardians of morality – which is to say, men – or worse, subject to arrest and imprisonment for even the slightest hint of perceived impropriety. *Persepolis* (2007) uses animation to show the deterioration in the condition of women following the 1979 Revolution. Finally, *This Is Not a Film* (2011) is director Jafar Panahi's clever (but dangerous) response to the Iranian government, which had prohibited him from making any more movies. His response was a (non)film depicting the drudgery of being under

*(Continued)*

**Box I.9: Continued**

house arrest. *This Is Not a Film* was smuggled out of Iran in a flashdrive hidden in a birthday cake and premiered at the Cannes Film Festival.

Special mention needs to be made of Joshua Oppenheimer's two outstanding documentaries that, almost single-handedly, brought the public's attention to the massive killings of upwards of 1 million "communists" by Indonesian authorities during the 1960s. *The Act of Killing* (2012) is certainly the louder version, as the camera follows Anwar Congo and some of his associates as they re-create some of the brutal murders they carried out at that time. It is only near the end of the film when Congo seems able to recognize and reflect on the nature of his actions. As its name might suggest, *The Look of Silence* (2014) tells much the same story, but in a much quieter way, this time through the eyes (figuratively) of Adi Rukun, an eye doctor whose brother was murdered before he was born, who tries to get his patients, government authorities, and even his aging parents to talk about this terrible period in Indonesian history.

Other outstanding films showing the cruelties of state terror and state oppression include *The Agronomist* (2003), displaying the courage of Jean Dominique, a radio announcer who was the voice of the Haitian resistance against the brutal dictatorships of "Papa Doc" and his son "Baby Doc" Duvalier. *Burma VJ* (2008) makes use of secretly recorded images of the abuses of the Burmese military that were then sent over the internet by way of Oslo, Norway. Ai Wei Wei's masterpiece *Never Sorry* (2010) provides a window into the oppressive practices of the Chinese government. Finally, Abderrahmane Sissako's film *Timbuktu* (2014) shows the manner in which oppressive fundamentalist rule sucks the very life out of a small village in North Africa.

## References

*Books and Articles*

Anthony J. Colangelo, "Constitutional Limits on Extraterritorial Jurisdiction: Terrorism and the Intersection of National and International Law," *Harvard International Law Journal* 48: 121–201 (2007)

Mark Gibney, "NSA Surveillance and Its Meaning for International Human Rights Law," in Thomas Gammeltoft-Hansen and Jens Vedsted-Hansen (eds.) *Human Rights and the Dark Side of Globalization: Transnational Law Enforcement and Migration Control*, London: Routledge (2017)

Mark Gibney et al., "The Political Terror Scale." Available at: www.politicalterror scale.org

Human Rights First, "Federal Courts Continue to Take Lead in Counterterrorism Prosecutions," (February 14, 2018). Available at: www.humanrightsfirst. org/resource/myth-v-fact-trying-terror-suspects-federal-courts

Naomi Roht-Arriaza, "State Responsibility to Investigate and Prosecute Grave Human Rights Violations in International Law," *California Law Review* 78: 449–513 (1990)

Stephen J. Schnably, "The Transformation of Human Rights Litigation: The Alien Tort Statute, The Antiterrorism Act, and JASTA," *University of Miami International and Comparative Law Review* 24: 285–438 (2017)


### U.N. Report

U.N. High Commissioner for Human Rights, *The Right to Privacy in the Digital Age*. Available at: www.ohchr.org/EN/Issues/DigitalAge/Pages/DigitalAge Index.aspx


### Cases

*Cicippio-Puleo v. Iran*, 353 F. 3d 1024 (D.C. Cir. 2004)

*Filartiga v. Pena-Irala*, 630 F. 2d 876 (2d. Cir. 1980)

*Flatow v. Iran*, 999 F. Supp. 1 (D.D.C. 1999)

*Google Spain SL v. Agencia Española de Protección de Datos*, European Court of Justice (2014)

*Humanitarian Law Project v. Holder*, 561 U.S. 1 (2010)

*In Re Terrorist Attacks IV*, 134 F. Supp. 3d 774 (S.D.N.Y. 2015)

*In Re Terrorist Attacks on September 11, 2001*, 538 F. 3d 71 (2d. Cir. 2008)

*Jesner v. Arab Bank*, 584 U.S. ____ (2018)

*John Doe (Also Known as Kidane) v. Ethiopia*, 851 F. 3d 7 (D.C. Cir. 2017)

*Klinghoffer v. S.N.C. Achille Lauro*, 739 F. Supp. 854 (S.D.N.Y. 1990), vacated by 937 F. 2d 44 (2d. Cir. 1991)

*Letelier v. Chile*, 488 F. Supp. 665 (D.D.C. 1980)

*Maximillian Schrems v. Data Protection Commissioner*, European Court of Justice (2015)

*McCann v. United Kingdom*, ECtHR, App. No. 18984/91 (1995)

*Schooner Exchange v. M'Faddon*, 7 Cranch 116 (1812)

*Tel-Oren v. Libyan Arab Republic*, 726 F. 2d 774 (D.C. Cir. 1984)

*Velasquez Rodriguez*, IACtHR (1988)


### International Agreements

International Covenant on Civil and Political Rights, ratified by General Assembly 16 December 1966, entry into force 23 March 1976

## Regional Law

American Convention on Human Rights, adopted 22 November 1969, entry into force 18 July 1978

European Convention for the Protection of Human Rights and Fundamental Freedoms, signed 4 November 1950, entry into force 3 September 1953

## Domestic Law

Alien Tort Statute (ATS), 28 U.S.C. Sec. 1350 (U.S.)

Antiterrorism Act of 1990, 18 U.S.C. Sec. 2333 (U.S.)

Authorization for the Use of Military Force, Public Law 107–40, codified at 115 Stat. 224, passed as S.J. Res 23 on 14 September 2001 (U.S.)

Foreign Sovereign Immunity Act (FSIA), 28 U.S.C. 1602–1611 (U.S.)

Justice Against Sponsors of Terrorism Act (JASTA), Public Law No. 114–222 (U.S.)

**2**

# Detaining "Enemy Combatants" and
# Suspected Terrorists

## The September 11 Detainees

In the days and weeks following the September 11 attacks, U.S. authorities detained approximately 1,200 foreign nationals, most on the basis of violations of their visa status, and held them as "special interest cases." Some were held for months without being charged with a crime. All were denied the opportunity to post bond and given very limited opportunities to communicate with family members or to seek legal counsel. The U.S. government even refused to release their names, arguing that disclosing such information would give terrorists a virtual roadmap to the government's investigation that could allow terrorists to chart a potentially deadly detour around such efforts.

Given the emotional nature of the September 11 attacks, there were strong concerns that the administration's increasingly broad authority to arrest and detain terror suspects would lead to racial profiling as well as physical and mental abuse of those being held. All this was detailed in an internal Justice Department investigation conducted by Inspector General Glenn Fine who reported "significant problems" with the treatment of the September 11 detainees (Office of the Inspector General 2003).

---

**Box 2.1: 9/11 Detainees Seek Justice**

A group of September 11 detainees who had been housed in the Metropolitan Detention Center (MDC) in Brooklyn, New York brought suit on the basis of their mistreatment while in custody. In their complaint they allege that they were held in

---

*(Continued)*

**Box 2.1: Continued**

tiny cells for over 23 hours a day with lights on continually; that they were denied any communication with the outside world; and were constantly subjected to being strip searched. They also claimed that they had been frequently beaten, resulting in broken bones and assorted other injuries.

The detainees sought what is known as a *Bivens*-style remedy, based on the U.S. Supreme Court ruling in *Bivens v. Six Unnamed Known Agents of Federal Bureau of Narcotics* (1971), which held that government officials could be sued in their personal capacity for particularly egregious constitutional violations. However, in *Ziglar v. Abbasi* (2017), the U.S. Supreme Court denied any form of relief, relying in large part on the need to give deference to the political branches in the conduct of the "war on terrorism." The majority opinion notes:

> Even if the action is confined to the conduct of a particular Executive Officer in a discrete instance, these claims would call into question the formulation and implementation of a general policy. This, in turn, would necessarily require inquiry and discovery into the whole course of the discussions and deliberations that led to the policies and governmental acts being challenged. These consequences counsel against allowing a *Bivens* action against the Executive Officials, for the burden and demand of litigation might well prevent them – or, to be more precise, future officials like them – from devoting the time and effort required for the proper discharge of their duties.
>
> They challenge as well major elements of the Government's whole response to the September 11 attacks, thus of necessity requiring an inquiry into sensitive issues of national security. Were this inquiry to be allowed in a private suit for damages, the *Bivens* action would assume dimensions far greater than those present in *Bivens* itself, or in either of its two follow-on cases, or indeed in any putative *Bivens* case yet to come before the Court.

Continuing:

> National-security policy is the prerogative of the Congress and President. Judicial inquiry into the national-security realm raises "concerns for the separation of powers in trenching on matters committed to the other branches." These concerns are even more pronounced when the judicial inquiry comes in the context of a claim seeking money damages rather than a claim seeking injunctive or other equitable relief. The risk of personal damages liability is more likely to cause an official to second-guess difficult but necessary decisions concerning national-security policy.
>
> For these and other reasons, courts have shown deference to what the Executive Branch "has determined . . . is 'essential to national security.'" Indeed, "courts traditionally have been reluctant to intrude upon the authority of the Executive in military and national security affairs" unless "Congress specifically has provided otherwise." Congress has not provided otherwise here.
>
> This silence is notable because it is likely that high-level policies will attract the attention of Congress. Thus, when Congress fails to provide a damages

remedy in circumstances like these, it is much more difficult to believe that "congressional inaction" was "inadvertent."

The dissent answers by stating that the abuse and mistreatment afforded the detainees is the basis of virtually all *Bivens*-style cases. In addition, the dissent points out that in the realm of national security, what is essential is not deference but additional vigilance.

> There may well be a particular need for *Bivens* remedies when security-related Government actions are at issue. History tells us of far too many instances where the Executive or Legislative Branch took actions during time of war that, on later examination, turned out unnecessarily and unreasonably to have deprived American citizens of basic constitutional rights. We have read about the Alien and Sedition Acts, the thousands of civilians imprisoned during the Civil War, and the suppression of civil liberties during World War I. The pages of the U. S. Reports themselves recite this Court's refusal to set aside the Government's World War II action removing more than 70,000 American citizens of Japanese origin from their west coast homes and interning them in camps – an action that at least some officials knew at the time was unnecessary. President Franklin Roosevelt's Attorney General, perhaps exaggerating, once said that "[t]he Constitution has not greatly bothered any wartime President."
>
>    Can we, in respect to actions taken during those periods, rely exclusively, as the Court seems to suggest, upon injunctive remedies or writs of habeas corpus, their retail equivalent? Complaints seeking that kind of relief typically come during the emergency itself, when emotions are strong, when courts may have too little or inaccurate information, and when courts may well prove particularly reluctant to interfere with even the least well-founded Executive Branch activity. That reluctance may itself set an unfortunate precedent, which, as Justice Jackson pointed out, can "li[e] about like a loaded weapon" awaiting discharge in another case.
>
>    A damages action, however, is typically brought after the emergency is over, after emotions have cooled, and at a time when more factual information is available. In such circumstances, courts have more time to exercise such judicial virtues as calm reflection and dispassionate application of the law to the facts. We have applied the Constitution to actions taken during periods of war and national-security emergency. I should think that the wisdom of permitting courts to consider *Bivens* actions, later granting monetary compensation to those wronged at the time, would follow *a fortiori*.

## Box 2.2: The Arrest of John Walker Lindh: The "American Taliban"

Soon after the invasion of Afghanistan, U.S. officials captured John Walker Lindh, an American citizen originally from Silver Spring, Maryland. Lindh became a convert

*(Continued)*

**B.2.2: Continued**

> b Sunni Islam when he was 16 and he had lived in Afghanistan since 2000. Lindh
> bught on behalf of the Taliban regime and was later involved in a prison upris-
> ng that killed hundreds of Taliban prisoners, but also Johnny "Mike" Spann, a CIA
> perative. Lindh claimed that he was not aware that the Taliban were fighting against
> U.S. forces. However, rather than go to trial where he would have faced multiple life
> entences, he accepted a plea deal of 20 years.

## "Enemy Combatants"

The war in Afghanistan produced a second category of detainees: enemy combat-ants. Starting on January 11, 2002, the U.S. military began transferring several hundred prisoners to an interrogation facility, dubbed "Camp X-Ray," at Guantanamo Bay, Cuba, purportedly representing the "worst of the worst" terrorist suspects. Although the great majority of these men were captured in Afghanistan in areas of conflict, a sizable number arrived after being turned over to the United States by governments from all over the globe based on their suspected ties to al-Qaeda.

The Bush administration took the position that the detainees at Guantanamo Bay should not have any access to U.S. courts nor should they receive any con-stitutional protections. This argument was based primarily on the grounds that this detention facility was outside the territorial borders of the United States. The Bush administration also claimed exemption from judicial oversight based on the president's powers as commander in chief. The U.S. government classified all of the Guantanamo Bay detainees as "enemy combatants," and it maintained the position that this designation, as well as the conditions under which these detainees were to be held, was outside the scope of any form of judicial review.

In addition to taking the position that the Guantanamo Bay detainees were without any form of protection under (U.S.) domestic law, the Bush administra-tion also argued that "enemy combatants" were not protected by international law generally and the Geneva Conventions in particular. The position of the Bush administration was that the Geneva Conventions, which we will return to in **Jus in Bello** (Chapter 5), were created to protect nonparticipating civilians and soldiers engaged in an inter-state military conflict, not the "unlawful combatants" who had been captured in Afghanistan. As described by White House counsel Alberto Gonzales, the war on terrorism represents a new kind of war, which rendered vari-ous provisions of the Conventions inoperative. Following protests by Secretary of State Colin Powell and his top legal aide William Howard Taft IV, the White House adopted the position that although the protection of the Geneva Conventions did not apply to captured al-Qaeda and Taliban fighters, the U.S. government would adhere to the conventions in its conduct of the war in Afghanistan "to the appropriate and consistent with military necessity."

Soon after the war in Afghanistan began, President Bush issued a milit. order that authorized creating military commissions to try any non-citizen captured in the armed conflict whom the president determines is or was a member of al-Qaeda, or else, has "engaged in, aided or abetted, or conspired to commit acts of international terrorism." As conceptualized, these military commissions would offer only scant protection to the accused, including the inability to know the evidence against them if this might compromise national security. In addition, the Order even permits indefinite detention without charge – including those who had been acquitted.

Legal challenges filed on behalf of the detainees ensued, but the initial question was whether non-citizen "enemy combatants" could invoke the federal (U.S.) habeas corpus statute. When the consolidated case of *Rasul v. Bush* came before the U.S. Supreme Court, the Bush administration argued that the case presented a nonjusticiable "political question." The Court rejected this position and it allowed this group of detainees to file a habeas petition in federal court in the United States.

---

## *Rasul v. Bush*, 542 U.S. 466 (2004)

### JUSTICE STEVENS DELIVERED THE OPINION OF THE COURT

On September 11, 2001, agents of the al Qaeda terrorist network hijacked four commercial airliners and used them as missiles to attack American targets. While one of the four attacks was foiled by the heroism of the plane's passengers, the other three killed approximately 3,000 innocent civilians, destroyed hundreds of millions of dollars of property, and severely damaged the U. S. economy. In response to the attacks, Congress passed a joint resolution authorizing the President to use "all necessary and appropriate force against those nations, organizations, or persons he determines planned, authorized, committed, or aided the terrorist attacks . . . or harbored such organizations or persons." *Authorization for Use of Military Force*. Acting pursuant to that authorization, the President sent U. S. Armed Forces into Afghanistan to wage a military campaign against al Qaeda and the Taliban regime that had supported it.

Petitioners in these cases are 2 Australian citizens and 12 Kuwaiti citizens who were captured abroad during hostilities between the United States and the Taliban. Since early 2002, the U.S. military has held them – along with, according to the Government's estimate, approximately 640 other non-Americans captured abroad – at the naval base at Guantanamo Bay. The United States occupies the base, which comprises 45 square miles of land and water along the southeast coast of Cuba, pursuant to a 1903 Lease Agreement executed with the newly independent Republic of Cuba in the aftermath of the Spanish-American War. Under the agreement, "the United States recognizes the continuance of the ultimate sovereignty of the Republic of Cuba over the [leased areas]," while "the Republic of Cuba consents that during the period of the occupation by the United States . . . the United States shall exercise complete jurisdiction and control over and within said areas." In 1934, the parties entered into a treaty providing that, absent an agreement to modify or abrogate the lease, the lease would remain in effect so long as the United States of America shall not abandon the . . . naval station of Guantanamo.

In 2002, petitioners, through relatives acting as their next friends, filed various actions in the U.S. District Court for the District of Columbia challenging the legality of their detention at the base. All alleged that none of the petitioners has ever been a combatant against the United States or has ever engaged in any terrorist acts. They also alleged that none has been charged with any wrongdoing, permitted to consult with counsel, or provided access to the courts or any other tribunal.

Construing all three actions as petitions for writs of habeas corpus, the District Court dismissed them for want of jurisdiction. The court held, in reliance on our opinion in *Johnson* v. *Eisentrager*, that "aliens detained outside the sovereign territory of the United States may not invoke a petition for a writ of habeas corpus." The Court of Appeals affirmed. Reading *Eisentrager* to hold that "'the privilege of litigation' does not extend to aliens in military custody who have no presence in 'any territory over which the United States is sovereign,'" it held that the District Court lacked jurisdiction over petitioners' habeas actions, as well as their remaining federal statutory claims that do not sound in habeas. We granted certiorari.

Congress has granted federal district courts, "within their respective jurisdictions," the authority to hear applications for habeas corpus by any person who claims to be held "in custody in violation of the Constitution or laws or treaties of the United States."

Executive imprisonment has been considered oppressive and lawless since John, at Runnymede, pledged that no free man should be imprisoned, dispossessed, outlawed, or exiled save by the judgment of his peers or by the law of the land. The judges of England developed the writ of habeas corpus largely to preserve these immunities from executive restraint.

Consistent with the historic purpose of the writ, this Court has recognized the federal courts' power to review applications for habeas relief in a wide variety of cases involving Executive detention, in wartime as well as in times of peace. The Court has, for example, entertained the habeas petitions of an American citizen who plotted an attack on military installations during the Civil War, *Ex parte Milligan*, and of admitted enemy aliens convicted of war crimes during a declared war and held in the United States.

The question now before us is whether the habeas statute confers a right to judicial review of the legality of Executive detention of aliens in a territory over which the United States exercises plenary and exclusive jurisdiction, but not "ultimate sovereignty."

Respondents' primary submission is that the answer to the jurisdictional question is controlled by our decision in *Eisentrager*. In that case, we held that a Federal District Court lacked authority to issue a writ of habeas corpus to 21 German citizens who had been captured by U.S. forces in China, tried and convicted of war crimes by an American military commission headquartered in Nanking, and incarcerated in the Landsberg Prison in occupied Germany. The Court of Appeals in *Eisentrager* had found jurisdiction, reasoning that "any person who is deprived of his liberty by officials of the United States, acting under purported authority of that Government, and who can show that his confinement is in violation of a prohibition of the Constitution, has a right to the writ." In reversing that determination, this Court summarized the six critical facts in the case:

> We are here confronted with a decision whose basic premise is that these prisoners are entitled, as a constitutional right, to sue in some court of the United States for a writ of *habeas corpus*. To support that assumption we must hold that a prisoner of our military authorities is constitutionally entitled to the writ,

even though he (a) is an enemy alien; (b) has never been or resided in the United States; (c) was captured outside of our territory and there held in military custody as a prisoner of war; (d) was tried and convicted by a Military Commission sitting outside the United States; (e) for offenses against laws of war committed outside the United States; (f) and is at all times imprisoned outside the United States.

On this set of facts, the Court concluded, no right to the writ of *habeas corpus* appears.

Petitioners in these cases differ from the *Eisentrager* detainees in important respects: They are not nationals of countries at war with the United States, and they deny that they have engaged in or plotted acts of aggression against the United States; they have never been afforded access to any tribunal, much less charged with and convicted of wrongdoing; and for more than two years they have been imprisoned in territory over which the United States exercises exclusive jurisdiction and control.

Not only are petitioners differently situated from the *Eisentrager* detainees, but the Court in *Eisentrager* made quite clear that all six of the facts critical to its disposition were relevant only to the question of the prisoners' *constitutional* entitlement to habeas corpus. The Court had far less to say on the question of the petitioners' *statutory* entitlement to habeas review. Its only statement on the subject was a passing reference to the absence of statutory authorization: "Nothing in the text of the Constitution extends such a right, nor does anything in our statutes."

Putting *Eisentrager* to one side, respondents contend that we can discern a limit on § 2241 through application of the "longstanding principle of American law" that congressional legislation is presumed not to have extraterritorial application unless such intent is clearly manifested. Whatever traction the presumption against extra-territoriality might have in other contexts, it certainly has no application to the operation of the habeas statute with respect to persons detained within "the territorial jurisdiction" of the United States. By the express terms of its agreements with Cuba, the United States exercises "complete jurisdiction and control" over the Guantanamo Bay Naval Base, and may continue to exercise such control permanently if it so chooses. Respondents themselves concede that the habeas statute would create federal-court jurisdiction over the claims of an American citizen held at the base. Considering that the statute draws no distinction between Americans and aliens held in federal custody, there is little reason to think that Congress intended the geographical coverage of the statute to vary depending on the detainee's citizenship. Aliens held at the base, no less than American citizens, are entitled to invoke the federal courts' authority under § 2241.

Application of the habeas statute to persons detained at the base is consistent with the historical reach of the writ of habeas corpus. At common law, courts exercised habeas jurisdiction over the claims of aliens detained within sovereign territory of the realm, as well as the claims of persons detained in the so-called "exempt jurisdictions," where ordinary writs did not run, and all other dominions under the sovereign's control. As Lord Mansfield wrote in 1759, even if a territory was "no part of the realm," there was "no doubt" as to the court's power to issue writs of habeas corpus if the territory was "under the subjection of the Crown." Later cases confirmed that the reach of the writ depended not on formal notions of territorial sovereignty, but rather on the practical question of "the exact extent and nature of the jurisdiction or dominion exercised in fact by the Crown." In the end, the answer to the question presented is clear. Petitioners contend that they are being held in federal custody in violation of the laws of the United States. No party questions the District Court's jurisdiction over petitioners' custodians. Section 2241, by its terms, requires nothing more. We therefore hold that § 2241 confers on the District Court jurisdiction to hear petitioners' habeas corpus challenges to the legality of their detention at the Guantanamo Bay Naval Base.

### JUSTICE KENNEDY, CONCURRING IN THE JUDGMENT

The Court is correct, in my view, to conclude that federal courts have jurisdiction to consider challenges to the legality of the detention of foreign nationals held at the Guantanamo Bay Naval Base in Cuba. In my view, the correct course is to follow the framework of *Eisentrager*.

*Eisentrager* considered the scope of the right to petition for a writ of habeas corpus against the backdrop of the constitutional command of the separation of powers. The issue before the Court was whether the Judiciary could exercise jurisdiction over the claims of German prisoners held in the Landsberg prison in Germany following the cessation of hostilities in Europe. The Court concluded the petition could not be entertained. The petition was not within the proper realm of the judicial power. It concerned matters within the exclusive province of the Executive, or the Executive and Congress, to determine.

The Court began by noting the "ascending scale of rights" that courts have recognized for individuals depending on their connection to the United States. Citizenship provides a longstanding basis for jurisdiction, the Court noted, and among aliens physical presence within the United States also "gave the Judiciary power to act." This contrasted with the "essential pattern for seasonable Executive constraint of enemy aliens." The place of the detention was also important to the jurisdictional question, the Court noted. Physical presence in the United States "implied protection," whereas in *Eisentrager* "the prisoners at no relevant time were within any territory over which the United States is sovereign," The Court next noted that the prisoners in *Eisentrager* "were actual enemies" of the United States, proven to be so at trial, and thus could not justify "a limited opening of our courts" to distinguish the "many [aliens] of friendly personal disposition to whom the status of enemy" was unproven. Finally, the Court considered the extent to which jurisdiction would "hamper the war effort and bring aid and comfort to the enemy." Because the prisoners in *Eisentrager* were proven enemy aliens found and detained outside the United States, and because the existence of jurisdiction would have had a clear harmful effect on the Nation's military affairs, the matter was appropriately left to the Executive Branch and there was no jurisdiction for the courts to hear the prisoner's claims.

The facts here are distinguishable from those in *Eisentrager* in two critical ways, leading to the conclusion that a federal court may entertain the petitions. First, Guantanamo Bay is in every practical respect a United States territory, and it is one far removed from any hostilities. The opinion of the Court well explains the history of its possession by the United States. In a formal sense, the United States leases the Bay; the 1903 lease agreement states that Cuba retains "ultimate sovereignty" over it. At the same time, this lease is no ordinary lease. Its term is indefinite and at the discretion of the United States. What matters is the unchallenged and indefinite control that the United States has long exercised over Guantanamo Bay. From a practical perspective, the indefinite lease of Guantanamo Bay has produced a place that belongs to the United States, extending the "implied protection" of the United States to it.

The second critical set of facts is that the detainees at Guantanamo Bay are being held indefinitely, and without benefit of any legal proceeding to determine their status. In *Eisentrager*, the prisoners were tried and convicted by a military commission of violating the laws of war and were sentenced to prison terms. Having already been subject to procedures establishing their status, they could not justify "a limited opening of our courts" to show that they were "of friendly personal disposition" and not enemy aliens. Indefinite detention without trial or other proceeding presents altogether different considerations. It allows friends and foes alike to remain in detention. It suggests a weaker case of military necessity and much greater alignment with the traditional function of habeas corpus. Perhaps, where detainees are taken from a zone of hostilities, detention without proceedings or trial would be justified by military necessity for a matter of weeks; but as the period of detention stretches from months to years, the case for continued detention to meet military exigencies becomes weaker.

In light of the status of Guantanamo Bay and the indefinite pretrial detention of the detainees, I would hold that federal-court jurisdiction is permitted in these cases. This approach would avoid creating automatic statutory authority to adjudicate the claims of persons located outside the United States, and remains true to the reasoning of *Eisentrager*. For these reasons, I concur in the judgment of the Court.

### JUSTICE SCALIA, WITH WHOM THE CHIEF JUSTICE AND JUSTICE THOMAS JOIN, DISSENTING

The Court today holds that the habeas statute, 28 U.S.C. § 2241, extends to aliens detained by the United States military overseas, outside the sovereign borders of the United States and beyond the territorial jurisdictions of all its courts. This is not only a novel holding; it contradicts a half-century-old precedent on which the military undoubtedly relied, *Johnson* v. *Eisentrager*.

In abandoning the venerable statutory line drawn in *Eisentrager*, the Court boldly extends the scope of the habeas statute to the four corners of the earth.

The consequence of this holding, as applied to aliens outside the country, is breathtaking. It permits an alien captured in a foreign theater of active combat to bring a § 2241 petition against the Secretary of Defense. Over the course of the last century, the United States has held millions of alien prisoners abroad. A great many of these prisoners would no doubt have complained about the circumstances of their capture and the terms of their confinement. The military is currently detaining over 600 prisoners at Guantanamo Bay alone; each detainee undoubtedly has complaints – real or contrived – about those terms and circumstances. The Court's unheralded expansion of federal-court jurisdiction is not even mitigated by a comforting assurance that the legion of ensuing claims will be easily resolved on the merits. To the contrary, the Court says that the "petitioners' allegations . . . unquestionably describe 'custody in violation of the Constitution or laws or treaties of the United States.'" From this point forward, federal courts will entertain petitions from these prisoners, and others like them around the world, challenging actions and events far away, and forcing the courts to oversee one aspect of the Executive's conduct of a foreign war.

---

## Notes and Comments:

1. In **Jus in Bello** (Chapter 5) we return to international humanitarian law, which is founded on the distinction between combatants and noncombatants. However, one of the essential elements of the Geneva Conventions is that everyone involved in warfare is deserving of some legal protection. Still, in your view, are those engaged in international terrorism "combatants" or "noncombatants"?

2. Upon entering into office, President Obama signed an Executive Order ordering the closure of the Guantanamo base within a year. This, of course, did

not occur. As of January 2018, of the 780 people who have been detained at Guantanamo Bay, Cuba, 730 have been transferred and 41 remain (the remaining number died while in captivity). Throughout the 2016 presidential campaign, Donald Trump promised to house more "enemy combatants" at this (infamous) facility.

3. The definitive book on the political side of the "war on terror" is Jane Mayer's, *The Dark Side: The Inside Story of How the War on Terror Turned Into a War on American Ideals* (2009), while an outstanding account of the daily terror at Guantanamo can be found in Moazzam Begg (with Victoria Brittain) *Enemy Combatant: A British Muslim's Journey to Guantanamo and Back* (2006).

4. The headline of a *New York Times* story on November 30, 2004 reads: "Red Cross Finds Detainee Abuse in Guantanamo." Because the ICRC operates in confidentiality, this charge could not be confirmed. Still, the Red Cross has long insisted that "humane treatment" of both civilians and combatants has always been a central feature of the laws of war, both treaty law but customary international law as well.

---

### Box 2.3: Citizenship Has Its Privileges: The Case of Yasser Esam Hamdi

One of the companion cases to *Rasul* involved the detention of Yasser Esam Hamdi who allegedly fought for the Taliban before being captured by Northern Alliance troops and turned over to American authorities. What differentiated Hamdi from the other "enemy combatants" was that he had been born in the United States and therefore was a U.S. citizen. After knowledge of this became known, Hamdi was transferred from Guantanamo to a military brig in Norfolk, Virginia. However, Hamdi was held without being charged and was not permitted to meet with his family or his attorneys.

In May 2002, Hamdi's attorneys filed a writ of habeas corpus in district court challenging his detention and designation as an "enemy combatant." The Supreme Court granted certiorari in this case and oral argument was conducted on April 28, 2004. One of the questions asked of Deputy Solicitor General Paul Clement was what constrained the administration's treatment of detainees if not federal courts, to which Clement responded: "where there is a war . . . you have to trust the executive to make the kind of quintessential military judgments that are involved in things like that." Ironically enough, that very evening, CBS News broadcast the first photos of the gross abuses at the Abu Ghraib prison in Iraq.

In terms of Hamdi's case, although no single opinion received a majority, the Supreme Court held squarely in favor of Hamdi, ruling that he had been denied certain due process protections. Similar to *Rasul*, the *Hamdi* decision placed severe limits on the manner in which the "war on terrorism" could be conducted. Hamdi was released to Saudi Arabia a short time later, after agreeing to relinquish his American citizenship.

Following the Court's decision in *Rasul*, in December 2005 Congress passed the *Detainee Treatment Act* (DTA), which added a new subsection to the habeas corpus statute that denied jurisdiction for claims from detainees held at Guantanamo Bay, Cuba. In addition, the DTA sought to limit the judiciary's role to the D.C. Circuit Court, and then only for the purpose of determining whether the designation of "enemy combatant" was supported by the evidence provided by the government. In addressing whether it had jurisdiction to even hear the case, the Court ruled (omitted here) that this did not apply to pending cases. In terms of the substantive issues raised, as it had in *Rasul* and *Hamdi*, the Supreme Court ruled against the Bush administration's detention policy.

---

### Box 2.4: Jose Padilla: The "Dirty Bomber"

Jose Padilla is yet another U.S. citizen held as an "enemy combatant." Padilla was arrested at O'Hare Airport on May 8, 2002 and originally held as a "material witness" on a warrant issued by the state of New York relating to the September 11 attacks. Government officials claimed that Padilla was planning on exploding a "dirty bomb" in the United States, thus the moniker.

One June 9, 2002, two days before there was to be a ruling on the validity of holding him as a material witness, President George W. Bush ordered that Padilla be charged as an "enemy combatant" and held in the military brig in Charleston, South Carolina. Through his lawyer, Padilla filed a petition for habeas corpus to the district court for the Southern District of New York, which ruled in his favor. The Court of Appeals held that without clear congressional approval, an American citizen arrested in the United States and away from a zone of combat cannot be held as an "illegal enemy combatant." However, on February 20, 2004 the U.S. Supreme Court dismissed Padilla's petition on the grounds that it was improperly filed in New York and not South Carolina.

After his case had been re-filed, Padilla's case was heard by the 4th Circuit Court of Appeals, which held that the president had the authority under the *Authorization for the Use of Military Force Against Terrorists* to detain Padilla. Thereafter, on November 22, 2005, Padilla was indicted in federal court on charges he "conspired to murder, kidnap, and maim people overseas." None of the original allegations made at the time of his arrest three years earlier were part of the indictment. After more legal wrangling, Padilla was finally put on trial and found guilty and sentenced on January 22, 2008 to 17 years and 4 months in federal prison.

---

## *Hamdan v. Rumsfeld*, 548 U.S. 557 (2006)

### JUSTICE STEVENS DELIVERED THE OPINION OF THE COURT

Petitioner Salim Ahmed Hamdan, a Yemeni national, is in custody at an American prison in Guantanamo Bay, Cuba. In November 2001, during hostilities between the United

States and the Taliban (which then governed Afghanistan), Hamdan was captured by militia forces and turned over to the U. S. military. In June 2002, he was transported to Guantanamo Bay. Over a year later, the President deemed him eligible for trial by military commission for then-unspecified crimes. After another year had passed, Hamdan was charged with one count of conspiracy "to commit . . . offenses triable by military commission."

Hamdan filed petitions for writs of habeas corpus and mandamus to challenge the Executive Branch's intended means of prosecuting this charge. He concedes that a court-martial constituted in accordance with the Uniform Code of Military Justice (UCMJ), 10 U. S. C. §801 *et seq*. would have authority to try him. His objection is that the military commission the President has convened lacks such authority, for two principal reasons: First, neither congressional Act nor the common law of war supports trial by this commission for the crime of conspiracy – an offense that, Hamdan says, is not a violation of the law of war. Second, Hamdan contends, the procedures that the President has adopted to try him violate the most basic tenets of military and international law, including the principle that a defendant must be permitted to see and hear the evidence against him.

Hamdan raises both general and particular objections to the procedures set forth in Commission Order No. 1. His general objection is that the procedures' admitted deviation from those governing courts-martial itself renders the commission illegal. Chief among his particular objections are that he may, under the Commission Order, be convicted based on evidence he has not seen or heard, and that any evidence admitted against him need not comply with the admissibility or relevance rules typically applicable in criminal trials and court-martial proceedings.

In part because the difference between military commissions and courts-martial originally was a difference of jurisdiction alone, and in part to protect against abuse and ensure evenhandedness under the pressures of war, the procedures governing trials by military commission historically have been the same as those governing courts-martial. As recently as the Korean and Vietnam wars, during which use of military commissions was contemplated but never made, the principle of procedural parity was espoused as a background assumption.

The uniformity principle is not an inflexible one; it does not preclude all departures from the procedures dictated for use by courts-martial. But any departure must be tailored to the exigency that necessitates it.

Article 36 places two restrictions on the President's power to promulgate rules of procedure for courts-martial and military commissions alike. First, no procedural rule he adopts may be "contrary to or inconsistent with" the UCMJ – however practical it may seem. Second, the rules adopted must be "uniform insofar as practicable." That is, the rules applied to military commissions must be the same as those applied to courts-martial unless such uniformity proves impracticable.

Nothing in the record before us demonstrates that it would be impracticable to apply court-martial rules in this case. There is no suggestion, for example, of any logistical difficulty in securing properly sworn and authenticated evidence or in applying the usual principles of relevance and admissibility. Assuming *arguendo* that the reasons articulated in the President's Article 36(a) determination ought to be considered in evaluating the impracticability of applying court-martial rules, the only reason offered in support of that determination is the danger posed by international terrorism. Without for one moment underestimating that danger, it is not evident to us why it should require, in the case of Hamdan's trial, any variance from the rules that govern courts-martial.

The absence of any showing of impracticability is particularly disturbing when considered in light of the clear and admitted failure to apply one of the most fundamental protections afforded not just by the Manual for Courts-Martial but also by the UCMJ itself: the right to be present. Whether or not that departure technically is "contrary to or inconsistent with" the terms of the UCMJ, 10 U. S. C. §836(a), the jettisoning of so basic a right cannot lightly be excused as "practicable."

Under the circumstances, then, the rules applicable in courts-martial must apply. Since it is undisputed that Commission Order No. 1 deviates in many significant respects from those rules, it necessarily violates Article 36(b).

The procedures adopted to try Hamdan also violate the Geneva Conventions. The conflict with al Qaeda is not, according to the Government, a conflict to which the full protections afforded detainees under the 1949 Geneva Conventions apply because Article 2 of those Conventions (which appears in all four Conventions) renders the full protections applicable only to "all cases of declared war or of any other armed conflict which may arise between two or more of the High Contracting Parties." Since Hamdan was captured and detained incident to the conflict with al Qaeda and not the conflict with the Taliban, and since al Qaeda, unlike Afghanistan, is not a "High Contracting Party" – i.e., a signatory of the Conventions, the protections of those Conventions are not, it is argued, applicable to Hamdan.

We need not decide the merits of this argument because there is at least one provision of the Geneva Conventions that applies here even if the relevant conflict is not one between signatories. Article 3, often referred to as Common Article 3 because, like Article 2, it appears in all four Geneva Conventions, provides that in a "conflict not of an international character occurring in the territory of one of the High Contracting Parties, each Party to the conflict shall be bound to apply, as a minimum," certain provisions protecting "[p]ersons taking no active part in the hostilities, including members of armed forces who have laid down their arms and those placed *hors de combat* by . . . detention." One such provision prohibits "the passing of sentences and the carrying out of executions without previous judgment pronounced by a regularly constituted court affording all the judicial guarantees which are recognized as indispensable by civilized peoples."

Common Article 3, then, is applicable here and, as indicated above, requires that Hamdan be tried by a "regularly constituted court affording all the judicial guarantees which are recognized as indispensable by civilized peoples." While the term "regularly constituted court" is not specifically defined in either Common Article 3 or its accompanying commentary, other sources disclose its core meaning. The commentary accompanying a provision of the Fourth Geneva Convention, for example, defines "'regularly constituted'" tribunals to include "ordinary military courts" and "definitely exclud[e] all special tribunals." And one of the Red Cross' own treatises defines "regularly constituted court" as used in Common Article 3 to mean "established and organized in accordance with the laws and procedures already in force in a country."

Common Article 3 obviously tolerates a great degree of flexibility in trying individuals captured during armed conflict; its requirements are general ones, crafted to accommodate a wide variety of legal systems. But *requirements* they are nonetheless. The commission that the President has convened to try Hamdan does not meet those requirements.

We have assumed, as we must, that the allegations made in the Government's charge against Hamdan are true. We have assumed, moreover, the truth of the message implicit in that charge – viz., that Hamdan is a dangerous individual whose beliefs, if acted upon, would cause great harm and even death to innocent civilians, and who would act upon those beliefs if given the opportunity. It bears emphasizing that Hamdan does not challenge, and we do not today address, the Government's power to detain him for the duration of active hostilities in order to prevent such harm. But in undertaking to try Hamdan and subject him to criminal punishment, the Executive is bound to comply with the Rule of Law that prevails in this jurisdiction.

---

**Box 2.5: Common Article 3(1) of the Geneva Conventions**

In the case of armed conflict not of an international character occurring in the territory of one of the High Contracting Parties, each Party to the conflict shall be bound to apply, as a minimum, the following provisions:

1) Persons taking no active part in the hostilities, including members of armed forces who have laid down their arms and those placed hors de combat by sickness, wounds, detention, or any other cause, shall in all circumstances be treated humanely, without any adverse distinction founded on race, colour, religion or faith, sex, birth or wealth, or any other similar criteria. To this end, the following acts are and shall remain prohibited at any time and in any place whatsoever with respect to the above-mentioned persons:
   a) violence to life and person, in particular murder of all kinds, mutilation, cruel treatment and torture;
   b) taking of hostages;
   c) outrages upon personal dignity, in particular, humiliating and degrading treatment;
   d) the passing of sentences and the carrying out of executions without previous judgment pronounced by a regularly constituted court affording all the judicial guarantees which are recognized as indispensable by civilized peoples.

---

**Note and Comments:**

1. Congress responded immediately to the *Hamdan* decision by passing the *Military Commissions Act of 2006* (MCA), which provides:

No court, justice or judge shall have jurisdiction to hear or consider an application for a writ of habeas corpus filed by or on behalf of an alien detained by the United States who has been determined by the United States to have been properly detained as an enemy combatant or is awaiting such determination.

And in a pointed response to the Court's ruling in *Hamdan*, a new subsection was added:

The Amendment . . . shall take effect on the date of the enactment of this Act, and shall apply to all cases, without exception, pending on or after the date of the enactment of this Act which relate to any aspect of the detention, transfer, trial, or conditions of detention of an alien detained by the United States since September 11, 2001.

However, as shown in *Boumediene*, the MCA not only did not deter the Supreme Court from deciding the case before it but, once again, the Court ruled against the Executive and Legislative branches.

---

## *Boumediene v. Bush*, 553 U.S. 723 (2008)

### JUSTICE KENNEDY DELIVERED THE OPINION OF THE COURT

Petitioners are aliens designated as enemy combatants and detained at the United States Naval Station at Guantanamo Bay, Cuba. There are others detained there, also aliens, who are not parties to this suit.

Petitioners present a question not resolved by our earlier cases relating to the detention of aliens at Guantanamo: whether they have the constitutional privilege of habeas corpus, a privilege not to be withdrawn except in conformance with the Suspension Clause, Art. I, §9, cl. 2. We hold these petitioners do have the habeas corpus privilege. Congress has enacted a statute, the Detainee Treatment Act of 2005 (DTA), that provides certain procedures for review of the detainees' status. We hold that those procedures are not an adequate and effective substitute for habeas corpus. Therefore §7 of the Military Commissions Act of 2006 (MCA) operates as an unconstitutional suspension of the writ. We do not address whether the President has authority to detain these petitioners nor do we hold that the writ must issue.

In considering both the procedural and substantive standards used to impose detention to prevent acts of terrorism, proper deference must be accorded to the political branches. Unlike the President and some designated Members of Congress, neither the Members of this Court nor most federal judges begin the day with briefings that may describe new and serious threats to our Nation and its people. The law must accord the Executive substantial authority to apprehend and detain those who pose a real danger to our security.

Officials charged with daily operational responsibility for our security may consider a judicial discourse on the history of the Habeas Corpus Act of 1679 and like matters to be far removed from the Nation's present, urgent concerns. Established legal doctrine, however, must be consulted for its teaching. Remote in time it may be; irrelevant to the present it is not. Security depends upon a sophisticated intelligence apparatus and the ability of our Armed Forces to act and to interdict. There are further considerations, however. Security subsists, too, in fidelity to freedom's first principles. Chief among these are freedom from arbitrary and unlawful restraint and the personal liberty that is secured by adherence to the separation of powers. It is from these principles that the judicial authority to consider petitions for habeas corpus relief derives.

Our opinion does not undermine the Executive's powers as Commander in Chief. On the contrary, the exercise of those powers is vindicated, not eroded, when confirmed by the Judicial Branch. Within the Constitution's separation-of-powers structure, few exercises of judicial power are as legitimate or as necessary as the responsibility to hear challenges to the authority of the Executive to imprison a person. Some of these petitioners have been in custody for six years with no definitive judicial determination as to the legality of their detention. Their access to the writ is a necessity to determine the lawfulness of their status, even if, in the end, they do not obtain the relief they seek.

Because our Nation's past military conflicts have been of limited duration, it has been possible to leave the outer boundaries of war powers undefined. If, as some fear, terrorism continues to pose dangerous threats to us for years to come, the Court might not have this luxury. This result is not inevitable, however. The political branches, consistent with their independent obligations to interpret and uphold the Constitution, can engage in a genuine debate about how best to preserve constitutional values while protecting the Nation from terrorism.

It bears repeating that our opinion does not address the content of the law that governs petitioners' detention. That is a matter yet to be determined. We hold that petitioners may invoke the fundamental procedural protections of habeas corpus. The laws and Constitution are designed to survive, and remain in force, in extraordinary times. Liberty and security can be reconciled; and in our system they are reconciled within the framework of the law. The Framers decided that habeas corpus, a right of first importance, must be a part of that framework, a part of that law.

It is so ordered.

### JUSTICE SCALIA, WITH WHOM THE CHIEF JUSTICE, JUSTICE THOMAS, AND JUSTICE ALITO JOIN, DISSENTING

Today, for the first time in our Nation's history, the Court confers a constitutional right to habeas corpus on alien enemies detained abroad by our military forces in the course of an ongoing war. The Chief Justice's dissent [omitted], which I join, shows that the procedures prescribed by Congress in the Detainee Treatment Act provide the essential protections that habeas corpus guarantees; there has thus been no suspension of the writ, and no basis exists for judicial intervention beyond what the Act allows. My problem with today's opinion is more fundamental still: The writ of habeas corpus does not, and never has, run in favor of aliens abroad; the Suspension Clause thus has no application, and the Court's intervention in this military matter is entirely *ultra vires*.

I shall devote most of what will be a lengthy opinion to the legal errors contained in the opinion of the Court. Contrary to my usual practice, however, I think it appropriate to begin with a description of the disastrous consequences of what the Court has done today.

America is at war with radical Islamists. The enemy began by killing Americans and American allies abroad: 241 at the Marine barracks in Lebanon, 19 at the Khobar Towers in Dhahran, 224 at our embassies in Dar es Salaam and Nairobi, and 17 on the USS Cole in Yemen. See National Commission on Terrorist Attacks upon the United States, The 9/11 Commission Report, pp. 60–61, 70, 190 (2004). On September 11, 2001, the enemy brought the battle to American soil, killing 2,749 at the Twin Towers in New York City, 184 at the Pentagon in Washington, D.C., and 40 in Pennsylvania. It has threatened further attacks against our homeland; one need only walk about buttressed and barricaded Washington, or board a plane anywhere in the country, to know that the threat is a serious one. Our Armed Forces are now in the field against the enemy, in Afghanistan and Iraq. Last week, 13 of our countrymen in arms were killed.

The game of bait-and-switch that today's opinion plays upon the Nation's Commander in Chief will make the war harder on us. It will almost certainly cause more Americans to be killed. That consequence would be tolerable if necessary to preserve a time-honored legal principle vital to our constitutional Republic. But it is this Court's blatant abandonment of such a principle that produces the decision today.

And today it is not just the military that the Court elbows aside. A mere two Terms ago in *Hamdan v. Rumsfeld* (2006), when the Court held (quite amazingly) that the Detainee Treatment Act of 2005 had not stripped habeas jurisdiction over Guantanamo petitioners' claims, four Members of today's five-Justice majority joined an opinion saying the following:

Nothing prevents the President from returning to Congress to seek the authority [for trial by military commission] he believes necessary.

Where, as here, no emergency prevents consultation with Congress, judicial insistence upon that consultation does not weaken our Nation's ability to deal with danger. To the contrary, that insistence strengthens the Nation's ability to determine – through democratic means – how best to do so. The Constitution places its faith in those democratic means.

Turns out they were just kidding. For in response, Congress, at the President's request, quickly enacted the Military Commissions Act, emphatically reasserting that it did not want these prisoners filing habeas petitions. It is therefore clear that Congress and the Executive – *both* political branches – have determined that limiting the role of civilian courts in adjudicating whether prisoners captured abroad are properly detained is important to success in the war that some 190,000 of our men and women are now fighting. As the Solicitor General argued, "the Military Commissions Act and the Detainee Treatment Act . . . . represent an effort by the political branches to strike an appropriate balance between the need to preserve liberty and the need to accommodate the weighty and sensitive governmental interests in ensuring that those who have in fact fought with the enemy during a war do not return to battle against the United States."

But it does not matter. The Court today decrees that no good reason to accept the judgment of the other two branches is "apparent." "The Government," it declares, "presents no credible arguments that the military mission at Guantanamo would be compromised if habeas corpus courts had jurisdiction to hear the detainees' claims." What competence does the Court have to second-guess the judgment of Congress and the President on such a point? None whatever. But the Court blunders in nonetheless. Henceforth, as today's opinion makes unnervingly clear, how to handle enemy prisoners in this war will ultimately lie with the branch that knows least about the national security concerns that the subject entails.

The Nation will live to regret what the Court has done today. I dissent.

---

### The Political Branches v. the Judiciary: Who Won?

*Boumediene* was met with much fanfare. Notwithstanding repeated efforts by Congress and the president, the Supreme Court refused to be sidelined by the government's conduct of the "war on terrorism." In addition, for arguably the first time ever, nonresident foreign nationals were recognized as having (some) constitutional rights.

However, at least two questions remain. One involves the evidence that is relied upon in determining a detainee's status, which is addressed in the next two cases from the Court of Appeals for the District of Columbia. Another issue is how far – literally – the rulings in *Rasul* et al. travel.

---

## *Al-Adahi v. Obama*, 613 F. 3d 1102 (D.C. Cir. 2010)

BEFORE HENDERSON AND KAVANAUGH, CIRCUIT JUDGES, AND RANDOLPH, SENIOR CIRCUIT JUDGE

In the summer of 2001, a thirty-nine year-old Yemeni security guard took a six-month leave of absence from his job to move to Afghanistan. Leaving his wife and his two children, he stayed at the Kandahar home of his brother-in-law, a close associate of Usama bin Laden. Twice he met personally with bin Laden. From Kandahar he moved into a guesthouse used as a staging area for al-Qaida recruits. He then attended al-Qaida's Al Farouq training camp, where many of the September 11th terrorists had trained. He traveled between Kabul, Khost, and Kandahar while American forces were launching attacks in Afghanistan. Among other explanations for his movements, he claimed that he had decided to take a vacation. After sustaining injuries requiring his hospitalization, he crossed the Pakistani border on a bus carrying wounded Arab and Pakistani fighters. This man, Mohammed Al-Adahi, who is now a detainee at Guantanamo Bay Naval Base, admits all of this but insists he was not a part of al-Qaida and never fought against the United States. Others identified him as a [redacted]. On his petition for a writ of habeas corpus, the district court ordered him released. We reverse.

Pakistani authorities captured Al-Adahi in late 2001. In 2004, a Combatant Status Review Tribunal determined, by a preponderance of evidence, that he was part of al-Qaida. Al-Adahi filed his habeas corpus petition in 2005. In 2008 the Supreme Court ruled that despite statutes depriving the federal courts of jurisdiction to hear habeas petitions from Guantanamo detainees, the Suspension Clause of the Constitution at least preserved the writ as it existed in 1789. *Boumediene v. Bush*, 553 U.S. 723 (2008).

Al-Adahi's habeas petition presented the question whether he was part of al-Qaida and therefore justifiably detained under the Authorization for Use of Military Force. The district court considered the government's two factual returns and Al-Adahi's three traverses, in addition to a substantial record that included intelligence reports, interrogation summaries, expert declarations, and Al-Adahi's direct and cross-examination (transmitted live from Guantanamo). The court found "no reliable evidence in the record that Petitioner was a member of al-Qaida" and ruled that he should be released. The government brought this appeal and Al-Adahi cross-appealed.

The Authorization for Use of Military Force empowers the President "to use all necessary and appropriate force against those nations, organizations, or persons he determines planned, authorized, committed, or aided the terrorist attacks that occurred on September 11, 2001, or harbored such organizations or persons, in order to prevent any future acts of international terrorism against the United States by such nations, organizations or persons." Pub.L. No. 107–40, § 2(a). "[A]ll necessary and appropriate force" includes the power to capture and detain those described in the congressional authorization. *Hamdi v. Rumsfeld*, 542 U.S. 507, 519 (2004). The government may therefore hold at Guantanamo and elsewhere those individuals who are "part of" al-Qaida, the Taliban, or associated forces.

Whether Al-Adahi fit that description was and is the ultimate issue. The obvious preliminary question is what sort of factual showing does the government, or the detainee, have to make? In this court the question is open. *Al-Bihani* held that the government does not have to prove the legality of detention "beyond a reasonable doubt" or by "clear and convincing evidence." *Al-Bihani* also decided that the preponderance-of-the-evidence standard is constitutionally permissible. But we have yet to decide whether that standard is required.

The district judge in this case adopted the preponderance standard. Other district judges in our circuit have done the same. Their rationale is unstated. After *Boumediene*, the district judges met in executive session and decided to coordinate proceedings in Guantanamo habeas cases. The Order stated, among other things, that the government should bear the burden of proving by a preponderance of the evidence that the petitioner's detention is lawful. In support, the Order cited *Boumediene*. But *Boumediene* held only that the "extent of the showing required of the Government in these cases is a matter to be determined."

[the court then went on to provide extensive analysis, placing Al-Adahi at bin Laden's training facility]

Al-Adahi was in Kabul when the September 11 attacks occurred. He said that he then decided to take a month long vacation and travel throughout the countryside. He said he went to Kabul because he was bored staying in Kandahar. When the United States began its military campaign in Afghanistan on October 7, 2001, Al-Adahi claimed he was still in Kabul. About a week and a half after the bombing began, he left for Khost, Afghanistan, where he stayed in a mosque for about two weeks. He said he then left Khost to return to Kandahar to search for his sister. He spent another two to three weeks in Kandahar, including two or three days in a hospital recuperating from injuries to his arm and side. Al-Adahi said he sustained his injuries in a motorcycle accident. He offered different versions of how the accident occurred: he hit a speed bump on his way to the market; he crashed into a cart as he was riding around Kandahar; he fell off his motorcycle while attempting to flee the United States bombing; he crashed trying to avoid a small car.

Al-Adahi left the hospital for Pakistan on a bus carrying wounded Arabs and Pakistanis. At one point in his interrogation, Al-Adahi described these fourteen men as Taliban soldiers; but he testified at the habeas proceeding that he learned this only from a newspaper article.

From Al-Adahi's movements in Afghanistan, his injuries, his shifting versions of his supposed motorcycle accident, and his capture on a bus loaded with wounded Taliban fighters, the government infers that Al-Adahi was complying with "bin Laden's order to persist in the jihad" after the American attacks. The district court, once again treating items of evidence in isolation, pronounced that "there is no evidence that [Al-Adahi] sought to join or was already part of a band of fighters fleeing the region." The court was wrong, and clearly so. Al-Adahi's capture on a bus carrying only himself and wounded Taliban fighters constituted such evidence, as did his injuries, his movements in the country, and the contradictions contained in his explanations. We do not say that any of these particular pieces of evidence are conclusive, but we do say that they add to the weight of the government's case against Al-Adahi and that the district court clearly erred in tossing them aside.

One of the oddest things about this case is that despite an extensive record and numerous factual disputes, the district court never made any findings about whether Al-Adahi was generally a credible witness or whether his particular explanations for his actions were worthy of belief. The court's omissions are particularly striking in light of the instructions in al-Qaida's training manuals for resisting interrogation. For those who belong to al-Qaida, "[c]onfronting the interrogator and defeating him is part of your jihad." To this end al-Qaida members are instructed to resist interrogation by developing a cover story, by refusing to answer questions, by recanting or changing answers already given, by giving as vague an answer as possible, and by claiming torture. Put bluntly, the instructions to detainees are to make up a story and lie. Despite this the district court displayed little skepticism about Al-Adahi's explanations for his actions. To the extent the court expressed any doubts, it addressed them to the government's case and did so on the mistaken view that each item of the government's evidence needed to prove the ultimate issue in the case.

We could go on, but what we have written thus far is enough to show that the district court clearly erred in its treatment of the evidence and in its view of the law. The court's conclusion was simply not a "permissible view of the evidence." And it reached this conclusion through a series of legal errors, as we have discussed. We have already mentioned the suggestion in *Al-Bihani* that attendance at either an al-Qaida training camp or an al-Qaida guesthouse "would seem too overwhelmingly, if not definitively, justify" detention. The evidence against Al-Adahi showed that he did both – stayed at an al-Qaida guesthouse and attended an al-Qaida training camp. And the evidence showed a good deal more, from his meetings with bin Laden, to his knowledge of those protecting bin Laden, to his wearing of a particular model of Casio watch, to his incredible explanations for his actions, to his capture on a bus carrying wounded Arabs and Pakistanis, and so on. One of the most damaging and powerful items of evidence against him is classified. In all there can be no doubt that Al-Adahi was more likely than not part of al-Qaida. We therefore reverse and remand with instructions to the district court to deny Al-Adahi's petition for a writ of habeas corpus.

So Ordered.

---

## Notes and Comments:

1. In a report entitled "No Hearing Habeas: D.C. Circuit Restricts Meaningful Review," several law professors at Seton Hall University Law School point to the *Al-Adahi* case as the turning point in terms of habeas petitions. Prior to this ruling, the petitioners had been successful in 59% of the first 34 habeas petitions. After *Al-Adahi* (until 2012 when the report was published), petitioners lost 92% of the next 12 cases brought.

2. In the next case, the issue is the degree to which a court of law should defer to a government report.

---

## *Latif v. Obama*, 677 F. 3d 1175 (D.D.C. 2012)

BROWN, CIRCUIT JUDGE

Latif is a Yemeni national who was apprehended near Pakistan's Afghan border in late 2001 and transferred to Guantanamo Bay in January 2002. The parties agree that Latif commenced his travels at the suggestion of a man named Ibrahim and that Latif set off from Yemen to Quetta, Pakistan, and from there to Kabul, Afghanistan. The parties also agree that after returning to Pakistan, Latif was seized by the Pakistani military without a passport. What the parties disagree about is the nature of Latif's trip. The Government says Latif was recruited and trained by the Taliban and then was stationed in Kabul on the front line against the Northern Alliance. Latif says he left Yemen in search of medical care and has never had anything to do with the Taliban.

The Government's case against Latif is based on a heavily redacted ("Report"). According to the story attributed to Latif in the Report, Ibrahim Al–Alawi began recruiting Latif for jihad in 2000. At Ibrahim's urging, Latif left home in early August 2001 and travelled to Afghanistan via Sana'a, Yemen; Karachi, Pakistan; and Quetta, Pakistan. Latif met Ibrahim at the Grand Mosque in Kandahar, Afghanistan, and stayed with him and his family for three days. From Kandahar, Ibrahim took Latif to the Taliban. The Taliban gave him weapons training and stationed him on the front line against the Northern Alliance, north of Kabul, under the command of Afghan leader Abu Fazl. While there, Latif reportedly "saw a lot of people killed during the bombings, but never fired a shot." While with the Taliban, Latif met Abu Hudayfa of Kuwait, Abu Hafs of Saudi Arabia, and Abu Bakr of the United Arab Emirates or Bahrain. Latif retreated to Pakistan via Jalalabad with fleeing Arabs, guided by an Afghan named Taqi Allah.

Latif does not deny being interviewed. Nor does he allege his statements were coerced or otherwise involuntary. But Latif says his statements were misunderstood or, alternatively, were misattributed to him. In a declaration filed with the district court in 2009, Latif denies ever being part of the Taliban and offers an innocent explanation for his journey.

At the heart of the Government's case is the Report in which Latif reportedly admitted being recruited for jihad, receiving weapons training from the Taliban, and serving on the front line with other Taliban troops. Latif's whole defense is that this official government record is unreliable – in other words, that the Government botched it. Latif says his interrogators so garbled his words that their summary bears no relation to what he actually said. Latif's case turns on this claim, because if the Report is an accurate summary of what Latif told his interrogators, then his detention is lawful. On this we all agree. The district court says it did not altogether disregard the Government's evidence, and for good reason: the Report has more than sufficient indicia of reliability to meet the Government's "minimum threshold of persuasiveness."

Ordinarily, at this point in our analysis, we would simply review the district court's comparison of the Government's evidence with the "detainee's facts and explanation," bearing in mind that the ultimate burden is on the Government to establish Latif's detention is legal. We pause here, however, because the district court expressly refused to accord a presumption of regularity to the Government's evidence, and on appeal the Government continues to assert its Report is entitled to such a presumption.

Since the problems Latif cites are typical of Guantanamo detainees' interrogation reports, the rule he proposes would subject all such documents to the he-said/she-said balancing of ordinary evidence. It is impossible to cure the conditions under which these documents were created, so Latif's proposed rule would render the traditional presumption of regularity wholly illusory in this context. We conclude first that intelligence documents of the sort at issue here are entitled to a presumption of regularity, and second that neither internal flaws nor external record evidence rebuts that presumption in this case.

Courts sensibly have anticipated that some sort of presumption is proper in the Guantanamo context, but until now we have not directly addressed the question. The dissent interprets our silence heretofore as disapproval and suggests that a presumption in favor of the Government's evidence in this case "inappropriately shift[s] the burden" of proof from the Government to the detainee.

A body of judge-made law is not born fully formed, like Athena from the head of Zeus. It grows gradually, developing little by little in response to the facts and circumstances of each new case. Until now, we have not had to decide whether the common-law presumption of regularity applies in Guantanamo habeas proceedings. This case finally forces the issue because Latif challenges only the reliability of the Report, and because the Government persists in its request for a presumption of regularity on appeal. We hold that in Guantanamo habeas proceedings a rebuttable presumption of regularity applies to official government records, including intelligence reports like the one at issue here.

Because the Report is entitled to a presumption of regularity, and because the Report, if reliable, proves the lawfulness of Latif's detention, we can only uphold the district court's grant of habeas if Latif has rebutted the Government's evidence with more convincing evidence of his own. Viewed together, both the internal flaws Latif identifies in the Report and the other evidence he uses to attack its reliability fail to meet this burden.

The quantum of incriminating detail in the Report could hardly be produced by good-faith mistake, and we will not infer bad-faith fabrication absent any evidence to that effect. The inconsistencies in the Report may suggest a document produced on the field by imperfect translators or transcribers, but they do not prove the Report's description of Latif's incriminating statements is fundamentally unreliable.

What makes Latif's current story so hard to swallow is not its intrinsic implausibility but its correspondence in so many respects with the Report he now repudiates. Like Dorothy Gale upon awakening at home in Kansas after her fantastic journey to the Land of Oz, Latif's current account of what transpired bears a striking resemblance to the familiar faces of his former narrative. Just as the Gales' farmhands were transformed by Dorothy's imagination into the Scarecrow, Tin Man, and Cowardly Lion, it is at least plausible that Latif, when his liberty was at stake, transformed his jihadi recruiter into a charity worker, his Taliban commander into an imam, his comrades-in-arms into roommates, and his military training camp into a center for religious study. Although the court noted Latif's "innocent explanations for the names that appear in the [Report]," and addressed them one by one, the court failed to consider the cumulative effect of all these uncanny coincidences as our precedent requires. Really, how likely is it that Latif's charity worker and imam just happened to have names virtually identical to those of a known Taliban recruiter and commander?

In light of the district court's expertise as a fact finder and judge of credibility, I am reluctant to reach the merits before the district court has had an opportunity to apply the controlling precedent. We therefore vacate and remand the district court's grant of habeas for further proceedings. On remand the district court must consider the evidence as a whole, bearing in mind that even details insufficiently probative by themselves may tip the balance of probability, that false exculpatory statements may be evidence of guilt, and that in the absence of other clear evidence a detainee's self-serving account must be credible – not just plausible – to overcome presumptively reliable government evidence.

So ordered.

### Tatel, Circuit Judge, Dissenting

All agree that this case turns on whether the district court correctly found that the government's key piece of evidence, the Report, was unreliable. And all agree that the "question whether evidence is sufficiently reliable to credit is one we review for clear error." Our disagreement centers on whether the district court was required to afford the Report a presumption of regularity.

The presumption of regularity stems from a humble proposition – that "[public officers] have properly discharged their official duties." The contours of the presumption are best understood by how courts typically apply it. These cases – in fact every case applying the presumption of regularity – have something in common: actions taken or documents produced within a process that is generally reliable because it is, for example, transparent, accessible, and often familiar.

By contrast, the Report at issue here was produced in the fog of war by a clandestine method that we know almost nothing about. It is not familiar, transparent, generally understood as reliable, or accessible; nor is it mundane, quotidian data entry akin to state court dockets or tax receipts. Its output, a [redactions] intelligence report, was, in this court's own words, "prepared in stressful and chaotic conditions, filtered through interpreters, subject to transcription errors, and heavily redacted for national security purposes." Needless to say, this is quite different from assuming the mail is delivered or that a court employee has accurately jotted down minutes from a meeting.

In its analysis, this court ignores a key step in the logic of applying a presumption of regularity, namely, that the challenged document emerged from a process that we can safely rely upon to produce accurate information. Reliability, not whether an official duty was performed, is the touchstone inquiry in every case this court cites.

One need imply neither bad faith nor lack of incentive nor ineptitude on the part of government officers to conclude that compiled in the field by in a [redactions] near an [redactions] that contain multiple layers of hearsay, depend on translators of unknown quality, and include cautionary disclaimers that are prone to significant errors; or, at a minimum, that such reports are insufficiently regular, reliable, transparent, or accessible to warrant an automatic presumption of regularity.

It is thus not at all surprising that our court has never before applied the presumption of regularity in Guantanamo Bay habeas cases despite numerous opportunities to do so.

The district court's opinion is by no means perfect. But clear error review demands a good deal less than perfection. That said, had the district court otherwise committed legal error or made some other mistake requiring remand, then I would have asked it to clarify whether it had indeed considered this evidence holistically. But nothing in our case law requires, nor would I now hold, that the mere fact that a district court that obviously and carefully considered the entire record failed to mention a couple items of tertiary importance reflects undue atomization of the evidence.

For the foregoing reasons, I would affirm the grant of the writ of habeas corpus.

---

## Note and Comments:

1. In January 2018, 11 of the 41 remaining prisoners at Guantanamo filed a habeas corpus petition on the grounds that the legal standards that had been in place from *Rasul* onwards had substantially changed under the Trump administration. Parts of the habeas petition are set forth here.

Petitioners are 11 Muslim men who have all been detained at Guantánamo without charge or trial, many of them for nearly 15 years or more. Their detention has spanned three presidential administrations and as many as five presidential terms. Many are suffering the devastating psychological and physiological consequences of indefinite detention in a remote prison camp where they have endured conditions devised to break human beings, and where the aura of forever hangs heavier than ever. Given President Donald Trump's proclamation against releasing any petitioners – driven by executive hubris and raw animus rather than by reason or deliberative national security concerns – these petitioners may never leave Guantánamo alive, absent judicial intervention.

Petitioners have participated in habeas corpus litigation that this Court and the higher courts have entertained for years, but this motion, brought by detainees collectively, is different – as it has to be. The two prior presidential administrations released a total of nearly 750 men. They did so by making case-by-case determinations based on an individual detainee's circumstances in a manner that was purportedly tailored to the executive branch's interest in national security. President Trump, in contrast to his predecessors, has declared and is carrying out his intention to keep all remaining detainees in Guantánamo, regardless of their individual circumstances – presumably even those the executive branch previously determined need no longer be detained. This defiant policy exceeds his authority under the 2001 Authorization for Use of Military Force ("AUMF"), which permits detention only for the narrow purpose of preventing the return of detainees to the battlefield. Instead, the policy is a symbolic, undifferentiated assertion of this President's expectation of absolute executive authority and a rejection of the policy framework that has governed Guantánamo detentions for years. Not least, it is a demonstration of his antipathy toward this prisoner population, all foreign-born Muslim men, and toward Muslims more broadly, of the kind courts have properly rejected in recent months.

For these 11 habeas petitioners, Guantánamo now sits in an even more precarious and dubious legal space than it did in 2002, when the executive branch resisted any legal constraints on its detention authority – a position the courts ultimately rejected in favor of judicial intervention. See *Rasul v. Bush*, 542 U.S. 466 (2004). Petitioners have all been detained between ten and sixteen years without charge or trial, and for much of that time, in subhuman conditions. Given the President's commitment, in fulfillment of a campaign promise, not to release any detainees during his administration, they face an arbitrary additional term of detention of four, or possibly eight, years. Such an additional term of years will mean irreparable harm for Petitioners. For the aging and unwell among them, including some on prolonged hunger strike, it may not be survivable. Habeas is a flexible, equitable remedy that at its core is meant to check arbitrary executive action. When fundamental legal principles – and human lives – are at stake, the judicial branch is compelled to act.

As the *Court in Boumediene v. Bush*, 533 U.S. 723 (2008), recognized, habeas developed to prevent arbitrary executive imprisonment and was constitutionally guaranteed by the Suspension Clause to prevent cyclical abuses of executive power. The President's apparent policy to detain for detention's sake, driven by religious animus, is unlawful. The obligation of the habeas court is clear. Because Petitioners' detentions violate the Constitution and the AUMF, their habeas petitions should be granted. And, should the President wish to detain Petitioners, the Constitution offers him one valid process to do so. The "Executive may . . . hand him over to the criminal authorities, whose detention for the purpose of prosecution will be lawful, or else must release him." Hamdi, 542 U.S. at 576 (Scalia, J., dissenting).

How would you rule on this petition?

## Beyond Guantanamo?

The second question alluded to earlier is whether *Rasul* et al. are "Guantana...o-only" cases because of the amount of authority exercised by U.S. officials. *Al Maqaleh* helps answer the question of the geographic scope of *Boumediene*.

---

## *Al Maqaleh v. Gates*, 605 F. 3d 84 (D.D.C. 2010)

All three petitioners are being held as unlawful enemy combatants at the Bagram Theater Internment Facility on the Bagram Airfield Military Base in Afghanistan. Petitioner Fadi Al-Maqaleh is a Yemeni citizen who alleges he was taken into custody in 2003. While Al-Maqaleh's petition asserts "on information and belief" that he was captured beyond Afghan borders, a sworn declaration from Colonel James W. Gray, Commander of Detention Operations, states that Al-Maqaleh was captured in Zabul, Afghanistan. Redha Al-Najar is a Tunisian citizen who alleges he was captured in Pakistan in 2002. Amin Al-Bakri is a Yemeni citizen who alleges he was captured in Thailand in 2002. Both Al-Najar and Al-Bakri allege they were first held in some other unknown location before being moved to Bagram.

Bagram Airfield Military Base is the largest military facility in Afghanistan occupied by United States and coalition forces. The United States entered into an "Accommodation Consignment Agreement for Lands and Facilities at Bagram Airfield" with the Islamic Republic of Afghanistan in 2006, which "consigns all facilities and land located at Bagram Airfield owned by [Afghanistan,] or Parwan Province, or private individuals, or others, for use by the United States and coalition forces for military purposes." The Agreement refers to Afghanistan as the "host nation" and the United States "as the lessee." The leasehold created by the agreement is to continue "until the United States or its successors determine that the premises are no longer required for its use."

Afghanistan remains a theater of active military combat. The United States and coalition forces conduct "an ongoing military campaign against al Qaeda, the Taliban regime, and their affiliates and supporters in Afghanistan." These operations are conducted in part from Bagram Airfield. Bagram has been subject to repeated attacks from the Taliban and al Qaeda, including a March 2009 suicide bombing striking the gates of the facility, and Taliban rocket attacks in June of 2009 resulting in death and injury to United States service members and other personnel.

Our duty, as explained above, is to determine the reach of the right to habeas corpus and therefore of the Suspension Clause to the factual context underlying the petitions we consider in the present appeal. In doing so, we are controlled by the Supreme Court's interpretation of the Constitution in Eisentrager as construed and explained in the Court's more recent opinion in Boumediene.

At the outset, we note that each of the parties has asserted both an extreme understanding of the law after Boumediene and a more nuanced set of arguments upon which each relies in anticipation of the possible rejection of the bright-line arguments. The United States would like us to hold that the Boumediene analysis has no application beyond territories that are, like Guantanamo, outside the de jure sovereignty of the United States but are subject to its de facto sovereignty. As the government puts it in its reply brief, "[t]he real question before this Court, therefore, is whether Bagram may be considered effectively part of the United States in light of the nature and history of the U.S. presence there." We disagree.

Relying upon three independent reasons, the Court in Boumediene expressly repudiated the argument of the United States in that case to the effect "that the Eisentrager Court adopted a formalistic, sovereignty-based test for determining the reach of the Suspension Clause."

For similar reasons, we reject the most extreme position offered by the petitioners. At various points, the petitioners seem to be arguing that the fact of United States control of Bagram under the lease of the military base is sufficient to trigger the extraterritorial application of the Suspension Clause, or at least satisfy the second factor of the three set forth in Boumediene. Again, we reject this extreme understanding. Such an interpretation would seem to create the potential for the extraterritorial extension of the Suspension Clause to noncitizens held in any United States military facility in the world, and perhaps to an undeterminable number of other United States-leased facilities as well. Significantly, the court engaged in an extended dialog with counsel for the petitioners in which we repeatedly sought some limiting principle that would distinguish Bagram from any other military installation. Counsel was able to produce no such distinction. Again, such an extended application is not a tenable interpretation of Boumediene. If it were the Supreme Court's intention to declare such a sweeping application, it would surely have said so. Just as we reject the extreme argument of the United States that would render most of the decision in Boumediene dicta, we reject the first line of argument offered by petitioners. Having rejected the bright-line arguments of both parties, we must proceed to their more nuanced arguments, and reach a conclusion based on the application of the Supreme Court's enumerated factors to the case before us.

The first of the enumerated factors is "the citizenship and status of the detainee and the adequacy of the process through which that status determination was made." Citizenship is, of course, an important factor in determining the constitutional rights of persons before the court. However, clearly the alien citizenship of the petitioners in this case does not weigh against their claim to protection of the right of habeas corpus under the Suspension Clause. So far as citizenship is concerned, they differ in no material respect from the petitioners at Guantanamo who prevailed in Boumediene. As to status, the petitioners before us are held as enemy aliens. But so were the Boumediene petitioners. While the Eisentrager petitioners were in a weaker position by having the status of war criminals, that is immaterial to the question before us. This question is governed by Boumediene and the status of the petitioners before us again is the same as the Guantanamo detainees, so this factor supports their argument for the extension of the availability of the writ.

The second factor, "the nature of the sites where apprehension and then detention took place," weighs heavily in favor of the United States. Like all petitioners in both Eisentrager and Boumediene, the petitioners here were apprehended abroad. While this in itself would appear to weigh against the extension of the writ, it obviously would not be sufficient, otherwise Boumediene would not have been decided as it was. However, the nature of the place where the detention takes place weighs more strongly in favor of the position argued by the United States and against the extension of habeas jurisdiction than was the case in either Boumediene or Eisentrager. In the first place, while de facto sovereignty is not determinative, for the reasons discussed above, the very fact that it was the subject of much discussion in Boumediene makes it obvious that it is not without relevance. As the Supreme Court set forth, Guantanamo Bay is "a territory that, while technically not part of the United States, is under the complete and total control of our Government." While it is true that the United States holds a leasehold interest in Bagram, and held a leasehold interest in Guantanamo, the surrounding circumstances are hardly the same. The United States has maintained its total control of Guantanamo Bay for over a century, even in the face of a hostile government maintaining de jure sovereignty over the property. In Bagram, while the United States has options as to duration of the lease agreement, there is no indication of any intent to occupy the base with permanence, nor is there hostility on the part of the "host" country. Therefore, the notion that de facto sovereignty extends to Bagram is no more real than would have been the same claim with respect to Landsberg in the Eisentrager case. While it is certainly realistic to assert that the United States has de facto sovereignty over Guantanamo, the same simply is not true with respect to Bagram. Though the site of detention analysis weighs in favor of the United States and against the petitioners, it is not determinative.

But we hold that the third factor, that is "the practical obstacles inherent in resolving the prisoner's entitlement to the writ," particularly when considered along with the second factor, weighs overwhelmingly in favor of the position of the United States. It is undisputed that Bagram, indeed the entire nation of Afghanistan, remains a theater of war. Not only does this suggest that the detention at Bagram is more like the detention at Landsberg than Guantanamo, the position of the United States is even stronger in this case than it was in Eisentrager. As the Supreme Court recognized in Boumediene, even though the active hostilities in the European theater had "c[o]me to an end," at the time of the Eisentrager decision, many of the problems of a theater of war remained:

In addition to supervising massive reconstruction and aid efforts the American forces stationed in Germany faced potential security threats from a defeated enemy. In retrospect the post-War occupation may seem uneventful. But at the time Eisentrager was decided, the Court was right to be concerned about judicial interference with the military's efforts to contain "enemy elements, guerilla fighters, and 'were-wolves.'"

In ruling for the extension of the writ to Guantanamo, the Supreme Court expressly noted that "[s]imilar threats are not apparent here." In the case before us, similar, if not greater, threats are indeed apparent. The United States asserts, and petitioners cannot credibly dispute, that all of the attributes of a facility exposed to the vagaries of war are present in Bagram.

We do not ignore the arguments of the detainees that the United States chose the place of detention and might be able "to evade judicial review of Executive detention decisions by transferring detainees into active conflict zones, thereby granting the Executive the power to switch the Constitution on or off at will." However, that is not what happened here. Indeed, without dismissing the legitimacy or sincerity of appellees' concerns, we doubt that this fact goes to either the second or third of the Supreme Court's enumerated factors. We need make no determination on the importance of this possibility, given that it remains only a possibility; its resolution can await a case in which the claim is a reality rather than a speculation. In so stating, we note that the Supreme Court did not dictate that the three enumerated factors are exhaustive. It only told us that "at least three factors" are relevant. Perhaps such manipulation by the Executive might constitute an additional factor in some case in which it is in fact present. However, the notion that the United States deliberately confined the detainees in the theater of war rather than at, for example, Guantanamo, is not only unsupported by the evidence, it is not supported by reason. To have made such a deliberate decision to "turn off the Constitution" would have required the military commanders or other Executive officials making the situs determination to anticipate the complex litigation history set forth above and predict the Boumediene decision long before it came down.

Also supportive of our decision that the third factor weighs heavily in favor of the United States, as the district court recognized, is the fact that the detention is within the sovereign territory of another nation, which itself creates practical difficulties. Indeed, it was on this factor that the district court relied in dismissing the fourth petition, which was filed by an Afghan citizen detainee. While that factor certainly weighed more heavily with respect to an Afghan citizen, it is not without force with respect to detainees who are alien to both the United States and Afghanistan. The United States holds the detainees pursuant to a cooperative arrangement with Afghanistan on territory as to which Afghanistan is sovereign. While we cannot say that extending our constitutional protections to the detainees would be in any way disruptive of that relationship, neither can we say with certainty what the reaction of the Afghan government would be.

In sum, taken together, the second and especially the third factors compel us to hold that the petitions should have been dismissed.

### CONCLUSION

For the reasons set forth above, we hold that the jurisdiction of the courts to afford the right to habeas relief and the protection of the Suspension Clause does not extend to aliens held in Executive detention in the Bagram detention facility in the Afghan theater of war. We therefore reverse the order of the district court denying the motion for dismissal of the United States and order that the petitions be dismissed for lack of jurisdiction.

## Note and Comments:

1. Would you have decided this case the same way? What factors would you consider in determining the rights of detainees? Geographic distance? Whether prisoners were being held in a "theater of war"? The nationality of the detainees? Who (and how) they were placed in detention? The length of time they had already served?

---

### Box 2.6: International Law at the Movies: The Wars in Afghanistan and Iraq

The invasion of Afghanistan followed by the war in Iraq have both been the focus of a number of outstanding documentaries and feature films. *Restrepo* (2010) is a documentary on life (and death) at this dangerous outpost in Afghanistan where American troops try to engage with local citizens and fight the Taliban – if only they could tell the difference between the two. *Armadillo* (2010) tells a similar story as the filmmakers travel with a contingent of Danish troops.

There are a host of insightful films about the ravages of the Iraq War as well. Laura Poitras' documentary *My Country, My Country* (2006) focuses on the effect the war had on civilian populations while *Gunner Palace* (2004) provides a thrilling and frightening account of daily life for U.S. soldiers in Baghdad. *No End in Sight* (2007) is a documentary directed by Charles Ferguson depicting the horrors of the Iraq occupation.

In terms of Hollywood's treatment of the subject, *The Hurt Locker* (2008) was awarded the Oscar for Best Picture for its harrowing portrayal of an Iraq Ordnance Disposal unit. Another feature film that drew a large audience is *American Sniper*

(2014), directed by Clint Eastwood, in which Bradley Cooper plays Chris Kyle, heralded as the "deadliest" sniper in U.S. military history.

*Why We Fight* (2005) is a documentary that takes its name from President Eisenhower's Farewell Address where he first coined the term "military-industrial complex," and it explores the large number of wars fought by the United States. And *Control Room* (2004) is the Iraq War as told through the eyes of Al Jazeera.

---

### Box 2.7: International Law at the Movies: Detention and Torture

There have been a number of outstanding documentaries made about the abuse of "enemy combatants," most notably those carried out at the Abu Ghraib prison in Iraq. *The Ghosts of Abu Ghraib* (2007) directed by Rory Kennedy provides a more traditional account, while Errol Morris's *Standard Operating Procedure* (2008) works hard to convince viewers that they do not necessarily "know" what we think we know from the unforgettable images. *Taxi to the Dark Side* (2007) directed by Alex Gibney was awarded the Oscar for Best Documentary for its investigation of the arrest, torture, and eventual murder of an Afghan taxi driver. Another documentary deserving of special mention is *The Prisoner or: How I Planned to Kill Tony Blair* (2006), a chilling documentary telling the story of an Iraqi journalist charged with attempting to assassinate the British Prime Minister. Finally, *The Road to Guantanamo* (2006) presents the saga of the "Tipton Three" – British citizens who went to Pakistan for a friend's wedding who decided to travel to Afghanistan for fun and excitement and who ended up in the custody of American authorities and shipped off to Guantanamo, before their eventual release.

**Photo 2.1** "Hooded Man"
*Source:* © Associated Press

## The Detention of Suspected Terrorists in the United Kingdom

The cases examined thus far have focused exclusively on the "enemy combatants" held in custody by the United States. As the following case shows, these same issues arose in other countries involved in the "war on terrorism."

---

# A. and others v. the UK, ECtHR, App. No. 3455/05 (2009)

On 11 September 2001 four commercial airplanes were hijacked over the United States of America. Two of them were flown directly at the Twin Towers of the World Trade Centre and a third at the Pentagon, causing great loss of life and destruction to property. The Islamist extremist terrorist organization al-Qaeda, led by Osama Bin Laden, claimed responsibility. The United Kingdom joined with the United States of America in military action in Afghanistan, which had been used as a base for al-Qaeda training camps.

The Government contended that the events of 11 September 2001 demonstrated that international terrorists, notably those associated with al-Qaeda, had the intention and capacity to mount attacks against civilian targets on an unprecedented scale. Further, given the loose-knit, global structure of al-Qaeda and its affiliates and their fanaticism, ruthlessness and determination, it would be difficult for the State to prevent future attacks. In the Government's assessment, the United Kingdom, because of its close links with the United States of America, was a particular target. They considered that there was an emergency of a most serious kind threatening the life of the nation. Moreover, they considered that the threat came principally, but not exclusively, from a number of foreign nationals present in the United Kingdom, who were providing a support network for Islamist terrorist operations linked to al-Qaeda. A number of these foreign nationals could not be deported because of the risk that they would suffer treatment contrary to Article 3 of the Convention in their countries of origin.

### ALLEGED VIOLATION OF ARTICLE 5 § 1 OF THE CONVENTION

The applicants contended that their detention was unlawful and incompatible with Article 5 § 1 of the Convention.

Article 5 § 1 of the Convention provides, in so far as relevant:

"1. Everyone has the right to liberty and security of person. No one shall be deprived of his liberty save in the following cases and in accordance with a procedure prescribed by law:

. . .

(f) the lawful arrest or detention of a person . . . against whom action is being taken with a view to deportation or extradition."

Article 5 enshrines a fundamental human right, namely the protection of the individual against arbitrary interference by the State with his or her right to liberty. The text of Article 5 makes it clear that the guarantees it contains apply to "everyone".

Sub-paragraphs (a) to (f) of Article 5 § 1 contain an exhaustive list of permissible grounds on which persons may be deprived of their liberty and no deprivation of liberty will be lawful unless it falls within one of those grounds. One of the exceptions, contained in sub-paragraph (f), permits the State to control the liberty of aliens in an immigration context. The Government contend that the applicants' detention was justified under the second limb of that sub-paragraph and that they were lawfully detained as persons "against whom action is being taken with a view to deportation or extradition".

Article 5 § 1 (f) does not demand that detention be reasonably considered necessary, for example to prevent the individual from committing an offence or fleeing. Any deprivation of liberty under the second limb of Article 5 § 1 (f) will be justified, however, only for as long as deportation or extradition proceedings are in progress. If such proceedings are not prosecuted with due diligence, the detention will cease to be permissible under Article 5 § 1 (f). The deprivation of liberty must also be "lawful". Where the "lawfulness" of detention is in issue, including the question whether "a procedure prescribed by law" has been followed, the Convention refers essentially to national law and lays down the obligation to conform to the substantive and procedural rules of national law. Compliance with national law is not, however, sufficient: Article 5 § 1 requires in addition that any deprivation of liberty should be in keeping with the purpose of protecting the individual from arbitrariness. It is a fundamental principle that no detention which is arbitrary can be compatible with Article 5 § 1 and the notion of "arbitrariness" in Article 5 § 1 extends beyond lack of conformity with national law, so that a deprivation of liberty may be lawful in terms of domestic law but still arbitrary and thus contrary to the Convention. To avoid being branded as arbitrary, detention under Article 5 § 1 (f) must be carried out in good faith; it must be closely connected to the ground of detention relied on by the Government; the place and conditions of detention should be appropriate; and the length of the detention should not exceed that reasonably required for the purpose pursued.

The choice by the Government and Parliament of an immigration measure to address what was essentially a security issue had the result of failing adequately to address the problem, while imposing a disproportionate and discriminatory burden of indefinite detention on one group of suspected terrorists. As the House of Lords found, there was no significant difference in the potential adverse impact of detention without charge on a national or on a non-national who in practice could not leave the country because of fear of torture abroad.

The Government advanced two arguments which the applicants claimed had not been relied on before the national courts. The first of the allegedly new arguments was that it was legitimate for the State, in confining the measures to non-nationals, to take into account the sensitivities of the British Muslim population in order to reduce the chances of recruitment among them by extremists. However, the Government have not placed before the Court any evidence to suggest that British Muslims were significantly more likely to react negatively to the detention without charge of national rather than foreign Muslims reasonably suspected of links to al-Qaeda. In this respect the Court notes that the system of control orders, put in place by the Prevention of Terrorism Act 2005, does not discriminate between national and non-national suspects.

The second allegedly new ground relied on by the Government was that the State could better respond to the terrorist threat if it were able to detain its most serious source, namely non-nationals. In this connection, again the Court has not been provided with any evidence which could persuade it to overturn the conclusion of the House of Lords that the difference in treatment was unjustified. Indeed, the Court notes that the national courts, including SIAC, which saw both the open and the closed material, were not convinced that the threat from non-nationals was more serious than that from nationals.

## Note and Comments:

1. One of the questions you might have is why the United Kingdom could not simply deport non-nationals who were suspected terrorists who were on its territory. In *Chahal v. United Kingdom*, the European Court of Human Rights held that the nonrefoulement principle protected all people, including those suspected of carrying out human rights violations.

### Protecting a State's Own Citizens?: The Case of Omar Khadr

The "war on terror" has truly been a global affair. Although it began with the invasion of Afghanistan and was then extended to Iraq, large numbers of foreign nationals from a host of other states were captured and sent to Guantanamo Bay, Cuba.

One of the foundational principles of international law is that states protect the security and interests of their own citizens. The following case raises this issue within the context of the war on terror and it addresses the question of the role a state could/should play when one of its nationals is subject to some form of abuse by another country.

**Photo 2.2** Omar Khadr Following His Release From Guantanamo

*Source:* © Associated Press

## *Canada v. Omar Ahmed Khadr*, 2010 SCC 3, [2010] 1 S.C.R. 44

### INTRODUCTION

Omar Khadr, a Canadian citizen, has been detained by the United States government at Guantanamo Bay, Cuba, for over seven years. The Prime Minister asks this Court to reverse the decision of the Federal Court of Appeal requiring the Canadian government to request the United States to return Mr. Khadr from Guantanamo Bay to Canada.

For the reasons that follow, we agree with the courts below that Mr. Khadr's rights under s. 7 of the *Canadian Charter of Rights and Freedoms* were violated. However, we conclude that the order made by the lower courts that the government request Mr. Khadr's return to Canada is not an appropriate remedy for that breach under s. 24(1) of the *Charter*. Consistent with the separation of powers and the well-grounded reluctance of courts to intervene in matters of foreign relations, the proper remedy is to grant Mr. Khadr a declaration that his *Charter* rights have been infringed, while leaving the government a measure of discretion in deciding how best to respond. We would therefore allow the appeal in part.

### BACKGROUND

Mr. Khadr was 15 years old when he was taken prisoner on July 27, 2002, by U.S. forces in Afghanistan. He was alleged to have thrown a grenade that killed an American soldier in the battle in which he was captured. About three months later, he was transferred to the U.S. military installation at Guantanamo Bay. He was placed in adult detention facilities.

On September 7, 2004, Mr. Khadr was brought before a Combatant Status Review Tribunal which affirmed a previous determination that he was an "enemy combatant". He was subsequently charged with war crimes and held for trial before a military commission. In light of a number of procedural delays and setbacks, that trial is still pending.

In February and September 2003, agents from the Canadian Security Intelligence Service ("CSIS") and the Foreign Intelligence Division of the Department of Foreign Affairs and International Trade ("DFAIT") questioned Mr. Khadr on matters connected to the charges pending against him and shared the product of these interviews with U.S. authorities. In March 2004, a DFAIT official interviewed Mr. Khadr again, with the knowledge that he had been subjected by U.S. authorities to a sleep deprivation technique, known as the "frequent flyer program", in an effort to make him less resistant to interrogation. During this interview, Mr. Khadr refused to answer questions. In 2005, von Finckenstein J. of the Federal Court issued an interim injunction preventing CSIS and DFAIT agents from further interviewing Mr. Khadr in order "to prevent a potential grave injustice" from occurring. In 2008, this Court ordered the Canadian government to disclose to Mr. Khadr the transcripts of the interviews he had given to CSIS and DFAIT in Guantanamo Bay, under s. 7 of the *Charter*:

Mr. Khadr has repeatedly requested that the Government of Canada ask the United States to return him to Canada: in March 2005 during a Canadian consular visit; on December 15, 2005, when a welfare report noted that "[Mr. Khadr] wants his government to bring him back home"

The Prime Minister announced his decision not to request Mr. Khadr's repatriation on July 10, 2008, during a media interview. The Prime Minister provided the following response to a journalist's question, posed in French, regarding whether the government would seek repatriation:

> [TRANSLATION] The answer is no, as I said the former Government, and our Government with the notification of the Minister of Justice had considered all these issues and the situation remains the same. . . . We keep on looking for [assurances] of good treatment of Mr. Khadr.

On August 8, 2008, Mr. Khadr applied to the Federal Court for judicial review of the government's "ongoing decision and policy" not to seek his repatriation. He alleged that the decision and policy infringed his rights under s. 7 of the *Charter*, which states:

Everyone has the right to life, liberty and security of the person and the right not to be deprived thereof except in accordance with the principles of fundamental justice.

After reviewing the history of Mr. Khadr's detention and applicable principles of Canadian and international law, O'Reilly J. concluded that in these special circumstances, Canada has a "duty to protect" Mr. Khadr. He found that "[t]he ongoing refusal of Canada to request Mr. Khadr's repatriation to Canada offends a principle of fundamental justice and violates Mr. Khadr's rights under s. 7 of the *Charter*" (para. 92). Also, he held that "[t]o mitigate the effect of that violation, Canada must present a request to the United States for Mr. Khadr's repatriation to Canada as soon as practicable" (para. 92).

The majority judgment of the Federal Court of Appeal upheld O'Reilly J.'s order, but defined the s. 7 breach more narrowly. The majority of the Court of Appeal found that it arose from the March 2004 interrogation conducted with the knowledge that Mr. Khadr had been subject to the "frequent flyer program", characterized by the majority as involving cruel and abusive treatment contrary to the principles of fundamental justice.

### The Issues

Mr. Khadr argues that the government has breached his rights under s. 7 of the *Charter*, and that the appropriate remedy for this breach is an order that the government request the United States to return him to Canada.

Mr. Khadr does not suggest that the government is obliged to request the repatriation of all Canadian citizens held abroad in suspect circumstances. Rather, his contention is that the conduct of the government of Canada in connection with his detention by the U.S. military in Guantanamo Bay, and in particular Canada's collaboration with the U.S. government in 2003 and 2004, violated his rights under the *Charter*, and requires as a remedy that the government now request his return to Canada.

The United States is holding Mr. Khadr for the purpose of trying him on charges of war crimes. The United States is thus the primary source of the deprivation of Mr. Khadr's liberty and security of the person. However, the allegation on which his claim rests is that Canada has also contributed to his past and continuing deprivation of liberty. To satisfy the requirements of s. 7, there must be "a sufficient causal connection between [the Canadian] government's participation and the deprivation [of liberty and security of the person] ultimately effected (sic)."

The record suggests that the interviews conducted by CSIS and DFAIT provided significant evidence in relation to these charges. During the February and September 2003 interrogations, CSIS officials repeatedly questioned Mr. Khadr about the central events at issue in his prosecution, extracting statements from him that could potentially prove inculpatory in the U.S. proceedings against him. A report of the Security Intelligence Review Committee titled *CSIS's Role in the Matter of Omar Khadr* (July 8, 2009), further indicated that CSIS assessed the interrogations of Mr. Khadr as being "highly successful, as evidenced by the quality intelligence information" elicited from Mr. Khadr. These statements were shared with U.S. authorities and were summarized in U.S. investigative reports. Mr. Khadr's statements to Canadian officials are potentially admissible against him in the U.S. proceedings, notwithstanding the oppressive circumstances under which they were obtained.

Mr. Khadr's *Charter* rights were breached when Canadian officials contributed to his detention by virtue of their interrogations at Guantanamo Bay knowing Mr. Khadr was a youth, did not have access to legal counsel or *habeas corpus* at that time and, at the time of the interview in March 2004, had been subjected to improper treatment by the U.S. authorities. As the information obtained by Canadian officials during the course of their interrogations may be used in the U.S. proceedings against Mr. Khadr, the effect of the breaches cannot be said to have been spent. It continues to this day. As discussed earlier, the material that Canadian officials gathered and turned over to the U.S. military authorities may form part of the case upon which he is currently being held. The evidence before us suggests that the material produced was relevant and useful. There has been no suggestion that it does not form part of the case against Mr. Khadr or that it will not be put forward at his ultimate trial. We therefore find that the breach of Mr. Khadr's s. 7 *Charter* rights remains ongoing and that the remedy sought could potentially vindicate those rights.

Is the remedy sought precluded by the fact that it touches on the Crown prerogative over foreign affairs? A connection between the remedy and the breach is not the only consideration. An appropriate and just remedy is also one that "must employ means that are legitimate within the framework of our constitutional democracy" and must be a "judicial one which vindicates the right while invoking the function and powers of a court". The government argues that courts have no power under the Constitution of Canada to require the executive branch of government to do anything in the area of foreign policy. It submits that the decision not to request the repatriation of Mr. Khadr falls directly within the prerogative powers of the Crown to conduct foreign relations, including the right to speak freely with a foreign state on all such matters.

The limited power of the courts to review exercises of the prerogative power for constitutionality reflects the fact that in a constitutional democracy, all government power must be exercised in accordance with the Constitution. This said, judicial review of the exercise of the prerogative power for constitutionality remains sensitive to the fact that the executive branch of government is responsible for decisions under this power, and that the executive is better placed to make such decisions within a range of constitutional options. The government must have flexibility in deciding how its duties under the power are to be discharged. But it is for the courts to determine the legal and constitutional limits within which such decisions are to be taken. It follows that in the case of refusal by a government to abide by constitutional constraints, courts are empowered to make orders ensuring that the government's foreign affairs prerogative is exercised in accordance with the constitution.

Having concluded that the courts possess a narrow power to review and intervene on matters of foreign affairs to ensure the constitutionality of executive action, the final question is whether O'Reilly J. misdirected himself in exercising that power in the circumstances of this case. If the record and legal principle support his decision, deference requires we not interfere. However, in our view that is not the case.

Our first concern is that the remedy ordered below gives too little weight to the constitutional responsibility of the executive to make decisions on matters of foreign affairs in the context of complex and ever-changing circumstances, taking into account Canada's broader national interests. For the following reasons, we conclude that the appropriate remedy is to declare that, on the record before the Court, Canada infringed Mr. Khadr's s. 7 rights, and to leave it to the government to decide how best to respond to this judgment in light of current information, its responsibility for foreign affairs, and in conformity with the *Charter*.

---

## Notes and Comments:

1. If you were the judge in this case would you have ordered Omar Khadr's repatriation to Canada – why or why not?

2. After spending a decade in captivity at Guantanamo Bay, Omar Khadr pleaded guilty of "murder in violation of the laws of war" for killing U.S. Army Sergeant 1st class Christopher Speer. In exchange for his guilty plea, Khadr was released and returned home to Canada. Khadr then appealed his conviction on the grounds that it was coerced and he sued the Canadian government. In July 2017, the Canadian government formally apologized to Khadr for violating his rights under the Canadian Charter of Rights and Freedoms and paid him $10 million in compensation for this.

3. Since it has been established that a Canadian citizen has been subjected to the "frequent flyer program" by U.S. officials, should Canada pursue a legal remedy against the United States? For example, should it pursue a claim before the International Court of Justice? Or file an inter-state complaint under Article 21 of the Torture Convention, which reads in part:

A State Party to this Convention may at any time declare under this article that it recognizes the competence of the Committee to receive and consider communications to the effect that a State Party claims that another State Party is not fulfilling its obligations under this Convention.

The United States and Canada have both agreed to receive inter-state complaints. Note, however, that not a single inter-state complaint has ever been filed under any of the U.N. international human rights treaties – including the Torture Convention.

---

**Box 2.8: International Law at the Movies: The Interrogation of Omar Khadr**

For those with a particular interest in Omar Khadr's case the documentary *You Don't Like the Truth: Four Days Inside of Guantanamo* (2010) is a must see. What the film presents are four days of Khadr being interrogated by Canadian security officials posing as diplomats who have traveled to Guantanamo ostensibly to help the young and scared 16-year-old. However, when he does not provide them with the information they want – thus the title – the "good cop" routine changes instantly. As far as I know, this is the only video of a Guantanamo Bay interrogation and the only reason for its public release is that this was ordered by the Canadian judiciary.

---

## References

### Books and Articles

Moazzam Begg (with Victoria Brittain), *Enemy Combatant: A British Muslim's Journey to Guantanamo and Back*, London: Free Press (2006)

Mark Denbeaux et al., "No Hearing Habeas: D.C. Circuit Restricts Meaningful Review." Available at: https://law.shu.edu/ProgramsCenters/PublicIntGovServ/policyresearch/upload/hearing-habeas.pdf

International Committee of the Red Cross, "Customary International Humanitarian Law." Available at: https://ihl-databases.icrc.org/customary-ihl/eng/docs/v1_cha_chapter32_rule100

Neil A. Lewis, "Red Cross Finds Detainee Abuse in Guantanamo," *New York Times*, (November 30, 2004). Available at: www.nytimes.com/2004/11/30/politics/red-cross-finds-detainee-abuse-in-guantanamo.html

Jane Mayer, *The Dark Side: The Inside Story of How the War on Terror Turned Into a War on American Ideals*, New York, NY: Anchor Books (2009)

### U.S. Government Report

Office of the Inspector General, *The September 11 Detainees: A Review of the Treatment of Aliens Held on Immigration Charges in Connection With the Investigation of the September 11 Attacks*, Washington, DC: U.S. Department of Justice (2003)

### Cases

*A (and Others) v. United Kingdom*, ECtHR, App. No. 3455/05 (2009)

*Al-Adahi v. Obama*, 613 F. 3d 1102 (D.C. Cir. 2010)

*Al Maqaleh v. Gates*, 605 F. 3d 84 (D.D.C. 2010)

*Bivens v. Six Unnamed Known Agents of Federal Bureau of Narcotics*, 403 U.S. 388 (1971)

*Boumediene v. Bush*, 553 U.S. 723 (2008)

*Chahal v. United Kingdom*, ECtHR, App. No. 22414/93 (1996)

*Hamdan v. Rumsfeld*, 548 U.S. 557 (2006)

*Hamdi v. Rumsfeld*, 542 U.S. 507 (2004)

*Canada v. Khadr*, 2010 SCC 3, [2010] 1 S.C.R. 44

*Latif v. Obama*, 677 F. 3d 1175 (D.D.C. 2012)

*Rasul v. Bush*, 542 U.S. 466 (2004)

*Ziglar v. Abbasi*, 582 U.S. ____ (2017)

### International Agreements

Convention Against Torture and Other Cruel, Inhuman or Degrading Treatment or Punishment, adopted and opened for signature 10 December 1984, entry into force 26 June 1987

Geneva Conventions, adopted on 12 August 1949, entry into force 21 October 1950

## Domestic Law

Authorization for the Use of Military Force, Public Law 107-40, codified at 115 Stat. 224, passed as S.J. Res 23 on 14 September 2001 (U.S.)

Detainee Treatment Act, 42 U.S.C. 21D (U.S.)

Military Commissions Act of 2006, Public Law No. 109-366 (U.S.)

# Extraordinary Rendition

## 54 States

The "war on terror" brought a new term into the public lexicon: extraordinary rendition. Extraordinary rendition is a practice where a suspected terrorist is kidnapped in one state and sent to another country where he is tortured (or worse). The *Open Society Justice Initiative* estimates that 54 countries played some role in extraordinary rendition practices, and what is perhaps even more astounding than the number itself is the fact that so many Western states (in bold) had portrayed themselves as strong proponents of human rights.

Afghanistan, *Albania*, Algeria, *Australia*, *Austria*, *Azerbaijan*, *Belgium*, *Bosnia-Herzegovina*, *Canada*, *Croatia*, *Cyprus*, the *Czech Republic*, *Denmark*, Djibouti, Egypt, Ethiopia, *Finland*, Gambia, *Georgia*, *Germany*, *Greece*, *Hong Kong*, *Iceland*, Indonesia, Iran, *Ireland*, *Italy*, Jordan, Kenya, Libya, *Lithuania*, *Macedonia*, Malawi, Malaysia, Mauritania, Morocco, Pakistan, *Poland*, *Portugal*, *Romania*, Saudi Arabia, Somalia, South Africa, *Spain*, Sri Lanka, *Sweden*, Syria, Thailand, *Turkey*, United Arab Emirates, *United Kingdom*, *Uzbekistan*, Yemen, and Zimbabwe.

Of course, not all of these states were involved in the same way. Some served as refueling sites and detention centers, while Syria and Egypt were places where some of the most brutal aspects of extraordinary rendition were carried out (New York City Bar 2004). The role and the responsibility of the United States raises a different set of questions. One of the oddities of the *Arar* and *El-Masri* cases set

113

forth in this chapter was the direct involvement of U.S. security personnel in both matters. For the most part, American involvement was much less evident, leaving the "dirty work," so to speak, to others.

We return to the issue of state responsibility in Chapter 9. However, this issue of state responsibility arises throughout the book. In the context of extraordinary rendition in particular, has a state that allows a "torture flight" to refuel on its territory violated international law? What about a state that allows such a flight to fly over its airspace?

The cases in this chapter do not get into these more nuanced issues. Rather, they all deal with situations of what we might call more direct state involvement. Still, as shown in the following two cases involving the United States, the road to responsibility is anything but straightforward (Guild, Bigo, and Gibney 2018). Thus, although the United States was the mastermind behind the extraordinary rendition program, not one victim has been successful in suing federal (U.S.) officials who directed and/or carried out these practices against them. In the *Arar* case, the court dismissed the action on the basis of a narrow reading of the *Bivens* doctrine (also see Box 2.1), while *El-Masri* does so on the grounds of "state secrets."

---

**Box 3.1: Feinstein Report**

**Photo 3.1** Senator Dianne Feinstein of the Senate Intelligence Committee
*Source*: © Associated Press

The U.S. Senate Intelligence Committee initiated a review of the CIA's Detention and Interrogation Program in March 2009, chaired by Senator Dianne Feinstein

(D-CA). The Committee approved the study on December 13, 2012 by a vote of 9–6. Following further discussions, including with the CIA, the Committee voted to declassify the study by a vote of 11–3. The executive summary of the study – which is more than 500 pages in length – has been released to the public. However, the study itself, which runs to 6,700 pages, has not been publicly released. According to the executive summary, the findings of the study fall into four main categories:

1. The CIA's "enhanced interrogation techniques" were not effective.
2. The CIA provided extensive misleading information about the operation of the program and its effectiveness to policymakers and the public.
3. The CIA's management of the program was inadequate and deeply flawed.
4. The CIA program was far more brutal than the CIA represented to policymakers and the American public (Guild 2018).

Although the Committee had been guaranteed full access to all CIA information on the extraordinary rendition program, it was quickly discovered that there were substantial gaps; most notably, videotapes of interrogations had been destroyed. And notwithstanding an agreement that the Committee would have unfettered access to the CIA computer system without surveillance, this agreement was breached on a number of occasions by the CIA, which searched the email exchanges of Committee members and its staff.

Finally, although torture is a violation of both domestic (U.S.) and international law, those involved in the design and implementation of the Detention and Interrogation Program were later immunized from prosecution by the Obama administration (Greenwald 2012).

In contrast to this, in *El-Masri v. Macedonia*, the ECtHR ruled that Macedonia had acted in violation of the European Convention not only for its own activities in carrying out torture, but also those subsequently carried out by American officials after he was turned over to CIA agents. In addition, in a stirring decision in *Zubaydah v. Poland*, the ECtHR condemned the Polish government both for allowing the CIA to set up a "black site" on Polish soil, but also for the government's apparent unwillingness to investigate the matter after these events became public knowledge.

The final case in this chapter raises the issue whether evidence obtained in another state, quite possibly by means of torture, could be introduced in a domestic trial in the United Kingdom.

**The American Judiciary**

---

## *Arar v. Ashcroft,* 585 F.3d 559 (2d Cir. 2009)

Arar is a dual citizen of Syria, where he was born and raised, and of Canada, to which his family immigrated when he was 17.

While on vacation in Tunisia in September 2002, Arar was called back to work in Montreal. His itinerary called for stops in Zurich and New York.

Arar landed at Kennedy Airport around noon on September 26. Between planes, Arar presented his Canadian passport to an immigration official who, after checking Arar's credentials, asked Arar to wait nearby. About two hours later, Arar was finger-printed and his bags searched. Between 4 p.m. and 9 p.m., Arar was interviewed by an agent from the Federal Bureau of Investigation ("FBI"), who asked about his relationships with certain individuals who were suspected of terrorist ties. Arar admitted knowing at least one of them, but denied being a member of a terrorist group. Following the FBI interview, Arar was questioned by an official from the Immigration and Naturalization Service ("INS") for three more hours; he continued to deny terrorist affiliations.

**Photo 3.2**  Maher Arar Following His Release From Captivity

*Source:* © Associated Press

Arar spent the night alone in a room at the airport. The next morning (September 27) he was questioned by FBI agents from approximately 9 a.m. until 2 p.m.; the agents asked him about Osama Bin Laden, Iraq, Palestine, and other things. That evening, Arar was given an opportunity to return voluntarily to Syria. He refused, citing a fear of torture, and asked instead to go to Canada or Switzerland. Later that evening, he was transferred to the Metropolitan Detention Center ("MDC") in Brooklyn, where he remained until October 8.

On October 1, the INS initiated removal proceedings, and served Arar with a document stating that he was inadmissible because he belonged to a terrorist organization. Later that day, he called his mother-in-law in Ottawa – his prior requests to place calls and speak to a lawyer having been denied or ignored. His family retained a lawyer to represent him and contacted the Canadian Consulate in New York.

A Canadian consular official visited Arar on October 3. The next day, immigration officers asked Arar to designate in writing the country to which he would want to be removed. He designated Canada. On the evening of October 5, Arar met with his attorney. The following evening, a Sunday, Arar was again questioned by INS officials. The INS District Director in New York left a voicemail message on the office phone of Arar's attorney that the interview would take place, but the attorney did not receive the message in time to attend. Arar was told that she chose not to attend. In days following, the attorney was given false information about Arar's whereabouts.

Arar was taken to New Jersey, whence he flew in a small jet to Washington, D.C., and then to Amman, Jordan. When he arrived in Amman on October 9, he was handed over to Jordanian authorities who treated him roughly and then delivered him to the custody of Syrian officials, who detained him at a Syrian Military Intelligence facility. Arar was in Syria for a year, the first ten months in an underground cell six feet by three, and seven feet high. He was interrogated for twelve days on his arrival in Syria, and in that period was beaten on his palms, hips, and lower back with a two-inch-thick electric cable and with bare hands. Arar alleges that United States officials conspired to send him to Syria for the purpose of interrogation under torture, and directed the interrogations from abroad by providing Syria with Arar's dossier, dictating questions for the Syrians to ask him, and receiving intelligence learned from the interviews.

On October 20, 2002, Canadian Embassy officials inquired of Syria as to Arar's whereabouts. The next day, Syria confirmed to Canada that Arar was in its custody; that same day, interrogation ceased. Arar remained in Syria, however, receiving visits from Canadian consular officials. On August 14, 2003, Arar defied his captors by telling the Canadians that he had been tortured and was confined to a small underground cell. Five days later, after signing a confession that he had trained as a terrorist in Afghanistan, Arar was moved to various locations. On October 5, 2003, Arar was released to the custody of a Canadian embassy official in Damascus, and was flown to Ottawa the next day.

In *Bivens v. Six Unknown Named Agents of Federal Bureau of Narcotics*, the Supreme Court recognized for the first time an implied private action for damages against federal officers alleged to have violated a citizen's constitutional rights. The plaintiff in *Bivens* had been subjected to an unlawful, warrantless search which resulted in his arrest. The Supreme Court allowed him to state a cause of action for money damages directly under the Fourth Amendment, thereby giving rise to a judicially-created remedy stemming directly from the Constitution itself.

The purpose of the *Bivens* remedy "is to deter individual federal officers from committing constitutional violations." So a *Bivens* action is brought against individuals, and any damages are payable by the offending officers. Notwithstanding the potential breadth of claims that would serve that objective, the Supreme Court has warned that the *Bivens* remedy is an extraordinary thing that should rarely if ever be applied in "new contexts."

This case requires us to examine whether allowing this *Bivens* action to proceed would extend *Bivens* to a new "context," and if so, whether such an extension is advisable.

"Context" is not defined in the case law. At a sufficiently high level of generality, any claim can be analogized to some other claim for which a *Bivens* action is afforded, just as at a sufficiently high level of particularity, every case has points of distinction.

We construe the word "context" as it is commonly used in law: to reflect a potentially recurring scenario that has similar legal and factual components.

The context of this case is international rendition, specifically, "extraordinary rendition." Extraordinary rendition is treated as a distinct phenomenon in international law. Indeed, law review articles that affirmatively advocate the creation of a remedy in cases like Arar's recognize "extraordinary rendition" as the context. More particularly, the context of extraordinary rendition in Arar's case is the complicity or cooperation of United States government officials in the delivery of a non-citizen to a foreign country for torture (or with the expectation that torture will take place). This is a "new context": no court has previously afforded a *Bivens* remedy for extraordinary rendition.

A suit seeking a damages remedy against senior officials who implement an extraordinary rendition policy would enmesh the courts ineluctably in an assessment of the validity and rationale of that policy and its implementation in this particular case, matters that directly affect significant diplomatic and national security concerns. It is clear from the face of the complaint that Arar explicitly targets the "policy" of extraordinary rendition; he cites the policy twice in his complaint, and submits documents and media reports concerning the practice. His claim cannot proceed without inquiry into the perceived need for the policy, the threats to which it responds, the substance and sources of the intelligence used to formulate it, and the propriety of adopting specific responses to particular threats in light of apparent geopolitical circumstances and our relations with foreign countries.

The Supreme Court has expressly counseled that matters touching upon foreign policy and national security fall within "an area of executive action 'in which courts have long been hesitant to intrude'" absent congressional authorization. It "has recognized 'the generally accepted view that foreign policy was the province and responsibility of the Executive. . . . Thus, unless Congress specifically has provided otherwise, courts traditionally have been *reluctant* to intrude upon the authority of the Executive in military and national security affairs.'"

---

## Notes and Comments:

1. If you were a judge in Arar's case, would you have issued the same kind of ruling?

2. For a short film clip of Maher Arar: www.youtube.com/watch?v=RFd Fvih F_NM

3. One of the interesting things to note is how vastly different the United States and Canada responded to Arar's situation. For their part, the Canadian government issued a state apology to Maher Arar and provided him with $10 million as a way of providing restitution to him. The American judiciary not only dismissed Arar's claim, but to this day Maher Arar remains on the U.S. government's terrorist "watchlist."

4. In Part IV we focus on violations of international human rights standards. Of course, extraordinary renditions are replete with any number of violations, beginning with the kidnapping, the imprisonment without any semblance of due process, and finally, the violation of the prohibition against torture.

5. One of the unique features of the Arar case is that it appears to be the only extraordinary rendition case where the victim had actually been on U.S. territory. In all other instances, the suspected terrorist was kidnapped someplace outside the United States and then transported to other states where the "enhanced interrogation" took place. The issue of whether the United States was "responsible" for committing an internationally wrongful act for essentially directing the extraordinary rendition program will be more fully addressed in Chapter 9. However, in the Maher Arar case it is clear the U.S. violated the *nonrefoulement* principle, which is that a state cannot send an individual to a country where that person's life or freedom might be threatened.

---

**Box 3.2: Double Victimization: The Denial of an "Effective Remedy"**

Article 2 (3) of the International Covenant on Civil and Political Rights provides: Each State Party to the present Covenant undertakes:

(a) To ensure that any person whose rights or freedoms as herein recognized are violated shall have an effective remedy, notwithstanding that the violation has been committed by persons acting in an official capacity;

(b) To ensure that any person claiming such a remedy shall have his right thereto determined by competent judicial, administrative or legislative authorities, or by any other competent authority provided for by the legal system of the State, and to develop the possibilities of judicial remedy;

(c) To ensure that the competent authorities shall enforce such remedies when granted.

---

While Maher Arar's lawsuit against various federal officials was dismissed on the basis of a narrow reading of the *Bivens* doctrine, the more common judicial response was to invoke the "state secrets" doctrine and dismiss the suit on that basis.

---

## *El-Masri v. United States*, 479 F.3d 296 (4th Cir. 2007)

On December 6, 2005, El-Masri, a German citizen of Lebanese descent, filed his Complaint in this case, alleging, in substance, as follows: on December 31, 2003, while travelling in Macedonia, he was detained by Macedonian law enforcement officials; after twenty-three days in Macedonian custody, he was handed over to CIA operatives, who flew him to a CIA-operated detention facility near Kabul, Afghanistan; he was held in

**Photo 3.3** Khalid El-Masri Following His Release From Captivity

*Source*: © Associated Press

this CIA facility until May 28, 2004, when he was transported to Albania and released in a remote area; and Albanian officials then picked him up and took him to an airport in Tirana, Albania, from which he travelled to his home in Germany. The Complaint asserted that El-Masri had not only been held against his will, but had also been mistreated in a number of other ways during his detention, including being beaten, drugged, bound, and blindfolded during transport; confined in a small, unsanitary cell; interrogated several times; and consistently prevented from communicating with anyone outside the detention facility, including his family or the German government. El-Masri alleged that his detention and interrogation were carried out pursuant to an unlawful policy and practice devised and implemented by defendant [CIA Director] Tenet known as "extraordinary rendition": the clandestine abduction and detention outside the United States of persons suspected of involvement in terrorist activities, and their subsequent interrogation using methods impermissible under U.S. and international laws.

The heart of El-Masri's appeal is his assertion that the facts essential to his Complaint have largely been made public, either in statements by United States officials or in reports by media outlets and foreign governmental entities. He maintains that the subject of this action is simply "a rendition and its consequences," and that its critical facts – the CIA's operation of a rendition program targeted at terrorism suspects, plus the tactics employed therein – have been so widely discussed that litigation concerning them could do no harm to national security. As a result, El-Masri contends that the district court should have allowed his case to move forward with discovery, perhaps with special procedures imposed to protect sensitive information.

El-Masri's contention in that regard, however, misapprehends the nature of our assessment of a dismissal on state secrets grounds. The controlling inquiry is not whether the general subject matter of an action can be described without resort to state secrets. Rather, we must ascertain whether an action can be *litigated* without threatening the disclosure of such state secrets. Thus, for purposes of the state secrets analysis, the "central facts" and "very subject matter" of an action are those facts that are essential to prosecuting the action or defending against it.

El-Masri is therefore incorrect in contending that the central facts of this proceeding are his allegations that he was detained and interrogated under abusive conditions, or that the CIA conducted the rendition program that has been acknowledged by United States officials. Facts such as those furnish the general terms in which El-Masri has related his story to the press, but advancing a case in the court of public opinion, against the United States at large, is an undertaking quite different from prevailing against specific defendants in a court of law. If El-Masri's civil action were to proceed, the facts central to its resolution would be the roles, if any, that the defendants played in the events he alleges. To establish a prima facie case, he would be obliged to produce admissible evidence not only that he was detained and interrogated, but that the defendants were involved in his detention and interrogation in a manner that renders them personally liable to him. Such a showing could be made only with evidence that exposes how the CIA organizes, staffs, and supervises its most sensitive intelligence operations. With regard to Director Tenet, for example, El-Masri would be obliged to show in detail how the head of the CIA participates in such operations, and how information concerning their progress is relayed to him. With respect to the defendant corporations and their unnamed employees, El-Masri would have to demonstrate the existence and details of CIA espionage contracts. Even marshalling the evidence necessary to make the requisite showings would implicate privileged state secrets, because El-Masri would need to rely on witnesses whose identities, and evidence the very existence of which, must remain confidential in the interest of national security.

Contrary to El-Masri's assertion, the state secrets doctrine does not represent a surrender of judicial control over access to the courts. As we have explained, it is the court, not the Executive that determines whether the state secrets privilege has been properly invoked. In order to successfully claim the state secrets privilege, the Executive must satisfy the court that disclosure of the information sought to be protected would expose matters that, in the interest of national security, ought to remain secret. Similarly, in order to win dismissal of an action on state secrets grounds, the Executive must persuade the court that state secrets are so central to the action that it cannot be fairly litigated without threatening their disclosure. The state secrets privilege cannot be successfully interposed, nor can it lead to dismissal of an action, based merely on the Executive's assertion that the pertinent standard has been met.

In this matter, the reasons for the United States' claim of the state secrets privilege and its motion to dismiss were explained largely in the Classified Declaration, which sets forth in detail the nature of the information that the Executive seeks to protect and explains why its disclosure would be detrimental to national security. We have reviewed the Classified Declaration, as did the district court, and the extensive information it contains is crucial to our decision in this matter. El-Masri's contention that his Complaint was dismissed based on the Executive's "unilateral assertion of a need for secrecy" is entirely unfounded. It is no doubt frustrating to El-Masri that many of the specific reasons for the dismissal of his Complaint are classified. An inherent feature of the state secrets privilege, however, is that the party against whom it is asserted will often not be privy to the information that the Executive seeks to protect. That El-Masri is unfamiliar with the Classified Declaration's explanation for the privilege claim does not imply, as he would have it, that no such explanation was required, or that the district court's ruling was simply an unthinking ratification of a conclusory demand by the executive branch.

---

### Box 3.3: International Law at the Movies: Extraordinary Rendition

*Rendition* (2007) is a feature film starring some of the biggest names in Hollywood – Meryl Streep, Reese Witherspoon, and Jake Gyllenhaal, to name a few – in

*(Continued)*

**Box 3.3: Continued**

its depiction of the rendition of an innocent man. *Rendition* is not to be confused with *Extraordinary Rendition* (2007), a feature film about an abduction on the streets of London and the horrors that soon follow.

## Notes and Comments:

1. The Court concedes that El-Masri might be "frustrated" because of his inability to see the evidence being used to dismiss his case. Is this the word you would use?
2. For a short film clip on Khalid El-Masri: www.youtube.com/watch?v=-Hh-877s01U
3. One of the questions you might have is what the response of the German government was to El-Masri's rendition. At the end of January 2007, a court in Munich issued arrest warrants for 13 CIA agents. These warrants were forwarded to Interpol, a move that apparently alarmed U.S. officials. However, a few years later Wikileaks published a cable that indicated that, a short time after the indictments were issued, the German government began cooperating with the United States and the matter was soon dropped. In light of this, would El-Masri have a cause of action against the German government as well?

**Box 3.4: Extraordinary Rendition and the CAT**

As a state party to the Torture Convention, the United States is required to file periodic reports with the Committee Against Torture (CAT), which in response provides its own Conclusions and Recommendations. In 2015, the CAT recognized President Obama's executive order (13491) ending the extraordinary rendition program. However, it criticized the continued lack of legal proceedings against the architects of the program.

> The Committee expresses its grave concern over the extraordinary rendition, secret detention and interrogation programme operated by the U.S. Central Intelligence Agency (CIA) between 2001 and 2008, which involved numerous human rights violations, including torture, ill-treatment and enforced disappearance of persons suspected of involvement in terrorism-related crimes. While noting the content and scope of Presidential E.O. 13491, the Committee regrets the scant information provided by the State party with regard to the now shuttered network of secret detention facilities, which formed part of the high-value detainee programme publicly referred to by President Bush

on 6 September 2006. It also regrets the lack of information provided on the practices of extraordinary rendition and enforced disappearance; and, on the extent of the CIA's abusive interrogation techniques used on suspected terrorists, such as water-boarding. In this regard, the Committee is closely following the declassification process of the U.S. Senate Select Committee on Intelligence's report [Feinstein Report] on the CIA's detention and interrogation programme.

## The European Response

The next case comes from the European Court of Human Rights (ECtHR), which not only afforded Khaled El-Masri his day in court, but ruled that Macedonia was responsible for the human rights violations carried out by CIA officials after he was turned over to the Americans. Also, notice how differently the facts are set forth here as opposed to the previous case.

## *El-Masri v. Macedonia,* ECtHR, App. No. 39630/09 (2012)

On 31 December 2003, the applicant boarded a bus in Ulm, Germany, with a view to visiting Skopje in order, as he stated, "to take a short vacation and some time off from a stressful home environment". At around 3 p.m., he arrived at the Serbian/Macedonian border crossing at Tabanovce. A suspicion arose as to the validity of his recently issued German passport. A border official checked his passport and asked him about the purpose of his trip and the length and location of his intended stay. A Macedonian entry stamp dated 31 December 2003 was affixed to his passport. On that occasion, his personal belongings were searched and he was questioned about possible ties with several Islamic organisations and groups. The interrogation ended at 10 p.m. Accompanied by men in civilian clothes who were armed, he was driven to a hotel, which later research indicated was the Skopski Merak Hotel in Skopje ("the hotel"). Upon his return to Germany, the applicant recognised, through photographs available on the hotel's website, the hotel building, the room where allegedly he had been held and one of the waiters who had served him food during his detention in the hotel.

The applicant was taken to a room on the top floor of the hotel. During his detention at the hotel, he was watched by a team of nine men, who changed shift every six hours. Three of them were with him at all times, even when he was sleeping. He was interrogated repeatedly throughout the course of his detention. He was questioned in English despite his limited proficiency in that language. His requests to contact the German embassy were refused. On one occasion, when he stated that he intended to leave, a gun was pointed at his head and he was threatened with being shot. After seven days of confinement, another official arrived and offered him a deal, namely that he would be sent back to Germany in return for a confession that he was a member of al-Qaeda.

On 23 January 2004 at around 8 p.m., the applicant was filmed by a video camera and instructed to say that he had been treated well, that he had not been harmed in any way and that he would shortly be flown back to Germany. Handcuffed and blindfolded, he was put in a car and taken to Skopje Airport.

Upon arrival, still handcuffed and blindfolded, he was initially placed in a chair, where he sat for one and a half hours. He was told that he would be taken into a room for a medical examination before being transferred to Germany. Then, two people violently pulled his arms back. On that occasion he was beaten severely from all sides. His clothes were sliced from his body with scissors or a knife. His underwear was forcibly removed. He was thrown to the floor, his hands were pulled back and a boot was placed on his back. He then felt a firm object being forced into his anus. As stated by the applicant's lawyers at the public hearing of 16 May 2012, of all the acts perpetrated against the applicant that had been the most degrading and shameful. A bag was placed over his head and a belt was put on him with chains attached to his wrists and ankles. He had difficulty breathing because of the bag that covered his head. Once inside the aircraft, he was thrown to the floor face down and his legs and arms were spread-eagled and secured to the sides of the aircraft. During the flight he received two injections.

Upon landing, the applicant disembarked. It was warmer outside than it had been in the former Yugoslav Republic of Macedonia, which was sufficient for him to conclude that he had not been returned to Germany. He deduced later that he was in Afghanistan and that he had been flown via Baghdad.

After landing in Afghanistan, the applicant was driven for about ten minutes, then dragged from the vehicle, slammed into the walls of a room, thrown to the floor, kicked and beaten. His head and neck were specifically targeted and stepped upon. He was left in a small, dirty, dark concrete cell. When he adjusted his eyes to the light, he saw that the walls were covered in Arabic, Urdu and Farsi handwriting. The cell did not contain a bed. Although it was cold, he had been provided with only one dirty, military-style blanket and some old, torn clothes bundled into a thin pillow. Later he understood that he had been transferred to a CIA-run facility which media reports have identified as the "Salt Pit", a brick factory north of the Kabul business district that was used by the CIA for detention and interrogation of some high-level terror suspects.

During his confinement, he was interrogated on three or four occasions, each time by the same man, who spoke Arabic with a south Lebanese accent, and each time at night. His interrogations were accompanied by threats, insults, pushing and shouting. His repeated requests to meet with a representative of the German government were ignored.

In March 2004 the applicant, together with several other inmates with whom he communicated through cell walls, commenced a hunger strike to protest about their continued confinement without charge. As a consequence of the conditions of his confinement and his hunger strike, the applicant's health deteriorated on a daily basis. He received no medical treatment during this time, although he had requested it on several occasions.

On 10 April 2004, the thirty-seventh day of his hunger strike, hooded men entered his cell, pulled him from his bed and bound his hands and feet. They dragged him into the interrogation room, sat him on a chair and tied him to it. A feeding tube was then forced through his nose to his stomach and a liquid was poured through it. After this procedure, the applicant was given some canned food, as well as some books to read.

Following his force-feeding, the applicant became extremely ill and suffered very severe pain. A doctor visited his cell in the middle of the night and administered medication, but he remained bedridden for several days.

On 28 May 2004 the applicant, blindfolded and handcuffed, was led out of his cell and locked in what seemed to be a shipping container until he heard the sound of an aircraft arriving. On that occasion, he was handed the suitcase that had been taken from him in Skopje. He was told to change back into the clothes he had worn upon his arrival in the former Yugoslav Republic of Macedonia and was given two new T-shirts, one of which he put on. He was then taken to the waiting aircraft, wearing a blindfold and earmuffs, and was chained to his seat there. "Sam" accompanied him on the aircraft. He said that the plane would land in a European country other than Germany, but that the applicant would eventually continue on to Germany.

When the aircraft landed, the applicant, still blindfolded, was placed in the back seat of a vehicle. He was not told where he was. He was driven in the vehicle up and down mountains, on paved and unpaved roads. He was taken from the car and his blindfold was removed. His captors gave him his belongings and passport, removed his handcuffs and directed him to walk down the path without turning back. It was dark and the road was deserted. He believed he would be shot in the back and left to die. He rounded a corner and came across three armed men. They immediately asked for his passport. They saw that his German passport had no visa in it and asked him why he was in Albania without legal permission. He replied that he had no idea where he was. He was told that he was near the Albanian borders with the former Yugoslav Republic of Macedonia and Serbia. The men led him to a small building with an Albanian flag and he was presented to a superior officer. The officer observed the applicant's long hair and long beard and told him that he looked like a terrorist. He was then driven to Mother Teresa Airport in Tirana. He was guided through customs and immigration control without inspection and put on a plane to Frankfurt, Germany. An Albanian exit stamp was affixed to the applicant's passport.

On 29 May 2004 at 8.40 a.m. the applicant arrived at Frankfurt International Airport. He was about eighteen kilograms lighter than when he had left Germany, his hair was long and unkempt, and he had not shaved since his arrival in the former Yugoslav Republic of Macedonia.

## THE LAW

### ALLEGED VIOLATION OF ARTICLE 3 OF THE CONVENTION

The applicant complained that the respondent State had been responsible for the ill-treatment to which he had been subjected while he was detained in the hotel and for the failure to prevent him from being subjected to "capture shock" treatment when transferred to the CIA rendition team at Skopje Airport. He further complained that the respondent State had been responsible for his ill-treatment during his detention in the "Salt Pit" in Afghanistan by having knowingly transferred him into the custody of US agents even though there had been substantial grounds for believing that there was a real risk of such ill-treatment. In this latter context, he complained that the conditions of detention, physical assaults, inadequate food and water, sleep deprivation, forced feeding and lack of any medical assistance during his detention in the "Salt Pit" amounted to treatment contrary to Article 3 of the Convention. Lastly, he complained that the investigation before the Macedonian authorities had not been effective within the meaning of this Article.

Article 3 of the Convention reads as follows:

"No one shall be subjected to torture or to inhuman or degrading treatment or punishment."

It is the settled case-law of the Court that the decision by a Contracting State to remove a fugitive – and, a fortiori, the actual removal itself – may give rise to an issue under Article 3, and hence engage the responsibility of that State under the Convention, where substantial grounds have been shown for believing that the person in question would, if extradited, face a real risk of being subjected to treatment contrary to

Article 3 in the receiving country. The establishment of such responsibility inevitably involves an assessment of conditions in the requesting country against the standards of Article 3 of the Convention. Nonetheless, there is no question of adjudicating on or establishing the responsibility of the receiving country, whether under general international law, under the Convention or otherwise. Insofar as any liability under the Convention is or may be incurred, it is liability incurred by the sending Contracting State by reason of its having taken action which has as a direct consequence the exposure of an individual to proscribed ill-treatment

On the basis of the facts already established to the required standard of proof, the Court must examine whether any responsibility may be attributed to the respondent State for having transferred the applicant into the custody of the US authorities.

In the first place, the Court notes that there is no evidence that the applicant's transfer into the custody of CIA agents was pursuant to a legitimate request for his extradition or any other legal procedure recognised in international law for the transfer of a prisoner to foreign authorities. Furthermore, no arrest warrant has been shown to have existed at the time authorising the delivery of the applicant into the hands of US agents.

Secondly, the evidence suggests that the Macedonian authorities had knowledge of the destination to which the applicant would be flown from Skopje Airport. Documents issued by the Civil Aviation Administration confirm that the aircraft N313P was allowed to land on 23 January 2004 at Skopje Airport. At 10.30 p.m. on the same day, permission was given for the aircraft to take off for Kabul. At 2.25 a.m. on 24 January 2004, the authorities authorised its onward route to Baghdad.

Thirdly, the Court attaches importance to the reports and relevant international and foreign jurisprudence, and – given the specific circumstances of the present case – to media articles, referred to above, which constitute reliable sources reporting practices that have been resorted to or tolerated by the US authorities and that are manifestly contrary to the principles of the Convention. The Court has already found some of these reports "worrying" and expressed its grave concerns about the interrogation methods used by the US authorities on persons suspected of involvement in international terrorism and detained in the naval base in Guantánamo Bay and in Bagram (Afghanistan). This material was in the public domain before the applicant's actual transfer into the custody of the US authorities. It is capable of proving that there were serious reasons to believe that if the applicant was to be transferred into US custody under the "rendition" programme, he would be exposed to a real risk of being subjected to treatment contrary to Article 3. Consequently, it must be concluded that the Macedonian authorities knew or ought to have known, at the relevant time, that there was a real risk that the applicant would be subjected to treatment contrary to Article 3 of the Convention. The Government failed to dispel any doubts in that regard. Material that came to light subsequent to the applicant's transfer confirms the existence of that risk.

Fourthly, the respondent State did not seek any assurances from the US authorities to avert the risk of the applicant being ill-treated.

In such circumstances, the Court considers that by transferring the applicant into the custody of the US authorities, the Macedonian authorities knowingly exposed him to a real risk of ill-treatment and to conditions of detention contrary to Article 3 of the Convention.

Having regard to the manner in which the applicant was transferred into the custody of the US authorities, the Court considers that he was subjected to "extraordinary rendition", that is, an "extrajudicial transfer of persons from one jurisdiction or State to another, for the purposes of detention and interrogation outside the normal legal system, where there was a real risk of torture or cruel, inhuman or degrading treatment".

Accordingly, the respondent State has violated Article 3 of the Convention on this account.

**Note and Comments:**

1. The ECtHR ruling in the *El-Masri* case is sometimes known for its reference to the "right to truth," which is referenced more in the joint concurring opinion of Judges Tulkens, Spielmann, Sicianos, and Keller:

> In relation to Article 13 of the Convention, which the Court unanimously found to have been breached in conjunction with Articles 3, 5 and 8, we would have liked the reasoning to extend to an aspect which in our view is fundamental. On account of the seriousness of the violations found, we consider that the Court should have acknowledged that in the absence of any effective remedies – as conceded by the Government – the applicant was denied the "right to the truth", that is, the right to an accurate account of the suffering endured and the role of those responsible for that ordeal.
>
> Obviously, this does not mean "truth" in the philosophical or metaphysical sense of the term but the right to ascertain and establish the true facts. As was pointed out by the United Nations High Commissioner for Human Rights, and also by Redress, Amnesty International and the International Commission of Jurists, in enforced disappearances cases the right to the truth is a particularly compelling norm in view of the secrecy surrounding the victims' fate.
>
> In addressing the applicant's complaint under Article 10 of the Convention that he "had a right to be informed of the truth regarding the circumstances that had led to the alleged violations", the Court considers that the issue raised overlaps with the merits of his Article 3 complaints and has already been dealt with in relation to those complaints. It could therefore be argued that the Court is implicitly acknowledging that the right to the truth has a place in the context of Article 3, although it does not really commit itself to such a finding, instead simply noting that there was an inadequate investigation which deprived the applicant of the possibility of being informed.
>
> In practice, the search for the truth is the objective purpose of the obligation to carry out an investigation and the raison d'être of the related quality requirements (transparency, diligence, independence, access, disclosure of results and scrutiny). For society in general, the desire to ascertain the truth plays a part in strengthening confidence in public institutions and hence the rule of law. For those concerned – the victims' families and close friends – establishing the true facts and securing an acknowledgment of serious breaches of human rights and humanitarian law constitute forms of redress that are just as important as compensation, and sometimes even more so. Ultimately, the wall of silence and the cloak of secrecy prevent these people

from making any sense of what they have experienced and are the greatest obstacles to their recovery.

What do you make of this "right to the truth"?

The final "extraordinary rendition" case we will examine also comes from the European Court of Human Rights and it involves one of the purported masterminds of the September 11 attacks.

---

## *Husayn (abu Zubydah) v. Poland*, ECtHR, App. No. 7511/13 (2014)

The applicant was born in 1971. He is currently detained in the Internment Facility at the United States Guantánamo Bay Naval Base in Cuba.

On 27 March 2002 agents of the United States and Pakistan seized the applicant from a house in Faisalabad, Pakistan. In the course of the operation, he was shot several times in the groin, thigh and stomach, which resulted in very serious wounds. He was taken into the custody of the CIA.

At the time of his capture the applicant was considered one of the key Al'Qaeda members and described by the American authorities as the "third or fourth man" in Al'Qaeda, who had had a role in its every major terrorist operation, including the role of a planner of the attacks on 11 September 2001. It was also alleged that he had been Osama bin Laden's senior lieutenant. As mentioned above, he was the first so-called "high-value detainee" ("the HVD") detained by the CIA at the beginning of the "war on terror" launched by President Bush after the 11 September 2001 attacks in the United States.

Subsequently – for more than four years from the day on which he was seized in Faisalabad until his transfer from the CIA's to the US Department of Defense's custody in September 2006 – the applicant was held in incommunicado detention in secret detention facilities, the so-called "black sites" run by the CIA around the world.

After his arrest, the applicant was transferred to a secret CIA detention facility in Thailand code-named "Cat's Eye" (often written as one word "Catseye" in CIA documents), where he was interrogated by CIA agents and where a variety of EITs were tested on him.

The applicant submitted that he had been transferred from Thailand to Poland under the HVD Programme on 5 December 2002.

The applicant's account of the abuse that he endured in CIA custody as rendered in the 2007 ICRC Report read, in so far as relevant, as follows:

I was then dragged from the small box, unable to walk properly and put on what looked like a hospital bed, and strapped down very tightly with belts. A black cloth was then placed over my face and the interrogators used a mineral water bottle to pour water on the cloth so that I could not breathe. After a few minutes the cloth was removed and the bed was rotated into an upright position. The pressure of the straps on my wounds was very painful. I vomited. The bed was then again lowered to horizontal position and the same torture carried out again with the black cloth over my face and water poured on from a bottle. On this occasion my head was in a more backward, downwards position and the water was poured on for a longer time. I struggled against the straps, trying to breathe, but it was hopeless. I thought I was going to die. I lost control of my urine. Since then I still lose control of my urine when under stress.

I was then placed again in the tall box. While I was inside the box loud music was played again and somebody kept banging repeatedly on the box from the outside. I tried to sit down on the floor, but because of the small space the bucket with urine tipped over and spilt over me. . . . I was then taken out and again a towel was wrapped around my neck and I was smashed into the wall with the plywood covering and repeatedly slapped in the face by the same two interrogators as before.

I was then made to sit on the floor with a black hood over my head until the next session of torture began. The room was always kept very cold. This went on for approximately one week. During this time the whole procedure was repeated five times. On each occasion, apart from one, I was suffocated once or twice and was put in the vertical position on the bed in between. On one occasion the suffocation was repeated three times. I vomited each time I was put in the vertical position between the suffocation.

During that week I was not given any solid food. I was only given ensure to drink. My head and beard were shaved every day.

I collapsed and lost consciousness on several occasions. Eventually the torture was stopped by the intervention of the doctor.

Since September 2006, the applicant has been held in the US Guantànamo Bay Naval Base in the highest security Camp 7 in extreme conditions of detention. Camp 7 was established to hold the High-Value Detainees transferred from the CIA to military custody.

The applicant's US counsel have been unable to provide many of the details of his physical and psychological injuries because all information obtained from him is presumed classified. They have stated that publicly available records described how prior injuries had been exacerbated by his ill-treatment and by his extended isolation, resulting in his permanent brain damage and physical impairment.

The applicant is suffering from blinding headaches and has developed an excruciating sensitivity to sound. Between 2008 and 2011 alone he experienced more than 300 seizures. At some point during his captivity, he lost his left eye. His physical pain has been compounded by his awareness that his mind has been slipping away. He suffers from partial amnesia and has difficulty remembering his family.

### PARLIAMENTARY INQUIRY IN POLAND

In November–December 2005 a brief parliamentary inquiry into allegations that a secret CIA detention site existed in the country was carried out in Poland. The inquiry was conducted by the Parliamentary Committee for Special Services (*Komisja do Spraw Służb Specjanych*) behind closed doors and none of its findings have been made public. The only public statement that the Polish Government made was at a press conference when they announced that the inquiry had not turned up anything "untoward".

The applicant's complaints under Article 3 of the Convention involved both substantive and procedural aspects of this provision.

1) As regards his alleged ill-treatment and detention in Poland, he complained that the Polish authorities had knowingly and intentionally enabled the CIA to hold him in secret detention at the Stare Kiejkuty site for more than nine months.

Poland had known about the CIA's rendition programme on its territory and of the real and immediate risk of torture to which High-Value Detainees under this programme had been subjected. Poland had actively agreed to establish a secret detention site and to facilitate the CIA unhindered use of that site.

2) Furthermore, the applicant alleged that Poland, by enabling the CIA to transfer him from its territory to its other secret black sites, had exposed him to years of further torture and ill-treatment. The Polish authorities had known, or should have known, of the real risk that he would continue to be held in the same detention regime as that to which he had been subjected until that point.

3) He also complained under Article 3 taken separately and in conjunction with Article 13 of the Convention that the Polish authorities had been in breach of the procedural obligations under Article 3 and that he had been denied the right to a remedy under Article 13, since they had failed to conduct an effective investigation into his into his allegations of torture, ill-treatment and secret detention in a CIA-run detention facility in Stare Kiejkuty and of being unlawfully transferred to places where he had faced further torture and ill-treatment.

Article 3 of the Convention states:

"No one shall be subjected to torture or to inhuman or degrading treatment or punishment."

The Court will first examine the applicant's complaint under the procedural aspect of Article 3 about the lack of an effective and thorough investigation into his allegations of ill-treatment when in CIA custody on Poland's territory.

### Applicable General Principles Deriving from the Court's Case-Law

Where an individual raises an arguable claim that he has suffered treatment infringing Article 3 at the hands of agents of the respondent State or, likewise, as a result of acts performed by foreign officials with that State's acquiescence or connivance, that provision, read in conjunction with the Contracting States' general duty under Article 1 of the Convention to "secure to everyone within their jurisdiction the rights and freedoms defined in. . . [the] Convention", requires by implication that there should be an effective official investigation. Such investigation should be capable of leading to the identification and punishment of those responsible. Otherwise, the general legal prohibition of torture and inhuman and degrading treatment and punishment would, despite its fundamental importance, be ineffective in practice and it would be possible in some cases for agents of the State to abuse the rights of those within their control with virtual impunity.

The investigation into serious allegations of ill-treatment must be both prompt and thorough. That means that the authorities must act of their own motion once the matter has come to their attention and must always make a serious attempt to find out what happened and should not rely on hasty or ill-founded conclusions to close their investigation or to use as the basis of their decisions. They must take all reasonable steps available to them to secure the evidence concerning the incident, including, *inter alia*, eyewitness testimony and forensic evidence. Any deficiency in the investigation which undermines its ability to establish the cause of injuries or the identity of the persons responsible will risk falling foul of this standard.

The investigation should be independent of the executive. Independence of the investigation implies not only the absence of a hierarchical or institutional connection, but also independence in practical terms. Furthermore, the victim should be able to participate effectively in the investigation in one form or another.

## Application of the Above Principles to the Present Case

The proceedings began as late as some 6 years after the applicant's detention and ill-treatment, despite the fact that the authorities must necessarily have been involved already at an early, preparatory stage of the implementation of the HVD Programme in Poland and that they knew of the nature and purposes of the CIA's activities on their territory between December 2002 and September 2003. However, at that time they did nothing to prevent those activities, let alone inquire into whether they were compatible with the national law and Poland's international obligations.

In the Court's view, this failure to inquire on the part of the Polish authorities, notwithstanding the abundance of publicly accessible information of widespread ill-treatment of al'Qaeda detainees in US custody emerging already in 2002–2003, could be explained in only one conceivable way. As shown by the sequence of the subsequent events, the nature of the CIA activities on Polish territory and Poland's complicity in those activities were to remain a secret shared exclusively by the intelligence services of the two cooperating countries.

The Court sees no other reason capable of explaining why, when in November 2005 Poland was for the first time publicly named as a country that had possibly hosted a CIA secret prison and received CIA-associated flights at the Szymany airport, there was no attempt to initiate any formal, meaningful procedure in order to clarify the circumstances surrounding the aircraft landings and the alleged CIA's use of, in the words of the 2005 [Human Rights Watch] Statement, "a large training facility and grounds near the Szymany airport" maintained by the Polish intelligence service. Nor did the inquiries instituted by the Council of Europe and the European Parliament prompt the Polish State to probe into those widely disseminated assertions of human rights violations. Indeed, the only response of the Polish authorities to the serious and *prima facie* credible allegations of their complicity in the CIA rendition and secret detention was to carry out a brief parliamentary inquiry in November-December 2005. The inquiry produced no results and was held behind closed doors. None of its findings have ever been made public and the only information that emerged afterwards was that the exercise did not entail anything "untoward."

### COURT'S CONCLUSION AS TO POLAND'S RESPONSIBILITY

The Court has already found that Poland knew of the nature and purposes of the CIA's activities on its territory at the material time and cooperated in the preparation and execution of the CIA rendition, secret detention and interrogation operations on its territory. It has also found that, given that knowledge and the emerging widespread public information about ill-treatment and abuse of detained terrorist suspects in the custody of the US authorities, it ought to have known that, by enabling the CIA to detain such persons on its territory, it exposed them to a serious risk of treatment contrary to the Convention.

It is true that, in the assessment of the experts – which the Court has accepted – the interrogations and, therefore, the torture inflicted on the applicant at the Stare Kiejkuty black site were the exclusive responsibility of the CIA and that it is unlikely that the Polish officials witnessed or knew exactly what happened inside the facility.

However, under Article 1 of the Convention, taken together with Article 3, Poland was required to take measures designed to ensure that individuals within its jurisdiction were not subjected to torture or inhuman or degrading treatment or punishment, including ill-treatment administered by private individuals.

Notwithstanding the above Convention obligation, Poland, for all practical purposes, facilitated the whole process, created the conditions for it to happen and made no attempt to prevent it from occurring. As the Court has already held above, on the basis of their own knowledge of the CIA activities deriving from Poland's complicity in the HVD Programme and from publicly accessible information on treatment applied in the context of the "war on terror" to terrorist suspects in US custody the authorities – even if they did not witness or participate in the specific acts of ill-treatment and abuse endured by the applicant – must have been aware of the serious risk of treatment contrary to Article 3 occurring on Polish territory.

Accordingly, the Polish State, on account of its "acquiescence and connivance" in the HVD Programme must be regarded as responsible for the violation of the applicant's rights under Article 3 of the Convention committed on its territory.

Furthermore, Poland was aware that the transfer of the applicant to and from its territory was effected by means of "extraordinary rendition", that is, "an extra-judicial transfer of persons from one jurisdiction or State to another, for the purposes of detention and interrogation outside the normal legal system, where there was a real risk of torture or cruel, inhuman or degrading treatment."

In these circumstances, the possibility of a breach of Article 3 was particularly strong and should have been considered intrinsic in the transfer. Consequently, by enabling the CIA to transfer the applicant to its other secret detention facilities, the Polish authorities exposed him to a foreseeable serious risk of further ill-treatment and conditions of detention in breach of Article 3 of the Convention.

---

## Notes and Comments:

1. How can you explain the stark differences in terms of how the U.S. judiciary has handled "extraordinary rendition" claims and the manner in which such cases have been handled by the European Court of Human Rights?

2. For an excellent treatment of the manner in which the Polish government did little to investigate these events, see Barbara Grabowska-Moroz (2018).

3. In many ways the *Zubydah* case is rather straightforward in the sense that he was tortured on Polish soil. However, as noted at the outset of this chapter, it has been estimated that upwards of 54 countries – more than a quarter of all the states in the world today – were involved, in one way or another, with extraordinary rendition practices. Should these "other" states be held legally responsible for their own involvement? If so, how should this be done? And to what extent should "responsibility" be determined?

4. In August 2017, two psychologists who were paid more than $80 million by the CIA to develop "enhanced interrogation" techniques reached an out-of-court settlement with three plaintiffs who alleged they had been tortured (Chappell 2017). In your view, what would be a "just" settlement? And should the U.S. government pay this?

---

### Box 3.5: The Rendition of Abu Omar

In addition to the *El-Masri* and *Zubydah* decisions, the European Court of Human Rights also handed down a ruling against Italy for the rendition of the Egyptian-born cleric Osama Mustafa Hassan Nar (better known as Abu Omar), who in February 2003 was abducted in broad daylight on the streets of Milan through a joint operation between Italian and American security officials (*Nasr and Ghali v. Italy*, ECtHR, App. No. 44883/09 (2016)). Abu Omar was first taken to a U.S. Air Force base in Germany and then transferred to Egypt where he was held for more than a year and interrogated throughout. The ECtHR ruled that Italy had violated a number of provisions of the European Convention, including the prohibition against torture.

One of the things that marks the Abu Omar situation are some of the attempts at holding both Italian and American security officials accountable. In terms of the latter, the office of the public prosecutor sought to have 22 CIA operatives arrested in order to be brought to trial. However, the Ministry of Justice declined to press for extradition. In response, the Milan District Court tried these individuals *in absentia*. What brought the case back into the public spotlight was that in 2016, one of those convicted, Sabrina de Sousa, a retired CIA operative, was arrested in Portugal and was about to be transferred to Italy to serve her sentence when the Italian government reduced her sentence, thereby allowing her to do community service in Portugal.

The second legal proceeding involved the arrest of two high-ranking officials of the Italian military intelligence agency. However, the Constitutional Court dismissed these charges on the basis of the state secrets doctrine.

## Introducing Evidence Obtained by Means of Torture

In the Introduction, we explored the definition of torture by focusing on whether "waterboarding" constituted "torture" under international law. In each of the preceding cases involving extraordinary rendition, suspected terrorists were not only abducted and sent to some far-flung place(s), but all claimed to have been tortured. In the case that follows, the question is whether evidence obtained in another country, perhaps through torture, can be introduced into a British judicial proceeding.

## *A (FC) and others (FC) v. Secretary of State for the Home Department* [2005] UKHL 71

May the Special Immigration Appeals Commission ("SIAC"), a superior court of record established by statute, when hearing an appeal under section 25 of the Anti-terrorism, Crime and Security Act 2001 by a person certified and detained under sections 21 and 23 of that Act, receive evidence which has or may have been procured by torture inflicted, in order to obtain evidence, by officials of a foreign state without the complicity of the British authorities? That is the central question which the House must answer in these appeals. The appellants, relying on the common law of England, on the European Convention on Human Rights and on principles of public international law, submit that the question must be answered with an emphatic negative. The Secretary of State agrees that this answer would be appropriate in any case where the torture had been inflicted by or with the complicity of the British authorities. He further states that it is not his intention to rely on, or present to SIAC or to the Administrative Court in relation to control orders, evidence which he knows or believes to have been obtained by a third country by torture. This intention is, however, based on policy and not on any acknowledged legal obligation.

### THE EUROPEAN CONVENTION ON HUMAN RIGHTS

The Secretary of State submits that under the Convention the admissibility of evidence is a matter left to be decided under national law; that under the relevant national law, namely, the 2001 Act and the Rules, the evidence which the Secretary of State seeks to adduce is admissible before SIAC; and that accordingly the admission of this evidence cannot be said to undermine the fairness of the proceedings. I shall consider the effect of the statutory scheme in more detail below. The first of these propositions is, however, only half true. It is correct that the European Court of Human Rights has consistently declined to articulate evidential rules to be applied in all member states and has preferred to leave such rules to be governed by national law. It has done so even where evidence was acknowledged to have been obtained unlawfully and in breach of another article of the Convention. But in these cases and others the court has also insisted on its responsibility to ensure that the proceedings, viewed overall on the particular facts, have been fair, and it has recognized that the way in which evidence has been obtained or used may be such as to render the proceedings unfair.

### PUBLIC INTERNATIONAL LAW

The appellants' submission has a further, more international, dimension. They accept, as they must, that a treaty, even if ratified by the United Kingdom, has no binding force in the domestic law of this country unless it is given effect by statute or expresses principles of customary international law. But they rely on the well-established principle that the words of a United Kingdom statute, passed after the date of a treaty and dealing with the same subject matter, are to be construed, if they are reasonably capable of bearing such a meaning, as intended to carry out the treaty obligation and not to be inconsistent with it. The courts are obliged under section 2 of the 1998 Act to take Strasbourg [European Court of Human Rights] jurisprudence into account in connection with a Convention right, their obligation under section 3 is to interpret and give effect to primary and subordinate legislation in a way which is compatible with Convention rights so far as possible to do so and it is their duty under section 6 not to act incompatibly with a Convention right. If, and to the extent that, development of the common law is called for, such development should ordinarily be in harmony with the United Kingdom's international obligations and not antithetical to them.

### ARTICLE 15 OF THE TORTURE CONVENTION

Article 15 of the Torture Convention:

> Each State Party shall ensure that any statement which is established to have been made as a result of torture shall not be invoked as evidence in any proceedings, except against a person accused of torture as evidence that the statement was made.

The additional qualification makes plain the blanket nature of this exclusionary rule. It cannot possibly be read, as counsel for the Secretary of State submits, as intended to apply only in criminal proceedings. Nor can it be understood to differentiate between confessions and accusatory statements, or to apply only where the state in whose jurisdiction the proceedings are held has inflicted or been complicit in the torture. It would indeed be remarkable if national courts, exercising universal jurisdiction, could try a foreign torturer for acts of torture committed abroad, but could nonetheless receive evidence obtained by such torture. The matter was succinctly put in the Report by Mr Alvaro Gil-Robles, the Council of Europe Commissioner for Human Rights, in his Report on his visit to the United Kingdom in November 2004:

> torture is torture whoever does it, judicial proceedings are judicial proceedings, whatever their purpose – the former can never be admissible in the latter.

A Committee against Torture was established under article 17 of the Torture Convention to monitor compliance by member states. The Committee has recognized a duty of states, if allegations of torture are made, to investigate them. The clear implication is that the evidence should have been excluded had the complaint been verified.

### THE BURDEN OF PROOF

The appellants contend that it is for a party seeking to adduce evidence to establish its admissibility if this is challenged. The Secretary of State submits that it is for a party seeking to challenge the admissibility of evidence to make good the factual grounds on which he bases his challenge. He supports this approach in the present context by pointing to the reference in article 15 of the Torture Convention to a statement "which is established to have been made as a result of torture." There is accordingly said to be a burden on the appellant in the SIAC proceedings to prove the truth of his assertion.

I do not for my part think that a conventional approach to the burden of proof is appropriate in a proceeding where the appellant may not know the name or identity of the author of an adverse statement relied on against him, may not see the statement or know what the statement says, may not be able to discuss the adverse evidence with the special advocate appointed (without responsibility) to represent his interests, and may have no means of knowing what witness he should call to rebut assertions of which he is unaware. It would, on the other hand, render section 25 appeals all but unmanageable if a generalized and unsubstantiated allegation of torture were in all cases to impose a duty on the Secretary of State to prove the absence of torture. It is necessary, in this very unusual forensic setting, to devise a procedure which affords some protection to an appellant without imposing on either party a burden which he cannot ordinarily discharge.

The appellant must ordinarily, by himself or his special advocate, advance some plausible reason why evidence may have been procured by torture. This will often be done by showing that evidence has, or is likely to have, come from one of those countries widely known or believed to practice torture (although they may well be parties to the Torture Convention and will, no doubt, disavow the practice publicly). Where such a plausible reason is given, or where SIAC with its knowledge and expertise in this field knows or suspects that evidence may have come from such a country, it is for SIAC to initiate or direct such inquiry as is necessary to enable it to form a fair judgment whether the evidence has, or whether there is a real risk that it may have been, obtained by torture or not. All will depend on the facts and circumstances of a particular case. If SIAC is unable to conclude that there is not a real risk that the evidence has been obtained by torture, it should refuse to admit the evidence. Otherwise it should admit it. It should throughout be guided by recognition of the important obligations laid down in articles 3 and 5(4) of the European Convention and, through them, article 15 of the Torture Convention, and also by recognition of the procedural handicaps to which an appellant is necessarily subject in proceedings from which he and his legal representatives are excluded.

## Note and Comments:

1. Amnesty International estimates that some 141 states still engage in torture, and that the overwhelming majority of these countries are state parties to the Torture Convention. In light of this situation, if you were a judge how would you determine whether torture abroad had been carried out or not? If a country had a record of committing torture, would you necessarily exclude any and all evidence from this state?

## References

### Books and Articles

Barbara Grabowska-Moroz, "The Polish roadmap to accountability: Why the implementation of Al Nashiri and Abu Zubaydah judggements is so highly problematic," in Elspeth Guild, Didier Bigo and Mark Gibney (eds.) *Extraordinary Rendition: Addressing the Challenges of Accountability*, London: Routledge (2018)

Bill Chappell, "Psychologists Behind CIA 'Enhanced Interrogation' Program Settle Detainees' Lawsuit," *NPR*, (August 17, 2017)

Glenn Greenwald, "Obama's Justice Department Grants Final Immunity to Bush's CIA Torturers," *The Guardian*, (August 31, 2012)

Elspeth Guild, "The U.S. Senate Select Intelligence Committee Report (Feinstein Report) on the CIA Extraordinary Rendition Programme–Perspectives from Europe," in Elspeth Guild, Didier Bigo and Mark Gibney (eds.) *Extraordinary Rendition: Addressing the Challenges of Accountability*, London: Routledge (2018)

New York City Bar, "Torture by Proxy: International and Domestic Law Applicable to 'Extraordinary Renditions'," (October 1, 2004). Available at: www.nycbar. org/member-and-career-services/committees/reports-listing/reports/detail/ torture-by-proxy-international-and-domestic-law-applicable-to-extraordinary-renditions

Open Society, *Globalizing Torture: CIA Secret Detention and Extraordinary Rendition* (2013). Available at: www.opensocietyfoundations.org/reports/globalizing-torture-cia-secret-detention-and-extraordinary-rendition

### U.N. Report

Committee against Torture, Fifty-third session 3–28 November 2014, observations on the third to fifth periodic reports of United States of America

3 Extraordinary Rendition • 137

## U.S. Government Report

U.S. Senate Select Committee on Intelligence, *CIA Torture Report (Feinstein Report)* (2014)

## Cases

*A (FC) v. Secretary of State for Home Department*, [2005] UKHL 71
*Arar v. Ashcroft*, 585 F. 3d 559 (2d. Cir. 2009)
*El-Masri v. Macedonia*, ECtHR, App. No. 39630/09 (2012)
*El-Masri v. U.S.*, 479 F. 3d 296 (4th Cir. 2007)
*Nasr and Ghali v. Italy*, ECtHR, App. No. 44883/09 (2016)
*Zubydah v. Poland*, ECtHR, App. No. 7511/13 (2014)

## International Agreements

Convention Against Torture and Other Cruel, Inhuman or Degrading Treatment or Punishment, adopted and opened for signature 10 December 1984, entry into force 26 June 1987
International Covenant on Civil and Political Rights, adopted 16 December 1966, entry into force 23 March 1976

# Part II
## Warfare

# 4
# Jus ad Bellum

The year 2018 marked the 90th anniversary of the Kellogg-Briand Pact – officially known as the *General Treaty for the Renunciation of War as an Instrument of National Policy* – which in a wonderful but perhaps naive way sought to outlaw war itself. This, of course, did not happen. Within three years, Japan invaded Manchuria and within seven years Italy attacked Ethiopia. World War II began in 1939 and when the fighting ended in 1945, upwards of 56 million people had been killed. With these unprecedented horrors serving as a backdrop, the United Nations was established on October 24, 1945. The Preamble of the *U.N. Charter* begins with these somber words: "*We the Peoples of the United Nations determined to save succeeding generations from the scourge of war, which twice in our lifetime has brought untold sorrow to mankind.*" Still, just pick up a newspaper and you will see that this promise has yet to be met.

In this chapter we will examine various aspects of how international law deals with the advent of war – jus ad bellum – and in the following chapter we take up the issue of the legal limitations on how wars are fought. Of course, if war could be eliminated there would be no need to concern ourselves with the latter, although, obviously, we have not been able to achieve this.

We begin with the *prohibition on the use of force,* best articulated by the International Court of Justice in the case of *Nicaragua v. United States.* Following that, we will address the issue of *genocide* and the duty of state parties to the Genocide Convention to "prevent" acts of genocide from taking place. In late December 2014, the *Arms Trade Treaty* (ATT) went into effect. Whether this international treaty will meet its goal of preventing the sales of arms to states that violate international humanitarian law remains to be seen. We examine this issue in the context of a suit that challenged British arms sales to Saudi Arabia for the use of these weapons in Yemen, a brutal conflict that was still ongoing in early 2019.

Humanitarian intervention is a longstanding principle under customary international law. Under this doctrine, states can lawfully intervene militarily in another country when massive human rights violations are occurring. There are, however, at least two problems with this. One involves when a "humanitarian" disaster is taking place and who gets to make this determination. The second problem is the converse of this: when outside states refuse to act. No doubt, the most egregious example of this failure to act occurred in 1994 involving the Rwandan genocide where an estimated 800,000 people were killed in a 100-day period. In the international realm, the response was the *Responsibility to Protect* (R2P) initiative, which has been heralded for its role in helping to guide the international intervention in Libya, although the ongoing conflict in Syria shows perhaps all too well the continuing inability of the international community to prevent, let alone respond to, massive levels of human rights violations.

The nature of warfare has changed over time. One change has been the advent of *cyberwarfare* where public and private actors in one state engage in a form of "warfare" against both public and private entities in another state. Is this war, albeit by different means? Another change has been the rise in the use of unmanned *drones*, especially in the airspace of countries that have not granted permission to do so. Once again the question: does the use of drones constitute an act of warfare against this other state?

Finally, one of the responses to the ravages of war has been the increasing use of *peacekeepers* as a way of trying to separate belligerent forces. What duty – if any – do peacekeeping forces have towards those who they are assigned to protect? We look at this issue in the context of one of the great peacekeeping failures of our time: the siege of Srebrenica.

### The Prohibition Against the Use of Force

We begin this chapter with the International Court of Justice's ruling in *Nicaragua v. United States* (1986). In this case, Nicaragua presented two different, but related, claims. One was that the United States had carried out aggressive actions against Nicaragua, such as mining the country's harbors, and thereby had violated the prohibition against the use of force. The second claim, which will be analyzed in Chapter 9, is that the United States should be held legally responsible for human rights violations committed by its contra allies.

## Box 4.1: Was the U.S.-led Invasion of Afghanistan Legal?

Article 2(4) of the *United Nations Charter* provides: "All Members shall refrain in their international relations from the threat or use of force against the territorial integrity or political independence of any state, or in any other manner inconsistent with the Purposes of the United Nations." There are, however, two exceptions to this rule. The first is self defense. Article 51 of the *U.N. Charter* states:

> Nothing in the present Charter shall impair the inherent right of individual or collective self-defence if an armed attack occurs against a Member of the United Nations, until the Security Council has taken measures necessary to maintain international peace and security. Measures taken by Members in the exercise of this right of self-defence shall be immediately reported to the Security Council and shall not in any way affect the authority and responsibility of the Security Council under the present Charter to take at any time such action as it deems necessary in order to maintain or restore international peace and security.

Was the U.S.-led invasion of Afghanistan simply a means of self defense? The problem with this is that the al-Qaeda organization was not affiliated with the Taliban-led Afghan government. In addition, the 19 hijackers – none of whom were Afghan citizens – were not state agents of Afghanistan. Can a state invade another state even if this state did not attack it? Perhaps the strongest argument in support of the invasion is that the Afghan government refused to turn Osama bin Laden over to U.S. officials. However, there is virtually no support under international law for this position.

The second exception to the prohibition is that the use of force has been authorized by the U.N. Security Council. However, there are some problems with this rationale, at least in this particular context. On September 12, 2001, the Security Council passed Resolution 1368. Paragraph 5 reads that the Security Council: "Expresses its readiness to take all necessary steps to respond to the terrorist attacks of 11 September 2001, and to combat all forms of terrorism, in accordance with its responsibilities under the Charter of the United Nations." Two weeks after this, the Security Council passed Resolution 1373, which calls on all states to: "Cooperate, particularly through bilateral and multilateral arrangements and agreements, to prevent and suppress terrorist attacks and take action against perpetrators of such acts." Note, however, that this language does not specifically authorize the invasion of Afghanistan. And as a final point, the war in Afghanistan continues to this day – although al-Qaeda has long ceased to exist as a potent force in that country.

# Case Concerning Military and Paramilitary Activities in and Against Nicaragua (Nicaragua v. U.S.) International Court of Justice, 27 June 1986

Before examining the complaint of Nicaragua against the United States that the United States is responsible for the military capacity, if not the very existence, of the *contra* forces, the Court will first deal with events which, in the submission of Nicaragua, involve the responsibility of the United States in a more direct manner. These are the mining of Nicaraguan ports or waters in early 1984; and certain attacks on, in particular, Nicaraguan port and oil installations in late 1983 and early 1984. It is the contention of Nicaragua that these were not acts committed by members of the *contras* with the assistance and support of United States agencies. Those directly concerned in the acts were, it is claimed, not Nicaraguan nationals or other members of the FDN or ARDE, but either United States military personnel or persons of the nationality of unidentified Latin American countries, paid by, and acting on the direct instructions of United States military or intelligence personnel. (These persons were apparently referred to in the vocabulary of the CIA as "UCLAs" – "Unilaterally Controlled Latino Assets", and this acronym will be used, purely for convenience, in what follows.) Furthermore, Nicaragua contends that such United States personnel, while they may have refrained from themselves entering Nicaraguan territory or recognized territorial waters, directed the operations and gave very close logistic, intelligence and practical support. A further complaint by Nicaragua which does not relate to *contra* activity is that of overflights of Nicaraguan territory and territorial waters by United States military aircraft. These complaints will now be examined.

The principle of non-intervention involves the right of every sovereign State to conduct its affairs without outside interference; though examples of trespass against this principle are not infrequent, the Court considers that it is part and parcel of customary international law. As the Court has observed: "Between independent States, respect for territorial sovereignty is an essential foundation of international relations, and international law requires political integrity also to be respected". Expressions of an *opinio juris* regarding the existence of the principle of non-intervention in customary international law are numerous and not difficult to find. Of course, statements whereby States avow their recognition of the principles of international law set forth in the United Nations Charter cannot strictly be interpreted as applying to the principle of non-intervention by States in the internal and external affairs of other States, since this principle is not, as such, spelt out in the Charter. But it was never intended that the Charter should embody written confirmation of every essential principle of international law in force. The existence in the *opinio juris* of States of the principle of non-intervention is backed by established and substantial practice. It has moreover been presented as a corollary of the principle of the sovereign equality of States.

Notwithstanding the multiplicity of declarations by States accepting the principle of non-intervention, there remain two questions: first, what is the exact content of the principle so accepted, and secondly, is the practice sufficiently in conformity with it for this to be a rule of customary international law? As regards the first problem – that of the content of the principle of non-intervention – the Court will define only those aspects of the principle which appear to be relevant to the resolution of the dispute. In this respect it notes that, in view of the generally accepted formulations, the principle forbids all States or groups of States to intervene directly or indirectly in internal or external affairs of other States. A prohibited intervention must accordingly be one bearing on matters in which each State is permitted, by the principle of State sovereignty, to decide freely. One of these is the choice of a political, economic, social and cultural system, and the formulation of foreign policy. Intervention is wrongful when it uses methods of coercion in regard to such choices, which must remain free ones. The element of coercion, which defines, and indeed forms the very essence of, prohibited intervention, is particularly obvious in the case of an intervention which uses force, either in the direct form of military action, or in the indirect form of support for subversive or terrorist armed activities within another State. As noted above, General Assembly resolution 2625 (XXV) equates assistance of this kind with the use of force by the assisting State when the acts committed in another State "involve a threat or use of force". These forms of action are therefore wrongful in the light of both the principle of non-use of force, and that of non-intervention. In view of the nature of Nicaragua's complaints against the United States, and those expressed by the United States in regard to Nicaragua's conduct towards El Salvador, it is primarily acts of intervention of this kind with which the Court is concerned in the present case.

## Note and Comments:

1. We will return to the *Nicarauga* opinion in Chapter 9 on the issue of state responsibility where the ICJ ruled that while the U.S. was responsible for violations of international law that its own agents had carried out directly, the United States was not responsible for human rights and humanitarian law violations carried out by its contra allies on the grounds that the U.S. had not exercised the requisite level of "effective control."

---

**Box 4.2: Anticipatory or Preemptive Self Defense**

The doctrine of self defense would make little sense if states had to actually wait until they were militarily attacked before they were able to respond. Thus, international law allows states to act prior to this – but what is subject to debate is how "preemptive" a preemptive attack can be and still be lawful. Michael Walzer has set forth these criteria in answering this question: 1) there is an intent to cause injury; 2) active preparations for a military attack are underway; and 3) the risk of injury will be increased if fighting is delayed (Walzer 1977).

One example of a lawful preemptive attack is Israel's attack on Egyptian soldiers massed on the Sinai Peninsula, which precipitated the advent of the Six-Day War in 1967. Prior to this, Egypt had taken a number of aggressive steps, making an invasion of Israel seem imminent. Contrast this with the U.S.-led invasion of Iraq in 2003. The constant refrain of the Bush administration was that the Saddam Hussein regime possessed weapons of mass destruction and that going to war was imperative to avoid the spectre of a "mushroom cloud." Of course, no weapons of mass destruction were ever found.

After assuming office in January 2017, the Trump administration began a war of words with North Korea, which throughout the year tested missile systems with an ever-increasing range. If the United States attacked North Korea in order to disable its nuclear weapons capabilities, would this be lawful as a form of preemptive self defense? Would it matter how such an attack unfolded? What if the U.S. had to resort to nuclear weapons itself?

---

## Genocide

A strong argument can be made that the first "human rights" treaty following World War II was the 1948 Genocide Convention. Yet, notwithstanding repeated vows of "Never Again!" genocide continues to be carried out, most notably in

Cambodia (1975–79), Guatemala (1981–83), Bosnia (1992), Somalia (1992), Rwanda (1994), and Sudan (2003).

Article 1 of the Genocide Convention provides: "The Contracting Parties confirm that genocide, whether committed in time of peace or in time of war, is a crime under international law which they undertake to prevent and to punish."

What constitutes genocide? Article 2 states:

> In the present Convention, genocide means any of the following acts committed with intent to destroy, in whole or in part, a national, ethnical, racial or religious group, as such:
>
> (a)  Killing members of the group;
> (b)  Causing serious bodily or mental harm to members of the group;
> (c)  Deliberately inflicting on the group conditions of life calculated to bring about its physical destruction in whole or in part;
> (d)  Imposing measures intended to prevent births within the group;
> (e)  Forcibly transferring children of the group to another group

What is punishable under the treaty? According to Article 3:

> The following acts shall be punishable:
>
> (a)  Genocide;
> (b)  Conspiracy to commit genocide;
> (c)  Direct and public incitement to commit genocide;
> (d)  Attempt to commit genocide;
> (e)  Complicity in genocide.

We will look at two different aspects of the crime of genocide. The first is an excerpt from *Prosecutor v. Akayesu*, which is the first conviction for genocide by an international court: the International Criminal Tribunal for Rwanda. The second case is from the International Court of Justice ruling in *Bosnia v. Serbia*, and it involves state responsibility for genocide (Gibney 2007).

---

## *Prosecutor v. Akayesu,* Trial Chamber, International Criminal Tribunal for Rwanda, Case No. ICTR-96–4-T Decision of: 2 September 1998

The Chamber notes that Rwanda acceded, by legislative decree, to the Convention on Genocide on 12 February 1975. Thus, punishment of the crime of genocide did exist in

Rwanda in 1994, at the time of the acts alleged in the Indictment, and the perpetrator was liable to be brought before the competent courts of Rwanda to answer for this crime.

Contrary to popular belief, the crime of genocide does not imply the actual extermination of group in its entirety, but is understood as such once any one of the acts mentioned in Article 2(2)(a) through 2(2)(e) is committed with the specific intent to destroy "in whole or in part" a national, ethnical, racial or religious group.

Genocide is distinct from other crimes inasmuch as it embodies a special intent or dolus specialis. Special intent of a crime is the specific intention, required as a constitutive element of the crime, which demands that the perpetrator clearly seeks to produce the act charged. Thus, the special intent in the crime of genocide lies in "the intent to destroy, in whole or in part, a national, ethnical, racial or religious group, as such".

Thus, for a crime of genocide to have been committed, it is necessary that one of the acts listed under Article 2(2) of the Statute be committed, that the particular act be committed against a specifically targeted group, it being a national, ethnical, racial or religious group.

Consequently, in order to clarify the constitutive elements of the crime of genocide, the Chamber will first state its findings on the acts provided for under Article 2(2)(a) through Article 2(2)(e) of the Statute, the groups protected by the Genocide Convention, and the special intent or dolus specialis necessary for genocide to take place.

On the issue of determining the offender's specific intent, the Chamber considers that intent is a mental factor which is difficult, even impossible, to determine. This is the reason why, in the absence of a confession from the accused, his intent can be inferred from a certain number of presumptions of fact. The Chamber considers that it is possible to deduce the genocidal intent inherent in a particular act charged from the general context of the perpetration of other culpable acts systematically directed against that same group, whether these acts were committed by the same offender or by others. Other factors, such as the scale of atrocities committed, their general nature, in a region or a country, or furthermore, the fact of deliberately and systematically targeting victims on account of their membership of a particular group, while excluding the members of other groups, can enable the Chamber to infer the genocidal intent of a particular act.

The Chamber finds that it has been established that, throughout the period covered in the Indictment, Akayesu, in his capacity as bourgmestre, was responsible for maintaining law and public order in the commune of Taba and that he had effective authority over the communal police. Moreover, as "leader" of Taba commune, of which he was one of the most prominent figures, the inhabitants respected him and followed his orders. Akayesu himself admitted before the Chamber that he had the power to assemble the population and that they obeyed his instructions. It has also been proven that a very large number of Tutsi were killed in Taba between 7 April and the end of June 1994, while Akayesu was bourgmestre of the Commune. Knowing of such killings, he opposed them and attempted to prevent them only until 18 April 1994, date after which he not only stopped trying to maintain law and order in his commune, but was also present during the acts of violence and killings, and sometimes even gave orders himself for bodily or mental harm to be caused to certain Tutsi, and endorsed and even ordered the killing of several Tutsi.

In the opinion of the Chamber, the said acts indeed incur the individual criminal responsibility of Akayesu for having ordered, committed, or otherwise aided and abetted in the preparation or execution of the killing of and causing serious bodily or mental harm to members of the Tutsi group. Indeed, the Chamber holds that the fact that Akayesu, as a local authority, failed to oppose such killings and serious bodily or mental harm constituted a form of tacit encouragement, which was compounded by being present to such criminal acts.

As stated in its findings on the law applicable to the crime of genocide, the Chamber holds the view that the intent underlying an act can be inferred from a number of facts. The Chamber is of the opinion that it is possible to infer the genocidal intention that presided over the commission of a particular act, inter alia, from all acts or utterances of the accused, or from the general context in which other culpable acts were perpetrated systematically against the same group, regardless of whether such other acts were committed by the same perpetrator or even by other perpetrators.

First of all, regarding Akayesu's acts and utterances during the period relating to the acts alleged in the Indictment, the Chamber is satisfied beyond reasonable doubt, on the basis of all evidence brought to its attention during the trial, that on several occasions the accused made speeches calling, more or less explicitly, for the commission of genocide. The Chamber, in particular, held in its findings on Count 4, that the accused incurred individual criminal responsibility for the crime of direct and public incitement to commit genocide. Yet, according to the Chamber, the crime of direct and public incitement to commit genocide lies in the intent to directly lead or provoke another to commit genocide, which implies that he who incites to commit genocide also has the specific intent to commit genocide: that is, to destroy, in whole or in part, a national, ethnical, racial or religious group, as such.

Furthermore, the Chamber has already established that genocide was committed against the Tutsi group in Rwanda in 1994, throughout the period covering the events alleged in the Indictment. Owing to the very high number of atrocities committed against the Tutsi, their widespread nature not only in the commune of Taba, but also throughout Rwanda, and to the fact that the victims were systematically and deliberately selected because they belonged to the Tutsi group, with persons belonging to other groups being excluded, the Chamber is also able to infer, beyond reasonable doubt, the genocidal intent of the accused in the commission of the above-mentioned crimes.

With regard, particularly, to the acts described in paragraphs 12(A) and 12(B) of the Indictment, that is, rape and sexual violence, the Chamber wishes to underscore the fact that in its opinion, they constitute genocide in the same way as any other act as long as they were committed with the specific intent to destroy, in whole or in part, a particular group, targeted as such. Indeed, rape and sexual violence certainly constitute infliction of serious bodily and mental harm on the victims and are even, according to the Chamber, one of the worst ways of inflict harm on the victim as he or she suffers both bodily and mental harm. In light of all the evidence before it, the Chamber is satisfied that the acts of rape and sexual violence described above were committed solely against Tutsi women, many of whom were subjected to the worst public humiliation, mutilated, and raped several times, often in public, in the Bureau Communal premises or in other public places, and often by more than one assailant. These rapes resulted in physical and psychological destruction of Tutsi women, their families and their communities. Sexual violence was an integral part of the process of destruction, specifically targeting Tutsi women and specifically contributing to their destruction and to the destruction of the Tutsi group as a whole.

---

*Bosnia v. Serbia* is the International Court of Justice's most definitive treatment of the meaning of the Genocide Convention as well as the responsibilities of the state parties. The decision itself created quite a stir, especially the Court's ruling that Serbia was not responsible for acts of genocide carried out by its Bosnian Serb allies, which will be examined in Chapter 9.

What in large part has been ignored is the Court's expansive notion of the responsibility of all state parties "to prevent" genocide. As you will read below, the ICJ ruled that all state parties have to do everything within their power to seek to prevent or halt acts of genocide – no matter where genocide is taking place; no matter if such efforts would be successful or not; and no matter if other state parties are fulfilling their own responsibilities under the Convention. Beyond this, the Court goes on to indicate that such a responsibility to prevent harm is to be found in all other international human rights treaties.

---

**Box 4.3: International Law at the Movies: Genocide**

Setting aside for the moment the multitude of films made on the Holocaust, which will be discussed in Chapter 6, there are a host of feature films and documentaries that take up some of the other genocides that have occurred.

The Cambodian genocide from 1975–79 brought about the deaths of upwards of a third of that country's population. In terms of feature films, *The Killing Fields* (1984) has not lost an ounce of power in its depiction of the relationship between *New York Times* reporter Sydney Schanberg (Sam Waterson) and his Cambodian interpreter Dith Pran (Haing S. Ngor), who survived unimagined horrors under the Khmer Rouge. *The Missing Picture* (2014) makes use of clay figures to tell one family's story of the Cambodian nightmare. Finally, *First They Killed My Father* (2017) was directed by Angelina Jolie based on a book written by Loung Ung.

The Rwandan genocide in 1994 is best known for the fact that upwards of 800,000 people – mainly Tutsis and moderate Hutus – were slaughtered in a 100-day period, with most killings carried out by hacking the victim to death with a machete. The Hollywood version of this story has been told in *Hotel Rwanda* (2004), while the "African" depiction has been best told in *Sometimes in April* (2005). One noteworthy documentary is *Shake Hands With the Devil* (2007), which tells the story of General Dellaire, the U.N. Commander in Rwanda at that time, who has said that with just a few thousand soldiers the genocide could have been prevented.

There remains some question whether genocide occurred in the Darfur region of the Sudan at the outset of this century. Setting this issue aside, there were massive killings that were systematically ignored until images appeared in Western publications, told in the documentary *The Devil Came on Horseback* (2007). Also noteworthy is the Don Cheadle–George Clooney produced documentary *Darfur Now* (2007), which ties together six different stories relating to genocide in the Sudan. Finally, the genocide in Somalia serves as the backdrop for the commercially successful *Black Hawk Down* (2001), although the film focuses almost exclusively on the fighting between U.S. and Somali militia forces, while the victims, unfortunately, remain an afterthought.

---

The disintegration of the former Yugoslavia serves as the backdrop for the following case. In 1991, the Republics of Slovenia and Croatia declared themselves independent, after which fighting broke out in both Republics. In response, the Security

Council in its Resolution 743 of February 21, 1992, set up the United Nations Protection Force (UNPROFOR). On March 3, 1992, the Republic of Bosnia-Herzegovina declared itself independent, which brought about fighting between the army of Bosnia-Herzegovina and the Bosnian Serb army. On June 8, 1992, the Security Council extended UNPROFOR's mandate to include Bosnia-Herzegovina. Fighting continued. On March 10, 1993, the commander of UNPROFOR visited Srebrenica, which was then under siege, and promised Bosnian Muslims living there that they were under the protection of the U.N. and they would not be abandoned. Unfortunately, this is exactly what took place. Perhaps the most gruesome illustration of this was when Bosnian Serb troops advanced into Srebrenica and took away a sizable proportion of fighting age men – most of whom were killed in the surrounding forests, a subject we return to at the close of the chapter. The Court's ruling that Serbia was not "responsible" for the genocide carried out by its Bosnian Serb allies was a stunning result and will be addressed in Chapter 9. In contrast to that conservative ruling is its liberal holding that Serbia had failed to meet its responsibility under the Genocide Convention to "prevent" genocide.

---

## Case Concerning Application of the Convention on the Prevention and Punishment of the Crime of Genocide (Bosnia and Herzegovina v. Serbia and Montenegro) (Bosnia v. Serbia), International Court of Justice, 26 Feb. 2007

As regards the obligation to prevent genocide, the Court thinks it necessary to begin with the following introductory remarks and clarifications, amplifying the observations already made above.

First, the Genocide Convention is not the only international instrument providing for an obligation on the States parties to it to take certain steps to prevent the acts it seeks to prohibit. Many other instruments include a similar obligation, in various forms: see, for example, the Convention against Torture and Other Cruel, Inhuman or Degrading Treatment or Punishment of 10 December 1984 (Art. 2); the Convention on the Prevention and Punishment of Crimes against Internationally Protected Persons, Including Diplomatic Agents, of 14 December 1973 (Art. 4); the Convention on the Safety of United Nations and Associated Personnel of 9 December 1994 (Art. 11); the International Convention on the Suppression of Terrorist Bombings of 15 December 1997 (Art. 15). The content of the duty to prevent varies from one instrument to another, according to the wording of the relevant provisions, and depending on the nature of the acts to be prevented.

The decision of the Court does not, in this case, purport to establish a general jurisprudence applicable to all cases where a treaty instrument, or other binding legal norm, includes an obligation for States to prevent certain acts. Still less does the decision of the Court purport to find whether, apart from the texts applicable to specific fields, there is a general obligation on States to prevent the commission by other persons or entities of acts contrary to certain norms of general international law. The Court will therefore confine itself to determining the specific scope of the duty to prevent in the Genocide Convention, and to the extent that such a determination is necessary to the decision to be given on the dispute before it. This will, of course, not absolve it of the need to refer, if need be, to the rules of law whose scope extends beyond the specific field covered by the Convention.

[I]t is clear that the obligation in question is one of conduct and not one of result, in the sense that a State cannot be under an obligation to succeed, whatever the circumstances, in preventing the commission of genocide: the obligation of States parties is rather to employ all means reasonably available to them, so as to prevent genocide so far as possible. A State does not incur responsibility simply because the desired result is not achieved; responsibility is however incurred if the State manifestly failed to take all measures to prevent genocide which were within its power, and which might have contributed to preventing the genocide. In this area the notion of "due diligence", which calls for an assessment *in concreto*, is of critical importance. Various parameters operate when assessing whether a State has duly discharged the obligation concerned. The first, which varies greatly from one State to another, is clearly the capacity to influence effectively the action of persons likely to commit or already committing, genocide. This capacity itself depends, among other things, on the geographical distance of the State concerned from the scene of the events, and on the strength of the political links, as well as links of all other kinds, between the authorities of that State and the main actors in the events. The State's capacity to influence must also be assessed by legal criteria, since it is clear that every State may only act within the limits permitted by international law; seen thus, a State's capacity to influence may vary depending on its particular legal position vis-à-vis the situations and persons facing the danger, or the reality, of genocide. On the other hand, it is irrelevant whether the State whose responsibility is in issue claims, or even proves, that even if it had employed all means reasonably at its disposal, they would not have sufficed to prevent the commission of genocide. As well as being generally difficult to prove, this is irrelevant to the breach of the obligation of conduct in question, the more so since the possibility remains that the combined efforts of several States, each complying with its obligation to prevent, might have achieved the result – averting the commission of genocide – which the efforts of only one State were insufficient to produce.

In light of the foregoing, the Court will now consider the facts of the case. For the reasons stated above, it will confine itself to the FRY's conduct vis-à-vis the Srebrenica massacres.

In view of their undeniable influence and of the information, voicing serious concern, in their possession, the Yugoslav federal authorities should, in the view of the Court, have made the best efforts within their power to try and prevent the tragic events then taking shape, whose scale, though it could not have been foreseen with certainty, might at least have been surmised. The FRY leadership, and President Milošević´ above all, were fully aware of the climate of deep-seated hatred which reigned between the Bosnian Serbs and the Muslims in the Srebrenica region. As the Court has noted above, it has not been shown that the decision to eliminate physically the whole of the adult male population of the Muslim community of Srebrenica was brought to the attention of the Belgrade authorities. Nevertheless, given all the international concern about what looked likely to happen at Srebrenica, given Milošević´'s own observations to Mladic´ [Bosnian Serb commander], which made it clear that the dangers were known and that these dangers seemed to be of an order that could suggest intent to commit genocide, unless brought under control, it must have been clear that there was a serious risk of genocide in Srebrenica. Yet the Respondent has not shown that it took any initiative to prevent what happened, or any action on its part to avert the atrocities which were committed. It must therefore be concluded that the organs of the Respondent did nothing to prevent the Srebrenica massacres, claiming that they were powerless to do so, which hardly tallies with their known influence over the VRS. As indicated above, for a State to be held responsible for breaching its obligation of prevention, it does not need to be proven that the State concerned definitely had the power to prevent the genocide; it is sufficient that it had the means to do so and that it manifestly refrained from using them.

Such is the case here. In view of the foregoing, the Court concludes that the Respondent violated its obligation to prevent the Srebrenica genocide in such a manner as to engage its international responsibility.

### Note and Comments:

1. What other countries also failed to meet their duty to prevent genocide in Bosnia? In Syria? In Rwanda? In the Sudan?

### Arming and Equipping

Until the Arms Trade Treaty (ATT) went into effect in late December 2014, international law failed to prohibit the sale of weapons to another state even if the sending state was fully aware that these weapons would be used to target civilians and to commit widespread human rights violations. What remains to be seen is whether the ATT will end such practices. The following case is not based on the ATT but a provision of British law that seeks to achieve this same end.

## *Campaign Against Arms Trade v. Secretary of State* [2017] EWHC 1726 (QB)

The issue in this claim for judicial review is whether the Secretary of State for International Trade, who since July 2016 has had responsibility for licensing the export of arms, is obliged by law to suspend extant export licences to the Kingdom of Saudi Arabia and cease granting new licences, to conform with Government policy to deny such licences where there is "a clear risk that the arms might be used in the commission of a serious violation of International Humanitarian Law". The claim springs from the conflict in Yemen and the border areas of Saudi Arabia. It focusses on airstrikes conducted by a coalition led by Saudi Arabia ("the Coalition") in support of the legitimate government of Yemen against the Houthi rebellion. The Claimant submits that the body of evidence available in the public domain, in particular from respected human rights organisations and international monitoring agencies, not only suggests but dictates the conclusion that such a clear risk exists. Since no other conclusion was rationally open to the Secretary of State, it is no longer lawful to license the sale of arms to Saudi Arabia.

This application for judicial review is primarily concerned with Criterion 2 of the Consolidated Criteria:

*The respect for human rights and fundamental freedoms in the country of final destination as well as respect by that country for international humanitarian law.*

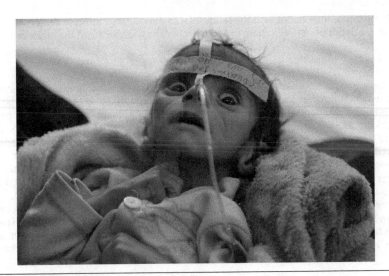

**Photo 4.1** "Collateral Damage"

*Source*: © Associated Press

Having assessed the recipient country's attitudes towards relevant principles established by international humanitarian rights instruments, the Government will:

c) *not grant a licence if there is a clear risk that the items might be used in the commission of a serious violation of international humanitarian law.*

The Claimant's case is that, given the available evidence, sub-criterion (c) of Criterion 2 is met.

BACKGROUND

## The Conflict in Yemen

Saudi Arabia and Yemen are contiguous and share a 1,800 km border. Since early 2015, Yemen's capital city, Sana'a, and parts of central and southern Yemen have been in the control of Houthi rebels backed by former Republican Guard Forces loyal to former President Saleh. The Houthi are a Shia-Zaydi movement from the north of Yemen.

Hostilities took place during 2015 and 2016, notwithstanding numerous ceasefire attempts, and continue to this day. Coalition military operations have taken the form primarily of airstrikes led by Saudi Arabia against the Houthis, together with some ground operations. The Saudis have reported numerous cross-border incursions and missile attacks by the Houthi, including use of SCUD missiles. There have been reports of attacks by Houthi forces on Coalition shipping in the Red Sea. As of early 2017, Houthi forces continue to occupy Sana'a, and ground fighting remains significant in the Northern Provinces and around Taizz. The Saudis have reported 745 Saudi soldiers and border guards killed along the Southern front, and over 10,000 injured since March 2015.

Terrorist organisations, such as Al-Qaeda in the Arabian Peninsula ("AQAP") and Daesh (also known as "ISIS"), have taken advantage of the on-going instability and ungoverned space in Yemen. This has complicated the picture and led to increased anti-terror operations in the region led by US forces.

There can be little doubt as to the seriousness of the military conflict in Yemen, and the threat which it is perceived to pose to Saudi Arabia and the stability of the wider region.

### ANALYSIS OF EVIDENCE CLAIMANT'S EVIDENCE

The Claimant relies upon a large volume of evidence which it submits demonstrates 'overwhelmingly' that Saudi Arabia has committed repeated and serious breaches of International Humanitarian Law during the conflict in Yemen, in particular, by committing indiscriminate or deliberate airstrikes against civilians. The Claimant's evidence runs to many hundreds of pages. It includes reports from the following bodies: United Nations; European Parliament; Council of the European Union; International Committee of the Red Cross; Médecins Sans Frontières; Amnesty International; Human Rights Watch; House of Commons Committee; and the press. For the most part, it does not distinguish between the activities of the different members of the Coalition.

The Claimant lists 72 reports of potential 'serious breaches' of International Humanitarian Law which are described as 'committed by' or 'attributed to' the Coalition. These include airstrikes which have killed civilians, airstrikes which have used 'cluster' munitions, airstrikes which have targeted schools and medical facilities, and a naval blockade.

### THE SECRETARY OF STATE'S EVIDENCE

## Defendant's Case

The Secretary of State takes issue with the essential reliability of the reports relied upon by the Claimant and Intervenors. He submits that the Government put in place a rigorous and comprehensive system for analysing reports of incidents and determining whether, at any stage, a "clear risk" of "serious" breaches of International Humanitarian Law existed such that arms sales to Saudi Arabia should be suspended or cancelled. The Secretary of State's case is that, at all material times, he was able and entitled rationally to conclude that, on the basis of open and closed material, notwithstanding the NGO and other reports, Criterion 2c was not satisfied.

## UK Engagement with Saudi Arabia

There has been extensive political and military engagement with Saudi Arabia with respect to the conduct of military operations in Yemen and International Humanitarian Law compliance.

It is clear from the evidence that, far from being immune to international criticism and concern as to civilian casualties alleged to have been caused by the Coalition in the Yemen conflict, Saudi Arabia has been mindful of concerns expressed, in particular, by the UK. It is also clear from the evidence that Saudi Arabia has sought positively to address these concerns, in particular by conducting investigations into incidents and setting up a permanent investigatory body.

## Claimant's Criticisms of Saudi Arabian Investigations

The Claimant submitted that there is little comfort to be gleaned from the existence of the Saudi investigatory procedures because (a) they have been too slow (as recognised in a statement to Parliament on 12th January 2017 by Tobias Ellwood MP, the Parliamentary Under Secretary for Foreign and Commonwealth Affairs), (b) they have been too few in number (the 14 JIAT reports to date amounted to only 5% of the total number of incidents reported), and (c) and the JIAT reports and methodology and the 'exiguous' published summaries have been the subject of criticism (in particular by Human Rights Watch in a letter to JIAT date 13th January 2017).

In our view, however, the Saudi's growing efforts to establish and operate procedures to investigate incidents of concern is of significance and a matter which the

Secretary of State was entitled to take into account as part of his overall assessment of the Saudi attitude and commitment to maintaining International Humanitarian Law standards.

It is clear why the Secretary of State took the view that he did that Criterion 2c was not triggered, notwithstanding the various third party reports that came to his, and his advisers', attention. His assessment of all the material in the light of the advice tendered by officials and fellow ministers was that the necessary risk was not established. We should add that it was not legally necessary for him to engage directly with everything that has been said by others on the topic.

In our view, the fact that senior officials were advising the Secretary of State that the decision was "finely balanced", and the Secretary of State himself expressly acknowledged that this was the case, is instructive. It points to the anxious scrutiny – indeed at what seems like anguished scrutiny at some stages – given to the matter and the essential rationality and rigour of the process in which the Secretary of State was engaged. The picture was acknowledged to be far from a black and white. The decision involved balancing a series of complex and competing factors. Such self-evidently finely balanced judgements are paradigm matters for evaluation and decision by the Executive in conformity with the scheme established by Parliament. They are, of course, subject to scrutiny in the High Court, but with a suitable recognition of the institutional competence of those charged with the decision-making process. So it is in this case. The Claimant appeared at one stage to suggest that because the Government themselves considered the decision to be finely balanced that would enable a Court more readily to interfere. On the contrary, in an area where the Court is not possessed of the institutional expertise to make the judgments in question, it should be especially cautious before interfering with a finely balanced decision reached after careful and anxious consideration by those who do have the relevant expertise to make the necessary judgements.

## Conclusion

In conclusion, in our judgment, the open and closed evidence demonstrates that the Secretary of State was rationally entitled to conclude as follows: (i) the Coalition were not deliberately targeting civilians; (ii) Saudi processes and procedures have been put in place to secure respect for the principles of International Humanitarian Law; (iii) the Coalition was investigating incidents of controversy, including those involving civilian casualties; (iv) the Saudi authorities have throughout engaged in constructive dialogue with the UK about both its processes and incidents of concern; (v) Saudi Arabia has been and remains genuinely committed to compliance with International Humanitarian Law; and (vi) that there was no "clear risk" that there might be "serious violations" of International Humanitarian Law (in its various manifestations) such that UK arms sales to Saudi Arabia should be suspended or cancelled under Criterion 2c.

## Note and Comments:

1. Will judicial bodies always be at a strong disadvantage in determining events on the ground such as in this case?
2. This case was overturned by an appeal court in June 2019 on the basis that the trial court decision had not given enough consideration to past violations by the Saudi government.

**Responsibility to Protect (R2P)**

The prohibition on the use of force is clearly established in Article 2(4) of the United Nations Charter: "All Members shall refrain in their international relations from the threat or use of force against the territorial sovereignty or political independence of any state." However, if force is necessary, Chapter VII of the Security Council is granted powers to engage in humanitarian intervention in order to maintain and restore international peace and security. Article 42 of the U.N. Charter provides:

> Should the Security Council consider that measures provided in Article 41 [relating to measures not involving armed force] would be inadequate or have proved to be inadequate, it may take such action by air, sea, or land forces as may be necessary to maintain or restore international peace and security. Such actions may include demonstrations, blockade, and other operations by air, sea, or land forces of Members of the United Nations.

There have been two fundamental problems with humanitarian intervention in practice. One is the inability or unwillingness of the Security Council to assume the role assigned to it in the Charter. The second is that when states have previously engaged in this practice – i.e., India in Pakistan (1971) and Vietnam in Cambodia (1978) – it is by no means clear whether political, rather than humanitarian, considerations predominated. However, a different problem, and arguably a much bigger one, are the myriad of cases where there is widespread human suffering and yet there has been no response by the international community. The most notable case of this at present would be the ongoing humanitarian disaster in Syria, but there is a long litany of situations where the international community has turned a blind eye to massive levels of human suffering.

In light of the myriad of problems associated with humanitarian intervention – that it infringes on state sovereignty; the unwillingness to intervene in many humanitarian disasters; the inability of the Security Council to lead; the manner in which intervention has occurred (i.e., the Kosovo bombings in 1999); and even the question whether intervention without Security Council authorization is legal – UN Secretary-General Kofi Annan raised this issue in his 2000 *Millennium Report*:

> If humanitarian intervention is, indeed, an unacceptable assault on state sovereignty, how should we respond to a Rwanda, to a Srebrenica – to gross and systematic violations of human rights that offend every precept of our common humanity?

Responding to the challenge, in 2000 the Canadian government, along with several international foundations, created the International Commission on Intervention and State Sovereignty (ICIS), which was made up of a body of distinguished academics and international policymakers. What ICIS drafted was the report: *The Responsibility to Protect*. At the 2005 UN World Summit, world leaders unanimously declared that all states have a responsibility to protect their citizens from genocide, war crimes, crimes against humanity, and ethnic cleansing and that as members of the international community they stand prepared to take collective action in cases where national authorities have failed to protect their populations. Furthermore, in April 2006 the UN Security Council reaffirmed the Responsibility to Protect (R2P), and in January 2009, the Secretary-General issued a report entitled *Implementing the responsibility to protect*.

One of the distinguishing features of R2P is how vastly different it conceives of state sovereignty itself, shifting the understanding from sovereignty as control to sovereignty as responsibility. In addition, sovereignty is not something that states are necessarily enshrined with automatically, but rather, under R2P sovereignty is something states must earn, and the way of doing this is by protecting their populations. Who has this responsibility? In the first instance it is the territorial state. However, if domestic authorities fail to meet this responsibility, this task is then placed in the hands of the international community.

But perhaps what most distinguishes R2P from humanitarian intervention is the nature and scope of state responsibility (Gibney 2011). Under the traditional approach, the emphasis was solely on the military intervention itself. Because of this, there was virtually no concern with events leading up to the humanitarian disaster, or any kind of subsequent obligation to help reconstruct a society after intervention has taken place. In contrast to this, *The Responsibility to Protect* proposal offers a much broader approach, setting forth three separate, but related, obligations: the responsibility to *prevent*; the responsibility to *react*; and finally, the responsibility to *rebuild*.

## Responsibility to Prevent

The first obligation of states is to prevent humanitarian disasters from arising in the first place. In the words of the *Report*: "Intervention should only be considered after prevention fails – and the best way of avoiding intervention is to ensure it doesn't fail." The primary responsibility for ensuring that no humanitarian disaster arises is the territorial state. However, if this state fails to meet this responsibility, then the states of the international community share a common obligation to take whatever resources are necessary: "more resources, more energy, more competence, more commitment."

The *Report* notes that there is an increasing reluctance of some states to accept any internationally endorsed preventive measures for fear that "internationalization" itself will naturally lead to further involvement in the affairs of other countries. However, it also points out that if preventive measures are not undertaken, this will eventually lead to even greater levels of international involvement – including military intervention itself. Thus, what R2P calls for is a change in mindset from a "culture of reaction" to a "culture of prevention," which can only be accomplished by holding states accountable for their actions and undertaking preventive measures at the local, national, regional and global levels. As the *Report* warns:

> Without a genuine commitment to conflict prevention at all levels – without new energy and momentum being devoted to the task – the world will continue to witness the needless slaughter of our fellow human beings, and the reckless waste of precious resources on conflict rather than social and economic development. The time has come for all of us to take practical responsibility to prevent the needless loss of human life, and to be ready to act in the cause of prevention and not just in the aftermath of disaster.

### Responsibility to React

The *Responsibility to Protect* initiative comes closest to traditional humanitarian intervention under the obligation to react, but only when all other efforts to avert disaster have failed. Applying "just war" principles, intervention under R2P should be guided by just cause; right intention; last resort; proportionate means; reasonable prospects; and finally, legitimate authority. In terms of the latter, the *Report* reiterates the central role the Security Council is expected to play in determining how and by whom military intervention should occur. However, what if the Security Council fails to act, as has happened so often in the past? Or as the *Report* states the problem: "There were too many occasions during the last decade when the Security Council, faced with conscience-shocking situations, failed to respond as it should have with timely authorization and support." In some instances, this role was taken over by others, such as NATO's intervention in Kosovo in 1999. However, in other instances – Rwanda in the 1990s and Syria today – the Security Council's inaction led directly to genocide and/or massive civilian deaths.

The Commission goes on to point out that such non-responses send two important messages to the United Nations. The first is that if the U.N. does not act, this vacuum will be filled by individual states. The second and broader message relates to the overall credibility of the institution itself if it cannot perform the most important task entrusted to it: maintaining international peace and security.

### Responsibility to Rebuild

The third and final duty under the R2P initiative is the responsibility to rebuild after military intervention has been completed. In many ways, the responsibility to rebuild is to be taken literally in the sense of the need to rebuild the infrastructure that has been destroyed. However, it is incumbent on the international community to provide security to allow these efforts to go forward. In addition, the rule of law needs to be established, although as the Commission Report points out, it would ultimately be self-defeating if this task was to be assumed solely by the international community, which would only lead to a situation where a "failed state" would, inexorably, fail once again. Thus, the country where the atrocities took place – even if this is a so-called "failed state" – has a crucial role to play in establishing a system of justice and protecting human rights. The role of the international community is to help the state to re-create itself.

We will close this section by asking whether R2P has become a customary norm under international law (Hakimi 2014). Another way of framing this is whether the failure to act in the face of gross and systematic human rights violations constitutes an internationally wrongful act. And to take this a step further, if you were a judge in a country whose government failed to act, how would you respond to a claim by victims from this other state?

## Cyberwarfare

Warfare used to be easy to determine. One state would physically attack another state with an array of bombs, bullets, and advancing soldiers and for centuries this is what would be known as "warfare." Warfare of this type is, of course, still prevalent. However, warfare has taken other forms as well. One is cyberwarfare, a practice by which a state, or more likely entities in this state, uses cyberware to hack into computer systems in other states as a means of disrupting business and/ or governmental practices.

Although the term "cyberwarfare" is commonly used, the initial question is whether this constitutes "warfare" or not. The answer international law has provided thus far is that it depends; and generally what it depends on is whether the cyberattack results in the loss of life or not. If it does, it will generally be treated as constituting "warfare." However, at least to date, nearly all cyberattacks do not result in the loss of life, although they can often result in enormous economic loss in the targeted state. A term used to describe this phenomenon is "cyber-disruptions," but the real question is how many and how severe can these "disruptions" be before warfare – cyber or otherwise – ensues?

A second issue is responsibility for these cyberattacks. The most definitive source of law is the *Tallinn Manual 2.0* (Schmitt 2017), the product of a group of experts who met in this Estonian city. The *Manual 2.0* by and large mirrors the International Law Commission's *Articles of State Responsibility* (Crawford 2002), which we will analyze more fully in Chapter 9. Rule 15 of the *Manual* states: "cyber operations conducted by organs of a State, or by persons or entities empowered by domestic law to exercise elements of governmental authority, are attributable to the State." Rule 17 states: "cyber operations conducted by a non-State actor are attributable to a State when: a) engaged in pursuant to its instructions or under its direction or control; or b) the State acknowledges and adopts the operations as its own."

---

### Box 4.4: Guardians of Peace

On November 24, 2014, the image in Photo 4.2 flashed onto every employee's computer screen at Sony Pictures Entertainment headquarters in Culver City, California. The group "Guardians of Peace" scrubbed more than a hundred terabytes of Sony's data and leaked thousands of confidential documents (Walton 2017). GOP threatened to release more documents if Sony did not halt the release of *The Interview*, a (black) comedy about the effort to assassinate the leader of North Korea. The U.S. State Department concluded that the hacking originated in North Korea. If you have never seen (or heard of) this film it is with good reason. After the hacking took place, a number of U.S. cinema chains canceled showing the film and the film went directly to digital release – but good luck finding it on Netflix.

Photo 4.2 Hacked by #GOP

---

There are at least two problems with this. The first is that, almost as a matter of course, states deny engaging in cyberattacks, and in this realm deciphering who is acting or not is decidedly much more difficult than in cases involving actual warfare (Kilovaty 2016). Related to this, a second problem is the degree of "direction or control" a state must exercise over non-state actors in order to be responsible under international law. The enormous disincentives in play here should be obvious. If a state does exercise sufficient "direction and control" of non-state actors engaged in cyberattacks this state will be responsible for committing an internationally wrongful act. The safer approach, at least in terms of establishing state responsibility, is to ensure that such direction or control is *not* exercised – or at least does not appear as such (Walton 2017).

---

**Box 4.5: The Iranian Nuclear Program and Russian Hacking in the 2016 U.S. Presidential Election**

As mentioned previously, states have seldom (perhaps have never) claimed to be engaging in cyberattacks against entities in another state. However, sometimes strong evidence points in this very direction. One example is the manner in which Iran's path to developing a nuclear weapon was stymied by a malware, referred to as Stuxnet, commonly attributed to the United States and/or Israel. If these rumors are true, have the U.S. and Israel violated Iran's sovereignty? Or would such actions be justified as some form of anticipatory self defense?

A second example involves the Russian interference with the 2016 presidential election in the United States (Ohlin 2017). Security officials in the United States are unanimous in their opinion (although President Trump takes the opposite position) that the Russian government, or at least operatives on Russian soil working on behalf of the Putin regime, was responsible for hacking the emails of the Democratic National Committee and then disseminating information obtained in these emails through Wikileaks. Assuming this is true, has the Russian government acted in violation of international law – or is this little more than the kind of routine spying that is a hallmark of diplomatic relations between countries?

---

## Drones

Another way that technology has challenged international law is the increasing use of drones. In its fight against international terrorism, the United States has increasingly made use of drone strikes, including attacks carried out in "neutral" states such as Pakistan. The question is whether drone strikes are consistent with international law – but also whether they are preferable to full-scale warfare. Are drones, by definition, an infringement on the sovereignty of another state? And do they violate the human rights of those individuals who they endlessly fly over?

In the case that follows, a victim from a drone attack is bringing suit against the United Kingdom for its part in passing along intelligence information to American operatives who carried out the drone attack.

## *Noor Khan v. The Secretary of State for Foreign and Commonwealth Affairs*, The Court of Appeal (Civil Division) (London), January 20, 2014

The claimant lives in Miranshah, North Waziristan Agency ("NWA"), in the Federally Administered Tribal Areas of Pakistan. His father was a member of the local Jirga, a peaceful council of tribal elders whose functions included the settling of commercial disputes. On 17 March, the claimant's father presided over a meeting of the Jirga held outdoors at Datta Khel, NWA. During the course of the meeting, a missile was fired from an unmanned aircraft or "drone" believed to have been operated by the US Central Intelligence Agency ("CIA"). The claimant's father was one of more than 40 people who were killed.

In 2010, it was reported in several media outlets, including *The Sunday Times*, on the basis of a briefing said to emanate from official sources, that the General Communications Headquarters ("GCHQ"), an agency for which the defendant Secretary of State is responsible, provides "locational intelligence" to the US authorities for use in drone strikes in various places, including Pakistan.

On 16 December 2011, the claimant's solicitors wrote to the Secretary of State seeking clarification of the policies and practices of the UK Government in relation to the passing of information to US agents for use in drone attacks in Pakistan. On 6 February 2012, the Treasury Solicitor replied saying that it would not be possible to make an exception to the long-standing policy of successive governments to give a "neither confirm nor deny" response to questions about matters the public disclosure of which would risk damaging important public interests, including national security and vital relations with international partners.

The claimant then issued these proceedings claiming judicial review of "a decision by the Defendant to provide intelligence to the US authorities for use in drone strikes in Pakistan, among other places". The relief claimed was a declaration that:

"(a) A person who passes to an agent of the United States Government intelligence on the location of an individual in Pakistan, foreseeing a serious risk that the information will be used by the Central Intelligence Agency to target or kill that individual:

    (i)  is not entitled to the defense of combatant immunity; and

    (ii) accordingly may be liable under domestic criminal law for soliciting, encouraging, persuading or proposing a murder or for aiding, abetting, counselling or procuring murder.

(b) Accordingly the Secretary of State has no power to direct or authorize GCHQ officers or other Crown servants in the United Kingdom to pass intelligence in the circumstances set out in (a) above.

(c) Alternatively, where a GCHQ officer or other Crown servant has information relating to the location of an individual, whom it knows or suspects the United States Government intends to target or kill, the officer may not pass the intelligence to an agent of the United States Government if there is a significant risk that doing so would facilitate the commission of a war crime or crimes against humanity contrary to the International Criminal Court Act 2001.

(d) Accordingly, before directing or authorizing the passing of intelligence relating to the location of such an individual to an agent of the United States Government, the Secretary of State must formulate, publish and apply a lawful policy setting out the circumstances in which such intelligence may be transferred."

In his witness statement Mr Morrison [representing the UK] explains why in his opinion if the court were to grant permission to the claimant to apply for judicial review, "the likely consequence would be serious harm to the national security and the international relations of the United Kingdom." He says that the UK's bilateral relationships with the US and Pakistan are critical to the UK's national security as they are both key partners in efforts to combat the very real threat of terrorism faced by the citizens of all three countries. A key feature of international relations is that law, politics and diplomacy are bound together and the assertion of legal arguments by a state is often regarded as a political act. The UK's international alliances could be damaged by the assertion of arguments under international law which might affect the position of those states. This is particularly so since this case raises difficult legal issues "such as the scope of a state's right under international law to use force in self-defense against non-state actors, which are the subject of intense international legal scrutiny and debate".

I shall start with the question of justiciability. It is common ground that our court will not decide whether the drone strikes committed by US officials are lawful. The principle is one which applies save in exceptional circumstances. One such exception is that it will not apply to foreign acts of state which are in breach of clearly established rules of international law or are contrary to English principles of public policy, as well as where there is a grave infringement of human rights.

How do these principles apply in the present case? Mr Chamberlain [the applicant's legal representative] accepts that our courts cannot adjudicate on the question of whether a CIA official who executes a drone strike is guilty of murder or indeed any other offence. His argument is that the principles have no application here. He is not asking the court to sit in judgment on the acts of CIA officials either by declaring that they are unlawful or by condemning them in any other way. He is not inviting the court to adjudicate on the legality or acceptability of the acts of the CIA officials either under our domestic law or under international law. He seeks relief on the basis that the acts of the CIA officials, *if committed by UK nationals*, would be unlawful in English law. The assumption that the operation of drone bombs by US nationals is treated as if executed by UK nationals is a necessary link in a chain of reasoning which comprises (i) a finding that the act of the principal who operates the bombs is murder in English law; (ii) a GCHQ employee who encourages or assists such an act is liable as a secondary party to murder; and (iii) the Secretary of State's practice and policy of providing locational guidance is unlawful.

It is true that the court will not be asked to make any finding that CIA officials are committing murder or acting unlawfully in some other way. Nor will the court be asked to say whether the US policy of drone bombing is unlawful as a matter of US law. As a matter of strict legal analysis, the court will be concerned with the hypothetical question of whether, subject to the defenses available in English law, a UK national who kills a person in a drone strike in Pakistan is guilty of murder.

In my view, a finding by our court that the notional UK operator of a drone bomb which caused a death was guilty of murder would inevitably be understood (and rightly understood) by the US as a condemnation of the US. In reality, it would be understood as a finding that (i) the US official who operated the drone was guilty of murder and (ii) the US policy of using drone bombs in Pakistan and other countries was unlawful. The fact that our courts have no jurisdiction to make findings on either of these issues is beside the point. What matters is that the findings would be understood by the US authorities as critical of them. Although the findings would have no legal effect, they would as a serious condemnation of the US by a court of this country.

**Notes and Comments:**

1. Would you have decided the case the same way?
2. In addition to drones, countries are also developing what have been called "killer robots" (Scharre 2018), autonomous weapons that might take the place of soldiers. Is this a good thing – or a nightmare waiting to happen?
3. Drones were at the center of rising tensions between the United States and Iran during the summer of 2019. In July, the United States destroyed an Iranin drone that was hovering over the Gulf of Hormuz, with the two countries squabbling over whether this occurred over Iranian airspace. In September, a Saudi oil refinery was attacked by drones that the Saudi government (as well as the United States) claimed were launched from Iran, which the Iranian government denies.

---

### Box 4.6: Mea Culpa and Ex Gratia

In January 2015, a U.S. drone strike in Pakistan accidentally killed Warren Weinstein, a U.S. citizen, and Giovanni Lo Porto, an Italian aid worker. As a response, President Obama paid compensation to the families and offered an apology. Similarly, in October 2017, a U.S. airstrike struck a Doctors Without Borders hospital in Kunduz, Afghanistan that resulted in the deaths of 22 people. President Obama issued an apology to Dr. Joanne Liu, the head of Doctors Without Borders, and promised a "full accounting" of the incident and a review of the rules of engagement. In addition, compensation was made to the families of those killed or injured.

However, the vast majority of civilian deaths caused by the security personnel of the United States do not receive such special treatment. Seldom has the U.S. directly acknowledged its causal responsibility or made a promise of non-repetition. On the other hand, it has often provided small monetary payments as an expression of sympathy for family members of the deceased, which are generally known as *ex gratia* or *solatia* payments (Wexler and Robbennolt 2017). As its name would indicate, such payments are not an admission of fault. Should international law demand such payments?

---

### Box 4.7: International Law at the Movies: Drone Warfare

*Unmanned: America's Drone Wars* (2013) is a documentary that is centered around the soldiers who have served as drone operators, while another documentary, *National Bird* (2016), focuses more on the ways in which drones have changed the nature of warfare. Finally, *Eye in the Sky* (2015) starring Helen Mirren is Hollywood's version of this new kind of warfare.

**Peacemaking and Peacekeeping**

We will close this chapter by examining what responsibilities peacekeeping forces have to those they have been assigned to protect. The claim made in the following case, brought before a Dutch domestic court, is that Dutch peacekeeping troops – Dutchbats – failed to protect civilian populations during the siege of Srebrenica.

By way of some background, United Nations peacekeeping began in 1948 when the Security Council authorized the deployment of U.N. military observers to the Middle East to monitor the Armistice Agreement between Israel and its Arab neighbors. Since then, 70 peacekeeping operations have been deployed, with most of these (57) since 1988. Initially U.N. peacekeeping forces consisted of either unarmed military observers or lightly armed troops. However, the nature of the peacekeeping forces has become increasingly militarized. At the present time, there are upwards of 110,000 military, police, and civilian staff serving in 15 peacekeeping missions.

---

## *Mothers of Srebrenica v. the Netherlands and the United Nations,* Supreme Court of the Netherlands, Case # 10/04437 (2012)

Claimants accuse Dutchbat of not or of not correctly implementing the formal order it received from Sarajevo on July 9th 1995 at 22:00 hours to take up *blocking positions* to prevent any further advance by the Bosnian Serbs towards the town of Srebrenica. In this connection Claimants point out that the commander of Dutchbat's B company Captain Groen interpreted incorrectly the order by instructing his men that only if there were a direct attack could they use self-defence and only then if it was necessary whereby initially they were to fire over the heads of the Bosnian Serbs. According to Claimants in doing so Dutchbat allowed its own safety to prevail over that of the task with which it had been charged namely to protect the populace in the *safe area* as is also evidenced by Karremans' statement in response to the current order namely, *"that he thought his troops were too good to be sacrificed"*. According to Claimants Dutchbat had abandoned the *blocking positions* too quickly and too easily and at the last *blocking position* taken had acted contrary to Gobilliard's order by leaving it unfortified.

[*The court then referenced the findings of the International Criminal Tribunal for the former Yugoslavia regarding the forced separation of all military aged men*]:

> *The Chamber accepts that, at the stage when the Bosnian Muslim men were divested of their identification en masse, it must have been apparent to any observer that the men were not being screened for war crimes. In the absence of personal documentation, these men could no longer be accurately identified for any purpose. Rather, the removal of their identification could only be an ominous signal of atrocities to come.*

(Krstić legal ground no 160).

The foregoing leads the District Court to conclude that where in the evening of July 12th 1995 Dutchbat could have suspected that the men who had been selected and carried off by the Bosnian Serbs ran a real risk of being killed or of being treated inhumanely on July 13th 1995 they knew that this would happen after they had seen the heap of identity papers lying about at the White House and in any case they had seen said heap burning as the men were carried off. Basing its opinion on statements by Franken, Rutten and Van Duijn the ICTY came to the same conclusion namely:

> At that point Dutch Bat soldiers were certain that the story about screening for war criminals could not be true: something more ominous was afoot.

(Krstić legal ground no 160).

### CONCLUSION REGARDING UNLAWFUL ACTS OF THE STATE

The District Court has determined that the following acts of Dutchbat attributable to the State are not unlawful:

(i) Abandoning the *blocking positions*
(ii) Not providing adequate medical care to the refugees
(iii) Handing over weapons and other equipment to the Bosnian Serbs
(iv) Upholding the decision throughout the transition period not to allow refugees entry to the compound
(vi) Separating the male refugees from the other refugees during the evacuation, in so far as this constitutes assistance by forming a lock and guiding the refugees to the buses in turns.

In a ground included for the sake of completeness, the District Court has held that even if it is established that Dutchbat advised the male refugees to flee to the woods, this advice – as well as the failure to raise the alarm about their fleeing – are not be deemed as unlawful. Whether or not this advice was indeed given does therefore not require further investigation.

The District Court deems Dutchbat's cooperation with the deportation in the late afternoon of July 13th 1995 of the able-bodied male refugees who had sought refuge at the compound an unlawful act for which the State is liable. It concerns about 320 men. The majority of these men were never seen alive again. A small number of them ended up in the Batkovici prison camp near Bijelina and were released in December 1995 under the Daytona Agreement, along with another group of men from Srebrenica.

The liability of the State extends to the family members of the men who were carried off from the compound and then killed by the Bosnian Serbs in the late afternoon of July 13th 1995, the starting point for which are the spouses and children of the adult men and the parents of the underage men. It should be noted that men who have reached the age of eighteen are deemed adults.

The foregoing entails that . . . on account of an unlawful act the State is liable for damages incurred by the . . . male refugees who in the late afternoon of July 13th 1995 were deported from the compound in Potočari by the Bosnian Serbs and subsequently killed.

## Note and Comments:

1. Several other U.N. peacekeeping missions have been charged with failing to protect. Arguably, the worst episode involved the cholera epidemic in Haiti introduced into the country by U.N. peacekeepers, which resulted in

the deaths of upwards of 10,000 people. In addition to this, there have been accusations that peacekeepers in Haiti have also operated a child sex ring. Who should bear responsibility in these kinds of situations? The United Nations or the states from which the peacekeeping forces came from?

---

### Box 4.8: International Law at the Movies: Peacekeeping

Rachel Weisz stars in *The Whistleblower* (2010), a feature film about a sex trafficking ring run by U.N. peacekeepers in postwar Bosnia. A (somewhat) more upbeat film is *No Man's Land* (2001), the setting of which is the war in Bosnia in the early 1990s. The plotline sounds like the start of a joke entailing enemy soldiers sharing the same foxhole, with one of them lying flat on his back on top of a landmine that will detonate if he is moved. Mix in the non-response of the head of UNPROFOR, who sees to it that the problem is ignored and the poor soldier left to his own devices, and you end up with an absurd result – truly reflecting the reality on the ground.

## References

*Books and Articles*

Mark Gibney, "Genocide and State Responsibility," *Human Rights Law Review* 7: 760–73 (2007)

Mark Gibney, "Universal Duties: The Responsibility to Protect, the Duty to Prevent (Genocide) and Extraterritorial Human Rights Obligations," *Global Responsibility to Protect* 3: 123–51 (2011)

Monica Hakimi, "Toward a Legal Theory on the Responsibility to Protect," *Yale Journal of International Law* 39: 247–81 (2014)

Ido Kilovaty, "Disruptive Cyberspace Operations as 'Attacks' Under International Humanitarian Law," *Michigan Telecommunications and Technology Law Review* 23: 113–47 (2016)

Jens David Ohlin, "Did Russian Cyber Interference in the 2016 Election Violate International Law?" *Texas Law Review* 95: 1579–98 (2017)

Paul Scharre, *Army of None: Autonomous Weapons and the Future of War*, New York, NY: Norton (2018)

Michael N. Schmitt (ed.), *Tallinn 2.0 on the International Law Applicable to Cyber Operations*, Cambridge: Cambridge University Press (2017)

Beatrice Walton, "Duties Owed: Low-intensity Cyber Attacks and Liability for Transboundary Torts in International Law," *Yale Law Journal* 126: 1460–519 (2017)

Michael Walzer, *Just and Unjust Wars: A Moral Argument With Historical Illustrations*, New York, NY: Basic Books (1977)

Lesley Wexler and Jennifer K. Robbennolt, "Designing Amends for Lawful Civilian Casualties," *Yale Journal of International Law* 42: 121–83 (2017)

## U.N. Reports

James Crawford, *The International Law Commission's Articles of State Responsibility: Introduction, Text and Commentaries*, Cambridge: Cambridge University Press (2002)

International Commission on Intervention and State Sovereignty, *The Responsibility to Protect* (2001)

Millennium Report of the U.N. Secretary General, *We the Peoples: The Role of the United Nations in the 21st Century* (2000)

Report of the Secretary General, *Implementing the Responsibility to Protect* (12 January 2009)

## Cases

*Bosnia v. Serbia*, ICJ (2007)

*Campaign Against Arms Trade v. Secretary of State*, [2017] EWHC 1726 (QB)

*Mothers of Srebrenica v. Netherlands and the United Nations*, Supreme Court of the Netherlands (2012)

*Nicaragua v. United States*, ICJ (1986)

*Noor Khan v. Secretary of State for Foreign and Commonwealth Affairs*, The Court of Appeal (Civil Division) (London), (20 January 2014)

*Prosecutor v. Akayesu*, Trial Chamber, ICTR (2 September 1998)

## International Agreements

Arms Trade Treaty, opened for signature 3 June 2013, entry into force 24 December 2014

Charter of the United Nations, signed 26 June 1945, entry into force 24 October 1945

Convention on the Prevention and Punishment of the Crime of Genocide, approved and proposed for signature 9 December 1948, entry into force 12 January 1951

Security Resolution 1368, adopted by the U.N. Security Council on 12 September 2001

Security Resolution 1373, adopted by the U.N. Security Council on 28 September 2001

Security Resolution 1674, adopted by the U.N. Security Council on 28 April 2006

# 5
# Jus in Bello

## Making the Inhumane – Humane?

The term Jus ad Bellum, which was the focus of the previous chapter, refers to the lawfulness of going to war while Jus in Bello, which will be the focus of the present chapter, refers to the means by which war is fought. We have already had some exposure to this issue in Chapter 2 dealing with the detention of "enemy combatants" at Guantanamo Bay, Cuba.

The appropriate place to begin this analysis is with the work of Henry Dunant, who after witnessing the brutality of the battle of Solferino (1859) became the driving force behind the adoption in 1864 of the Geneva Convention for the Amelioration of the Condition of the Wounded in Armies in the Field. These "laws of war" were further codified at the Hague Conferences of 1899 and 1907. Following World War II, in 1949 the four Geneva Conventions were adopted concerning the: I) wounded and sick on land; II) wounded, sick and shipwrecked members of the armed forces at sea; III) prisoners of war; and IV) civilians. These were further refined in 1977 with the adoption of two Additional Protocols.

The foundational principle of the Geneva Conventions is the distinction between combatants and noncombatants, but also the humane treatment of both. One of the central issues in the "war on terrorism" has been whether "terrorists" are covered by international humanitarian law. Among the arguments set forward against this are: there is no discernible command structure within terrorist networks; terrorists do not signify themselves as soldiers; they do not carry their arms openly; and finally, they do not conduct operations in accordance with the laws and customs of war. A perfect example of the latter would be the September 11, 2001 attacks on the World Trade Centers in New York, which had no military significance whatsoever. On the other hand, the Geneva Conventions were intended to provide protection to everyone involved in warfare, intentionally or otherwise, so that if suspected terrorists are not to be treated as combatants they should then be accorded protection as noncombatants – not "enemy combatants" afforded virtually no legal protections at all.

Much of the law protecting civilians in wartime and under occupation is analyzed in various places throughout this chapter, especially in the Goldstone Report and the ICJ ruling on the Israeli security wall at the close of the chapter. However, special mention should be made of two essential principles that serve as the foundation of international humanitarian law. The first is the principle of *distinction* between civilian populations and combatants. Combatants are fair game; civilians are not. This does not mean that it is illegal to kill civilians. What it does mean is that the only targets that are permissible are those that have some military purpose, such as a munitions factory that might employ civilian workers.

---

### Box 5.1: My Lai Massacre

The My Lai massacre, which occurred on March 16, 1968, resulted in the slaughter of upwards of 500 Vietnamese civilians, including children and infants. The event was initially portrayed as a firefight between U.S. and Viet Cong forces. However, in November 1969 journalist Seymour Hersh broke the true story of the slaughter of innocent civilians. Twenty-two American servicemen were charged with various criminal offenses, although only the platoon leader, William Calley, was convicted. Calley was sentenced to life imprisonment but his sentence was repeatedly shortened and he ended up serving 3 ½ years under house arrest.

---

The second principle is *proportionality*, which serves as an additional means of protecting civilian populations. Due to the very real prospects of causing "collateral damage," there are limitations to the amount of force that can be deployed in achieving military advantages.

International humanitarian law has increasingly attended to the means by which warfare is conducted. The year 2017 marked the 20th anniversary of the entry into force of the *Chemical Weapons Convention*, which all but five states are party to. It was also the 20th anniversary of the signing of the *Anti-Personnel Mine Ban Convention*. At present, 162 states are party to this Convention.

---

### Box 5.2: Syria and the Use of Chemical Weapons

On April 6, 2017, the United States launched 59 U.S. Navy Tomahawk Land Missiles against the Al Shayrat airfield in Syria as a response to the Syrian government's use of chemical weapons two days earlier, which killed approximately 100 civilians. Almost exactly a year later, the Trump administration launched another attack following revelations of another chemical attack by the Syrian military.

Chemical weapons have been outlawed since 1925 under the Geneva Gas Protocol and, more recently, the *Chemical Weapons Convention*, to which both Syria and the United States are state parties to. Although these military responses both met with worldwide acclaim, they raise a number of questions. One is whether such attacks violate the prohibition against the use of force. The ready answer, of course, is that Syria (and Russia) have massively violated this principle of international law already. Yet, does this allow other states to do so themselves?

On the other hand, what is puzzling is how (and why) the use of chemical weapons by the Assad regime would prompt this swift military response, while the much larger humanitarian disaster in that country has not (Schmitt and Ford 2017). Perhaps only a cynic would suggest that the message to the Syrian government was this: you can kill your civilian population with impunity, but not by chemical weapons.

## Nuclear Weapons

If chemical weapons are prohibited under international law, what about nuclear weapons? At present, nine countries are known to have nuclear weapons: United States, Russia, China, France, United Kingdom, Pakistan, India, Israel, and North Korea. The apartheid government of South Africa had also built nuclear weapons; however, these bombs were destroyed and the entire nuclear program scrapped just before the country underwent democratic transformation.

One of the great fears after the breakup of the Soviet Union was that nuclear weapons would fall into the "wrong" hands – although it is by no means clear, in this context at least, what the "right" hands would be. With the exception of the nuclear bombs dropped on Hiroshima and Nagasaki at the end of World War II, no country has ever used a nuclear weapon. However, North Korea has repeatedly tested missile systems with an ever-increasing range, while President Donald Trump repeatedly threatened to wipe North Korea from the face of the earth. However, not all news on this front was negative. On July 7, 2017, 122 states adopted the Treaty on the Prohibition of Nuclear Weapons.

The question addressed by the International Court of Justice in the following advisory opinion is whether it would be lawful to use nuclear weapons – or even to threaten to do so. As you will see, in many respects the ICJ's "answer" is no answer at all.

### Box 5.3: ICJ Advisory Opinions

In addition to ruling on contentious cases, the International Court of Justice also has jurisdiction to issue advisory opinions on specific matters of international law.

*(Continued)*

**Box 5.3: Continued**

The advisory opinion jurisdiction can only be invoked by the organs of the United Nations and its specialized agencies. Although advisory opinions are non-binding, they do carry a substantial amount of weight in terms of the interpretation of international law.

## *Legality of the Threat or Use of Nuclear Weapons,* ICJ, Advisory Opinion of 8 July 1996

Some of the proponents of the illegality of the use of nuclear weapons have argued that such use would violate the right to life as guaranteed in Article 6 of the International Covenant on Civil and Political Rights, as well as in certain regional instruments for the protection of human rights. Article 6, paragraph 1, of the International Covenant provides as follows: "Every human being has the inherent right to life. This right shall be protected by law. No one shall be arbitrarily deprived of his life." In reply, others contended that the International Covenant on Civil and Political Rights made no mention of war or weapons, and it had never been envisaged that the legality of nuclear weapons was regulated by that instrument. It was suggested that the Covenant was directed to the protection of human rights in peacetime, but that questions relating to unlawful loss of life in hostilities were governed by the law applicable in armed conflict.

The Court observes that the protection of the International Covenant of Civil and Political Rights does not cease in times of war, except by operation of Article 4 of the Covenant whereby certain provisions may be derogated from in a time of national emergency. Respect for the right to life is not, however, such a provision. In principle, the right not arbitrarily to be deprived of one's life applies also in hostilities. The test of what is an arbitrary deprivation of life, however, then falls to be determined by the applicable lex specialis, namely, the law applicable in armed conflict which is designed to regulate the conduct of hostilities. Thus whether a particular loss of life, through the use of a certain weapon in warfare, is to be considered an arbitrary deprivation of life contrary to Article 6 of the Covenant, can only be decided by reference to the law applicable in armed conflict and not deduced from the terms of the Covenant itself.

*[The ICJ then turned to the issue of whether the use of nuclear weapons would be in violation of laws intended to protect the environment.]*

In both their written and oral statements, some States furthermore argued that any use of nuclear weapons would be unlawful by reference to existing norms relating to the safeguarding and protection of the environment, in view of their essential importance.

However, the Court is of the view that the issue is not whether the treaties relating to the protection of the environment are or are not applicable during an armed conflict, but rather whether the obligations stemming from these treaties were intended to be obligations of total restraint during military conflict. The Court does not consider that the treaties in question could have intended to deprive a State of the exercise of its right of self-defence under international law because of its obligations to protect the environment. Nonetheless, States must take environmental considerations into account when assessing what is necessary and proportionate in the pursuit of legitimate military objectives. Respect for the environment is one of the elements that go to assessing whether an action is in conformity with the principles of necessity and proportionality.

The Court thus finds that while the existing international law relating to the protection and safeguarding of the environment does not specifically prohibit the use of nuclear weapons, it indicates important environmental factors that are properly to be taken into account in the context of the implementation of the principles and rules of the law applicable in armed conflict.

***

In the light of the foregoing the Court concludes that the most directly relevant applicable law governing the question of which it was seised, is that relating to the use of force enshrined in the United Nations Charter and the law applicable in armed conflict which regulates the conduct of hostilities, together with any specific treaties on nuclear weapons that the Court might determine to be relevant.

In applying this law to the present case, the Court cannot however fail to take into account certain unique characteristics of nuclear weapons. The Court has noted the definitions of nuclear weapons contained in various treaties and accords. It also notes that nuclear weapons are explosive devices whose energy results from the fusion or fission of the atom. By its very nature, that process, in nuclear weapons as they exist today, releases not only immense quantities of heat and energy, but also powerful and prolonged radiation. According to the material before the Court, the first two causes of damage are vastly more powerful than the damage caused by other weapons, while the phenomenon of radiation is said to be peculiar to nuclear weapons. These characteristics render the nuclear weapon potentially catastrophic. The destructive power of nuclear weapons cannot be contained in either space or time. They have the potential to destroy all civilization and the entire ecosystem of the planet. The radiation released by a nuclear explosion would affect health, agriculture, natural resources and demography over a very wide area. Further, the use of nuclear weapons would be a serious danger to future generations. Ionizing radiation has the potential to damage the future environment, food and marine ecosystem, and to cause genetic defects and illness in future generations.

The Court will now address the question of the legality or illegality of recourse to nuclear weapons in the light of the provisions of the Charter relating to the threat or use of force.

The Charter contains several provisions relating to the threat and use of force. In Article 2, paragraph 4, the threat or use of force against the territorial integrity or political independence of another State or in any other manner inconsistent with the purposes of the United Nations is prohibited. That paragraph provides: "All Members shall refrain in their international relations from the threat or use of force against the territorial integrity or political independence of any State, or in any other manner inconsistent with the Purposes of the United Nations." This prohibition of the use of force is to be considered in the light of other relevant provisions of the Charter. In Article 51, the Charter recognizes the inherent right of individual or collective self-defence if an armed attack occurs. A further lawful use of force is envisaged in Article 42, whereby the Security Council may take military enforcement measures in conformity with Chapter VII of the Charter.

These provisions do not refer to specific weapons. They apply to any use of force, regardless of the weapons employed. The Charter neither expressly prohibits, nor permits, the use of any specific weapon, including nuclear weapons. A weapon that is already unlawful per se, whether by treaty or custom, does not become lawful by reason of its being used for a legitimate purpose under the Charter.

Some States put forward the argument that possession of nuclear weapons is itself an unlawful threat to use force. Possession of nuclear weapons may indeed justify an inference of preparedness to use them. In order to be effective, the policy of deterrence, by which those States possessing or under the umbrella of nuclear weapons seek to discourage military aggression by demonstrating that it will serve no purpose, necessitates that the intention to use nuclear weapons be credible. Whether this is a "threat" contrary to Article 2, paragraph 4, depends upon whether the particular use of force envisaged would be directed against the territorial integrity or political independence of a State, or against the Purposes of the United Nations or whether, in the event that it were intended as a means of defence, it would necessarily violate the principles of necessity and proportionality. In any of these circumstances the use of force, and the threat to use it, would be unlawful under the law of the Charter.

The Court notes by way of introduction that international customary and treaty law does not contain any specific prescription authorizing the threat or use of nuclear weapons or any other weapon in general or in certain circumstances, in particular those of the exercise of legitimate self defence. Nor, however, is there any principle or rule of international law which would make the legality of the threat or use of nuclear weapons or of any other weapons dependent on a specific authorization. State practice shows that the illegality of the use of certain weapons as such does not result from an absence of authorization but, on the contrary, is formulated in terms of prohibition.

The Court will now turn to an examination of customary international law to determine whether a prohibition of the threat or use of nuclear weapons as such flows from that source of law.

States which hold the view that the use of nuclear weapons is illegal have endeavoured to demonstrate the existence of a customary rule prohibiting this use. They refer to a consistent practice of non-utilization of nuclear weapons by States since 1945 and they would see in that practice the expression of an opinio juris on the part of those who possess such weapons.

Some other States, which assert the legality of the threat and use of nuclear weapons in certain circumstances, invoked the doctrine and practice of deterrence in support of their argument. They recall that they have always, in concert with certain other States, reserved the right to use those weapons in the exercise of the right to self-defence against an armed attack threatening their vital security interests. In their view, if nuclear weapons have not been used since 1945, it is not on account of an existing or nascent custom but merely because circumstances that might justify their use have fortunately not arisen.

The Court does not intend to pronounce here upon the practice known as the "policy of deterrence". It notes that it is a fact that a number of States adhered to that practice during the greater part of the Cold War and continue to adhere to it. Furthermore, the members of the international community are profoundly divided on the matter of whether non-recourse to nuclear weapons over the past 50 years constitutes the expression of an opinio juris. Under these circumstances the Court does not consider itself able to find that there is such an opinio juris.

According to certain States, the important series of General Assembly resolutions, beginning with resolution 1653 (XVI) of 24 November 1961, that deal with nuclear weapons and that affirm, with consistent regularity, the illegality of nuclear weapons, signify the existence of a rule of international customary law which prohibits recourse to those weapons. According to other States, however, the resolutions in question have no binding character on their own account and are not declaratory of any customary rule of prohibition of nuclear weapons; some of these States have also pointed out that this series of resolutions not only did not meet with the approval of all of the nuclear-weapon States but of many other States as well.

States which consider that the use of nuclear weapons is illegal indicated that those resolutions did not claim to create any new rules, but were confined to a confirmation of customary law relating to the prohibition of means or methods of warfare which, by their use, overstepped the bounds of what is permissible in the conduct of hostilities. In their view, the resolutions in question did no more than apply to nuclear weapons the existing rules of international law applicable in armed conflict; they were no more than the "envelope" or instrumentum containing certain pre-existing customary rules of international law. For those States it is accordingly of little importance that the instrumentum should have occasioned negative votes, which cannot have the effect of obliterating those customary rules which have been confirmed by treaty law.

Having said this, the Court points out that the adoption each year by the General Assembly, by a large majority, of resolutions recalling the content of resolution 1653 (XVI), and requesting the member States to conclude a convention prohibiting the use of nuclear weapons in any circumstance, reveals the desire of a very large section of the international community to take, by a specific and express prohibition of the use of nuclear weapons, a significant step forward along the road to complete nuclear disarmament. The emergence, as lex lata, of a customary rule specifically prohibiting the use of nuclear weapons as such is hampered by the continuing tensions between the nascent opinio juris on the one hand, and the still strong adherence to the practice of deterrence on the other.

The Court not having found a conventional rule of general scope, nor a customary rule specifically proscribing the threat or use of nuclear weapons per se, it will now deal with the question whether recourse to nuclear weapons must be considered as illegal in the light of the principles and rules of international humanitarian law applicable in armed conflict and of the law of neutrality.

The cardinal principles contained in the texts constituting the fabric of humanitarian law are the following. The first is aimed at the protection of the civilian population and civilian objects and establishes the distinction between combatants and non-combatants; States must never make civilians the object of attack and must consequently never use weapons that are incapable of distinguishing between civilian and military targets. According to the second principle, it is prohibited to cause unnecessary suffering to combatants: it is accordingly prohibited to use weapons causing them such harm or uselessly aggravating their suffering. In application of that second principle, States do not have unlimited freedom of choice of means in the weapons they use.

Although the applicability of the principles and rules of humanitarian law and of the principle of neutrality to nuclear weapons is hardly disputed, the conclusions to be drawn from this applicability are, on the other hand, controversial.

According to one point of view, the fact that recourse to nuclear weapons is subject to and regulated by the law of armed conflict does not necessarily mean that such recourse is as such prohibited.

Another view holds that recourse to nuclear weapons could never be compatible with the principles and rules of humanitarian law and is therefore prohibited. In the event of their use, nuclear weapons would in all circumstances be unable to draw any distinction between the civilian population and combatants, or between civilian objects and military objectives, and their effects, largely uncontrollable, could not be restricted, either in time or in space, to lawful military targets. Such weapons would kill and destroy in a necessarily indiscriminate manner, on account of the blast, heat and radiation occasioned by the nuclear explosion and the effects induced; and the number of casualties which would ensue would be enormous. The use of nuclear weapons would therefore be prohibited in any circumstance, notwithstanding the absence of any explicit conventional prohibition. That view lay at the basis of the assertions by certain States before the Court that nuclear weapons are by their nature illegal under customary international law, by virtue of the fundamental principle of humanity.

Accordingly, in view of the present state of international law viewed as a whole, as examined above by the Court, and of the elements of fact at its disposal, the Court is led to observe that it cannot reach a definitive conclusion as to the legality or illegality of the use of nuclear weapons by a State in an extreme circumstance of self-defence, in which its very survival would be at stake.

Given the eminently difficult issues that arise in applying the law on the use of force and above all the law applicable in armed conflict to nuclear weapons, the Court considers that it now needs to examine one further aspect of the question before it, seen in a broader context. In the long run, international law, and with it the stability of the international order which it is intended to govern, are bound to suffer from the continuing difference of views with regard to the legal status of weapons as deadly as nuclear weapons. It is consequently important to put an end to this state of affairs: the long-promised complete nuclear disarmament appears to be the most appropriate means of achieving that result.

In these circumstances, the Court appreciates the full importance of the recognition by Article VI of the Treaty on the Non-Proliferation of Nuclear Weapons of an obligation to negotiate in good faith a nuclear disarmament. This provision is worded as follows: "Each of the Parties to the Treaty undertakes to pursue negotiations in good faith on effective measures relating to cessation of the nuclear arms race at an early date and to nuclear disarmament, and on a treaty on general and complete disarmament under strict and effective international control." The legal import of that obligation goes beyond that of a mere obligation of conduct; the obligation involved here is an obligation to achieve a precise result – nuclear disarmament in all its aspects – by adopting a particular course of conduct, namely, the pursuit of negotiations on the matter in good faith.

---

**Notes and Comments:**

1. How satisfied are you with the Court's ruling – or its analysis?

2. At the close of its ruling the ICJ puts in a strong plug for strengthening the Treaty on the Non-Proliferation of Nuclear Weapons (NPT), which came into force in 1970 and presently has 191 state parties – more than any other arms control treaty – although three of the states that possess nuclear weapons (India, Pakistan, and Israel) are not parties to the treaty, and in 2003 North Korea announced its withdrawal from the treaty. The NPT seeks to halt the proliferation of nuclear weapons, while also encouraging the sharing of the benefits of peaceful nuclear technology. Has the NPT been successful?

3. French nuclear testing in the ocean in South Asia has been the centerpiece of two important international law claims. The first involved a case brought before the International Court of Justice by New Zealand and Australia. However, before a judgment could be rendered, the French ceased its nuclear testing. In 1985, the French government announced its plan to resume such testing, which prompted Greenpeace to send the ship the *Rainbow Warrior* to Auckland, New Zealand in order to stage a protest. While in harbor, a

bomb was detonated, sinking the ship and killing one crewman. Although France originally denied any responsibility for the act, it soon admitted the involvement of French security agents. When the two countries could not reach an amicable agreement, the case was referred to the U.N. Secretary-General for a binding ruling. The arbitration award generally favored New Zealand, although the two French agents responsible for setting the bomb were allowed to serve the majority of their sentence on a French naval base before they were released.

4. In its Advisory Opinion, the ICJ states that human rights treaties continue even in times of war. Previous to this, many international lawyers thought that according to the doctrine of *lex specialis*, wartime was governed exclusively by international humanitarian law. However, what remains unclear is when one takes precedence over the other.

---

**Box 5.4: International Law at the Movies: Nuclear Warfare**

*The War Game* (1962) is a black and white film depicting what a nuclear attack on Great Britain would look like. I saw the film as an undergraduate and it has never left me. *White Light, Black Rain: The Destruction of Hiroshima and Nagasaki* (2007) is a documentary providing the most horrifying images of the destructive capabilities of nuclear weapons.

Nuclear war is certainly not a likely backdrop for humor. There are, however, exceptions. Peter Sellers plays three different roles, including the namesake of the film, in *Dr. Strangelove: Or How I Learned to Stop Worrying and Learned to Love the Bomb* (1964). *Atomic Café* (1982) looks back, somewhat whimsically, at when the U.S. government would instruct young students to "duck and cover" as a way of (somehow) surviving a nuclear attack.

Finally, one of the most widely viewed programs in U.S. television history was the made-for-TV film *The Day After* (1983) shown at the height of tensions between the United States and the former Soviet Union. The day after, of course, refers to the complete devastation of life on this planet from any kind of nuclear attack.

---

**Box 5.5: International Law at the Movies: Diamonds, Arms, and the Child Soldiers**

Wars used to be fought to gain territory but increasingly they are fought over minerals in the ground, including diamonds. In *Blood Diamond* (2006), Leonardo DiCaprio uses his star power to show the evils that are fought for in the name of fashion. In *Lord of War* (2004), Nicolas Cage plays Yuri Orlov, one of the world's most successful private arms dealers, who turns to the camera at the outset of the film and announces that there are 550 million firearms in circulation – or approximately 1 in 12 people have a gun – and his goal is to arm the other 11.

*(Continued)*

## Box 5.5: Continued

There are a wide array of international law instruments prohibiting the recruitment of child soldiers, most notably the Rome Statute of the International Criminal Court, the Convention on the Rights of the Child, and the Optional Protocol on the Rights of the Child on the Involvement of Children in Armed Conflict (OPAC). In addition, the first prosecution by the International Criminal Court (ICC), discussed further in Chapter 6, was against Thomas Lubanga based on his recruitment of child soldiers. Yet, these practices still continue. A disturbing portrait of this is shown in *Beasts of No Nation* (2015) starring Idris Elba as a completely amoral warlord.

## Assassination

Under the U.N. Charter there are only two lawful means for going to war: either as a means of self defense or where there has been Security Council approval. But events on the ground are changing rapidly. For example, before the onset of the Iraq war there were massive efforts to assassinate Iraqi dictator Saddam Hussein. If successful, would this have averted war altogether? But is assassination consonant with international law? The U.S. government was later successful in assassinating Osama bin Laden in a mountainous region of Pakistan. What follows is a legal challenge to the assassination plot, or so it is alleged, to kill Nasser Al-Aulaqi, a U.S. citizen.

## *Nasser Al-Aulaqi v. Obama,* 727 F.Supp.2d 1 (D.D.C. 2010)

On August 30, 2010, plaintiff Nasser Al-Aulaqi ("plaintiff") filed this action, claiming that the President, the Secretary of Defense, and the Director of the CIA (collectively, "defendants") have unlawfully authorized the targeted killing of plaintiff's son, Anwar Al-Aulaqi, a dual U.S.-Yemeni citizen currently hiding in Yemen who has alleged ties to al Qaeda in the Arabian Peninsula ("AQAP"). Plaintiff seeks an injunction prohibiting defendants from intentionally killing Anwar Al-Aulaqi "unless he presents a concrete, specific, and imminent threat to life or physical safety, and there are no means other than lethal force that could reasonably be employed to neutralize the threat." This is a unique and extraordinary case.

Stark, and perplexing, questions readily come to mind, including the following: How is it that judicial approval is required when the United States decides to target a U.S. citizen overseas for electronic surveillance, but that, according to defendants, judicial scrutiny is prohibited when the United States decides to target a U.S. citizen overseas for death? Can a U.S. citizen – himself or through another – use the U.S. judicial system to vindicate his constitutional rights while simultaneously evading U.S. law enforcement authorities, calling for "jihad against the West," and engaging in operational planning for an organization that has already carried out numerous terrorist attacks against the United States? Can the Executive order the assassination of a U.S. citizen without first affording him any form of judicial process whatsoever, based on the mere assertion that he is a dangerous member of a terrorist organization? How can the courts, as plaintiff proposes, make real-time assessments of the nature and severity of alleged threats to national security, determine the imminence of those threats, weigh the benefits and costs of possible diplomatic and military responses, and ultimately decide whether, and under what circumstances, the use of military force against such threats is justified? When would it ever make sense for the United States to disclose in advance to the "target" of contemplated military action the precise standards under which it will take that military action? And how does the evolving AQAP relate to core al Qaeda for purposes of assessing the legality of targeting AQAP (or its principals) under the September 18, 2001 Authorization for the Use of Military Force?

This case arises from the United States's alleged policy of "authorizing, planning, and carrying out targeted killings, including of U.S. citizens, outside the context of armed conflict." Specifically, plaintiff, a Yemeni citizen, claims that the United States has authorized the targeted killing of plaintiff's son, Anwar Al-Aulaqi, in violation of the Constitution and international law.

Anwar Al-Aulaqi is a Muslim cleric with dual U.S.-Yemeni citizenship, who is currently believed to be in hiding in Yemen. Anwar Al-Aulaqi was born in New Mexico in 1971, and spent much of his early life in the United States, attending college at Colorado State University and receiving his master's degree from San Diego State University before moving to Yemen in 2004. On July 16, 2010, the U.S. Treasury Department's Office of Foreign Assets Control ("OFAC") designated Anwar Al-Aulaqi as a Specially Designated Global Terrorist ("SDGT") in light of evidence that he was "acting for or on behalf of al-Qa'ida in the Arabian Peninsula (AQAP)" and "providing financial, material or technological support for, or other services to or in support of, acts of terrorism[.]" In its designation, OFAC explained that Anwar Al-Aulaqi had "taken on an increasingly operational role" in AQAP since late 2009, as he "facilitated training camps in Yemen in support of acts of terrorism" and provided "instructions" to Umar Farouk Abdulmutallab, the man accused of attempting to detonate a bomb aboard a Detroit bound Northwest Airlines flight on Christmas Day 2009. Media sources have also reported ties between Anwar Al-Aulaqi and Nidal Malik Hasan, the U.S. Army Major suspected of killing 13 people in a November 2009 shooting at Fort Hood, Texas. According to a January 2010 *Los Angeles Times* article, unnamed "U.S. officials" have discovered that Anwar Al-Aulaqi and Hasan exchanged as many as eighteen emails prior to the Fort Hood shootings.

Recently, Anwar Al-Aulaqi has made numerous public statements calling for "jihad against the West."

Plaintiff does not deny his son's affiliation with AQAP or his designation as a SDGT. Rather, plaintiff challenges his son's alleged unlawful inclusion on so-called "kill lists" that he contends are maintained by the CIA and the Joint Special Operations Command ("JSOC"). In support of his claim that the United States has placed Anwar Al-Aulaqi on "kill lists," plaintiff cites a number of media reports, which attribute their information to anonymous U.S. military and intelligence sources.

Based on these news reports, plaintiff claims that the United States has placed Anwar Al-Aulaqi on the CIA and JSOC "kill lists" without "charge, trial, or conviction." Plaintiff alleges that individuals like his son are placed on "kill lists" after a "closed executive process" in which defendants and other executive officials determine that "secret criteria" have been satisfied. Plaintiff further avers "[u]pon information and belief" that once an individual is placed on a "kill list," he remains there for "months at a time." Consequently, plaintiff argues, Anwar Al-Aulaqi is "now subject to a standing order that permits the CIA and JSOC to kill him . . . without regard to whether, at the time lethal force will be used, he presents a concrete, specific, and imminent threat to life, or whether there are reasonable means short of lethal force that could be used to address any such threat."

The United States has neither confirmed nor denied the allegation that it has issued a "standing order" authorizing the CIA and JSOC to kill plaintiff's son. Additionally, the United States has neither confirmed nor denied whether – if it has, in fact, authorized the use of lethal force against plaintiff's son – the authorization was made with regard to whether Anwar Al-Aulaqi presents a concrete, specific, and imminent threat to life, or whether there were reasonable means short of lethal force that could be used to address any such threat. The United States has, however, repeatedly stated that if Anwar Al-Aulaqi "were to surrender or otherwise present himself to the proper authorities in a peaceful and appropriate manner, legal principles with which the United States has traditionally and uniformly complied would prohibit using lethal force or other violence against him in such circumstances."

Before this Court may entertain the merits of his claims, plaintiff, as the party invoking federal jurisdiction, must establish that he has the requisite standing to sue.

"Next friend" standing originated in connection with petitions for habeas corpus, as early American courts allowed "next friends" to appear "on behalf of detained prisoners who [were] unable, usually because of mental incompetence or inaccessibility, to seek relief themselves." Congress statutorily authorized "next friend" standing in the habeas corpus context in 1948, amending the habeas corpus statute to allow petitions to be " 'signed and verified by the person for whose relief it is intended *or by someone acting in his behalf.*' " The Court noted, however, that to the extent parties may ever invoke a "federal doctrine of 'next friend' standing" in non-habeas proceedings, the scope of that doctrine "is no broader than what is permitted by the habeas corpus statute, which codified the historical practice."

Plaintiff has failed to provide an adequate explanation for his son's inability to appear on his own behalf, which is fatal to plaintiff's attempt to establish "next friend" standing. In his complaint, plaintiff maintains that his son cannot bring suit on his own behalf because he is "in hiding under threat of death" and any attempt to access counsel or the courts would "expos[e] him to possible attack by Defendants." But while Anwar Al-Aulaqi may have chosen to "hide" from U.S. law enforcement authorities, there is nothing preventing him from peacefully presenting himself at the U.S. Embassy in Yemen and expressing a desire to vindicate his constitutional rights in U.S. courts. Defendants have made clear – and indeed, both international and domestic law would require – that if Anwar Al-Aulaqi were to present himself in that manner, the United States would be "prohibit[ed] [from] using lethal force or other violence against him in such circumstances."

The Court's conclusion that Anwar Al-Aulaqi can access the U.S. judicial system by presenting himself in a peaceful manner implies no judgment as to Anwar Al-Aulaqi's status as a potential terrorist. *All* U.S. citizens may avail themselves of the U.S. judicial system if they present themselves peacefully, and *no* U.S. citizen may simultaneously avail himself of the U.S. judicial system and evade U.S. law enforcement authorities. Anwar Al-Aulaqi is thus faced with the same choice presented to all U.S. citizens.

---

## Notes and Comments:

1. Al-Aulaqi was assassinated on September 30, 2011. Two weeks later, his 16-year-old son Abdulrahman was killed in a drone attack, and on January 29, 2017, his 8-year-old daughter, Namar Al-Aulaqi, was killed in a drone attack in the early days of the Trump administration.

2. International law scholar Marko Milanovic (2015) has questioned citizenship as a basis of possessing certain rights. Using the assassination of Al-Aulaqi as a point of reference, he questions the following logic:

[I]t is normatively incoherent to say that before being killed by the U.S. government 1) a U.S. national on U.S. soil is entitled to due process; 2) a non-U.S national lawfully on U.S. soil (e.g. a tourist) is entitled to due process; 3) a non-U.S. national *unlawfully* on U.S. soil is entitled to due process; 4) a U.S. national *outside* U.S. soil is also entitled to due process; but that *only* 5) a non-U.S. national outside U.S. territory has no entitlement to due process.

Milanovic continues:

It seems impossible to identify a principle whereby 5) can truly be distinguished from 1–4, and I have never seen it persuasively explained why this should be the case – this distinction is all too often assumed rather than argued, and even when it is argued this is usually done in a perfunctory way.

Do you agree or disagree with Milanovic's position? Or with the court's disposition of this case?

---

### Box 5.6: International Law at the Movies: The Killing of Osama bin Laden

The feature film *Zero Dark Thirty* (2012), starring Jessica Chastain, is Kathryn Bigelow's *tour de force* on the decade-long hunt for Osama bin Laden. The film won the Oscar for Best Picture and Chastain was nominated for Best Actress.

---

### Box 5.7: The Assassination of Osama bin Laden: Was This Lawful?

On May 2, 2011, Osama bin Laden, the mastermind behind the September 11 attacks on the United States, was killed in his hiding place in Pakistan during a nighttime raid conducted by a group of Special Forces. Certainly, the reaction in the United States was one of near-universal glee. However, was the assassination legal? Executive Order 12333 provides: "No employee of the United States Government shall engage in, or conspire to engage in, political assassination." This EO was issued following revelations by what was known as the Church Committee in the U.S. Senate, under the chairmanship of Senator Frank Church, which unveiled a series of assassination plots concocted by the CIA.

In terms of the bin Laden assassination, the U.S. government presented two defenses. The first was that Osama bin Laden was still at war with the United States

*(Continued)*

**Box 5.7: Continued**

and therefore still a valid military target. The second rationale was that bin Laden did not surrender to U.S. military forces, thereby justifying his killing and that of four of his associates, including his son. However, what perhaps will never be known is whether bin Laden was even given the opportunity to disarm and surrender.

### International Humanitarian Law: The Israeli-Palestinian Conflict

The year 2017 marked the 50th anniversary of the 1967 war between Israel and neighboring Arab countries. As a result of the conflict, Israel took control of what is known as the Occupied Territories consisting of land on the West Bank of the Jordan River and, until 2005, the Gaza Strip. Much has ensued over the past half century, including another war between Israel and its Arab neighbors (1973), two intifada uprisings, a series of suicide bombings, repeated rocket attacks, a rather ill-advised war in southern Lebanon in 1982, but also some efforts at achieving peace, most notably through the Oslo Peace Accords (1993).

The Israeli-Palestinian conflict will be used as a prism through which various aspects of international humanitarian law are examined. We begin with two different interpretations of the responsibilities of an occupying power within the context of Israel's "security wall." The first is from the Israeli Supreme Court and the second is an Advisory Opinion from the International Court of Justice. Following this, the contentious Goldstone Report on Israel's invasion of Gaza in 2009 serves as a useful vehicle for understanding the "laws of war." This chapter closes with a case brought against the Caterpillar corporation which manufactures equipment that is used to bulldoze the homes of alleged terrorists, but in this instance a bulldozer crushed one of the protesters, who also happens to be a U.S. citizen.

---

## Beit Sourik Village Council v. The Government of Israel, HCJ 2056/04

### J U D G M E N T  PRESIDENT A. BARAK

The Commander of the IDF Forces in Judea and Samaria issued orders to take possession of plots of land in the area of Judea and Samaria. The purpose of the seizure was to erect a separation fence on the land. The question before us is whether the orders and the fence are legal.

#### BACKGROUND

Since 1967, Israel has been holding the areas of Judea and Samaria [hereinafter – the area] in belligerent occupation. In 1993 Israel began a political process with the PLO, and signed a number of agreements transferring control over parts of the area to the Palestinian Authority. Israel and the PLO continued political negotiations in an attempt to solve the remaining problems. The negotiations, whose final stages took place at Camp David in Maryland, USA, failed in July 2000.

From respondents' affidavit in answer to order nisi we learned that, a short time after the failure of the Camp David talks, the Israeli-Palestinian conflict reached new heights of violence. In September 2000, the Palestinian side began a campaign of terror against Israel and Israelis. Terror attacks take place both in the area and in Israel. They are directed against citizens and soldiers, men and women, elderly and infants, regular citizens and public figures. Terror attacks are carried out everywhere: in public transportation, in shopping centers and markets, in coffee houses and in restaurants. Terror organizations use gunfire attacks, suicide attacks, mortar fire, Katyusha rocket fire, and car bombs. From September 2000 until the beginning of April 2004, more than 780 attacks were carried out within Israel. During the same period, more than 8200 attacks were carried out in the area.

The armed conflict claimed (as of April 2004) the lives of 900 Israeli citizens and residents. More than 6000 were injured, some with serious wounds that have left them severely handicapped. The armed conflict has left many dead and wounded on the Palestinian side as well. Bereavement and pain wash over us.

These terror acts have caused Israel to take security precautions on several levels. The government, for example, decided to carry out various military operations, such as Operation Defensive Wall (March 2002) and Operation Determined Path (June 2002). The objective of these military actions was to defeat the Palestinian terrorist infrastructure and to prevent terror attacks. These combat operations – which are not regular police operations, but embody all the characteristics of armed conflict – did not provide a sufficient answer to the immediate need to stop the terror. The Ministers' Committee on National Security considered a list of steps intended to prevent additional terror acts and to deter potential terrorists from participating in such acts. Despite all these measures, the terror did not come to an end. The attacks did not cease. Innocent people paid with both life and limb. This is the background behind the decision to construct the separation fence.

### THE SEIZURE PROCEEDINGS

Parts of the separation fence are being erected on land which is not privately owned. Other parts are being erected on private land. In such circumstances – and in light of the security necessities – an order of seizure is issued by the Commander of the IDF Forces in the area of Judea and Samaria. Pursuant to standard procedure, every land owner whose land is seized will receive compensation for the use of his land. After the order of seizure is signed, it is brought to the attention of the public, and the proper liaison body of the Palestinian Authority is contacted. An announcement is relayed to the residents, and each interested party is invited to participate in a survey of the area affected by the order of seizure, in order to present the planned location of the fence. A few days after the order is issued, a survey is taken of the area, with the participation of the landowners, in order to point out the land which is about to be seized.

After the survey, a one week leave is granted to the landowners, so that they may submit an appeal to the military commander. The substance of the appeals is examined. Where it is possible, an attempt is made to reach understandings with the landowners. If the appeal is denied, leave of one additional week is given to the landowner, so that he may petition the High Court of Justice.

Petitioners' argument is that the orders are illegal in light of Israeli administrative law, and in light of the principles of public international law which apply to the dispute before us. First, petitioners claim that respondent lacks the authority to issue the orders of seizure. Were the route of the separation fence to pass along Israel's border, they would have no complaint. However, this is not the case. The route of the separation fence, as per the orders of seizure, passes through areas of Judea and Samaria. According to their argument, these orders alter the borders of the West Bank with no express legal authority. It is claimed that the separation fence annexes areas to Israel in violation of international law. The separation fence serves the needs of the occupying power and not the needs of the occupied area. The objective of the fence is to prevent the infiltration of terrorists into Israel; as such, the fence is not intended to serve the interests of the local population in the occupied area, or the needs of the occupying power in the occupied area. Moreover, military necessity does not require construction of the separation fence along the planned route. The security arguments guiding respondents disguise the real objective: the annexation of areas to Israel. As such, there is no legal basis for the construction of the fence, and the orders of seizure which were intended to make it possible are illegal. Second, petitioners argue that the procedure for the determination of the route of the separation fence was illegal. The orders were not published and were not brought to the knowledge of most of the affected landowners; petitioners learned of them by chance, and they were granted extensions of only a few days for the submission of appeals. Thus, they were not allowed to participate in the determination of the route of the separation fence, and their arguments were not heard.

Third, the separation fence violates many fundamental rights of the local inhabitants, illegally and without authority. Their right to property is violated by the very taking of possession of the lands and by the prevention of access to their lands. In addition, their freedom of movement is impeded. Their livelihoods are hurt and their freedom of occupation is restricted. Beyond the difficulties in working the land, the fence will make the trade of farm produce difficult. The fence detracts from the educational opportunities of village children, and throws local family and community life into disarray. Freedom of religion is violated, as access to holy places is prevented. Nature and landscape features are defaced. Petitioners argue that these violations are disproportionate and are not justified under the circumstances. The separation fence route reflects collective punishment, prohibited by international law. Thus, respondent neglects the obligation, set upon his shoulders by international law, to make normal and proper life possible for the inhabitants of Judea and Samaria. The security considerations guiding him cannot, they claim, justify such severe injury to the local inhabitants. This injury does not fulfill the requirements of proportionality. According to their argument, despite the language of the orders of seizure, it is clear that the fence is not of a temporary character, and the critical wound it inflicts upon the local population far outweighs its benefits.

### THE RESPONSE TO THE PETITION

Respondents, in their first response, argued that the orders of seizure and the route through which the separation fence passes are legal. The separation fence is a project of utmost national importance. Israel is in the midst of actual combat against a wave of terror, supported by the Palestinian population and leadership. At issue are the lives of the citizens and residents of Israel, who are threatened by terrorists who infiltrate into the territory of Israel. At issue are the lives of Israeli citizens residing in the area.

Respondents explain that, in planning the route of the separation fence, great weight was given to the interests of the residents of the area, in order to minimize, to the extent possible, the injury to them.

The power to seize land for the obstacle is a consequence of the natural right of the State of Israel to defend herself against threats from outside her borders. Likewise, security officials have the power to seize lands for combat purposes, and by the laws of belligerent occupation. Respondents do not deny the need to be considerate of the injury to the local population and to keep that injury proportionate; their claim is that they fulfill these obligations. Respondents deny the severity of the injury claimed by petitioners. The extent of the areas to be seized for the building of the fence, the injury to agricultural areas, and the injury to trees and groves, are lesser – by far – than claimed. All the villages are connected to water systems and, as such, damage to wells cannot prevent the supply of water for agricultural and other purposes. The marketing of agricultural produce will be possible even after the construction of the fence. In each village there is a medical clinic, and there is a central clinic in Bidu. A few archeological sites will find themselves beyond the fence, but these sites are neglected and not regularly visited. The educational needs of the local population will also be taken into account. Respondents also note that, in places where the separation fence causes injury to the local population, efforts are being made to minimize that injury. In light of all this, respondents argue that the petitions should be denied.

The principle of proportionality applies to our examination of the legality of the separation fence. This approach is accepted by respondents. It is reflected in the government decision (of October 1, 2003) that during the planning, every effort shall be made to minimize, to the extent possible, the disturbance to the daily lives of the Palestinians due to the construction of the obstacle. The argument that the damage caused by the separation fence route is proportionate was the central argument of respondents. Indeed, our point of departure is that the separation fence is intended to realize a security objective which the military commander is authorized to achieve. The key question regarding the route of the fence is: is the route of the separation fence proportionate? The proportionality of the separation fence must be decided by the three following questions, which reflect the three subtests of proportionality. First, does the route pass the "appropriate means" test (or the "rational means" test)? The question is whether there is a rational connection between the route of the fence and the goal of the construction of the separation fence. Second, does it pass the test of the "least injurious" means? The question is whether, among the various routes which would achieve the objective of the separation fence, is the chosen one the least injurious. Third, does it pass the test of proportionality in the narrow sense? The question is whether the separation fence route, as set out by the military commander, injures the local inhabitants to the extent that there is no proper proportion between this injury and the security benefit of the fence. According to the "relative" examination of this test, the separation fence will be found disproportionate if an alternate route for the fence is suggested that has a smaller security advantage than the route chosen by respondent, but which will cause significantly less damage than that original route.

*[The Court then proceeded to examine where the separation fence was to be laid out and deemed certain areas where the "proportionate" standard had not been met, while approving most of where the fence was to be located.]*

During the hearings, we asked respondent whether it would be possible to compensate petitioners by offering them other lands in exchange for the lands that were taken to build the fence and the lands that they will be separated from. We did not receive a satisfactory answer. This petition concerns farmers that make their living from the land. Taking petitioners' lands obligates the respondent, under the circumstances, to attempt to find other lands in exchange for the lands taken from the petitioners. Monetary compensation may only be offered if there are no substitute lands.

The injury caused by the separation fence is not restricted to the lands of the inhabitants and to their access to these lands. The injury is of a far wider scope. It strikes across the fabric of life of the entire population. In many locations, the separation fence passes right by their homes. In certain places (like Beit Sourik), the separation fence surrounds the village from the west, the south and the east. The fence directly affects the links between the local inhabitants and the urban centers (Bir Nabbala and Ramallah). This link is difficult even without the separation fence. This difficulty is multiplied sevenfold by the construction of the fence.

The task of the military commander is not easy. He must delicately balance between security needs and the needs of the local inhabitants. We were impressed by the sincere desire of the military commander to find this balance, and his willingness to change the original plan in order to reach a more proportionate solution. We found no stubbornness on his part. Despite all this, we are of the opinion that the balance determined by the military commander is not proportionate. There is no escaping, therefore, a renewed examination of the route of the fence, according to the standards of proportionality that we have set out.

### Epilogue

Our task is difficult. We are members of Israeli society. Although we are sometimes in an ivory tower, that tower is in the heart of Jerusalem, which is not infrequently hit by ruthless terror. We are aware of the killing and destruction wrought by the terror against the state and its citizens. As any other Israelis, we too recognize the need to defend the country and its citizens against the wounds inflicted by terror. We are aware that in the short term, this judgment will not make the state's struggle against those rising up against it easier. But we are judges. When we sit in judgment, we are subject to judgment. We act according to our best conscience and understanding. Regarding the state's struggle against the terror that rises up against it, we are convinced that at the end of the day, a struggle according to the law will strengthen her power and her spirit. There is no security without law. Satisfying the provisions of the law is an aspect of national security.

Only a separation fence built on a base of law will grant security to the state and its citizens. Only a separation route based on the path of law, will lead the state to the security so yearned for.

---

## Note and Comments:

1. Has justice been done in this case? Have the strictures of international law been met?

A short time after the ruling by the Israeli Supreme Court in *Beit Sourik Village Council v. Israel*, the U.N. General Assembly requested an advisory opinion by the International Court of Justice on essentially this same matter. As you will see, the ICJ interpreted international humanitarian law much differently than the Israeli high court. In addition to this, this ruling places the Israeli-Palestinian conflict into a broader historical context. And finally, the ICJ also addresses the relationship between international human rights law and international humanitarian law.

## Legal Consequences of the Construction of a Wall in the Occupied Palestinian Territory, ICJ Advisory Opinion (2004)

In the present instance, if the General Assembly requests the Court to state the "legal consequences" arising from the construction of the wall, the use of these terms necessarily encompasses an assessment of whether that construction is or is not in breach of certain rules and principles of international law. Thus, the Court is first called upon to determine whether such rules and principles have been and are still being breached by the construction of the wall along the planned route.

As regards the request for an advisory opinion now before it, the Court acknowledges that Israel and Palestine have expressed radically divergent views on the legal consequences of Israel's construction of the wall, on which the Court has itself noted, "Differences of views . . . on legal issues have existed in practically every advisory proceeding."

Furthermore, the Court does not consider that the subject-matter of the General Assembly's request can be regarded as only a bilateral matter between Israel and Palestine. Given the powers and responsibilities of the United Nations in questions relating to international peace and security, it is the Court's view that the construction of the wall must be deemed to be directly of concern to the United Nations. The responsibility of the United Nations in this matter also has its origin in the Mandate and the Partition Resolution concerning Palestine. This responsibility has been described by the General Assembly as "a permanent responsibility towards the question of Palestine until the question is resolved in all its aspects in a satisfactory manner in accordance with international legitimacy." Within the institutional framework of the Organization, this responsibility has been manifested by the adoption of many Security Council and General Assembly resolutions, and by the creation of several subsidiary bodies specifically established to assist in the realization of the inalienable rights of the Palestinian people.

The question put by the General Assembly concerns the legal consequences of the construction of the wall in the Occupied Palestinian Territory. However, in order to indicate those consequences to the General Assembly the Court must first determine whether or not the construction of that wall breaches international law. It will therefore make this determination before dealing with the consequences of the construction.

Palestine was part of the Ottoman Empire. At the end of the First World War, a class "A" Mandate for Palestine was entrusted to Great Britain by the League of Nations. The territorial boundaries of the Mandate for Palestine were laid down by various instruments, in particular on the eastern border by a British memorandum of 16 September 1922 and an Anglo-Transjordanian Treaty of 20 February 1928.

In 1947 the United Kingdom announced its intention to complete evacuation of the mandated territory by 1 August 1948, subsequently advancing that date to 15 May 1948. In the meantime, the General Assembly had on 29 November 1947 adopted resolution 181 (II) on the future Kingdom government . . . and of Palestine, which "Recommends to all other Members of the to the United Nations the adoption and implementation . . . of the Plan of Partition" of the territory, as set forth in the resolution, between two independent States, one Arab, the other Jewish, as well as the creation of a special international régime for the City of Jerusalem. The Arab population of Palestine and the Arab States rejected this plan, contending that it was unbalanced; on 14 May 1948, Israel proclaimed its independence on the strength of the General Assembly resolution; armed conflict then broke out between Israel and a number of Arab States and the Plan of Partition was not implemented.

By resolution 62 (1948) of 16 November 1948, the Security Council decided that "an armistice shall be established in all sectors of Palestine" and called upon the parties directly involved in the conflict to seek agreement to this end. In conformity with this decision, general armistice agreements were concluded in 1949 between Israel and the neighboring States through mediation by the United Nations.

In the 1967 armed conflict, Israeli forces occupied all the territories which had constituted Palestine under British Mandate (including those known as the West Bank, lying to the east of the Green Line). On 22 November 1967, the Security Council unanimously adopted resolution 242 (1967), which emphasized the inadmissibility of acquisition of territory by war and called for the "Withdrawal of Israel armed forces from territories occupied in the recent conflict", and "Termination of all claims or states of belligerency". From 1967 onwards, Israel took a number of measures in these territories aimed at changing the status of the City of Jerusalem. The Security Council, after recalling on a number of occasions "the principle that acquisition of territory by military conquest is inadmissible", condemned those measures.

Later, following the adoption by Israel on 30 July 1980 of the Basic Law making Jerusalem the "complete and united" capital of Israel, the Security Council, by resolution 478 (1980) of 20 August 1980, stated that the enactment of that Law constituted a violation of international law and that "all legislative and administrative measures and actions taken by Israel, the occupying Power, which have altered or purport to alter the character and status of the Holy City of Jerusalem . . . are null and void". It further decided "not to recognize the 'basic law' and such other actions by Israel that, as a result of this law, seek to alter the character and status of Jerusalem".

Lastly, a number of agreements have been signed since 1993 between Israel and the Palestine Liberation Organization imposing various obligations on each Party. Those agreements inter alia required Israel to transfer to Palestinian authorities certain powers and responsibilities exercised in the Occupied Palestinian Territory by its military authorities and civil administration. Such transfers have taken place, but, as a result of subsequent events, they remained partial and limited.

The Court would observe that, under customary international law territory is considered occupied when it is actually placed under the authority of the hostile army, and the occupation extends only to the territory where such authority has been established and can be exercised.

The territories situated between the Green Line and the former eastern boundary of Palestine under the Mandate were occupied by Israel in 1967 during the armed conflict between Israel and Jordan. Under customary international law, these were therefore occupied territories in which Israel had the status of occupying Power. Subsequent events in these territories have done nothing to alter this situation. All these territories (including East Jerusalem) remain occupied territories and Israel has continued to have the status of occupying Power. It is essentially in these territories that Israel has constructed or plans to construct the works described in the report of the Secretary-General.

The Court will now determine the rules and principles of international law which are relevant in assessing the legality of the measures taken by Israel. Such rules and principles can be found in the United Nations Charter and certain other treaties, in customary international law and in the relevant resolutions adopted pursuant to the Charter by the General Assembly and the Security Council. However, doubts have been expressed by Israel as to the applicability in the Occupied Palestinian Territory of certain rules of international humanitarian law and human rights instruments. The Court will now consider these various questions.

The Court notes that the principle of self-determination of peoples has been enshrined in the United Nations Charter and reaffirmed by the General Assembly in resolution 2625 (XXV) cited above, pursuant to which "Every State has the duty to refrain from any forcible action which deprives peoples referred to [in that resolution] . . . of their right to self-determination." Article 1 common to the International Covenant on Economic, Social and Cultural Rights and the International Covenant on Civil and Political Rights reaffirms the right of all peoples to self-determination, and lays upon the States parties the obligation to promote the realization of that right and to respect it, in conformity with the provisions of the United Nations Charter.

The participants in the proceedings before the Court also disagree whether the international human rights conventions to which Israel is party apply within the Occupied Palestinian Territory. Annex 1 to the report of the Secretary-General States:

> 4. Israel denies that the International Covenant on Civil and Political Rights and the International Covenant on Economic, Social and Cultural Rights, both of which it has signed, are applicable to the occupied Palestinian territory. It asserts that humanitarian law is the protection granted in a conflict situation such as the one in the West Bank and Gaza Strip, whereas human rights treaties were intended for the protection of citizens from their own Government in times of peace.

Of the other participants in the proceedings, those who addressed this issue contend that, on the contrary, both Covenants are applicable within the Occupied Palestinian Territory. More generally, the Court considers that the protection offered by human rights conventions does not cease in case of armed conflict, save through the effect of provisions for derogation of the kind to be found in Article 4 of the International Covenant on Civil and Political Rights. As regards the relationship between international humanitarian law and human rights law, there are thus three possible situations: some rights may be exclusively matters of international humanitarian law; others may be exclusively matters of human rights law; yet others may be matters of both these branches of international law. In order to answer the question put to it, the Court will have to take into consideration both these branches of international law, namely human rights law and, as lex specialis, international humanitarian law.

It remains to be determined whether the two international Covenants and the Convention on the Rights of the Child are applicable only on the territories of the States parties thereto or whether they are also applicable outside those territories and, if so, in what circumstances. The scope of application of the International Covenant on Civil and Political Rights is defined by Article 2, paragraph 1, thereof, which provides:

> Each State Party to the present Covenant undertakes to respect and to ensure to all individuals within its territory and subject to its jurisdiction the rights recognized in the present Covenant, without distinction of any kind, such as race, color, sex, language, religion, political or other opinion, national or social origin, property, birth or other status.

This provision can be interpreted as covering only individuals who are both present within a State's territory and subject to that State's jurisdiction. It can also be construed as covering both individuals present within a State's territory and those outside that territory but subject to that State's jurisdiction. The Court will thus seek to determine the meaning to be given to this text.

The Court would observe that, while the jurisdiction of States is primarily territorial, it may sometimes be exercised outside the national territory. Considering the object and purpose of the International Covenant on Civil and Political Rights, it would seem natural that, even when such is the case, States parties to the Covenant should be bound to comply with its provisions.

In conclusion, the Court considers that the International Covenant on Civil and Political Rights is applicable in respect of acts done by a State in the exercise of its jurisdiction outside its own territory.

The International Covenant on Economic, Social and Cultural Rights contains no pro-vision on its scope of application. This may be explicable by the fact that this Covenant guarantees rights which are essentially territorial. However, it is not to be excluded that it applies both to territories over which a State party has sovereignty and to those over which that State exercises territorial jurisdiction.

It is not without relevance to recall in this regard the position taken by Israel in its reports to the Committee on Economic, Social and Cultural Rights. In its initial report to the Committee of 4 December 1998, Israel provided "statistics indicating the enjoyment of the rights enshrined in the Covenant by Israeli settlers in the occupied Territories". The Committee noted that, according to Israel, "the Palestinian population within the same jurisdictional areas were excluded from both the report and the protection of the Covenant." The Committee expressed its concern in this regard, to which Israel replied in a further report of 19 October 2001 that it has "consistently maintained that the Covenant does not apply to areas that are not subject to its sovereign territory and jurisdiction" (a formula inspired by the language of the International Covenant on Civil and Political Rights). This position, continued Israel, is "based on the well-established distinction between human rights and humanitarian law under international law". It added: "the Committee's mandate cannot relate to events in the West Bank and the Gaza Strip, inasmuch as they are part and parcel of the context of armed conflict as distinct from a relationship of human rights." In view of these observations, the Commit-tee reiterated its concern about Israel's position and reaffirmed "its view that the State party's obligations under the Covenant apply to all territories and populations under its effective control."

For the reasons explained above, the Court cannot accept Israel's view. It would also observe that the territories occupied by Israel have for over 37 years been subject to its territorial jurisdiction as the occupying Power. In the exercise of the powers available to it on this basis, Israel is bound by the provisions of the International Covenant on Economic, Social and Cultural Rights. Furthermore, it is under an obligation not to raise any obstacle to the exercise of such rights in those fields where competence has been transferred to Palestinian authorities.

Having determined the rules and principles of international law relevant to reply to the question posed by the General Assembly, and having ruled in particular on the applicability within the Occupied Palestinian Territory of international humanitarian law and human rights law, the Court will now seek to ascertain whether the construc-tion of the wall has violated those rules and principles.

In this regard, Annex II to the report of the Secretary-General, entitled "Summary Legal Position of the Palestine Liberation Organization", states that "The construction of the Barrier is an attempt to annex the territory contrary to international law" and that "The de facto annexation of land interferes with the territorial sovereignty and consequently with the right of the Palestinians to self-determination." This view was echoed in certain of the written statements submitted to the Court and in the views expressed at the hearings. Inter alia, it was contended that:

> The wall severs the territorial sphere over which the Palestinian people are en-titled to exercise their right of self-determination and constitutes a violation of the legal principle prohibiting the acquisition of territory by the use of force.

In this connection, it was in particular emphasized that "the route of the wall is designed to change the demographic composition of the Occupied Palestinian Terri-tory, including East Jerusalem, by reinforcing the Israeli settlements' illegally established on the Occupied Palestinian Territory. It was further contended that the wall aimed at "reducing and parceling out the territorial sphere over which the Palestinian people are entitled to exercise their right of Self-determination."

For its part, Israel has argued that the wall's sole purpose is to enable it effectively to combat terrorist attacks launched from the West Bank. Furthermore, Israel has repeatedly stated that the Barrier is a temporary measure. The Court notes that the route of the wall as fixed by the Israeli Government includes within the "Closed Area" some 80 percent of the settlers living in the Occupied Palestinian Territory. Moreover, it is apparent from an examination of the map mentioned above that the wall's sinuous route has been traced in such a way as to include within that area the great majority of the Israeli settlements in the occupied Palestinian Territory (including East Jerusalem).

As regards these settlements, the Court notes that Article 49, paragraph 6, of the Fourth Geneva Convention provides: "The Occupying Power shall not deport or transfer parts of its own civilian population into the territory it occupies." That provision prohibits not only deportations or forced transfers of population such as those carried out during the Second World War, but also any measures taken by an occupying Power in order to organize or encourage transfers of parts of its own population into the occupied territory.

In this respect, the information provided to the Court shows that, since 1977, Israel has conducted a policy and developed practices involving the establishment of Settlements in the Occupied Palestinian Territory, contrary to the terms of Article 49, paragraph 6, just cited.

The Security Council has thus taken the view that such policy and practices "have no legal validity". It has also called upon "Israel, as the occupying Power, to abide scrupulously" by the Fourth Geneva Convention and:

> to rescind its previous measures and to desist from taking any action which would result in changing the legal status and geographical nature and materially affecting the demographic composition of the Arab territories occupied since 1967, including Jerusalem and, in particular, not to transfer parts of its own civilian population into the occupied Arab territories.

The Council reaffirmed its position in resolutions 452 (1979) of 20 July 1979 and 465 (1980) of 1 March 1980. Indeed, in the latter case it described "Israel's policy and practices of settling parts of its population and new immigrants in [the occupied] territories" as a "flagrant violation" of the Fourth Geneva Convention.

The Court concludes that the Israeli settlements in the Occupied Palestinian Territory (including East Jerusalem) have been established in breach of international law. Whilst the Court notes the assurance given by Israel that the construction of the wall does not amount to annexation and that the wall is of a temporary nature, it nevertheless cannot remain indifferent to certain fears expressed to it that the route of the wall will prejudge the future frontier between Israel and Palestine, and the fear that Israel may integrate the settlements and their means of access. The Court considers that the construction of the wall and its associated régime create a "fait accompli" on the ground that could well become permanent, in which case, and notwithstanding the formal characterization of the wall by Israel, it would be tantamount to de facto annexation.

To sum up, the Court, from the material available to it, is not convinced that the specific course Israel has chosen for the wall was necessary to attain its security objectives. The wall, along the route chosen, and its associated régime gravely infringe a number of rights of Palestinians residing in the territory occupied by Israel, and the infringements resulting from that route cannot be justified by military exigencies or by the requirements of national security or public order. The construction of such a wall accordingly constitutes breaches by Israel of various of its obligations under the applicable international humanitarian law and human rights instruments.

The Court has thus concluded that the construction of the wall constitutes action not in conformity with various international legal obligations incumbent upon Israel. However, Annex 1 to the report of the Secretary-General states that, according to Israel:

"the construction of the Barrier is consistent with Article 51 of the Charter of the United Nations, its inherent right to self-defense and Security Council resolutions 1368 (2001) and 1373 (2001)". More specifically, Israel's Permanent Representative to the United Nations asserted in the General Assembly on 20 October 2003 that "the fence is a measure wholly consistent with the right of States to self-defense enshrined in Article 51 of the Charter"; the Security Council resolutions referred to, he continued, "have clearly recognized the right of States to use force in self-defense against terrorist attacks", and therefore surely recognize the right to use non-forcible measures to that end.

Under the terms of Article 51 of the Charter of the United Nations: "Nothing in the present Charter shall impair the inherent right of individual or collective self-defense if an armed attack occurs against a Member of the United Nations, until the Security Council has taken measures necessary to maintain international peace and security." Article 51 of the Charter thus recognizes the existence of an inherent right of self-defense in the case of armed attack by one State against another State. However, Israel does not claim that the attacks against it are imputable to a foreign State.

The Court also notes that Israel exercises control in the Occupied Palestinian Territory and that, as Israel itself states, the threat which it regards as justifying the construction of the wall originates within, and not outside, that territory. The situation is thus different from that contemplated by Security Council resolutions 1368 (2001) and 1373 (2001), and therefore Israel could not in any event invoke those resolutions in support of its claim to be exercising a right of self-defense.

Consequently, the Court concludes that Article 51 of the Charter has no relevance in this case. The Court having concluded that, by the construction of the wall in the Occupied Palestinian Territory, including in and around East Jerusalem, and by adopting its associated régime, Israel has violated various international obligations incumbent upon it, it must now, in order to reply to the question posed by the General Assembly, examine the consequences of those violations [omitted].

## Notes and Comments:

1. Which opinion – the Israeli Supreme Court or the International Court of Justice – do you agree with the most?
2. In 2005, the Israeli Supreme Court revisited this issue in *Mara'abe v. Prime Minister of Israel*, HCJ 7957/04, where the Court ruled, as it had in *Beit Sourik Village Council*, that portions of the separation wall violated international law. However, the Court also addressed the ICJ advisory opinion and held that this ruling had no domestic effect.

---

### Box 5.8: International Law at the Movies: The Israeli-Palestinian Conflict

One of the difficulties in picking out the "best" documentaries and feature films on the Israeli-Palestinian conflict is that there are so many to choose from. Listed are some of my personal favorites.

*Arna's Children* (2004) is one of the most powerful films I have ever seen perhaps because of the juxtaposition of watching old videos of Palestinian children joyously playing theatrical roles as part of a children's acting troupe – and then seeing these same individuals, now as young adults, making their farewell video before they are about to embark on a terrorist attack. Along these same lines, *Paradise Now* (2005) is a feature film that tells the story of two young Palestinians who are about to embark on a suicide mission in Israel. *5 Broken Cameras* (2011) is a documentary that tells the story of the Israeli occupation through the lens (literally) of a Palestinian man.

*Waltz with Bashir* (2008) is a stunningly effective animated film that explores the Israeli invasion of Lebanon in 1982 and the humanitarian law violations committed there. There is only one small moment when the film shifts to "real" mode – and it is devastating. *Budrus* (2009) is a documentary about acts of civil disobedience carried out by ordinary citizens when Palestinian villagers are about to be separated from their olive groves. The title of the documentary *To See if I'm Smiling* (2007) is a question asked by a former female member of the Israeli Defense Force who reflects on camera regarding some of the things she did to civilian populations while she served as a soldier in the Occupied Territories.

Turning to international law directly, *The Gatekeepers* (2012) is a remarkable documentary consisting of interviews with former heads of Shin Bet, Israel's security agency. Equally striking is *The Law in These Parts* (2011), which consists of interviews with judges who served in the Occupied Territories and the manner in which they viewed the law and how (differently) they applied the law – in these parts.

## The Goldstone Report

The United Nations Fact-Finding Mission on the Gaza Conflict, better known as the Goldstone Report, named for its chair, Richard Goldstone, was established in April 2009 to investigate war crimes during the January 2009 Gaza Conflict. Parts of the conclusion of this extensive report are set forth in the following. As you will see, the Goldstone Report charged that members of the Israel Defense Force were responsible for carrying out various war crimes. In an interesting twist, on April 1, 2011, Goldstone retracted his claim that the Israeli government deliberately targeted civilians. However, the three other members of the committee released a joint communication criticizing Goldstone and reaffirming the findings in the report.

United Nations Human Rights Council, *Human Rights in Palestine and Other Occupied Arab Territories, Report of the United Nations Fact-Finding Mission on the Gaza Conflict* (2009)

The international community as well as the State of Israel and, to the extent determined by their authority and means, Palestinian authorities, have the responsibility to protect victims of violations and ensure that they do not continue to suffer the scourge of war or the oppression and humiliations of occupation or indiscriminate rocket attacks. People of Palestine have the right to freely determine their

own political and economic system, including the right to resist forcible deprivation of their right to self-determination and the right to live, in peace and freedom,
in their own State. The people of Israel have the right to live in peace and security.
Both peoples are entitled to justice in accordance with international law.

The Mission is of the view that Israel's military operation in Gaza between 27
December 2008 and 18 January 2009 and its impact cannot be understood and
assessed in isolation from developments prior and subsequent to it. The operation
fits into a continuum of policies aimed at pursuing Israel's political objectives with
regard to Gaza and the Occupied Palestinian Territory as a whole. Many such policies are based on or result in violations of international human rights and humanitarian law. Military objectives as stated by the government of Israel do not explain
the facts ascertained by the Mission, nor are they congruous with the patterns
identified by the Mission during the investigation.

The continuum is evident most immediately with the policy of blockade that
preceded the operations and that in the Mission's view amounts to collective punishment intentionally inflicted by the Government of Israel on the people of the
Gaza Strip. When the operations began, the Gaza Strip had been for almost three
years under a severe regime of closures and restrictions on the movement of people,
goods and services. This included basic life necessities such as food and medical
supplies, and products required for the ordinary conduct of daily life such as fuel,
electricity, school items, and repair and construction material. These measures
were imposed by the State of Israel purportedly to isolate and weaken Hamas after
its electoral victory in view of the perceived continuing threat to Israel's security
that it represented. Their effect was compounded by the withholding of financial
and other assistance by some donors on similar grounds. Adding hardship to the
already difficult situation in the Gaza Strip, the effects of the prolonged blockade
did not spare any aspect of the life of Gazans. Prior to the military operation the
Gaza economy had been depleted, the health sector beleaguered, the population
had been made dependent on humanitarian assistance for survival and the conduct of daily life. Men, women, and children were psychologically suffering from
longstanding poverty, insecurity, and violence, and enforced confinement in a
heavily overcrowded territory. The dignity of the people of Gaza had been severely
eroded. This was the situation in the Gaza Strip when the Israeli armed forces
launched their offensive in December 2008. The military operations and the manner in which they were conducted considerably exacerbated the aforementioned
effects of the blockade. The result, in a very short time was unprecedented long-
term damage both to the people and their development and recovery prospects.

When the Mission conducted its first visit to the Gaza Strip in early June 2009,
almost five months had passed since the end of the Israeli military operations.
The devastating effects of the operations on the population were, however,

unequivocally manifest. In addition to the visible destruction of houses, factories, wells, schools, hospitals, police stations, and other public buildings, the sight of families, including the elderly and children, still living amid the rubble of their former dwellings – no reconstruction possible due to the continuing blockade – was evidence of the protracted impact of the operations on the living conditions of the Gaza population. Reports of the trauma suffered during the attacks, the stress due to the uncertainty about the future, the hardship of life and the fear of further attacks, pointed to less tangible but not less real long-term effects.

The Gaza military operations were, according to the Israeli Government, thoroughly and extensively planned. While the Israeli Government has sought to portray its operations as essentially a response to rocket attacks in the exercise of its right to self defense, the Mission considers the plan to have been directed, at least in part, at a different target: the people of Gaza as a whole.

In this respect, the operations were in furtherance of an overall policy aimed at punishing the Gaza population for its resilience and for its apparent support for Hamas, and possibly with the intent of forcing a change in such support. The Mission considers this position to be firmly based in fact, bearing in mind what it saw and heard on the ground, what it read in the accounts of soldiers who served in the campaign, and what it heard and read from current and former military officers and political leaders whom the Mission considers to be representative of the thinking that informed the policy and strategy of the military operations.

The Mission recognizes that the principal focus in the aftermath of military operations will often be on the people who have been killed – more than 1,400 in just three weeks. This is rightly so. Part of the functions of reports such as this is to attempt, albeit in a very small way, to restore the dignity of those whose rights have been violated in the most fundamental way of all – the arbitrary deprivation of life. It is important that the international community asserts formally and unequivocally that such violence to the most basic fundamental rights and freedoms of individuals should not be overlooked and should be condemned.

In this respect, the Mission recognizes that not all deaths constitute violations of international humanitarian law. The principle of proportionality acknowledges that under certain strict conditions, actions resulting in the loss of civilian life may not be unlawful. What makes the application and assessment of proportionality difficult in respect of many of the events investigated by the Mission is that deeds by Israeli forces and words of military and political leaders prior to and during the operations indicate that as a whole they were premised on a deliberate policy of disproportionate force aimed not at the enemy but at the "supporting infrastructure." In practice, this appears to have meant the civilian population.

The timing of the first Israeli attack, at 11:30 am on a week day, when children were returning from school and the streets of Gaza were crowded with people going about their daily business, appears to have been calculated to create the greatest disruption and widespread panic among the civilian population. The treatment of many civilians detained or even killed while trying to surrender is one manifestation of the way in which the effective rules of engagement, standard operating procedures and instructions to the troops on the ground appear to have been framed in order to create an environment in which due regard for civilian lives and basic human dignity was replaced with the disregard for basic international humanitarian law and human rights norms.

The repeated failure to distinguish between combatants and civilians appears to the Mission to have been the result of deliberate guidance issued to soldiers, as described by some of them, and not the result of occasional lapses.

The Mission recognizes that some of those killed were combatants directly engaged in hostilities against Israel, but many were not. The outcome and the modalities of the operations indicate, in the Mission's view, that they were only partially aimed at killing leaders and members of Hamas, Qassam Brigades and other armed groups. They were also to a large degree aimed at destroying or incapacitating civilian property and the means of subsistence of the civilian population.

It is clear from evidence gathered by the Mission that the destruction of food supply installations, water sanitation systems, concrete factories and residential houses was the result of a deliberate and systematic policy by the Israeli armed forces. It was not carried out because those objects presented a military threat or opportunity but to make the daily process of living, and dignified living, more difficult for the civilian population.

Allied to the systematic destruction of the economic capacity of the Gaza Strip, there appears also to have been an assault on the dignity of the people. This was seen not only in the use of human shields and unlawful detentions sometimes in unacceptable conditions, but also in the vandalizing of houses when occupied and the way in which people were treated when their houses were entered. The graffiti on the walls, the obscenities and often racist slogans all constituted an overall image of humiliation and dehumanization of the Palestinian population.

The operations were carefully planned in all their phases. Legal opinions and advice were given throughout the planning stages and at certain operational levels during the campaign. There were almost no mistakes made according to the Government of Israel. It is in these circumstances that the Mission concludes that what occurred in just over three weeks at the end of 2008 and the beginning of 2009 was a deliberately disproportionate attack designed to punish, humiliate and terrorize a civilian population, radically diminish its local economic capacity both to work and to provide for itself, and to force upon it an ever increasing sense of dependency and vulnerability.

The Mission has noted with concern public statements by Israeli officials, including senior military officials, to the effect that the use of disproportionate force, attacks on civilian population and destruction of civilian property are legitimate means to achieve Israel's military and political objectives. The Mission believes that such statements not only undermine the entire regime of international law, they are inconsistent with the spirit of the United Nations Charter and, therefore, deserve to be categorically denounced.

Whatever violations of international humanitarian and human rights law may have been committed, the systematic and deliberate nature of the activities described in this report leave the Mission in no doubt that responsibility lies in the first place with those who designed, planned, ordered and oversaw the operations.

Palestinian armed groups have launched thousands of rockets and mortars into Israel since April 2001. These have succeeded in causing terror within Israel's civilian population, as evidenced by the high rates of psychological trauma within the affected communities. The attacks have also led to erosion of the social, cultural and economic lives of the communities in southern Israel, and have affected the rights to education of the tens of thousands of children and young adults who attend classes in the affected areas.

Within the mandated period of the Mission, these attacks have left 4 people dead and hundreds injured. That there have not been more casualties is due to a combination of luck and measures taken by the Israeli government, including the fortification of public buildings, construction of shelters and, in times of escalated hostilities, the closure of schools.

The Mission notes, with concern, that Israel has not provided the same level of protection from rockets and mortars to affected Palestinian citizens as it has to Jewish citizens. In particular, it has failed to provide public shelters or fortification of schools, for example, to the Palestinian community living in the unrecognised villages and some of the recognized communities. It ought to go without saying that the thousands of Palestinian Israelis – including a significant number of children – who live within the range of rocket fire, deserve the same protection as the Israeli Government provides to its Jewish citizens.

Both the Palestinians and the Israelis are legitimately angered at the lives that they are forced to lead: For the Palestinians, the anger about individual events – the civilian casualties, injuries and destruction in Gaza following from military attacks, the blockade, the continued construction of the Wall outside of the 1967 borders – feed into an underlying anger about the continuing Israeli occupation, its daily humiliations and their as-yet-unfulfilled right to self determination. For the Israelis, the public statements of Palestinian armed groups celebrating rocket and mortar attacks on civilians strengthen a deep-rooted concern that negotiation will yield little and that their nation remains under existential threat from which only it can protect its people. In this way, both the Israelis and the Palestinians share a secret fear – for some, a belief – that each has no intention of accepting the other's right to a country of their own. This anger and fear are unfortunately ably represented by many politicians.

The Mission is firmly convinced that justice and respect for the rule of law are the indispensable basis for peace. The prolonged situation of impunity has created a justice crisis in the OPT that warrants action.

After reviewing Israel's system of investigation and prosecution of serious violations of human rights and humanitarian law, in particular of suspected war crimes and crimes against humanity, the Mission found major structural flaws that in its view make the system inconsistent with international standards. With military "operational debriefings" at the core of the system, there is the absence of any effective and impartial investigation mechanism and victims of such alleged violations are deprived of any effective or prompt remedy. Furthermore, such investigations being internal to the Israeli military authority, do not comply with international standards of independence and impartiality. The Mission believes that the few investigations conducted by the Israeli authorities on alleged serious violations of international human rights and humanitarian law and, in particular, alleged war crimes, in the context of the military operations in Gaza between 27 December 2008 and 18 January 2009, are affected by the defects in the system, have been unduly delayed despite the gravity of the allegations, and, therefore, lack the required credibility and conformity with international standards. The Mission is concerned that investigations of relatively less serious violations that the GOI claims to be investigating have also been unduly protracted.

The Mission noted the pattern of delays, inaction or otherwise unsatisfactory handling by Israeli authorities of investigations, prosecutions and convictions of military personnel and settlers for violence and offences against Palestinians, including in the West Bank, as well as their discriminatory outcome. Additionally, the current constitutional and legal framework in Israel provides very limited possibilities, if any, for Palestinians to seek compensation and reparations.

In light of the information reviewed and its analysis, the Mission concludes that there are serious doubts about the willingness of Israel to carry out genuine investigations in an impartial, independent, prompt and effective way as required by international law. The Mission is also of the view that the system presents inherently discriminatory features that make the pursuit of justice for Palestinian victims extremely difficult.

With regard to allegations of violations of international humanitarian law falling within the jurisdiction of responsible Palestinian authorities in Gaza, the Mission finds that these allegations have not been investigated.

The Mission notes that the responsibility to investigate violations of international human rights and humanitarian law, prosecute if appropriate and try perpetrators belongs in the first place to domestic authorities and institutions. This is a legal obligation incumbent on States and state-like entities. However, where domestic authorities are unable or unwilling to comply with this obligation, international justice mechanisms must be activated to prevent impunity.

The Mission believes that, in the circumstances, there is little potential for accountability for serious violations of international humanitarian and human rights law through domestic institutions in Israel and even less in Gaza. The Mission is of the view that longstanding impunity has been a key factor in the perpetuation of violence in the region and in the reoccurrence of violations, as well as in the erosion of confidence among Palestinians and many Israelis concerning prospects for justice and a peaceful solution to the conflict.

The Mission considers that several of the violations referred to in this report amount to grave breaches of the Fourth Geneva Convention. It notes that there is a duty imposed by the Geneva Conventions on all High Contracting Parties to search for and bring before their courts those responsible for the alleged violations. The Mission considers that the serious violations of International Humanitarian Law recounted in this report fall within the subject-matter jurisdiction of the International Criminal Court (ICC). The Mission notes that the United Nations Security Council has long recognized the impact of the situation in the Middle East, including the Palestinian question, on international peace and security and that it regularly considers and reviews this situation. The Mission is persuaded that, in the light of the longstanding nature of the conflict, the frequent and consistent allegations of violations of international humanitarian law against all parties, the apparent increase in intensity of such violations in the recent military operations, and the regrettable possibility of a return to further violence, meaningful and practical steps to end impunity for such violations would offer an effective way to deter such violations recurring in the future. The Mission is of the view that the prosecution of persons responsible for serious violations of international humanitarian law would contribute to ending such violations, to the protection of civilians and to the restoration and maintenance of peace.

*****

**Note and Comments:**

1. Is there any venue where the victims of the violations catalogued in the Goldstone Report could present their claims (Kamminga 2007)?

The next case involves a suit brought by the family of an American citizen, Rachel Corrie, who was killed while protesting Israel's policy of destroying the homes of suspected Palestinian terrorists. The suit is against the Caterpillar corporation, which built the bulldozer that was used in the demolition that resulted in Corrie's death.

---

## *Corrie v. Caterpillar*, 503 F. 3d 974 (9th Cir. 2007)

Following the Six Day War in 1967, Israel occupied and took control of the West Bank and Gaza Strip. Caterpillar is the world's leading manufacturer of heavy construction and mining equipment. Among its customers is the IDF, which since 1967 has utilized Caterpillar bulldozers to demolish homes in the Palestinian Territories. According to plaintiffs' complaint, Caterpillar sold the bulldozers to the IDF despite its actual and constructive notice that the IDF would use them to further its home destruction policy in the Palestinian Territories; a policy plaintiffs contend violates international law. Seventeen members of plaintiffs' families – sixteen Palestinians and one American – were killed or injured in the course of the demolitions.

The complaint alleges that Caterpillar sold bulldozers to the IDF, but it does not explain how those bulldozers were financed. There is undisputed evidence in the record, however, that the United States government paid for every bulldozer that Caterpillar transferred to the IDF.

The decisive factor here is that Caterpillar's sales to Israel were paid for by the United States. Though mindful that we must analyze each of the plaintiffs' "individual claims," each claim unavoidably rests on the singular premise that Caterpillar should not have sold its bulldozers to the IDF. Yet these sales were financed by the executive branch pursuant to a congressionally enacted program calling for executive discretion as to what lies in the foreign policy and national security interests of the United States.

Allowing this action to proceed would necessarily require the judicial branch of our government to question the political branches' decision to grant extensive military aid to Israel. It is difficult to see how we could impose liability on Caterpillar without at least implicitly deciding the propriety of the United States' decision to pay for the bulldozers which allegedly killed the plaintiffs' family members.

We cannot intrude into our government's decision to grant military assistance to Israel, even indirectly by deciding this challenge to a defense contractor's sales. Plaintiffs' claims can succeed only if a court ultimately decides that Caterpillar should not have sold its bulldozers to the IDF. Because that foreign policy decision is committed under the Constitution to the legislative and executive branches, we hold that plaintiffs' claims are nonjusticiable under the first Baker test.

In this regard, we are mindful of the potential for causing international embarrassment were a federal court to undermine foreign policy decisions in the sensitive context of the Israeli-Palestinian conflict. Plaintiffs argue that the United States government has already criticized Israel's home demolitions in the Palestinian Territories. They point, for example, to former Secretary of State Powell's statement that "[w]e oppose the destruction of [Palestinian] homes-we don't think that is productive." But that language is different in kind from a declaration that the IDF has systematically committed grave violations of international law, none of which the United States has ever accused Israel of, so far as the record reveals. Diplomats choose their words carefully, and we cannot subvert United States foreign policy by latching onto such mildly critical language by the Secretary of State.

It is not the role of the courts to indirectly indict Israel for violating international law with military equipment the United States government provided and continues to provide. Plaintiffs may purport to look no further than Caterpillar itself, but resolving their suit will necessarily require us to look beyond the lone defendant in this case and toward the foreign policy interests and judgments of the United States government itself.

We therefore hold that the district court did not err in dismissing the suit under the political question doctrine. Because we affirm on this ground, we do not reach the other issues raised on appeal.

---

## Note and Comments:

1. Do you agree with the holding? Would the Corrie family have a cause of action against the United States?

## References

### Books and Articles

Menno T. Kamminga, "Towards a Permanent International Claims Commission for Victims of Violations of International Humanitarian Law," *Windsor Yearbook of Access to Justice* 25: 23–30 (2007)

Marko Milanovic, "Human Rights Treaties and Foreign Surveillance: Privacy in the Digital Age," *Harvard International Law Journal* 56: 81–146 (2015)

Michael N. Schmitt and Christopher M. Ford, "Assessing U.S. Justifications for Using Force in Response to Syria's Chemical Attacks: An International Law Perspective," *Journal of National Security Law & Policy* 9: 1–19 (2017)

### U.N. Report

United Nations Human Rights Council, *Human Rights in Palestine and Other Occupied Arab Territories, Report of the United Nations Fact-Finding Mission on the Gaza Conflict* (Goldstone Report) (2009)

### Cases

*Al-Aulauqi v. Obama*, 727 F. Supp. 2d 1 (D.D.C. 2010)
*Beit Sourik Village Council*, HCJ 2056/04 (2004)
*Corrie v. Caterpillar*, 503 F. 3d 974 (9th Cir. 2007)
*Legal Consequences of the Construction of a Wall in OPT*, ICJ Advisory Opinion (2004)

*Legality of the Threat or Use of Nuclear Weapons*, ICJ Advisory Opinion (8 July 1996)

*Nuclear Tests Case (New Zealand v. France)*, ICJ (20 December 1974)

*Rainbow Warrior (New Zealand v. France)*, France-New Zealand Arbitration Tribunal (30 April 1990)

### International Agreements

Chemical Weapons Convention, opened for signature 13 January 1993, entry into force 29 April 1997

Convention on the Prohibition of the Use, Stockpiling, Production and Transfer of Anti-Personnel Mines and on Their Destruction (Landmine Convention), signed 3 December 1997, entry into force 1 March 1999

Protocol Additional to the Geneva Conventions of 12 August 1949, and Relating to the Protection of Victims of Non-International Armed Conflicts of 8 June 1977

Protocol for the Prohibition of the Use in War of Asphyxiating, Poisonous or Other Gases, and of Bacteriological Methods of Warfare (Geneva Protocol), signed 17 June 1925, entry into force 8 February 1928

Treaty on the Non-Proliferation of Nuclear Weapons (NPT), signed 1 July 1968, entry into force 5 March 1970

Treaty on the Prohibition of Nuclear Weapons, signed 20 September 2017

# Part III
## Accountability,
## Responsibility, and Immunity

# 6

# Individual Accountability

Part III explores the consequences of violating international law. The present chapter focuses on individual accountability for violations of the laws of war or international human rights standards, while **International Crimes** (Chapter 7) takes up the issue of transgressions that traverse national borders including drug trafficking and corruption, but also the extradition of criminals from one state to another.

One of the more interesting aspects of **Corporate Accountability** (Chapter 8) is that it appears to be heading in two different directions at the same time. On the one hand, in *Jesner v. Arab Bank* (2018), the U.S. Supreme Court has seemingly closed the door in terms of applying the Alien Tort Statute to corporate malfeasance in foreign lands. Yet, at the same time, there have been other initiatives not only to hold corporations accountable but placing an obligation on the "home" state to do so.

## The Nuremberg Legacy

A strong argument can be made that the genesis of the present day "human rights revolution" was the Nuremberg trials against a select group of Nazi military, political, and economic leaders following World War II. For the first time ever, alleged war criminals, including many top-ranking Nazi leaders, were tried by an international tribunal made up of the occupying powers: United States, Soviet Union, France, and Great Britain. In his opening statement, the chief American prosecutor, Robert Jackson, spoke of the historical importance of the proceedings that were about to be undertaken:

The wrongs which we seek to condemn and punish have been so calculated, so malignant, and so devastating, that civilization cannot tolerate their being ignored, because it cannot survive their being repeated. That four great nations, flush with victory and stung with injury stay the hand of vengeance and voluntarily submit their captive enemies to the judgment of the law is one of the most significant tributes that Power has ever paid to Reason.

Of the 22 defendants put on trial, guilty verdicts were returned against 19 of them. Of these, 12 were sentenced to hang and the others received prison terms of various lengths. Although the London Charter, which established the International Military Tribunal (IMT), had not placed a limit on the number of proceedings, these were the only ones conducted by the IMT itself, although there were "subsequent proceedings" carried out by the occupying powers. In total, 177 defendants were tried resulting in 142 convictions. Although oftentimes overlooked, war crimes trials were carried out against 25 Japanese war leaders. All were convicted by the 11-nation International Military Tribunal of the Far East, and seven sentenced to death.

It would take decades before the Nuremberg/Tokyo precedent would be more fully carried out – first, through the establishment of international criminal tribunals for Yugoslavia (ICTY) and for Rwanda (ICTR), followed by the establishment of the International Criminal Court (ICC). However, what helped keep the sparks of justice alive were two cases that drew worldwide attention. The first was the abduction in Argentina and subsequent prosecution in Israel of former Nazi operative Adolf Eichmann, while the second occurred more than a quarter century later involving the international effort to extradite and prosecute former Chilean dictator Augusto Pinochet.

---

**Box 6.1: International Law at the Movies: The Holocaust**

There are so many "great" films on the Holocaust that it is not clear where to begin, but perhaps the most appropriate place to start is with the 32-minute documentary *Night and Fog* (1956) released fully a decade after the end of World War II, and providing some of the first publicly released video images of the death camps. *Night and Fog* is extraordinarily difficult to watch because of the haunting images of piles of emaciated bodies that bear only a slight resemblance to human beings. Although there are no gruesome images in *Shoah* (1985), which plays for more than nine hours, what makes the viewer squirm is the means by which individuals living around the concentration camps continue to deny that they were aware of the genocide taking place right by where they were living throughout the war. The last documentary I will mention is *A Film Unfinished* (2010). The fascinating story behind this project is that it reexamines the making of a German propaganda film that sought to show that many Jews lived comfortably during World War II. However, what gives lie to this film are the repeated "takes," showing that this was anything but a documentary.

In terms of feature films, it is difficult to argue that there has ever been a greater movie than *Schindler's List* (1993), Steven Spielberg's masterpiece starring Liam Neeson as Oskar Schindler, who begins the film as a self-serving businessman trying to make money by exploiting cheap Jewish labor – and evolves into a complete human being who desperately tries to save the lives of as many as possible. In *The Pianist* (2002), Adrien Brody gives an Academy Award-winning performance as Wladyslaw Szpilman, a professional musician, who is somehow able to survive the war in hiding. Finally, two favorites of mine are *Sophie's Choice* (1982) and *Au Revoir, Les Enfants* (1987). The former stars Meryl Streep as a refugee from Poland who is forced to make two wrenching decisions in her life. The latter is Louis Malle's autobiographical portrayal of the school he attended during the war where a few Jewish students were hidden as Christians – until they were discovered and taken away by the German authorities.

---

## *The Attorney-General of the Government of Israel v. Eichmann,* The District Court of Jerusalem, December 11, 1961

Adolf Eichmann was abducted from Argentina and brought to trial in Israel under the Nazi Collaborators (Punishment) Law, enacted after Israel became a state and after the events charged against Eichmann during the Nazi era in Germany.

Section 1(a) of the Law provides:

"A person who has committed one of the following offences:

(1) during the period of the Nazi regime in a hostile country, carried out an act constituting a crime against the Jewish People;
(2) during the period of the Nazi regime, carried out an act constituting a crime against humanity, in a hostile country;
(3) during the period of the Second World War, carried out an act constituting a war crime, in a hostile country; is liable to the death penalty."

Counsel for Eichmann objected to the jurisdiction of the Court, *inter alia*, on grounds based on international law.

Learned Counsel does not ignore the fact that the Israeli Law applicable to the acts attributed to the Accused vests in us the jurisdiction to try this case. His contention against the jurisdiction of the Court is not based on this Law, but on international law. He contends:

(a) that the Israeli Law, by inflicting punishment for acts committed outside the boundaries of the state and before its establishment, against persons who were not Israeli citizens, and by a person who acted in the course of duty on behalf of a foreign country ("Act of State") conflicts with international law and exceeds the powers of the Israeli legislator;
(b) that the prosecution of the Accused in Israel upon his abduction from a foreign country conflicts with international law and exceeds the jurisdiction of the Court.

**Photo 6.1** Adolf Eichmann Pictured During His Trial in Israel

*Source:* © Associated Press

Before entering upon an analysis of these two contentions and the legal questions involved, we will clarify the relation between them.

The first contention of Counsel that Israel Law is in conflict with international law, and that therefore it cannot vest jurisdiction in this Court, raises the preliminary question as to the validity of international law in Israel and as to whether, in the event of a conflict between it and the laws of the land, it is to be preferred to the laws of the land.

Our jurisdiction to try this case is based on the Nazis and Nazi Collaborators (Punishment) Law, a statutory law the provisions of which are unequivocal. The Court has to give effect to the law of the Knesset, and we cannot entertain the contention that this law conflicts with the principles of international law. For this reason alone, Counsel's first contention must be rejected.

But we have also perused the sources of international law, including the numerous authorities mentioned by learned Counsel in his comprehensive written brief upon which he based his oral pleadings, and by the learned Attorney General in his comprehensive oral pleadings, and have failed to find any foundation for the contention that Israeli law is in conflict with the principles of international law. On the contrary, we have reached the conclusion that the Law in question conforms to the best traditions of the law of nations.

The power of the State of Israel to enact the Law in question or Israel's "right to punish" is based, with respect to the offences in question, from the point of view of international law, on a dual foundation: The universal character of the crimes in question and their specific character as being designed to exterminate the Jewish People. In what follows, we shall deal with each of these two aspects separately.

The abhorrent crimes defined in this Law are crimes not under Israeli law alone. These crimes which offended the whole of mankind and shocked the conscience of nations are grave offences against the law of nations itself ("delicta juris gentium"). Therefore, so far from international law negating or limiting the jurisdiction of countries with respect to such crimes, in the absence of an International Court, the international law is in need of the judicial and legislative authorities of every country, to give effect to its penal injunctions and to bring criminals to trial. The jurisdiction to try crimes under international law is universal.

It is therefore the moral duty of every sovereign state (of "kings and any who have rights equal to the rights of kings") to enforce the natural right to punish, possessed by the victims of the crime whoever they may be, against criminals whose acts have violated in extreme form the law of nature or the law of nations. By these pronouncements the father of international law laid the foundations for the future definition of the "crime against humanity" as a "crime under the law of nations" and to universal jurisdiction over such crimes.

We have said that the crimes dealt with in this case are not crimes under Israeli law alone, but are in essence offences against the law of nations. Indeed, the crimes in question are not a free creation of the legislator who enacted the law for the punishment of Nazis and Nazi collaborators, but have been stated and defined in that law according to a precise pattern of international laws and conventions which define crimes under the law of nations.

The "crime against the Jewish People" is defined on the pattern of the genocide crime defined in the "Convention for the prevention and punishment of genocide" which was adopted by the United Nations Assembly on 9 December 1948.

The State of Israel's "right to punish" the Accused derives, in our view, from two cumulative sources: a universal source (pertaining to the whole of mankind) which vests the right to prosecute and punish crimes of this order in every state within the family of nations; and a specific or national source which gives the victim nation the right to try any who assault its existence.

Notwithstanding the difference of opinion as to the closeness of the requisite link, the very term "connection" or "linking point" is useful for the elucidation of the problem before us. The question is: What is the special connection between the State of Israel and the offences attributed to the Accused, and whether this connection is sufficiently close to form a foundation for Israel's right of punishment against the Accused. This is no merely technical question but a wide and universal one; for the principles of international law are wide and universal principles and not articles in an express code.

When the question is presented in its wider form, as stated above, it seems to us that there can be no doubt what the answer will be. The "linking point" between Israel and the Accused (and for that matter between Israel and any person accused of a crime against the Jewish People under this law) is striking in the "crime against the Jewish People," a crime that postulates an intention to exterminate the Jewish People in whole or in part. Indeed, even without such specific definition – and it must be noted that the draft law only defined "crimes against humanity" and "war crimes" – there was a subsisting "linking point," since most of the Nazi crimes of this kind were perpetrated against the Jewish People; but viewed in the light of the definition of "crime against the Jewish People," as defined in the Law, constitutes in effect an attempt to exterminate the Jewish People, or a partial extermination of the Jewish People. If there is an effective link (and not necessarily identity) between the State of Israel and the Jewish People, then a crime intended to exterminate the Jewish People has an obvious connection with the State of Israel.

The retroactive application of the Law to a period precedent to the establishment of the State of Israel is not, in respect to the Accused (and, for that matter, to any accused under this Law), a problem different from that of the usual retrospectivity on which we have already dwelt above. Goodhart states in his "The Legality of the Nuremberg Trial," inter alia:

> Many of the national courts now functioning in the liberated countries have been established recently, but no one has argued that they are not competent to try the cases that arose before their establishment . . . No defendant can complain that he is being tried by a court which did not exist when he committed the act.

What is said here of a court which did not exist at the time of the commission of the crime, is also valid with respect to a state which was not sovereign at the time of the commission of the crime. The whole political landscape of the continent of occupied Europe has changed after the War; boundaries have changed, as has also changed the very identity of states that had existed before. But all this does not concern the Accused.

---

**Notes and Comments:**

1. There are any number of aspects to the Eichmann case that are noteworthy under international law. One involves how he came to stand trial in the first place. After years spent hunting for Eichmann, members of the Mossad, Israel's intelligence service, located him in Buenos Aires, where he was captured. Eichmann was interrogated for nine days before being flown to Israel. Argentina requested an emergency meeting of the U.N. Security Council, which passed Resolution 138 agreeing that Argentina's sovereignty had been violated by Eichmann's capture. Subsequent to this, Israel did acknowledge this violation of Argentina's sovereignty.

2. The trial of Eichmann drew worldwide attention. Not only was Eichmann, the Nazi operative, brought to trial but, in a way, the Holocaust itself was as well. Certainly, the most renowned analysis of the Eichmann case came from Hannah Arendt (1963) who coined the term the "banality of evil" to describe the bureaucratic mindset that led to such horrors.

**Nuremberg Reborn?**

The Eichmann trial was followed a few years later by a series of prosecutions of mid-level German guards who had served in various concentration camps during the war. After this, however, the practice of individual accountability for violations of humanitarian law seemed to be halted, whether due to Cold War politics or simply the disinterest or exhaustion of the international community. However, this was to change in the face of the brutalities of the fighting in the Balkans. Perhaps in reaction to the international community's unwillingness to intervene militarily, in 1993 the U.N. Security Council voted to establish the International Criminal Tribunal for Yugoslavia (ICTY) with a mandate to investigate and prosecute four crimes: grave breaches of the Geneva Conventions; war crimes; genocide; and crimes against humanity. Among those prosecuted was former Serbian leader Slobodan Milosevic, who had been arrested by Serbian authorities in 2001 and handed over to the ICTY, where he defended himself before he died in 2006 before his trial was completed. Another noteworthy prosecution was of Ratko Mladic, the commander of the Bosnian Serb forces, who was extradited to the Hague in 2011 and eventually convicted in November 2017.

The success of the ICTY also resulted in the creation of the International Criminal Tribunal for Rwanda (ICTR) in 1994 to prosecute war crimes, crimes against humanity, and genocide carried out in Rwanda in 1994. Once again, one of the possible explanations for the establishment of the Court relates to the unwillingness of the international community to intervene to halt the genocide. There have been several criticisms of the ICTR. One is that the proceedings were held in Arusha, Tanzania rather than in-country, thereby failing to engage the Rwandan people. Another criticism, one also directed at the ICTY, relates to the deliberateness of the proceedings as well as the costs. More recently, there have been U.N.-backed courts in Sierra Leone and Cambodia.

However, the most significant achievement since the Nuremberg and Tokyo proceedings was the 1998 *Rome Statute*, which established the International Criminal Court. The ICC can undertake prosecution for four international crimes: war crimes, crimes against humanity, genocide, and aggression. The Court has jurisdiction only if the crime was committed on the territory of a state party; if committed by a national of a state party; or finally, if authorized by the U.N. Security Council. The ICC works under the "complementarity" principle under which it will take up a matter only if the appropriate state either refuses to do so or if its prosecution is not undertaken in good faith. What also needs to be pointed out is that the ICC does not have a law enforcement unit of its own. In that way, it is dependent on the cooperation of states parties.

---

**Box 6.2: The "Hague Invasion" Act**

As is well known, the United States was one of a handful of states not to become a state party to the *Rome Statute*. More than this, in 2002 Congress passed the American Service-Members' Protection Act – which is perhaps better known as the "Hague Invasion Act" – which authorizes the President to use "all means necessary and appropriate to bring about the release of any U.S. or allied personnel being detained or imprisoned by, on behalf of, or at the request of the International Criminal Court." To date, no U.S. invasion of the Netherlands has occurred.

---

One of the great victories in the realm of human rights – or so it was thought – was the international effort to prosecute former Chilean dictator Augusto Pinochet in Spain, resulting in what came to be known as the Pinochet Principle. However, subsequent to this the International Court of Justice ruled that heads of state (as well as current ministers) could not be tried before the domestic courts of another state. On the other hand, recent litigation involving Hissene Habre, the former Chad dictator, seems to offer some hope for establishing accountability and justice.

## Regina v. Bartle and Commissioner of Police, Ex Parte Pinochet [1999] UKHL

### Lord Browne-Wilkinson

On 11 September 1973 a right-wing coup evicted the left-wing regime of President Allende. The coup was led by a military junta, of whom Senator (then General) Pinochet was the leader. At some stage he became head of state. The Pinochet regime remained in power until 11 March 1990 when Senator Pinochet resigned.

There is no real dispute that during the period of the Senator Pinochet regime appalling acts of barbarism were committed in Chile and elsewhere in the world: torture, murder and the unexplained disappearance of individuals, all on a large scale. Although it is not alleged that Senator Pinochet himself committed any of those acts, it is alleged that they were done in pursuance of a conspiracy to which he was a party, at his instigation and with his knowledge. He denies these allegations. None of the conduct alleged was committed by or against citizens of the United Kingdom or in the United Kingdom.

In 1998 Senator Pinochet came to the United Kingdom for medical treatment. The judicial authorities in Spain sought to extradite him in order to stand trial in Spain on a large number of charges. Some of those charges had links with Spain. But most of the charges had no connection with Spain. The background to the case is that to those of left-wing political convictions Senator Pinochet is seen as an arch-devil: to those of right-wing persuasions he is seen as the saviour of Chile. It may well be thought that the trial of Senator Pinochet in Spain for offences all of which related to the state of Chile and most of which occurred in Chile is not calculated to achieve the best justice. But I cannot emphasise too strongly that that is no concern of your Lordships.

### State Immunity

This is the point around which most of the argument turned. It is of considerable general importance internationally since, if Senator Pinochet is not entitled to immunity in relation to the acts of torture alleged to have occurred after 29 September 1988, it will be the first time so far as counsel have discovered when a local domestic court has refused to afford immunity to a head of state or former head of state on the grounds that there can be no immunity against prosecution for certain international crimes.

Given the importance of the point, it is surprising how narrow is the area of dispute. There is general agreement between the parties as to the rules of statutory immunity and the rationale which underlies them. The issue is whether international law grants state immunity in relation to the international crime of torture and, if so, whether the Republic of Chile is entitled to claim such immunity even though Chile, Spain and the United Kingdom are all parties to the Torture Convention and therefore "contractually" bound to give effect to its provisions from 8 December 1988 at the latest.

It is a basic principle of international law that one sovereign state (the forum state) does not adjudicate on the conduct of a foreign state. The foreign state is entitled to procedural immunity from the processes of the forum state. This immunity extends to both criminal and civil liability. State immunity probably grew from the historical immunity of the person of the monarch. In any event, such personal immunity of the head of state persists to the present day: the head of state is entitled to the same immunity as the state itself. The diplomatic representative of the foreign state in the forum state is also afforded the same immunity in recognition of the dignity of the state which he represents. This immunity enjoyed by a head of state in power and an ambassador in post is a complete immunity attaching to the person of the head of state or ambassador and rendering him immune from all actions or prosecutions whether or not they relate to matters done for the benefit of the state. Such immunity is said to be granted ratione personae.

What then when the ambassador leaves his post or the head of state is deposed? The position of the ambassador is covered by the Vienna Convention on Diplomatic Relations, 1961. After providing for immunity from arrest (Article 29) and from criminal and civil jurisdiction (Article 31), Article 39(1) provides that the ambassador's privileges shall be enjoyed from the moment he takes up post; and subsection (2) provides:

> (2) When the functions of a person enjoying privileges and immunities have come to an end, such privileges and immunities shall normally cease at the moment when he leaves the country, or on expiry of a reasonable period in which to do so, but shall subsist until that time, even in case of armed conflict. However, with respect to acts performed by such a person in the exercise of his functions as a member of the mission, immunity shall continue to subsist.

The continuing partial immunity of the ambassador after leaving post is of a different kind from that enjoyed ratione personae while he was in post. Since he is no longer the representative of the foreign state he merits no particular privileges or immunities as a person. However in order to preserve the integrity of the activities of the foreign state during the period when he was ambassador, it is necessary to provide that immunity is afforded to his *official* acts during his tenure in post. If this were not done the sovereign immunity of the state could be evaded by calling in question acts done during the previous ambassador's time. Accordingly under Article 39(2) the ambassador, like any other official of the state, enjoys immunity in relation to his official acts done while he was an official. This limited immunity, ratione materiae, is to be contrasted with the former immunity ratione personae which gave complete immunity to all activities whether public or private.

In my judgment at common law a former head of state enjoys similar immunities, ratione materiae, once he ceases to be head of state. He too loses immunity ratione personae on ceasing to be head of state. As ex head of state he cannot be sued in respect of acts performed whilst head of state in his public capacity. Thus, at common law, the position of the former ambassador and the former head of state appears to be much the same: both enjoy immunity for acts done in performance of their respective functions whilst in office.

The question then which has to be answered is whether the alleged organisation of state torture by Senator Pinochet (if proved) would constitute an act committed by Senator Pinochet as part of his official functions as head of state. It is not enough to say that it cannot be part of the functions of the head of state to commit a crime. Actions which are criminal under the local law can still have been done officially and therefore give rise to immunity ratione materiae. The case needs to be analysed more closely.

Can it be said that the commission of a crime which is an international crime against humanity and jus cogens is an act done in an official capacity on behalf of the state? I believe there to be strong ground for saying that the implementation of torture as defined by the Torture Convention cannot be a state function.

I have doubts whether, before the coming into force of the Torture Convention, the existence of the international crime of torture as jus cogens was enough to justify the conclusion that the organisation of state torture could not rank for immunity purposes as performance of an official function. At that stage there was no international tribunal to punish torture and no general jurisdiction to permit or require its punishment in domestic courts. Not until there was some form of universal jurisdiction for the punishment of the crime of torture could it really be talked about as a fully constituted international crime. But in my judgment the Torture Convention did provide what was missing: a worldwide universal jurisdiction. Further, it required all member states to ban and outlaw torture: Article 2. How can it be for international law purposes an official function to do something which international law itself prohibits and criminalises? Thirdly, an essential feature of the international crime of torture is that it must be committed "by or with the acquiesence of a public official or other person acting in an official capacity." As a result all defendants in torture cases will be state officials. Yet, if the former head of state has immunity, the man most responsible will escape liability while his inferiors (the chiefs of police, junior army officers) who carried out his orders will be liable. I find it impossible to accept that this was the intention.

For these reasons in my judgment if, as alleged, Senator Pinochet organised and authorised torture after 8 December 1988, he was not acting in any capacity which gives rise to immunity ratione materiae because such actions were contrary to international law, Chile had agreed to outlaw such conduct and Chile had agreed with the other parties to the Torture Convention that all signatory states should have jurisdiction to try official torture (as defined in the Convention) even if such torture were committed in Chile.

---

### Note and Comments:

1. The "Pinochet Principle" established an important precedent in international law. In terms of General Pinochet himself, rather than allowing for his extradition to Spain to be carried out, Jack Straw, the British Home Secretary, allowed him to return to Chile on "humanitarian grounds." Although never tried and convicted back in his home country, Pinochet spent the last years of his life fending off various legal challenges, although other members of his dictatorship were eventually brought to justice.

---

**Box 6.3: International Law at the Movies: International Justice**

*Judgment at Nuremberg* (1961) is a fictionalized account of an actual trial brought against a group of German judges who enforced the Nazis' Aryan race laws. Spencer Tracy plays Dan Haywood, an "ordinary" American judge pressed into the service of delivering international justice in the aftermath of the war. However, the film is stolen by the riveting performance by Maximilian Schell, a defense attorney who repeatedly puts the prosecution on its heels by referencing similar racial laws in the United States. Although no justice follows, still, Errol Morris' *Fog of War* (2003) is an indelible documentary where Robert McNamara, the former U.S. Defense Secretary, mulls over his role in the firebombing of Japan during World War II and later the indiscriminate bombing of Vietnam.

The backdrop for the documentary *War Don Don* (War Is Over) (2010) is the bloody civil conflict in Sierra Leone and the Special Court created by the United Nations. What is surprising is the conflicting views that are expressed, as many of the survivors are of the belief that all this money could have been better spent addressing the abject poverty of this country. For something much different, *My Neighbor, My Killer* (2009) provides special insight into the gacaca proceedings in Rwanda as victims of the country's genocide confront some of the perpetrators, oftentimes people who they had lived alongside of for years.

The International Criminal Court is the subject of Pamela Yates' film *The Reckoning: The Battle for the International Criminal Court* (2008) which provides more insight into the establishment of the ICC than on how it operates. The most famous prosecution to date was of the former Serbian strongman Slobodan Milosevic, on display in the documentary *Milosevic on Trial* (2007). *Carla's List* (2006) is a rather breathless account of the busy world of former ICC Chief Prosecutor Carla Del Ponte.

The Extraordinary Chambers in the Courts of Cambodia, otherwise known as the Cambodia Tribunal Court, is a U.N.-backed international tribunal that was created to bring former Khmer Rouge leaders to justice. *Enemies of the People* (2009) is an extraordinary documentary that tells the story of the efforts of Cambodian journalist Thet Sambath to make some sense of the country's genocide. Through these efforts he is able to locate and even befriend Nuon Chea, Brother Number Two behind Pol Pot among the Khmer Rouge leadership. The film closes with Nuon Chea being led away to face prosecution.

*Brother Number One* (2011) is not referring to Pol Pot but Kerry Hamill, an Australian citizen and the brother of Olympic rower Rob Hamill. Kerry Hamill's yacht mistakenly entered into Cambodian territorial waters, where he was arrested and later tortured and killed at the infamous S-21 concentration camp. Rob Hamill serves as the conscience of this film about the prosecution of Comrade Duch, the head of S-21.

For something completely different, *Breaker Morant* (1980) is a deeply moving feature film that tells the story of the 1902 court-martial of three Australian soldiers serving in the British army during the Boer War in South Africa.

---

## Box 6.4: International Law at the Movies: The Pinochet Dictatorship

The military coup that overthrew the democratically elected government of Salvador Allende has been the focus of much of Patricio Guzman's work. *The Battle for Chile* is a three-part series that provides an important backdrop of the country's political struggles between the left and the right. *The Pinochet Case* (2001) focuses on the attempt to extradite General Augusto Pinochet to Spain to face trial for human rights violations carried out under his dictatorship. One of the classic scenes is when Pinochet, who

*(Continued)*

**Box 6.4: Continued**

was allowed to return back home based on humanitarian grounds, is being wheeled on the tarmac in Santiago – when he suddenly, and quite magically, bolts from his chair, no longer the enfeebled old man he apparently had convinced British officials he was. In their own quiet way, *Chile, Obstinate Memory* (1997) and *Nostalgia for the Light* (2010) both deal with the aftermath of the country's experience with the Pinochet dictatorship and the unanswered questions that continue to this day.

In the wake of the Pinochet proceedings, a number of states, including Belgium, enacted "universal jurisdiction" statutes. However, the euphoria from the Pinochet case was tempered considerably with the International Court of Justice ruling in the *Arrest Warrant* case.

## Democratic Republic of Congo v. Belgium (Case Concerning the Arrest Warrant of 11 April 2000), ICJ (2002)

On 11 April 2000 an investigating judge of the Brussels tribunal de première instance issued "an international arrest warrant in absentia" against Mr. Abdulaye Yerodia Ndombasi, charging him, as perpetrator or co-perpetrator, with offences constituting grave breaches of the Geneva Conventions of 1949 and of the Additional Protocols thereto, and with crimes against humanity. At the time when the arrest warrant was issued Mr. Yerodia was the Minister for Foreign Affairs of the Congo.

In the arrest warrant, Mr. Yerodia is accused of having made various speeches inciting racial hatred during the month of August 1998. The crimes with which Mr. Yerodia was charged were punishable in Belgium under the Law of 16 June 1993 "concerning the Punishment of Grave Breaches of the International Geneva Conventions of 12 August 1949 and of Protocols I and II of 8 June 1977 Additional Thereto", as amended by the Law of 19 February 1999 "concerning the Punishment of Serious Violations of International Humanitarian Law" (hereinafter referred to as the "Belgian Law").

Article 7 of the Belgian Law provides that "The Belgian courts shall have jurisdiction in respect of the offences provided for in the present Law, wheresoever they may have been committed". In the present case, according to Belgium, the complaints that initiated the proceedings as a result of which the arrest warrant was issued emanated from 12 individuals all resident in Belgium, five of whom were of Belgian nationality. It is not contested by Belgium, however, that the alleged acts to which the arrest warrant relates were committed outside Belgian territory, that Mr. Yerodia was not a Belgian national at the time of those acts, and that Mr. Yerodia was not in Belgian territory at the time that the arrest warrant was issued and circulated. That no Belgian nationals were victims of the violence that was said to have resulted from Mr. Yerodia's alleged offences was also uncontested.

The Congo maintains that, during his or her term of office, a Minister for Foreign Affairs of a sovereign State is entitled to inviolability and to immunity from criminal process being "absolute or complete", that is to say, they are subject to no exception. Accordingly, the Congo contends that no criminal prosecution may be brought against a Minister for Foreign Affairs in a foreign court as long as he or she remains in office, and that any finding of criminal responsibility by a domestic court in a foreign country, or any act of investigation undertaken with a view to bringing him or her to court, would contravene the principle of immunity from jurisdiction. According to the Congo, the basis of such criminal immunity is purely functional, and immunity is accorded under customary international law simply in order to enable the foreign State representative enjoying such immunity to perform his or her functions freely and without hindrance. The Congo adds that the immunity thus accorded to Ministers for Foreign Affairs when in office covers all their acts, including any committed before they took office, and that it is irrelevant whether the acts done whilst in office may be characterized or not as "official acts".

The Congo states further that it does not deny the existence of a principle of international criminal law, deriving from the decisions of the Nuremberg and Tokyo international military tribunals, that the accused's official capacity at the time of the acts cannot, before any court, whether domestic or international, constitute a ground of exemption from his criminal responsibility or a ground for mitigation of sentence. The Congo then stresses that the fact that an immunity might bar prosecution before a specific court or over a specific period does not mean that the same prosecution cannot be brought, if appropriate, before another court which is not bound by that immunity, or at another time when the immunity need no longer be taken into account. It concludes that immunity does not mean impunity.

Belgium maintains for its part that, while Ministers for Foreign Affairs in office generally enjoy an immunity from jurisdiction before the courts of a foreign State, such immunity applies only to acts carried out in the course of their official functions, and cannot protect such persons in respect of private acts or when they are acting otherwise than in the performance of their official functions.

Belgium further states that, in the circumstances of the present case, Mr. Yerodia enjoyed no immunity at the time when he is alleged to have committed the acts of which he is accused, and that there is no evidence that he was then acting in any official capacity. It observes that the arrest warrant was issued against Mr. Yerodia personally.

The Court would observe at the outset that in international law it is firmly established that, as also diplomatic and consular agents, certain holders of high-ranking office in a State, such as the Head of State, Head of Government and Minister for Foreign Affairs, enjoy immunities from jurisdiction in other States, both civil and criminal. For the purposes of the present case, it is only the immunity from criminal jurisdiction and the inviolability of an incumbent Minister for Foreign Affairs that fall for the Court to consider.

All of the conventions mentioned by the Parties provide useful guidance on certain aspects of the question of immunities. They do not, however, contain any provision specifically defining the immunities enjoyed by Ministers for Foreign Affairs. It is consequently on the basis of customary international law that the Court must decide the questions relating to the immunities of such Ministers raised in the present case.

In customary international law, the immunities accorded to Ministers for Foreign Affairs are not granted for their personal benefit, but to ensure the effective performance of their functions on behalf of their respective States. In order to determine the extent of these immunities, the Court must therefore first consider the nature of the functions exercised by a Minister for Foreign Affairs. He or she is in charge of his or her Government's diplomatic activities and generally acts as its representative in international negotiations and intergovernmental meetings. Ambassadors and other diplomatic agents carry out their duties under his or her authority. His or her acts may bind the State represented, and there is a presumption that a Minister for Foreign Affairs, simply by virtue of that office, has full powers to act on behalf of the State (see, e.g., Art. 7, para. 2 (a), of the 1969 Vienna Convention on the Law of Treaties). In the performance of these functions, he or she is frequently required to travel internationally, and thus must be in a position freely to do so whenever the need should arise. He or she must also be in constant communication with the Government, and with its diplomatic missions around the world, and be capable at any time of communicating with representatives of other States. The Court further observes that a Minister for Foreign Affairs, responsible for the conduct of his or her State's relations with all other States, occupies a position such that, like the Head of State or the Head of Government, he or she is recognized under international law as representative of the State solely by virtue of his or her office. He or she does not have to present letters of credence: to the contrary, it is generally the Minister who determines the authority to be conferred upon diplomatic agents and countersigns their letters of credence. Finally, it is to the Minister for Foreign Affairs that chargés d'affaires are accredited.

The Court accordingly concludes that the functions of a Minister for Foreign Affairs are such that, throughout the duration of his or her office, he or she when abroad enjoys full immunity from criminal jurisdiction and inviolability. That immunity and that inviolability protects the individual concerned against any act of authority of another State which would hinder him or her in the performance of his or her duties.

In this respect, no distinction can be drawn between acts performed by a Minister for Foreign Affairs in an "official" capacity, and those claimed to have been performed in a "private capacity", or, for that matter, between acts performed before the person concerned assumed office as Minister for Foreign Affairs and acts committed during the period of office. Thus, if a Minister for Foreign Affairs is arrested in another State on a criminal charge, he or she is clearly thereby prevented from exercising the functions of his or her office. The consequences of such impediment to the exercise of those official functions are equally serious, regardless of whether the Minister for Foreign Affairs was, at the time of arrest, present in the territory of the arresting State on an "official" visit or a "private" visit, regardless of whether the arrest relates to acts allegedly performed before the person became the Minister for Foreign Affairs or to acts performed while in office, and regardless of whether the arrest relates to alleged acts performed in an "official" capacity or a "private" capacity. Furthermore, even the mere risk that, by travelling to or transiting another State a Minister for Foreign Affairs might be exposing himself or herself to legal proceedings could deter the Minister from travelling internationally when required to do so for the purposes of the performance of his or her official functions.

The Court has carefully examined State practice, including national legislation and those few decisions of national higher courts, such as the House of Lords or the French Court of Cassation. It has been unable to deduce from this practice that there exists under customary international law any form of exception to the rule according immunity from criminal jurisdiction and inviolability to incumbent Ministers for Foreign Affairs, where they are suspected of having committed war crimes or crimes against humanity.

The Court has also examined the rules concerning the immunity or criminal responsibility of persons having an official capacity contained in the legal instruments creating international criminal tribunals, and which are specifically applicable to the latter (see Charter of the International Military Tribunal of Nuremberg, Art. 7; Charter of the International Military Tribunal of Tokyo, Art. 6; Statute of the International Criminal Tribunal for the former Yugoslavia, Art. 7, para. 2; Statute of the International Criminal Tribunal for Rwanda, Art. 6, para. 2; Statute of the International Criminal Court, Art. 27). It finds that these rules likewise do not enable it to conclude that any such an exception exists in customary international law in regard to national courts.

Finally, none of the decisions of the Nuremberg and Tokyo international military tribunals, or of the International Criminal Tribunal for the former Yugoslavia, cited by Belgium deal with the question of the immunities of incumbent Ministers for Foreign Affairs before national courts where they are accused of having committed war crimes or crimes against humanity. The Court accordingly notes that those decisions are in no way at variance with the findings it has reached above.

## Notes and Comments:

1. There are a few things to note about the *Arrest Warrant* ruling. The first is that the prohibition only applies to domestic courts in other countries and not international tribunals. Theoretically, war criminals can still be tried by the International Criminal Court or by an internationally created regional court, such as the ICTY or the ICTR. However, what remains unclear is how far the privilege extends. For example, under the *Torture Convention*, each state party obligates itself to either "prosecute or extradite" any alleged torturer who is within its territorial borders – even if the torture did not take place there; even if this person is not a citizen of that state; and even if victims are not nationals as well. But does this mean that a state has a legal obligation to try (or extradite) those who engaged in torture – yet they are prohibited from bringing criminal proceedings against the very government officials who were architects of this policy?

2. Showing sensitivity toward the charge of impunity, the ICJ pointed out that the prosecution of the defendant was still possible, if either: 1) the Democratic Republic of the Congo carried out the prosecution; 2) the DRC waived immunity; 3) the accused leaves office; or 4) proceedings against this individual are brought before an international criminal tribunal. What do you make of this argument?

3. In May 2012, Charles Taylor, the former president of Liberia, was convicted by the U.N.-backed special tribunal in Sierra Leone of war crimes and crimes against humanity for the atrocities committed in his country's civil war. In the words of the court, Taylor was responsible for: "aiding and abetting, as well as planning, some of the most heinous and brutal crimes recorded in human history."

In the case that follows, Belgium has brought a claim against Senegal on the basis that the latter has failed to prosecute Hissène Habré, the former dictator of Chad who had been living in Senegal for a considerable period of time after he fled from his home land.

# Belgium v. Senegal, ICJ (2012)

*[After taking power in a military coup on 7 June 1982, Mr. Hissène Habré assumed the position of president of the Republic of Chad and remained there for eight years during which time large-scale violations of human rights were committed, including arrests of actual or presumed political opponents, detentions without trial, mistreatment, torture, extrajudicial executions, and enforced disappearances. Mr. Habré was overthrown on December 1, 1990. After a brief stay in Cameroon, he requested political asylum from the Senegalese Government, a request which was granted. He then settled in Dakar and it is the non-response to his presence that is the legal issue in the following ruling by the International Court of Justice.]*

On 19 February 2009, the Kingdom of Belgium (hereinafter "Belgium") led in the Registry of the Court an Application instituting proceedings against the Republic of Senegal (hereinafter "Senegal") in respect of a dispute concerning "Senegal's compliance with its obligation to prosecute Mr. Hissène Habré, former President of the Republic of Chad, or to extradite him to Belgium for the purposes of criminal proceedings". Belgium based its claims on the United Nations Convention against Torture and Other Cruel, Inhuman or Degrading Treatment or Punishment of 10 December 1984 (hereinafter "the Convention against Torture" or the "Convention"), as well as on customary international law.

### ADMISSIBILITY OF BELGIUM'S CLAIMS

Senegal objects to the admissibility of Belgium's claims. In particular, Senegal contends that none of the alleged victims of the acts said to be attributable to Mr. Habré was of Belgian nationality at the time when the acts were committed.

The Court will first consider whether being a party to the Convention is sufficient for a State to be entitled to bring a claim to the Court concerning the cessation of alleged violations by another State party of its obligations under that instrument.

As stated in its Preamble, the object and purpose of the Convention is "to make more effective the struggle against torture . . . throughout the world". The States parties to the Convention have a common interest to ensure, in view of their shared values, that acts of torture are prevented and that, if they occur, their authors do not enjoy impunity. The obligations of a State party to conduct a preliminary inquiry into the facts and to submit the case to its competent authorities for prosecution are triggered by the presence of the alleged offender in its territory, regardless of the nationality of the offender or the victims, or of the place where the alleged offences occurred. All the other States parties have a common interest in compliance with these obligations by the State in whose territory the alleged offender is present. That common interest implies that the obligations in question are owed by any State party to all the other States parties to the Convention. All the States parties "have a legal interest" in the protection of the rights involved. These obligations may be defined as "obligations *erga omnes partes*" in the sense that each State party has an interest in compliance with them in any given case. In this respect, the relevant provisions of the Convention against Torture are similar to those of the Convention on the Prevention and Punishment of the Crime of Genocide, with regard to which the Court observed that

> In such a convention the contracting States do not have any interests of their own; they merely have, one and all, a common interest, namely, the accomplishment of those high purposes which are the *raison d'être* of the Convention.
> *(Reservations to the Convention on the Prevention and Punishment of the Crime of Genocide, Advisory Opinion, I.C.J. Reports 1951*, p. 23.)

THE ALLEGED VIOLATIONS OF THE CONVENTION AGAINST TORTURE

Article 7, paragraph 1, of the Convention provides:

> The State Party in the territory under whose jurisdiction a person alleged to have committed any offence referred to in Article 4 is found shall in the cases contemplated in Article 5, if it does not extradite him, submit the case to its competent authorities for the purpose of prosecution.

Belgium, while recognizing that the time frame for implementation of the obligation to prosecute depends on the circumstances of each case, and in particular on the evidence gathered, considers that the State in whose territory the suspect is present cannot indefinitely delay performing the obligation incumbent upon it to submit the matter to its competent authorities for the purpose of prosecution. Procrastination on the latter's part could, according to Belgium, violate both the rights of the victims and those of the accused.

REMEDIES

The Court notes that, in its final submissions, Belgium requests the Court to adjudge and declare, first, that Senegal breached its international obligations by failing to incorporate in due time into its domestic law the provisions necessary to enable the Senegalese judicial authorities to exercise the universal jurisdiction provided for in Article 5, paragraph 2, of the Convention against Torture, and that it has breached and continues to breach its international obligations under Article 6, paragraph 2, and Article 7, paragraph 1, of the Convention by failing to bring criminal proceedings against Mr. Habré for the crimes he is alleged to have committed, or, otherwise, to extradite him to Belgium for the purposes of such criminal proceedings. Secondly, Belgium requests the Court to adjudge and declare that Senegal is required to cease these internationally wrongful acts by submitting without delay the "Hissène Habré case" to its competent authorities for the purpose of prosecution, or, failing that, by extraditing Mr. Habré to Belgium without further ado.

The purpose of these treaty provisions is to prevent alleged perpetrators of acts of torture from going unpunished, by ensuring that they cannot find refuge in any State party. The State in whose territory the suspect is present does indeed have the option of extraditing him to a country which has made such a request, but on the condition that it is to a State which has jurisdiction in some capacity, pursuant to Article 5 of the Convention, to prosecute and try him.

The Court emphasizes that, in failing to comply with its obligations under Article 6, paragraph 2, and Article 7, paragraph 1, of the Convention, Senegal has engaged its international responsibility. Consequently, Senegal is required to cease this continuing wrongful act, in accordance with general international law on the responsibility of States for internationally wrongful acts. Senegal must therefore take without further delay the necessary measures to submit the case to its competent authorities for the purpose of prosecution, if it does not extradite Mr. Habré.

---

## Notes and Comments:

1. Twenty-five years after he fled Senegal and after repeated attempts to bring him to justice, on May 30, 2016 Hissène Habré was finally convicted by the

Extraordinary African Chambers in the Senegalese court system of crimes against humanity, war crimes, and torture, including sexual violence and rape.

2. You might be curious about Belgium's involvement in all these matters. On June 16, 1993, Belgium passed the most far-ranging "universal jurisdiction" statute in the world, allowing an individual (Belgian or not) to file a criminal complaint in a Belgian court against any person for international crimes in violation of the 1949 Geneva Conventions and their additional protocols, even if these acts were carried out outside Belgian territory and against non-Belgians. In 1999, the law was amended to cover genocide and crimes against humanity. In addition, the 1999 amendment provided no immunity based on "official capacity" that would preclude application of the law.

During its first decade, some 30 complaints were filed against a host of government officials including PLO leader Yasser Arafat and Israeli Prime Minister Ariel Sharon, Cuban President Fidel Castro, and Iraqi dictator Saddam Hussein. A number of complaints were also filed against U.S. officials, including one against former President George H.W. Bush for actions that occurred during the Persian Gulf War in 1991 as well as President George W. Bush and U.K. Prime Minister Tony Blair for alleged war crimes carried out in the Iraq War.

After U.S. officials threatened that the Belgian universal jurisdiction statute could negatively affect Belgium's status as the host of the North Atlantic Treaty Organization (NATO), the law was amended significantly. The new law limited the filing of a criminal complaint to situations where either the suspect is a Belgian citizen or someone residing in Belgium, or the victim is either a Belgian or a non-national who has lived in Belgium for at least three years. In addition, the revised law exempts complaints against sitting heads of state and foreign ministers as well as other individuals enjoying immunity based on treaties. Based on this revised statute, in September 2003 the Belgian Supreme Court dismissed all pending charges against American officials (Murphy 2006: 248–49).

---

### Box 6.5: The Prosecution of Thomas Lubanga

The International Criminal Court's first prosecution was of Thomas Lubanga Dyilo, the leader of the Union of Congolese Patriots, who was convicted of conscripting and enlisting children under the age of 15. Lubanga was arrested in 2006 and then sent by the Democratic Republic of the Congo to the Prosecutor's Office of the ICC. Lubanga was convicted in 2012.

**Photo 6.2** Thomas Lubanga During Trial Proceedings Before the ICC

*Source:* © Associated Press

---

**Box 6.6: International Law at the Movies: Prosecuting Hissène Habré**

The international effort to prosecute Hissène Habré has been told in two fine documentaries. One is *The Dictator Hunter* (2007) in which the viewer witnesses the tireless efforts of Reed Brody of Human Rights Watch. More recently, *Hissene Habre: A Chadian Tragedy* (2016) continues this story, which, after so many years and so much effort, finally succeeded.

---

**Box 6.7: Omar al-Bashir in South Africa**

In March 2009, Omar al-Bashir, the president of the Sudan, became the first head of state to be indicted by the International Criminal Court for directing a ruthless campaign of mass killing in the Darfur region of that country. In April 2019, al-Bashir was overthrown in a military coup, although it is not clear whether the new Sudanese government will cooperate with the ICC and turn him over for prosecution.

One of the more interesting developments in his case involved a trip he took to South Africa in June 2015. Although the ICC sent an urgent request to South African government officials to arrest Bashir, this was not done and he was able to return to Sudan. In a subsequent proceeding initiated by the ICC, South Africa defended

*(Continued)*

## Box 6.7: Continued

its position on the grounds that under customary international law, a head of state enjoys immunity from criminal proceedings, including arrest, and this immunity had not been waived by the Sudanese government. The ICC soundly rejected this position:

**Photo 6.3** Omar al-Bashir Pictured With Syrian President Bashar al-Assad

*Source:* © Associated Press

The Chamber concludes that, by not arresting Omar al-Bashir while he was on its territory between 13 and 15 June 2015, South Africa failed to comply with the Court's request for the arrest and surrender of Omar al-Bashir contrary to the provisions of the [Rome] Statute, thereby preventing the Court from exercising its functions and powers under the Statute in connection with the criminal proceedings instituted against Omar al-Bashir.

However, the Court declined to issue a formal finding of noncompliance by South Africa.

## A (New) Duty to Punish?

Under Article 1 of the *Genocide Convention* state parties have a responsibility "to prevent and to punish" acts of genocide. Prior to the case of *Bosnia v. Serbia*, it had been common to treat these two obligations as being one in the same. However, in this case the ICJ addressed these separately and treated them as two separate and distinct responsibilities. Earlier in Chapter 4 we analyzed the far-ranging responsibility "to prevent" genocide and in the next chapter we will come back to *Bosnia v. Serbia* for the Court's treatment of state responsibility for "complicity" or "aiding and assisting" in genocide. What we turn to now is the Court's analysis of the responsibility "to punish" acts of genocide. As you will see, the ICJ not only holds that state parties (or at least certain state parties) to the *Genocide Convention* have a responsibility to punish, but the Court goes so far as to suggest that a similar duty exists in most, if not all other, international human rights treaties.

---

## *Bosnia v. Serbia*, ICJ (2007)

The Court now turns to the question of the Respondent's compliance with its obligation to punish the crime of genocide stemming from Article I and the other relevant provisions of the Convention.

In its fifth final submission, Bosnia and Herzegovina requests the Court to adjudge and declare:

> That Serbia and Montenegro has violated and is violating its obligations under the Convention on the Prevention and Punishment of the Crime of Genocide for having failed and for failing to punish acts of genocide or any other act prohibited by the Convention on the Prevention and Punishment of the Crime of Genocide, and for having failed and for failing to transfer individuals accused of genocide or any other act prohibited by the Convention to the International Criminal Tribunal for the former Yugoslavia and to fully co-operate with this Tribunal.

This submission implicitly refers to Article VI of the Convention, according to which:

> Persons charged with genocide or any of the other acts enumerated in article III shall be tried by a competent tribunal of the State in the territory of which the act was committed, or by such international penal tribunal as may have jurisdiction with respect to those Contracting Parties which shall have accepted its jurisdiction.

The Court would first recall that the genocide in Srebrenica, the commission of which it has established above, was not carried out in the Respondent's territory. It concludes from this that the Respondent cannot be charged with not having tried before its own courts those accused of having participated in the Srebrenica genocide, either as principal perpetrators or as accomplices, or of having committed one of the other acts mentioned in Article III of the Convention in connection with the Srebrenica genocide. Even if Serbian domestic law granted jurisdiction to its criminal courts to try those accused, and even supposing such proceedings were compatible with Serbia's other international obligations, *inter alia* its obligation to co-operate with the ICTY, to which the Court will revert below, an obligation to try the perpetrators of the Srebrenica massacre in Serbia's domestic courts cannot be deduced from Article VI. Article VI only obliges the Contracting Parties to institute and exercise territorial criminal jurisdiction; while it certainly does not prohibit States, with respect to genocide, from conferring jurisdiction on their criminal courts based on criteria other than where the crime was committed which are compatible with international law, in particular the nationality of the accused, it does not oblige them to do so.

It is thus to the obligation for States parties to co-operate with the "international penal tribunal" mentioned in the above provision that the Court must now turn its attention. For it is certain that once such a court has been established, Article VI obliges the Contracting Parties "which shall have accepted its jurisdiction" to co-operate with it, which implies that they will arrest persons accused of genocide who are in their territory – even if the crime of which they are accused was committed outside it – and, failing prosecution of them in the parties' own courts, that they will hand them over for trial by the competent international tribunal.

In order to determine whether the Respondent has fulfilled its obligations in this respect, the Court must first answer two preliminary questions: does the ICTY constitute an "international penal tribunal" within the meaning of Article VI? And must the Respondent be regarded as having "accepted the jurisdiction" of the tribunal within the meaning of that provision?

As regards the first question, the Court considers that the reply must definitely be in the affirmative. The notion of an "international penal tribunal" within the meaning of Article VI must at least cover all international criminal courts created after the adoption of the Convention (at which date no such court existed) of potentially universal scope, and competent to try the perpetrators of genocide or any of the other acts enumerated in Article III. The nature of the legal instrument by which such a court is established is without importance in this respect. When drafting the Genocide Convention, its authors probably thought that such a court would be created by treaty: a clear pointer to this lies in the reference to "those Contracting Parties which shall have accepted [the] jurisdiction" of the international penal tribunal. Yet, it would be contrary to the object of the provision to interpret the notion of "international penal tribunal" restrictively in order to exclude from it a court which, as in the case of the ICTY, was created pursuant to a United Nations Security Council resolution adopted under Chapter VII of the Charter. The Court has found nothing to suggest that such a possibility was considered by the authors of the Convention, but no intention of seeking to exclude it can be imputed to them.

The question whether the Respondent must be regarded as having "accepted the jurisdiction" of the ICTY within the meaning of Article VI must consequently be formulated as follows: is the Respondent obliged to accept the jurisdiction of the ICTY, and to co-operate with the Tribunal by virtue of the Security Council resolution which established it, or of some other rule of international law? If so, it would have to be concluded that, for the Respondent, co-operation with the ICTY constitutes both an obligation stemming from the resolution concerned and from the United Nations Charter, or from another norm of international law obliging the Respondent to co-operate, and an obligation arising from its status as a party to the Genocide Convention, this last clearly being the only one of direct relevance in the present case.

Turning now to the facts of the case, the question the Court must answer is whether the Respondent has fully co-operated with the ICTY, in particular by arresting and handing over to the Tribunal any persons accused of genocide as a result of the Srebrenica genocide and finding themselves on its territory. In this connection, the Court would first observe that, during the oral proceedings, the Respondent asserted that the duty to co-operate had been complied with following the régime change in Belgrade in the year 2000, thus implicitly admitting that such had not been the case during the preceding period. The conduct of the organs of the FRY before the régime change however engages the Respondent's international responsibility just as much as it does that of its State authorities from that date. Further, the Court cannot but attach a certain weight to the plentiful, and mutually corroborative, information suggesting that General Mladić, indicted by the ICTY for genocide, as one of those principally responsible for the Srebrenica massacres, was on the territory of the Respondent at least on several occasions and for substantial periods during the last few years and is still there now, without the Serb authorities doing what they could and can reasonably do to ascertain exactly where he is living and arrest him. In particular, counsel for the Applicant referred during the hearings to recent statements made by the Respondent's Minister for Foreign Affairs, reproduced in the national press in April 2006, and according to which the intelligence services of that State knew where Mladic´ was living in Serbia, but refrained from informing the authorities competent to order his arrest because certain members of those services had allegedly remained loyal to the fugitive. The authenticity and accuracy of those statements has not been disputed by the Respondent at any time.

It therefore appears to the Court sufficiently established that the Respondent failed in its duty to co-operate fully with the ICTY. This failure constitutes a violation by the Respondent of its duties as a party to the Dayton Agreement, and as a Member of the United Nations, and accordingly a violation of its obligations under Article VI of the Genocide Convention. The Court is of course without jurisdiction in the present case to declare that the Respondent has breached any obligations other than those under the Convention. But as the Court has jurisdiction to declare a breach of Article VI insofar as it obliges States to co-operate with the "international penal tribunal", the Court may find for that purpose that the requirements for the existence of such a breach have been met. One of those requirements is that the State whose responsibility is in issue must have "accepted [the] jurisdiction" of that "international penal tribunal"; the Court thus finds that the Respondent was under a duty to co-operate with the tribunal concerned pursuant to international instruments other than the Convention, and failed in that duty. On this point, the Applicant's submissions relating to the violation by the Respondent of Articles I and VI of the Convention must therefore be upheld.

It follows from the foregoing considerations that the Respondent failed to comply both with its obligation to prevent and its obligation to punish genocide deriving from the Convention, and that its international responsibility is thereby engaged.

---

## Note and Comments:

1. What do you make of this "duty to punish"? Do some states have a stronger duty than others, and if so, on what basis?

## References

### Books and Articles

Hannah Arendt, *Eichmann in Jerusalem: A Report on the Banality of Evil*, New York, NY: Viking (1963)

Sean Murphy, *Principles of International Law*, St. Paul, MN: Thomson/West (2006)

### Cases

*The Attorney General of Israel v. Eichmann*, The District Court of Jerusalem (11 December 1961)

*Belgium v. Senegal*, ICJ (2012)

*Bosnia v. Serbia*, ICJ (2007)

*DRC v. Belgium*, ICJ (2002)
*Ex Parte Pinochet* [1999] UKHL

## International Agreements

Convention Against Torture and Other Cruel, Inhuman or Degrading Treatment or Punishment, adopted and opened for signature 10 December 1984, entry into force 26 June 1987

Convention on the Prevention and Punishment of the Crime of Genocide, approved and proposed for signature 9 December 1948, entry into force 12 January 1951

Rome Statute of the International Criminal Court, adopted on 17 July 1998, entry into force 1 July 2002

## Domestic Law

American Service Members Protection Act, Public Law No. 107–206 (U.S.)

# 7

# International Crimes

This chapter focuses on crimes that transcend national borders. We begin with *drug trafficking* and analyze two cases from the United States. There is certainly good reason to look at the practices of the United States because no country enforces its criminal laws outside its own national borders like the United States, especially in the realm of the country's decades-long "war on drugs." The first case is *United States v. Verdugo-Urquidez* and the question is whether a drug search conducted by U.S. Drug Enforcement Agents (DEA) in Mexico was governed by the Constitution. This is followed by *United States v. Perez-Oviedo*, which highlights the extent to which the U.S. government extends the enforcement of its laws.

Quite often, *corruption* has an international element to it and we will examine some of the efforts to shine a light on these illicit and expensive crimes. *Extradition* is a central component of fighting crime and we examine three cases involving the United States. *U.S. v. Alvarez-Machain* involves the kidnapping of a Mexican national in the U.S. "war on drugs," where federal (U.S.) authorities operate outside the bounds of an extradition treaty between the United States and Mexico. The *Noriega* case was a rather bizarre situation where the self-proclaimed leader of Panama, Manuel Noriega, was arrested after an American military invasion of that country. Finally, we look at what is called the "non-inquiry" principle under extradition law.

---

### Box 7.1: Extradition Treaties

Under international law, states are presumed to have jurisdiction over all individuals, citizens and foreign nationals alike, who are within their territorial boundaries. Thus, if some other state wishes to prosecute a criminal defendant in another country, it must do so under an extradition treaty with this other state. Although the United States has extradition treaties with most countries, it has no such treaty with the Russian Republic (think Edward Snowden), North Korea, or China.

There are certain basic provisions to extradition treaties. One is the requirement that the alleged criminal act is a crime in both states (*dual criminality*). Another is the *rule of speciality*, which requires that the individual who is extradited only be tried for the crime he was extradited for. And finally, there is exception for what are deemed to be *political offenses*, although differentiating between a common crime and a crime based on political convictions will not always be easy. Beyond this, some states, such as Brazil and France, refuse to extradite their own citizens. And finally, some countries, such as Canada and New Zealand, refuse to extradite criminal defendants to countries (most notably, the United States) that have the death penalty in the absence of a diplomatic assurance that this particular penalty will not be applied.

---

## Drug Trafficking

---

## *U.S. v. Verdugo-Urquidez,* 494 U.S. 259 (1990)

### CHIEF JUSTICE REHNQUIST DELIVERED THE OPINION OF THE COURT

The question presented by this case is whether the Fourth Amendment applies to the search and seizure by United States agents of property that is owned by a non-resident alien and located in a foreign country. We hold that it does not.

Respondent Rene Martin Verdugo-Urquidez is a citizen and resident of Mexico. He is believed by the United States Drug Enforcement Agency (DEA) to be one of the leaders of a large and violent organization in Mexico that smuggles narcotics into the United States. Based on a complaint charging respondent with various narcotics-related offenses, the Government obtained a warrant for his arrest on August 3, 1985. In January 1986, Mexican police officers, after discussions with United States marshals, apprehended Verdugo-Urquidez in Mexico and transported him to the United States Border Patrol station in Calexico, California. There, United States marshals arrested respondent and eventually moved him to a correctional center in San Diego, California, where he remains incarcerated pending trial.

Following respondent's arrest, Terry Bowen, a DEA agent assigned to the Calexico DEA office, decided to arrange for searches of Verdugo-Urquidez's Mexican residences located in Mexicali and San Felipe. Bowen believed that the searches would reveal evidence related to respondent's alleged narcotics trafficking activities and his involvement in the kidnaping and torture-murder of DEA Special Agent Enrique Camarena Salazar (for which respondent subsequently has been convicted in a separate prosecution). Bowen telephoned Walter White, the Assistant Special Agent in charge of the DEA office in Mexico City, and asked him to seek authorization for the search from the Director General of the Mexican Federal Judicial Police (MFJP). After several attempts to reach high ranking Mexican officials, White eventually contacted the Director General, who authorized the searches and promised the cooperation of Mexican authorities. Thereafter, DEA agents working in concert with officers of the MFJP searched respondent's properties in Mexicali and San Felipe and seized certain documents. In particular, the search of the Mexicali residence uncovered a tally sheet, which the Government believes reflects the quantities of marijuana smuggled by Verdugo-Urquidez into the United States.

The District Court granted respondent's motion to suppress evidence seized during the searches, concluding that the Fourth Amendment applied to the searches and that the DEA agents had failed to justify searching respondent's premises without a warrant.

The Fourth Amendment provides:

> The right of the people to be secure in their persons, houses, papers, and effects, against unreasonable searches and seizures, shall not be violated, and no Warrants shall issue, but upon probable cause, supported by Oath or affirmation, and particularly describing the place to be searched, and the persons or things to be seized.

That text, by contrast with the Fifth and Sixth Amendments, extends its reach only on "the people." Contrary to the suggestion of amici curiae that the Framers used this phrase "simply to avoid an awkward rhetorical redundancy," "the people" seems to have been a term of art employed in select parts of the Constitution. The Preamble declares that the Constitution is ordained and established by "the people of the United States." The second Amendments projects "the right of the people to keep and bear Arms," and the Ninth and Tenth Amendments provide that certain rights and powers are retained by and reserved to "the people". While this textual exegesis is by no means conclusive, it suggests that "the people" protected by the Fourth Amendment, and by the First and Second Amendments, and to whom rights and powers are reserved in the Ninth and Tenth Amendments, refers to a class of persons who are part of a national community or who have otherwise developed sufficient connection with this country to be considered part of that community. The language of these Amendments contrasts with the words "person" and "accused" used in the Fifth and Sixth Amendments regulating procedure in criminal cases.

Indeed, we have rejected the claim that aliens are entitled to Fifth Amendment rights outside the sovereign territory of the United States. In Johnson v. Eisentrager (1950), the Court held that enemy aliens arrested in China and imprisoned in Germany after World War II could not obtain writs of habeas corpus in our federal courts on the ground that their convictions for war crimes had violated the Fifth Amendment and other constitutional provisions. The Eisentrager opinion acknowledged that in some cases constitutional provisions extend beyond the citizenry; "[t]he alien . . . has been accorded a generous and ascending scale of rights as he increases his identity with our society." But our rejection of extraterritorial application of the Fifth Amendment was emphatic:

> Such extraterritorial application of organic law would have been so significant an innovation in the practice of governments that, if intended or apprehended, it could scarcely have failed to excite contemporary comment. Not one word can be cited. No decision of this Court supports such a view. None of the learned

commentators on our Constitution has even hinted at it. The practice of every modern government is opposed to it.

For better or for worse, we live in a world of nation-states in which our Government must be able to "functio[n] effectively in the company of sovereign nations." Perez v. Brownell (1958). Some who violate our laws may live outside our borders under a regime quite different from that which obtains in this country. Situations threatening to important American interests may arise halfway around the globe, situations which in the view of the political branches of our Government require an American response with armed force. If there are to be restrictions on searches and seizures which occur incident to such American action, they must be imposed by the political branches through diplomatic understanding, treaty, or legislation.

The judgment of the Court of Appeals is accordingly

Reversed.

### JUSTICE KENNEDY, CONCURRING

I agree that no violation of the Fourth Amendment has occurred and that we must reverse the judgment of the Court of Appeals. Although some explanation of my views is appropriate given the difficulties of this case, I do not believe they depart in fundamental respects from the opinion of the Court, which I join.

In cases involving the extraterritorial application of the Constitution, we have taken care to state whether the person claiming its protection is a citizen or an alien. The distinction between citizens and aliens follows from the undoubted proposition that the Constitution does not create, nor do general principles of law create, any juridical relation between our country and some undefined, limitless class of noncitizens who are beyond our territory. We should note, however, that the absence of this relation does not depend on the idea that only a limited class of persons ratified the instrument that formed our Government. Though it must be beyond dispute that persons outside the United States did not and could not assent to the Constitution, that is quite irrelevant to any construction of the powers conferred or the limitations imposed by it. As Justice Story explained in his Commentaries:

> A government may originate in the voluntary compact or assent of the people of several states, or of a people never before united, and yet when adopted and ratified by them, be no longer a matter resting in compact; but become an executed government or constitution, a fundamental law, and not a mere league. But the difficulty in asserting it to be a compact between the people of each state, and all the people of the other states is, that the constitution itself contains no such expression, and no such designation of parties.

1 Commentaries on the Constitution 365, p. 335 (1833) (footnote omitted).

The force of the Constitution is not confined because it was brought into being by certain persons who gave their immediate assent to its terms.

For somewhat similar reasons, I cannot place any weight on the reference to "the people" in the Fourth Amendment as a source of restricting its protections. With respect, I submit these words do not detract from its force or its reach. Given the history of our Nation's concern over warrantless and unreasonable searches, explicit recognition of "the right of the people" to Fourth Amendment protection may be interpreted to underscore the importance of the right, rather than to restrict the category of persons who may assert it. The restrictions that the United States must observe with reference to aliens beyond its territory or jurisdiction depend, as a consequence, on general principles of interpretation, not on an inquiry as to who formed the Constitution or a construction that some rights are mentioned as being those of "the people."

I take it to be correct that the Government may act only as the Constitution authorizes, whether the actions in question are foreign or domestic. But this principle is only a first step in resolving this case. The question before us then becomes what constitutional standards apply when the Government acts, in reference to an alien, within its sphere of foreign operations.

The conditions and considerations of this case would make adherence to the Fourth Amendment's warrant requirement impracticable and anomalous. If the search had occurred in a residence within the United States, I have little doubt that the full protections of the Fourth Amendment would apply. But that is not this case. The absence of local judges or magistrates available to issue warrants, the differing and perhaps unascertainable conceptions of reasonableness and privacy that prevail abroad, and the need to cooperate with foreign officials all indicate that the Fourth Amendment's warrant requirement should not apply in Mexico as it does in this country. For this reason, in addition to the other persuasive justifications stated by the Court, I agree that no violation of the Fourth Amendment has occurred in the case before us. The rights of a citizen, as to whom the United States has continuing obligations, are not presented by this case.

I do not mean to imply, and the Court has not decided, that persons in the position of the respondent have no constitutional protection. The United States is prosecuting a foreign national in a court established under Article III, and all of the trial proceedings are governed by the Constitution. All would agree, for instance, that the dictates of the Due Process Clause of the Fifth Amendment protect the defendant. Indeed, as Justice Harlan put it, "the question of which specific safeguards . . . are appropriately to be applied in a particular context . . . can be reduced to the issue of what process is 'due' a defendant in the particular circumstances of a particular case." Nothing approaching a violation of due process has occurred in this case.

### Justice Brennan, with Whom Justice Marshall Joins, Dissenting

Today the Court holds that although foreign nationals must abide by our laws even when in their own countries, our Government need not abide by the Fourth Amendment when it investigates them for violations of our laws. I respectfully dissent.

Particularly in the past decade, our Government has sought, successfully, to hold foreign nationals criminally liable under federal laws for conduct committed entirely beyond the territorial limits of the United States that nevertheless has effects in this country. Foreign nationals must now take care not to violate our drug laws, our antitrust laws, our securities laws, and a host of other federal criminal statutes. The enormous expansion of federal criminal jurisdiction outside our Nation's boundaries has led one commentator to suggest that our country's three largest exports are now "rock music, blue jeans, and United States law."

The Constitution is the source of Congress' authority to criminalize conduct, whether here or abroad, and of the Executive's authority to investigate and prosecute such conduct. But the same Constitution also prescribes limits on our Government's authority to investigate, prosecute, and punish criminal conduct, whether foreign or domestic.

The Court today creates an antilogy: the Constitution authorizes our Government to enforce our criminal laws abroad, but when Government agents exercise this authority, the Fourth Amendment does not travel with them. This cannot be. At the very least, the Fourth Amendment is an unavoidable correlative of the Government's power to enforce the criminal law.

The Fourth Amendment guarantees the right of "the people" to be free from unreasonable searches and seizures and provides that a warrant shall issue only upon presentation of an oath or affirmation demonstrating probable cause and particularly describing the place to be searched and the persons or things to be seized. According to the majority, the term "the people" refers to "a class of persons who are part of a national community or who have otherwise developed sufficient connection with this country to be considered part of that community." The Court admits that "the people" extends beyond the citizenry, but leaves the precise contours of its "sufficient connection" test unclear. At one point the majority hints that aliens are protected by the Fourth Amendment only when they come within the United States and develop "substantial connections" with our country. At other junctures, the Court suggests that an alien's presence in the United States must be voluntary and that the alien must have "accepted some societal obligations." At yet other points, the majority implies that respondent would be protected by the Fourth Amendment if the place searched were in the United States.

What the majority ignores, however, is the most obvious connection between Verdugo-Urquidez and the United States: he was investigated and is being prosecuted for violations of United States law and may well spend the rest of his life in a United States prison. The "sufficient connection" is supplied not by Verdugo-Urquidez, but by the Government. Respondent is entitled to the protections of the Fourth Amendment because our Government, by investigating him and attempting to hold him accountable under United States criminal laws, has treated him as a member of our community for purposes of enforcing our laws. He has become, quite literally, one of the governed. Fundamental fairness and the ideals underlying our Bill of Rights compel the conclusion that when we impose "societal obligations," such as the obligation to comply with our criminal laws, on foreign nationals, we in turn are obliged to respect certain correlative rights, among them the Fourth Amendment.

By concluding that respondent is not one of "the people" protected by the Fourth Amendment, the majority disregards basic notions of mutuality. If we expect aliens to obey our laws, aliens should be able to expect that we will obey our Constitution when we investigate, prosecute, and punish them.

The majority's rejection of respondent's claim to Fourth Amendment protection is apparently motivated by its fear that application of the Amendment to law enforcement searches against foreign nationals overseas "could significantly disrupt the ability of the political branches to respond to foreign situations involving our national interest." The majority's doomsday scenario – that American Armed Forces conducting a mission to protect our national security with no law enforcement objective "would have to articulate specific facts giving them probable cause to undertake a search or seizure," – is fanciful. Verdugo-Urquidez is protected by the Fourth Amendment because our Government, by investigating and prosecuting him, has made him one of "the governed." Accepting respondent as one of "the governed," however, hardly requires the Court to accept enemy aliens in wartime as among "the governed" entitled to invoke the protection of the Fourth Amendment.

Moreover, with respect to non-law-enforcement activities not directed against enemy aliens in wartime but nevertheless implicating national security, doctrinal exceptions to the general requirements of a warrant and probable cause likely would be applicable more frequently abroad, thus lessening the purported tension between the Fourth Amendment's strictures and the Executive's foreign affairs power. Many situations involving sensitive operations abroad likely would involve exigent circumstances such that the warrant requirement would be excused. Therefore, the Government's conduct would be assessed only under the reasonableness standard, the application of which depends on context.

When our Government conducts a law enforcement search against a foreign national outside of the United States and its territories, it must comply with the Fourth Amendment. Absent exigent circumstances or consent, it must obtain a search warrant from a United States court. When we tell the world that we expect all people, wherever they may be, to abide by our laws, we cannot in the same breath tell the world that our law enforcement officers need not do the same. Because we cannot expect others to respect our laws until we respect our Constitution, I respectfully dissent.

## Notes and Comments:

1. Which opinion – if any – do you agree with?
2. One of the odd features of this case is that U.S. DEA agents carried out the search, rather than Mexican security personnel. Would this matter? Should this matter (Gibney 1990)?
3. What should determine the kinds of rights enjoyed by citizens of one country vis-à-vis another state (Keitner 2011)?

The following case raises the issue of whether American officials must establish a "nexus" to the United States in order to proceed with an arrest that takes place on the high seas. As discussed in the case, all of the U.S. circuit courts that have heard this matter, with the exception of the 9th circuit, do not require proof that drugs seized on the high seas were heading to the United States.

## *United States v. Perez-Oviedo*, 281 F. 3d. 400 (3d. Cir. 2002)

Jose Luis Perez-Oviedo ("Perez-Oviedo") [*a citizen of Colombia*] agreed to be the captain of the Adriatik, a Panamanian registered vessel. In October of 1999, the Adriatik left the port of Cartagena, Colombia and arrived in Barranquilla, Colombia, where it was loaded with 800 tons of sugar. The ship left Barranquilla and at the mouth of the Magdalena River over 2 tons of cocaine were loaded from a fishing boat. The vessel then proceeded toward its intended final destination of Canada.

On November 11, 1999, the HMS Northumberland, on board which there was a United States Coast Guard law enforcement detachment, intercepted the Adriatik north of Trinidad and Tobago. Upon observing signs suggesting narcotics smuggling, a Statement of No Objection was requested from the Panamanian government for permission to search the Adriatik and, if need be, escort it to a United States port for an intrusive and destructive search. The Panamanian government granted the request.

The Adriatik arrived in the Virgin Islands on November 13, 1999. Prior to the search, Perez-Oviedo informed a Special Agent of the Coast Guard that the cocaine was located in the Number 3 starboard tank. A preliminary search revealed 400 kilograms of cocaine; a second search uncovered another 1700 kilograms.

An Information was filed, charging Perez-Oviedo with two violations of the Maritime Drug Law Enforcement Act ("MDLEA"): one count of knowingly and intentionally conspiring to distribute cocaine on board a vessel subject to the jurisdiction of the United States (in violation of 46 U.S.C.App. §§ 1903(a) and 1903(j)) and one count of aiding and abetting to knowingly and intentionally possessing with the intent to distribute cocaine on board a vessel subject to the jurisdiction of the United States (in violation of 46 U.S.C.App. § 1903(a)). Perez-Oviedo pled guilty to the first count, preserving the issue of jurisdiction. Prior to sentencing, a motion was filed to dismiss for lack of jurisdiction. The District Court denied the motion, and sentenced Perez-Oviedo to 120 months imprisonment.

Perez-Oviedo raises four issues on appeal: 1) whether there was a sufficient factual basis for the charge to which he pled guilty; 2) whether a nexus to the United States is an element of the charge; 3) whether the Due Process limits on jurisdiction were exceeded; and 4) whether the conviction and sentencing before an Article IV Court were unlawful where the allegations involved only Article I high seas offenses without any nexus to the Article IV territories.

We address Perez-Oviedo's first two issues together, as our analysis of both is identical. Under the first issue, Perez-Oviedo argues that he lacked the requisite *mens rea* for conspiracy because he did not intend for the Adriatik or the smuggled cocaine to have any connection to, or to fall within the jurisdiction of, the United States. He contends on the second issue that a nexus with the United States was required under international law.

Sections 1903(a) and (j) of the MDLEA state:

(a) Vessels of United States or vessels subject to jurisdiction of United States
    It is unlawful for any person on board a vessel of the United States, or on board a vessel subject to the jurisdiction of the United States, or who is a citizen of the United States or a resident alien of the United States on board any vessel, to knowingly or intentionally manufacture or distribute, or to possess with intent to manufacture or distribute, a controlled substance.
(j) Attempt or conspiracy
    Any person who attempts or conspires to commit any offense defined in this chapter shall be subject to the same penalties as those prescribed for the offense, the commission of which was the object of the attempt or conspiracy.

In *Martinez-Hidalgo*, we held that the District Court had jurisdiction to adjudicate the criminal charges despite the fact that the vessel in question had no nationality (Colombia had disclaimed its registry of the vessel) and the final destination for the drugs was likely to be Puerto Rico or St. Croix. The critical factual distinction to be made in Perez-Oviedo's case is that the Adriatik did have nationality, it was registered in Panama. Since Panama consented to the search of the Adriatik, we hold that the government satisfied its jurisdictional requirements under the MDLEA.

While the issue previously has not been squarely before us, we explained in *Martinez-Hidalgo* that our holding in that case did not depend upon the vessel being stateless. We stated that "our holding obviously applies to any prosecution under the Maritime Drug Law Enforcement Act." We acknowledged in our discussion that our holding in *Martinez-Hidalgo* was not joining the holding of the Court of Appeals for the Ninth Circuit in *United States v. Davis* (199), which read into the MDLEA a nexus requirement with respect to foreign-registered vessels.

In holding that there was no nexus requirement in the MDLEA, we refused to distinguish *Martinez-Hidalgo* from *Davis* on the basis of whether the ship involved was stateless or actually registered in another country. Our conclusion rested upon the fact that "46 U.S.C. app. § 1903(d) expresses the necessary congressional intent to override international law to the extent that international law might require a nexus to the United States for the prosecution of the offenses defined in the [MDLEA]."

Other Courts of Appeal have likewise taken issue with the holding in *Davis*. They have held that no nexus is needed between a defendant's criminal conduct and the United States in order for there to be jurisdiction, even when the vessel at issue is registered in a foreign country (as opposed to being stateless). Perez-Oviedo's first two issues are without merit. The vessel's final destination of Canada and lack of a nexus to the United States are wholly irrelevant to our analysis of the jurisdiction of the United States to prosecute him under the MDLEA given that the Panamanian government consented to the search.

With regard to Perez-Oviedo's third issue, we previously held in *Martinez-Hidalgo* that no due process violation occurs in an extraterritorial prosecution under the MDLEA when there is no nexus between the defendant's conduct and the United States. Since drug trafficking is condemned universally by law-abiding nations, we reasoned that there was no reason for us to conclude that it is " 'fundamentally unfair' for Congress to provide for the punishment of a person apprehended with narcotics on the high seas." Perez-Oviedo's state of facts presents an even stronger case for concluding that no due process violation occurred. The Panamanian government expressly consented to the application of the MDLEA (unlike the stateless vessel in *Martinez-Hidalgo*). Such consent from the flag nation eliminates a concern that the application of the MDLEA may be arbitrary or fundamentally unfair.

Perez-Oviedo's fourth issue can be disposed of in short order. In *United States v. Canel*, we declined to hold that only an Article III judge could preside over the trial where the charge was a violation of the criminal law of the United States. We also held that no due process violation occurs when the trial of a criminal charge takes place before a judge enjoying the limited tenure afforded to judges of the District Court of the Virgin Islands. Perez-Oviedo's position that his conviction and sentencing before an Article IV Court was unlawful because the allegations involved only Article I high seas offenses without any nexus to the Article IV territories also fails.

---

## Notes and Comments:

1. As indicated in this case, in 1986 Congress passed the *Maritime Drug Law Enforcement Act* which defined drug smuggling in international waters as a crime against the U.S. even if it could not be established that the drugs were on their way to the United States. In the 1990s and 2000s, maritime detentions averaged around 200 a year. However, in 2012, the Department of Defense's Southern Command was given the mission to halt the interdiction of drugs from this part of the globe and the number of arrests skyrocketed. Perhaps what is even more noteworthy is that those arrested spend months literally chained to the railing of the ship they are on – described in the title of a *New York Times Magazine* article as "floating Guantanamos" – before eventually being brought before a federal district court judge, invariably, *not* on the West Coast, which is the jurisdiction of the 9th Circuit, which has demanded such a nexus (Wessler 2017).

2. You might recall from the Introduction (Box I.8) the five sources for a state to exercise criminal jurisdiction: territory (the crime occurred within the

territory of that state); nationality (the perpetrator is a citizen of that state); passive personality (the victims are nationals of that state); protective (the illicit actions negatively affect the security of the state); and universal (for crimes such as piracy or torture). In this case, which jurisdictional basis do you think the U.S. government could rely on?

---

**Box 7.2: International Law at the Movies: The International Drug Trade**

International drug trafficking is fertile ground for filmmakers so no list can be complete, but here are a few outstanding movies. *The French Connection* (1971) was one of Gene Hackman's first roles as a lead actor and his portrayal of Popeye Doyle, a New York City detective leading a fight against an international drug cartel, remains the gold standard. Although car chase scenes are now standard fare in films, none are as thrilling as the one with Doyle behind the wheel. In *Blow* (2001), Johnny Depp becomes dangerously involved in the Latin American drug trade. More recently, in *American Made* (2017), Tom Cruise plays Barry Seal, a former commercial airline pilot who does some work for the CIA – but then discovers a more lucrative (but dangerous) line of work smuggling drugs for the Medellin Cartel.

---

## Corruption

Corruption quite often has an international element to it. As a way of combating this, in October 2003 the U.N. General Assembly adopted the Convention Against Corruption, which as of October 2017 had 183 states parties. The Convention sets forth certain anti-corruption measures that states are required to undertake, and it also requires criminalization of certain practices, including embezzlement and bribery.

One of the signature events in the fight against international corruption was the passage in the United States of the Foreign Corrupt Practices Act (FCPA) in 1977, which criminalizes the payment of bribes to foreign officials. At the time of its passage, the FCPA was criticized for putting American business interests at a competitive disadvantage. Note, however, that its provisions apply not only to U.S. nationals but to foreign businesses that sell shares in the United States. The list of prosecutions in 2017 posted on the Security and Exchange Commission website reflects the far-ranging application of the FCPA:

- Telia: The Sweden-based telecommunications provider agreed to pay $965 million in a global settlement to resolve violations of the FCPA to win business in Uzbekistan. (9/21/17)

- Halliburton: The U.S.-based company agreed to pay $29.2 million, and a former vice president agreed to pay a $75,000 penalty, to settle charges related to payments made to a local company in Angola in the course of winning lucrative oilfield services contracts. (7/27/17)
- Michael L. Cohen and Vanja Baros: The former Och-Ziff executives were charged with being the driving forces behind a far-reaching bribery scheme that paid tens of millions of dollars in bribes to high-level government officials in Africa. (1/26/17)
- Orthofix International: The Texas-based medical device company agreed to pay more than $6 million to settle charges that its subsidiary in Brazil used high discounts and improper payments to induce doctors under government employment to use Orthofix products. (1/18/17)
- SQM: Chilean-based chemical and mining company Sociedad Quimica y Minera de Chile S.A. agreed to pay more than $30 million to resolve parallel civil and criminal cases finding that it violated the FCPA by making improper payments to Chilean political figures and others. (1/13/17)
- Biomet: The Warsaw, Indiana-based medical device manufacturer agreed to pay more than $30 million to resolve SEC and Justice Department investigations into the company's anti-bribery violations in Brazil and Mexico. (1/12/17)
- Cadbury Limited/Mondelez International: The global snacking business agreed to pay a $13 million penalty for FCPA violations occurring after Mondelez (then Kraft Foods Inc.) acquired Cadbury and its subsidiaries, including one in India that proceeded to make illicit payments to obtain government licenses and approvals for a chocolate factory in Baddi, India. (1/6/17)

Available at: *www.sec.gov/spotlight/fcpa/fcpa-cases.shtml.*

In the 1990s, European states also took up this issue of transnational corruption resulting in the *Convention on Combating Bribery of Foreign Public Officials and Development* (OECD Convention). Article 4 provides that the state parties shall "take measures as may be necessary to establish its jurisdiction over the bribery of a foreign public official when the offense is committed in whole or in part in its territory." However, the Commentary accompanying the text states that the provision should be interpreted "broadly so that an extensive physical connection to the bribery act is not required." Furthermore, in a 2009 OECD Recommendation on the implementation of the Convention, state parties are instructed that legal persons "cannot avoid responsibility by using intermediaries," a direct reference to the standard practice of hiding behind shell corporations and foreign subsidiaries (Skogly and Osim forthcoming).

## Box 7.3: Panama Papers/Paradise Papers

The scale of international corruption is perhaps best shown in the release of two sets of documents involving offshore accounts. The first was the release in 2015 of what came to be called the Panama Papers, which were comprised of 11.5 million files that had been in the possession of the Panamanian law firm Mossack Fonseca. Twelve national leaders and 143 politicians were implicated in this tax avoidance scheme.

Two years later there was the clandestine release of the Paradise Papers, which showed the extent to which some of the largest corporations in the world – Nike, Apple, Facebook, Twitter, McDonald's – but also the likes of Queen Elizabeth and her son Charles used offshore accounts as a means of avoiding taxes.

## Box 7.4: The Ever-Expanding Reach of U.S. Criminal Law: FIFA Corruption Charges

At the same time that the *Alien Tort Statute*, which provided the basis for *civil* actions against a range of entities from all over the world, has been reduced substantially by the U.S. Supreme Court's ruling in *Jesner* (Chapter 8), the application of American criminal law has gone in the opposite direction. An example of this would be the indictments handed down in May 2016 by the U.S. Department of Justice against 14 officials of FIFA, the world soccer governing body that has its headquarters in Switzerland, on the grounds that the defendants had used some element of the U.S. banking system in its operations. However, couldn't this be said about just about any financial transfers?

## Box 7.5: International Law at the Movies: International Corruption

*Big Men* (2013) is a documentary that gets the viewer into the high stakes world of oil drilling off the coast of Western Africa and the massive corruption that goes with this. For a documentary more in the style of Michael Moore, in *The Ambassador* (2011), Mads Brugger, a (white) Danish journalist, poses as a Liberian diplomat who uses his position to engage in all kinds of deals involving arms and diamonds.

## Box 7.6: Corruption and the Denial of a Right to Education

Socio-Economic Rights and Accountability Project (SERAP) is a Nigerian-based NGO that sued the Nigerian government, claiming that the country's massive corruption had the effect of causing a denial of the right to education in that country. The Economic Community of West African States (ECOWAS) Community Court of Justice ruled that the matter was to be handled through domestic and not international law.

Funds stolen by officers charged with the responsibility of providing basic education to the people should be treated as crime, pure and simple or the culprits may be dealt with in accordance with the applicable civil laws of the country to recover the funds. Unless this is done, every case of theft or embezzlement of public funds will be treated as a denial of human rights of the people in respect of the project for which the funds were allocated.

Would you agree with this or would you see this as implicating international law as well?

## Box 7.7: Cybercrime

In Chapter 4 there was discussion of cyberattacks, but a related phenomenon is cybercrime. Notwithstanding its transnational nature, cybercrime continues to be treated as a purely "domestic" matter. One great problem with this approach is the nature of the internet itself, where because of the "packet system" that places a premium on speed, it is impossible to determine beforehand what particular route a message will travel. In addition, most cybercrime laws, including those of the United States, do not apply extraterritorially. In her critique of this territorial approach to a transnational crime, Perloff-Giles writes:

> The jurisdictional rules developed for the nineteenth-century world of Westphalian nation-states are in many ways at odds with the network architecture of modern computing and the inherently cross-border character of transnational cyber offenses.
>
> (Perloff-Giles 2018: 226)

## Extradition

Extradition is the practice where a prisoner is transferred between states. We will see an example of this in the *Soering* case (Chapter 9), where law enforcement officials in Virginia sought to have Jens Soering extradited in order to face double murder charges. The issue there was whether the United Kingdom, where Soering was being detained, would be responsible for the harms the defendant might suffer if the extradition went through and he was exposed to what the European Court of Human Rights termed the "death row" phenomenon.

Our first case involves an extradition treaty between the United States and Mexico that was essentially ignored by American officials. One question you might ask is why a state would enter into an extradition treaty if it felt free to bypass its provisions. Following this, the U.S. invasion of Panama and the eventual arrest of Manuel Noriega provides a unique setting for quite a different form of "extradition." The third case, *Ahmad v. Wigen*, is an example of what is known as the "non-inquiry" principle.

---

## U.S. v. Alvarez-Machain, 504 U.S. 655 (1992)

### CHIEF JUSTICE REHNQUIST DELIVERED THE OPINION OF THE COURT

The issue in this case is whether a criminal defendant, abducted to the United States from a nation with which it has an extradition treaty, thereby acquires a defense to the jurisdiction of this country's courts. We hold that he does not, and that he may be tried in federal district court for violations of the criminal law of the United States.

Respondent, Humberto Alvarez-Machain, is a citizen and resident of Mexico. He was indicted for participating in the kidnap and murder of United States Drug Enforcement Administration (DEA) special agent Enrique Camarena-Salazar and a Mexican pilot working with Camarena, Alfredo Zavala Avelar. The DEA believes that respondent, a medical doctor, participated in the murder by prolonging Agent Camarena's life so that others could further torture and interrogate him. On April 2, 1990, respondent was forcibly kidnaped from his medical office in Guadalajara, Mexico, to be flown by private plane to El Paso, Texas, where he was arrested by DEA officials.

Respondent moved to dismiss the indictment, claiming that his abduction consti- tuted outrageous governmental conduct, and that the District Court lacked jurisdiction to try him because he was abducted in violation of the extradition treaty between the United States and Mexico. Extradition Treaty, May 4, 1978, [1979] United States-United Mexican States, 31 U. S. T. 5059, T. I. A. S. No. 9656 (Extradition Treaty or Treaty). The District Court rejected the outrageous governmental conduct claim, but held that it lacked jurisdiction to try respondent because his abduction violated the Extradition Treaty. The District Court discharged respondent and ordered that he be repatriated to Mexico.

In the instant case, the Court of Appeals affirmed the District Court's finding that the United States had authorized the abduction of respondent, and that letters from the Mexican Government to the United States Government served as an official protest of the Treaty violation. Therefore, the Court of Appeals ordered that the indictment against respondent be dismissed and that respondent be repatriated to Mexico. We granted certiorari, and now reverse.

Although we have never before addressed the precise issue raised in the present case, we have previously considered proceedings in claimed violation of an extradi- tion treaty and proceedings against a defendant brought before a court by means of a forcible abduction. We addressed the former issue in *United States* v. *Rauscher* (1886); more precisely, the issue whether the Webster-Ashburton Treaty of 1842, 8 Stat. 576, which governed extraditions between England and the United States, prohibited the prosecution of defendant Rauscher for a crime other than the crime for which he had been extradited. Whether this prohibition, known as the doctrine of specialty, was an intended part of the treaty had been disputed between the two nations for some time. Justice Miller delivered the opinion of the Court, which carefully examined the terms and history of the treaty; the practice of nations in regards to extradition treaties; the case law from the States; and the writings of commentators, and reached the following conclusion:

"[A] person who has been brought within the jurisdiction of the court *by virtue of proceedings under an extradition treaty*, can only be tried for one of the offences described in that treaty, and for the offence with which he is charged in the proceedings for his extradition, until a reasonable time and opportunity have been given him, after his release or trial upon such charge, to return to the country from whose asylum he had been forcibly taken under those proceedings." In addition, Justice Miller's opinion noted that any doubt as to this interpretation was put to rest by two federal statutes which imposed the doctrine of specialty upon extradition treaties to which the United States was a party. Unlike the case before us today, the defendant in *Rauscher* had been brought to the United States by way of an extradition treaty; there was no issue of a forcible abduction.

In *Ker* v. *Illinois* (1886), also written by Justice Miller and decided the same day as *Rauscher*, we addressed the issue of a defendant brought before the court by way of a forcible abduction. Frederick Ker had been tried and convicted in an Illinois court for larceny; his presence before the court was procured by means of forcible abduction from Peru. A messenger was sent to Lima with the proper warrant to demand Ker by virtue of the extradition treaty between Peru and the United States. The messenger, however, disdained reliance on the treaty processes, and instead forcibly kidnaped Ker and brought him to the United States. We distinguished Ker's case from *Rauscher*, on the basis that Ker was not brought into the United States by virtue of the extradition treaty between the United States and Peru, and rejected Ker's argument that he had a right under the extradition treaty to be returned to this country only in accordance with its terms. We rejected Ker's due process argument more broadly, holding in line with "the highest authorities" that "such forcible abduction is no sufficient reason why the party should not answer when brought within the jurisdiction of the court which has the right to try him for such an offence, and presents no valid objection to his trial in such court."

In *Frisbie* v. *Collins*, we applied the rule in *Ker* to a case in which the defendant had been kidnapped in Chicago by Michigan officers and brought to trial in Michigan. We upheld the conviction over objections based on the Due Process Clause and the federal Kidnapping Act and stated:

> This Court has never departed from the rule announced in *[Ker]* that the power of a court to try a person for crime is not impaired by the fact that he had been brought within the court's jurisdiction by reason of a 'forcible abduction.' No persuasive reasons are now presented to justify overruling this line of cases. They rest on the sound basis that due process of law is satisfied when one present in court is convicted of crime after having been fairly apprised of the charges against him and after a fair trial in accordance with constitutional procedural safeguards. There is nothing in the Constitution that requires a court to permit a guilty person rightfully convicted to escape justice because he was brought to trial against his will.

The only differences between *Ker* and the present case are that *Ker* was decided on the premise that there was no governmental involvement in the abduction; and Peru, from which Ker was abducted, did not object to his prosecution. Respondent finds these differences to be dispositive, as did the Court of Appeals in *Verdugo* contending that they show that respondent's prosecution, like the prosecution of Rauscher, violates the implied terms of a valid extradition treaty. The Government, on the other hand, argues that *Rauscher* stands as an "exception" to the rule in *Ker* only when an extradition treaty is invoked, and the terms of the treaty provide that its breach will limit the jurisdiction of a court. Therefore, our first inquiry must be whether the abduction of respondent from Mexico violated the Extradition Treaty between the United States and Mexico. If we conclude that the Treaty does not prohibit respondent's abduction, the rule in *Ker* applies, and the court need not inquire as to how respondent came before it.

In construing a treaty, as in construing a statute, we first look to its terms to determine its meaning. The Treaty says nothing about the obligations of the United States and Mexico to refrain from forcible abductions of people from the territory of the other nation, or the consequences under the Treaty if such an abduction occurs. Respondent submits that Article 22(1) of the Treaty, which states that it "shall apply to offenses specified in Article 2 [including murder] committed before and after this Treaty enters into force," evidences an intent to make application of the Treaty mandatory for those offenses. However, the more natural conclusion is that Article 22 was included to ensure that the Treaty was applied to extraditions requested after the Treaty went into force, regardless of when the crime of extradition occurred.

More critical to respondent's argument is Article 9 of the Treaty, which provides:

1. Neither Contracting Party shall be bound to deliver up its own nationals, but the executive authority of the requested Party shall, if not prevented by the laws of that Party, have the power to deliver them up if, in its discretion, it be deemed proper to do so.

2. If extradition is not granted pursuant to paragraph 1 of this Article, the requested Party shall submit the case to its competent authorities for the purpose of prosecution, provided that Party has jurisdiction over the offense.

According to respondent, Article 9 embodies the terms of the bargain which the United States struck: If the United States wishes to prosecute a Mexican national, it may request that individual's extradition. Upon a request from the United States, Mexico may either extradite the individual or submit the case to the proper authorities for prosecution in Mexico. In this way, respondent reasons, each nation preserved its right to choose whether its nationals would be tried in its own courts or by the courts of the other nation. This preservation of rights would be frustrated if either nation were free to abduct nationals of the other nation for the purposes of prosecution. More broadly, respondent reasons, as did the Court of Appeals, that all the processes and restrictions on the obligation to extradite established by the Treaty would make no sense if either nation were free to resort to forcible kidnaping to gain the presence of an individual for prosecution in a manner not contemplated by the Treaty.

We do not read the Treaty in such a fashion. Article 9 does not purport to specify the only way in which one country may gain custody of a national of the other country for the purposes of prosecution.

Respondent contends that the Treaty must be interpreted against the backdrop of customary international law, and that international abductions are "so clearly prohibited in international law" that there was no reason to include such a clause in the Treaty itself. The international censure of international abductions is further evidenced, according to respondent, by the United Nations Charter and the Charter of the Organization of American States. Respondent does not argue that these sources of international law provide an independent basis for the right respondent asserts not to be tried in the United States, but rather that they should inform the interpretation of the Treaty terms.

Respondent and his *amici* may be correct that respondent's abduction was "shocking," and that it may be in violation of general international law principles. Mexico has protested the abduction of respondent through diplomatic notes, and the decision of whether respondent should be returned to Mexico, as a matter outside of the Treaty, is a matter for the Executive Branch. We conclude, however, that respondent's abduction was not in violation of the Extradition Treaty between the United States and Mexico, and therefore the rule of *Ker* v. *Illinois* is fully applicable to this case. The fact of respondent's forcible abduction does not therefore prohibit his trial in a court in the United States for violations of the criminal laws of the United States.

The judgment of the Court of Appeals is therefore reversed, and the case is remanded for further proceedings consistent with this opinion.

### JUSTICE STEVENS, WITH WHOM JUSTICE BLACKMUN AND JUSTICE O'CONNOR JOIN, DISSENTING

The Court correctly observes that this case raises a question of first impression. The case is unique for several reasons. It does not involve an ordinary abduction by a private kidnaper, or bounty hunter, as in *Ker* v. *Illinois* (1886); nor does it involve the apprehension of an American fugitive who committed a crime in one State and sought asylum in another, as in *Frisbie* v. *Collins* (1952). Rather, it involves this country's abduction of another country's citizen; it also involves a violation of the territorial integrity of that other country, with which this country has signed an extradition treaty.

The extradition treaty with Mexico is a comprehensive document containing 23 articles and an appendix listing the extraditable offenses covered by the agreement. The parties announced their purpose in the preamble: The two governments desire "to cooperate more closely in the fight against crime and, to this end, to mutually render better assistance in matters of extradition." From the preamble, through the description of the parties' obligations with respect to offenses committed within as well as beyond the territory of a requesting party, the delineation of the procedures and evidentiary requirements for extradition, the special provisions for political offenses and capital punishment, and other details, the Treaty appears to have been designed to cover the entire subject of extradition. Thus, Article 22, entitled "Scope of Application," states that the "Treaty shall apply to offenses specified in Article 2 committed before and after this Treaty enters into force," and Article 2 directs that "extradition shall take place, subject to this Treaty, for willful acts which fall within any of [the extraditable offenses listed in] the clauses of the Appendix." Moreover, as noted by the Court, Article 9 expressly provides that neither contracting party is bound to deliver up its own nationals, although it may do so in its discretion, but if it does not do so, it "shall submit the case to its competent authorities for purposes of prosecution."

It is true, as the Court notes, that there is no express promise by either party to refrain from forcible abductions in the territory of the other nation. Relying on that omission, the Court, in effect, concludes that the Treaty merely creates an optional method of obtaining jurisdiction over alleged offenders, and that the parties silently reserved the right to resort to self-help whenever they deem force more expeditious than legal process. If the United States, for example, thought it more expedient to torture or simply to execute a person rather than to attempt extradition, these options would be equally available because they, too, were not explicitly prohibited by the Treaty. That, however, is a highly improbable interpretation of a consensual agreement, which on its face appears to have been intended to set forth comprehensive and exclusive rules concerning the subject of extradition. In my opinion, "the manifest scope and object of the treaty itself," plainly imply a mutual undertaking to respect the territorial integrity of the other contracting party. That opinion is confirmed by a consideration of the "legal context" in which the Treaty was negotiated.

A critical flaw pervades the Court's entire opinion. It fails to differentiate between the conduct of private citizens, which does not violate any treaty obligation, and conduct expressly authorized by the Executive Branch of the Government, which unquestionably constitutes a flagrant violation of international law, and in my opinion, also constitutes a breach of our treaty obligations. Thus, at the outset of its opinion, the Court states the issue as "whether a criminal defendant, abducted to the United States from a nation with which it has an extradition treaty, thereby acquires a defense to the jurisdiction of this country's courts." That, of course, is the question decided in *Ker v. Illinois* (1886); it is not, however, the question presented for decision today.

As the Court observes at the outset of its opinion, there is reason to believe that respondent participated in an especially brutal murder of an American law enforcement agent. That fact, if true, may explain the Executive's intense interest in punishing respondent in our courts. Such an explanation, however, provides no justification for disregarding the Rule of Law that this Court has a duty to uphold. That the Executive may wish to reinterpret the Treaty to allow for an action that the Treaty in no way authorizes should not influence this Court's interpretation. Indeed, the desire for revenge exerts "a kind of hydraulic pressure . . . before which even well settled principles of law will bend," but it is precisely at such moments that we should remember and be guided by our duty "to render judgment evenly and dispassionately according to law, as each is given understanding to ascertain and apply it." The way that we perform that duty in a case of this kind sets an example that other tribunals in other countries are sure to emulate.

The significance of this Court's precedents is illustrated by a recent decision of the Court of Appeal of the Republic of South Africa. Based largely on its understanding of the import of this Court's cases – including our decision in *Ker* – that court held that the prosecution of a defendant kidnaped by agents of South Africa in another country must be dismissed. The Court of Appeal of South Africa – indeed, I suspect most courts throughout the civilized world – will be deeply disturbed by the "monstrous" decision the Court announces today. For every nation that has an interest in preserving the Rule of Law is affected, directly or indirectly, by a decision of this character. As Thomas Paine warned, an "avidity to punish is always dangerous to liberty" because it leads a nation "to stretch, to misinterpret, and to misapply even the best of laws." To counter that tendency, he reminds us: "He that would make his own liberty secure must guard even his enemy from oppression; for if he violates this duty he establishes a precedent that will reach to himself." I respectfully dissent.

---

## Notes and Comments:

1. This is an unusual opinion – is it not? But is the Court correct? Or does this interpretation totally defeat why the extradition treaty exists in the first place?

2. The dissent suggests that the majority does not make the appropriate distinction between a foreign abduction carried out by the state and one by a private actor. Do you agree that this should matter?

3. Dr. Humberto Alvarez-Machain was tried in the United States for his alleged role in the torture and murder of a federal DEA agent. However, the district court directed a verdict of not guilty based on the lack of evidence. Alvarez-Machain then brought an *Alien Tort Statute* suit against Francisco Sosa, a former Mexican police officer who he alleges was one of his kidnappers. However, the U.S. Supreme Court ruled that his claim of arbitrary arrest was not a "specific, universal, and obligatory" norm of international law (*Sosa v. Alvarez-Machain*, 542 U.S. 692 (2004)).

# U.S. v. Noriega, 746 F.Supp. 1506 (S.D. FLA. 1990)

**Photo 7.1** Former Panamanian Strongman Manuel Noriega Following His Capture

*Source:* © Associated Press

### HOEVELER, DISTRICT JUDGE

This case comes before the Court on the several motions of Defendants General Manuel Antonio Noriega and Lt. Col. Luis Del Cid to dismiss for lack of jurisdiction the indictment which charges them with various narcotics-related offenses.

The case at bar presents the Court with a drama of international proportions, considering the status of the principal defendant and the difficult circumstances under which he was brought before this Court. The pertinent facts are as follows:

On February 14, 1988, a federal grand jury sitting in Miami, Florida returned a twelve-count indictment charging General Manuel Antonio Noriega with participating in an international conspiracy to import cocaine and materials used in producing cocaine into and out of the United States. Noriega is alleged to have exploited his official position as head of the intelligence branch of the Panamanian National Guard, and then as Commander-in-Chief of the Panamanian Defense Forces, to receive payoffs in return for assisting and protecting international drug traffickers, including various members of the Medellin Cartel, in conducting narcotics and money laundering operations in Panama.

Specifically, the indictment charges that General Noriega protected cocaine shipments from Colombia through Panama to the United States; arranged for the transshipment and sale to the Medellin Cartel of ether and acetone, including such chemicals previously seized by the Panamanian Defense Forces; provided refuge and a base for continued operations for the members of the Medellin Cartel after the Colombian government's crackdown on drug traffickers following the murder of the Colombian Minister of Justice, Rodrigo Lara-Bonilla; agreed to protect a cocaine laboratory in Darien

Province, Panama; and assured the safe passage of millions of dollars of narcotic proceeds from the United States into Panamanian banks. Noriega also allegedly traveled to Havana, Cuba and met with Cuban president Fidel Castro, who, according to the indictment, mediated a dispute between Noriega and the Cartel caused by the Panamanian troops' seizure of a drug laboratory that Noriega was paid to protect. All of these activities were allegedly undertaken for General Noriega's own personal profit. Defendant Del Cid, in addition to being an officer in the Panamanian Defense Forces, was General Noriega's personal secretary. He is charged with acting as liaison, courier, and emissary for Noriega in his transactions with Cartel members and other drug traffickers.

In the interval between the time the indictment was issued and Defendants were arrested, relations between the United States and General Noriega deteriorated considerably. Shortly after charges against Noriega were brought, the General delivered a widely publicized speech in which he brought a machete crashing down on a podium while denouncing the United States. On December 15, 1989, Noriega declared that a "state of war" existed between Panama and the United States. Tensions between the two countries further increased the next day, when U.S. military forces in Panama were put on alert after Panamanian troops shot and killed an American soldier, wounded another, and beat a Navy couple. Three days later, on December 20, 1989, President Bush ordered U.S. troops into combat in Panama City on a mission whose stated goals were to safeguard American lives, restore democracy, preserve the Panama Canal treaties, and seize General Noriega to face federal drug charges in the United States. Before U.S. troops were engaged, American officials arranged a ceremony in which Guillermo Endara was sworn in as president and recognized by the United States as the legitimate head of the government of Panama. Endara was reported to have won the Panamanian presidential election held several months earlier, the results of which were nullified and disregarded by General Noriega.

Not long after the invasion commenced, Defendant Del Cid, the commander of about two thousand Panamanian troops located in the Chiriqui Province, surrendered to American forces. He was then transferred into the custody of agents from the United States Drug Enforcement Agency, who thereupon arrested Del Cid for the offenses for which he is under indictment in this Court. The apprehension of General Noriega was not quite so easy. He successfully eluded American forces for several days, prompting the United States government to offer a one million dollar bounty for his capture. Eventually, the General took sanctuary in the Papal Nunciature in Panama City, where he apparently hoped to be granted political asylum. Noriega's presence in the Papal Nunciature touched off a diplomatic impasse and a round of intense negotiations involving several countries. Vatican officials initially refused to turn Noriega over to the United States. While he was still ensconced in the nunciature, American troops stationed outside pelted the building with loud rock-and-roll music blasted through loudspeakers. The music was played continuously for three days until church authorities protested the action as offensive. After an eleven-day standoff, Noriega finally surrendered to American forces, apparently under pressure from the papal nuncio and influenced by a threatening crowd of about 15,000 angry Panamanian citizens who had gathered outside the residence. On January 3, 1990, two weeks after the invasion began, Noriega walked out of the Papal Nunciature and surrendered himself to U.S. military officials waiting outside. He was flown by helicopter to Howard Air Force Base, where he was ushered into a plane bound for Florida and formally arrested by agents of the Drug Enforcement Agency. During the course of this litigation, which has included several hearings, no evidence was presented nor suggestion made that Noriega was in any way physically mistreated.

As is evident from the unusual factual background underlying this case, the Court is presented with several issues of first impression. This is the first time that a leader or de facto leader of a sovereign nation has been forcibly brought to the United States to face criminal charges. The fact that General Noriega's apprehension occurred in the course of a military action only further underscores the complexity of the issues involved. In addition to Defendant Noriega's motion to dismiss based on lack of jurisdiction over the offense and sovereign immunity, Defendants Noriega and Del Cid argue that they are prisoners of war pursuant to the Geneva Convention. This status, Defendants maintain, deprives the Court of jurisdiction to proceed with the case. Additionally, Noriega contends that the military action which brought about his arrest is "shocking to the conscience", and that due process considerations require the Court to divest itself of jurisdiction over his person. Noriega also asserts that the invasion occurred in violation of international law. Finally, Noriega argues that, even in the absence of constitutional or treaty violations, the Court should dismiss the indictment pursuant to its supervisory powers so as to prevent the judicial system from being party to and tainted by the government's alleged misconduct in arresting Noriega. The Court examines each of these issues, in turn, below.

The first issue confronting the Court is whether the United States may exercise jurisdiction over Noriega's alleged criminal activities. Noriega maintains that "the extraterritorial application of the criminal law is unreasonable under the unique facts of this case, and cannot be relied upon to secure jurisdiction over a leader of a sovereign nation who has personally performed no illegal acts within the borders of the United States." Although the defendant attempts to weave his asserted status as a foreign leader into his challenge to the extraterritorial application of this country's criminal laws, the question of whether the United States may proscribe conduct which occurs beyond its borders is separate from the question of whether Noriega is immune from prosecution as a head of state. This distinction is made clear in the defendant's own discussion of the applicable international law on extraterritorial jurisdiction, which does not look to a foreign defendant's official status but rather to the nature and effect of the conduct at issue. The Court therefore reserves analysis of Noriega's claim to head of state immunity and confines its discussion here to the ability of the United States to reach and prosecute acts committed by aliens outside its territorial borders. While the indictment cites specific instances of conduct occurring within the United States, including the shipment of cocaine from Panama to Miami and several flights to and from Miami by Noriega's alleged co-conspirators, the activity ascribed to Noriega occurred solely in Panama with the exception of the one trip to Cuba. Noriega is charged with providing safe haven to international narcotic traffickers by allowing Panama to be used as a location for the manufacture and shipment of cocaine destined for this country's shores.

Where a court is faced with the issue of extraterritorial jurisdiction, the analysis to be applied is 1) whether the United States has the power to reach the conduct in question under traditional principles of international law; and 2) whether the statutes under which the defendant is charged are intended to have extraterritorial effect. As Noriega concedes, the United States has long possessed the ability to attach criminal consequences to acts occurring outside this country which produce effects within the United States.

In the drug smuggling context, the 'intent doctrine' has resulted in jurisdiction over persons who attempted to import narcotics into the United States but never actually succeeded in entering the United States or delivering drugs within its borders. The fact that no act was committed and no repercussions were felt within the United States did not preclude jurisdiction over conduct that was clearly directed at the United States.

These principles unequivocally support jurisdiction in this case. The indictment charges Noriega with conspiracy to import cocaine into the United States and alleges several overt acts performed within the United States in furtherance of the conspiracy.

The Court next turns to Noriega's assertion that he is immune from prosecution based on head of state immunity, the act of state doctrine, and diplomatic immunity. Grounded in customary international law, the doctrine of head of state immunity provides that a head of state is not subject to the jurisdiction of foreign courts, at least as to official acts taken during the ruler's term of office.

In order to assert head of state immunity, a government official must be recognized as a head of state. Noriega has never been recognized as Panama's Head of State either under the Panamanian Constitution or by the United States. Title VI, Article 170 of the Panamanian Constitution provides for an executive branch composed of the President and Ministers of State, neither of which applies to Noriega. Officially, Noriega is the *Commandante* of the Panamanian Defense Forces, but he was never elected to head Panama's government and in fact abrogated the Panamanian presidential elections of May 7, 1989. More importantly, the United States government has never accorded Noriega head of state status, but rather continued to recognize President Eric Arturo Delvalle as the legitimate leader of Panama while Noriega was in power.

Noriega next argues that the act of state doctrine prohibits the Court from adjudicating the legality of his official actions in Panama. Unlike head of state immunity, the act of state doctrine presents no jurisdictional question but instead addresses the Court's permissible scope of inquiry into certain governmental acts. It is more properly understood as an issue preclusion device rather than an immunity prohibiting prosecution.

The classic expression of the doctrine is stated in *Underhill v. Hernandez*: "Every sovereign is bound to respect the independence of every other sovereign State, and the courts of one country will not sit in judgement on the acts of the government of another done within its own territory."

Although stated in terms of acts of the "State" or "sovereign," the doctrine also extends to governmental acts of State officials vested with sovereign authority.

In order for the act of state doctrine to apply, the defendant must establish that his activities are "acts of state," i.e., that they were taken on behalf of the state and not, as private acts, on behalf of the actor himself. Though the distinction between the public and private acts of government officials may prove elusive, this difficulty has not prevented courts from scrutinizing the character of the conduct in question.

The Court fails to see how Noriega's alleged drug trafficking and protection of money launderers could conceivably constitute public action taken on behalf of the Panamanian state.

Defendant does little more than state that, as the de facto ruler of Panama, his actions constitute acts of state. This sweeping position completely ignores the public/private distinction and suggests that government leaders are, as such, incapable of engaging in private, unofficial conduct.

Noriega also moves to dismiss the indictment on the ground that the manner in which he was brought before this Court – as a result of the United States government's invasion of Panama – is "shocking to the conscience and in violation of the laws and norms of humanity." He argues that the Court should therefore divest itself of jurisdiction over his person. In support of this claim, Noriega alleges that the invasion of Panama violated the Due Process Clause of the Fifth Amendment of the United States Constitution, as well as international law. Alternatively, he argues that even in the absence of constitutional or treaty violations, this Court should nevertheless exercise its supervisory authority and dismiss the indictment so as to prevent the Court from becoming a party to the government's alleged misconduct in bringing Noriega to trial.

It is well settled that the manner by which a defendant is brought before the court normally does not affect the ability of the government to try him. The Ker-Frisbie doctrine, as this rule has come to be known, provides that a court is not deprived of jurisdiction to try a defendant on the ground that the defendant's presence before the court was procured by unlawful means.

Noriega does not challenge the validity of the Ker-Frisbie rule but instead relies on what is commonly referred to as the Toscanino exception carved out by the Second Circuit. *United States v. Toscanino* (1974). In that case, which also involved a challenge to a court's exercise of personal jurisdiction, the defendant contended that his presence was illegally obtained through torture and abuse. In support of his claim, the defendant offered to prove that United States officials abducted him from Uruguay and subjected him to extensive and continuous torture, including pinching his fingers with metal pliers, flushing alcohol into his eyes and nose, forcing other fluids up his anal passage, and attaching electrodes to his extremities and genitals. Confronted with these allegations, the court refused to permit the government the fruits of its misconduct, holding that "we view due process as now requiring a court to divest itself of jurisdiction over the person of a defendant where it has been acquired as the result of the government's deliberate, unnecessary and unreasonable invasion of the accused's constitutional rights." Noriega asserts that the deaths, casualties, and destruction of property caused by the United States military action in Panama was "shocking to the conscience" and therefore falls within the Toscanino exception as narrowed by *Lujan v. Gengler*.

The case at bar, however, does not present such a situation, since Noriega does not, and presumably cannot, allege that the Government's invasion of Panama violated any right personal to him, as required by the Due Process Clause of the Fifth Amendment. The defendant does not claim that he was personally mistreated in any manner incident to his arrest, at least not in any manner nearly approaching the egregious physical abuse stated in Toscanino. Rather, Noriega bases his due process claim on the rights of third parties, to wit, those Panamanian citizens who were killed, injured, or had their property destroyed as a consequence of the invasion. The applicable cases suggest, however, that the limitations of the Due Process Clause "come into play only when the Government activity in question violated some protected right of the *defendant*.

In addition to his due process claim, Noriega asserts that the invasion of Panama violated international treaties and principles of customary international law. Initially, it is important to note that individuals lack standing to assert violations of international treaties in the absence of a protest from the offended government. Moreover, the Ker-Frisbie doctrine establishes that violations of international law alone do not deprive a court of jurisdiction over a defendant in the absence of specific treaty language to that effect. To defeat the Court's personal jurisdiction, Noriega must therefore establish that the treaty in question is self-executing in the sense that it confers individual rights upon citizens of the signatory nations, and that it by its terms expresses "a self-imposed limitation on the jurisdiction of the United States and hence on its courts."

As a general principle of international law, individuals have no standing to challenge violations of international treaties in the absence of a protest by the sovereign involved.

It can perhaps be argued that reliance on the above body of law, under the unusual circumstances of this case, is a form of legal bootstrapping. Noriega, it can be asserted, is the government of Panama or at least its de facto head of state, and as such he is the appropriate person to protest alleged treaty violations; to permit removal of him and his associates from power and reject his complaint because a new and friendly government is installed, he can further urge, turns the doctrine of sovereign standing on its head. This argument is not without force, yet there are more persuasive answers in response. First, as stated earlier, the United States has consistently refused to recognize the Noriega regime as Panama's legitimate government, a fact which considerably undermines Noriega's position. Second, Noriega nullified the results of the Panamanian presidential election held shortly before the alleged treaty violations occurred. The suggestion that his removal from power somehow robs the true government of the opportunity to object under the applicable treaties is therefore weak indeed. Finally, there is no provision or suggestion in the treaties cited which would permit the Court to ignore the absence of complaint or demand from the present duly constituted government of Panama. The current government of the Republic of Panama led by Guillermo Endara is therefore the appropriate entity to object to treaty violations. In light of Noriega's lack of standing to object, this Court therefore does not reach the question of whether these treaties were violated by the United States military action in Panama.

---

### Note and Comments:

1. Would you have dismissed Noriega's claim that the invasion of Panama "shocked the conscience" of the court? Or to state this another way: think of all the death and destruction that ensued in what was, essentially, a drug bust.

The following case is an example of what is called the "non-inquiry" principle. To what extent should the sending state concern itself with issues involving the fairness of proceedings in the receiving state?

---

## *Ahmad v. Wigen*, 910 F.2d 1063 (2d. Cir. 1990)

### Van Graafeiland, Circuit Judge

Mahmoud El-Abed Ahmad, also known as Mahmoud Abed Atta, appeals from a judgment of the United States District Court for the Eastern District of New York (Weinstein, J.), dismissing Ahmad's petition for a writ of habeas corpus, by means of which he hoped to escape extradition to Israel. The United States seeks to extradite Ahmad to Israel to stand trial for his alleged terrorist attack on a bus. After a hearing, Judge Korman of the United States District Court for the Eastern District of New York granted the Government's application for the certification to the Secretary of State of Ahmad's extraditability. Ahmad then petitioned unsuccessfully for habeas corpus. We affirm.

Although we affirm, we do not necessarily subscribe to the district court's dicta concerning the expanded role of habeas corpus in an extradition proceeding, which led to the district court's extensive exploration of Israel's system of justice.

Since the facts in the instant case already have been recounted in the two district judges' opinions, a brief summary will suffice for our purposes. In April 1986, three men attacked a commercial Israeli bus in the West Bank with molotov cocktails and automatic weapons fire. The attackers killed the bus driver and wounded one passenger, both civilians. Israeli authorities apprehended two of the attackers, and they implicated Ahmad as their accomplice.

About a year later, Ahmad was located in Venezuela where he was being detained on charges relating to his involvement with the Abu Nidal Organization, an international terrorist group. Upon being advised that Venezuela was going to deport Ahmad to the United States where he was a naturalized citizen, the United States Attorney for the Eastern District of New York filed a section 3184 complaint, and Magistrate Caden issued a warrant for Ahmad's provisional arrest. When Venezuela placed Ahmad on a commercial plane headed for New York, FBI agents on the plane executed the arrest warrant. On June 26, 1987, Israel requested that the United States extradite Ahmad to Israel to stand trial for murder, attempted murder, attempted arson, and other crimes.

After conducting a section 3184 hearing, Magistrate Caden denied the extradition request on the grounds that the attack on the bus was a political act for which Ahmad was immune from extradition and that Ahmad had been brought into the United States illegally. The Government then brought a new extradition proceeding that was heard by Judge Korman. Judge Korman granted certification, stating as he did so that Caden had applied erroneous legal standards and made plainly erroneous findings of fact. Thereafter, Judge Weinstein dismissed Ahmad's petition for habeas corpus relief.

Seven pages of Ahmad's brief are devoted to the argument that the evidence submitted in support of extradition failed to establish probable cause to believe that appellant committed the offense with which he was charged. This extensive discussion demonstrates either a misunderstanding or a misapplication of the law. Judge Korman's function was to determine whether there was competent evidence to justify certifying Ahmad for extradition, not to predict that an Israeli court would convict him. If the evidence would support a reasonable belief that Ahmad was guilty of the crime charged, it sufficed. Judge Weinstein correctly held that there was no ground to reverse Judge Korman's finding of probable cause.

Article VI of the United States-Israel Extradition Treaty provides that extradition shall not be granted if

> the offense is regarded by the requested Party as one of a political character or if the person sought proves that the request for his extradition has, in fact, been made with a view to trying or punishing him for an offense of a political character.

Whether an extraditee is accused of an offense of a political nature is an issue for judicial determination. Moreover, because Judge Korman ruled that Ahmad's alleged offense was not political in nature and therefore fell within the terms of the Treaty, his ruling was subject to habeas corpus review. Whether such review should be a completely *de novo* review as Judge Weinstein suggests is a question we need not now answer. Judge Weinstein reached the same result as had Judge Korman. We find the analyses of both judges persuasive and note that their reasoning is similar to that of the State Department on this issue. We agree that an attack on a commercial bus carrying civilian passengers on a regular route is not a political offense. Political motivation does not convert every crime into a political offense.

We have no problem with the district court's rejection of Ahmad's remaining argument to the effect that, if he is returned to Israel, he probably will be mistreated, denied a fair trial, and deprived of his constitutional and human rights. We do, however, question the district court's decision to explore the merits of this contention in the manner that it did. The Supreme Court's above-cited cases dealing with the scope of habeas corpus review carefully prescribe the limits of such review. Habeas corpus is not a writ of error, and it is not a means of rehearing what the certification judge or magistrate already has decided. A consideration of the procedures that will or may occur in the requesting country is not within the purview of a habeas corpus judge. Indeed, there is substantial authority for the proposition that this is not a proper matter for consideration by the certifying judicial officer.

Notwithstanding the above described judicial roadblocks, the district court proceeded to take testimony from both expert and fact witnesses and received extensive reports, affidavits, and other documentation concerning Israel's law enforcement procedures and its treatment of prisoners. This, we think, was improper. The interests of international comity are ill-served by requiring a foreign nation such as Israel to satisfy a United States district judge concerning the fairness of its laws and the manner in which they are enforced. It is the function of the Secretary of State to determine whether extradition should be denied on humanitarian grounds. So far as we know, the Secretary never has directed extradition in the face of proof that the extraditee would be subjected to procedures or punishment antipathetic to a federal court's sense of decency. Indeed, it is difficult to conceive of a situation in which a Secretary of State would do so.

Affirmed.

---

## Notes and Comments:

1. Is the "non-inquiry" principle consistent with international human rights law?

2. One of the most famous/infamous extradition cases involved John Demjanjuk, a retired autoworker who had been living in the United States since 1952. Demjanjuk's original name was Ivan – thus, the moniker "Ivan the Terrible" – when he was born in the Ukraine. Demjanjuk served in the Red Army during World War II but was captured by the Nazis where he served as a guard at the Treblinka concentration camp. In 1986, Demjanjuk was extradited to Israel where he was convicted of war crimes. However, the Israeli Supreme Court eventually overturned his conviction on the grounds that there was not enough evidence against him. Demjanjuk was then returned to the United States and had his U.S. citizenship restored. In 2001, Israel again sought to have him extradited but this never came to pass, although his American citizenship was removed and he died a stateless person.

## Piracy

Piracy is the oldest international crime and for centuries it was the only international crime that called for universal jurisdiction – so that any pirate found anywhere in the world could be prosecuted by any state. Of course, the "normal" way of dealing with pirates, at least until the 20th century, was to treat them as a hostile enemy and to immediately resort to lethal force. Although it is common to only associate maritime piracy with events of long ago – Jack Sparrow and his ilk – this phenomenon remains a present day reality that international law has attempted to deal with, most notably in the *U.N. Convention on the Law of the Seas* (UNCLOS), provisions of which are set forth in the *Ali* case that follows.

One of the unusual aspects of the *Ali* case is that the alleged pirate was prosecuted in the United States after he was tricked into coming to this country. Although UNCLOS only speaks of prosecution by the captor state, in virtually all cases, the prosecution – assuming there is a prosecution – takes place in one of the states in the Horn of Africa region, where most piracy occurs. However, what this masks are important differences in penalties depending on where the legal proceedings take place. For example, someone convicted of piracy in a U.S. court will almost always be handed a life sentence; however, if U.S. authorities transferred him to Kenya for prosecution, the average sentence there is nine years. And when China was in the business of prosecuting pirates in the late 1990s and early 2000s, the death penalty was often applied (Kontorovich 2012).

---

## United States v. Ali Mohamed Ali, (D.C. Cir 2013)

### Before BROWN, Circuit Judge, and EDWARDS and
### SILBERMAN, Senior Circuit Judges

The government says Ali is a pirate; he protests that he is not. Though a trial will determine whether he is in fact a pirate, the question before us is whether the government's allegations are legally sufficient. And the answer to that question is complicated by a factor the district court deemed critical: Ali's alleged involvement was limited to acts he committed on land and in territorial waters – not upon the high seas. Thus, the district court restricted the charge of aiding and abetting piracy to his conduct on the high seas and dismissed the charge of conspiracy to commit piracy. Eventually, the district court also dismissed the hostage taking charges, concluding that prosecuting him for his acts abroad would violate his right to due process. On appeal, we affirm dismissal of the charge of conspiracy to commit piracy. We reverse, however, the district court's dismissal of the hostage taking charges, as well as its decision to limit the aiding and abetting piracy charge.

### I. Background

## A. Modern Piracy

Mention "pirates" to most Americans and you are more likely to evoke Johnny Depp's droll depiction of Captain Jack Sparrow than concern about the international scourge of piracy that long ago led most civilized states to declare such marauders the enemy of all mankind. In unstable parts of the world, piracy is serious business, and these troubled waters have seen a resurgence in pirate attacks, both successful and attempted. These predatory activities have proven especially lucrative in the Gulf of Aden (situated between the Arabian Peninsula and the Horn of Africa and bounded by a long stretch of Somalia's coast), where pirates can exploit a key trade route undeterred by Somalia's unstable government.

## B. Ali's Offense and Prosecution

Ali is a member of Somalia's Warsengeli clan, which, together with the Majertein clan, plotted the capture of the CEC Future, a Danish-owned merchant ship that flew a Bahamian flag and carried cargo owned by a U.S. corporation. On November 7, 2008, the CEC Future was traveling in the Gulf of Aden on the "high seas" – i.e., outside any nation's territorial waters. Wielding AK-47s and a rocket-propelled grenade, the raiders fired warning shots, boarded the ship, and seized the crew. They then forced crewmembers at gunpoint to reroute the ship to Point Ras Binna, off the coast of Somalia, where, on November 9, Ali came aboard and assumed the role of interpreter. The ship traveled that same day to Eyl, a Somali port, and remained at anchor there until it was ransomed the following January.

Except for a brief period of "minutes" during which the CEC Future entered the high seas, the ship traversed exclusively territorial waters while Ali was aboard. Ali promptly began negotiating with the owners of the CEC Future, starting with an initial demand of $7 million for the release of the ship, its crew, and its cargo. Discussions continued into January 2009, when Ali and the CEC Future's owners agreed to a $1.7 million ransom. As payment for his assistance, Ali also demanded $100,000 (a figure he later reduced to $75,000) be placed in a personal bank account. On January 14, the pirates received the agreed-upon $1.7 million, and two days later Ali and his cohorts left the ship. Ali's share amounted to $16,500 – one percent of the total ransom less expenses. He later received his separate $75,000 payment via wire transfer to the account he had previously specified.

As it happens, "pirate hostage negotiator" is not the only line on Ali's resume. In June 2010, he was appointed Director General of the Ministry of Education for the Republic of Somaliland, a self-proclaimed sovereign state within Somalia. When he received an email in March 2011 inviting him to attend an education conference in Raleigh, North Carolina, he agreed. Little did he know it was all an elaborate ruse. For some time, federal prosecutors had been busy building a case against Ali, charging him via criminal complaint and later obtaining a formal indictment. When Ali landed at Dulles International Airport on April 20, 2011, to attend the sham conference, he was promptly arrested.

II. THE PIRACY CHARGES

In most cases, the criminal law of the United States does not reach crimes committed by foreign nationals in foreign locations against foreign interests. Two judicial presumptions promote this outcome. The first is the presumption against the extraterritorial effect of statutes: "When a statute gives no clear indication of an extraterritorial application, it has none." The second is the judicial presumption that "an act of Congress ought never to be construed to violate the law of nations if any other possible construction remains," Murray v. Schooner Charming Betsy – the so-called Charming Betsy canon. Because international law itself limits a state's authority to apply its laws beyond its borders, Charming Betsy operates alongside the presumption against extraterritorial effect to check the exercise of U.S. criminal jurisdiction. Neither presumption imposes a substantive limit on Congress's legislative authority, but they do constrain judicial inquiry into a statute's scope.

Piracy, however, is no ordinary offense. The federal piracy statute clearly applies extraterritorially to "[w]hoever, on the high seas, commits the crime of piracy as defined by the law of nations," even though that person is only "afterwards brought into or found in the United States." 18 U.S.C. § 1651. Likewise, through the principle of universal jurisdiction, international law permits states to "define and prescribe punishment for certain offenses recognized by the community of nations as of universal concern." And of all such universal crimes, piracy is the oldest and most widely acknowledged. "Because he commits hostilities upon the subjects and property of any or all nations, without any regard to right or duty, or any presence of public authority," the pirate is "hostis humani generis," – in other words, "an enemy of the human race." Thus, "all nations [may punish] all persons, whether natives or foreigners, who have committed this offence against any persons whatsoever, with whom they are in amity."

Universal jurisdiction is not some idiosyncratic domestic invention but a creature of international law. Unlike the average criminal, a pirate may easily find himself before an American court despite committing his offense on the other side of the globe. Ali's situation is a bit more complicated, though. His indictment contains no straightforward charge of piracy. Rather, the government accuses him of two inchoate offenses relating to piracy: conspiracy to commit piracy and aiding and abetting piracy.

## 1. Piracy and the Charming Betsy Canon

Section 1651 criminalizes "the crime of piracy as defined by the law of nations." Correspondence between the domestic and international definitions is essential to exercising universal jurisdiction. Otherwise, invocation of the magic word "piracy" would confer universal jurisdiction on a nation and vest its actions with the authority of international law. As a domestic matter, doing so may be perfectly legal. But because Charming Betsy counsels against interpreting federal statutes to contravene international law, we must satisfy ourselves that prosecuting Ali for aiding and abetting piracy would be consistent with the law of nations.

Though § 1651's invocation of universal jurisdiction may comport with international law, that does not tell us whether § 2's broad aider and abettor liability covers conduct neither within U.S. territory nor on the high seas. Resolving that difficult question requires examining precisely what conduct constitutes piracy under the law of nations. Luckily, defining piracy is a fairly straightforward exercise. Despite not being a signatory, the United States has recognized, via United Nations Security Council resolution, that the U.N. Convention on the Law of the Sea ("UNCLOS") "sets out the legal framework applicable to combating piracy and armed robbery at sea." According to UNCLOS:

Piracy consists of any of the following acts:

(a) any illegal acts of violence or detention, or any act of depredation, committed for private ends by the crew or the passengers of a private ship and directed:
(i) on the high seas, against another ship or against persons or property on board such ship;
(ii) against a ship, persons or property in a place outside the jurisdiction of any State;
(b) any act of voluntary participation in the operation of a ship with knowledge of facts making it a pirate ship;
(c) any act of inciting or of intentionally facilitating an act described in subparagraph (a) or (b).

UNCLOS, art. 101, Dec. 10, 1982, 1833 U.N.T.S. 397, 436. By including "intentionally facilitating" a piratical act within its definition of piracy, article 101(c) puts to rest any worry that American notions of aider and abettor liability might fail to respect the international understanding of piracy. One question remains: does international law require facilitative acts take place on the high seas?

Ali contends that even if facilitative acts count as piracy, a nation's universal jurisdiction over piracy offenses is limited to high seas conduct. In support of this claim, Ali invokes UNCLOS article 105, which reads,

> On the high seas, or in any other place outside the jurisdiction of any State, every State may seize a pirate ship or aircraft, or a ship or aircraft taken by piracy and under the control of pirates and arrest the persons and seize the property on board. The courts of the State which carried out the seizure may decide upon the penalties to be imposed.

1833 U.N.T.S. at 437. Ali understands article 105's preface to govern the actual enforcement of antipiracy law – and, by extension, to restrict universal jurisdiction to the high seas – even if the definition of piracy is more expansive. In fact, Ali gets it backward. Rather than curtailing the categories of persons who may be prosecuted as pirates, the provision's reference to the high seas highlights the broad authority of nations to apprehend pirates even in international waters. His reading also proves too much, leaving nations incapable of prosecuting even those undisputed pirates they discover within their own borders – a far cry from "universal" jurisdiction. Article 105 is therefore no indication international law limits the liability of aiders and abettors to their conduct on the high seas.

Of course, § 1651's high seas language could also be read as Congress's decision to narrow the scope of the international definition of piracy to encompass only those actions committed on the high seas. But Ali's preferred interpretation has some problems. Most damningly, to understand § 1651 as a circumscription of the law of nations would itself run afoul of Charming Betsy, requiring a construction in conflict with international law. Ultimately, we think it most prudent to read the statute the way it tells us to. It is titled "[p]iracy under law of nations," after all.

Like the Charming Betsy canon, the presumption against extraterritorial effect does not constrain trying Ali for aiding and abetting piracy. While the offense he aided and abetted must have involved acts of piracy committed on the high seas, his own criminal liability is not contingent on his having facilitated these acts while in international waters himself.

[Analysis of other criminal charges against Ali are omitted and the case was remanded.]

---

## Notes and Comments:

1. Following the circuit court ruling, Ali was tried in district court for hostage taking and piracy facilitation, charges that the district court had originally dropped but which were added by the D.C. Circuit. However, the jury found Ali not guilty of the charge of piracy but deadlocked on the less serious charge of hostage taking. Prosecutors had originally sought a retrial on the hostage taking charges, but in early 2014 dropped all charges against Ali. Would such a result influence U.S. officials in terms of whether to try pirates in the United States?

2. Another kind of piracy today is internet piracy. Although the pirating of films, television shows, and music is oftentimes associated with developing countries, the worldwide leader of this is Sweden, particularly due to the (illegal) work of The Pirate Bay, the hub for illegal file-sharing which has been in existence since 2003. According to a report by Sweden's Film and

TV Industry Cooperation Committee, nearly a third of the Swedish public regularly watches pirated films and television shows, and among those aged 16 to 29, fully two-thirds of this population does so (Heyman 2015).

---

**Box 7.8: International Law at the Movies: Piracy**

I will forgo *Pirates of the Caribbean* and its innumerable sequels and make mention of a single film that captures well the political, legal, and economic complexities of piracy. This is *Captain Phillips* (2013), a thriller starring Tom Hanks who plays the captain of the *MV Maersk Alabama*, which is hijacked by a group of Somali pirates.

---

## References

### Books and Articles

Mark Gibney, "Policing the World: The Long Reach of U.S. Law and the Short Arm of the Constitution," *Connecticut Journal of International Law* 6: 103–26 (1990)

Stephen Heyman, "Sweden's Notorious Distinction as a Haven for Online Pirates," *New York Times*, (June 17, 2015) Available at: www.nytimes.com/2015/06/18/arts/international/swedens-notorious-distinction-as-a-haven-for-online-pirates.html

Chimene I. Keitner, "Rights Beyond Borders," *Yale Journal of International Law* 36: 55–114 (2011)

Eugene Kontorovich, "The Penalties for Piracy: An Empirical Study of National Prosecution of International Crime," Northwestern University, faculty working papers (2012)

Alexandra Perloff-Giles, "Transnational Cyber Offenses: Overcoming Jurisdictional Challenges," *Yale Journal of International Law* 43: 191–227 (2018)

Sigrun Skogly and Philippa Osim, "States' Reluctance to Exercise Extraterritorial Jurisdiction: A Barrier to Compliance With the Extraterritorial Obligations to Protect Against Human Rights Abuses by Non-State Actors," (forthcoming)

Seth Freed Wessler, "The Coast Guard's Floating Guantanamos, Prisoners at Sea," *New York Times Magazine*, (November 20, 2017)

### Cases

*Ahmad v. Wigen*, 910 F. 2d 1063 (2d. Cir. 1990)

*Rantsev v. Cyprus and Russia*, ECtHR, App. No. 25965/04 (2010)

*SERAP v. Nigeria*, ECOWAS Community Court of Justice No. ECW/CCJ/JUD/07/10 (2010)

*Sosa v. Alvarez-Machain*, 542 U.S. 692 (2004)
*U.S. v. Ali Mohamed Ali*, 718 (D.C. Cir. 2013)
*U.S. v. Alvarez-Machain*, 504 U.S. 655 (1992)
*U.S. v. Noriega*, 746 F. Supp. 1506 (S.D. FLA. 1990)
*U.S. v. Perez-Oviendo*, 281 F. 3d. 400 (3d. Cir. 2002)
*U.S. v. Verdugo-Urquidez*, 494 U.S. 259 (1990)

### International Agreements

Convention Against Corruption, adopted by U.N. General Assembly 31 October 2003, entry into force 14 December 2005
Convention on the Law of the Sea, opened for signature on 10 December 1982, entry into force November 1994

### Regional Law

Convention on Combating Bribery of Foreign Public Officials and Development in International Business Transactions, 17 December 1997, S. Treaty Doc. No. 104–43

### Domestic Laws

Alien Tort Statute (ATS), 28 U.S.C. Sec. 1350 (U.S.)
Foreign Corrupt Practices Act, 15 U.S.C. Chapter 26, Sec 78a et seq, (U.S.)
Maritime Drug Law Enforcement Act of 1988, 46 U.S.C. Secs. 70501–70505 (U.S.)

# 8

# Corporate Accountability

In the landmark ruling of *Filartiga v. Pena-Irala* (1980) referenced earlier in Chapter 1, the Second Circuit Court of Appeals ruled that the 1789 Alien Tort Statute (ATS) could serve as the jurisdictional basis for foreign nationals to pursue claims involving violations of international law that occurred outside the United States. The case involved the torture and death of Joelito Filartiga, the son of a prominent Paraguayan dissident, at the hands of Americo Roberto Pena-Irala, the Inspector General of Asuncion, Paraguay in March 1976. Not only were no criminal proceedings brought against Pena-Irala in Paraguay, which at the time was under a dictatorship, but the attorney hired by the Filartiga family was imprisoned, tortured, and later disbarred. In short, justice – at least in Paraguay – was denied.

In 1978, Joelito's sister, Dolly, had applied for asylum and was living in the United States. Pena-Irala was also in the U.S. having overstayed a visitor's visa. During the course of the immigration proceedings brought against Pena-Irala, Dolly Filartiga learned about the whereabouts of her brother's murderer and, working with the Center for Constitutional Rights, she filed a civil action against him on the basis of the ATS, which reads in its entirety: "The district courts shall have original jurisdiction of any civil action by an alien for a tort only, committed in violation of the law of nations or a treaty of the United States." The district court dismissed this case, but in what became a landmark decision, the Second Circuit ruled that torture constituted a violation of international law and awarded the Filartiga family more than $10 million in damages.

Following this ruling, there was a veritable explosion in cases brought against individuals who had also violated international human rights and humanitarian law standards, including such "luminaries" as Ferdinand Marcos (former President of the Philippines), Guillermo Suarez-Mason (former Argentine military leader during the country's "Dirty War"), Radovan Karadzic (former president of the Republika Srpska), and Hector Gramajo (former Guatemalan defense minister). To be clear, not one of these cases actually went to trial. Instead, as in *Filartiga*, the defendant would invariably leave the United States (the ATS is a civil and not criminal proceeding) and go back home, leaving the plaintiff with a default judgment. Still, in case after case against individual defendants, federal courts refused to dismiss the ATS-based complaints brought before them. Moreover, in 2004 in *Sosa v. Alvarez-Machain*, the U.S. Supreme Court upheld the application of the ATS, at least as applied to individuals, although at the same time it limited the scope of its application to violations of the law of nations that were a "specific, universal, and obligatory norm." In this case, the Court ruled that a single illegal abduction for less than a day did not meet this standard.

The ATS has also been the basis of suits brought against corporations, which is the focus of the present chapter, and here the reception by federal courts was much more uneven. In many instances, especially in actions brought against U.S.-based corporations, the case would be dismissed on the basis of *forum non conveniens* – which essentially means this is not the appropriate forum. However, the biggest change began with the Court's ruling in *Kiobel* (2013), where it upheld dismissal of a case brought in U.S. federal district court against a foreign corporation for events taking place in Nigeria, ruling that the cause of action was too attenuated to the United States. Five years later, the Court went a step further in *Jesner* (2018), holding that, absent congressional consent, suits against multinational corporations can no longer be brought under the ATS.

---

## *Kiobel v. Royal Dutch Petroleum Co. et al.*, 569 U.S. 108 (2013)

### CHIEF JUSTICE ROBERTS DELIVERED THE OPINION OF THE COURT

Petitioners, a group of Nigerian nationals residing in the United States, filed suit in federal court against certain Dutch, British, and Nigerian corporations. Petitioners sued under the Alien Tort Statute, 28 U. S. C. §1350, alleging that the corporations aided and abetted the Nigerian Government in committing violations of the law of nations in Nigeria. The question presented is whether and under what circumstances courts may recognize a cause of action under the Alien Tort Statute, for violations of the law of nations occurring within the territory of a sovereign other than the United States.

Petitioners were residents of Ogoniland, an area of 250 square miles located in the Niger delta area of Nigeria and populated by roughly half a million people. When the complaint was filed, respondents Royal Dutch Petroleum Company and Shell Transport and Trading Company, p.l.c., were holding companies incorporated in the Netherlands and England, respectively. Their joint subsidiary, respondent Shell Petroleum

Development Company of Nigeria, Ltd. (SPDC), was incorporated in Nigeria, and engaged in oil exploration and production in Ogoniland. According to the complaint, after concerned residents of Ogoniland began protesting the environmental effects of SPDC's practices, respondents enlisted the Nigerian Government to violently suppress the burgeoning demonstrations. Throughout the early 1990's, the complaint alleges, Nigerian military and police forces attacked Ogoni villages, beating, raping, killing, and arresting residents and destroying or looting property. Petitioners further allege that respondents aided and abetted these atrocities by, among other things, providing the Nigerian forces with food, transportation, and compensation, as well as by allowing the Nigerian military to use respondents' property as a staging ground for attacks.

Passed as part of the Judiciary Act of 1789, the ATS was invoked twice in the late 18th century, but then only once more over the next 167 years. The statute provides district courts with jurisdiction to hear certain claims, but does not expressly provide any causes of action. We held in *Sosa v. Alvarez-Machain*, however, that the First Congress did not intend the provision to be "stillborn." The grant of jurisdiction is instead "best read as having been enacted on the understanding that the common law would provide a cause of action for [a] modest number of international law violations." We thus held that federal courts may "recognize private claims [for such violations] under federal common law." The Court in Sosa rejected the plaintiff's claim in that case for "arbitrary arrest and detention," on the ground that it failed to state a violation of the law of nations with the requisite "definite content and acceptance among civilized nations."

The question here is not whether petitioners have stated a proper claim under the ATS, but whether a claim may reach conduct occurring in the territory of a foreign sovereign. Respondents contend that claims under the ATS do not, relying primarily on a canon of statutory interpretation known as the presumption against extraterritorial application. That canon provides that "[w]hen a statute gives no clear indication of an extraterritorial application, it has none," and reflects the "presumption that United States law governs domestically but does not rule the world." This presumption "serves to protect against unintended clashes between our laws and those of other nations which could result in international discord."

We typically apply the presumption to discern whether an Act of Congress regulating conduct applies abroad. The ATS, on the other hand, is "strictly jurisdictional." It does not directly regulate conduct or afford relief. It instead allows federal courts to recognize certain causes of action based on sufficiently definite norms of international law. But we think the principles underlying the canon of interpretation similarly constrain courts considering causes of action that may be brought under the ATS.

Indeed, the danger of unwarranted judicial interference in the conduct of foreign policy is magnified in the context of the ATS, because the question is not what Congress has done but instead what courts may do. This Court in *Sosa* repeatedly stressed the need for judicial caution in considering which claims could be brought under the ATS, in light of foreign policy concerns. As the Court explained, "the potential [foreign policy] implications . . . of recognizing . . . causes [under the ATS] should make courts particularly wary of impinging on the discretion of the Legislative and Executive Branches in managing foreign affairs."

These concerns are not diminished by the fact that *Sosa* limited federal courts to recognizing causes of action only for alleged violations of international law norms that are "'specific, universal, and obligatory.'" The principles underlying the presumption against extraterritoriality thus constrain courts exercising their power under the ATS.

Petitioners contend that even if the presumption applies, the text, history, and purposes of the ATS rebut it for causes of action brought under that statute. It is true that Congress, even in a jurisdictional provision, can indicate that it intends federal law to apply to conduct occurring abroad (providing jurisdiction over the offense of genocide "regardless of where the offense is committed" if the alleged offender is, among other things, "present in the United States"). But to rebut the presumption, the ATS would need to evince a "clear indication of extraterritoriality." It does not.

There is no indication that the ATS was passed to make the United States a uniquely hospitable forum for the enforcement of international norms. As Justice Story put it, "No nation has ever yet pretended to be the custos morum of the whole world. . . ." It is implausible to suppose that the First Congress wanted their fledgling Republic – struggling to receive international recognition – to be the first. Indeed, the parties offer no evidence that any nation, meek or mighty, presumed to do such a thing.

The United States was, however, embarrassed by its potential inability to provide judicial relief to foreign officials injured in the United States. Such offenses against ambassadors violated the law of nations, "and if not adequately redressed could rise to an issue of war." The ATS ensured that the United States could provide a forum for adjudicating such incidents. Nothing about this historical context suggests that Congress also intended federal common law under the ATS to provide a cause of action for conduct occurring in the territory of another sovereign.

Indeed, far from avoiding diplomatic strife, providing such a cause of action could have generated it. Recent experience bears this out. Moreover, accepting petitioners' view would imply that other nations, also applying the law of nations, could hale our citizens into their courts for alleged violations of the law of nations occurring in the United States, or anywhere else in the world. The presumption against extraterritoriality guards against our courts triggering such serious foreign policy consequences, and instead defers such decisions, quite appropriately, to the political branches.

We therefore conclude that the presumption against extraterritoriality applies to claims under the ATS, and that nothing in the statute rebuts that presumption. "[T]here is no clear indication of extraterritoriality here," and petitioners' case seeking relief for violations of the law of nations occurring outside the United States is barred.

On these facts, all the relevant conduct took place outside the United States. And even where the claims touch and concern the territory of the United States, they must do so with sufficient force to displace the presumption against extraterritorial application. Corporations are often present in many countries, and it would reach too far to say that mere corporate presence suffices. If Congress were to determine otherwise, a statute more specific than the ATS would be required.

JUSTICE BREYER, WITH WHOM JUSTICE GINSBURG, JUSTICE SOTOMAYOR AND JUSTICE KAGAN JOIN,
CONCURRING IN THE JUDGMENT

I agree with the Court's conclusion but not with its reasoning. Unlike the Court, I would not invoke the presumption against extraterritoriality. Rather, guided in part by principles and practices of foreign relations law, I would find jurisdiction under this statute where (1) the alleged tort occurs on American soil, (2) the defendant is an American national, or (3) the defendant's conduct substantially and adversely affects an important American national interest, and that includes a distinct interest in preventing the United States from becoming a safe harbor (free of civil as well as criminal liability) for a torturer or other common enemy of mankind. In this case, however, the parties and relevant conduct lack sufficient ties to the United States for the ATS to provide jurisdiction.

Our decision in Sosa frames the question. In Sosa the Court specified that the Alien Tort Statute (ATS), when enacted in 1789, "was intended as jurisdictional." We added that the statute gives today's courts the power to apply certain "judge-made" damages law to victims of certain foreign affairs-related misconduct, including "three specific offenses" to which "Blackstone referred," namely "violation of safe conducts, infringement of the rights of ambassadors, and piracy." We held that the statute provides today's federal judges with the power to fashion "a cause of action" for a "modest number" of claims, "based on the present-day law of nations," and which "rest on a norm of international character accepted by the civilized world and defined with a specificity comparable to the features" of those three "18th-century paradigms."

Recognizing that Congress enacted the ATS to permit recovery of damages from pirates and others who violated basic international law norms as understood in 1789, *Sosa* essentially leads today's judges to ask: Who are today's pirates? We provided a framework for answering that question by setting down principles drawn from international norms and designed to limit ATS claims to those that are similar in character and specificity to piracy.

In this case we must decide the extent to which this jurisdictional statute opens a federal court's doors to those harmed by activities belonging to the limited class that Sosa set forth when those activities take place abroad. In my view the majority's effort to answer the question by referring to the "presumption against extraterritoriality" does not work well. That presumption "rests on the perception that Congress ordinarily legislates with respect to domestic, not foreign matters." The ATS, however, was enacted with "foreign matters" in mind. The statute's text refers explicitly to "alien[s]," "treat[ies]," and "the law of nations."

The statute's purpose was to address violations of the law of nations, admitting of a judicial remedy and at the same time threatening serious consequences in international affairs. And at least one of the three kinds of activities that we found to fall within the statute's scope, namely piracy, normally takes place abroad.

The majority cannot wish this piracy example away by emphasizing that piracy takes place on the high seas. That is because the robbery and murder that make up piracy do not normally take place in the water; they take place on a ship. And a ship is like land, in that it falls within the jurisdiction of the nation whose flag it flies. Indeed, in the early 19th century Chief Justice Marshall described piracy as an "offenc[e] against the nation under whose flag the vessel sails, and within whose particular jurisdiction all on board the vessel are."

The majority nonetheless tries to find a distinction between piracy at sea and similar cases on land. It writes, "Applying U. S. law to pirates . . . does not typically impose the sovereign will of the United States onto conduct occurring within the territorial jurisdiction of another sovereign and therefore carries less direct foreign policy consequences." But, as I have just pointed out, "[a]pplying U. S. law to pirates" does typically involve applying our law to acts taking place within the jurisdiction of another sovereign.

Thus the Court's reasoning, as applied to the narrow class of cases that *Sosa* described, fails to provide significant support for the use of any presumption against extraterritoriality; rather, it suggests the contrary. In any event, as the Court uses its presumption against extraterritorial application, it offers only limited help in deciding the question presented, namely "under what circumstances the Alien Tort Statute . . . allows courts to recognize a cause of action for violations of the law of nations occurring within the territory of a sovereign other than the United States." The majority echoes in this jurisdictional context *Sosa's* warning to use "caution" in shaping federal common-law causes of action. But it also makes clear that a statutory claim might sometimes "touch and concern the territory of the United States . . . with sufficient force to displace the presumption." It leaves for another day the determination of just when the presumption against extraterritoriality might be "overcome."

Considering these jurisdictional norms in light of both the ATS's basic purpose (to provide compensation for those injured by today's pirates) and *Sosa's* basic caution (to avoid international friction), I believe that the statute provides jurisdiction where (1) the alleged tort occurs on American soil, (2) the defendant is an American national, or (3) the defendant's conduct substantially and adversely affects an important American national interest, and that includes a distinct interest in preventing the United States from becoming a safe harbor (free of civil as well as criminal liability) for a torturer or other common enemy of mankind.

As I have indicated, we should treat this Nation's interest in not becoming a safe harbor for violators of the most fundamental international norms as an important jurisdiction-related interest justifying application of the ATS in light of the statute's basic purposes – in particular that of compensating those who have suffered harm at the hands of, e.g., torturers or other modern pirates. Nothing in the statute or its history suggests that our courts should turn a blind eye to the plight of victims in that "handful of heinous actions." To the contrary, the statute's language, history, and purposes suggest that the statute was to be a weapon in the "war" against those modern pirates who, by their conduct, have "declar[ed] war against all mankind."

Applying these jurisdictional principles to this case, however, I agree with the Court that jurisdiction does not lie. The defendants are two foreign corporations. Their shares, like those of many foreign corporations, are traded on the New York Stock Exchange. Their only presence in the United States consists of an office in New York City (actually owned by a separate but affiliated company) that helps to explain their business to potential investors. The plaintiffs are not United States nationals but nationals of other nations. The conduct at issue took place abroad. And the plaintiffs allege, not that the defendants directly engaged in acts of torture, genocide, or the equivalent, but that they helped others (who are not American nationals) to do so.

Under these circumstances, even if the New York office were a sufficient basis for asserting general jurisdiction, it would be farfetched to believe, based solely upon the defendants' minimal and indirect American presence, that this legal action helps to vindicate a distinct American interest, such as in not providing a safe harbor for an "enemy of all mankind." Thus I agree with the Court that here it would "reach too far to say" that such "mere corporate presence suffices."

I consequently join the Court's judgment but not its opinion.

---

## Notes and Comments:

1. Which human rights claims do you feel "touch and concern" the United States so that the plaintiffs can proceed under the ATS? What about a situation comparable to *Filartiga* (Steinhardt 2014)?

2. The ATS is a federal (U.S.) statute and as you can see from *Kiobel* as well as the *Jesner* case that follows, this avenue of relief for victims of human rights claims is closing – and perhaps might already be closed. But what about state courts in the United States? Can they be used as a forum for claims based on state law (Davis and Whytock 2018)?

---

## *Jesner v. Arab Bank*, 584 U.S. ___ (2018)

### JUSTICE KENNEDY DELIVERED THE OPINION OF THE COURT

Petitioners in this case, or the persons on whose behalf petitioners now assert claims, allegedly were injured or killed by terrorist acts committed abroad. Those terrorist acts, it is contended, were in part caused or facilitated by a foreign corporation. The foreign corporation charged with liability in these ATS suits is Arab Bank, PLC. Some of Arab Bank's officials, it is alleged, allowed the Bank to be used to transfer funds to terrorist groups in the Middle East, which in turn enabled or facilitated criminal acts of terrorism, causing the deaths or injuries for which petitioners now seek compensation. Petitioners seek to prove Arab Bank helped the terrorists receive the moneys in part by means of currency clearances and bank transactions passing through its New York City offices, all by means of electronic transfers.

Petitioners contend that international and domestic laws impose responsibility and liability on a corporation if its human agents use the corporation to commit crimes in violation of international laws that protect human rights. The question here is whether the Judiciary has the authority, in an ATS action, to make that determination and then to enforce that liability in ATS suits, all without any explicit authorization from Congress to do so.

A significant majority of the plaintiffs in these lawsuits – about 6,000 of them – are foreign nationals whose claims arise under the ATS. These foreign nationals are petitioners here. They allege that they or their family members were injured by terrorist attacks in the Middle East over a 10-year period. Two of the five lawsuits also included claims brought by American nationals under the Anti-Terrorism Act, 18 U. S. C. §2333(a), but those claims are not at issue.

Arab Bank is a major Jordanian financial institution with branches throughout the world, including in New York. Petitioners allege that Arab Bank helped finance attacks by Hamas and other terrorist groups. Among other claims, petitioners allege that Arab Bank maintained bank accounts for terrorists and their front groups and allowed the accounts to be used to pay the families of suicide bombers.

Most of petitioners' allegations involve conduct that occurred in the Middle East. Yet petitioners allege as well that Arab Bank used its New York branch to clear dollar-denominated transactions through the Clearing House Interbank Payments System. That elaborate system is commonly referred to as CHIPS. It is alleged that some of these CHIPS transactions benefited terrorists.

Under the Articles of Confederation, the Continental Congress lacked authority to "cause infractions of treaties, or of the law of nations to be punished. " The Continental Congress urged the States to authorize suits for damages sustained by foreign citizens as a result of violations of international law; but the state courts' vindication of the law of nations remained unsatisfactory.

The Framers addressed these matters at the 1787 Philadelphia Convention; and, as a result, Article III of the Constitution extends the federal judicial power to "all cases affecting ambassadors, other public ministers and consuls," and "to controversies . . . between a state, or the citizens thereof, and foreign states, citizens, or subjects."

The First Congress passed a statute to implement these provisions. The Judiciary Act of 1789 authorized federal jurisdiction over suits involving disputes between aliens and United States citizens and suits involving diplomats. As noted, the ATS is central to this case and its brief text bears repeating. Its full text is: "The district courts shall have original jurisdiction of any civil action by an alien for a tort only, committed in violation of the law of nations or a treaty of the United States."

The ATS is "strictly jurisdictional" and does not by its own terms provide or delineate the definition of a cause of action for violations of international law. But the statute was not enacted to sit on a shelf awaiting further legislation. Rather, Congress enacted it against the backdrop of the general common law, which in 1789 recognized a limited category of "torts in violation of the law of nations."

In the 18th century, international law primarily governed relationships between and among nation-states, but in a few instances it governed individual conduct occurring outside national borders (for example, "disputes relating to prizes, to shipwrecks, to hostages, and ransom bills"). There was, furthermore, a narrow domain in which "rules binding individuals for the benefit of other individuals over-lapped with" the rules governing the relationships between nation-states. As understood by Blackstone, this domain included "three specific offenses against the law of nations addressed by the criminal law of England: violation of safe conducts, infringement of the rights of ambassadors, and piracy." It was this narrow set of violations of the law of nations, admitting of a judicial remedy and at the same time threatening serious consequences in international affairs, that was probably on the minds of the men who drafted the ATS.

This history teaches that Congress drafted the ATS "to furnish jurisdiction for a relatively modest set of actions alleging violations of the law of nations." The principal objective of the statute, when first enacted, was to avoid foreign entanglements by ensuring the availability of a federal forum where the failure to provide one might cause another nation to hold the United States responsible for an injury to a foreign citizen.

With that introduction, it is proper now to turn first to the question whether there is an international-law norm imposing liability on corporations for acts of their employees that contravene fundamental human rights.

Petitioners and Arab Bank disagree as to whether corporate liability is a question of international law or only a question of judicial authority and discretion under domestic law.

In modern times, there is no doubt, of course, that "the international community has come to recognize the common danger posed by the flagrant disregard of basic human rights," leading "the nations of the world to recognize that respect for fundamental human rights is in their individual and collective interest." That principle and commitment support the conclusion that human-rights norms must bind the individual men and women responsible for committing humanity's most terrible crimes, not just nation-states in their interactions with one another.

It does not follow, however, that current principles of international law extend liability – civil or criminal – for human-rights violations to corporations or other artificial entities. This is confirmed by the fact that the charters of respective international criminal tribunals often exclude corporations from their jurisdictional reach.

The Charter for the Nuremberg Tribunal, created by the Allies after World War II, provided that the Tribunal had jurisdiction over natural persons only. Later, a United States Military Tribunal prosecuted 24 executives of the German corporation IG Farben. Among other crimes, Farben's employees had operated a slave-labor camp at Auschwitz. Although the Military Tribunal "used the term 'Farben' as descriptive of the instrumentality of cohesion in the name of which" the crimes were committed, the Tribunal noted that "corporations act through individuals." Farben itself was not held liable.

The jurisdictional reach of more recent international tribunals also has been limited to "natural persons." See Statute of the International Criminal Tribunal for the Former Yugoslavia; Statute of the International Tribunal for Rwanda. The Rome Statute of the International Criminal Court, for example, limits that tribunal's jurisdiction to "natural persons." The drafters of the Rome Statute considered, but rejected, a proposal to give the International Criminal Court jurisdiction over corporations. The international community's conscious decision to limit the authority of these international tribunals to natural persons counsels against a broad holding that there is a specific, universal, and obligatory norm of corporate liability under currently prevailing international law.

In light of the sources just discussed, the sources petitioners rely on to support their contention that liability for corporations is well established as a matter of international law lend weak support to their position.

It must be remembered that international law is distinct from domestic law in its domain as well as its objectives. International human-rights norms prohibit acts repugnant to all civilized peoples – crimes like genocide, torture, and slavery, that make their perpetrators "enem[ies] of all mankind." In the American legal system, of course, corporations are often subject to liability for the conduct of their human employees, and so it may seem necessary and natural that corporate entities are liable for violations of international law under the ATS. It is true, furthermore, that the enormity of the offenses that can be committed against persons in violation of international human-rights protections can be cited to show that corporations should be subject to liability for the crimes of their human agents.

But the international community has not yet taken that step, at least in the specific, universal, and obligatory manner required by *Sosa*. Indeed, there is precedent to the contrary in the statement during the Nuremberg proceedings that "[c]rimes against international law are committed by men, not by abstract entities, and only by punishing individuals who commit such crimes can the provisions of international law be enforced."

In any event, the Court need not resolve the questions whether corporate liability is a question that is governed by international law, or, if so, whether international law imposes liability on corporations. There is at least sufficient doubt on the point to turn to *Sosa*'s second question – whether the Judiciary must defer to Congress, allowing it to determine in the first instance whether that universal norm has been recognized and, if so, whether it is prudent and necessary to direct its enforcement in suits under the ATS.

*Sosa* is consistent with this Court's general reluctance to extend judicially created private rights of action. That is because "the Legislature is in the better position to consider if the public interest would be served by imposing a new substantive legal liability."

The ATS was intended to promote harmony in international relations by ensuring foreign plaintiffs a remedy for international-law violations in circumstances where the absence of such a remedy might provoke foreign nations to hold the United States accountable. But here, and in similar cases, the opposite is occurring.

Petitioners are foreign nationals seeking hundreds of millions of dollars in damages from a major Jordanian financial institution for injuries suffered in attacks by foreign terrorists in the Middle East. The only alleged connections to the United States are the CHIPS transactions in Arab Bank's New York branch and a brief allegation regarding a charity in Texas. At a minimum, the relatively minor connection between the terrorist attacks at issue in this case and the alleged conduct in the United States well illustrates the perils of extending the scope of ATS liability to foreign multinational corporations like Arab Bank. For 13 years, this litigation has "caused significant diplomatic tensions" with Jordan, a critical ally in one of the world's most sensitive regions. Jordan considers the instant litigation to be a "grave affront" to its sovereignty.

Petitioners insist that whatever the faults of this litigation – for example, its tenuous connections to the United States and the prolonged diplomatic disruptions it has caused – the fact that Arab Bank is a foreign corporate entity, as distinct from a natural person, is not one of them. That misses the point. As demonstrated by this litigation, foreign corporate defendants create unique problems. And courts are not well suited to make the required policy judgments that are implicated by corporate liability in cases like this one. If, in light of all the concerns that must be weighed before imposing liability on foreign corporations via ATS suits, the Court were to hold that it has the discretion to make that determination, then the cautionary language of *Sosa* would be little more than empty rhetoric. Accordingly, the Court holds that foreign corporations may not be defendants in suits brought under the ATS.

JUSTICE SOTOMAYOR, WITH WHOM JUSTICE GINSBURG, JUSTICE BREYER,
AND JUSTICE KAGAN JOIN, DISSENTING

The Court today holds that the Alien Tort Statute (ATS), 28 U. S. C. §1350, categorically forecloses foreign corporate liability. In so doing, it absolves corporations from responsibility under the ATS for conscience-shocking behavior. I disagree both with the Court's conclusion and its analytic approach. The text, history, and purpose of the ATS, as well as the long and consistent history of corporate liability in tort, confirm that tort claims for law-of-nations violations may be brought against corporations under the ATS. Nothing about the corporate form in itself raises foreign-policy concerns that require the Court, as a matter of common-law discretion, to immunize all foreign corporations from liability under the ATS, regardless of the specific law-of-nations violations alleged. I respectfully dissent.

The plurality assumes without deciding that whether corporations can be permissible defendants under the ATS turns on the first step of the two-part inquiry set out in *Sosa* v. *Alvarez-Machain*, 542 U. S. 692 (2004). But by asking whether there is "a specific, universal, and obligatory norm of liability for corporations" in international law, the plurality fundamentally misconceives how international law works and so misapplies the first step of *Sosa*.

*Sosa* does not . . . demand that there be sufficient international consensus with regard to the mechanisms of enforcing these norms, for enforcement is not a question with which customary international law is concerned. Although international law determines what substantive conduct violates the law of nations, it leaves the specific rules of how to enforce international-law norms and remedy their violation to states, which may act to impose liability collectively through treaties or independently via their domestic legal systems.

The international-law norm against genocide, for example, imposes obligations on all actors. Acts of genocide thus violate the norm irrespective of whether they are committed privately or in concert with the state. In contrast, other norms, like the prohibition on torture, require state action. Conduct thus qualifies as torture and violates the norm only when done "by or at the instigation of or with the consent or acquiescence of a public official or other person acting in an official capacity."

Again, the question of who must undertake the prohibited conduct for there to be a violation of an international-law norm is one of international law, but how a particular actor is held liable for a given law-of-nations violation generally is a question of enforcement left up to individual states. Sometimes, states act collectively and establish international tribunals to punish certain international-law violations. Each such tribunal is individually negotiated, and the limitations placed on its jurisdiction are typically driven by strategic considerations and resource constraints.

For example, the Allies elected not to prosecute corporations at Nuremberg because of pragmatic factors. More recently, the delegations that negotiated the Rome Statute of the International Criminal Court in the 1990's elected not to extend that tribunal's jurisdiction to corporations in part because states had varying domestic practices as to whether and how to impose criminal liability on corporations. Ultimately, the evidence on which the plurality relies does not prove that international law distinguishes between corporations and natural persons as a categorical matter. To the contrary, it proves only that states' collective efforts to enforce various international-law norms have, to date, often focused on natural rather than corporate defendants.

In fact, careful review of states' collective and individual enforcement efforts makes clear that corporations are subject to certain obligations under international law. For instance, the United States Military Tribunal that prosecuted several corporate executives of IG Farben declared that corporations could violate international law.

In addition, various international agreements require signatory states to impose liability on corporations for certain conduct. Of particular relevance here, the International Convention for the Suppression of the Financing of Terrorism provides: "Any person commits an offence within the meaning of this Convention if that person by any means, directly or indirectly, unlawfully and wilfully, provides or collects funds with the intention that they should be used or in the knowledge that they are to be used, in full or in part, in order to carry out" an act of terrorism.

The plurality dismisses the relevance of this Convention because it does not require states parties to hold corporations liable in common-law tort actions, but rather permits them to "fulfill their obligations . . . by adopting detailed regulatory regimes governing financial institutions." That critique misses the point. The significance of the Convention is that the international community agreed that financing terrorism is unacceptable conduct and that such conduct violates the Convention when undertaken by corporations. Finally, a number of states, acting individually, have imposed criminal and civil liability on corporations for law-of-nations violations through their domestic legal systems.

Instead of asking whether there exists a specific, universal, and obligatory norm of corporate liability under international law, the relevant inquiry in response to the question presented here is whether there is any reason – under either international law or our domestic law – to distinguish between a corporation and a natural person who is alleged to have violated the law of nations under the ATS. As explained above, international law provides no such reason. Nor does domestic law. The text, history, and purpose of the ATS plainly support the conclusion that corporations may be held liable.

Moreover, our Nation has an interest not only in providing a remedy when our own citizens commit law of nations violations, but also in preventing our Nation from serving as a safe harbor for today's pirates. To that end, Congress has ratified treaties requiring the United States "to punish or extradite offenders, even when the offense was not committed . . . by a national." see Torture Convention, Arts. 5, 7; Convention on the Prevention and Punishment of Crimes Against Internationally Protected Persons, Including Diplomatic Agents; Convention for the Suppression of Unlawful Acts Against the Safety of Civil Aviation; Convention for the Suppression of Unlawful Seizure of Aircraft; Geneva Convention Relative to the Treatment of Prisoners of War.

At its second step, Sosa cautions that courts should consider whether permitting a case to proceed is an appropriate exercise of judicial discretion in light of potential foreign-policy implications. The plurality only assumes without deciding that international law does not impose liability on corporations, so it necessarily proceeds to Sosa's second step. Here, too, its analysis is flawed.

Nothing about the corporate form in itself justifies categorically foreclosing corporate liability in all ATS actions. Each source of diplomatic friction that respondent Arab Bank and the plurality identify can be addressed with a tool more tailored to the source of the problem than a blanket ban on corporate liability.

Arab Bank contends that foreign citizens should not be able "to sue a Jordanian corporation in New York for events taking place in the Middle East." The heart of that qualm was already addressed in Kiobel, which held that the presumption against extraterritoriality applies to the ATS. Only where the claims "touch and concern the territory of the United States . . . with sufficient force" can the presumption be displaced. "[M]ere corporate presence" does not suffice. Thus, contrary to the majority's contention, "the relatively minor connection between the terrorist attacks at issue in this case and the alleged conduct in the United States" does not "well illustrat[e] the perils of extending the scope of ATS liability to foreign multinational corporations," but merely illustrates the risks of extending the scope of ATS liability extraterritorially absent sufficient connection to the United States.

Finally, the plurality offers a set of "[o]ther considerations relevant to the exercise of judicial discretion" that it concludes "counsel against allowing liability under the ATS for foreign corporations." None is persuasive.

First, the plurality asserts that "[i]t has not been shown that corporate liability under the ATS is essential to serve the goals of the statute" because "the ATS will seldom be the only way for plaintiffs to hold the perpetrators liable," and because "plaintiffs still can sue the individual corporate employees responsible for a violation of international law under the ATS." This Court has never previously required that, to maintain an ATS action, a plaintiff must show that the ATS is the exclusive means by which to hold the alleged perpetrator liable and that no relief can be had from other parties. Such requirements extend far beyond the inquiry *Sosa* contemplated and are without any basis in the statutory text.

Moreover, even if there are other grounds on which a suit alleging conduct constituting a law-of-nations violation can be brought, such as a state-law tort claim, the First Congress created the ATS because it wanted foreign plaintiffs to be able to bring their claims in federal court and sue for law-of-nations violations. A suit for state-law battery, even if based on the same alleged conduct, is not the equivalent of a federal suit for torture; the latter contributes to the uptake of international human rights norms, and the former does not.

Furthermore, holding corporations accountable for violating the human rights of foreign citizens when those violations touch and concern the United States may well be necessary to avoid the international tension with which the First Congress was concerned. Would the diplomatic strife that followed really have been any less charged if a corporation had sent its agent to accost the Secretary? Or, consider piracy. If a corporation owned a fleet of vessels and directed them to seize other ships in U. S. waters, there no doubt would be calls to hold the corporation to account. Finally, take, for example, a corporation posing as a job-placement agency that actually traffics in persons, forcibly transporting foreign nationals to the United States for exploitation and profiting from their abuse. Not only are the individual employees of that business less likely to be able fully to compensate successful ATS plaintiffs, but holding only individual employees liable does not impose accountability for the institution-wide disregard for human rights. Absent a corporate sanction, that harm will persist unremedied. Immunizing the corporation from suit under the ATS merely because it is a corporation, even though the violations stemmed directly from corporate policy and practice, might cause serious diplomatic friction.

Second, the plurality expresses concern that if foreign corporations are subject to liability under the ATS, other nations could hale American corporations into court and subject them "to an immediate, constant risk of claims seeking to impose massive liability for the alleged conduct of their employees and subsidiaries around the world," a prospect that will deter American corporations from investing in developing economies. The plurality offers no empirical evidence to support these alarmist conjectures, which is especially telling given that plaintiffs have been filing ATS suits against foreign corporations in United States courts for years.

In categorically barring all suits against foreign corporations under the ATS, the Court ensures that foreign corporations – entities capable of wrongdoing under our domestic law – remain immune from liability for human rights abuses, however egregious they may be.

Corporations can be and often are a force for innovation and growth. Many of their contributions to society should be celebrated. But the unique power that corporations wield can be used both for good and for bad. Just as corporations can increase the capacity for production, so, too, some can increase the capacity for suffering. Consider the genocide that took upwards of 800,000 lives in Rwanda in 1994, which was fueled by incendiary rhetoric delivered via a private radio station, the Radio Télévision Libre des Mille Collines (RTLM). Men spoke the hateful words, but the RTLM made their widespread influence possible.

There can be, and sometimes is, a profit motive for these types of abuses. Although the market does not price all externalities, the law does. We recognize as much when

we permit a civil suit to proceed against a paint company that long knew its product contained lead yet continued to sell it to families, or against an oil company that
failed to undertake the requisite safety checks on a pipeline that subsequently burst.
There is no reason why a different approach should obtain in the human rights context.
Immunizing corporations that violate human rights from liability under the ATS undermines the system of accountability for law-of-nations violations that the First Congress
endeavored to impose. It allows these entities to take advantage of the significant benefits of the corporate form and enjoy fundamental rights.

I respectfully dissent.

---

## Notes and Comments:

1. Which opinion do you agree with? Would there be the same result for a suit
   brought against a U.S.-based corporation?
2. What are the prospects that the U.S. Congress will pass a law allowing suits
   against foreign corporations?

The next two cases take up the issue of the relationship between a parent corporation and its subsidiaries. Which result do you agree with – and why?

---

## *Lubbe and Others,* UK House of Lords, 2000

### LORD BINGHAM OF CORNHILL

My Lords,
    The central issue between the plaintiffs and the defendant in these interlocutory
appeals is whether proceedings brought by the plaintiffs against the defendant should
be tried in this country or in South Africa.
    There are at present over 3,000 plaintiffs. All the plaintiffs claim damages for per-
sonal injuries (and in some cases death) allegedly suffered as the result of exposure to
asbestos and its related products in South Africa. In some cases the exposure is said to
have occurred in the course of the plaintiff's employment, in others as a result of living
in a contaminated area. The exposure is said to have taken place in different places in
South Africa and over varying, but sometimes lengthy, periods of time, ending for claim
purposes in 1979. One of the plaintiffs (Mrs. Pauline Nel, suing as personal representative of her deceased husband) is a British citizen resident in England. All the others are
South African citizens resident in South Africa. Most of the plaintiffs are black and of
modest means. Instructions to sue have been given to English solicitors by more than
800 additional claimants.

*[The defendant is a limited public company incorporated in England and has been
doing business in South Africa and in other countries since 1893.]*

Some of the claims made in these actions date back to times when the defendant was
itself operating in Northern Cape Province. But the central thrust of the claims made by
each of the plaintiffs is not against the defendant as the employer of that plaintiff or
as the occupier of the factory where that plaintiff worked, or as the immediate source

of the contamination in the area where that plaintiff lived. Rather, the claim is made against the defendant as a parent company which, knowing (so it is said) that exposure to asbestos was gravely injurious to health, failed to take proper steps to ensure that proper working practices were followed and proper safety precautions observed throughout the group. In this way, it is alleged, the defendant breached a duty of care which it owed to those working for its subsidiaries or living in the area of their operations (with the result that the plaintiffs thereby suffered personal injury and loss). Some 360 claims are made by personal representatives of deceased victims. As reformulated during the first Court of Appeal hearing the main issue raised by the plaintiffs' claim was put in this way:

> Whether a parent company which is proved to exercise de facto control over the operations of a (foreign) subsidiary and which knows, through its directors, that those operations involve risks to the health of workers employed by the subsidiary and/or persons in the vicinity of its factory or other business premises, owes a duty of care to those workers and/or other persons in relation to the control which it exercises over and the advice which it gives to the subsidiary company?

The issues in the present cases fall into two segments. The first segment concerns the responsibility of the defendant as a parent company for ensuring the observance of proper standards of health and safety by its overseas subsidiaries. Resolution of this issue will be likely to involve an inquiry into what part the defendant played in controlling the operations of the group, what its directors and employees knew or ought to have known, what action was taken and not taken, whether the defendant owed a duty of care to employees of group companies overseas and whether, if so, that duty was broken. Much of the evidence material to this inquiry would, in the ordinary way, be documentary and much of it would be found in the offices of the parent company, including minutes of meetings, reports by directors and employees on visits overseas and correspondence.

The second segment of the cases involves the personal injury issues relevant to each individual: diagnosis, prognosis, causation (including the contribution made to a plaintiff's condition by any sources of contamination for which the defendant was not responsible) and special damage. Investigation of these issues would necessarily involve the evidence and medical examination of each plaintiff and an inquiry into the conditions in which that plaintiff worked or lived and the period for which he did so. Where the claim is made on behalf of a deceased person the inquiry would be essentially the same, although probably more difficult.

The emergence of over 3,000 new plaintiffs following the decision of the first Court of Appeal had an obvious and significant effect on the balance of the proceedings. While the parent company responsibility issue remained very much what it had always been, the personal injury issues assumed very much greater significance. To investigate, prepare and resolve these issues, in relation to each of the plaintiffs, would plainly involve a careful, detailed and cumbersome factual inquiry and, at least potentially, a very large body of expert evidence.

---

## Note and Comments:

1. The court concluded that South Africa, and not the United Kingdom, was the appropriate forum. Do you agree with this result? Would it matter how much control the parent corporation exercised over various subsidiaries?

A different result was reached in a case brought by a group of Zambians against the British parent corporation Vedata Resources for the environmental harms caused by Konkola Copper Mines, a subsidiary of Vedata Resources. In upholding the High Court ruling, the Supreme Court held that Vedata Resources had exercised enough control over Konkola's operations that there was a real legal issue to be resolved in the United Kingdom. In addition, the Court questioned whether the claimants would be able to sufficiently proceed with the case if brought in Zambia. *Vedanta Resources v. Lungowe and Others* [2019] UKSC 20.

---

## *Choc. v. Hudbay Minerals,* Superior Court of Justice – Ontario, 2013 ONSC 1414

The plaintiffs are indigenous Mayan Q'eqchi' from El Estor, Guatemala. They bring three related actions against Canadian mining company, Hudbay Minerals, and its wholly-controlled subsidiaries. They allege that security personnel working for Hudbay's subsidiaries, who were allegedly under the control and supervision of Hudbay, the parent company, committed human rights abuses. The allegations of abuse include a shooting, a killing and gang-rapes committed in the vicinity of the former Fenix mining project, a proposed open-pit nickel mining operation located in eastern Guatemala.

### THE DEFENDANTS

Hudbay Minerals is a Canadian mining company headquartered in Toronto, incorporated under the Canadian Business Corporations Act, R.S.C. 1985, c. C-44, with mining properties in South and North America. During the times relevant to the Choc and Chub actions, Hudbay Minerals owned the Fenix mining project through CGN.

CGN owned and operated the Fenix mining project in El Estor, Guatemala. At all material times, CGN was a wholly-controlled and 98.2% owned subsidiary of Hudbay Minerals. In August of 2011, Hudbay Minerals sold CGN and the Fenix project. However, it agreed, as part of the purchase and sale agreement, to remain responsible for and retain control over the conduct of any litigation against CGN regarding the events of September 27, 2009, regardless of where it occurs. CGN, by agreement, is required to cooperate with Hudbay Minerals, including by making employees available and providing records and information to Hudbay as required. In other words, Hudbay, as a matter of contract, controls the conduct of any litigation against CGN regarding the death of Adolfo Ich.

### THE CONTESTED LANDS

The factual context from which these actions arise, as set forth in the pleadings, is as follows. Several indigenous Mayan Q'eqchi' farming communities were located on a portion of the Fenix property. At all material times, the defendants maintained that they had a valid legal right to this land, while the Mayan communities claimed that the Mayan Q'eqchi' were the rightful owners of the lands, which they considered to be their ancestral homeland. The plaintiffs allege in their pleadings that any claim to ownership by the defendants is illegitimate, as rights to those lands were first granted to the defendants by a dictatorial military government during the Guatemalan Civil War, during the time when the Mayan Q'eqchi' were being massacred and driven off their lands.

On February 8, 2011, the Constitutional Court of Guatemala, the highest court in the country, ruled that Mayan Q'eqchi' communities had valid legal rights to the contested lands and ordered the government of Guatemala to formally recognize the community's collective property rights.

### THE POSITION OF THE DEFENDANTS/MOVING PARTIES

The defendants make several overarching arguments. Firstly, they argue that the plaintiffs are implicitly asking the Court to ignore the separate corporate personalities of Hudbay, HMI and CGN. Secondly, they argue that the negligence claim is an attempt to use the common law to impose absolute supervisory liability on parent and grand-parent companies regarding the operations of their subsidiaries in foreign countries. Thirdly, they argue that even if there is a duty of care owed, the alleged conduct was not foreseeable based on the facts as pleaded in the Statement of Claim.

On the issue of negligence, the defendants submit that there is no recognized duty of care owed by a parent company to ensure that the commercial activities carried on by its subsidiary in a foreign country are conducted in a manner designed to protect those people with whom the subsidiary interacts. The defendants further submit that there is no foreseeability or proximity to establish a novel duty of care, and that policy considerations militate against recognizing any such duty.

On the issue of separate legal personality, the defendants argue that the law is clear that one corporation cannot be responsible for the actions of another and, particularly, that a parent corporation cannot be responsible for the actions of its subsidiary. They submit that the narrow exceptions under which the corporate veil may be pierced have not been met. They argue that the plaintiffs are implicitly requesting that the Court ignore the separate corporate identity of Hudbay's subsidiary, CGN, and impose absolute supervisory liability on the parent company. They argue that permitting these actions to proceed would result in the overturn of one hundred years of corporate law.

The plaintiffs argue that the pleadings are not based primarily on the theories of piercing the corporate veil or vicarious liability, although those are also pled in the Choc action. Rather, the pleadings rely predominantly on Hudbay's direct liability for actions leading to the human rights abuses, shootings, killing and gang rapes alleged in the Statements of Claim.

The plaintiffs submit that the primary cause of action in all three cases is negligence based on the direct actions and omissions of Hudbay, and not on share ownership or vicarious liability of the parent corporation for the actions of its subsidiary, as argued by the defendants. This direct negligence includes Hudbay/Skye's wrongdoing in its on-the-ground management of the Fenix project, and in particular, its negligent management of the Fenix security personnel who allegedly shot the plaintiffs in the Choc and Chub actions and raped the plaintiffs in the Caal action.

The Statements of Claim in the three cases include detailed allegations regarding the alleged direct negligence of Hudbay. In all three actions, the plaintiffs plead that:

> Hudbay/Skye voluntarily retained considerable direct responsibility and control over key aspects of on-the-ground operations at the Fenix mining project, including control and responsibility over security policy and security personnel, as well as the corporate response to ongoing land conflicts with local Mayan communities;
>
> Hudbay/Skye retained ultimate control over the forced removal of Mayan subsistence farming villages, including those in which the plaintiffs resided;

Hudbay/Skye continually acknowledged direct responsibility for security practices at the Fenix project with public statements committing to the implementation of detailed standards of conduct applicable to security personnel. These statements included a commitment to adhere to Guatemalan and international law and to the Voluntary Principles on Security and Human Rights. It further committed to extensive training of security personnel on the Fenix site; and

Hudbay/Skye created a high risk of violence by retaining undertrained and inadequately supervised security personnel. It failed to implement and enforce standards of conduct with respect to those security personnel. Hudbay/Skye knew that the Fenix security personnel were armed with unlicensed and illegal weapons, and were providing security services without authorization from the Guatemalan state.

The plaintiffs plead that Hudbay/Skye's detailed on-the-ground management and control was achieved through managers employed by Hudbay/Skye. These managers were responsible for the day-to-day operation and management of the Fenix project in Guatemala.

### THE SUBMISSIONS OF AMNESTY INTERNATIONAL CANADA

Pursuant to my Order of February 14, 2013, Amnesty made submissions with respect to international norms, authorities and standards which, it argued, support the view that a duty of care may exist in circumstances where a parent company's subsidiary is alleged to be involved in gross human rights abuses. Amnesty submits that transnational corporations can owe a duty of care to those who may be harmed by the activities of subsidiaries, particularly where the business is operating in conflict-affected or high-risk areas, such as Guatemala. Amnesty also argued that the transnational character of the dispute should not exempt the defendants from the application of established principles of tort law.

The human rights implications of transnational corporate activity have received the attention of numerous international and intergovernmental organizations over the past few decades and have resulted in a range of voluntary codes of conduct developed in conjunction with multinational corporations. Such codes of conduct include the Voluntary Principles on Security and Human Rights, which were established in 2000 and elaborate norms for corporate conduct in the extractive industry when engaging public and private security forces to protect business interests in areas with a potential for violence or conflict. The Voluntary Principles call for a risk assessment of the human rights impacts of security forces and require corporations to screen and train security personnel and establish clear parameters for their use of force. Hudbay stated that this code guided their corporate conduct.

Amnesty submits that the existence of these international norms and standards of conduct demonstrate the recognition by corporations in the extractive industries of the risks of security forces, both public and private, violating human rights and otherwise causing injury to members of local communities in high risk areas.

Amnesty further argues, as do the plaintiffs, that the concept of direct parent liability is not new to tort law, and Canadian courts have recognized that a parent company may be directly liable for its own negligent conduct with respect to managing or failing to properly manage the actions of its subsidiaries.

Amnesty argues, based on the international norms and standards and on the foregoing authorities, that a reasonable cause of action may be found to exist where a parent company is alleged to have knowledge of risks to others posed by a subsidiary and has a degree of control over its response to those risks. It submits that the transnational character of the dispute should have no bearing on the application of these well-established principles of law.

Finally, Amnesty makes submissions with respect to policy reasons for recognizing a duty of care in these circumstances. It states that the essence of the defendants'
argument on this issue is that the plaintiffs are proposing a radical departure in the
common law and that the issue of accountability for corporate human rights abuses
abroad should be left to legislative reform. Amnesty submits that cases involving parent corporation liability have been upheld in the U.K. courts, including the House of
Lords; that issues of access to justice must be considered; and that, in order to preserve
Canada's reputation, Canadian society has a strong interest in ensuring that Canadian
corporations respect human rights, wherever they may operate and whatever ownership and business structure they may put in place to advance their operations in foreign
countries.

The plaintiffs argue that a parent corporation can be liable in negligence for its own
actions and omissions in another country. They argue that the actions involve a straightforward application of established and well-recognized tort law. Further, they argue
that a parent corporation can be found jointly and severally liable with the subsidiary
where the direct actions of each result in damage.

Similarly, in this case, the plaintiffs are not claiming that Hudbay is responsible for
the torts of the security personnel, but that Hudbay was, itself, negligent in failing to
prevent the harms that they committed. As in any ordinary direct negligence action, it
must be considered whether the pleadings disclose a claim that Hudbay owed a duty of
care to the plaintiffs.

In the circumstances of this case and based on the foregoing analysis and caselaw, it
cannot be said that the Statements of Claim plainly and obviously disclose no cause of
action. A novel claim of negligence should only be struck at the pleadings stage where
it is clearly unsustainable. In this case, it cannot be said that it is clearly unsustainable or
untenable. The plaintiffs have properly pleaded the elements necessary to recognize a
novel duty of care. The plaintiffs have also pleaded that the defendants breached the
duty of care and that the breach caused the plaintiffs' losses. Accordingly, I find that
it is not plain and obvious that the three Statements of Claim disclose no reasonable
cause of action in negligence. The defendants' motion to strike the plaintiffs' actions
is dismissed.

---

## Notes and Comments:

1. Under what circumstances – if any – should a parent corporation be responsible for acts of commission or omission by its subsidiaries?

2. Should multinational corporations have human rights obligations – or
should this be limited to states? According to the *UN Guiding Principles
on Business and Human Rights* (OHCR 2011) – better known as the Ruggie Principles – corporations have a responsibility to respect human rights.
What, exactly, does this mean?

3. At the time of this writing, there are ongoing efforts underway to draft a
legally binding treaty on business and human rights. In your view, what
should this look like?

## Box 8.1: "Home State" Responsibility?

Does a "home state" have a legal responsibility to ensure that multinational corporations headquartered in that country do not harm individuals in other lands? According to the Ruggie Principles, the home state *may* so regulate, but it is not required by international law to do so.

The *Maastricht Principles on Extraterritorial Obligations of States in the Area of Economic, Social and Cultural Rights* (de Schutter et al. 2012) provide a different interpretation of international law. In fact, Article 24 of the Maastricht ETO Principles places such a burden not only on the "home" state, but any state which is in a position to regulate the harmful practices of private actors, including MNCs. Article 24 reads in part:

> All States must take necessary measures to ensure that non-State actors which they are in a position to regulate . . . such as private individuals and organisations, and transnational corporations and other business enterprises, do not nullify or impair the enjoyment of economic, social and cultural rights.

This same issue has been the subject of a fair amount of parliamentary debate in Canada (Seck 2008). The precipitating event centered around the mining operations of TVI Pacific, a Canadian-based corporation, that has a mining operation in the Siocon Zamboanga del Norte municipality in the Philippines. Local residents claim that TVI Pacific's operations have caused widespread levels of environmental degradation. In November 2004, a delegation from this community traveled to Canada and met with a Parliamentary subcommittee, which issued a report that concluded:

> Mining activities in some developing countries have had adverse effects on local communities, especially where regulations governing the mining sector and its impact on the economic and social wellbeing of employees and local residents, as well as on the environment, are weak or non-existent, or where they are not enforced.

Noting that Canada does not have any legislation to help ensure that Canadian mining companies in developing countries conform to human rights standards, the Subcommittee recommended that the government put in place stronger incentives to encourage compliance with international human rights standards as well as stronger monitoring and complaint mechanisms. The report also called for the establishment of "clear legal norms" to ensure that Canadian corporations and residents were held accountable for environmental and human rights violations. However, in October 2005, the government tabled a response that rejected many of the recommendations in the SCFAIT Report. According to this government report, the international community is still in the early stages of defining and measuring corporate social responsibility, especially in terms of human rights standards. Moreover, the recommendation to establish clear legal norms to hold Canadian corporations accountable was rejected, with a commitment only to examining the "best practices"

*(Continued)*

## Box 8.1: Continued

of states. The government report noted that Canadian law does not generally provide for extraterritorial application, and to do so would raise several problems including "conflict with the sovereignty of foreign states; conflicts where states have legislation that differs from that of Canada; and difficulties with Canadian official taking enforcement action in foreign states."

In sum, the Canadian government refuses to regulate the extraterritorial activities of Canadian mining corporations, even in the face of the lack of regulation and protection by the "host" state and even after being presented with first-hand accounts of the violations carried out by TVI Pacific and other Canadian mining companies. In that way, Canada – like other industrial countries – has adopted a narrow interpretation of state responsibility under international human rights law.

## References

### Books and Articles

Seth Davis and Christopher A. Whytock, "State Remedies for Human Rights," *Boston University Law Review* 98: 397–484 (2018)

Olivier de Schutter et al., "Commentary to the Maastricht Principles on Extraterritorial Obligations of States in the Area of Economic, Social and Cultural Rights," *Human Rights Quarterly* 34: 1084–169 (2012)

Sara Seck, "Home State Responsibility and Local Communities: The Case of Global Mining," *Yale Human Rights and Development Law Journal* 11: 177–206 (2008)

Ralph Steinhardt, "Determining Which Human Rights Claims 'Touch and Concern' the United States: Justice Kennedy's 'Filartiga'," *Notre Dame Law Review* 89: 1695–717 (2014)

### U.N. Report

Office of the High Commissioner for Human Rights, *UN Guiding Principles on Business and Human Rights: Implementing the United Nations "Protect, Respect and Remedy" Framework* (2011)

### Cases

*Choc. v. Hudbay Minerals Inc.*, Superior Court of Justice–Ontario, 2013 ONSC 1414 (2013)

*Filartiga v. Pena-Irala*, 630 F. 2d 876 (2d. Cir. 1980)

*Jesner v. Arab Bank*, 584 U.S. ___ (2018)

*Kiobel v. Royal Dutch Shell*, 569 U.S. 108 (2013)

*Lubbe and Others*, UK House of Lords (2000)
*Sosa v. Alvarez-Machain*, 542 U.S. 692 (2004)
*Vedanta Resources v. Lungowe and Others* [2019] UKSC 20

### Domestic Law

Alien Tort Statute (ATS), 28 U.S.C. Sec. 1350 (U.S.)

# 9
# State Responsibility and Jurisdictional Limitations

In the previous chapter we examined the issue of individual accountability for violations of humanitarian law or human rights standards. In this chapter we turn our attention to two matters. The first is the issue of state responsibility. Or to phrase this even more concretely: when are states responsible for violations of international law standards? In most instances, this will not be an issue. A state whose agents torture a political dissident will be violating various provisions of international human rights law. However, where state responsibility seems more problematic is when states act outside their own borders, and especially when they act by and through outside actors.

This is exactly the situation involved in extraordinary rendition, which we discussed in Chapter 3. In nearly all extraordinary rendition cases, the kidnapping of a suspected terrorist occurs in one country, but this individual is then transported to some other state (or many different states) during which time he is imprisoned and tortured. Who bears responsibility in these situations? There is every reason to believe that the United States was the moving force behind every instance of extraordinary rendition and in some cases it has been alleged that American security personnel were present during interrogation sessions. Yet, notwithstanding the deep involvement of the U.S., it is not clear whether international law would assign "responsibility" to the United States. The reason for this is that, with almost no exception, the kidnappings and torture occurred outside the territorial boundaries of the U.S. and the acts of torture were generally (but not always) carried out by foreign nationals. One might even go so far as to say that extraordinary rendition was designed in such a way so as to avoid state responsibility – or at least U.S. responsibility.

In order to get a better sense of state responsibility, consider the following scenario involving State A, which routinely tortures its own political dissidents, and the actions of other states. State B provides the torture equipment used by State A; State C trains agents of State A in the "art" of torture; and finally, agents of State D are present during "interrogation" sessions in State A and even provide intelligence to those conducting these interrogations. Are States B, C, and D responsible for violating the prohibition against torture?

The second issue we take up in this chapter involves jurisdictional limitations. To be clear, state responsibility is not the same as the issue of jurisdiction, although the two are oftentimes conflated. As we will see later in this chapter, there will be instances where state responsibility has been clearly established in the sense that a state has acted in violation of some human rights standard. However, the question is whether the victims of these violations are within the "jurisdiction" of the offending state for purposes of a particular treaty, the European Convention in the cases we analyze.

## Direct Actions

We begin with a ruling by the U.N. Human Rights Committee that involves direct actions by one state but acting within the territorial borders of another country. In this case, Uruguayan agents had kidnapped and detained one of the country's dissidents – but had done so in Argentina, not Uruguay. The question addressed by the HRC is whether Uruguay had acted in violation of the International Covenant on Civil and Political Rights. Note that the ICCPR, like most other international human rights treaties, has language specifying "territory" and/or "jurisdiction." Article 2 provides:

> Each State Party to the present Covenant undertakes to respect and to ensure to all individuals within its *territory* and subject to its *jurisdiction* the rights recognized in the present Covenant, without distinction of any kind, such as race, colour, sex, language, religion, political or other opinion, national or social origin, property, birth or other status.
>
> (emphases supplied)

How is Article 2 to be interpreted? Does this language mean that a state only has responsibilities to individuals who are within its territorial borders (and who are within its jurisdiction) – but that it has no obligations to those outside its borders (or at least those who are not citizens of that state)? That, essentially, is the argument made by Uruguay in the following case.

## Sergio Euben Lopez Burgos v. Uruguay, Communication No. R.12/52, U.N. Doc. Supp. No. 40 (A/36/40) at 176 (1981), Human Rights Committee

### FACTS OF THE CASE

Delia Saldias de Lopez, the author of the communication (referred to as the author), is a political refugee of Uruguayan nationality residing in Austria. She submits the communication on behalf of her husband, Sergio Ruben Lopez Burgos, a worker and trade-union leader in Uruguay.

The author states that mainly because of the alleged victim's active participation in the trade union movement, he was subjected to various forms of harassment by the authorities from the beginning of his trade union involvement. Thus, he was arrested in December 1974 and held without charges for four months. In May 1975, shortly after his release and while still subjected to harassment by the authorities, he moved to Argentina. In September 1975 he obtained recognition as a political refugee by the Office of the United Nations High Commissioner for Refugees.

The author claims that on 13 July 1976 her husband was kidnapped in Buenos Aires by members of the "Uruguayan security and intelligence forces" who were aided by Argentine paramilitary groups, and was secretly detained in Buenos Aires for about two weeks. On 26 July 1976 Mr. Lopez Burgos, together with several other Uruguayan nationals, was illegally and clandestinely transported to Uruguay, where he was detained incommunicado by the special security forces at a secret prison for three months. During his detention of approximately four months both in Argentina and Uruguay, he was continuously subjected to physical and mental torture and other cruel, inhuman or degrading treatment.

The author asserts that her husband was subjected to torture and ill-treatment as a consequence of which he suffered a broken jawbone and perforation of the eardrums.

The author further states that her husband was transferred from the secret prison and held "at the disposition of military justice", first at a military hospital where for several months he had to undergo treatment because of the physical and mental effects of the torture applied to him prior to his "official" arrest, and subsequently at Libertad prison in San Jose. After a delay of 14 months his trial started in April 1978. At the time of writing, Mr. Lopez was still waiting for final judgement to be passed by the military court.

### THE HUMAN RIGHTS COMMITTEE OBSERVATIONS

The Human Rights Committee observes that although the arrest and initial detention and mistreatment of Lopez Burgos allegedly took place on foreign territory, the Committee is not barred either by virtue of article 1 of the Optional Protocol ("individuals subject to its jurisdiction") or by virtue of article 2 (1) of the Covenant ("individuals within its territory and subject to its jurisdiction") from considering these allegations, together with the claim of subsequent abduction into Uruguayan territory, inasmuch as these acts were perpetrated by Uruguayan agents acting on foreign soil.

The reference to 'individuals subject to its jurisdiction" does not affect the above conclusion because the reference in that article is not to the place where the violation occurred, but rather to the relationship between the individual and the State in relation to a violation of any of the rights set forth in the Covenant, wherever they occurred.

Article 2 (1) of the Covenant places an obligation upon a State party to respect and to ensure rights "to all individuals within its territory and subject to its jurisdiction", but it does not imply that the State party concerned cannot be held accountable for violations of rights under the Covenant which its agents commit upon the territory of another State, whether with the acquiescence of the Government of that State or in opposition to it. According to article 5 (1) of the Covenant:

> Nothing in the present Covenant may be interpreted as implying for any State, group or person any right to engage in any activity or perform any act aimed at the destruction of any of the rights and freedoms recognized herein or at their limitation to a greater extent than is provided for in the present Covenant.

In line with this, it would be unconscionable to so interpret the responsibility under article 2 of the Covenant as to permit a State party to perpetrate violations of the Covenant on the territory of another State, which violations it could not perpetrate on its own territory.

### INDIVIDUAL OPINION APPENDED TO THE COMMITTEE'S VIEWS AT THE REQUEST OF MR. CHRISTIAN TOMUSCHAT

I concur in the views expressed by the majority. Nonetheless, the arguments affirming the applicability of the Covenant also with regard to those events which have taken place outside Uruguay need to be clarified and expanded. Indeed, the view expressed in the decision according to which article 2 (1) of the Covenant does not imply that a State party "cannot be held accountable for violations of rights under the Covenant which its agents commit upon the territory of another State", is too broadly framed and might therefore give rise to misleading conclusions. In principle, the scope of application of the Covenant is not susceptible to being extended by reference to article 5, a provision designed to cover instances where formally rules under the Covenant seem to legitimize actions which substantially run counter to its purposes and general spirit. Thus, governments may never use the limitation clauses supplementing the protected rights and freedoms to such an extent that the very substance of those rights and freedoms would be annihilated.

Individuals are legally barred from availing themselves of the same rights and freedoms with a view to overthrowing the regime of the rule of law which constitutes the basic philosophy of the Covenant. In the present case, however, the Covenant does not even provide the pretext for a 'right' to perpetrate the criminal acts which, according to the Committee's conviction, have been perpetrated by the Uruguayan authorities. To construe the words "within its territory" pursuant to their strict literal meaning as excluding any responsibility for conduct occurring beyond the national boundaries would, however, lead to utterly absurd results.

The formula was intended to take care of objective difficulties which might impede the implementation of the Covenant in specific situations. Thus, a State party is normally unable to ensure the effective enjoyment of the rights under the Covenant to its citizens abroad, having at its disposal only the tools of diplomatic protection with their limited potential. Instances of occupation of foreign territory offer another example of situations which the drafters of the Covenant had in mind when they confined the obligation of States parties to their own territory.

All these factual patterns have in common, however, that they provide plausible grounds for denying the protection of the Covenant. It may be concluded, therefore, that it was the intention of the drafters, whose sovereign decision cannot be challenged, "to restrict the territorial scope of the Covenant in view of such situations where enforcing the Covenant would be likely to encounter exceptional obstacles. Never was it envisaged, however, to grant States parties unfettered discretionary power to carry out willful and deliberate attacks against the freedom and personal integrity against their citizens living abroad. Consequently, despite the wording of article 2 (1), the events which took place outside Uruguay come within the purview of the Covenant.

### Note and Comments:

1. In some respects, *Lopez Burgos* is an "easy" case in the sense that the kidnapping and detention were carried out by Uruguayan agents, albeit within Argentina's territorial borders. Would/should the HRC come up with the same result if agents of Argentina had carried out these same actions instead, albeit at the behest of Uruguay?

### Indirect Actions: Aiding and Assisting

*Nicaragua v. United States* is a landmark ruling handed down by the International Court of Justice in 1986. The case was referenced in Chapter 4 in the context of the prohibition against the use of force. You might recall that the ICJ ruled that through its *direct* actions, such as mining Nicaragua's harbors, the United States had violated the prohibition against the use of force under international law.

The issue we turn to now is related but different. In its attempts to remove the Sandinista-controlled government, the United States acted on its own, but it primarily relied upon various paramilitary groups, collectively known as the contras, providing these forces with massive amounts of economic, military, and political support. President Ronald Reagan went so far as to describe the contras as the "moral equivalent of the founding fathers." Notwithstanding this, the contras carried out widespread human rights violations and the question was whether the United States was "responsible" for these violations. As you will see in what follows, the ICJ ruled that under the circumstances of this case the U.S. was not responsible due to the fact that the United States had not exercised the prerequisite level of "effective control."

---

## *Nicaragua v. United States,* ICJ (1986)

It appears to be recognized by Nicaragua that, with the exception of some of the operations, operations on Nicaraguan territory were carried out by the *contras* alone, all United States trainers and advisers remaining on the other side of the frontier, or in international waters. It is however claimed by Nicaragua that the United States Government has devised the strategy and directed the tactics of the *contra* force, and provided direct combat support for its military operations.

In support of the claim that the United States devised the strategy and directed the tactics of the *contras*, counsel for Nicaragua referred to the successive stages of the United States legislative authorization for funding the *contras* and observed that every offensive by the *contras* was preceded by a new infusion of funds from the United States. From this, it is argued, the conclusion follows that the timing of each of those offensives was determined by the United States. In the sense that an offensive could not be launched until the funds were available, that may well be so; but, in the Court's view, it does not follow that each provision of funds by the United States was made in order to set in motion a particular offensive, and that that offensive was planned by the United States.

Despite the large quantity of documentary evidence and testimony which it has examined, the Court has not been able to satisfy itself that the respondent State "created" the *contra* force in Nicaragua. It seems certain that members of the former Somoza National Guard, together with civilian opponents to the Sandinista régime, withdrew from Nicaragua soon after that régime was installed in Managua, and sought to continue their struggle against it, even if in a disorganized way and with limited and ineffectual resources, before the Respondent took advantage of the existence of these opponents and incorporated this fact into its policies vis-à-vis the régime of the Applicant. Nor does the evidence warrant a finding that the United States gave "direct and critical combat support", at least if that form of words is taken to mean that this support was tantamount to direct intervention by the United States combat forces, or that all *contra* operations reflected strategy and tactics wholly devised by the United States. On the other hand, the Court holds it established that the United States authorities largely financed, trained, equipped, armed and organized the FDN.

What the Court has to determine at this point is whether or not the relationship of the *contras* to the United States Government was so much one of dependence on the one side and control on the other that it would be right to equate the *contras*, for legal purposes, with an organ of the United States Government, or as acting on behalf of that Government. Here it is relevant to note that in May 1983 the assessment of the Intelligence Committee in the Report (mentioned in the full version of the Court's opinion), was that the *contras* "constitute[d] an independent force" and that the "only element of control that could be exercised by the United States" was "cessation of aid". Paradoxically this assessment serves to underline, *a contrario*, the potential for control inherent in the degree of the *contras'* dependence on aid. Yet despite the heavy subsidies and other support provided to them by the United States, there is no clear evidence of the United States having actually exercised such a degree of control in all fields as to justify treating the *contras* as acting on its behalf.

The Court has taken the view that United States participation, even if preponderant or decisive, in the financing, organizing, training, supplying and equipping of the *contras*, the selection of its military or paramilitary targets, and the planning of the whole of its operation, is still insufficient in itself, on the basis of the evidence in the possession of the Court, for the purpose of attributing to the United States the acts committed by the *contras* in the course of their military or paramilitary operations in Nicaragua. All the forms of United States participation mentioned above, and even the general control by the respondent State over a force with a high degree of dependency on it, would not in themselves mean, without further evidence, that the United States directed or enforced the perpetration of the acts contrary to human rights and humanitarian law alleged by the applicant State. Such acts could well be committed by members of the *contras* without the control of the United States. For this conduct to give rise to legal responsibility of the United States, it would in principle have to be proved that that State had effective control of the military or paramilitary operations in the course of which the alleged violations were committed.

The Court does not consider that the assistance given by the United States to the *contras* warrants the conclusion that these forces are subject to the United States to such an extent that any acts they have committed are imputable to that State. It takes the view that the *contras* remain responsible for their acts, and that the United States is not responsible for the acts of the *contras*, but for its own conduct vis-à-vis Nicaragua, including conduct related to the acts of the *contras*. What the Court has to investigate is not the complaints relating to alleged violations of humanitarian law by the *contras*, regarded by Nicaragua as imputable to the United States, but rather unlawful acts for which the United States may be responsible directly in connection with the activities of the *contras*. The lawfulness or otherwise of such acts of the United States is a question different from the violations of humanitarian law of which the *contras* may or may not have been guilty. It is for this reason that the Court does not have to determine whether the violations of humanitarian law attributed to the *contras* were in fact committed by them. At the same time, the question whether the United States Government was, or must have been, aware at the relevant time that allegations of breaches of humanitarian law were being made against the *contras* is relevant to an assessment of the lawfulness of the action of the United States. In this respect, the material facts are primarily those connected with the issue in 1983 of a manual of psychological operations.

---

**Notes and Comments:**

1. Where does the "effective control" standard come from (Tzevelekos 2014)? Is this the standard that you would apply – why or why not? Under what conditions would you hold states responsible under international law? Would it matter what was involved? For example, would you be more (or less) willing to hold a state responsible for providing material support (arms in particular) to a government that was engaging in torture or carrying out massive levels of human rights violations – but less apt to hold a state responsible when the stakes, the human costs in particular, were a lot less evident?

2. There is little question that if a country provided massive amounts of military assistance to a domestic group that carried out gross and systematic human rights violations, this state would be responsible for committing an internationally wrongful act. Why such a difference when national borders are crossed (Raustiala 2005)?

3. Prior to *Nicaragua*, the United States had recognized the jurisdiction of the International Court of Justice as compulsory, but before the proceedings began in this case it withdrew its declaration and refused to participate. Nonetheless, the ICJ proceeded with the case. At the present time 73 states have agreed to compulsory jurisdiction – although the United States still has not.

## Overall Control: The ICTY Responds to *Nicaragua*

The *Nicaragua* ruling certainly drew its share of criticism (Gibney, Tomasevski and Vedsted-Hansen 1999). Not only was the "effective control" standard a demanding one, but the ICJ treated the issue of "state responsibility" as an either/or matter. Either a state was fully responsible – or else it was not responsible at all. The International Criminal Tribunal for the Former Yugoslavia addressed the appropriateness of this standard in *Tadic´* and offered up an "overall control" test instead.

---

### *Prosecutor v. Tadic´*, ICTY, Appeals Chamber, 15 July 1999 (Case no. IT-94–1-A)

International humanitarian law does not contain any criteria unique to this body of law for establishing when a group of individuals may be regarded as being under the control of a State, that is, as acting as de facto State officials. Consequently, it is necessary to examine the notion of control by a State over individuals, laid down in general international law, for the purpose of establishing whether those individuals may be regarded as acting as de facto State officials. This notion can be found in those general international rules on State responsibility which set out the legal criteria for attributing to a State acts performed by individuals not having the formal status of State officials.

#### THE NOTION OF CONTROL SET OUT BY THE INTERNATIONAL COURT OF JUSTICE IN NICARAGUA

In dealing with the question of the legal conditions required for individuals to be considered as acting on behalf of a State, i.e., as de facto State officials, a high degree of control has been authoritatively suggested by the International Court of Justice in Nicaragua.

The issue brought before the International Court of Justice was whether a foreign State, the United States, because of its financing, organising, training, equipping and planning of the operations of organised military and paramilitary groups of Nicaraguan rebels (the so-called contras) in Nicaragua, was responsible for violations of international humanitarian law committed by those rebels. The Court held that a high degree of control was necessary for this to be the case. It required that (i) a Party not only be in effective control of a military or paramilitary group, but that (ii) the control be exercised with respect to the specific operation in the course of which breaches may have been committed. The Court went so far as to state that in order to establish that the United States was responsible for "acts contrary to human rights and humanitarian law" allegedly perpetrated by the Nicaraguan contras, it was necessary to prove that the United States had specifically "directed or enforced" the perpetration of those acts.

As is apparent, the issue brought before the International Court of Justice revolved around State responsibility; what was at stake was not the criminal culpability of the contras for serious violations of international humanitarian law, but rather the question of whether or not the contras had acted as de facto organs of the United States on its request, thus generating the international responsibility of that State.

### THE NICARAGUA TEST WOULD NOT SEEM TO BE CONSONANT WITH THE LOGIC OF THE LAW OF STATE RESPONSIBILITY

A first ground on which the Nicaragua test as such may be held to be unconvincing is based on the very logic of the entire system of international law on State responsibility.

The principles of international law concerning the attribution to States of acts performed by private individuals are not based on rigid and uniform criteria. These principles are reflected in Article 8 of the Draft on State Responsibility adopted on first reading by the United Nations International Law Commission and, even more clearly, in the text of the same provisions as provisionally adopted in 1998 by the ILC Drafting Committee. Under this Article, if it is proved that individuals who are not regarded as organs of a State by its legislation nevertheless do in fact act on behalf of that State, their acts are attributable to the State. The rationale behind this rule is to prevent States from escaping international responsibility by having private individuals carry out tasks that may not or should not be performed by State officials, or by claiming that individuals actually participating in governmental authority are not classified as State organs under national legislation and therefore do not engage State responsibility. In other words, States are not allowed on the one hand to act de facto through individuals and on the other to disassociate themselves from such conduct when these individuals breach international law. The requirement of international law for the attribution to States of acts performed by private individuals is that the State exercises control over the individuals. The degree of control may, however, vary according to the factual circumstances of each case. The Appeals Chamber fails to see why in each and every circumstance international law should require a high threshold for the test of control. Rather, various situations may be distinguished.

One situation is the case of a private individual who is engaged by a State to perform some specific illegal acts in the territory of another State (for instance, kidnapping a State official, murdering a dignitary or a high-ranking State official, blowing up a power station or, especially in times of war, carrying out acts of sabotage). In such a case, it would be necessary to show that the State issued specific instructions concerning the commission of the breach in order to prove – if only by necessary implication – that the individual acted as a de facto State agent. Alternatively it would be necessary to show that the State has publicly given retroactive approval to the action of that individual. A generic authority over the individual would not be sufficient to engage the international responsibility of the State. A similar situation may come about when an unorganised group of individuals commits acts contrary to international law. For these acts to be attributed to the State it would seem necessary to prove not only that the State exercised some measure of authority over those individuals but also that it issued specific instructions to them concerning the performance of the acts at issue, or that it ex post facto publicly endorsed those acts.

To these situations another one may be added, which arises when a State entrusts a private individual (or group of individuals) with the specific task of performing lawful actions on its behalf, but then the individuals, in discharging that task, breach an international obligation of the State (for instance, a private detective is requested by State authorities to protect a senior foreign diplomat but he instead seriously mistreats him while performing that task). In this case, by analogy with the rules concerning State responsibility for acts of State officials acting ultra vires, it can be held that the State incurs responsibility on account of its specific request to the private individual or individuals to discharge a task on its behalf.

One should distinguish the situation of individuals acting on behalf of a State without specific instructions, from that of individuals making up an organised and hierarchically structured group, such as a military unit or, in case of war or civil strife, armed bands of irregulars or rebels. Plainly, an organised group differs from an individual in that the former normally has a structure, a chain of command and a set of rules as well as the outward symbols of authority. Normally a member of the group does not act on his own but conforms to the standards prevailing in the group and is subject to the authority of the head of the group. Consequently, for the attribution to a State of acts of these groups it is sufficient to require that the group as a whole be under the overall control of the State.

This kind of State control over a military group and the fact that the State is held responsible for acts performed by a group independently of any State instructions, or even contrary to instructions, to some extent equates the group with State organs proper. Under the rules of State responsibility, as restated in Article 10 of the Draft on State Responsibility as provisionally adopted by the International Law Commission, a State is internationally accountable for ultra vires acts or transactions of its organs. In other words it incurs responsibility even for acts committed by its officials outside their remit or contrary to its behest. The rationale behind this provision is that a State must be held accountable for acts of its organs whether or not these organs complied with instructions, if any, from the higher authorities. Generally speaking, it can be maintained that the whole body of international law on State responsibility is based on a realistic concept of accountability, which disregards legal formalities and aims at ensuring that States entrusting some functions to individuals or groups of individuals must answer for their actions, even when they act contrary to their directives.

The same logic should apply to the situation under discussion. As noted above, the situation of an organised group is different from that of a single private individual performing a specific act on behalf of a State. In the case of an organised group, the group normally engages in a series of activities. If it is under the overall control of a State, it must perforce engage the responsibility of that State for its activities, whether or not each of them was specifically imposed, requested or directed by the State.

What has just been said should not, of course, blur the necessary distinction between the various legal situations described. In the case envisaged by Article 10 of the Draft on State Responsibility (as well as in the situation envisaged in Article 7 of the same Draft), State responsibility objectively follows from the fact that the individuals who engage in certain internationally wrongful acts possess, under the relevant legislation, the status of State officials or of officials of a State's public entity. In the case under discussion here, that of organised groups, State responsibility is instead the objective corollary of the overall control exercised by the State over the group. Despite these legal differences, the fact nevertheless remains that international law renders any State responsible for acts in breach of international law performed (i) by individuals having the formal status of organs of a State (and this occurs even when these organs act ultra vires or contra legem), or (ii) by individuals who make up organised groups subject to the State's control. International law does so regardless of whether or not the State has issued specific instructions to those individuals. Clearly, the rationale behind this legal regulation is that otherwise, States might easily shelter behind, or use as a pretext, their internal legal system or the lack of any specific instructions in order to disclaim international responsibility.

## THE NICARAGUA TEST IS AT VARIANCE WITH JUDICIAL AND STATE PRACTICE

There is a second ground – of a similarly general nature as the one just expounded – on which the Nicaragua test as such may be held to be unpersuasive. This ground is determinative of the issue. The "effective control" test propounded by the International Court of Justice as an exclusive and all-embracing test is at variance with international judicial and State practice: such practice has envisaged State responsibility in circumstances where a lower degree of control than that demanded by the Nicaragua test was exercised. In short, as shall be seen, this practice has upheld the Nicaragua test with regard to individuals or unorganised groups of individuals acting on behalf of States. By contrast, it has applied a different test with regard to military or paramilitary groups.

Precisely what measure of State control does international law require for organised military groups? Judging from international case law and State practice, it would seem that for such control to come about, it is not sufficient for the group to be financially or even militarily assisted by a State. This proposition is confirmed by the international practice concerning national liberation movements. Although some States provided movements such as the PLO, SWAPO or the ANC with a territorial base or with economic and military assistance (short of sending their own troops to aid them), other States, including those against which these movements were fighting, did not attribute international responsibility for the acts of the movements to the assisting States. Nicaragua also supports this proposition, since the United States, although it aided the contras financially, and otherwise, was not held responsible for their acts (whereas on account of this financial and other assistance to the contras, the United States was held by the Court to be responsible for breaching the principle of non-intervention as well as "its obligation not to use force against another State.")

In order to attribute the acts of a military or paramilitary group to a State, it must be proved that the State wields overall control over the group, not only by equipping and financing the group, but also by coordinating or helping in the general planning of its military activity. Only then can the State be held internationally accountable for any misconduct of the group. However, it is not necessary that, in addition, the State should also issue, either to the head or to members of the group, instructions for the commission of specific acts contrary to international law.

In sum, the Appeals Chamber holds the view that international rules do not always require the same degree of control over armed groups or private individuals for the purpose of determining whether an individual not having the status of a State official under internal legislation can be regarded as a de facto organ of the State. The extent of the requisite State control varies. Where the question at issue is whether a single private individual or a group that is not militarily organised has acted as a de facto State organ when performing a specific act, it is necessary to ascertain whether specific instructions concerning the commission of that particular act had been issued by that State to the individual or group in question; alternatively, it must be established whether the unlawful act had been publicly endorsed or approved ex post facto by the State at issue. By contrast, control by a State over subordinate armed forces or militias or paramilitary units may be of an overall character (and must comprise more than the mere provision of financial assistance or military equipment or training). This requirement, however, does not go so far as to include the issuing of specific orders by the State, or its direction of each individual operation. Under international law it is by no means necessary that the controlling authorities should plan all the operations of the units dependent on them, choose their targets, or give specific instructions concerning the conduct of military operations and any alleged violations of international humanitarian law. The control required by international law may be deemed to exist when a State (or, in the context of an armed conflict, the Party to the conflict) has a role in organising, coordinating or planning the military actions of the military group, in addition to financing, training and equipping or providing operational support to that group. Acts performed by the group or members thereof may be regarded as acts of de facto State organs regardless of any specific instruction by the controlling State concerning the commission of each of those acts.

It now falls to the Appeals Chamber to establish whether, in the circumstances of the case, the Yugoslav Army exercised in 1992 the requisite measure of control over the Bosnian Serb Army. The answer must be in the affirmative.

As the Appeals Chamber has already pointed out, international law does not require that the particular acts in question should be the subject of specific instructions or directives by a foreign State to certain armed forces in order for these armed forces to be held to be acting as de facto organs of that State. It follows that in the circumstances of the case it was not necessary to show that those specific operations carried out by the Bosnian Serb forces which were the object of the trial (the attacks on Kozarac and more generally within opština Prijedor) had been specifically ordered or planned by the Yugoslav Army. It is sufficient to show that this Army exercised overall control over the Bosnian Serb Forces. This showing has been made by the Prosecution before the Trial Chamber. Such control manifested itself not only in financial, logistical and other assistance and support, but also, and more importantly, in terms of participation in the general direction, coordination and supervision of the activities and operations of the VRS. This sort of control is sufficient for the purposes of the legal criteria required by international law.

---

### Note and Comments:

1. In your view, which test is better? The "effective control" standard from *Nicaragua* or the "overall control" test enunciated in *Tadic´*? Or can you think of some other test that would more appropriately reflect the degree to which a state ought to be deemed "responsible"?

### The ICJ Reaffirms the *Nicaragua* Standard

In 2007, the International Court of Justice returned to the issue of (indirect) state responsibility in a case remarkably similar to *Nicaragua v. United States*, which had been decided nearly two decades earlier. In a case brought under the Genocide Convention, Bosnia claimed that the Serbian government was "responsible" for the acts of genocide carried out by various Bosnian Serb paramilitary groups it had provided massive amounts of military, economic, and political support to. In addressing this matter, the ICJ immediately turned to the International Law Commission's Draft Article on State Responsibility, which was completed (and renumbered) between the time of the *Nicaragua* ruling and *Bosnia v. Serbia*.

The ICJ first applied Article 4 (Conduct of Organs of a State) and maintained that in order for the Bosnian Serb forces to be considered as "state organs" of Serbia what would have to be established is their "complete dependence" on the Serbian state, which the ICJ concluded did not exist. The ICJ then turned to Article 8 (Conduct directed and controlled by a State), which provides: "The conduct of a person or group of persons shall be considered an act of a State under international law if the person or group of persons is in fact acting on the instructions of, or under the direction or control of, that State in carrying out the conduct." As you will see, the ICJ rejected the *Tadic'* "overall control" standard and reaffirmed the "effective control" test from *Nicaragua* and in doing so it ruled that Serbia had not "directed or controlled" its Bosnian Serb allies.

---

## *Bosnia v. Serbia,* ICJ (2007)

This provision [Article 8] must be understood in the light of the Court's jurisprudence on the subject, particularly that of the 1986 Judgment in the case concerning *Military and Paramilitary Activities in and against Nicaragua (Nicaragua v. United States of America).* In that Judgment the Court, as noted above, after having rejected the argument that the *contras* were to be equated with organs of the United States because they were "completely dependent" on it, added that the responsibility of the Respondent could still arise if it were proved that it had itself "directed or enforced the perpetration of the acts contrary to human rights and humanitarian law alleged by the applicant State" (*I.C.J. Reports 1986*, p. 64, para. 115); this led to the following significant conclusion:

> For this conduct to give rise to legal responsibility of the United States, it would in principle have to be proved that that State had effective control of the military or paramilitary operations in the course of which the alleged violations were committed.

The test thus formulated differs in two respects from the test – described above – to determine whether a person or entity may be equated with a State organ even if not having that status under internal law. First, in this context it is not necessary to show that the persons who performed the acts alleged to have violated international law were in general in a relationship of "complete dependence" on the respondent State; it has to be proved that they acted in accordance with that State's instructions or under its "effective control". It must however be shown that this "effective control" was exercised, or that the State's instructions were given, in respect of each operation in which the alleged violations occurred, not generally in respect of the overall actions taken by the persons or groups of persons having committed the violations.

The Applicant has, it is true, contended that the crime of genocide has a particular nature, in that it may be composed of a considerable number of specific acts separate, to a greater or lesser extent, in time and space. According to the Applicant, this particular nature would justify, among other consequences, assessing the "effective control" of the State allegedly responsible, not in relation to each of these specific acts, but in relation to the whole body of operations carried out by the direct perpetrators of the genocide. The Court is however of the view that the particular characteristics of genocide do not justify the Court in departing from the criterion elaborated in the Judgment in the case concerning *Military and Paramilitary Activities in and against Nicaragua (Nicaragua v. United States of America).* The rules for attributing alleged internationally wrongful conduct to a State do not vary with the nature of the wrongful act in question in the absence of a clearly expressed *lex specialis.* Genocide will be considered as attributable to a State if and to the extent that the physical acts constitutive of genocide that have been committed by organs or persons other than the State's own agents were carried out, wholly or in part, on the instructions or directions of the State, or under its effective control. This is the state of customary international law, as reflected in the ILC Articles on State Responsibility.

The Court notes however that the Applicant has further questioned the validity of applying, in the present case, the criterion adopted in the *Military and Paramilitary Activities* Judgment. It has drawn attention to the Judgment of the ICTY Appeals Chamber in the *Tadic´* case. In that case the Chamber did not follow the jurisprudence of the Court in the *Military and Paramilitary Activities* case: it held that the appropriate criterion, applicable in its view both to the characterization of the armed conflict in Bosnia and Herzegovina as international, and to imputing the acts committed by Bosnian Serbs to the FRY under the law of State responsibility, was that of the "overall control" exercised over the Bosnian Serbs by the FRY; and further that that criterion was satisfied in the case, In other words, the Appeals Chamber took the view that acts committed by Bosnian Serbs could give rise to international responsibility of the FRY on the basis of the overall control exercised by the FRY over the Republika Srpska and the VRS, without there being any need to prove that each operation during which acts were committed in breach of international law was carried out on the FRY's instructions, or under its effective control.

The Court has given careful consideration to the Appeals Chamber's reasoning in support of the foregoing conclusion, but finds itself unable to subscribe to the Chamber's view. First, the Court observes that the ICTY was not called upon in the *Tadic´* case, nor is it in general called upon, to rule on questions of State responsibility, since its jurisdiction is criminal and extends over persons only. Thus, in that Judgment the Tribunal addressed an issue which was not indispensable for the exercise of its jurisdiction. As stated above, the Court attaches the utmost importance to the factual and legal findings made by the ICTY in ruling on the criminal liability of the accused before it and, in the present case, the Court takes fullest account of the ICTY's trial and appellate judgments dealing with the events underlying the dispute. The situation is not the same for positions adopted by the ICTY on issues of general international law which do not lie within the specific purview of its jurisdiction and, moreover, the resolution of which is not always necessary for deciding the criminal cases before it.

This is the case of the doctrine laid down in the *Tadic´* Judgment. Insofar as the "overall control" test is employed to determine whether or not an armed conflict is international, which was the sole question which the Appeals Chamber was called upon to decide, it may well be that the test is applicable and suitable; the Court does not however think it appropriate to take a position on the point in the present case, as there is no need to resolve it for purposes of the present Judgment. On the other hand, the ICTY presented the "overall control" test as equally applicable under the law of State responsibility for the purpose of determining – as the Court is required to do in the present case – when a State is responsible for acts committed by paramilitary units, armed forces which are not among its official organs. In this context, the argument in favour of that test is unpersuasive.

It should first be observed that logic does not require the same test to be adopted in resolving the two issues, which are very different in nature: the degree and nature of a State's involvement in an armed conflict on another State's territory which is required for the conflict to be characterized as international, can very well, and without logical inconsistency, differ from the degree and nature of involvement required to give rise to that State's responsibility for a specific act committed in the course of the conflict.

It must next be noted that the "overall control" test has the major drawback of broadening the scope of State responsibility well beyond the fundamental principle governing the law of international responsibility: a State is responsible only for its own conduct, that is to say the conduct of persons acting, on whatever basis, on its behalf. That is true of acts carried out by its official organs, and also by persons or entities which are not formally recognized as official organs under internal law but which must nevertheless be equated with State organs because they are in a relationship of complete dependence on the State. Apart from these cases, a State's responsibility can be incurred for acts committed by persons or groups of persons – neither State organs nor to be equated with such organs – only if, assuming those acts to be internationally wrongful, they are attributable to it under the rule of customary international law reflected in Article 8 cited above. This is so where an organ of the State gave the instructions or provided the direction pursuant to which the perpetrators of the wrongful act acted or where it exercised effective control over the action during which the wrong was committed. In this regard the "overall control" test is unsuitable, for it stretches too far, almost to breaking point, the connection which must exist between the conduct of a State's organs and its international responsibility.

---

After ruling that Serbia had not acted in violation of either Article 4 or 8 of the DASR, the Court then turned to Article 16 (Aid or assistance in the commission of an internationally wrongful act), which provides:

A State which aids or assists another State in the commission of an internationally wrongful act by the latter is internationally responsible for doing so if:

(a) That State does so with knowledge of the circumstances of the internationally wrongful act; and

(b) The act would be internationally wrongful if committed by that State.

We now turn to the ICJ's interpretation of Article 16.

---

## Bosnia v. Serbia, ICJ (2007)

Although this provision [Article 16], because it concerns a situation characterized by a relationship between two States, is not directly relevant to the present case, it nevertheless merits consideration. The Court sees no reason to make any distinction of substance between "complicity in genocide", within the meaning of Article III, paragraph (e), of the Convention, and the "aid or assistance" of a State in the commission of a wrongful act by another State within the meaning of the aforementioned Article 16 – setting aside the hypothesis of the issue of instructions or directions or the exercise of effective control, the effects of which, in the law of international responsibility, extend beyond complicity. In other words, to ascertain whether the Respondent is responsible for "complicity in genocide" within the meaning of Article III, paragraph (e), which is what the Court now has to do, it must examine whether organs of the respondent State, or persons acting on its instructions or under its direction or effective control, furnished "aid or assistance" in the commission of the genocide in Srebrenica, in a sense not significantly different from that of those concepts in the general law of international responsibility.

Before the Court turns to an examination of the facts, one further comment is required. It concerns the link between the specific intent (dolus specialis) which characterizes the crime of genocide and the motives which inspire the actions of an accomplice (meaning a person providing aid or assistance to the direct perpetrators of the crime): the question arises whether complicity presupposes that the accomplice shares the specific intent *(dolus specialis)* of the principal perpetrator. But whatever the reply to this question, there is no doubt that the conduct of an organ or a person furnishing aid or assistance to a perpetrator of the crime of genocide cannot be treated as complicity in genocide unless at the least that organ or person acted knowingly, that is to say, in particular, was aware of the specific intent *(dolus specialis)* of the principal perpetrator. If that condition is not fulfilled, that is sufficient to exclude categorization as complicity. The Court will thus first consider whether this latter condition is met in the present case. It is only if it replies to that question of fact in the affirmative that it will need to determine the legal point referred to above.

The Court is not convinced by the evidence furnished by the Applicant that the above conditions were met. Undoubtedly, the quite substantial aid of a political, military and financial nature provided by the FRY to the Republika Srpska and the VRS, beginning long before the tragic events of Srebrenica, continued during those events. There is thus little doubt that the atrocities in Srebrenica were committed, at least in part, with the resources which the perpetrators of those acts possessed as a result of the general policy of aid and assistance pursued towards them by the FRY. However, the sole task of the Court is to establish the legal responsibility of the Respondent, a responsibility which is subject to very specific conditions. One of those conditions is not fulfilled, because it is not established beyond any doubt in the argument between the Parties whether the authorities of the FRY supplied – and continued to supply – the VRS leaders who decided upon and carried out those acts of genocide with their aid and assistance, at a time when those authorities were clearly aware that genocide was about to take place or was under way; in other words that not only were massacres about to be carried out or already under way, but that their perpetrators had the specific intent characterizing genocide, namely, the intent to destroy, in whole or in part, a human group, as such.

A point which is clearly decisive in this connection is that it was not conclusively shown that the decision to eliminate physically the adult male population of the Muslim community from Srebrenica was brought to the attention of the Belgrade authorities when it was taken; the Court has found that that decision was taken shortly before it was actually carried out, a process which took a very short time (essentially between 13 and 16 July 1995), despite the exceptionally high number of victims. It has therefore not been conclusively established that, at the crucial time, the FRY supplied aid to the perpetrators of the genocide in full awareness that the aid supplied would be used to commit genocide.

The Court concludes from the above that the international responsibility of the Respondent is not engaged for acts of complicity in genocide mentioned in Article III, paragraph *(e)*, of the Convention. In the light of this finding, and of the findings above relating to the other paragraphs of Article III, the international responsibility of the Respondent is not engaged under Article III as a whole.

---

## Notes and Comments:

1. Unlike domestic courts where there is a hierarchy of authority between various levels of courts, international law does not operate in the same fashion, which is also to say that, at least in theory, the International Court of Justice

is not "superior" to the Appeals Chamber of the ICTY – or any other international tribunal, for that matter.

2. After *Nicaragua* and *Bosnia*, can you imagine a situation where a state that provides "aid and assistance" to another government or entities in another state would ever be "responsible" for the harms carried out by the recipients (Gibney 2007)? In many respects this approach to state responsibility is directly counter to how states approach the issue of terrorism. You might recall the *Flatow* case in Chapter 1, which ruled that under U.S. law, Iran was a state sponsor of terrorism – and thereby deprived of sovereign immunity protection – due to the fact that it provided a relatively small amount of money (approximately $2 million a year) to what was considered to be a "terrorist organization." Furthermore, there was no indication that Iran exercised any form of "effective control" over the recipients of these funds. Compare this with *Bosnia v. Serbia*. In this case, Serbia provided vastly more sums of money and training to its Bosnian Serb allies, and yet Serbia was found not to be responsible for the acts of genocide carried out by the recipients of this aid. What explains the different results?

## Shared Responsibility

One of the basic premises of this book is that nearly all of the world's problems can only be addressed through international assistance and cooperation. Unfortunately, international law has long struggled with the notion of shared responsibility in large part because of the primacy of state sovereignty (Nollkaemper and Jacobs 2013). The following case involves a sex trafficking ring where young Russians are enticed to travel to Cyprus where they are forced into prostitution. In this case, a young woman in this situation commits suicide and her father brings a claim against both Russia and Cyprus for their (joint) failure to protect his daughter.

---

## *Rantsev v. Cyprus and Russia*, ECtHR, App. No. 25965/04 (2010)

The applicant complained under Articles 2, 3, 4, 5 and 8 of the Convention about the lack of sufficient investigation into the circumstances of the death of his daughter, the lack of adequate protection of his daughter by the Cypriot police while she was still alive and the failure of the Cypriot authorities to take steps to punish those responsible for his daughter's death and ill-treatment. He also complained under Articles 2 and 4 about the failure of the Russian authorities to investigate his daughter's alleged trafficking and subsequent death and to take steps to protect her from the risk of trafficking. Finally, he complained under Article 6 of the Convention about the inquest proceedings and an alleged lack of access to court in Cyprus.

The applicant, Mr Nikolay Mikhaylovich Rantsev, is a Russian national who was born in 1938 and lives in Svetlogorsk, Russia. He is the father of Ms Oxana Rantseva, also a Russian national, born in 1980.

The facts of the case, as established by the submissions of the parties and the material submitted by them, in particular the witness statements taken by the Cypriot police, may be summarised as follows.

Oxana Rantseva arrived in Cyprus on 5 March 2001. On 13 February 2001, X.A., the owner of a cabaret in Limassol, had applied for an "artiste" visa and work permit for Ms Rantseva to allow her to work as an artiste in his cabaret (see further paragraph 115 below). The application was accompanied by a copy of Ms Rantseva's passport, a medical certificate, a copy of an employment contract (apparently not yet signed by Ms Rantseva) and a bond.

Ms Rantseva was granted a temporary residence permit as a visitor until 9 March 2001. She stayed in an apartment with other young women working in X.A.'s cabaret. On 12 March 2001 she was granted a permit to work until 8 June 2001 as an artiste in a cabaret owned by X.A. and managed by his brother, M.A. She began work on 16 March 2001.

On 19 March 2001, at around 11a.m., M.A. was informed by the other women living with Ms Rantseva that she had left the apartment and taken all her belongings with her. The women told him that she had left a note in Russian saying that she was tired and wanted to return to Russia. On the same date M.A. informed the Immigration Office in Limassol that Ms Rantseva had abandoned her place of work and residence. According to M.A.'s subsequent witness statement, he wanted Ms Rantseva to be arrested and expelled from Cyprus so that he could bring another girl to work in the cabaret. However, Ms Rantseva's name was not entered on the list of persons wanted by the police.

> *[On 28 March 2001, Ms Rantseva was seen at a disco and M.A. was summoned and brought her to the police station. Although the police did not arrest her, as M.A. had requested, she was released in his custody where she was taken to the home of D.P., an associate of M.A., where she was placed in a second story bedroom. At around 6:30 a.m. Ms Rantseva's body was found on the ground outside the apartment, apparently having fallen in an attempt to leave D.P.'s apartment.]*

**\*\*\***

*Ex Officio report of the Cypriot Ombudsman on the regime regarding entry and employment of alien women as artistes in entertainment places in Cyprus, 24 November 2003*

In November 2003, the Cypriot Ombudsman published a report on "artistes" in Cyprus. The Ombudsman's report considered the history of the employment of young foreign women as cabaret artistes, noting that the word "artiste" in Cyprus has become synonymous with "prostitute". Her report explained that since the mid-1970s, thousands of young women had legally entered Cyprus to work as artistes but had in fact worked as prostitutes in one of the many cabarets in Cyprus. Since the beginning of the 1980s, efforts had been made by the authorities to introduce a stricter regime in order to guarantee effective immigration monitoring and to limit the "well-known and commonly acknowledged phenomenon of women who arrived in Cyprus to work as artistes". However, a number of the measures proposed had not been implemented due to objections from cabaret managers and artistic agents.

The Ombudsman's report noted that in the 1990s, the prostitution market in Cyprus started to be served by women coming mainly from former States of the Soviet Union. She concluded that:

> During the same period, one could observe a certain improvement regarding the implementation of those measures and the policy being adopted. However, there

*was not improvement regarding sexual exploitation, trafficking and mobility of women under a regime of modern slavery.*

As regards the living and working conditions of artistes, the report stated:

*The majority of the women entering the country to work as artistes come from poor families of the post socialist countries. Most of them are educated. . . . Few are the real artistes. Usually they are aware that they will be compelled to prostitute themselves. However, they do not always know about the working conditions under which they will exercise this job. There are also cases of alien women who come to Cyprus, having the impression that they will work as waitresses or dancers and that they will only have drinks with clients ('consomation'). They are made by force and threats to comply with the real terms of their work. . . .*

*The alien artistes from the moment of their entry into the Republic of Cyprus to their departure are under constant surveillance and guard of their employers. After finishing their work, they are not allowed to go wherever they want. There are serious complaints even about cases of artistes who remain locked in their residence place. Moreover, their passports and other personal documents are retained by their employers or artistic agents. Those who refuse to obey are punished by means of violence or by being imposed fees which usually consist in deducting percentages of drinks, 'consommation' or commercial sex. Of course these amounts are included in the contracts signed by the artistes.*

*. . .*

*Generally, artistes stay at one or zero star hotels, flats or guest-houses situated near or above the cabarets, whose owners are the artistic agents or the cabaret owners. These places are constantly guarded. Three or four women sleep in each room. According to reports given by the Police, many of these buildings are inappropriate and lack sufficient sanitation facilities.*

*. . . Finally, it is noted that at the point of their arrival in Cyprus alien artistes are charged with debts, for instance with traveling expenses, commissions deducted by the artistic agent who brought them in Cyprus or with commissions deducted by the agent who located them in their country etc. Therefore, they are obliged to work under whichever conditions to pay off at least their debts.*

Concerning the recruitment of women in their countries of origin, the report noted:

*Locating women who come to work in Cyprus is usually undertaken by local artistic agents in cooperation with their homologues in different countries and arrangements are made between both of them. After having worked for six months maximum in Cyprus, a number of these artistes are sent to Lebanon, Syria, Greece or Germany.*

### ALLEGED VIOLATION OF ARTICLE 2 OF THE CONVENTION

The applicant contended that there had been a violation of Article 2 of the Convention by both the Russian and Cypriot authorities on account of the failure of the Cypriot authorities to take steps to protect the life of his daughter and the failure of the authorities of both States to conduct an effective investigation into her death. Article 2 provides, *inter alia*, that:

1. Everyone's right to life shall be protected by law. No one shall be deprived of his life intentionally save in the execution of a sentence of a court following his conviction of a crime for which this penalty is provided by law. . . .

It is clear that Article 2 enjoins the State not only to refrain from the intentional and unlawful taking of life but also to take appropriate steps to safeguard the lives of those within its jurisdiction. In the first place, this obligation requires the State to secure the right to life by putting in place effective criminal law provisions to deter the commission of offences against the person backed up by law enforcement machinery for the prevention, suppression and punishment of breaches of such provisions. However, it also implies, in appropriate circumstances, a positive obligation on the authorities to take preventive operational measures to protect an individual whose life is at risk from the criminal acts of another individual.

The Court reiterates that the scope of any positive obligation must be interpreted in a way which does not impose an impossible or disproportionate burden on the authorities, bearing in mind the difficulties in policing modern societies, the unpredictability of human conduct and the operational choices which must be made in terms of priorities and resources. Not every claimed risk to life can entail for the authorities a Convention requirement to take operational measures to prevent that risk from materialising. For the Court to find a violation of the positive obligation to protect life, it must be established that the authorities knew or ought to have known at the time of the existence of a real and immediate risk to the life of an identified individual from the criminal acts of a third party and that they failed to take measures within the scope of their powers which, judged reasonably, might have been expected to avoid that risk.

Although it is undisputed that victims of trafficking and exploitation are often forced to live and work in cruel conditions and may suffer violence and ill-treatment at the hands of their employers, in the absence of any specific indications in a particular case, the general risk of ill-treatment and violence cannot constitute a real and immediate risk to life. In the present case, even if the police ought to have been aware that Ms Rantseva might have been a victim of trafficking, there were no indications during the time spent at the police station that Ms Rantseva's life was at real and immediate risk. The Court considers that particular chain of events leading to Ms Rantseva's death could not have been foreseeable to the police officers when they released her into M.A.'s custody. Accordingly, the Court concludes that no obligation to take operational measures to prevent a risk to life arose in the present case.

For the above reasons, the Court concludes that there has been no violation of the Cypriot authorities' positive obligation to protect Ms Rantseva's right to life under Article 2 of the Convention.

### ALLEGED VIOLATION OF ARTICLE 4 OF THE CONVENTION

## Cyprus

In assessing whether there has been a violation of Article 4, the relevant legal or regulatory framework in place must be taken into account. The Court considers that the spectrum of safeguards set out in national legislation must be adequate to ensure the practical and effective protection of the rights of victims or potential victims of trafficking. Accordingly, in addition to criminal law measures to punish traffickers, Article 4 requires member States to put in place adequate measures regulating businesses often used as a cover for human trafficking. Furthermore, a State's immigration rules must address relevant concerns relating to encouragement, facilitation or tolerance of trafficking.

Bearing in mind the difficulties involved in policing modern societies and the operational choices which must be made in terms of priorities and resources, the obligation to take operational measures must, however, be interpreted in a way which does not impose an impossible or disproportionate burden on the authorities. It is relevant to the consideration of the proportionality of any positive obligation arising in the present case that the Palermo Protocol, signed by both Cyprus and the Russian Federation in 2000, requires States to endeavour to provide for the physical safety of victims of trafficking while in their territories and to establish comprehensive policies and programmes to prevent and combat trafficking. States are also required to provide relevant training for law enforcement and immigration officials.

Article 4 also entails a procedural obligation to investigate situations of potential trafficking. The requirement to investigate does not depend on a complaint from the victim or next-of-kin: once the matter has come to the attention of the authorities they must act of their own motion. For an investigation to be effective, it must be independent from those implicated in the events. It must also be capable of leading to the identification and punishment of individuals responsible, an obligation not of result but of means. A requirement of promptness and reasonable expedition is implicit in all cases but where the possibility of removing the individual from the harmful situation is available, the investigation must be undertaken as a matter of urgency.

Finally, the Court reiterates that trafficking is a problem which is often not confined to the domestic arena. When a person is trafficked from one State to another, trafficking offences may occur in the State of origin, any State of transit and the State of destination. Relevant evidence and witnesses may be located in all States. Although the Palermo Protocol is silent on the question of jurisdiction, the Anti-Trafficking Convention explicitly requires each member State to establish jurisdiction over any trafficking offence committed in its territory. Such an approach is, in the Court's view, only logical in light of the general obligation, outlined above, incumbent on all States under Article 4 of the Convention to investigate alleged trafficking offences. In addition to the obligation to conduct a domestic investigation into events occurring on their own territories, member States are also subject to a duty in cross-border trafficking cases to cooperate effectively with the relevant authorities of other States concerned in the investigation of events which occurred outside their territories. Such a duty is in keeping with the objectives of the member States, as expressed in the preamble to the Palermo Protocol, to adopt a comprehensive international approach to trafficking in the countries of origin, transit and destination. It is also consistent with international agreements on mutual legal assistance in which the respondent States participate in the present case.

In the present case, the failures of the police authorities were multiple. First, they failed to make immediate further inquiries into whether Ms Rantseva had been trafficked. Second, they did not release her but decided to confide her to the custody of M.A. Third, no attempt was made to comply with the provisions of Law 3(1) of 2000 and to take any of the measures in section 7 of that law (see paragraph 130 above) to protect her. The Court accordingly concludes that these deficiencies, in circumstances which gave rise to a credible suspicion that Ms Rantseva might have been trafficked or exploited, resulted in a failure by the Cypriot authorities to take measures to protect Ms Rantseva. There has accordingly been a violation of Article 4 in this respect also.

RUSSIA

## Procedural Obligation to Investigate Potential Trafficking

The Court recalls that, in cases involving cross-border trafficking, trafficking offences may take place in the country of origin as well as in the country of destination. In the case of Cyprus, as the Ombudsman pointed out in her report, the recruitment of victims is usually undertaken by artistic agents in Cyprus working with agents in other countries. The failure to investigate the recruitment aspect of alleged trafficking would allow an important part of the trafficking chain to act with impunity. In this regard, the Court highlights that the definition of trafficking adopted in both the Palermo Protocol and the Anti-Trafficking Convention expressly includes the recruitment of victims. The need for a full and effective investigation covering all aspects of trafficking allegations from recruitment to exploitation is indisputable. The Russian authorities therefore had an obligation to investigate the possibility that individual agents or networks operating in Russia were involved in trafficking Ms Rantseva to Cyprus.

However, the Court observes that the Russian authorities undertook no investigation into how and where Ms Rantseva was recruited. In particular, the authorities took no steps to identify those involved in Ms Rantseva's recruitment or the methods of recruitment used. The recruitment having occurred on Russian territory, the Russian authorities were best placed to conduct an effective investigation into Ms Rantseva's recruitment. The failure to do so in the present case was all the more serious in light of Ms Rantseva's subsequent death and the resulting mystery surrounding the circumstances of her departure from Russia.

There has accordingly been a violation by the Russian authorities of their procedural obligation under Article 4 to investigate alleged trafficking.

---

### Notes and Comments:

1. Do you think the Court would have reached the same result absent Rantseva's death?

2. Notwithstanding the novelty of this holding, there is little likelihood that sex trafficking between Russia and Cyprus has been curtailed. What, if anything, does this say about international law?

3. If you were to assign a number to reflect the degree of wrongdoing in this scenario, what part would you assign to Cyprus and what part to Russia?

4. Contrary to what emerges from the *Rantsev* case, countries oftentimes work in cooperation with other countries and many have entered into formal agreements generally known as "mutual legal assistance in criminal matters treaties" (MLATs). According to the U.S. State Department website:

   Mutual Legal Assistance Treaties (MLATs) allow generally for the exchange of evidence and information in criminal and related matters. In money laundering cases, they can be extremely useful as a means of obtaining banking and other financial records from our treaty partners. MLATs, which are negotiated by the Department of State in cooperation with the Department of Justice to facilitate cooperation in criminal matters, are in force with the following countries. . . [listing 60 states the U.S. has a MLAT with].

   In addition to creating a formal tie in which to jointly undertake criminal investigations, the MLAT will oftentimes specify when cooperation will not take place, for example, for particular kinds of searches or crimes.

5. In addition to its contribution to international law, the *Rantsev* case also highlights the vulnerability of women, a topic that is touched upon in other parts of this book, particularly the last section, Human Rights.

> **Box 9.1: International Law at the Movies: Sex Trafficking**
>
> In *Lilya 4-Ever* (2002), a young Ukrainian girl is lured to Sweden where she is brutally forced into prostitution. This feature film is certainly not for the faint of heart. *The Price of Sex* (2011) is a documentary with parallels to the *Rantsev* case showing how Eastern European women are tricked into prostitution. Finally, *Trapped* (2007) is a powerful documentary that focuses on two Nigerian women who are being held as sex slaves in Copenhagen.

## Jurisdictional Limitations

Jurisdictional limitations in international agreements have often had the effect of limiting the ability of victims to pursue their claims on the grounds that this individual was not within the "jurisdiction" of one of the state parties to a particular human rights treaty. This does not necessarily mean that this state is not responsible for violating international law standards. Rather, what it does mean is that the victims cannot proceed with their claim under a particular human rights treaty. It is easy to conclude from this that the state is not responsible. But with so few fora available to victims, what this also means is that the offending state will nearly always remain beyond legal sanction. One other thing that needs to be pointed out, and which only adds to the confusion between "state responsibility" and "within its jurisdiction," is that the same language – effective control – is used in both realms.

**Photo 9.1** Jens Soering in Custody in the United States

*Source:* © Associated Press

We begin with the landmark *Soering* decision where the European Court of Human Rights applied a fairly liberal reading of when one of the contracting states (the United Kingdom) would be responsible for "torture" in another country (the United States in this case). One of the questions to consider is whether in subsequent cases the ECtHR has applied both the letter and the spirit of *Soering*.

---

## *Soering v. The United Kingdom,* ECtHR (1989)

The applicant, Mr Jens Soering, was born on 1 August 1966 and is a German national. He is currently detained in prison in England pending extradition to the United States of America to face charges of murder in the Commonwealth of Virginia.

The homicides in question were committed in Bedford County, Virginia, in March 1985. The victims, William Reginald Haysom and Nancy Astor Haysom, were the parents of the applicant's girlfriend, Elizabeth Haysom, who is a Canadian national. Death in each case was the result of multiple and massive stab and slash wounds to the neck, throat and body. At the time the applicant and Elizabeth Haysom, aged 18 and 20 respectively, were students at the University of Virginia. They disappeared together from Virginia in October 1985, but were arrested in England in April 1986 in connection with cheque fraud.

The applicant was interviewed in England between 5 and 8 June 1986 by a police investigator from the Sheriff's Department of Bedford County. In a sworn affidavit dated 24 July 1986 the investigator recorded the applicant as having admitted the killings in his presence and in that of two United Kingdom police officers. The applicant had stated that he was in love with Miss Haysom but that her parents were opposed to the relationship. He and Miss Haysom had therefore planned to kill them. They rented a car in Charlottesville and travelled to Washington where they set up an alibi. The applicant then went to the parents' house, discussed the relationship with them and, when they told him that they would do anything to prevent it, a row developed during which he killed them with a knife.

On 13 June 1986 a grand jury of the Circuit Court of Bedford County indicted him on charges of murdering the Haysom parents. The charges alleged capital murder of both of them and the separate non-capital murders of each.

On 11 August 1986 the Government of the United States of America requested the applicant's and Miss Haysom's extradition under the terms of the Extradition Treaty of 1972 between the United States and the United Kingdom.

### PRISON CONDITIONS IN MECKLENBURG CORRECTIONAL CENTER

There are currently 40 people under sentence of death in Virginia. The size of a death row inmate's cell is 3m by 2.2m. Prisoners have an opportunity for approximately 7½ hours' recreation per week in summer and approximately 6 hours' per week, weather permitting, in winter. The death row area has two recreation yards, both of which are equipped with basketball courts and one of which is equipped with weights and weight benches. Inmates are also permitted to leave their cells on other occasions, such as to receive visits, to visit the law library or to attend the prison infirmary. In addition, death row inmates are given one hour out-of-cell time in the morning in a common area. Each death row inmate is eligible for work assignments, such as cleaning duties. When prisoners move around the prison they are handcuffed, with special shackles around the waist.

When not in their cells, death row inmates are housed in a common area called "the pod". The guards are not within this area and remain in a box outside. In the event of disturbance or inter-inmate assault, the guards are not allowed to intervene until instructed to do so by the ranking officer present.

The applicant adduced much evidence of extreme stress, psychological deterioration and risk of homosexual abuse and physical attack undergone by prisoners on death row, including Mecklenburg Correctional Center. This evidence was strongly contested by the United Kingdom Government on the basis of affidavits sworn by administrators from the Virginia Department of Corrections.

### ALLEGED BREACH OF ARTICLE 3 (ART. 3)

The applicant alleged that the decision by the Secretary of State for the Home Department to surrender him to the authorities of the United States of America would, if implemented, give rise to a breach by the United Kingdom of Article 3 (art. 3) of the Convention, which provides:

> No one shall be subjected to torture or to inhuman or degrading treatment or punishment.

### APPLICABILITY OF ARTICLE 3 (ART. 3) IN CASES OF EXTRADITION

The alleged breach derives from the applicant's exposure to the so-called "death row phenomenon". This phenomenon may be described as consisting in a combination of circumstances to which the applicant would be exposed if, after having been extradited to Virginia to face a capital murder charge, he were sentenced to death.

The question remains whether the extradition of a fugitive to another State where he would be subjected or be likely to be subjected to torture or to inhuman or degrading treatment or punishment would itself engage the responsibility of a Contracting State under Article 3 (art. 3). That the abhorrence of torture has such implications is recognised in Article 3 of the United Nations Convention Against Torture and Other Cruel, Inhuman or Degrading Treatment or Punishment, which provides that "no State Party shall . . . extradite a person where there are substantial grounds for believing that he would be in danger of being subjected to torture". The fact that a specialised treaty should spell out in detail a specific obligation attaching to the prohibition of torture does not mean that an essentially similar obligation is not already inherent in the general terms of Article 3 (art. 3) of the European Convention. It would hardly be compatible with the underlying values of the Convention, that "common heritage of political traditions, ideals, freedom and the rule of law" to which the Preamble refers, were a Contracting State knowingly to surrender a fugitive to another State where there were substantial grounds for believing that he would be in danger of being subjected to torture, however heinous the crime allegedly committed. Extradition in such circumstances, while not explicitly referred to in the brief and general wording of Article 3 (art. 3), would plainly be contrary to the spirit and intendment of the Article, and in the Court's view this inherent obligation not to extradite also extends to cases in which the fugitive would be faced in the receiving State by a real risk of exposure to inhuman or degrading treatment or punishment proscribed by that Article (art. 3).

It is not normally for the Convention institutions to pronounce on the existence or otherwise of potential violations of the Convention. However, where an applicant claims that a decision to extradite him would, if implemented, be contrary to Article 3 (art. 3) by reason of its foreseeable consequences in the requesting country, a departure from this principle is necessary, in view of the serious and irreparable nature of the alleged suffering risked, in order to ensure the effectiveness of the safeguard provided by that Article (art. 3).

In sum, the decision by a Contracting State to extradite a fugitive may give rise to an issue under Article 3 (art. 3), and hence engage the responsibility of that State under the Convention, where substantial grounds have been shown for believing that the person concerned, if extradited, faces a real risk of being subjected to torture or to inhuman or degrading treatment or punishment in the requesting country. The establishment of such responsibility inevitably involves an assessment of conditions in the requesting country against the standards of Article 3 (art. 3) of the Convention. Nonetheless, there is no question of adjudicating on or establishing the responsibility of the receiving country, whether under general international law, under the Convention or otherwise. Insofar as any liability under the Convention is or may be incurred, it is liability incurred by the extraditing Contracting State by reason of its having taken action which has as a direct consequence the exposure of an individual to proscribed ill-treatment.

---

**Note and Comments:**

1. Consider how far ranging the holding in *Soering* is: A state is held responsible for violating the prohibition against torture under Article 3 of the European Convention even though the violations have not yet occurred (and might never occur), and if they do, this will happen within the territory of another state and will be carried out by agents of this other country.

We now turn to *Bankovic v. Belgium*, another landmark decision of the ECtHR. One thing that differentiates these two cases is that in *Soering* agents of the offending state (United Kingdom) never entered onto the territory of this other country (United States), while in *Bankovic* the European states that comprise NATO had bombed Serbia, which at the time was not a state party to the European Convention. However, notwithstanding this, the results are much different, although the ECtHR maintains in *Bankovic* that the result is consistent with *Soering*.

---

## *Bankovic et al. v. Belgium et al.*, ECtHR, App. No. 52207/99 [2001]

[*NATO forces undertook a bombing mission of Serbia, which at the time (1999) was not a state party to the European Convention, resulting in the deaths of 16 civilians and injury to that same number. Survivors and decedents of the victims brought suit claiming violations of the Convention. In previous cases, the European Court of Human Rights had given the Convention an extraterritorial reading, mainly in cases involving Turkey's occupation of parts of Cyprus. The issue in this case is whether these civilians were "within the jurisdiction" of the Contracting States at the time of the bombing.*]

*Whether the applicants and their deceased relatives came within the "jurisdiction" of the respondent States within the meaning of Article 1 of the Convention*

This is the principal basis upon which the Governments contest the admissibility of the application and the Court will consider first this question. Article 1 of the Convention reads as follows:

> The High Contracting Parties shall secure to everyone within their jurisdiction the rights and freedoms defined in Section I of [the] Convention.

The Governments contend that the applicants and their deceased relatives were not, at the relevant time, within the "jurisdiction" of the respondent States and that the application is therefore incompatible *ratione personae* with the provisions of the Convention.

As to the precise meaning of "jurisdiction", they suggest that it should be interpreted in accordance with the ordinary and well-established meaning of that term in public international law. The exercise of "jurisdiction" therefore involves the assertion or exercise of legal authority, actual or purported, over persons owing some form of allegiance to that State or who have been brought within that State's control. They also suggest that the term "jurisdiction" generally entails some form of structured relationship normally existing over a period of time.

The Court notes that the real connection between the applicants and the respondent States is the impugned act which, wherever decided, was performed, or had effects, outside of the territory of those States ("the extra-territorial act"). It considers that the essential question to be examined therefore is whether the applicants and their deceased relatives were, as a result of that extra-territorial act, capable of falling within the jurisdiction of the respondent States.

#### THE MEANING OF THE WORDS "WITHIN THEIR JURISDICTION"

As to the "ordinary meaning" of the relevant term in Article 1 of the Convention, the Court is satisfied that, from the standpoint of public international law, the jurisdictional competence of a State is primarily territorial. While international law does not exclude a State's exercise of jurisdiction extra-territorially, the suggested bases of such jurisdiction (including nationality, flag, diplomatic and consular relations, effect, protection, passive personality and universality) are, as a general rule, defined and limited by the sovereign territorial rights of the other relevant States.

Accordingly, for example, a State's competence to exercise jurisdiction over its own nationals abroad is subordinate to that State's and other States' territorial competence. In addition, a State may not actually exercise jurisdiction on the territory of another without the latter's consent, invitation or acquiescence, unless the former is an occupying State in which case it can be found to exercise jurisdiction in that territory, at least in certain.

The Court is of the view, therefore, that Article 1 of the Convention must be considered to reflect this ordinary and essentially territorial notion of jurisdiction, other bases of jurisdiction being exceptional and requiring special justification in the particular circumstances of each case.

The Court finds State practice in the application of the Convention since its ratification to be indicative of a lack of any apprehension on the part of the Contracting States of their extra-territorial responsibility in contexts similar to the present case. Although there have been a number of military missions involving Contracting States acting extra-territorially since their ratification of the Convention (*inter alia*, in the Gulf, in Bosnia and Herzegovina and in the FRY), no State has indicated a belief that its extra-territorial actions involved an exercise of jurisdiction within the meaning of Article 1 of the Convention by making a derogation pursuant to Article 15 of the Convention.

In keeping with the essentially territorial notion of jurisdiction, the Court has accepted only in exceptional cases that acts of the Contracting States performed, or producing effects, outside their territories can constitute an exercise of jurisdiction by them within the meaning of Article 1 of the Convention.

However, the Court notes that liability is incurred in such cases by an action of the respondent State concerning a person while he or she is on its territory, clearly within its jurisdiction, and that such cases do not concern the actual exercise of a State's competence or jurisdiction abroad.

Moreover, in that first Loizidou judgment (*preliminary objections*), the Court found that, bearing in mind the object and purpose of the Convention, the responsibility of a Contracting Party was capable of being engaged when as a consequence of military action (lawful or unlawful) it exercised effective control of an area outside its national territory. The obligation to secure, in such an area, the Convention rights and freedoms was found to derive from the fact of such control whether it was exercised directly, through the respondent State's armed forces, or through a subordinate local administration. The Court concluded that the acts of which the applicant complained were capable of falling within Turkish jurisdiction within the meaning of Article 1 of the Convention.

On the merits, the Court found that it was not necessary to determine whether Turkey actually exercised detailed control over the policies and actions of the authorities of the "Turkish Republic of Northern Cyprus" ("TRNC"). It was obvious from the large number of troops engaged in active duties in northern Cyprus that Turkey's army exercised "effective overall control over that part of the island". Such control, according to the relevant test and in the circumstances of the case, was found to entail the responsibility of Turkey for the policies and actions of the "TRNC". The Court concluded that those affected by such policies or actions therefore came within the "jurisdiction" of Turkey for the purposes of Article 1 of the Convention. Turkey's obligation to secure the rights and freedoms set out in the Convention was found therefore to extend to northern Cyprus.

In its subsequent *Cyprus v. Turkey* judgment, the Court added that since Turkey had such "effective control", its responsibility could not be confined to the acts of its own agents therein but was engaged by the acts of the local administration which survived by virtue of Turkish support. Turkey's "jurisdiction" under Article 1 was therefore considered to extend to securing the entire range of substantive Convention rights in northern Cyprus.

In sum, the case-law of the Court demonstrates that its recognition of the exercise of extra-territorial jurisdiction by a Contracting State is exceptional: it has done so when the respondent State, through the effective control of the relevant territory and its inhabitants abroad as a consequence of military occupation or through the consent, invitation or acquiescence of the Government of that territory, exercises all or some of the public powers normally to be exercised by that Government.

Additionally, the Court notes that other recognised instances of the extra-territorial exercise of jurisdiction by a State include cases involving the activities of its diplomatic or consular agents abroad and on board craft and vessels registered in, or flying the flag of, that State. In these specific situations, customary international law and treaty provisions have recognised the extra-territorial exercise of jurisdiction by the relevant State.

## WERE THE PRESENT APPLICANTS THEREFORE CAPABLE OF COMING WITHIN THE "JURISDICTION" OF THE RESPONDENT STATES?

The applicants maintain that the bombing of RTS by the respondent States constitutes yet a further example of an extra-territorial act which can be accommodated by the notion of "jurisdiction" in Article 1 of the Convention, and are thereby proposing a further specification of the ordinary meaning of the term "jurisdiction" in Article 1 of the Convention. The Court must be satisfied that equally exceptional circumstances exist in the present case which could amount to the extra-territorial exercise of jurisdiction by a Contracting State.

The Court is inclined to agree with the Governments' submission that the text of Article 1 does not accommodate such an approach to "jurisdiction". Admittedly, the applicants accept that jurisdiction, and any consequent State Convention responsibility, would be limited in the circumstances to the commission and consequences of that particular act. However, the Court is of the view that the wording of Article 1 does not provide any support for the applicants' suggestion that the positive obligation in Article 1 to secure "the rights and freedoms defined in Section I of this Convention" can be divided and tailored in accordance with the particular circumstances of the extra-territorial act in question and, it considers its view in this respect supported by the text of Article 19 of the Convention. Indeed the applicants' approach does not explain the application of the words "within their jurisdiction" in Article 1 and it even goes so far as to render those words superfluous and devoid of any purpose. Had the drafters of the Convention wished to ensure jurisdiction as extensive as that advocated by the applicants, they could have adopted a text the same as or similar to the contemporaneous Articles 1 of the four Geneva Conventions of 1949.

Furthermore, the applicants' notion of jurisdiction equates the determination of whether an individual falls within the jurisdiction of a Contracting State with the question of whether that person can be considered to be a victim of a violation of rights guaranteed by the Convention. These are separate and distinct admissibility conditions, each of which has to be satisfied in the aforementioned order, before an individual can invoke the Convention provisions against a Contracting State.

In short, the Convention is a multilateral treaty operating in an essentially regional context and notably in the legal space (*espace juridique*) of the Contracting States. The FRY clearly does not fall within this legal space. The Convention was not designed to be applied throughout the world, even in respect of the conduct of Contracting States. Accordingly, the desirability of avoiding a gap or vacuum in human rights' protection has so far been relied on by the Court in favour of establishing jurisdiction only when the territory in question was one that, but for the specific circumstances, would normally be covered by the Convention.

## THE COURT'S CONCLUSION

The Court is not therefore persuaded that there was any jurisdictional link between the persons who were victims of the act complained of and the respondent States. Accordingly, it is not satisfied that the applicants and their deceased relatives were capable of coming within the jurisdiction of the respondent States on account of the extra-territorial act in question.

**Note and Comments:**

1. The *Bankovic* case was a landmark ruling by the European Court of Human Rights, although it has been subjected to repeated criticism (Roxström, Gibney and Einarsen 2005). Since then, although the ECtHR repeatedly refers to the case as "settled law," it has retreated considerably. In *Ocalan v. Turkey* (2000), the Court held that the former PKK leader who was arrested by Turkish officials at the airport in Nairobi, Kenya was within Turkey's "jurisdiction." In *Ilascu v. Russia and Moldova* (2004), the ECtHR ruled that both countries were responsible for human rights violations in a contested area of Moldova. Russian responsibility was premised on the fact that it continued to exercise "effective control" over this area of one of the former Soviet republics; Moldova because these events occurred within its own territorial borders, although it did not exercise any authority or control there. And finally, in *Issa v. Turkey* (2005), a group of Iraqi civilians claimed that Turkish officials, operating on Iraqi territory, had mutilated and killed relatives of theirs, in violation of the European Convention. The Court seemed willing to enunciate a new legal standard for establishing "jurisdiction" – "temporary effective control" – however, it then went on to dismiss the case on the basis that there was not sufficient proof that Turkish troops had carried out these unlawful killings.

This leads to *Al-Skeini v. United Kingdom*. The case revolves around the deaths of six Iraqi civilians caused by British forces in the Basra region of Iraq. Five of the deaths occurred on the "street," while the sixth was while the defendant was in the custody of British forces. In domestic litigation in the U.K., only the individual who died in a British prison was found to be "within the jurisdiction" of one of the Contracting States to the European Convention. In the case that follows, the ECtHR ruled that all six Iraqi civilians were within the "jurisdiction" of the United Kingdom and thus governed by the European Convention.

---

## Al-Skeini and Others v. The United Kingdom, ECtHR, App. No. 55721/07 (2011)

The facts of the case may be summarised as follows.

*The occupation of Iraq from 1 May 2003 to 28 June 2004*
*Background: United Nations Security Council Resolution 1441*

On 8 November 2002 the United Nations Security Council, acting under Chapter VII of the Charter of the United Nations, adopted Resolution 1441. The Resolution decided, *inter alia*, that Iraq had been and remained in material breach of its obligations under previous United Nations Security Council resolutions to disarm and to cooperate with United Nations and International Atomic Energy Agency weapons inspectors. Resolution 1441 decided to afford Iraq a final opportunity to comply with its disarmament obligations and set up an enhanced inspection regime. It requested the Secretary-General of the United Nations immediately to notify Iraq of the Resolution and demanded that Iraq cooperate immediately, unconditionally, and actively with the inspectors. Resolution 1441 concluded by recalling that the Security Council had "repeatedly warned Iraq that it would face serious consequences as a result of its continued violations of its obligations". The Security Council decided to remain seized of the matter.

#### MAJOR COMBAT OPERATIONS: 20 MARCH TO 1 MAY 2003

On 20 March 2003 a Coalition of armed forces under unified command, led by the United States of America with a large force from the United Kingdom and small contingents from Australia, Denmark and Poland, commenced the invasion of Iraq. By 5 April 2003 the British had captured Basra and by 9 April 2003 United States troops had gained control of Baghdad. Major combat operations in Iraq were declared complete on 1 May 2003. Thereafter, other States sent personnel to help with the reconstruction effort.

#### LEGAL AND POLITICAL DEVELOPMENTS IN MAY 2003

The occupying States, acting through the Commander of Coalition Forces, created the Coalition Provisional Authority (CPA) to act as a "caretaker administration" until an Iraqi government could be established. It had power, *inter alia*, to issue legislation. On 13 May 2003 the US Secretary of Defense, Donald Rumsfeld, issued a memorandum formally appointing Ambassador Paul Bremer as Administrator of the CPA with responsibility for the temporary governance of Iraq.

#### GENERAL PRINCIPLES RELEVANT TO JURISDICTION UNDER ARTICLE 1
#### OF THE CONVENTION

Article 1 of the Convention reads as follows:

> "The High Contracting Parties shall secure to everyone within their jurisdiction the rights and freedoms defined in Section I of [the] Convention."

As provided by this Article, the engagement undertaken by a Contracting State is confined to "securing" ("*reconnaître*" in the French text) the listed rights and freedoms to persons within its own "jurisdiction." "Jurisdiction" under Article 1 is a threshold criterion. The exercise of jurisdiction is a necessary condition for a Contracting State to be able to be held responsible for acts or omissions imputable to it which give rise to an allegation of the infringement of rights and freedoms set forth in the Convention.

#### THE TERRITORIAL PRINCIPLE

A State's jurisdictional competence under Article 1 is primarily territorial. Jurisdiction is presumed to be exercised normally throughout the State's territory. Conversely, acts of the Contracting States performed, or producing effects, outside their territories can constitute an exercise of jurisdiction within the meaning of Article 1 only in exceptional cases.

To date, the Court in its case-law has recognized a number of exceptional circumstances capable of giving rise to the exercise of jurisdiction by a Contracting State outside its own territorial boundaries. In each case, the question whether exceptional circumstances exist which require and justify a finding by the Court that the State was exercising jurisdiction extraterritorially must be determined with reference to the particular facts.

### THE LEGAL SPACE ("ESPACE JURIDIQUE") OF THE CONVENTION

The Convention is a constitutional instrument of European public order. It does not govern the actions of States not Parties to it, nor does it purport to be a means of requiring the Contracting States to impose Convention standards on other States.

The Court has emphasized that, where the territory of one Convention State is occupied by the armed forces of another, the occupying State should in principle be held accountable under the Convention for breaches of human rights within the occupied territory, because to hold otherwise would be to deprive the population of that territory of the rights and freedoms hitherto enjoyed and would result in a "vacuum" of protection within the "legal space of the Convention". However, the importance of establishing the occupying State's jurisdiction in such cases does not imply, a contrario, that jurisdiction under Article 1 of the Convention can never exist outside the territory covered by the Council of Europe member States. The Court has not in its case-law applied any such restriction.

### APPLICATION OF THESE PRINCIPLES TO THE FACTS OF THE CASE

In determining whether the United Kingdom had jurisdiction over any of the applicants' relatives when they died, the Court takes as its starting-point that, on 20 March 2003, the United Kingdom together with the United States of America and their Coalition partners, through their armed forces, entered Iraq with the aim of displacing the Ba'ath regime then in power. This aim was achieved by 1 May 2003, when major combat operations were declared to be complete and the United States of America and the United Kingdom became Occupying Powers within the meaning of Article 42 of the Hague Regulations.

As explained in the letter dated 8 May 2003 sent jointly by the Permanent Representatives of the United Kingdom and the United States of America to the President of the United Nations Security Council, United States of America and the United Kingdom, having displaced the previous regime, created the CPA "to exercise powers of government temporarily". One of the powers of government specifically referred to in the letter of 8 May 2003 to be exercised by the United States of America and the United Kingdom through the CPA was the provision of security in Iraq, including the maintenance of civil law and order. The letter further stated that "[t]he United States, the United Kingdom and Coalition partners, working through the Coalition Provisional Authority, shall, *inter alia*, provide for security in and for the provisional administration of Iraq, including by . . . assuming immediate control of Iraqi institutions responsible for military and security matters".

In its first legislative act, CPA Regulation No. 1 of 16 May 2003, the CPA declared that it would "exercise powers of government temporarily in order to provide for the effective administration of Iraq during the period of transitional administration, to restore conditions of security and stability" (see paragraph 12 above).

It can be seen that following the removal from power of the Ba'ath regime and until the accession of the interim Iraqi government, the United Kingdom (together with the United States of America) assumed in Iraq the exercise of some of the public powers normally to be exercised by a sovereign government. In particular, the United Kingdom assumed authority and responsibility for the maintenance of security in south-east

Iraq. In these exceptional circumstances, the Court considers that the United Kingdom, through its soldiers engaged in security operations in Basra during the period in question, exercised authority and control over individuals killed in the course of such security operations, so as to establish a jurisdictional link between the deceased and the United Kingdom for the purposes of Article 1 of the Convention.

The Court is conscious that the deaths in the present case occurred in Basra City in south-east Iraq in the aftermath of the invasion, during a period when crime and violence were endemic. Although major combat operations had ceased on 1 May 2003, the Coalition Forces in south-east Iraq, including British soldiers and military police, were the target of over a thousand violent attacks in the subsequent thirteen months. In tandem with the security problems, there were serious breakdowns in the civilian infrastructure, including the law enforcement and criminal justice systems.

While remaining fully aware of this context, the Court's approach must be guided by the knowledge that the object and purpose of the Convention as an instrument for the protection of individual human beings requires that its provisions be interpreted and applied so as to make its safeguards practical and effective. Article 2, which protects the right to life and sets out the circumstances when deprivation of life may be justified, ranks as one of the most fundamental provisions of the Convention. No derogation from it is permitted under Article 15, "except in respect of deaths resulting from lawful acts of war". Article 2 covers both intentional killing and also the situations in which it is permitted to use force which may result, as an unintended outcome, in the deprivation of life. Any use of force must be no more than "absolutely necessary" for the achievement of one or more of the purposes set out above.

The general legal prohibition of arbitrary killing by agents of the State would be ineffective in practice if there existed no procedure for reviewing the lawfulness of the use of lethal force by State authorities. The obligation to protect the right to life under this provision, read in conjunction with the State's general duty under Article 1 of the Convention to "secure to everyone within their jurisdiction the rights and freedoms defined in [the] Convention", requires by implication that there should be some form of effective official investigation when individuals have been killed as a result of the use of force by, *inter alios*, agents of the State. The essential purpose of such an investigation is to secure the effective implementation of the domestic laws safeguarding the right to life and, in those cases involving State agents or bodies, to ensure their accountability for deaths occurring under their responsibility.

However, the investigation should also be broad enough to permit the investigating authorities to take into consideration not only the actions of the State agents who directly used lethal force but also all the surrounding circumstances, including such matters as the planning and control of the operations in question, where this is necessary in order to determine whether the State complied with its obligation under Article 2 to protect life.

---

### Notes and Comments:

1. How much of the decision is premised on the formal occupation of the Basra region by British troops?

2. Under what circumstances are individuals in one state "within the jurisdiction" of an outside state? What about economic sanctions applied against North Korea? Could we say that the citizens of North Korea are "within the

jurisdiction" of the states applying such sanctions? Or what about Russian involvement in Syria? Are Syrian civilians "within the jurisdiction" of the Russian Republic?

3. Finally, how are individuals outside of Europe who are harmed by the policies and practices of the European states able to hold these governments accountable?

## References

### Books and Articles

Mark Gibney, "Genocide and State Responsibility," *Human Rights Law Review* 7: 760–73 (2007)

Mark Gibney, Katarina Tomasevski and Jens Vedsted-Hansen, "Transnational State Responsibility for Violations of Human Rights," *Harvard Human Rights Journal* 12: 267–96 (1999)

Andre Nollkaemper and Dov Jacobs, "Shared Responsibility in International Law: A Conceptual Framework," *Michigan Journal of International Law* 34: 359–438 (2013)

Kal Raustiala, "The Geography of Justice," *Fordham Law Review* 73: 2501–60 (2005)

Erik Roxström, Mark Gibney and Terje Einarsen, "The NATO Bombing Case and the Limits of Western Human Rights Protection," *Boston University International Law Journal* 23: 55–136 (2005)

Vassilis P. Tzevelekos, "Reconstructing the Effective Control Criterion in Extraterritorial Human Rights Breaches: Direct Attribution of Wrongfulness, Due Diligence, and Concurrent Responsibility," *Michigan Journal of International Law* 36: 129–78 (2014)

### U.N. Report

James Crawford, *The International Law Commission's Articles of State Responsibility: Introduction, Text and Commentaries*, Cambridge: Cambridge University Press (2002)

### Cases

*Al-Skeini v. United Kingdom*, ECtHR, App. No. 55721/07 (2011)

*Bankovic et al. v. Belgium et al.*, ECtHR, App. No. 52207/99 (2001)

*Bosnia v. Serbia*, ICJ (2007)

*Ilascu v. Russia and Moldova*, ECtHR, App. No. 48787/99 (2004)

*Issa v. Turkey*, ECtHR, App. No. 31821/96 (2005)

*Lopez Burgos v. Uruguay*, Communication No. R.12/52, U.N. Doc. Supp. No. 40 (A/36/40) at 176 (1981), Human Rights Committee

*Nicaragua v. United States*, ICJ (1986)

*Ocalan v. Turkey*, ECtHR, App. No. 46221/99 (2000) (dec. on admiss.)

*Prosecutor v. Tadic´*, ICTY, Appeals Chamber (15 July 1999) (Case No. IT-94–1-A)

*Rantsev v. Cyprus and Russia*, ECtHR, App. No. 29565/04 (2010)

*Soering v. United Kingdom*, ECtHR (1989)

### International Agreements

Convention on the Prevention and Punishment of the Crime of Genocide, approved and proposed for signature 9 December 1948, entry into force 12 January 1951

International Covenant on Civil and Political Rights, adopted 16 December 1966, entry into force 23 March 1976

# 10

## Foreign and Domestic Immunities

In this chapter our focus turns to state immunities. Foreign immunity refers to the immunity that one state provides to other states, while domestic immunity refers to the immunity that a state provides under its own law to itself. Although state immunity has been a fundamental principle in international law, there is no international treaty governing this practice. Rather, such immunities are established by each state under its own domestic laws and through a particular reading of customary international law. However, there are cracks in the armor. Some of this is because of the changing nature of the state, but also because of changes in international law itself, especially the rise of international human rights law.

### Act of State Doctrine

Under the Act of State doctrine, judicial bodies in one country decline to sit in judgment of policies and actions carried out by foreign governments. An example of this is *Banco Nacional de Cuba v. Sabbatino* (1964), a case challenging the expropriation practices of the Cuban government. The U.S. Supreme Court dismissed this action on the basis that one state should not sit in judgment of the policy decisions of another sovereign state.

However, as shown in *Belhaj v. Straw*, the "war on terrorism" might help work to change or at least modify this principle. In this case the U.K. government sought to have a case challenging its own actions in a rendition case dismissed on the grounds that a reviewing court would first have to pass judgment on the legality of the actions of a number of other states – which would constitute a violation of the Act of State doctrine. In a complicated ruling, only a small portion of which

**Photo 10.1**  Abdelhakim Belhaj
*Source*: © Associated Press

is reproduced below, the U.K. Supreme Court unanimously rejected this argument, holding that what was at issue were the actions of the U.K. government. In addition, the Court held that the Act of State doctrine is based on international comity rather than being based on international law principles, which also means that the "public policy" exception to the Act of State doctrine is perfectly consonant with international law.

## *Belhaj v. United Kingdom,* UKSC 3 [2017]

The appeals now before the Supreme Court in *Belhaj and Boudchar v. Straw* and *Ministry of Defence v. Rahmatullah* concern the alleged complicity of United Kingdom authorities and officials in various torts, allegedly committed by various other states in various overseas jurisdictions. The torts alleged include unlawful detention and rendition, torture or cruel and inhuman treatment and assault. The defences include in both appeals state immunity and the doctrine of foreign act of state.

Both cases originate with events in February/March 2004. In *Belhaj*, Mr Belhaj, a Libyan national and opponent of Colonel Gaddafi, and his wife, Mrs Boudchar, a Moroccan national, attempted (under, it seems likely, other names) to take a commercial flight from Beijing to London, but were instead and for whatever reason deported by the Chinese authorities to Kuala Lumpur. There they were detained. MI6 is alleged to have become aware of their detention and on 1 March 2004 to have sent the Libyan intelligence services a facsimile reporting their whereabouts. This is said to have led to a plan being developed to render them against their will to Libya. Thereafter, they allege, they were unlawfully detained first by Malaysian officials in Kuala Lumpur and then by Thai officials and United States agents in Bangkok, before being put on board a US airplane which took them to Libya. There they were further detained, in the case of Mrs Boudchar until 21 June 2004, in the case of Mr Belhaj until 23 March 2010.

Mr Belhaj and Mrs Boudchar allege that the United Kingdom procured this detention in all these places "by common design with the Libyan and US authorities". They allege that they suffered mistreatment amounting to torture at the hands of US agents in Bangkok and in the airplane and at the hands of Libyan officials in Libya. They allege that the United Kingdom "by common design arranged, assisted and encouraged [their] unlawful rendition . . . to Libya". They rely in this connection upon a letter dated 18 March 2004 alleged to have been written by the second appellant, Sir Mark Allen, allegedly a senior official of the Secret Intelligence Service ("SIS") to Mr Moussa Koussa, Head of the Libyan External Security Organisation. The letter congratulated Mr Moussa Koussa "on the safe arrival of [Mr Belhaj]". It said that "This was the least we could do for you and for Libya to demonstrate the remarkable relationship we have built over recent years". It indicated that British intelligence had led to Mr Belhaj's transfer to Libya, although the British services "did not pay for the air cargo". Mr Belhaj and Mrs Boudchar further allege that the United Kingdom: "conspired in, assisted and acquiesced in torture, inhumane and degrading treatment, batteries and assaults inflicted upon [them] by the US and Libyan authorities".

The appellants' case in both proceedings is that the issues now before the Supreme Court are inadmissible or non-justiciable on their merits by reason of principles governing state immunity and/or foreign act of state. More specifically, the appellants submit that the claims are based on conduct where the prime actors were foreign state officials, and they either implead the foreign states or would require the English courts to adjudicate upon foreign acts of state. I use the phrase "foreign act of state" loosely at this point to cover various bases on which it is submitted that the English court cannot or should not adjudicate upon proceedings against the United Kingdom, its authorities or officials when the proceedings would also involve adjudicating upon the conduct of a foreign state, even though state immunity is not established on the part of the United Kingdom and the relevant foreign state is not impleaded in the proceedings. The appellants submit that the principles governing foreign act of state dovetail naturally with those governing state immunity, and that underpinning both are conceptions of mutual international respect and comity. That said, there are, as will appear, also differences, not least that state immunity is firmly based on customary international law, whereas foreign act of state in most if not all of its strands has been developed doctrinally in domestic law. State immunity qualifies the jurisdiction of domestic courts. Foreign act of state in one sense requires a domestic court to accept without challenge the validity of certain foreign state acts, but in another sense it is a broader principle of non-justiciability, whereby the domestic court must simply declare itself incompetent to adjudicate. The difficulties which exist in separating or aligning these strands are considerable.

Sovereign states who without justification and without permitting access to justice detain or mistreat individuals in the course or in relation to their conduct of foreign relations or affairs have sovereign immunity in foreign domestic courts. But I see no reason why English law should refrain from scrutinising their conduct in the course of adjudicating upon claims against other parties involved who enjoy no such immunity here, where the alleged conduct involves almost indefinite detention, combined with deprivation of any form of access to justice and, for good measure, torture or persistent ill-treatment of an individual.

Turning to *Belhaj*, on the assumed facts, this appeal too cannot in my view be regarded as raising any issues of a sovereign, international or inter-state nature upon which a domestic court cannot or should not appropriately adjudicate. A hint of the underlying reasons why the United Kingdom may have been willing to supply information to Libya about Mr Belhaj is present in the alleged letter reference to demonstrating "the remarkable relationship we have built over the years", and the respondents themselves add to this an allegation that "the renditions took place as part of a co-ordinated strategy designed to secure diplomatic and intelligence advantages from Colonel Gaddafi". As to this, there is, as I have noted no suggestion that general foreign policy advantages of this nature could justify a plea of Crown act of state. Any attempt to rely on them to support a plea of foreign act of state in respect of the present claims against the United Kingdom for collaboration or connivance in the alleged false imprisonment, rendition from one country to another or mistreatment of individuals such as Mr Belhaj and Mrs Boudchar would at once meet the difficulty that the United Kingdom would be advancing its own breaches of the fundamental rights of those individuals. The letter reference and the respondents' allegation do not therefore represent any basis for regarding the claims as non-justiciable.

---

## Note and Comments:

1. Note that if the plaintiffs had brought suit against the other states involved (i.e., Malaysia, Thailand, United States, and Libya), in all likelihood the case would be dismissed, either on the basis of the Act of State doctrine, or on the basis of Foreign Sovereign Immunity, which we will turn to next.

## Foreign Sovereign Immunity

We addressed foreign sovereign immunity in Chapter 1 in the context of the "terrorism" exception to the *Foreign Sovereign Immunity Act* (FSIA). As mentioned then, for a long period of time states enjoyed absolute immunity in the courts of other countries, a remnant of a time when kings ruled by divine right. During the course of the last century, the doctrine came to be modified, particularly as states began to engage in commercial activities. However, even in the face of the international human rights revolution from the post-World War II period on, the doctrine of sovereign immunity has not changed substantially (Chilton and Whytock 2015). This has led to an odd, even hypocritical, result. Thus, while individuals who either direct or carry out torture can be – actually, *must be* – prosecuted not only in their own state, but wherever they are found, the state these individuals work for and whose policies they are implementing remains immune.

In the following case the U.S. Supreme Court takes up a case of an American citizen, Scott Nelson, who has been tortured in Saudi Arabia and who is filing a claim against the Saudi government. Note that if the individuals who had tortured Nelson happened to travel to the United States and were found (and properly served), he would have a cause of action against them under the Torture Victim Protection Act, which essentially extended the Alien Tort Statute to U.S. nationals. This, however, did not happen, and his only cause of action was against Saudi Arabia itself.

One other thing to note is that although torture is a *jus cogens* norm under international law, this preferred position under international law apparently played no role in the Supreme Court's decision. More than this, the Court spent virtually no time addressing torture as a universal crime under international law. Instead, the Court's analysis extended no further than analyzing whether Saudi Arabia had engaged in a "commercial activity" within the United States.

---

## *Saudi Arabia et al. v. Nelson* 507 U.S. 349 (1993)

[*The respondents Nelson, a married couple, filed this action for damages against petitioners, the Kingdom of Saudi Arabia, a Saudi hospital, and the hospital's purchasing agent in the United States. They alleged, among other things, that respondent husband suffered personal injuries as a result of the Saudi Government's unlawful detention and torture of him and petitioners' negligent failure to warn him of the possibility of severe retaliatory action if he attempted to report on-the-job hazards.*]

### JUSTICE SOUTER DELIVERED THE OPINION OF THE COURT

The Foreign Sovereign Immunities Act of 1976 entitles foreign states to immunity from the jurisdiction of courts in the United States, 28 U. S. C. § 1604, subject to certain enumerated exceptions. § 1605. One is that a foreign state shall not be immune in any case "in which the action is based upon a commercial activity carried on in the United States by the foreign state." §1605(a)(2). We hold that respondents' action alleging personal injury resulting from unlawful detention and torture by the Saudi Government is not "based upon a commercial activity" within the meaning of the Act, which consequently confers no jurisdiction over respondents' suit.

Because this case comes to us on a motion to dismiss the complaint, we assume that we have truthful factual allegations before us, though many of those allegations are subject to dispute. Petitioner Kingdom of Saudi Arabia owns and operates petitioner King Faisal Specialist Hospital in Riyadh, as well as petitioner Royspec Purchasing Services, the hospital's corporate purchasing agent in the United States. The Hospital Corporation of America, Ltd. (HCA), an independent corporation existing under the laws of the Cayman Islands, recruits Americans for employment at the hospital under an agreement signed with Saudi Arabia in 1973.

In its recruitment effort, HCA placed an advertisement in a trade periodical seeking applications for a position as a monitoring systems engineer at the hospital. The advertisement drew the attention of respondent Scott Nelson in September 1983, while Nelson was in the United States. After interviewing for the position in Saudi Arabia, Nelson returned to the United States, where he signed an employment contract with the hospital, satisfied personnel processing requirements, and attended an orientation session that HCA conducted for hospital employees. In the course of that program, HCA identified Royspec as the point of contact in the United States for family members who might wish to reach Nelson in an emergency.

In December 1983, Nelson went to Saudi Arabia and began work at the hospital, monitoring all facilities, equipment, utilities and maintenance systems to insure the safety of patients, hospital staff, and others. He did his job without significant incident until March 1984, when he discovered safety defects in the hospital's oxygen and nitrous oxide lines that posed fire hazards and otherwise endangered patients' lives. Over a period of several months, Nelson repeatedly advised hospital officials of the safety defects and reported the defects to a Saudi Government commission as well. Hospital officials instructed Nelson to ignore the problems.

The hospital's response to Nelson's reports changed, however, on September 27, 1984, when certain hospital employees summoned him to the hospital's security office where agents of the Saudi Government arrested him. The agents transported Nelson to a jail cell, in which they shackled, tortured and beat him, and kept him four days without food. Although Nelson did not understand Arabic, government agents forced him to sign a statement written in that language, the content of which he did not know; a hospital employee who was supposed to act as Nelson's interpreter advised him to sign "anything" the agents gave him to avoid further beatings. Two days later, government agents transferred Nelson to the Al Sijan Prison to await trial on unknown charges.

At the prison, Nelson was confined in an overcrowded cell area infested with rats, where he had to fight other prisoners for food and from which he was taken only once a week for fresh air and exercise. Although police interrogators repeatedly questioned him in Arabic, Nelson did not learn the nature of the charges, if any, against him. For several days, the Saudi Government failed to advise Nelson's family of his whereabouts, though a Saudi official eventually told Nelson's wife, respondent Vivian Nelson, that he could arrange for her husband's release if she provided sexual favors.

Although officials from the United States Embassy visited Nelson twice during his detention, they concluded that his allegations of Saudi mistreatment were "not credible" and made no protest to Saudi authorities. It was only at the personal request of a United States Senator that the Saudi Government released Nelson, 39 days after his arrest, on November 5, 1984. Seven days later, after failing to convince him to return to work at the hospital, the Saudi Government allowed Nelson to leave the country.

The Foreign Sovereign Immunities Act "provides the sole basis for obtaining jurisdiction over a foreign state in the courts of this country." *Argentine Republic* v. *Amerada Hess Shipping Corp.* Under the Act, a foreign state is presumptively immune from the jurisdiction of United States courts; unless a specified exception applies, a federal court lacks subject-matter jurisdiction over a claim against a foreign state.

Only one such exception is said to apply here. The first clause of §1605(a)(2) of the Act provides that a foreign state shall not be immune from the jurisdiction of United States courts in any case "in which the action is based upon a commercial activity carried on in the United States by the foreign state." The Act defines such activity as "commercial activity carried on by such state and having substantial contact with the United States," §1603(e), and provides that a commercial activity may be "either a regular course of commercial conduct or a particular commercial transaction or act," the "commercial character of [which] shall be determined by reference to" its "nature," rather than its "purpose" §1603(d).

There is no dispute here that Saudi Arabia, the hospital, and Royspec all qualify as "foreign state[s]" within the meaning of the Act. For there to be jurisdiction in this case, therefore, the Nelsons' action must be "based upon" some "commercial activity" by petitioners that had "substantial contact" with the United States within the meaning of the Act. Because we conclude that the suit is not based upon any commercial activity by petitioners, we need not reach the issue of substantial contact with the United States.

In this case, the Nelsons have alleged that petitioners recruited Scott Nelson for work at the hospital, signed an employment contract with him, and subsequently employed him. While these activities led to the conduct that eventually injured the Nelsons, they are not the basis for the Nelsons' suit. Even taking each of the Nelsons' allegations about Scott Nelson's recruitment and employment as true, those facts alone entitle the Nelsons to nothing under their theory of the case. The Nelsons have not, after all, alleged breach of contract, but personal injuries caused by petitioners' intentional wrongs and by petitioners' negligent failure to warn Scott Nelson that they might commit those wrongs. Those torts, and not the arguably commercial activities that preceded their commission, form the basis for the Nelsons' suit.

The Nelsons and their *amici* urge us to give significance to their assertion that the Saudi Government subjected Nelson to the abuse alleged as retaliation for his persistence in reporting hospital safety violations, and argue that the character of the mistreatment was consequently commercial. One *amicus*, indeed, goes so far as to suggest that the Saudi Government "often uses detention and torture to resolve commercial disputes." Brief for Human Rights Watch as *Amicus Curiae* 6. But this argument does not alter the fact that the powers allegedly abused were those of police and penal officers. In any event, the argument is off the point, for it goes to purpose, the very fact the Act renders irrelevant to the question of an activity's commercial character. Whatever may have been the Saudi Government's motivation for its allegedly abusive treatment of Nelson, it remains the case that the Nelsons' action is based upon a sovereign activity immune from the subject-matter jurisdiction of United States courts under the Act.

The Nelsons' action is not "based upon a commercial activity" within the meaning of the first clause of §1605(a)(2) of the Act, and the judgment of the Court of Appeals is accordingly reversed.

It is So Ordered.

### JUSTICE WHITE, WITH WHOM JUSTICE BLACKMUN JOINS, CONCURRING IN THE JUDGMENT

According to respondents' complaint, Scott Nelson's employer retaliated against him for reporting safety problems by "summon[ing him] . . . to the hospital's security office from which he was transported to a jail cell." Once there, he allegedly was "shackled, tortured and beaten by persons acting at the direction, instigation, provocation, instruction or request of" petitioners – Saudi Arabia, King Faisal Specialist Hospital, and Royspec. The majority concludes that petitioners enjoy sovereign immunity because respondents' action is not "based upon a commercial activity." I disagree. I nonetheless concur in the judgment because in my view the commercial conduct upon which respondents base their complaint was not "carried on in the United States."

To run and operate a hospital, even a public hospital, is to engage in a commercial enterprise. The majority never concedes this point, but it does not deny it either, and to my mind the matter is self-evident. By the same token, warning an employee when he blows the whistle and taking retaliatory action, such as harassment, involuntary transfer, discharge, or other tortious behavior, although not prototypical commercial acts, are certainly well within the bounds of commercial activity. The House and Senate Reports accompanying the legislation virtually compel this conclusion, explaining as they do that "a foreign government's . . . employment or engagement of laborers, clerical staff or marketing agents . . . would be among those included within" the definition of commercial activity. Nelson alleges that petitioners harmed him in the course of engaging in their commercial enterprise, as a direct result of their commercial acts. His claim, in other words, is "based upon commercial activity."

Nevertheless, I reach the same conclusion as the majority because petitioners' commercial activity was not "carried on in the United States." The Act defines such conduct as "commercial activity . . . having substantial contact with the United States." Respondents point to the hospital's recruitment efforts in the United States, including advertising in the American media, and the signing of the employment contract in Miami. As

I earlier noted, while these may very well qualify as commercial activity in the United States, they do not constitute the commercial activity upon which respondents' action is based. Conversely, petitioners' commercial conduct in Saudi Arabia, though constituting the basis of the Nelsons' suit, lacks a sufficient nexus to the United States. Neither the hospital's employment practices, nor its disciplinary procedures, has any apparent connection to this country. On that basis, I agree that the Act does not grant the Nelsons access to our courts.

### JUSTICE STEVENS, DISSENTING

Under the Foreign Sovereign Immunities Act of 1976 (FSIA), a foreign state is subject to the jurisdiction of American courts if two conditions are met: The action must be "based upon a commercial activity" and that activity must have a "substantial contact with the United States." These two conditions should be separately analyzed because they serve two different purposes. The former excludes commercial activity from the scope of the foreign sovereign's immunity from suit; the second identifies the contacts with the United States that support the assertion of jurisdiction over the defendant.

In this case, as Justice White has demonstrated, petitioner Kingdom of Saudi Arabia's operation of the hospital and its employment practices and disciplinary procedures are "commercial activities" within the meaning of the statute, and respondent Scott Nelson's claim that he was punished for acts performed in the course of his employment was unquestionably "based upon" those activities. Thus, the first statutory condition is satisfied; petitioner is not entitled to immunity from the claims asserted by respondent.

Unlike Justice White, however, I am also convinced that petitioner's commercial activities – whether defined as the regular course of conduct of operating a hospital or, more specifically, as the commercial transaction of engaging respondent "as an employee with specific responsibilities in that enterprise," have sufficient contact with the United States to justify the exercise of federal jurisdiction. Petitioner Royspec maintains an office in Maryland and purchases hospital supplies and equipment in this country. For nearly two decades the hospital's American agent has maintained an office in the United States and regularly engaged in the recruitment of personnel in this country. Respondent himself was recruited in the United States and entered into his employment contract with the hospital in the United States. Before traveling to Saudi Arabia to assume his position at the hospital, respondent attended an orientation program in Tennessee. The position for which respondent was recruited and ultimately hired was that of a monitoring systems manager, a troubleshooter, and, taking respondent's allegations as true, it was precisely respondent's performance of those responsibilities that led to the hospital's retaliatory actions against him.

Whether the first clause of §1605(a)(2) broadly authorizes "general" jurisdiction over foreign entities that engage in substantial commercial activity in this country, or, more narrowly, authorizes only "specific" jurisdiction over particular commercial claims that have a substantial contact with the United States, petitioners' contacts with the United States in this case are, in my view, plainly sufficient to subject petitioners to suit in this country on a claim arising out of their nonimmune commercial activity relating to respondent. If the same activities had been performed by a private business, I have no doubt jurisdiction would be upheld. And that, of course, should be a touchstone of our inquiry; for as Justice White explains, when a foreign nation sheds its uniquely sovereign status and seeks out the benefits of the private marketplace, it must, like any private party, bear the burdens and responsibilities imposed by that marketplace. I would therefore affirm the judgment of the Court of Appeals.

**Notes and Comments:**

1. Which opinion – if any – do you agree with the most?
2. Although foreign sovereign immunity is treated as a longstanding principle under international law, it is important to point out that there is no international treaty as such that governs this practice. Instead, each state has its own law on sovereign immunity, although there certainly is some commonality among the various states.
3. Recall in Chapter 1 our discussion of the attempts to hold Saudi Arabia responsible for its involvement in the terrorist attacks on the United States on September 11, 2001. After a series of unsuccessful lawsuits brought by victims and families of the victims, Congress passed the *Justice Against Sponsors of Terrorism Act* (JASTA), which would allow American nationals the ability to bring suit against states that sponsor terrorism – even if these countries are not on the U.S. State Department's official States Sponsors of Terrorism list and even if the "entire tort" did not occur in the United States. What remains unclear is whether JASTA will ever be fully implemented. However, there is little likelihood that JASTA or any of the other provisions of the *Foreign Sovereign Immunity Act* would prove useful to someone like Scott Nelson.

When I give talks on human rights I almost always reference the next court case. I argue that if just one judge in this 9–8 ruling by the European Court of Human Rights had held in favor of the applicant, this would have fundamentally changed the nature of human rights protection. The reason for saying this is that one reason – and I would say the main reason – why states are able to violate international human rights standards with impunity is the fact that they are provided impunity by other states. But if this were to change?

---

## *Al-Adsani v. The United Kingdom,* ECtHR, App. No. 35763/97 (2001)

The applicant made the following allegations concerning the events underlying the dispute he submitted to the English courts. The Government stated that they were not in a position to comment on the accuracy of these claims.

The applicant, who is a trained pilot, went to Kuwait in 1991 to assist in its defense against Iraq. During the Gulf War he served as a member of the Kuwaiti Air Force and, after the Iraqi invasion, he remained behind as a member of the resistance movement. During that period he came into possession of sex videotapes involving Sheikh Jaber Al-Sabah Al-Saud Al-Sabah ("the Sheikh"), who is related to the Emir of Kuwait and is said to have an influential position in Kuwait. By some means these tapes entered general circulation, for which the applicant was held responsible by the Sheikh.

After the Iraqi armed forces were expelled from Kuwait, on or about 2 May 1991, the Sheikh and two others gained entry to the applicant's house, beat him and took him at gunpoint in a government jeep to the Kuwaiti State Security Prison. The applicant was falsely imprisoned there for several days during which he was repeatedly beaten by security guards. He was released on 5 May 1991, having been forced to sign a false confession.

On or about 7 May 1991 the Sheikh took the applicant at gunpoint in a government car to the palace of the Emir of Kuwait's brother. At first the applicant's head was repeatedly held underwater in a swimming-pool containing corpses, and he was then dragged into a small room where the Sheikh set fire to mattresses soaked in petrol, as a result of which the applicant was seriously burnt.

Initially the applicant was treated in a Kuwaiti hospital, and on 17 May 1991 he returned to England where he spent six weeks in hospital being treated for burns covering 25% of his total body surface area. He also suffered psychological damage and has been diagnosed as suffering from a severe form of post-traumatic stress disorder, aggravated by the fact that, once in England, he received threats warning him not to take action or give publicity to his plight.

[Al-Adsani brought a claim against Kuwait in domestic (UK) courts but his suit was dismissed on the basis of the country's sovereign immunity statute. He then filed the present action against the UK on the basis that, in doing so, the United Kingdom had violated his rights under the European Convention.]

### Alleged Violation of Article 3 of the Convention

The applicant contended that the United Kingdom had failed to secure his right not to be tortured, contrary to Article 3 of the Convention read in conjunction with Articles 1 and 13.

Article 3 provides:

No one shall be subjected to torture or to inhuman or degrading treatment or punishment.

Article 1 provides:

The High Contracting Parties shall secure to everyone within their jurisdiction the rights and freedoms defined in Section I of [the] Convention.

Article 13 provides:

Everyone whose rights and freedoms as set forth in [the] Convention are violated shall have an effective remedy before a national authority notwithstanding that the violation has been committed by persons acting in an official capacity.

He submitted that, correctly interpreted, the above provisions taken together required the United Kingdom to assist one of its citizens in obtaining an effective remedy for torture against another State. The grant of immunity from civil suit to the State of Kuwait had, however, frustrated this purpose.

It is true that, taken together, Articles 1 and 3 place a number of positive obligations on the High Contracting Parties, designed to prevent and provide redress for torture and other forms of ill-treatment. However, in each case the State's obligation applies only in relation to ill-treatment allegedly committed within its jurisdiction.

In *Soering*, the Court recognized that Article 3 has some, limited, extraterritorial application, to the extent that the decision by a Contracting State to expel an individual might engage the responsibility of that State under the Convention, where substantial grounds had been shown for believing that the person concerned, if expelled, faced a real risk of being subjected to torture or to inhuman or degrading treatment or punishment in the receiving country. In the judgment it was emphasized, however, that in so far as any liability under the Convention might be incurred in such circumstances, it would be incurred by the expelling Contracting State by reason of its having taken action which had as a direct consequence the exposure of an individual to proscribed ill-treatment.

The applicant does not contend that the alleged torture took place within the jurisdiction of the United Kingdom or that the United Kingdom authorities had any causal connection with its occurrence. In these circumstances, it cannot be said that the High Contracting Party was under a duty to provide a civil remedy to the applicant in respect of torture allegedly carried out by the Kuwaiti authorities.

It follows that there has been no violation of Article 3 of the Convention in the present case.

### ALLEGED VIOLATION OF ARTICLE 6 § 1 OF THE CONVENTION

The applicant alleged that he was denied access to a court in the determination of his claim against the State of Kuwait and that this constituted a violation of Article 6 § 1 of the Convention, which provides in its first sentence:

> In the determination of his civil rights and obligations or of any criminal charge against him, everyone is entitled to a fair and public hearing within a reasonable time by an independent and impartial tribunal established by law.

The Government submitted that Article 6 § 1 did not apply to the proceedings, but that, even if it did, any interference with the right of access to a court was compatible with its provisions.

Within the Convention system it has long been recognized that the right under Article 3 not to be subjected to torture or to inhuman or degrading treatment or punishment enshrines one of the fundamental values of democratic society. It is an absolute right, permitting of no exception in any circumstances. Of all the categories of ill-treatment prohibited by Article 3, "torture" has a special stigma, attaching only to deliberate inhuman treatment causing very serious and cruel suffering.

While the Court accepts, on the basis of these authorities, that the prohibition of torture has achieved the status of a peremptory norm in international law, it observes that the present case concerns not, as in *Furundzija* and *Pinochet*, the criminal liability of an individual for alleged acts of torture, but the immunity of a State in a civil suit for damages in respect of acts of torture within the territory of that State. Notwithstanding the special character of the prohibition of torture in international law, the Court is unable to discern in the international instruments, judicial authorities or other materials before it any firm basis for concluding that, as a matter of international law, a State no longer enjoys immunity from civil suit in the courts of another State where acts of torture are alleged. In particular, the Court observes that none of the primary international instruments referred to (Article 5 of the Universal Declaration of Human Rights, Article 7 of the International Covenant on Civil and Political Rights and Articles 2 and 4 of the UN Convention) relates to civil proceedings or to State immunity.

The Court, while noting the growing recognition of the overriding importance of the prohibition of torture, does not accordingly find it established that there is yet acceptance in international law of the proposition that States are not entitled to immunity in respect of civil claims for damages for alleged torture committed outside the forum State.

FOR THESE REASONS, THE COURT

1. *Holds* unanimously that there has been no violation of Article 3 of the Convention;
2. *Holds* by nine votes to eight that there has been no violation of Article 6 § 1 of the Convention.

CONCURRING OPINION OF JUDGE PELLONPÄÄ, JOINED BY
JUDGE SIR NICOLAS BRATZA

The somewhat paradoxical result, had the minority's view prevailed, could have been that precisely those States which so far have been most liberal in accepting refugees and asylum-seekers, would have had imposed upon them the additional burden of guaranteeing access to a court for the determination of perhaps hundreds of refugees' civil claims for compensation for alleged torture.

Although giving absolute priority to the prohibition of torture may at first sight seem very "progressive", a more careful consideration tends to confirm that such a step would also run the risk of proving a sort of "Pyrrhic victory". International cooperation, including cooperation with a view to eradicating the vice of torture, presupposes the continuing existence of certain elements of a basic framework for the conduct of international relations. Principles concerning State immunity belong to that regulatory framework, and I believe it is more conducive to orderly international cooperation to leave this framework intact than to follow another course.

In my view this case leaves us with at least two important lessons. First, although consequences should not alone determine the interpretation of a given rule, one should never totally lose sight of the consequences of a particular interpretation one is about to adopt. Secondly, when having to touch upon central questions of general international law, this Court should be very cautious before taking upon itself the role of a forerunner.

DISSENTING OPINION OF JUDGE FERRARI BRAVO

What a pity! The Court, whose task in this case was to rule whether there had been a violation of Article 6 § 1, had a golden opportunity to issue a clear and forceful condemnation of all acts of torture. To do so, it need only have upheld the thrust of the House of Lords' judgment in *Regina v. Bow Street Metropolitan Stipendiary and Others, ex parte Pinochet Ugarte (No. 3)* to the effect that the prohibition of torture is now *jus cogens*, so that torture is a crime under international law. It follows that every State has a duty to *contribute* to the punishment of torture and cannot hide behind formalist arguments to avoid having to give judgment.

I say to "contribute" to punishment, and not, obviously, to punish, since it was clear that the acts of torture had not taken place in the United Kingdom but elsewhere, in a State over which the Court did not have jurisdiction.

But it is precisely one of those old formalist arguments which the Court endorsed when it said that it was unable to discern any rules of international law requiring it not to apply the rule of immunity from civil suit where acts of torture were alleged. And the Court went further, notwithstanding its analysis of the cases, concluding sadly that the contrary rule was not *yet* accepted. *Quousque tandem . . . !* [How long. . . !]

There will be other such cases, but the Court has unfortunately missed a very good opportunity to deliver a courageous judgment.

**Note and Comments:**

1. *Al-Adsani* poses the question of state responsibility in a rather stark way: are states that provide sovereign immunity protection to states that violate international human rights standards thereby complicit (Gibney and Roxström 2012)? What do you think?

**Domestic Sovereign Immunity**

We turn from foreign sovereign immunity to domestic sovereign immunity by examining U.S. law under the Federal Tort Claims Act (FTCA). Foreign sovereign immunity involves one state providing immunity to other states – while domestic sovereign immunity involves a state providing sovereign immunity to itself. In the case that follows, a U.S. warship that was protecting Iraqi oil tankers (note that this was at a time when the United States actively supported Saddam Hussein) shot down an Iranian commercial aircraft thereby killing all aboard. The heirs of those killed then brought this case against the U.S. government and federal (U.S.) officials.

---

## *Koohi v. United States,* 976 F. 2d. 1328 (9th Cir. 1992)

### REINHARDT, CIRCUIT JUDGE

The tragedy that gives rise to this lawsuit – the shooting down of a civilian aircraft by a United States warship – occurred in the midst of the undeclared "tanker war" that was a part of the larger hostilities between the nations of Iran and Iraq. During the tanker war, each of those nations attacked vessels carrying the other's oil. In August, 1986, Iran began to concentrate its attacks on ships calling at Kuwaiti ports, especially those flying the Kuwaiti flag. Those ships, according to Iran, were carrying Iraqi-produced cargo, primarily oil, as well as cargo destined for Iraq. Kuwait appealed to the United States for help in protecting its shipping.

In March of 1987, the United States announced that it would allow qualifying Kuwaiti tankers to re-register under the American flag and that the United States Navy would then provide those tankers with protection. Because at that time Kuwait was closely allied with Iraq, the decision had the effect of aiding Iraq in its war with Iran. Shortly after the March announcement, American naval forces commenced protecting ships carrying Iraqi oil and products destined for Iraq against attacks by Iranian forces. Not surprisingly, the United States Navy soon began to engage in combat with Iranian naval vessels.

The incident that underlies this lawsuit occurred on July 3, 1988. Early that morning, the USS Vincennes, a naval cruiser equipped with the computerized Aegis air defense system, dispatched a reconnaissance helicopter to investigate reported activity by Iranian gunboats. The helicopter was allegedly fired upon by antiaircraft guns. The Vincennes in turn crossed into Iranian territorial waters and fired upon the gunboats.

Minutes later, a civilian Iranian Airbus, Iran Air Flight 655, took off from a joint com-mercial-military airport at Bandar Abbas, Iran. The Vincennes was in the vicinity of the aircraft's flight path. Its crew mistook the civilian aircraft for an Iranian F-14 and shot it down over the Persian Gulf. All 290 persons aboard the Iranian Airbus died.

Briefs recently filed by the Department of Justice in the International Court of Jus-tice report that the Vincennes was in Iranian waters at the time of the incident. Certain other events preceding the downing of the Iranian civilian plane remain the subject of controversy. Official government reports state the facts in the manner described in the text. Other sources suggest that the U.S. Navy deliberately provoked the conflict with the gunboats in order to create an opportunity to destroy Iran's remaining naval forces.

The outcome of this case is not affected by the truth of these matters. The result would be the same regardless of which side precipitated the naval encounter, and regardless of the Vincennes' location when it shot down the civilian plane.

Plaintiffs are the heirs of some of the deceased passengers and crew. They seek compensation from the United States and several private companies involved in the construction of the Aegis Air Defense System, which was deployed on the Vincennes. They assert two different types of claims: claims against the United States for the neg-ligent operation of the Vincennes and claims against the weapons manufacturers for design defects in the Aegis system. Essentially, they contend that the defendants were, for differing reasons and to differing degrees, each responsible for the misidentifica-tion of the civilian Airbus as an F-14 and the consequent decision to shoot it down. They contend that various statutes impose liability on the defendants. Following the district court's dismissal of their lawsuits, the plaintiffs appealed. We affirm.

### Sovereign Immunity

As a general matter, the federal courts may not entertain an action against the federal government without its consent. We conclude that neither act provides a waiver of sovereign immunity for the plaintiffs' action.

The waiver of sovereign immunity enacted in the FTCA [Federal Torts Claims Act] contains an explicit exception for "[a]ny claim arising out of combatant activities of the military or naval forces, or the Coast Guard, during time of war."

It seems clear that the purpose of the exception we are construing is to ensure that the government will not be liable for negligent conduct by our armed forces in times of combat. Whether that combat is formally authorized by the Congress or follows less formal actions of the Executive and Legislative branches would seem to be irrelevant to Congress's objectives. We perceive three principal reasons for the combatant activi-ties exception. First, tort law is based in part on the theory that the prospect of liability makes the actor more careful.

Here, Congress certainly did not want our military personnel to exercise great cau-tion at a time when bold and imaginative measures might be necessary to overcome enemy forces; nor did it want our soldiers, sailors, or airmen to be concerned about the possibility of tort liability when making life or death decisions in the midst of combat. Second, tort law is based in part on a desire to secure justice – to provide a remedy for the innocent victim of wrongful conduct.

War produces innumerable innocent victims of harmful conduct – on all sides. It would make little sense to single out for special compensation a few of these persons – usually enemy citizens – on the basis that they have suffered from the negligence of our military forces rather than from the overwhelming and pervasive violence which each side intentionally inflicts on the other. Third, there is a punitive aspect to tort law. Society believes tortfeasors should suffer for their sins. It is unlikely that there are many Americans who would favor punishing our servicemen for injuring members of the enemy military or civilian population as a result of actions taken in order to preserve their own lives and limbs. For these and other reasons, tort law, in toto, is an inappropriate subject for injection into the area of military engagements. The FTCA clearly recognizes this principle, and we see no reason why Congress would want to differentiate in this respect between declared and undeclared wars.

In sum, we have no difficulty in concluding that when, as a result of a deliberate decision by the executive branch, United States armed forces engage in an organized series of hostile encounters on a significant scale with the military forces of another nation, the FTCA exception applies. Under those circumstances, a "time of war" exists, at least for purposes of domestic tort law.

There can be no doubt that during the "tanker war" a "time of war" existed. The United States' involvement in naval combat while the Iran-Iraq war was in progress was the result of a deliberate decision on the part of the executive branch to engage in hostile military activities vis-a-vis Iran in order to protect Gulf shipping. Our activities included not only the defense of reflagged tankers servicing Iraq's needs, but ultimately attacks upon Iranian gunboats and oil platforms. The Vincennes' actions constituted a part of our military involvement in the Persian Gulf. The act of shooting down the Iranian civilian aircraft, although a result of tragic error, was committed in order to further the perceived interests of the United States in its involvement in the tanker war. Moreover, we believe that the ill-fated Iranian Airbus may fairly be said to have been operating "during time of war" both temporally and spatially. The aircraft took off from an Iranian airport used for both civilian and military purposes. Its flight path was in the general area in which hostilities had occurred with regularity over the past year. The United States had issued warnings to all aircraft operations in the region notifying them of the dangers. The pilots of the Iranian aircraft should not have been surprised to encounter conditions of "war". Under the circumstances, we believe that the shooting down of the Airbus by the Vincennes falls within the FTCA's exception for combatant activities during time of war. Accordingly, the plaintiffs' FTCA action against the Vincennes is barred by the doctrine of sovereign immunity.

The result would be no different if the downing of the civilian plane had been deliberate rather than the result of error. The combatant activities exception applies whether U.S. military forces hit a prescribed or an unintended target, whether those selecting the target act wisely or foolishly, whether the missiles we employ turn out to be "smart" or dumb, whether the target we choose performs the function we believe it does or whether our choice of an object for destruction is a result of error or miscalculation. In other words, it simply does not matter for purposes of the "time of war" exception whether the military makes or executes its decisions carefully or negligently, properly or improperly. It is the nature of the act and not the manner of its performance that counts. Thus, for purposes of liability under the FTCA, it is of no significance whether a plane that is shot down is civilian or military, so long as the person giving the order or firing the weapon does so for the purpose of furthering our military objectives or of defending lives, property, or other interests. To put it in the terms of the statute, the only question that need be answered is whether the challenged action constituted combatant activity during time of war.

---

**Notes and Comments:**

1. Do you agree with the court that even if the downing of the civilian aircraft had been "deliberate" the United States would enjoy sovereign immunity protection under the FTCA?

2. The aftermath of *Koohi* is also interesting to note from an international law perspective. Immediately after the event, the United States government offered to make *ex gratia* payments – but directly to the victims and not the Iranian government, which it viewed then (as it does now) as a state sponsor of terrorism.

The next two cases involve U.S. activities in Central America during the 1980s. These opinions were written by Judge Antonin Scalia before he was appointed to the U.S. Supreme Court. This was an extraordinarily volatile period of time with civil conflicts in Nicaragua, El Salvador, Honduras, and Guatemala.

## *Ramirez de Arellano v. Weinberger,* 724 F.2d 143 (D.C. Cir. 1983)

### SCALIA, CIRCUIT JUDGE

This is an appeal by plaintiffs Ramirez, two Puerto Rican corporations, and four Honduran corporations from dismissal of their suit against the Secretary of Defense claiming wrongful occupation of their property in Honduras for use as a training facility for Salvadoran soldiers. The district court granted defendants' motion to dismiss, on the ground that the case presented a nonjusticiable political question. We disagree with that basis of dismissal but affirm because in other respects the plaintiffs have failed to present a claim upon which injunctive or other relief can be granted.

Accepting as true the allegations contained in plaintiffs' pleadings and affidavits,] the facts of the case are as follows: One of the plaintiff Honduran corporations owns a large tract of land in the northern portion of Honduras, on which the two other Honduran corporations conduct, respectively, a cattle ranching and shrimp packing business. These three Honduran corporations are owned by the fourth Honduran corporation, which is in turn owned by one of the plaintiff Puerto Rican corporations, which, finally, is owned by the second Puerto Rican corporation (owned by plaintiff Ramirez) and by Ramirez, an American citizen. The plaintiffs' total investment in the property is approximately $13,000,000.

Still accepting the plaintiffs' view of the facts: In late March 1983, the Defense Department decided to establish in Honduras a Regional Military Training Center at which American military specialists would train Salvadoran soldiers. The Defense Department selected the site, which turned out to be the plaintiffs' ranch. While the fact of its private ownership may not have been known initially, after that came to light the Department still refused to change its plans, and proceeded with construction. The base was originally to be located on 1,500–2,000 acres, but it has expanded onto an additional 5,300 acres, so that it occupies about half of the total ranch and about 90% of the year-round grazing land. Permanent facilities include a tent camp, buildings, ammunition storage areas, and a firing range. About one hundred Green Berets and 1,000 other soldiers, including Honduran troops who are participating in the exercises, are now living and training on the land. As a consequence of the construction of the base and the conduct of its activities, prime grazing land and fences have been bulldozed, the flow of water to the meat packing plant has been interrupted, cattle have been shot by stray bullets, the animals in the occupied area have become undernourished, and ranch employees have refused to work in areas where the training is taking place. No eminent domain proceedings, Honduran or American, have been conducted, and no compensation paid plaintiffs, although Honduran proceedings have been discussed with plaintiff Ramirez by Honduran officials.

The plaintiffs filed a complaint in the United States District Court for the District of Columbia. They requested an injunction, a declaratory judgment and such other relief as the court deems just and proper.

The district court found that these allegations presented a nonjusticiable political question, because, to repeat the most salient concrete points, (1) " 'it is not the function of the Judiciary to entertain private litigation – even by a citizen – which challenges the legality, the wisdom, or the propriety of the Commander-in-Chief in sending our armed forces abroad or to any particular region,' "; (2) adjudication of the matter would "necessarily involve sensitive and confidential communications between the highest members of the Executive branch and officials of a foreign power that are not judicially discoverable,"; and (3) judicial intervention would interfere with the conduct of our foreign affairs in Central America. We do not agree with this basis of dismissal.

The plaintiffs do not seek adjudication of the propriety of the American military presence in Honduras, but of a narrower issue: whether United States officials have, by their actions, unlawfully deprived them of the use of their land. To be sure, because this case involves land in Central America, and because United States military activities in that region are currently the subject of national interest and debate, the issue is presented in a more politically charged context. That may make it, in a sense, a political *case* – but as the Court noted in *Baker v. Carr* (1962), "[t]he doctrine . . . is one of 'political questions,' not one of 'political cases.' "

The district court's concern about interfering with our foreign policy of providing assistance to threatened governments of Central America is a valid one. Such damage would arise, however, not from our mere resolution of the issue whether United States forces are in possession of the plaintiffs' land, but from injunctive relief, should we choose to provide it, which would bring the present operation to a halt. It is relevant, as we shall discuss below, to the nature of the remedy which plaintiffs can obtain – but not to the "political" character of the question we have been asked to resolve.

The dissent accuses us of not only error but apparently even of prejudgment, asserting that we have "gone to extraordinary lengths to deprive plaintiff Ramirez of an opportunity for relief," and that essential portions of our analysis are "only advanced . . . to make the denial of this citizen's constitutional rights more palatable." We of course reject that imputation, as we reject the dissent's more demonstrable distortions of our position. We do not, for example, maintain that "the U.S. plaintiffs should be forced to bring their claims in the foreign courts of Honduras," (though since they have been injured only in their capacity as shareholders of the other plaintiffs, the four Honduran corporations, with respect to land acquired and activities undertaken in Honduras, that would hardly seem outrageous); to the extent they have valid claims they may bring them here, but must be content with the ordinary remedy of monetary compensation – for what is, after all, a monetary injury, despite the dissent's romantic characterization of this $13 million, corporate-owned, multinational agribusiness-packery as "a U.S. citizen's private ranch." Similarly, we have not remotely said that the foreign affairs context of Executive action can shield unlawful conduct from judicial inquiry, only that this particular foreign affairs context, plus many other factors, precludes the extraordinary remedy of injunction in this case.

The dissent invokes "the great tradition of judicial protection of individual rights against unconstitutional governmental activities." But that tradition has not come to us from La Mancha, and does not impel us to right the unrightable wrong by thrusting the sharpest of our judicial lances heedlessly and in perilous directions. It acknowledges the need to craft judicial protection in such fashion as to preserve the proper functions of government. We are therefore perplexed rather than inspired by the dissent's uncompromising pronouncement that it "do[es] not accept the proposition that a United States district court is powerless to stop a continuing violation of a U.S. citizen's constitutional rights," or "should decline for prudential considerations to intervene to arrest ongoing constitutional violations, when the alleged perpetrators are officials of the Executive Branch, amenable to process and supervision here in Washington, D.C." Such a vision of judicial supremacy, not only in interpreting the Constitution but in controlling every aspect of Executive activity bearing upon citizens' constitutional rights, does not comport with our understanding of the separation of powers. It is a vision that obscures not merely the common-law tradition that injunction is an extraordinary remedy, but also the political truth that society has many other needs that must be accommodated with proper protection of individual rights, and the related constitutional reality that we serve beside the officers of two other coequal branches, whose responsibilities, no less important than our own, require knowledge and judgment we do not possess. If the traditional and hence limited relief we have found available in this case, based upon a more modest conception of our abilities and powers, lends itself less to stirring eulogy of the judicial role in vindicating individual liberties, we are consoled by the fact that it lends itself more to preservation of the Constitution.

For the reasons stated, the judgment of the district court is
Affirmed.

### WILKEY, Circuit Judge, Dissenting

Plaintiff Temistocles Ramirez de Arellano, a citizen of the United States, sought to invoke the remedial powers of the federal Judiciary to halt an allegedly unconstitutional seizure and destruction of his cattle ranch by officers of the United States. Because plaintiff Ramirez sought equitable relief in the federal district court, a majority of this panel affirms the dismissal of his claim at the threshold of litigation. I cannot agree that the district court is powerless to give this citizen the relief he seeks. Accordingly, I dissent from that portion of the majority opinion which holds that the plaintiff has failed to state a claim for relief. I would remand this case to the district court for factual development on the merits.

The location of the plaintiffs' land in a foreign country does not prevent the district court from granting relief. Courts often properly issue equitable decrees involving property outside the jurisdiction of the court. When, as here, the court adjudicating the controversy has personal jurisdiction over the defendants, the extraterritorial nature of the property involved in the litigation is not a bar to equitable relief. Under such circumstances, courts in equity do not hesitate to order the defendants, who are present before the court, to do or refrain from doing something directly involving foreign property.

A conclusion that the enforcement of any equitable decree would require an impermissible degree of judicial supervision rests entirely on assumed facts neither presented nor suggested by plaintiffs' complaint. The court should assume that the defendants, all officers of the United States present in Washington, D.C., will obey a decree of the district court. This country has a long tradition of government reliance on the military to uphold and enforce judicial decrees, which belies an assumption that the defendants will flout an equitable order of the federal Judiciary. Furthermore, there is simply no factual basis for concluding that an equitable decree would involve this court in numerous or even any compliance disputes.

The plaintiffs' pleadings outline a classic case for injunctive or declaratory relief entitling them to go forward on the merits in the federal district court. Instead, the majority has gone to extraordinary lengths to deprive plaintiff Ramirez of an opportunity for relief from the continuing unconstitutional invasion of his property rights alleged here.

In affirming the dismissal of the plaintiffs' claim, the majority departs from a long tradition of the exercise of federal remedial powers to vindicate individual rights overridden by specific, unconstitutional military actions. It ignores the Nation's historic commitment to protecting private citizens' rights against military excesses, the spirit of which is embodied in the Third Amendment's express prohibition against the forced quartering of soldiers in private homes. Charges that U.S. military officers are unconstitutionally housing over 1,000 soldiers on a U.S. citizen's private ranch cannot conscionably be nullified by this court for failure to state a claim for relief.

The majority errs gravely when it announces that the thwarting of such unconstitutional military activity is beyond the remedial authority of the federal Judiciary. I do not accept the proposition that a United States district court is powerless to stop a continuing violation of a U.S. citizen's constitutional rights, and that instead the citizen can only obtain monetary relief after the event in the Claims Court. Nor do I accept the proposition that a United States district court should decline for prudential considerations to intervene to arrest ongoing constitutional violations, when the alleged perpetrators are officials of the Executive Branch, amenable to process and supervision here in Washington, D.C. It simply cannot be the law that this American plaintiff is relegated to damages or to the courts of a foreign country for redress of injuries caused by United States officials' ongoing, unconstitutional destruction of his ranch, his property, his livelihood, and his personal safety as claimed.

I respectfully but emphatically dissent.

---

In earlier chapters we examined the International Court of Justice's ruling in *Nicaragua v. United States* (1986) where the Court held that the United States had violated international law for its "direct" actions in attempting to overthrow the Sandinista-led government in that country (but not for its "indirect" actions in arming and equipping the *contras*). The following case is, in a way, an attempt to implement this ruling of an international tribunal in a domestic (U.S.) court.

---

## *Sanchez-Espinoza v. Reagan*, 770 F. 2d 202 (D.C. Cir. 1985)

### SCALIA, CIRCUIT JUDGE

The complaint at issue in this appeal recites various causes of action arising out of appellees' alleged support of forces bearing arms against the government of Nicaragua (so-called "Contra" forces). The United States District Court for the District of Columbia granted a motion to dismiss, primarily on the ground that the case presented a nonjusticiable political question. The issues presented by the appeal include whether the Alien Tort Statute, 28 U.S.C. § 1350 (1982), confers jurisdiction over suits against officers of the United States alleging violation of international law by this country; whether the nonresident alien appellants can maintain an action for damages to vindicate their asserted rights under the fourth and fifth amendments to the United States

Constitution or under any of several statutes relating to United States foreign and military affairs; whether those appellants who are members of Congress can obtain judicial relief for the Executive Branch's alleged violation of the constitutional provision reserving to Congress the power to declare war; and whether, in the circumstances of this case, discretionary judicial remedies can properly be invoked.

The appellants can be divided into three groups: First, twelve citizens of Nicaragua, nine of whom reside there, two of whom reside in Germany, and one in France (the "Nicaraguan appellants"), who sue for redress of tortious injuries to themselves or their families at the hands of the Contras in Nicaragua. Second, twelve members of the United States House of Representatives (the "congressional appellants"), who sue to end appellees' alleged disregard of Congress's right to declare war and of a prohibition against supporting the Contras imposed by Congress through statute. Third, two residents of Dade County, Florida, who sue to enjoin an alleged nuisance created by the maintenance and operation of paramilitary camps at that location.

The appellees can also be divided into three groups: First, nine present or former United States executive officials (the "federal appellees"), most of whom are sued both individually and in their official capacities. Second, two organizations – Alpha 66, Inc., and Bay of Pigs Veterans Association, Brigade 2506, Inc. – which are alleged to operate paramilitary training camps in the United States. Third, Max Vargas, a Nicaraguan exile and resident of the State of Florida, who is alleged to be leader of the Nicaraguan Democratic Union-Revolutionary Armed Forces of Nicaragua, which operates paramilitary camps in Nicaragua and elsewhere.

The principal assertions, in addition to those alluded to above, are as follows: That the federal appellees, acting in concert and conspiracy with the other defendants and others unknown, have authorized, financed, trained, directed and knowingly provided substantial assistance for the performance of activities which terrorize and otherwise injure the civilian population of the Republic of Nicaragua. That in November 1981 President Reagan, various members of the National Security Council, and others approved a plan submitted by the CIA for covert activities to destabilize and overthrow the government of Nicaragua. That pursuant to that plan, the United States has provided financial assistance of at least $19 million, training by mobile teams of United States military personnel, and other forms of support to paramilitary groups in their operations against Nicaragua. That the federal appellees are providing financial, technical, and other support to anti-Nicaraguan terrorist groups operating military training camps in the United States, Honduras, Costa Rica, and Nicaragua. And that as a result of this assistance the Contras have carried out scores of attacks upon innocent Nicaraguan civilians" which have "resulted in summary execution, murder, abduction, torture, rape, wounding, and the destruction of private property and public facilities. The complaint recounts the specific instances of attacks on Nicaraguan towns and villages that caused harm to the Nicaraguan appellants, and alleges that the raids are continuing on a regular basis.

Without necessarily disapproving the District Court's conclusion that all aspects of the present case present a nonjusticiable political question, we choose not to resort to that doctrine for most of the claims.

The Nicaraguan appellants allege three causes of action assertedly coming within the Alien Tort Statute, 28 U.S.C. § 1350 (1982). They state that the acts of the appellees "constitute torts in violation of the law of nations as evinced by [a number of international declarations and agreements]," "constitute violations of the tort law of Nicaragua, several States, and the District of Columbia," and "constitute violations of international law."

The Alien Tort Statute provides that "[t]he district courts shall have original jurisdiction of any civil action by an alien for a tort only, committed in violation of the law of nations or a treaty of the United States." We are aware of no treaty that purports to make the activities at issue here unlawful when conducted by private individuals. As for the law of nations – so-called "customary international law," arising from "the customs and usages of civilized nations," – we conclude that this also does not reach private, non-state conduct of this sort. Assuming, however, that the Alien Tort Statute covers state acts as well, then it embraces this suit only insofar as the federal appellees are sued in their official, as opposed to their personal, capacities – *i.e.*, to the extent that appellants are seeking to hold them to account for, or to prevent them from implementing in the future, *actions of the United States*. It would make a mockery of the doctrine of sovereign immunity if federal courts were authorized to sanction or enjoin, by judgments nominally against present or former Executive officers, actions that are, *concededly and as a jurisdictional necessity*, official actions of the United States. These consequences are tolerated when the officer's action is unauthorized because contrary to statutory or constitutional prescription, but we think that exception can have no application when the basis for jurisdiction requires action authorized by the sovereign as opposed to private wrongdoing. A waiver of sovereign immunity must therefore be found. Insofar as the claim for money damages is concerned, there is none. The Alien Tort Statute itself is not a waiver of sovereign immunity.

The Nicaraguan appellants assert that the appellees' actions violate the fourth and fifth amendments to the United States Constitution. We do not reach the question whether the protections of the Constitution extend to noncitizens abroad since we conclude that no relief is in any event available, and that this portion of the complaint therefore was properly dismissed under Fed.R.Civ.P. 12(b)(6).

Under *Bivens v. Six Unknown Named Agents of the FBI*, in appropriate situations the federal courts may fashion a damages remedy for violation of constitutional rights. The Supreme Court "has expressly cautioned, however, that such a remedy will not be available when 'special factors counselling hesitation' are present." We have no doubt that these considerations of institutional competence preclude judicial creation of damage remedies here. Just as the special needs of the armed forces require the courts to leave to Congress the creation of damage remedies against military officers for allegedly unconstitutional treatment of soldiers, so also the special needs of foreign affairs must stay our hand in the creation of damage remedies against military and foreign policy officials for allegedly unconstitutional treatment of foreign subjects causing injury abroad. The foreign affairs implications of suits such as this cannot be ignored – their ability to produce what the Supreme Court has called in another context "embarrassment of our government abroad" through "multifarious pronouncements by various departments on one question." Whether or not the present litigation is motivated by considerations of geopolitics rather than personal harm, we think that as a general matter the danger of foreign citizens' using the courts in situations such as this to obstruct the foreign policy of our government is sufficiently acute that we must leave to Congress the judgment whether a damage remedy should exist.

The congressional appellants allege two causes of action. First, they assert that the federal appellees have violated the so-called Boland Amendment, which forbids the provision of assistance by the CIA or the Department of Defense "to any group or individual, not part of a country's armed forces, for the purpose of overthrowing the Government of Nicaragua. . . . " But the appropriations, and hence the operative effect of the limiting rider, expired on September 30, 1983, the end of the fiscal year. Since the congressional appellants seek relief of only prospective effect (declaratory judgment and injunction), we must dismiss this cause of action as moot.

The congressional appellants also allege that assistance to the Contras is tantamount to waging war, so that they "have been deprived of their right to participate in the decision to declare war" in violation of the war powers clause of the Constitution, art. I, § 8, cl. 11. Dismissal of this claim is required by our decision in *Crockett v. Reagan* (1983), which upheld dismissal of a similar claim by twenty-nine members of Congress relating to alleged military activity in El Salvador on the ground that the war powers issue presented a nonjusticiable political question.

The Florida appellants allege that the defendants have violated Florida nuisance law by maintaining "[a]t least five paramilitary training camps" in Florida. Since the federal claims supporting that jurisdiction were, as we have found, properly dismissed, this claim was properly dismissed as well.

Since the doctrine of foreign sovereign immunity is quite distinct from the doctrine of domestic sovereign immunity that we apply here, being based upon considerations of international comity, rather than separation of powers, it does not necessarily follow that an Alien Tort Statute suit filed against the officer of a foreign sovereign would have to be dismissed. Thus, nothing in today's decision necessarily conflicts with the decision of the Second Circuit in *Filartiga v. Pena-Irala*.

---

### Note and Comments:

1. When, if ever, should a state enjoy sovereign immunity protection in its own courts?

### Corporate Actors

One of the most noteworthy aspects of the Iraq War is that there were as many private contractors serving there as there were military personnel. The most infamous of these was Blackwater, which has since changed its name to Xe, no doubt as a way of trying to disassociate itself from the criminal behavior of some of its employees. The question is this: when should private contractors be protected under the same immunities afforded governments and officials from those governments?

---

## *Suhail Najim Abdullah Al Shimari, et al. v. CACI PREMIER TECH, Inc.,* U.S. District Court for the Eastern District of Virginia, 28 June 2017

Plaintiffs Suhail Al Shimari, Salah Al-Ejaili, and Asa'ad Al-Zuba'e, all Iraqi nationals, were detained in the custody of the U.S. Army at Abu Ghraib prison in Iraq in 2003 and 2004. In 2008, they brought a civil action under the ATS [Alien Tort Statute] against CACI Premier Technology, Inc. ("CACI" or "defendant"), which provided interrogation services for the U.S. military at Abu Ghraib at the time of the relevant events. Plaintiffs allege that defendant violated the law of nations by committing acts involving torture, CIDT, and war crimes.

This civil action has been before the Fourth Circuit four times, most recently after plaintiffs' Third Amended Complaint was dismissed on the grounds that it presented a non-justiciable political question. The district court had reasoned that according to the chain of command "the military exercised 'plenary' and 'direct' control over how Defendants interrogated detainees at Abu Ghraib" and that "[t]o consider Plaintiffs' claims would require the Court to impose state tort duties onto an active war zone, raising a broad array of interferences by the judiciary into the military functions textually committed by our Constitution to Congress, the President, and the Executive Branch." On appeal, the Fourth Circuit found that the district court erred by focusing on formal control and "failing to determine whether the military exercised actual control over any of CACI's alleged conduct" and explained that "irrespective [of] whether that conduct occurred under the actual control of the military," "conduct by CACI employees that was unlawful when committed is justiciable." In keeping with this principle, the acts committed by CACI "are shielded from judicial review under the political question doctrine" only if they "were not unlawful when committed and occurred under the actual control of the military or involved sensitive military judgments."

Accordingly, the Fourth Circuit vacated the district court's judgment and remanded the case with the explanation that on remand, the district court will be required to determine which of the alleged acts, or constellations of alleged acts, violated settled international law and criminal law governing CACI's conduct and, therefore, are subject to judicial review. The district court will also be required to identify any 'grey area' conduct that was committed under the actual control of the military or involved sensitive military judgments and, thus, is protected under the political question doctrine.

To the extent that the alleged conduct was lawful, CACI will be shielded from judicial review under the political question doctrine if the lawful action occurred under the "*actual control* of the military."

In defining the content of the prohibition against torture, the Court looks first to congressionally authorized statutes, and any case law interpreting or applying those statutes. In the context of torture, relevant statutes defining "torture" include the Anti-Torture Act and the TVPA [Torture Victim Protection Act]. According to the Anti-Torture Act, " 'torture' means an act committed by a person acting under the color of law specifically intended to inflict severe physical or mental pain or suffering (other than pain or suffering incidental to lawful sanctions) upon another person within his custody or physical control." Similarly, the TVPA, which applies to individuals who act "under actual or apparent authority, or color of law, of any foreign nation."

Notwithstanding the limitation to state actors, an ostensibly private organization may be found to have acted under color of law when, for example, "there is such a 'close nexus between the State and the challenged action' that seemingly private behavior 'may be fairly treated as that of the State itself.' " [*The court proceeded to review several cases addressing this issue.*]

Applying these cases, a court in this circuit [*Al-Qurashi*] found that contractors operating alongside the military as interpreters for non-English speaking detainees at Abu Ghraib performed a public function. That finding was premised on the observation that "[o]peration of a military force is one of the most basic governmental functions, and one for which there is no privatized equivalent." "While certain discreet military tasks, such as translation services in this case, may be delegated to contractors, the military still has need to understand, digest, and act upon information taken from enemy (or suspected enemy) prisoners who speak a language other than English." Because defendants were "alleged to have operated alongside the military, carrying out a military task which likely would have been performed by the military itself under other circumstances," the court concluded that their work could be viewed as a public function. Turning to the alternative, "willful participant" standard, the court found that based on plaintiffs' allegations that "certain members of the military, indisputably state actors, conspired and acted together with Defendants to commit the alleged acts of torture" plaintiffs had "properly alleged joint action between Defendants and state actors such that Defendants may be deemed to have acted under color of law." Although this Court does not currently decide the color-of-law question, it finds *Al-Qurashi's* analysis persuasive and the parties should treat it as controlling precedent.

## War Crimes

Counts VII, VIII, and IX of the Third Amended Complaint allege war crimes offenses, including "torture, cruel, inhuman and degrading treatment, and willfully causing great suffering and serious bodily injury to Plaintiffs," as well as civil conspiracy to commit war crimes and aiding and abetting the commission of war crimes.

Defendant acknowledges that "[a]s with torture, a general proscription on war crimes existed in 2003–04" and that "courts have recognized war crimes as actionable ATS claims." The content of this norm is provided by the War Crimes Act of 1996, which states that a war crime includes any conduct "defined as a grave breach" of any of the Geneva Conventions of August 12, 1949 or prohibited by select articles of the Hague Convention IV. The grave breaches of the Geneva Conventions defined by the statute include "torture" and "cruel or inhuman treatment," as well as "intentionally causing serious bodily injury."

Importantly, the Fourth Geneva Convention, which covers treatment of civilians in war zones and occupied territories, "does not limit its application based on the identity of the perpetrator of the war crimes," suggesting that there is no distinction between state and private actors when it comes to liability for war crimes. The most influential decision recognizing this principle is the Second Circuit's decision in *Kadic*, which explained that "[t]he liability of private individuals for committing war crimes has been recognized since World War I and was confirmed at Nuremberg after World War II, and remains today an important aspect of international law." Consistent with this history, the War Crimes Act "does not provide that non-state actors are exempt from prosecution," and current government regulations specifically instruct contractors to notify their employees that they can be held liable under that statute. In addition, "[t]he weight of authority . . . shows that a claim of war crimes may be asserted against private actors."

Notwithstanding the consensus that war crimes are clearly defined and actionable against private actors under the ATS, defendant argues that the norm prohibiting war crimes does not provide a cause of action in this case because "the claim involves U.S. military operations and conditions of detention approved by the military chain of command." This argument is contradicted by *Al Shimari IV's* holding that "the military cannot lawfully exercise its authority by directing a contractor to engage in unlawful activity." In keeping with the Fourth Circuit's opinion, whether the U.S. military approved the conditions of detention has no bearing on whether war crimes claims are actionable under the ATS.

Next, defendant argues that because the War Crimes Act does not create a private right of action, it cannot support a claim brought under the ATS. This argument, which mirrors defendant's contentions regarding torture and CIDT, is similarly unavailing and demonstrates a fundamental failure to understand that common law provides the cause of action for all actionable ATS claims.

---

## Note and Comments:

1. In August 2017, an out-of-court settlement was reached in a lawsuit brought by a group of former prisoners at a CIA detention facility who claimed they

had been tortured. The action was brought against Dr. Bruce Jessen and Dr. James Mitchell, who were architects of the CIA's interrogation policy. In 2002, these two psychologists produced a memo proposing various "interrogation" methods against terrorist suspects, including waterboarding, stuffing prisoners into small boxes, forcing them to hold painful positions for hours, and slamming them into flexible walls.

## References

### Books and Articles

Adam S. Chilton and Christopher A. Whytock, "Foreign Sovereign Immunity and Comparative Institutional Competence," *University of Pennsylvania Law Review* 163: 411–86 (2015)

Mark Gibney and Erik Roxström, "What a Pity! Sovereign Immunity, State Responsibility and the Diminution of Accountability Under International Human Rights Law," *Journal of Human Rights* 11: 443–59 (2012)

### Cases

*Al-Adsani v. United Kingdom*, ECtHR, App. No. 35763/97 (2001)

*Al-Shimari v. CACI*, (D.C. Cir. E.D. VA. 2017)

*Banco Nacional de Cuba v. Sabbatino*, 376 U.S. 398 (1964)

*Belhaj v. United Kingdom*, UKSC 3 [2017]

*Koohi v. United States*, 976 F. 2d 1328 (9th Cir. 1992)

*Ramirez de Arellano v. Weinberger*, 724 F. 2d 143 (D.C. Cir. 1983)

*Sanchez-Espinoza v. Reagan*, 770 F. 2d 202 (D.C. Cir. 1985)

*Saudi Arabia v. Nelson*, 507 U.S. 349 (1993)

### Regional Law

European Convention on Human Rights, signed 4 November 1950, entry into force 3 September 1953

### Domestic Law

Federal Tort Claims Act, 28 U.S.C. Chapter 171 (U.S.)

Foreign Sovereign Immunity Act (FSIA), 28 U.S.C. 1602–1611 (U.S.)

Justice Against Sponsors of Terrorism Act (JASTA), Public Law No. 114–222 (U.S.)

Torture Victim Protection Act of 1991, Public Law No. 102–256 (U.S.)

# Part IV
## Human Rights

# 11
## Poverty and Disease

### The Necessities of Life

In this chapter we will be focusing on what are commonly referred to as subsistence rights – the right to food, water, shelter, health care, and a clean environment – in order to understand the degree to which international law protects these necessities of life, and perhaps even helps to ensure them as well. Article 2 (1) of the International Covenant on Economic, Social, and Cultural Rights (ICESCR) states:

> Each State Party to the present Covenant undertakes to take steps, individually and through international assistance and co-operation, especially economic and technical, to the maximum of its available resources, with a view to achieving progressively the full realization of the rights recognized in the present Covenant by all appropriate means, including particularly the adoption of legislative measures.

The ICESCR differs from nearly all other international and regional human rights treaties in several important ways. For one, there is no mention of either "territory" or "jurisdiction." In addition, the treaty demands that the state parties engage in "international assistance and cooperation." On this basis, a strong argument could be made that the state parties have obligations that go beyond their own national borders.

Another thing to note about the ICESCR is that states are only required to "take steps" toward the "progressive realization" of the rights set forth in the

Covenant. What this means is that international law does not demand that states protect ESCR immediately, as they must with respect to civil and political rights. For example, the prohibition against torture demands that states stop torturing now – not to reduce the incidents of torture or to stop torturing at some point in the future. Economic, social, and cultural rights are different. However, the U.N. Committee on Economic, Social, and Cultural Rights has specified that there are "core minimum obligations" that all states are bound by immediately. In addition, the Committee has also demanded of states that there be no retrogression in terms of meeting ESCR.

---

### Box 11.1: MDGs and SDGs

In September 2000, leaders of 189 countries convened at the United Nations head-quarters and signed the Millennium Declaration, in which they committed to achieving a set of eight *Millennium Development Goals* (MDGs) by 2015, including halving extreme poverty and hunger, promoting gender equality, and reducing child mortality.

The *Sustainable Development Goals* (SDGs) followed from this, but they also go beyond the MDGs. For one thing, there are 17 different SDGs. Another distinction is the absolute nature of some of goals, including: "zero poverty" and "zero hunger." While the MDGs were premised on increased levels of Official Development Assistance (ODA), which never really materialized, the SDGs put sustainable, inclusive economic development at the core of the project.

MDGs and SDGs would fall into the category of "soft law" in the sense that states have not bound themselves legally to achieve these standards. On the other hand, perhaps these could be viewed as evidence of customary international law, which would be binding on all states.

---

There are, of course, resource limitations. The question, then, is what resources are "available"? This issue has posed problems within the domestic realm but what is equally vexing is the measurement of "available resources" from other states when they provide the "international assistance and cooperation" mandated by the ICESCR. This, however, begs the question whether states have a legal obligation to provide such assistance in the first place.

---

### Box 11.2: Is There a Legal Obligation to Provide Foreign Assistance?

In a country study of Sweden, the former U.N. Special Rapporteur on the Right to Health (Paul Hunt) asked government officials in that country whether Sweden – arguably the most "generous" country in the world in terms of amount of foreign aid it provides per capita – has a legal obligation to provide any form of aid. Swedish government officials answered that it did not. Hunt responds:

> If there is no legal obligation underpinning the human rights responsibility of international assistance and cooperation, inescapably all international assistance and cooperation is based fundamentally upon charity. While such a position might have been tenable 100 years ago, it is unacceptable in the twenty-first century.
>
> (Hunt 2007: 28)

In her definitive study of the drafting of the ICESCR, Sigrun Skogly found that there was little controversy about the scope of the Convention. Rather, "international assistance and cooperation" meant exactly that.

> [I]t seems that the delegations were quite agreed that international assistance and cooperation is needed for the full implementation of the rights, and that the resources available based upon this co-operation and assistance should be part of the resources used for the full realization of these rights.
>
> (Skogly 2006: 86)

The list of rights specified in the ICESCR is far ranging. Without attempting to be exhaustive, this includes the right to work (Art. 6) under just and favorable conditions (Art. 7), with the ability to form trade unions (Art. 8). All individuals have a right to social security or social insurance (Art. 9). Article 10 specifies the importance of the family unit and it sets forth a number of protections to help guard the special role of families in all societies. The right to an education is set forth in Article 13 and it specifies that this right:

> shall be directed to the full development of the human personality and the sense of its dignity, and shall strengthen the respect for human rights and fundamental freedoms.

Our primary focus in this chapter will be on the sets of rights in Articles 11 and 12. Article 11 (1) provides:

> The States Parties to the present Covenant recognize the right of everyone to an adequate standard of living for himself and his family, including adequate food, clothing and housing, and to the continuous improvement of living conditions. The States Parties will take appropriate steps to ensure the realization of this right, recognizing to this effect the essential importance of international co-operation based on free consent.

Article 12 (1) provides:

> The States Parties to the present Covenant recognize the right of everyone to the enjoyment of the highest attainable standard of physical and mental health.

We now turn to see how these rights under international human rights law have (or have not) been met. Many of the cases that follow are from the South African Constitutional Court. The reason for this, quite simply, is that the country's post-apartheid Constitution is the most "progressive" one in the world. On the other hand, as we will soon see, these human rights have often been tempered by realities on the ground, most notably, the country's dire poverty.

**The Right to Water**

We begin with the right to water. Although Article 11 makes no mention of such a right (only the right to food), the U.N. treaty body administering the ICESCR has recognized such a right in its *General Comment 15 (right to water)*. In the *Mazibuko* case that follows, the Constitutional Court of South Africa provides some insight into how this right might be implemented. The plaintiffs in this case are a group of residents from Johannesburg who challenge the government's water allocation.

---

## *Mazibuko and Others v. Johannesburg and Others,* Constitutional Court of South Africa, 2009

This application for leave to appeal against a judgment of the Supreme Court of Appeal raises, for the first time in this Court, the proper interpretation of section 27(1)(b) of the Constitution which provides that everyone has the right to have access to sufficient water. Cultures in all parts of the world acknowledge the importance of water. Water is life. Without it, nothing organic grows. Human beings need water to drink, to cook, to wash and to grow our food. Without it, we will die. It is not surprising then that our Constitution entrenches the right of access to water.

Although rain falls everywhere, access to water has long been grossly unequal. This inequality is evident in South Africa. While piped water is plentifully available to mines, industries, some large farms and wealthy families, millions of people, especially women, spend hours laboriously collecting their daily supply of water from streams, pools and distant taps. In 1994, it was estimated that 12 million people (approximately a quarter of the population), did not have adequate access to water. By the end of 2006, this number had shrunk to 8 million, with 3.3 million of that number having no access to a basic water supply at all. Yet, despite the significant improvement in the first fifteen years of democratic government, deep inequality remains and for many the task of obtaining sufficient water for their families remains a tiring daily burden. The achievement of equality, one of the founding values of our Constitution, will not be accomplished while water is abundantly available to the wealthy, but not to the poor.

At the same time, ours is a largely arid country, often assailed by drought. Redeeming the constitutional promise of access to sufficient water for all will require careful management of a scarce resource. The need to preserve water is a responsibility that affects all spheres of government.

Section 27 of the Constitution provides as follows:

(1) Everyone has the right to have access to –
   (a) health care services, including reproductive health care;
   (b) sufficient food and water; and
   (c) social security, including, if they are unable to support themselves and their dependents, appropriate social assistance.
(2) The state must take reasonable legislative and other measures, within its available resources, to achieve the progressive realization of each of these rights.
(3) No one may be refused emergency medical treatment.

Traditionally, constitutional rights (especially civil and political rights) are understood as imposing an obligation upon the state to refrain from interfering with the exercise of the right by citizens (the so-called negative obligation or the duty to respect). As this Court has held, social and economic rights are no different. The state bears a duty to refrain from interfering with social and economic rights just as it does with civil and political rights.

At the time the Constitution was adopted, millions of South Africans did not have access to the basic necessities of life, including water. The purpose of the constitutional entrenchment of social and economic rights was thus to ensure that the state continue to take reasonable legislative and other measures progressively to achieve the realization of the rights to the basic necessities of life. It was not expected, nor could it have been, that the state would be able to furnish citizens immediately with all the basic necessities of life. Social and economic rights empower citizens to demand of the state that it acts reasonably and progressively to ensure that all enjoy the basic necessities of life. In so doing, the social and economic rights enable citizens to hold government to account for the manner in which it seeks to pursue the achievement of social and economic rights.

Moreover, what the right requires will vary over time and context. Fixing a quantified content might, in a rigid and counter-productive manner, prevent an analysis of context. The concept of reasonableness places context at the center of the enquiry and permits an assessment of context to determine whether a government program is indeed reasonable.

The Constitution envisages that legislative and other measures will be the primary instrument for the achievement of social and economic rights. Thus it places a positive obligation upon the state to respond to the basic social and economic needs of the people by adopting reasonable legislative and other measures. By adopting such measures, the rights set out in the Constitution acquire content, and that content is subject to the constitutional standard of reasonableness.

Thus the positive obligations imposed upon government by the social and economic rights in our Constitution will be enforced by courts in at least the following ways. If government takes no steps to realize the rights, the courts will require government to take steps. If government's adopted measures are unreasonable, the courts will similarly require that they be reviewed so as to meet the constitutional standard of reasonableness.

The outcome of the case is that the applicants have not persuaded this Court to specify what quantity of water is "sufficient water" within the meaning of section 27 of the Constitution. Nor have they persuaded the Court that the City's policy is unreasonable. The applicants submitted during argument that if this were to be the result, litigation in respect of the positive obligations imposed by social and economic rights would be futile. It is necessary to consider this submission.

The purpose of litigation concerning the positive obligations imposed by social and economic rights should be to hold the democratic arms of government to account through litigation. In so doing, litigation of this sort fosters a form of participative democracy that holds government accountable and requires it to account between elections over specific aspects of government policy.

## Notes and Comments:

1. Johannesburg is certainly not the only city in South Africa experiencing a severe water shortage. In spring 2018, Cape Town established a date – Day Zero – when government officials predicted the city would be depleted of water. This was originally set for late April 2018, but after some small amounts of rainfall, this was moved back to July 9. The more important point is that the situation in South Africa is dangerous at best.

2. The issue in *Mazibuko* involves the domestic distribution of water. However, another issue that will only continue to grow in importance relates to the international distribution of this precious resource. Consider that of the 54 African countries, 51 depend on water resources of shared rivers. Moreover, at least 34 rivers on the African continent are shared by two countries and 28 are shared by three or more states (Bulto 2014). Under customary international law, codified in the 1997 Convention on the Law of the Non-Navigational Uses of International Watercourses, states are guided by the principle of "equitable and reasonable utilization." Another way of putting this is that states are to be mindful of those downstream and only take the water resources they need.

### Box 11.3: Land Grabbing

Land grabbing is a term used to describe a governmental policy through which individuals are dispossessed from their homes, and the government then sells this land to private developers. Cambodia is one of the countries where massive land grabbing has taken place. The 2001 Land Law of Cambodia allows the government to expropriate private land from citizens for "economic land concessions" (ELCs). However, many ELCs are unlawful in that they involve forced evictions of landowners without fair and equitable compensation and many superceded the 10,000 hectares limit specified by law.

From an international law perspective, an interesting development involves a lawsuit filed in the United Kingdom by residents of Cambodia's Koh Kong province claiming that sugar cane from their confiscated land was then unlawfully sold to Tate & Lyle, a British multinational corporation (Mohan 2014).

---

**Box 11.4: International Law at the Movies: Subsistence Rights**

In my book *Watching Human Rights: The 101 Best Films*, I rank order what I feel are the "best" feature films and documentaries that deal with human rights issues. In terms of the latter category, my two highest rated documentaries are *Darwin's Nightmare* (2004) and *Nero's Guests* (2009). The former takes place in an impoverished village in Tanzania on the shores of Lake Victoria where the inhabitants attempt to make a living fishing for Nile perch, a predatory creature that was mistakenly introduced into the lake some years ago and which is now killing all the other life forms – and, ultimately, Lake Victoria itself. The story that eventually emerges in the film is that Tanzania is facing a famine that could cause the death of an estimated 2 million people – all while the country continues to export massive amounts of Nile perch to European markets. Moreover, the planes that arrive each day are not empty as so many claim. Instead, they are filled with military weapons that will arm and equip the various civil conflicts on the African continent.

The title of *Nero's Guests* only becomes clear near the close of the film and when it does the emotional impact is enormous. On one level, the film is about farmer suicides in India. However, as the film progresses, what the viewer comes to understand is the manner in which these distant events are not distant at all.

---

**Health Care**

Article 12 of the ICESCR speaks of "the right of everyone to the enjoyment of the highest attainable standard of physical and mental health." Yet, as we will see in the next two cases, both from South Africa, this right has to be read within the larger context of a country's national budget as well as the limited resources oftentimes allocated to health care.

---

## *Soobramoney v. Minister of Health (Kwazulu-Natal)*, Constitutional Court of South Africa, 1997

The appellant (Soobramoney), a 41 year-old unemployed man, is a diabetic who suffers from ischaemic heart disease and cerebro-vascular disease which caused him to have a stroke during 1996. In 1996 his kidneys also failed. Sadly, his condition is irreversible and he is now in the final stages of chronic renal failure. His life could be prolonged by means of regular renal dialysis. He has sought such treatment from the renal unit of the Addington state hospital in Durban. The hospital can, however, only provide dialysis treatment to a limited number of patients. The renal unit has 20 dialysis machines available to it, and some of these machines are in poor condition. Each treatment takes four hours and a further two hours have to be allowed for the cleaning of a machine, before it can be used again for other treatment. Because of the limited facilities that are available for kidney dialysis the hospital has been unable to provide the appellant with the treatment he has requested.

The reasons given by the hospital for this are set out in the respondent's answering affidavit deposed to by Doctor Saraladevi Naicker, a specialist physician and nephrologist in the field of renal medicine who has worked at Addington Hospital for 18 years and who is currently the President of the South African Renal Society. In her affidavit Dr Naicker says that Addington Hospital does not have enough resources to provide dialysis treatment for all patients suffering from chronic renal failure. Additional dialysis machines and more trained nursing staff are required to enable it to do this, but the hospital budget does not make provision for such expenditure. The hospital would like to have its budget increased but it has been told by the provincial health department that funds are not available for this purpose.

Because of the shortage of resources the hospital follows a set policy in regard to the use of the dialysis resources. Only patients who suffer from acute renal failure, which can be treated and remedied by renal dialysis, are given automatic access to renal dialysis at the hospital. Those patients who, like the appellant, suffer from chronic renal failure which is irreversible are not admitted automatically to the renal programme. A set of guidelines has been drawn up and adopted to determine which applicants who have chronic renal failure will be given dialysis treatment. According to the guidelines the primary requirement for admission of such persons to the dialysis programme is that the patient must be eligible for a kidney transplant. A patient who is eligible for a transplant will be provided with dialysis treatment until an organ donor is found and a kidney transplant has been completed.

The guidelines provide that an applicant is not eligible for a transplant unless he or she is "free of significant vascular or cardiac disease." The appellant suffers from ischaemic heart disease and cerebro-vascular disease and he is therefore not eligible for a kidney transplant.

We live in a society in which there are great disparities in wealth. Millions of people are living in deplorable conditions and in great poverty. There is a high level of unemployment, inadequate social security, and many do not have access to clean water or to adequate health services. These conditions already existed when the Constitution was adopted and a commitment to address them, and to transform our society into one in which there will be human dignity, freedom and equality, lies at the heart of our new constitutional order. For as long as these conditions continue to exist that aspiration will have a hollow ring.

The constitutional commitment to address these conditions is expressed in the preamble which, after giving recognition to the injustices of the past, states:

> We therefore, through our freely elected representatives, adopt this Constitution as the supreme law of the Republic so as to –
> Heal the divisions of the past and establish a society based on democratic values, social justice and fundamental human rights;
> . . . .
> Improve the quality of life of all citizens and free the potential of each person.

This commitment is also reflected in various provisions of the bill of rights and in particular section 27:

27. Health care, food, water and social security

(1) Everyone has the right to have access to –
    (a) health care services, including reproductive health care;
    (b) sufficient food and water; and
    (c) social security, including, if they are unable to support themselves and their dependants, appropriate social assistance.
(2) The state must take reasonable legislative and other measures, within its available resources, to achieve the progressive realisation of each of these rights.
(3) No one may be refused emergency medical treatment.

At present the Department of Health in KwaZulu-Natal does not have sufficient funds to cover the cost of the services which are being provided to the public. In 1996–1997 it overspent its budget by R152 million, and in the current year it is anticipated that the overspending will be R700 million rand unless a serious cutback is made in the services which it provides. The renal unit at the Addington Hospital has to serve the whole of KwaZulu-Natal and also takes patients from parts of the Eastern Cape. There are many more patients suffering from chronic renal failure than there are dialysis machines to treat such patients. This is a nation-wide problem and resources are stretched in all renal clinics throughout the land. Guidelines have therefore been established to assist the persons working in these clinics to make the agonizing choices which have to be made in deciding who should receive treatment, and who not. These guidelines were applied in the present case.

By using the available dialysis machines in accordance with the guidelines more patients are benefited than would be the case if they were used to keep alive persons with chronic renal failure, and the outcome of the treatment is also likely to be more beneficial because it is directed to curing patients, and not simply to maintaining them in a chronically ill condition. It has not been suggested that these guidelines are unreasonable or that they were not applied fairly and rationally when the decision was taken by the Addington Hospital that the appellant did not qualify for dialysis.

The appellant avers in his affidavits that better use could be made of the dialysis machines at the Addington Hospital by keeping the clinic open for longer hours. He says that some of the nurses "moonlight" at other hospitals after their normal working hours in order to earn extra income, and that if they were given overtime opportunities at the Addington Hospital more people could be treated.

The appellant's case must be seen in the context of the needs which the health services have to meet, for if treatment has to be provided to the appellant it would also have to be provided to all other persons similarly placed. Although the renal clinic could be kept open for longer hours, it would involve additional expense in having to pay the clinic personnel at overtime rates, or in having to employ additional personnel working on a shift basis. It would also put a great strain on the existing dialysis machines which are already showing signs of wear. It is estimated that the cost to the state of treating one chronically ill patient by means of renal dialysis provided twice a week at a state hospital is approximately R60 000 per annum. If all the persons in South Africa who suffer from chronic renal failure were to be provided with dialysis treatment – and many of them, as the appellant does, would require treatment three times a week – the cost of doing so would make substantial inroads into the health budget. And if this principle were to be applied to all patients claiming access to expensive medical treatment or expensive drugs, the health budget would have to be dramatically increased to the prejudice of other needs which the state has to meet.

One cannot but have sympathy for the appellant and his family, who face the cruel dilemma of having to impoverish themselves in order to secure the treatment that the appellant seeks in order to prolong his life. The hard and unpalatable fact is that if the appellant were a wealthy man he would be able to procure such treatment from private sources; he is not and has to look to the state to provide him with the treatment. But the state's resources are limited and the appellant does not meet the criteria for admission to the renal dialysis programme. Unfortunately, this is true not only of the appellant but of many others who need access to renal dialysis units or to other health services. There are also those who need access to housing, food and water, employment opportunities, and social security. These too are aspects of the right to

> human life: the right to live as a human being, to be part of a broader community, to share in the experience of humanity.

The state has to manage its limited resources in order to address all these claims. There will be times when this requires it to adopt a holistic approach to the larger needs of society rather than to focus on the specific needs of particular individuals within society.

---

**Note and Comments:**

1. Would you have written a similar opinion? Should the court have looked at all other government expenditures – military spending, for example – before arriving at its conclusion?

The next case also interprets Article 27 of the South African Constitution, but it comes out with a different result.

---

**Box 11.5: International Law at the Movies: Health**

*Contagion* (2011) is an international thriller starring Matt Damon depicting a world ravaged by a killer disease – all from a single unsanitary transaction in Asia and a cheating spouse. *The Constant Gardener* (2009) starring Ralph Fiennes and Rachel Weisz is another Hollywood thriller that centers around unethical pharmaceutical testing practices in Africa.

---

## *Minister of Health and Others v. Treatment Action Campaign and Others,* Constitutional Court of South Africa, 2002

The HIV/AIDS pandemic in South Africa has been described as "an incomprehensible calamity" and "the most important challenge facing South Africa since the birth of our new democracy" and government's fight against "this scourge" as "a top priority". It "has claimed millions of lives, inflicting pain and grief, causing fear and uncertainty, and threatening the economy". These are not the words of alarmists but are taken from a Department of Health publication in 2000 and a ministerial foreword to an earlier departmental publication.

It is the applicants' case that the measures adopted by government to provide access to health care services to HIV-positive pregnant women were deficient in two material respects: first, because they prohibited the administration of nevirapine at public hospitals and clinics outside the research and training sites; and second, because they failed to implement a comprehensive program for the prevention of mother-to-child transmission of HIV.

The two questions are interrelated and a consequence of government's policy as it was when these proceedings were instituted. The use of nevirapine to reduce the risk of mother-to-child transmission of HIV was confined to mothers and newborn children at hospitals and clinics included in the research and training sites. At all other public hospitals and clinics the use of nevirapine for this purpose was not provided for. Public hospitals and clinics outside the research and training sites were not supplied with nevirapine for doctors to prescribe for the prevention of mother-to-child transmission. Only later would a decision be taken as to whether nevirapine and the rest of the package would be made available elsewhere in the health system. That decision would depend upon the results at the research and training sites. The applicants contend that this is not reasonable and that government ought to have had a comprehensive national program to prevent mother-to-child transmission of HIV, including voluntary counselling and testing, antiretroviral therapy and the option of substitute feeding.

In the present case this Court has the duty to determine whether the measures taken in respect of the prevention of mother-to-child transmission of HIV are reasonable. We know that throughout the country health services are overextended. HIV/AIDS is but one of many illnesses that require attention. It is, however, the greatest threat to public health in our country. As the government's *HIV/AIDS & STD strategic plan for South Africa 2000–2005* states:

> During the last two decades, the HIV pandemic has entered our consciousness as an incomprehensible calamity. HIV/AIDS has claimed millions of lives, inflicting pain and grief, causing fear and uncertainty, and threatening the economy.

We are also conscious of the daunting problems confronting government as a result of the pandemic. And besides the pandemic, the state faces huge demands in relation to access to education, land, housing, health care, food, water and social security. These are the socio-economic rights entrenched in the Constitution, and the state is obliged to take reasonable legislative and other measures within its available resources to achieve the progressive realization of each of them. In the light of our history this is an extraordinarily difficult task. Nonetheless it is an obligation imposed on the state by the Constitution.

A dispute concerning socio-economic rights is . . . likely to require a court to evaluate state policy and to give judgment on whether or not it is consistent with the Constitution. If it finds that policy is inconsistent with the Constitution it is obliged to make a declaration to that effect. But that is not all. Section 38 of the Constitution contemplates that where it is established that a right in the Bill of Rights has been infringed a court will grant "appropriate relief". It has wide powers to do so and in addition to the declaration a court may also "make any order that is just and equitable".

We thus reject the argument that the only power that this Court has in the present case is to issue a declaratory order. Where a breach of any right has taken place, including a socio-economic right, a court is under a duty to ensure that effective relief is granted. The nature of the right infringed and the nature of the infringement will provide guidance as to the appropriate relief in a particular case. Where necessary this may include both the issuing of a mandamus and the exercise of supervisory jurisdiction.

In the present case we have identified aspects of government policy that are inconsistent with the Constitution. The decision not to make nevirapine available at hospitals and clinics other than the research and training sites is central to the entire policy. Once that restriction is removed, government will be able to devise and implement a more comprehensive policy that will give access to health care services to HIV-positive mothers and their newborn children, and will include the administration of nevirapine where that is appropriate. The policy as reformulated must meet the constitutional requirement of providing reasonable measures within available resources for the progressive realization of the rights of such women and newborn children.

What remains to be considered is whether it is appropriate in the circumstances of the present case to grant further relief. We have come to the conclusion that it is appropriate to do so, though in terms differing from the orders made by the High Court.

It is essential that there be a concerted national effort to combat the HIV/AIDS pandemic. The government has committed itself to such an effort. We have held that its policy fails to meet constitutional standards because it excludes those who could reasonably be included where such treatment is medically indicated to combat mother-to-child transmission of HIV. That does not mean that everyone can immediately claim access to such treatment, although the ideal, as Dr Ntsaluba says, is to achieve that goal. Every effort must, however, be made to do so as soon as reasonably possible. The increases in the budget to which we have referred will facilitate this.

We do not underestimate the nature and extent of the problem facing government in its fight to combat HIV/AIDS and, in particular, to reduce the transmission of HIV from mother to child. We also understand the need to exercise caution when dealing with a potent and a relatively unknown drug. But the nature of the problem is such that it demands urgent attention. Nevirapine is a potentially lifesaving drug. Its safety and efficacy have been established. There is a need to assess operational challenges for the best possible use of nevirapine on a comprehensive scale to reduce the risk of mother-to-child transmission of HIV. There is an additional need to monitor issues relevant to the safety and efficacy of and resistance to the use of nevirapine for this purpose. There is, however, also a pressing need to ensure that where possible loss of life is prevented in the meantime.

*[The Court then ordered that government to expand the use of nevirapine to women in all parts of the country.]*

---

### Note and Comments:

1. Can these two cases be reconciled with one another?

---

### Box 11.6: AIDS Medicine and South Africa

An April 20, 2001 article from *The New York Times* describes the settlement of a lawsuit that had been filed against South Africa based on a domestic law that allowed for the importation of generic drugs to fight AIDS.

Bowing to mounting public pressure, the pharmaceutical industry today dropped its legal effort to prevent South Africa from importing cheaper anti-AIDS drugs and other medicines.

All 39 drug makers that had sued South Africa in 1998 conceded today that a South African law allowing the government to purchase brand-name drugs at the lowest rates available anywhere in the world complied with international trade agreements. During its three-year fight, the industry had closed factories here, canceled investments and said that health officials were intent on destroying international treaties intended to protect drug patents – an issue that has created a clash with AIDS activists.

But in ending its legal efforts today, the companies agreed that the law could be enforced as written and said that they would pay the government's legal costs. The companies that began the negotiations that led to today's settlement were Bristol-Myers Squibb and Merck, both of the United States, GlaxoSmithKline of Britain, Hoffmann-La Roche of Switzerland, and Boehringer Ingelheim of Germany.

## Shelter

Housing is a human right and like many other ESCR, in South Africa this right is enshrined in the country's constitution.

---

## *Government of South Africa and Others v. Grootboom and Others,* Constitutional Court of South Africa, 2000

The people of South Africa are committed to the attainment of social justice and the improvement of the quality of life for everyone. The Preamble to our Constitution records this commitment. The Constitution declares the founding values of our society to be "[h]uman dignity, the achievement of equality and the advancement of human rights and freedoms." This case grapples with the realization of these aspirations for it concerns the state's constitutional obligations in relation to housing: a constitutional issue of fundamental importance to the development of South Africa's new constitutional order.

The issues here remind us of the intolerable conditions under which many of our people are still living. The respondents are but a fraction of them. It is also a reminder that unless the plight of these communities is alleviated, people may be tempted to take the law into their own hands in order to escape these conditions. The case brings home the harsh reality that the Constitution's promise of dignity and equality for all remains for many a distant dream. People should not be impelled by intolerable living conditions to resort to land invasions. Self-help of this kind cannot be tolerated, for the unavailability of land suitable for housing development is a key factor in the fight against the country's housing shortage.

The group of people with whom we are concerned in these proceedings lived in appalling conditions, decided to move out and illegally occupied someone else's land. They were evicted and left homeless. The root cause of their problems is the intolerable conditions under which they were living while waiting in the queue for their turn to be allocated low-cost housing. They are the people whose constitutional rights have to be determined in this case.

The cause of the acute housing shortage lies in apartheid. Colonial dispossession and a rigidly enforced racial distribution of land in the rural areas had dislocated the rural economy and rendered sustainable and independent African farming increasingly precarious. Given the absence of formal housing, large numbers of people moved into informal settlements throughout the Cape peninsula. The cycle of the apartheid era, therefore, was one of untenable restrictions on the movement of African people into urban areas, the inexorable tide of the rural poor to the cities, inadequate housing, resultant overcrowding, mushrooming squatter settlements, constant harassment by officials and intermittent forced removals.

The key constitutional provisions at issue in this case are section 26 and section 28(1)(c).

Section 26 provides:

(1) Everyone has the right to have access to adequate housing.
(2) The state must take reasonable legislative and other measures, within its available resources, to achieve the progressive realization of this right.
(3) No one may be evicted from their home, or have their home demolished, without an order of court made after considering all the relevant circumstances. No legislation may permit arbitrary evictions.

Section 28(1)(c) provides:

(1) Every child has the right – . . . (c) to basic nutrition, shelter, basic health care services and social services.

These rights need to be considered in the context of the cluster of socio-economic rights enshrined in the Constitution. They entrench the right of access to land, to adequate housing and to healthcare, food, water and social security. They also protect the rights of the child and the right to education.

Socio-economic rights are expressly included in the Bill of Rights; they cannot be said to exist on paper only. Section 7(2) of the Constitution requires the state "to respect, protect, promote and fulfil the rights in the Bill of Rights" and the courts are constitutionally bound to ensure that they are protected and fulfilled. The question is therefore not whether socio-economic rights are justiciable under our Constitution, but how to enforce them in a given case.

Consideration is now given to whether the state action (or inaction) in relation to the respondents met the required constitutional standard. It is a central feature of this judgment that the housing shortage in the area of the Cape Metro in general and Oostenberg in particular had reached crisis proportions. Wallacedene was obviously bursting and it was probable that people in desperation were going to find it difficult to resist the temptation to move out of the shack settlement onto unoccupied land in an effort to improve their position. This is what the respondents apparently did.

Whether the conduct of Mrs Grootboom and the other respondents constituted a land invasion was disputed on the papers. There was no suggestion however that the respondents' circumstances before their move to New Rust was anything but desperate. There is nothing in the papers to indicate any plan by the municipality to deal with the occupation of vacant land if it occurred. If there had been such a plan the appellants might well have acted differently.

The respondents began to move onto the New Rust Land during September 1998 and the number of people on this land continued to grow relentlessly. I would have expected officials of the municipality responsible for housing to engage with these people as soon as they became aware of the occupation. I would also have thought that some effort would have been made by the municipality to resolve the difficulty on a case-by-case basis after an investigation of their circumstances before the matter got out of hand. The municipality did nothing and the settlement grew by leaps and bounds.

Summary and conclusion of this case shows the desperation of hundreds of thousands of people living in deplorable conditions throughout the country. The Constitution obliges the state to act positively to ameliorate these conditions. The obligation is to provide access to housing, health-care, sufficient food and water, and social security to those unable to support themselves and their dependants. The state must also foster conditions to enable citizens to gain access to land on an equitable basis. Those in need have a corresponding right to demand that this be done.

I am conscious that it is an extremely difficult task for the state to meet these obligations in the conditions that prevail in our country. This is recognised by the Constitution which expressly provides that the state is not obliged to go beyond available resources or to realise these rights immediately. I stress however, that despite all these qualifications, these are rights, and the Constitution obliges the state to give effect to them. This is an obligation that courts can, and in appropriate circumstances, must enforce.

Neither section 26 nor section 28 entitles the respondents to claim shelter or housing immediately upon demand. The High Court order ought therefore not to have been made. However, section 26 does oblige the state to devise and implement a coherent, co-ordinated programme designed to meet its section 26 obligations. The programme that has been adopted and was in force in the Cape Metro at the time that this application was brought fell short of the obligations imposed upon the state by section 26(2) in that it failed to provide for any form of relief to those desperately in need of access to housing.

In the light of the conclusions I have reached, it is necessary and appropriate to make a declaratory order. The order requires the state to act to meet the obligation imposed upon it by section 26(2) of the Constitution. This includes the obligation to devise, fund, implement and supervise measures to provide relief to those in desperate need.

---

### Box 11.7: International Law at the Movies: Land Grabbing and the Right to Housing

With its unforgettable title, *Dead Donkeys Fear No Hyenas* (2017) is a documentary set in Ethiopia where the national government is leasing out massive amounts of (supposedly) unused land to foreign investors in order to grow export crops and in the process dispossessing thousands of people who were already living there. A small segment of the land grabbing problem in Cambodia is told in *A Cambodian Spring* (2016). Finally, the denial of the right to housing in South Africa is the basis of the documentary *Dear Mandela* (2012).

## Clean and Healthy Environment

The final right we will examine is the right to a clean and healthy environment, which is implicit in a number of ESCR. In the first case, a nongovernmental organization in Nigeria is claiming that the government is turning a blind eye to the environmental devastation involved in oil exploration. The two cases that follow involve the issue of climate change and both were brought in domestic courts – one in the Netherlands and the other in the United States.

## Social and Economic Rights Action Centre and the Centre for Economic and Social Rights v. Nigeria, African Commission on Human and Peoples' Rights, 155/96 (2001)

The Communication alleges that the oil consortium has exploited oil reserves in Ogoniland with no regard for the health or environment of the local communities, disposing toxic wastes into the environment and local waterways in violation of applicable international environmental standards. The consortium also neglected and/or failed to maintain its facilities causing numerous avoidable spills in the proximity of villages. The resulting contamination of water, soil and air has had serious short and long-term health impacts, including skin infections, gastrointestinal and respiratory ailments, and increased risk of cancers, and neurological and reproductive problems.

The Complainants allege that the Nigerian government violated the right to health and the right to clean environment as recognized under Articles 16 and 24 of the African Charter by failing to fulfill the minimum duties required by these rights. This, the Complainants allege, the government has done by directly participating in the contamination of air, water and soil and thereby harming the health of the Ogoni population, and failing to protect the Ogoni population from the harm caused by the NNPC Shell Consortium but instead using its security forces to facilitate the damage. Article 16 of the African Charter reads:

> (1) Every individual shall have the right to enjoy the best attainable state of physical and mental health. (2) States Parties to the present Charter shall take the necessary measures to protect the health of their people and to ensure that they receive medical attention when they are sick.

Article 24 of the African Charter reads:

> All peoples shall have the right to a general satisfactory environment favourable to their development.

The right to a general satisfactory environment, as guaranteed under Article 24 of the African Charter or the right to a healthy environment, as it is widely known, imposes clear obligations upon a government. It requires the State to take reasonable and other measures to prevent pollution and ecological degradation, to promote conservation, and to secure an ecologically sustainable development and use of natural resources. Article 12 of the International Covenant on Economic, Social and Cultural Rights (ICESCR), to which Nigeria is a party, requires governments to take necessary steps for the improvement of all aspects of environmental and industrial hygiene.

The Complainants also allege a violation of Article 21 of the African Charter by the government of Nigeria. The Complainants allege that the Military government of Nigeria was involved in oil production and thus did not monitor or regulate the operations of the oil companies and in so doing paved a way for the Oil Consortiums to exploit oil reserves in Ogoniland. Furthermore, in all their dealings with the Oil Consortiums, the government did not involve the Ogoni Communities in the decisions that affected the development of Ogoniland. The destructive and selfish role-played by oil development in Ogoniland, closely tied with repressive tactics of the Nigerian Government, and the lack of material benefits accruing to the local population, may well be said to constitute a violation of Article 21. Article 21 provides

> 1. All peoples shall freely dispose of their wealth and natural resources. This right shall be exercised in the exclusive interest of the people. In no case shall a people be deprived of it. 2. In case of spoliation the dispossessed people shall have the

right to the lawful recovery of its property as well as to an adequate compensation. 3. The free disposal of wealth and natural resources shall be exercised without prejudice to the obligation of promoting international economic co-operation based on mutual respect, equitable exchange and the principles of international law. 4. States parties to the present Charter shall individually and collectively exercise the right to free disposal of their wealth and natural resources with a view to strengthening African unity and solidarity. 5. States Parties to the present Charter shall undertake to eliminate all forms of foreign economic exploitation particularly that practised by international monopolies so as to enable their peoples to fully benefit from the advantages derived from their national resources.

The origin of this provision may be traced to colonialism, during which the human and material resources of Africa were largely exploited for the benefit of outside powers, creating tragedy for Africans themselves, depriving them of their birthright and alienating them from the land. The aftermath of colonial exploitation has left Africa's precious resources and people still vulnerable to foreign misappropriation. The drafters of the Charter obviously wanted to remind African governments of the continent's painful legacy and restore co-operative economic development to its traditional place at the heart of African Society.

The Commission notes that in the present case, despite its obligation to protect persons against interferences in the enjoyment of their rights, the Government of Nigeria facilitated the destruction of the Ogoniland. Contrary to its Charter obligations and despite such internationally established principles, the Nigerian Government has given the green light to private actors, and the oil Companies in particular, to devastatingly affect the well-being of the Ogonis. By any measure of standards, its practice falls short of the minimum conduct expected of governments, and therefore, is in violation of Article 21 of the African Charter.

---

## Notes and Comments:

1. The *Serac v. Nigeria* case examined the meaning of the right to a healthy environment within a domestic setting although these rights are firmly based on international law principles. There is also the issue of transboundary pollution. The leading case in this area is *Trail Smelter Arbitration (U.S. v. Canada)* (1941), which involved a smelter physically located in Canada that spewed sulphur dioxide that ultimately landed in the state of Washington. In ruling for the United States, the arbitration panel held:

   The Tribunal ... finds that ... under the principles of international law, as well as of the law of the United States, no State has the right to use or permit the use of its territory in such a manner as to cause injury by fumes in or to the territory of another of the properties or persons therein, when the case is of serious consequence and the injury is established by clear and convincing evidence.

2. The same general principle of international law articulated in the *Trail Smelter* ruling – that states have an obligation to prevent harm to other states – was reinforced in the *Corfu Channel* (1949) case, one of the landmark rulings

of the International Court of Justice. The background of this case involved mines that had been placed in Albania's territorial waters, which caused damage to British Navy ships passing through these straits. The Court ruled that even if Albania had not actually laid the mines, as they claimed, it was aware of their existence, and thus had a duty to warn other states.

3. In 2008, Ecuador filed a claim against Colombia before the International Court of Justice regarding aerial spraying of dangerous chemicals at or near the Ecuadorian border. The aerial spraying was directed at Colombia's cocoa production, which it was carrying out largely at the behest of the United States. Ecuador maintained that the "spraying has already caused serious damage to people, to crops, to animals, and to the natural environment" in Ecuador. Following negotiations between the two countries, an out-of-court settlement was reached in 2013.

---

### Box 11.8: Global Warming: The Inuit Petition

In late 2005, the Inuit Circumpolar Conference (ICC) submitted a petition to the Washington D.C.-based Inter-American Commission on Human Rights seeking relief from violations of the human rights of Inuits resulting from global warming caused by greenhouse gas emissions from the United States of America. In the petition, the ICC alleged that global warming was having a devastating effect on the Arctic and the Inuit people who live there. The rationale behind suing the United States is that although the U.S. population comprises only 5% of the world's population, it produces a quarter of the greenhouse gases responsible for global warming. Nearly a year later, the IACHR declined to rule on the case on the grounds that there was not sufficient evidence of harm.

How would you have ruled in this case?

---

### Box 11.9: The Environment and International Law

There is little doubt that the greatest challenge of our age is climate change. What has international law done in this regard – and what must it do now and in the future? Starting off on an optimistic note, one of the great achievements in international law was the *Montreal Protocol on Substances the Deplete the Ozone Layer*, which has started to reverse the hole in the earth's ozone layer.

However, there has been less success in terms of tackling climate change. The two most notable achievements have been the *Kyoto Protocol* and the *Paris Agreement*, both of which attempt to reduce the levels of greenhouse gas emissions. The Protocol is based on the differentiation between industrialized states and developing countries (which includes China), with the former legally obligated to reduce emissions, but which were only voluntary for developing states. One of the great advances of the *Paris Agreement* is that this distinction between industrial and developing states was discarded, although the removal of the United States from the Agreement casts strong doubt on whether worldwide reduction targets can and will be met.

---

**Box 11.10: International Law at the Movies: Environmental Degradation and Global Warming**

Al Gore's award-winning documentary *An Inconvenient Truth* (2006) on the devastating prospects of climate change did much to raise this issue politically. A decade later *An Inconvenient Sequel* (2017) was released – at the advent of the Trump administration – detailing both the enormous advances that have been made in the interim period, but also the continuing concerns, especially in the absence of U.S. leadership on this issue. *The Age of Stupid* (2009) is a clever documentary set in the future where the question asked by succeeding generations is why our present generation did not take global warming much more seriously than it is doing.

On a more localized level, *Manufactured Landscapes* (2006) shows us where the "things" in our (Western) lives come from, but also where the trash is discarded and the negative effect all this has on "other" people. *Crude* (2009) is a documentary that focuses on environmental devastation in the Ecuadorian rainforest and the lawsuit brought against Texaco/Chevron for these harms.

---

The next case is brought by a Dutch NGO, Urgenda Foundation, seeking to get a judicial order to order the Dutch government to reduce CO2 emissions in that country.

---

## *Urgenda Foundation v. the Netherlands,* Hague District Court (2015)

This case is essentially about the question whether the State has a legal obligation towards Urgenda to place further limits on greenhouse gas emissions – particularly CO2 emissions – in addition to those arising from the plans of the Dutch government, acting on behalf of the State. Urgenda argues that the State does not pursue an adequate climate policy and therefore acts contrary to its duty of care towards Urgenda and the parties it represents as well as, more generally speaking, Dutch society. Urgenda also argues that because of the Dutch contribution to the climate policy, the State wrongly exposes the international community to the risk of dangerous climate change, resulting in serious and irreversible damage to human health and the environment. Based on these grounds, which are briefly summarised here, Urgenda claims, except for several declaratory decisions, that the State should be ordered to limit, or have limited, the joint volume of the annual greenhouse gas emissions of the Netherlands so that these emissions will have been reduced by 40% and at least by 25% in 2020, compared to

1990. In case this claim is denied, Urgenda argues for an order to have this volume limited by 40% in 2030, also compared to 1990.

For its part, the State argues that the Netherlands – also based on European agreements – pursues an adequate climate policy. Therefore, and for many other reasons, the State believes Urgenda's claims cannot succeed.

Article 21 of the Dutch Constitution imposes a duty of care on the State relating to the liveability of the country and the protection and improvement of the living environment. For the densely populated and low–lying Netherlands, this duty of care concerns important issues, such as the water defences, water management and the living environment. This rule and its background do not provide certainty about the manner in which this duty of care should be exercised nor about the outcome of the consideration in case of conflicting stipulations. The manner in which this task should be carried out is covered by the government's own discretionary powers.

The realisation that climate change is an extra–territorial, global problem and fighting it requires a worldwide approach has prompted heads of state and government leaders to contribute to the development of legal instruments for combating climate change by means of mitigating greenhouse gas emissions as well as by making their countries "climate–proof" by means of taking mitigating measures. These instruments have been developed in an international context (in the UN), European context (in the EU) and in a national context. The Dutch climate policy is based on these instruments to a great extent.

The question whether the State is in breach of its duty of care for taking insufficient measures to prevent dangerous climate change is a legal issue which has never before been answered in Dutch proceedings and for which jurisprudence does not provide a ready–made framework. The answer to the question whether or not the State is taking sufficient mitigation measures depends on many factors, with two aspects having particular relevance. In the first place, it has to be assessed whether there is a unlawful hazardous negligence on the part of the State. Secondly, the State's discretionary power is relevant in assessing the government's actions. From case law about government liability it follows that the court has to assess fully whether or not the State has exercised or exercises sufficient care, but that this does not alter the fact that the State has the discretion to determine how it fulfils its duty of care. However, this discretionary power vested in the State is not unlimited: the State's care may not be below standard. However, the test of due care required here and the discretionary power of the State are not wholly distinguishable. After all, the detailing of the duty of care of the person called to account will also have been included in his specific position in view of the special nature of his duty or authority. The standard of care has been attuned to this accordingly.

The State has argued that allowing Urgenda's claim, which is aimed at a higher reduction of greenhouse gas emission in the Netherlands, would not be effective on a global scale, as such a target would result in a very minor, if not negligible, reduction of global greenhouse gas emissions. After all, whether or not the 2°C target is achieved will mainly depend on the reduction targets of other countries with high emissions. More specifically, the States relies on the fact that the Dutch contribution to worldwide emissions is currently only 0.5%.

This argument does not succeed. It is an established fact that climate change is a global problem and therefore requires global accountability. This means that more reduction measures have to be taken on an international level. It compels all countries, including the Netherlands, to implement the reduction measures to the fullest extent as possible. The fact that the amount of the Dutch emissions is small compared to other countries does not affect the obligation to take precautionary measures in view of the State's obligation to exercise care. After all, it has been established that any anthropogenic greenhouse gas emission, no matter how minor, contributes to an increase of CO2 levels in the atmosphere and therefore to hazardous climate change. Emission reduction therefore concerns both a joint and individual responsibility of the signatories to the UN Climate Change Convention.

Due to the severity of the consequences of climate change and the great risk of hazardous climate change occurring – without mitigating measures – the court concludes that the State has a duty of care to take mitigation measures. The circumstance that the Dutch contribution to the present global greenhouse gas emissions is currently small does not affect this.

Based on the foregoing, the court concludes that the State has acted negligently and therefore unlawfully towards Urgenda by starting from a reduction target for 2020 of less than 25% compared to the year 1990.

### THE RULING

The court: orders the State to limit the joint volume of Dutch annual greenhouse gas emissions, or have them limited, so that this volume will have reduced by at least 25% at the end of 2020 compared to the level of the year 1990, as claimed by Urgenda, in so far as acting on its own behalf.

---

## Notes and Comments:

1. Is *Urgenda* an important case – or much ado about nothing?
2. The Urgenda Foundation is a Dutch nongovernmental organization. Do you think the court would have granted standing (the ability to present a claim) if it was a foreign organization? What about a foreign government?
3. Current international law is largely based on the notion of independent international responsibility – rather than shared responsibility (Nollkaemper and Jacobs 2013). Yet, isn't climate change, by definition, based on "shared responsibility" (Faure and Nollkaemper 2007)?
4. Even if you agree with the court's ruling (which I will assume many of you will), is this country-by-country approach the "best" or most "efficient" way of addressing the issue of climate change?

---

### Box 11.11: The Trafigura Case

In 2006, a ship (*Probo Koala*) filled with toxic waste was taken to Amsterdam harbor for processing but government officials refused to allow the material to be unloaded due to its hazardous nature. In violation of a number of international environmental treaties including the 1989 Basel Convention on the Control of Transboundary Movements of Hazardous Wastes and their Disposal, the material was taken to Abidjan, Ivory Coast and dumped in various locations around the city, harming thousands. In 2008, Dutch prosecutors began proceedings against Trafigura, the company that had chartered the *Probo Koala*, and a class action suit was filed against the company in the United Kingdom (van Wingerde 2015).

*(Continued)*

**Box 11.11: Continued**

**Photo 11.1** Toxic Waste From the Trafigura

*Source:* © Associated Press

*Juliana v. United States* is a case brought in federal district by a group of young Americans challenging U.S. environmental policy. The case has caught the eye of many for several reasons, but particularly because of the special "standing" treatment the court gives to young people in various locales throughout the United States.

## *Juliana v. United States,* District Court for Oregon, Nov. 2016

Plaintiffs in this civil rights action are a group of young people between the ages of eight and nineteen ("youth plaintiffs,); Earth Guardians, an association of young environmental activists; and Dr. James Hansen, acting as guardian for future generations. Plaintiffs filed this action against defendants the United States, President Barack Obama, and numerous executive agencies. Plaintiffs allege defendants have known for more than fifty years that the carbon dioxide ("$CO_2$") produced by burning fossil fuels was destabilizing the climate system in a way that would "significantly endanger plaintiffs, with the damage persisting for millenia." Despite that knowledge, plaintiffs assert defendants, "[b]y their exercise of sovereign authority over our country's atmosphere and fossil fuel resources, . . . permitted, encouraged, and otherwise enabled continued exploitation, production, and combustion of fossil fuels, . . . deliberately allow[ing] atmospheric C02 concentrations to escalate to levels unprecedented in human history."

This is no ordinary lawsuit. Plaintiffs challenge the policies, acts, and omissions of the President of the United States, the Council on Environmental Quality, the Office of Management and Budget, the Office of Science and Technology Policy, the Department of Energy, the Department of the Interior, the Department of Transportation ("DOT"), the

Department of Agriculture, the Department of Commerce, the Department of Defense, the Department of State, and the Environmental Protection Agency ("EPA"). This lawsuit challenges decisions defendants have made across a vast set of topics – decisions like whether and to what extent to regulate $CO_2$ emissions from power plants and vehicles, whether to permit fossil fuel extraction and development to take place on federal lands, how much to charge for use of those lands, whether to give tax breaks to the fossil fuel industry, whether to subsidize or directly fund that industry, whether to fund the construction of fossil fuel infrastructure such as natural gas pipelines at home and abroad, whether to authorize new marine coal terminal projects. Plaintiffs assert defendants' decisions on these topics have substantially caused the planet to warm and the oceans to rise. They draw a direct causal line between defendants' policy choices and floods, food shortages, destruction of property, species extinction, and a host of other harms.

This lawsuit is not about proving that climate change is happening or that human activity is driving it. For the purposes of this motion, those facts are undisputed. The questions before the Court are whether defendants are responsible for some of the harm caused by climate change, whether plaintiffs may challenge defendants' climate change policy in court, and whether this Court can direct defendants to change their policy without running afoul of the separation of powers doctrine.

### STANDING TO SUE

A threshold question in every federal case is whether at least one plaintiff has standing. To demonstrate standing, a plaintiff must show (1) she suffered an injury in fact that is concrete, particularized, and actual or imminent; (2) the injury is fairly traceable to the defendant's challenged conduct; and (3) the injury is likely to be redressed by a favorable court decision. A plaintiff must support each element of the standing test "with the manner and degree of evidence required at the successive stages of the litigation." Accordingly, at the motion to dismiss stage "general allegations" suffice to establish standing because those allegations are presumed to "embrace those specific facts that are necessary to support the claim."

### INJURY IN FACT

In an environmental case, a plaintiff cannot demonstrate injury in fact merely by alleging injury to the environment; there must be an allegation that the challenged conduct is harming (or imminently will harm) the plaintiff. For example, a plaintiff may meet the injury in fact requirement by alleging the challenged activity" impairs his or her economic interests or aesthetic and environmental well-being."

Plaintiffs adequately allege injury in fact. Lead plaintiff Kelsey Juliana alleges algae blooms harm the water she drinks, and low water levels caused by drought kill the wild salmon she eats. Plaintiff Xiuhtezcatl Roske-Martinez alleges increased wildfires and extreme flooding jeopardize his personal safety. Plaintiff Alexander Loznak alleges record- setting temperatures harm the health of the hazelnut orchard on his family farm, an important source of both revenue and food for him and his family. Plaintiff Jacob Lebel alleges drought conditions required his family to install an irrigation system at their farm.

The government contends these injuries are not particular to plaintiffs because they are caused by climate change, which broadly affects the entire planet (and all people on it) in some way. According to the government, this renders plaintiffs' injuries nonjusticiable generalized grievances. The government misunderstands the generalized grievance rule. As the Ninth Circuit recently explained, federal courts lack jurisdiction to hear a case when the harm at issue is "not only widely shared, but is also of an abstract and indefinite nature-for example, harm to the common concern for obedience to the law." Standing alone, "the fact that a harm is widely shared does not necessarily render it a generalized grievance." Because plaintiffs seek injunctive relief, they must show their injuries are "ongoing or likely to recur." They have met this requirement.

The complaint alleges that "the present level of C02 and its warming, both realized and latent, are already in the zone of danger." It also alleges that "our country is now in a period of carbon overshoot, with early consequences that are already threatening and that will, in the short term, rise to unbearable unless Defendants take immediate action. Youth plaintiffs each allege harm that is ongoing and likely to continue in the future. By alleging injuries that are concrete, particularized, and actual or imminent, plaintiffs have satisfied the first prong of the standing test.

### CAUSATION

The second requirement of standing is causation. A plaintiff must show the injury alleged is "fairly traceable" to the challenged action of the defendant and not the result of "the independent action of some third party not before the court." Although a defendant's action need not be the sole source of injury to support standing, "the line of causation between the defendant's action and the plaintiffs harm must be more than attenuated. However, a "causal chain does not fail simply because it has several links, provided those links are not hypothetical or tenuous and remain plausible." Here, by contrast, plaintiffs' chain of causation rests on the core allegation that defendants are responsible for a substantial share of worldwide greenhouse gas emissions. Plaintiffs allege that over the 263 years between 1751 and 2014, the United States produced more than twenty-five percent of global C02 emissions. Greenhouse gas emissions produced in the United States continue to increase. In 2012, the United States was the second largest producer and consumer of energy in the world.

The causal chain alleged by plaintiffs here is conclusionary, but that is because they have not yet had the opportunity to present evidence. At oral argument, plaintiffs explained that their theory of causation has two components. The first relates to defendants' affirmative acts. Specifically, plaintiffs allege that fossil fuel combustion accounts for approximately ninety-four percent of United States C02 emissions. Defendants lease public lands for oil, gas, and coal production; undercharge royalties in connection with those leases; provide tax breaks to companies to encourage fossil fuel development; permit the import and export of fossil fuels; and incentivize the purchase of sport utility vehicles. Here, the chain of causation is: fossil fuel combustion accounts for the lion's share of greenhouse gas emissions produced in the United States; defendants have the power to increase or decrease those emissions; and defendants use that power to engage in a variety of activities that actively cause and promote higher levels of fossil fuel combustion.

The second component of plaintiffs' causation themy involves defendants' failure to act in areas where they have authority to do so. Plaintiffs allege that together, power plants and transportation produce nearly two-thirds of C02 emissions in the United States. Plaintiffs also allege DOT and EPA have broad power to set emissions standards in these sectors. So the chain of causation is: DOT and EPA have jurisdiction over sectors producing sixty-four percent of United States emissions, which in turn constitute roughly fourteen percent of emissions worldwide; they allow high emissions levels by failing to set demanding standards; high emissions levels cause climate change; and climate change causes plaintiffs' injuries.

Each link in these causal chains may be difficult to prove, but the "spectre of difficulty down the road does not inform [the] justiciability determination at this early stage of the proceedings." At the pleading stage, plaintiffs have adequately alleged a causal link between defendants' conduct and the asserted injuries.

The final prong of the standing inquiry is redressability. A plaintiff need not show a favorable decision is certain to redress his injury, but must show a substantial likelihood it will do so. It is sufficient for the redressability inquiry to show that the requested remedy would "slow or reduce" the harm. The declaratory and injunctive relief plaintiffs request meets this standard. Most notably, plaintiffs ask this Court to "order Defendants to prepare and implement an enforceable national remedial plan to phase out fossil fuel emissions and draw down excess atmospheric $CO_2$. If plaintiffs can show, as they have alleged, that defendants have control over a quarter of the planet's greenhouse gas emissions, and that a reduction in those emissions would reduce atmospheric $CO_2$ and slow climate change, then plaintiffs' requested relief would redress their injuries.

Defendants and intervenors essentially argue that because many entities contribute to global warming, an injunction operating on one entity – even a major player – would offer no guarantee of an overall reduction in greenhouse gas emissions. But whether the Court could guarantee an overall reduction in greenhouse gas emissions is the wrong inquiry for at least two reasons. First, redressability does not require certainty, it requires only a substantial likelihood that the Court could provide meaningful relief. Second, the possibility that some other individual or entity might later cause the same injury does not defeat standing – the question is whether the injury *caused by the defendant* can be redressed.

Redressability in this case is scientifically complex, particularly in light of the specter of "irreversible climate change," wherein greenhouse gas emissions above a certain level push the planet past "points of no return, beyond which irreversible consequences become inevitable, out of humanity's control." This raises a host of questions, among them: What part of plaintiffs' injuries are attributable to causes beyond this Court's control? Even if emissions increase elsewhere, will the magnitude of plaintiffs' injuries be less if they obtain the relief they seek in this lawsuit? When would we reach this point of no return, and do defendants have it within their power to avert reaching it even without cooperation from third parties? All of these questions are inextricably bound up in the causation inquiry, and none of them can be answered at the motion to dismiss stage.

Plaintiffs ask this Court to "order Defendants to cease their permitting, authorizing, and subsidizing of fossil fuels and, instead, move to swiftly phase out $CO_2$ emissions, as well as take such other action necessary to ensure that atmospheric $CO_2$ is no more concentrated than 350 ppm by 2100, including to develop a national plan to restore Earth's energy balance, and implement that national plan so as to stabilize the climate system." Construing the complaint in plaintiffs' favor, they allege that this relief would at least partially redress their asserted injuries. Youth plaintiffs have adequately alleged they have standing to sue.

Throughout their objections, defendants and intervenors attempt to subject a lawsuit alleging constitutional injuries to case law governing statutory and common-law environmental claims. They are correct that plaintiffs likely could not obtain the relief they seek through citizen suits brought under the Clean Air Act, the Clean Water Act, or other environmental laws. But that argument misses the point. This action is of a different order than the typical environmental case. It alleges that defendants' actions and inactions – whether or not they violate any specific statutory duty – have so profoundly damaged our home planet that they threaten plaintiffs' fundamental constitutional rights to life and liberty.

This lawsuit may be groundbreaking, but that fact does not alter the legal standards governing the motions to dismiss. Indeed, the seriousness of plaintiffs' allegations underscores how vitally important it is for this Court to apply those standards carefully and correctly.

Federal courts too often have been cautious and overly deferential in the arena of environmental law, and the world has suffered for it. "A strong and independent judiciary is the cornerstone of our liberties." These words, spoken by Oregon Senator Mark 0. Hatfield, are etched into the walls of the Portland United States courthouse for the District of Oregon. The words appear on the first floor, a daily reminder that it is "emphatically the province and duty of the judicial department to say what the law is." *Marbury v. Madison.* Even when a case implicates hotly contested political issues, the judiciary must not shrink from its role as a coequal branch of government.

---

## Notes and Comments:

1. Although many of the plaintiffs were relatively young, still, all were alive at the time that suit was filed. Should a judge also grant "standing" for future generations – those not (yet) born but who will be severely affected by actions taken now (Hiskes 2017)? In addition, all of the plaintiffs in this case lived in the United States. Would it be appropriate to grant standing to non-nationals living in other countries as well? Why or why not?

2. Perhaps heeding the sentiment at the close of the *Juliana* case, there has been a surge of environmental cases being brought. For example, in November 2015, Saúl Luciano Lliuya, a Peruvian farmer who lives in Huaraz, Peru, filed claims for declaratory judgment and damages in a German court against RWE, Germany's largest electricity producer. Lliuya's suit alleged that RWE, having knowingly contributed to climate change by emitting substantial volumes of greenhouse gases (GHGs), bears some measure of responsibility for the melting of mountain glaciers near his town of Huaraz.

3. One of the most important judicial rulings in this area was the Inter-American Court of Human Rights' Advisory Opinion on *The Environment and Human Rights* (2018). The question addressed by the Court was whether a state has "jurisdiction" over a person situated outside the territory of that State Party if his or her human rights have been violated as a result of damage to the environment or of the risk of environmental damage that could be attributed to that state. The Court held:

> It would be unconscionable to so interpret the responsibility under article 2 of the Covenant as to permit a State party to perpetrate

violations of the Covenant on the territory of another State, which violations it could not perpetrate on its own territory.

## References

### Books and Articles

Takele Bulto, *The Extraterritorial Application of the Human Right to Water in Africa*, Cambridge: Cambridge University Press (2014)

Michael G. Faure and Andre Nollkaemper, "Climate Change Liability and the Allocation of Risk: International Liability as an Instrument to Prevent and Compensate for Climate Change," *Stanford Journal of International Law* 43: 123–79 (2007)

Richard Hiskes, "With Apologies to the Future: Environmental Human Rights and the Politics of Communal Responsibility," *The International Journal of Human Rights* 21: 1401–16 (2017)

Mahdev Mohan, "The Road to Song Mao: Transnational Litigation from Southeast Asia to the United Kingdom," *American Journal of International Law* (2014)

Andre Nollkaemper and Dov Jacobs, "Shared Responsibility in International Law: A Conceptual Framework," *Michigan Journal of International Law* 34: 359–438 (2013)

Sigrun Skogly, *Beyond National Borders: States' Human Rights Obligations in International Cooperation*, Antwerp: Intersentia (2006)

C.G. van Wingerde, "The Limits of Environmental Regulation in a Globalized Economy: Lessons from the Probo Koala Case," in J.G. van Erp and W. Huisman (eds.) *Routledge Handbook of White-Collar and Corporate Crime in Europe*, Oxford: Routledge (2015)

### U.N. Reports

U.N. Committee on Economic, Social and Cultural Rights, *General Comment 15 (The Right to Water (arts. 11 and 12 of the International Covenant on Economic, Social and Cultural Rights)*, (20 January 2003)

Paul Hunt, *Report of the Special Rapporteur on the Right to Everyone to the Enjoyment of the Highest Attainable Standard of Physical and Mental Health, Paul Hunt Addendum, Mission to Sweden*, UN Human Rights Council, A/HRC/4/28/Add.2 (2007)

### Cases

*Advisory Opinion on The Environment and Human Rights*, IACtHR (7 February 2018)

*Corfu Channel (United Kingdom v. Albania)*, ICJ (1949)

*Government of the South Africa and Others v. Grootboom and Others*, Constitutional Court of South Africa (2000)

*Juliana v. United States*, 217 F. Supp. 3d 1224 (D.C. Ore. 2016)

*Mazibuko and Others v. Johannesburg and Others*, Constitutional Court of South Africa (2009)

*Minister of Health and Others v. Treatment Action Campaign and Others*, Constitutional Court of South Africa (2002)

*Social and Economic Rights Action Centre and the Centre for Economic and Social Rights v. Nigeria*, African Commission on Human and Peoples' Rights, 155/96 (2001)

*Soobramoney v. Minister of Health (Kwazulu-Natal)*, Constitutional Court of South Africa (1997)

*Trail Smelter Arbitration (U.S. v. Canada)* (1941)

*Urgenda Foundation v. the Netherlands*, Hague District Court (2015)


### International Agreements

Basel Convention on the Control of Transboundary Movements of Hazardous Wastes and Their Disposal, adopted 22 March 1989, entry into force 5 May 1992

Convention on the Law of the Non-Navigational Uses of International Watercourses, adopted by the U.N. General Assembly 21 May 1997, entry into force 17 August 2014

International Covenant on Economic, Social and Economic Rights, adopted by the U.N. General Assembly on 16 December 1966, entry into force 3 January 1976

Kyoto Protocol to the United Nations Framework Convention on Climate Change, 10 December 1997, U.N. Doc FCCC/CP/1997/7/Add.1, 37 I.L.M. 22 (1998)

Millennium Development Goals. Available at: www.un.org/millenniumgoals/

Paris Agreement, signed on 12 December 2015, entry into force 4 November 2016

Sustainable Development Goals. Available at: www.un.org/sustainabledevelopment/sustainable-development-goals/


### Domestic Law

South African Constitution

# 12
# Vulnerable Populations

In this final chapter we analyze the degree to which marginalized populations – refugees, women, children, indigenous populations, and sexual minorities – are protected (or not) by international law. We begin with those displaced from their homes by violence, which at the close of 2017 numbered 65.6 million, of which 22.5 million are refugees. To provide some additional context to this unprecedented wave of individuals in need, 55% of the world's refugees come from just one of three counties: Syria (5.5 million), Afghanistan (2.5 million), and South Sudan (1.4 million). And in terms of hosting states, the most generous are the following: Turkey (2.9 million), Pakistan (1.4 million), Lebanon (1.0 million), Iran (979,400), Uganda (940,800), and Ethiopia (791,600).

## Refugees and Asylum Seekers

International law is premised on the principle that each state has a responsibility to protect its own people. However, as we know from the numbers, there are many instances when this does not occur and protection has to be provided by some other state. Under the 1951 Refugee Convention, individuals have the right to apply for asylum. However, no state has an obligation to provide refugee protection. Instead, the only obligation that state parties have is not to return an individual to a country where his/her life or freedom would be threatened. This is called the *nonrefoulement* principle. The following two cases take up the issue of when (and where) a state's legal responsibility to asylum seekers arises.

## Sale v. Haitian Ctrs. Council, 509 U.S. 155 (1993)

### JUSTICE STEVENS, DELIVERED THE OPINION OF THE COURT

The President has directed the Coast Guard to intercept vessels illegally transporting passengers from Haiti to the United States and to return those passengers to Haiti without first determining whether they may qualify as refugees. The question presented in this case is whether such forced repatriation, "authorized to be undertaken only beyond the territorial sea of the United States," violates § 243(h)(1) of the Immigration and Nationality Act of 1952 (INA or Act). We hold that neither § 243(h) nor Article 33 of the United Nations Protocol Relating to the Status of Refugees applies to action taken by the Coast Guard on the high seas.

Aliens residing illegally in the United States are subject to deportation after a formal hearing. Aliens arriving at the border, or those who are temporarily paroled into the country, are subject to an exclusion hearing, the less formal process by which they, too, may eventually be removed from the United States. In either a deportation or exclusion proceeding the alien may seek asylum as a political refugee for whom removal to a particular country may threaten his life or freedom. Requests that the Attorney General grant asylum or withhold deportation to a particular country are typically, but not necessarily, advanced as parallel claims in either a deportation or an exclusion proceeding. When an alien proves that he is a "refugee," the Attorney General has discretion to grant him asylum pursuant to § 208 of the Act. If the proof shows that it is more likely than not that the alien's life or freedom would be threatened in a particular country because of his political or religious beliefs, under § 243(h) the Attorney General must not send him to that country. The INA offers these statutory protections only to aliens who reside in or have arrived at the border of the United States. For 12 years, in one form or another, the interdiction program challenged here has prevented Haitians such as respondents from reaching our shores and invoking those protections.

Both parties argue that the plain language of § 243(h)(1) is dispositive. It reads as follows:

> The Attorney General shall not deport or return any alien (other than an alien described in section 1251(a)(4)(D) of this title) to a country if the Attorney General determines that such alien's life or freedom would be threatened in such country on account of race, religion, nationality, membership in a particular social group, or political opinion.

Respondents emphasize the words "any alien" and "return"; neither term is limited to aliens within the United States. Respondents also contend that the 1980 amendment deleting the words "within the United States" from the prior text of § 243(h), obviously gave the statute an extraterritorial effect. This change, they further argue, was required in order to conform the statute to the text of Article 33.1 of the Convention, which they find as unambiguous as the present statutory text.

Petitioners' response is that a fair reading of the INA as a whole demonstrates that § 243(h) does not apply to actions taken by the President or Coast Guard outside the United States; that the legislative history of the 1980 amendment supports their reading; and that both the text and the negotiating history of Article 33 of the Convention indicate that it was not intended to have any extraterritorial effect.

Two aspects of Article 33's text are persuasive. The first is the explicit reference in Article 33.2 to the country in which the alien is located; the second is the parallel use of the terms "expel or return," the latter term explained by the French word "refouler."

The full text of Article 33 reads as follows:

*Article 33. – Prohibition of Expulsion or Return ('refoulement')*

1. No Contracting State shall expel or return *('re- fouler')* a refugee in any manner whatsoever to the frontiers of territories where his life or freedom would be threatened on account of his race, religion, nationality, membership of a particular social group or political opinion.

2. The benefit of the present provision may not, however, be claimed by a refugee whom there are reasonable grounds for regarding as a danger to the security of *the country in which he is*, or who, having been convicted by a final judgment of a particularly serious crime, constitutes a danger to the community of that country.

Under the second paragraph of Article 33 an alien may not claim the benefit of the first paragraph if he poses a danger to the country in which he is located. If the first paragraph did apply on the high seas, no nation could invoke the second paragraph's exception with respect to an alien there: An alien intercepted on the high seas is in no country at all. If Article 33.1 applied extraterritorially, therefore, Article 33.2 would create an absurd anomaly: Dangerous aliens on the high seas would be entitled to the benefits of 33.1 while those residing in the country that sought to expel them would not. It is more reasonable to assume that the coverage of 33.2 was limited to those already in the country because it was understood that 33.1 obligated the signatory state only with respect to aliens within its territory.

Article 33.1 uses the words "expel or return ('refouler')" as an obvious parallel to the words "deport or return" in § 243(h)(1). There is no dispute that "expel" has the same meaning as "deport"; it refers to the deportation or expulsion of an alien who is already present in the host country. The dual reference identified and explained in our opinion in *Leng May Ma* v. *Barber* suggests that the term "return ('refouler')" refers to the exclusion of aliens who are merely "'on the threshold of initial entry.'"

This suggestion – that "return" has a legal meaning narrower than its common meaning – is reinforced by the parenthetical reference to *"refouler,"* a French word that is *not* an exact synonym for the English word "return." Indeed, neither of two respected English-French dictionaries mentions *"refouler"* as one of many possible French translations of "return." Conversely, the English translations of *"refouler"* do not include the word "return." They do, however, include words like "repulse," "repel," "drive back," and even "expel." To the extent that they are relevant, these translations imply that "return" means a defensive act of resistance or exclusion at a border rather than an act of transporting someone to a particular destination. In the context of the Convention, to "return" means to "repulse" rather than to "reinstate."

The text of Article 33 thus fits with Judge Edwards' understanding that "'expulsion' would refer to a 'refugee already admitted into a country' and that 'return' would refer to a 'refugee already within the territory but not yet resident there.' Thus, the Protocol was not intended to govern parties' conduct outside of their national borders." From the time of the Convention, commentators have consistently agreed with this view.

The drafters of the Convention and the parties to the Protocol – like the drafters of § 243(h) – may not have contemplated that any nation would gather fleeing refugees and return them to the one country they had desperately sought to escape; such actions may even violate the spirit of Article 33; but a treaty cannot impose uncontemplated extraterritorial obligations on those who ratify it through no more than its general humanitarian intent. Because the text of Article 33 cannot reasonably be read to say anything at all about a nation's actions toward aliens outside its own territory, it does not prohibit such actions.

Respondents contend that the dangers faced by Haitians who are unwillingly repatriated demonstrate that the judgment of the Court of Appeals fulfilled the central purpose of the Convention and the Refugee Act of 1980. While we must, of course, be guided by the high purpose of both the treaty and the statute, we are not persuaded that either one places any limit on the President's authority to repatriate aliens interdicted beyond the territorial seas of the United States.

The judgment of the Court of Appeals is reversed.

*It is so ordered.*

### JUSTICE BLACKMUN, DISSENTING

When, in 1968, the United States acceded to the United Nations Protocol Relating to the Status of Refugees, it pledged not to "return (*'refouler'*) a refugee in any manner whatsoever" to a place where he would face political persecution. In 1980, Congress amended our immigration law to reflect the Protocol's directives. Today's majority nevertheless decides that the forced repatriation of the Haitian refugees is perfectly legal, because the word "return" does not mean return, because the opposite of "within the United States" is not outside the United States, and because the official charged with controlling immigration has no role in enforcing an order to control immigration.

I believe that the duty of nonreturn expressed in both the Protocol and the statute is clear. The majority finds it "extraordinary," that Congress would have intended the ban on returning "any alien" to apply to aliens at sea. That Congress would have meant what it said is not remarkable. What is extraordinary in this case is that the Executive, in disregard of the law, would take to the seas to intercept fleeing refugees and force them back to their persecutors – and that the Court would strain to sanction that conduct.

Article 33.1 of the Convention states categorically and without geographical limitation:

> No Contracting State shall expel or return (*'refouler'*) a refugee in any manner whatsoever to the frontiers of territories where his life or freedom would be threatened on account of his race, religion, nationality, membership of a particular social group or political opinion.

The terms are unambiguous. Vulnerable refugees shall not be returned. The language is clear, and the command is straightforward; that should be the end of the inquiry.

The majority, however, has difficulty with the treaty's use of the term "return (*'refouler'*)." "Return," it claims, does not mean return, but instead has a distinctive legal meaning.

The text of the Convention does not ban the "exclusion" of aliens who have reached some indeterminate "threshold"; it bans their "return." It is well settled that a treaty must first be construed according to its "ordinary meaning." The ordinary meaning of "return" is "to bring, send, or put (a person or thing) back to or in a former position." Webster's Third New International Dictionary 1941 (1986). That describes precisely what petitioners are doing to the Haitians. By dispensing with ordinary meaning at the outset, and by taking instead as its starting point the assumption that "return," as used in the treaty, "has a legal meaning narrower than its common meaning," the majority leads itself astray.

The straightforward interpretation of the duty of nonreturn is strongly reinforced by the Convention's use of the French term "*refouler*." The ordinary meaning of "*refouler*," as the majority concedes, is "[t]o repulse, . . . to drive back, to repel." Thus construed, Article 33.1 of the Convention reads: "No contracting state shall expel or [repulse, drive back, or repel] a refugee in any manner whatsoever to the frontiers of territories where his life or freedom would be threatened. . . ." That, of course, is exactly what the Government is doing.

And yet the majority insists that what has occurred is not, in fact, "*refoulement*." It reaches this conclusion in a peculiar fashion. After acknowledging that the ordinary meaning of "*refouler*" is "repulse," "repel," and "drive back," the majority without elaboration declares: "To the extent that they are relevant, these translations imply that 'return' means a defensive act of resistance or exclusion at a border. . ." I am at a loss to find the narrow notion of "exclusion at a border" in broad terms like "repulse," "repel," and "drive back." Gage was repulsed (initially) at Bunker Hill. Lee was repelled at Gettysburg. Rommel was driven back across North Africa. The majority's puzzling progression ("*refouler*" means repel or drive back; therefore "return" means only exclude at a border; therefore the treaty does not apply) hardly justifies a departure from the path of ordinary meaning. The text of Article 33.1 is clear, and whether the operative term is "return" or "*refouler*," it prohibits the Government's actions.

Article 33.1 is clear not only in what it says, but also in what it does not say: It does not include any geographical limitation. It limits only where a refugee may be sent "to," not where he may be sent from. This is not surprising, given that the aim of the provision is to protect refugees against persecution.

Article 33.2, by contrast, *does* contain a geographical reference, and the majority seizes upon this as evidence that the section as a whole applies only within a signatory's borders. That inference is flawed. Article 33.2 states that the benefit of Article 33.1

> may not . . . be claimed by a refugee whom there are reasonable grounds for regarding as a danger to the security of the country in which he is, or who, having been convicted by a final judgment of a particularly serious crime, constitutes a danger to the community of that country.

The signatories' understandable decision to allow nations to deport criminal aliens who have entered their territory hardly suggests an intent to permit the apprehension and return of noncriminal aliens who have not entered their territory, and who may have no desire ever to enter it. One wonders what the majority would make of an exception that removed from the Article's protection all refugees who "constitute a danger to their families." By the majority's logic, the inclusion of such an exception presumably would render Article 33.1 applicable only to refugees with families.

Far from constituting "an absurd anomaly," the fact that a state is permitted to "expel or return" a small class of refugees found within its territory but may not seize and return refugees who remain outside its frontiers expresses precisely the objectives and concerns of the Convention. Nonreturn is the rule; the sole exception (neither applicable nor invoked here) is that a nation endangered by a refugee's very presence may "expel or return" him to an unsafe country if it chooses. The tautological observation that only a refugee already in a country can pose a danger to the country "in which he is" proves nothing.

That the clarity of the text and the implausibility of its theories do not give the majority more pause is due, I think, to the majority's heavy reliance on the presumption against extraterritoriality. The presumption runs throughout the majority's opinion, and it stacks the deck by requiring the Haitians to produce "affirmative evidence" that when Congress prohibited the return of "any" alien, it indeed meant to prohibit the interception and return of aliens at sea.

The judicially created canon of statutory construction against extraterritorial application of United States law has no role here, however. It applies only where congressional intent is "unexpressed." Here there is no room for doubt: A territorial restriction has been deliberately deleted from the statute.

Even where congressional intent is unexpressed, however, a statute must be assessed according to its intended scope. The primary basis for the application of the presumption (besides the desire – not relevant here – to avoid conflict with the laws of other nations) is "the commonsense notion that Congress generally legislates with domestic concerns in mind." Where that notion seems unjustified or unenlightening, however, generally worded laws covering varying subject matters are routinely applied extraterritorially.

In this case we deal with a statute that regulates a distinctively international subject matter: immigration, nationalities, and refugees. Whatever force the presumption may have with regard to a primarily domestic statute evaporates in this context. There is no danger that the Congress that enacted the Refugee Act was blind to the fact that the laws it was crafting had implications beyond this Nation's borders. The "commonsense notion" that Congress was looking inwards – perfectly valid in a case involving the Federal Tort Claims Act, such as *Smith* – cannot be reasonably applied to the Refugee Act of 1980.

The Convention that the Refugee Act embodies was enacted largely in response to the experience of Jewish refugees in Europe during the period of World War II. The tragic consequences of the world's indifference at that time are well known. The resulting ban on *refoulement*, as broad as the humanitarian purpose that inspired it, is easily applicable here, the Court's protestations of impotence and regret notwithstanding.

The refugees attempting to escape from Haiti do not claim a right of admission to this country. They do not even argue that the Government has no right to intercept their boats. They demand only that the United States, land of refugees and guardian of freedom, cease forcibly driving them back to detention, abuse, and death. That is a modest plea, vindicated by the treaty and the statute. We should not close our ears to it.

I dissent.

## Notes and Comments:

1. Which opinion do you agree with?
2. If the majority is correct that *nonrefoulement* protection only begins at U.S. borders, what other international human rights treaties also have a "territorial" basis – and what would be the implications of this?

---

### Box 12.1: International Law at the Movies: The Plight of Refugees

Although the vast majority of Syrian refugees have remained in the Middle East, a substantial number have attempted to gain entry into Europe. *On the Bride's Side* (2014) is a documentary that follows a group posing as a wedding party trying to make their way through Europe in order to get to Sweden. *Fire at Sea* (2016) takes the viewer to the unassuming island of Lampedusa, south of Sicily, which has now become a refugee destination. *4.1 Miles* (2016) is only 20 minutes long but its power belies its brevity as it shows both heroism and tragedy on the Mediterranean Sea. Two earlier feature films dealing with Third World migrants attempting to gain entry into "Fortress Europe" are *Journey of Hope* (1990) and *In This World* (2002).

In terms of the United States, *Well-Founded Fear* (2000) is a documentary that takes the viewer through the vagaries of the asylum determination process. *Sentenced Home* (2006) shows all too clearly, and cruelly, the deportation consequences of three Cambodians who are forced to return to a country they had left as children and had never known – until now. *El Norte* (1983) is an earlier feature film following a brother and sister who make their way north away from the violence that had engulfed their family in Guatemala.

**Photo 12.1** The "Lucky" Ones Who Have Made Their Way to Safety

*Source*: © Associated Press

Finally, the *Sierra Leone Refugee All Stars* (2005) tells a "feel good" story of how a now-famous band was formed in refugee camps in Western Africa, but underlying all this is a story marred by death and destruction.

Like the *Sale* ruling, the following case involves states enforcing their immigration laws some distance away from the country's borders and the question is whether legal protection also follows.

## *Hirsi Jamaa and Others v. Italy,* ECtHR, App. No. 27765/09 (2012)

The applicants, eleven Somali nationals and thirteen Eritrean nationals, were part of a group of about two hundred individuals who left Libya aboard three vessels with the aim of reaching the Italian coast.

On 6 May 2009, when the vessels were 35 nautical miles south of Lampedusa (Agrigento), that is, within the Maltese Search and Rescue Region of responsibility, they were intercepted by three ships from the Italian Revenue Police (*Guardia di finanza*) and the Coastguard.

The occupants of the intercepted vessels were transferred onto Italian military ships and returned to Tripoli. The applicants alleged that during that voyage the Italian authorities did not inform them of their real destination and took no steps to identify them.

All their personal effects, including documents confirming their identity, were confiscated by the military personnel.

On arrival in the port of Tripoli, following a ten-hour voyage, the migrants were handed over to the Libyan authorities. According to the applicants' version of events, they objected to being handed over to the Libyan authorities but were forced to leave the Italian ships.

At a press conference held on 7 May 2009, the Italian Minister of the Interior stated that the operation to intercept the vessels on the high seas and to push the migrants back to Libya was the consequence of the entry into force on 4 February 2009 of bilateral agreements concluded with Libya, and represented an important turning point in the fight against clandestine immigration. In a speech to the Senate on 25 May 2009, the Minister stated that between 6 and 10 May 2009 more than 471 irregular migrants had been intercepted on the high seas and transferred to Libya in accordance with those bilateral agreements. After explaining that the operations had been carried out in application of the principle of cooperation between States, the Minister stated that the push-back policy was very effective in combating illegal immigration. According to the Minister of the Interior, that policy discouraged criminal gangs involved in people smuggling and trafficking, helped save lives at sea and substantially reduced landings of irregular migrants along the Italian coast, which had decreased fivefold in May 2009 as compared with May 2008.

On 29 December 2007 Italy and Libya signed a bilateral cooperation agreement in Tripoli to combat clandestine immigration. On the same date the two countries signed an Additional Protocol setting out the operational and technical arrangements for implementing the said Agreement. Under Article 2 of the Agreement:

Italy and the 'Great Socialist People's Libyan Arab Jamahiriya' undertake to organise maritime patrols using six ships made available on a temporary basis by Italy. Mixed crews shall be present on ships, made up of Libyan personnel and Italian police officers, who shall provide training, guidance and technical assistance on the use and handling of the ships. Surveillance, search and rescue operations shall be conducted in the departure and transit areas of vessels used to transport clandestine immigrants, both in Libyan territorial waters and in international waters, in compliance with the international conventions in force and in accordance with the operational arrangements to be decided by the two countries.

### THE ISSUE OF JURISDICTION UNDER ARTICLE 1 OF THE CONVENTION

Article 1 of the Convention provides:

The High Contracting Parties shall secure to everyone within their jurisdiction the rights and freedoms defined in Section I of [the] Convention.

The Government acknowledged that the events in question had taken place on board Italian military ships. However, they denied that the Italian authorities had exercised "absolute and exclusive control" over the applicants. They submitted that the vessels carrying the applicants had been intercepted in the context of the rescue on the high seas of persons in distress – which is an obligation imposed by international law, namely, the United Nations Convention on the Law of the Sea ("the Montego Bay Convention") – and could in no circumstances be described as a maritime police operation.

The Italian ships had confined themselves to intervening to assist the three vessels in distress and ensuring the safety of the persons on board. They had then accompanied the intercepted migrants to Libya in accordance with the bilateral agreements of 2007 and 2009. The Government argued that the obligation to save human lives on the high seas did not in itself create a link between the State and the persons concerned establishing the State's jurisdiction.

Whenever the State through its agents operating outside its territory exercises control and authority over an individual, and thus jurisdiction, the State is under an obligation under Article 1 to secure to that individual the rights and freedoms under Section I of the Convention that are relevant to the situation of that individual.

There are other instances in the Court's case-law of the extraterritorial exercise of jurisdiction by a State in cases involving the activities of its diplomatic or consular agents abroad and on board craft and vessels registered in, or flying the flag of, that State. In these specific situations, the Court, basing itself on customary international law and treaty provisions, has recognized the extraterritorial exercise of jurisdiction by the relevant State.

The Court observes that in the instant case the events took place entirely on board ships of the Italian armed forces, the crews of which were composed exclusively of Italian military personnel. In the Court's opinion, in the period between boarding the ships of the Italian armed forces and being handed over to the Libyan authorities, the applicants were under the continuous and exclusive *de jure* and *de facto* control of the Italian authorities. Speculation as to the nature and purpose of the intervention of the Italian ships on the high seas would not lead the Court to any other conclusion. Accordingly, the events giving rise to the alleged violations fall within Italy's "jurisdiction" within the meaning of Article 1 of the Convention.

### ALLEGED VIOLATIONS OF ARTICLE 3 OF THE CONVENTION

The applicants complained that they had been exposed to the risk of torture or inhuman or degrading treatment in Libya and in their respective countries of origin, namely Eritrea and Somalia, as a result of having been returned. They relied on Article 3 of the Convention which provides: "No one shall be subjected to torture or to inhuman or degrading treatment or punishment."

According to the Court's established case-law, Contracting States have the right, as a matter of well-established international law and subject to their treaty obligations, including the Convention, to control the entry, residence and expulsion of aliens. The Court also notes that the right to political asylum is not contained in either the Convention or its Protocols.

However, expulsion, extradition or any other measure to remove an alien may give rise to an issue under Article 3 of the Convention, and hence engage the responsibility of the expelling State under the Convention, where substantial grounds have been shown for believing that the person in question, if expelled, would face a real risk of being subjected to treatment contrary to Article 3 in the receiving country.

In order to ascertain whether or not there was a risk of ill-treatment, the Court must examine the foreseeable consequences of the removal of an applicant to the receiving country in the light of the general situation there as well as his or her personal circumstances.

The Court has already had occasion to note that the States which form the external borders of the European Union are currently experiencing considerable difficulties in coping with the increasing influx of migrants and asylum-seekers. It does not underestimate the burden and pressure this situation places on the States concerned, which are all the greater in the present context of economic crisis. It is particularly aware of the difficulties related to the phenomenon of migration by sea, involving for States additional complications in controlling the borders in southern Europe. However, having regard to the absolute character of the rights secured by Article 3, that cannot absolve a State of its obligations under that provision.

The Court reiterates that protection against the treatment prohibited by Article 3 imposes on States the obligation not to remove any person who, in the receiving country, would run the real risk of being subjected to such treatment. It notes that the numerous reports by international bodies and non-governmental organizations paint a disturbing picture of the treatment meted out to clandestine immigrants in Libya at the material time. The conclusions of those documents are moreover corroborated by the CPT [Convention on the Prevention of Torture] report of 28 April 2010.

According to the various reports mentioned above, during the period in question no rule governing the protection of refugees was complied with by Libya. Any person entering the country by illegal means was deemed to be clandestine and no distinction was made between irregular migrants and asylum-seekers. Consequently, those persons were systematically arrested and detained in conditions that outside visitors, such as delegations from UNHCR, Human Rights Watch and Amnesty International, could only describe as inhuman. Many cases of torture, poor hygiene conditions and lack of appropriate medical care were denounced by all the observers. Clandestine migrants were at risk of being returned to their countries of origin at any time and, if they managed to regain their freedom, were subjected to particularly precarious living conditions as a result of their irregular situation. Irregular immigrants, such as the applicants, were destined to occupy a marginal and isolated position in Libyan society, rendering them extremely vulnerable to xenophobic and racist acts.

Having regard to the foregoing, the Court considers that in the present case substantial grounds have been shown for believing that there was a real risk that the applicants would be subjected to treatment in Libya contrary to Article 3. The fact that a large number of irregular immigrants in Libya found themselves in the same situation as the applicants does not make the risk concerned any less individual where it is sufficiently real and probable.

Relying on these conclusions and the obligations on States under Article 3, the Court considers that, by transferring the applicants to Libya, the Italian authorities, in full knowledge of the facts, exposed them to treatment proscribed by the Convention.

Accordingly, the Government's objection concerning the applicants' lack of victim status must be rejected and it must be concluded that there has been a violation of Article 3 of the Convention.

---

## Notes and Comments:

1. What if the crew was made up of both Italian and Libyan crewmen? Would this change the result? Or what about an all-Libyan crew, but patrolling on a ship provided by the Italian government?

2. Providing assistance to those in distress at sea is a longstanding obligation reflected in both customary international law but also in a number of treaties, including the *Convention of the Law of the Sea*. Yet, as shown in *Hirsi Jamaa*, there are certain legal obligations that go along with this, but which might also provide strong disincentives to provide help in the first place (Wilson 2016).

## Women

Women are not a numerical minority; however, in one country after another they are marginalized in terms of what they earn, issues surrounding personal safety, and in terms of political power.

The following case involves a woman who is seeking asylum in the United States. In order to meet the refugee standard, an individual who is outside her country of nationality or residence must establish a "well-founded fear" of persecution on account of one of five factors: race, religion, nationality, political opinion, or membership of a particular social group. The first four nexus requirements are rather self-evident. The following case involving the prospects of the applicant being forced to undergo female genital mutilation (FGM) if forced to return to her native country (Togo) provides some insight into the meaning of "social group."

**Photo 12.2** Fauziya Kasinga
*Source*: © Associated Press

## *In Re Fauziya KASINGA,* Board of Immigration Appeals

### SCHMIDT, Chairman:

The applicant is a 19-year-old native and citizen of Togo. She attended 2 years of high school. She is a member of the Tchamba-Kunsuntu Tribe of northern Togo. She testified that young women of her tribe normally undergo FGM at age 15. However, she did not because she initially was protected from FGM by her influential, but now deceased, father.

The applicant stated that upon her father's death in 1993, under tribal custom her aunt, her father's sister, became the primary authority figure in the family. The applicant's mother was driven from the family home, left Togo, and went to live with her family in Benin. The applicant testified that she does not currently know her mother's exact whereabouts.

The applicant further testified that her aunt forced her into a polygamous marriage in October 1994, when she was 17. The husband selected by her aunt was 45 years old and had three other wives at the time of marriage. The applicant testified that, under tribal custom, her aunt and her husband planned to force her to submit to FGM before the marriage was consummated.

The applicant testified that she feared imminent mutilation. With the help of her older sister, she fled Togo for Ghana. However, she was afraid that her aunt and her husband would locate her there. Consequently, using money from her mother, the applicant embarked for Germany by airplane.

Upon arrival in Germany, the applicant testified that she was somewhat disoriented and spent several hours wandering around the airport looking for fellow Africans who might help her. Finally, she struck up a conversation, in English, with a German woman. After hearing the applicant's story, the woman offered to give the applicant temporary shelter in her home until the applicant decided what to do next. For the next 2 months, the applicant slept in the woman's living room, while performing cooking and cleaning duties.

The applicant further stated that in December 1994, while on her way to a shopping center, she met a young Nigerian man. He was the first person from Africa she had spoken to since arriving in Germany. They struck up a conversation, during which the applicant told the man about her situation. He offered to sell the applicant his sister's British passport so that she could seek asylum in the United States, where she has an aunt, an uncle, and a cousin. The applicant followed the man's suggestion, purchasing the passport and the ticket with money given to her by her sister.

The applicant did not attempt a fraudulent entry into the United States. Rather, upon arrival at Newark International Airport on December 17, 1994, she immediately requested asylum. She remained in detention by the Immigration and Naturalization Service ("INS") until April 1996.

The applicant testified that the Togolese police and the Government of Togo were aware of FGM and would take no steps to protect her from the practice. She further testified that her aunt had reported her to the Togolese police. Upon return, she would be taken back to her husband by the police and forced to undergo FGM. She testified at several points that there would be nobody to protect her from FGM in Togo.

The applicant testified that she could not find protection anywhere in Togo. She stated that Togo is a very small country and her husband and aunt, with the help of the police, could locate her anywhere she went. She also stated that her husband is well known in Togo and is a friend of the police. On cross-examination she stated that it would not be possible for her to live with another tribe in Togo.

The applicant also testified that the Togolese police could locate her in Ghana. She indicated that she did not seek asylum in Germany because she could not speak German and therefore could not continue her education there. She stated that she did not have relatives in Germany as she does in the United States.

According to the applicant's testimony, the FGM practiced by her tribe, the Tchamba-Kunsuntu is of an extreme type involving cutting the genitalia with knives, extensive bleeding, and a 40-day recovery period. The background materials confirm that the FGM practiced in some African countries, such as Togo, is of an extreme nature causing permanent damage, and not just a minor form of genital ritual.

The record material establishes that FGM in its extreme forms is a practice in which portions of the female genitalia are cut away. In some cases, the vagina is sutured partially closed. This practice clearly inflicts harm or suffering upon the girl or woman who undergoes it.

FGM is extremely painful and at least temporarily incapacitating. It permanently disfigures the female genitalia. FGM exposes the girl or woman to the risk of serious, potentially life-threatening complications. These include, among others, bleeding, infection, urine retention, stress, shock, psychological trauma, and damage to the urethra and anus. It can result in permanent loss of genital sensation and can adversely affect sexual and erotic functions.

The *FGM Alert*, compiled and distributed by the INS Resource Information Center, notes that "few African countries have officially condemned female genital mutilation and still fewer have enacted legislation against the practice". Further, according to the *FGM Alert*, even in those few African countries where legislative efforts have been made, they are usually ineffective to protect women against FGM. The *FGM Alert* notes that "it remains practically true that [African] women have little legal recourse and may face threats to their freedom, threats or acts of physical violence, or social ostracization for refusing to undergo this harmful traditional practice or attempting to protect their female children." Togo is not listed in the *FGM Alert* as among the African countries that have made even minimal efforts to protect women from FGM.

For the purposes of this case, we adopt the description of FGM drawn from the record and summarized in Part I.B.4. of this opinion. We agree with the parties that this level of harm can constitute "persecution" within the meaning of section 101(a)(42)(A) of the Act, 8 U.S.C. § 1101(a)(42)(A) (1994).

While a number of descriptions of persecution have been formulated in our past decisions, we have recognized that persecution can consist of the infliction of harm or suffering by a government, or persons a government is unwilling or unable to control, to overcome a characteristic of the victim.

As observed by the INS, many of our past cases involved actors who had a subjective intent to punish their victims. However, this subjective "punitive" or "malignant" intent is not required for harm to constitute persecution. Our characterization of FGM as persecution is consistent with our past definitions of that term. We therefore reach the conclusion that FGM can be persecution without passing on the INS's proposed "shocks the conscience" test.

To be a basis for a grant of asylum, persecution must relate to one of five categories described in section 101(a)(42)(A) of the Act. The parties agree that the relevant category in this case is "particular social group." Each party has advanced several formulations of the "particular social group" at issue in this case. However, each party urges the Board to adopt only that definition of social group necessary to decide this individual case.

In the context of this case, we find the particular social group to be the following: young women of the Tchamba-Kunsuntu Tribe who have not had FGM, as practiced by that tribe, and who oppose the practice. This is very similar to the formulations suggested by the parties.

The burden of proof is upon an applicant for asylum to establish that a "reasonable person" in her circumstances would fear persecution upon return to Togo. The applicant has met this burden through a combination of her credible testimony and the introduction of documentary evidence and background information that supports her claim.

To be eligible for asylum, the applicant must establish that her well-founded fear of persecution is "on account of" one of the five grounds specified in the Act, here, her membership in a "particular social group."

We agree with the parties that, as described and documented in this record, FGM is practiced, at least in some significant part, to overcome sexual characteristics of young women of the tribe who have not been, and do not wish to be, subjected to FGM. We therefore find that the persecution the applicant fears in Togo is "on account of" her status as a member of the defined social group.

**Notes and Comments:**

1. Realistically, how many women facing the prospect of female genital mutilation will be able to travel to the United States in order to file an asylum claim?

2. *Kasinga* involves a woman who had not been subjected to FGM. Would the result have been the same – should the result have been the same – if she already had?

3. What about other situations that many women face? Should women who fear persecution if they do not wear a chador qualify as refugees? Women who experience domestic violence and who do not receive adequate protection from the state?

4. In the *Kasinga* case any persecution would be from the hands of non-state actors, although states have an obligation to protect their citizens from such private harms. In *Matter of A-R-C-G et al.*, 26 I&N (BIA 2014), the Board of Immigration Appeals held that a married Guatemalan woman who was repeatedly beaten by her husband, but who was not able to leave her relationship with him, qualified for refugee status. However, in *Matter of A-B-*, 27 I&N 316 (A.G. 2018), Attorney General Jeff Sessions overturned this ruling on the basis that the previous opinion did not provide a "clear benchmark for determining who falls within the group." Moreover, Sessions went on to state that this was a problem with crafting a "social group" in situations involving private criminal activity.

---

**Box 12.2: Exporting Despair**

Under the "Mexico City Policy" – or what is better known as the "global gag order rule" – the U.S. government prohibits funding for any facility that performs or even promotes abortion as part of its family planning services. Going back to the Reagan administration, this has been a political football between Republicans and Democrats, with Republican presidents reinstituting the ban (invariably within the first week of coming into office), while Democratic presidents have removed the ban (invariably within the first week of coming into office). Consistent with this pattern, in January 2017, President Trump re-instituted this rule.

The Crowley Program for International Human Rights conducted a study of the effects of this policy on the right to health in Kenya. At the time the study was conducted in the early 2000s, outside donors paid for a substantial portion of the country's health budget and the single biggest donor was USAID. When the gag order was implemented at the outset of the George W. Bush administration, a number of health facilities in Kenya that provided abortion services were hit hard by the resulting loss of aid, which in turn resulted in increased levels of maternal mortality rates.

According to the authors of this study, Kenya had failed to meet its obligations under international human rights law. But what about the United States? The "Exporting Despair" report frames the issue this way:

> Holding Kenya responsible for the effects of a policy instituted by the United States may appear beside the point in any setting other than international law. As this Report notes, Kenya has assumed binding obligations to realize the right to health, the elimination of discrimination based upon gender, and freedom of expression. As this Report further documents, the impact of the Mexico City restrictions within the country suggest that, in the first instance, the Kenyan government has failed to make good on these legal obligations. This legal conclusion, however, begs the practical reality. But for the Mexico City Policy, the reductions in health and reproductive care, disproportionate impact on women, and attempted censorship of reproductive medical information described here would not have occurred. This is not to say the Kenyan government was powerless to anticipate and mitigate these effects. Yet at the end of the day, the effective causes for the challenges under review comprise the funding restrictions, USAID, and the United States.

What is your view on this? Has the United States committed an internationally wrongful act? Or to state this more simply, has it violated international human rights law by taking away money knowing that this would have severe human consequences?

## Children

Due to their age but also their political powerlessness, children are almost the prototype of a "vulnerable population." Although the *Convention on the Rights of the Child* is the most ratified international human rights treaty, there is not a single country where children enjoy the rights the CRC proclaims that children possess. In the case that follows, a young boy has been beaten by his stepfather. Under international human rights law, states have three sets of responsibilities. The first is the duty to *respect*, which means that the state itself should not violate human rights standards. The second, which is the basis for the decision in the *Case of A.*, is that states have an obligation to *protect* individuals from harm by private actors. Finally, states have a duty to *fulfill*, which means that in order to protect human rights, the state might have to provide something. For example, the right to a fair trial is premised on the principle that a judicial system exists and the state provides fair and unbiased judges.

---

# Case of A. v. United Kingdom, ECtHR (1997)

### THE APPLICANT IS A BRITISH CITIZEN, BORN IN 1984

In May 1990 he and his brother were placed on the local child protection register because of "known physical abuse". The cohabitant of the boys' mother was given a police caution after he admitted hitting A. with a cane. Both boys were removed from the child protection register in November 1991. The cohabitant subsequently married the applicant's mother and became his stepfather.

In February 1993, the head teacher at A.'s school reported to the local Social Services Department that A.'s brother had disclosed that A. was being hit with a stick by his stepfather. The stepfather was arrested on 5 February 1993 and released on bail the next day.

On 5 February 1993 the applicant was examined by a consultant paediatrician, who found the following marks on his body, *inter alia*: (1) a fresh red linear bruise on the back of the right thigh, consistent with a blow from a garden cane, probably within the preceding twenty-four hours; (2) a double linear bruise on the back of the left calf, consistent with two separate blows given some time before the first injury; (3) two lines on the back of the left thigh, probably caused by two blows inflicted one or two days previously; (4) three linear bruises on the right bottom, consistent with three blows, possibly given at different times and up to one week old; (5) a fading linear bruise, probably several days old.

The paediatrician considered that the bruising was consistent with the use of a garden cane applied with considerable force on more than one occasion.

The stepfather was charged with assault occasioning actual bodily harm and tried in February 1994. It was not disputed by the defence that the stepfather had caned the boy on a number of occasions, but it was argued that this had been necessary and reasonable since A. was a difficult boy who did not respond to parental or school discipline.

In summing up, the judge advised the jury on the law as follows:

> What is it the prosecution must prove? If a man deliberately and unjustifiably hits another and causes some bodily injury, bruising or swelling will do, he is guilty of actual bodily harm. What does 'unjustifiably' mean in the context of this case? It is a perfectly good defence that the alleged assault was merely the correcting of a child by its parent, in this case the stepfather, provided that the correction be moderate in the manner, the instrument and the quantity of it. Or, put another way, reasonable. It is not for the defendant to prove it was lawful correction. It is for the prosecution to prove it was not.
>
> This case is not about whether you should punish a very difficult boy. It is about whether what was done here was reasonable or not and you must judge that.

The jury found by a majority verdict that the applicant's stepfather was not guilty of assault occasioning actual bodily harm.

ALLEGED VIOLATION OF ARTICLE 3 OF THE CONVENTION

The applicant asked the Court to find a violation of Article 3 of the Convention, which provides: "No one shall be subjected to torture or to inhuman or degrading treatment or punishment."

The Court recalls that ill-treatment must attain a minimum level of severity if it is to fall within the scope of Article 3. The assessment of this minimum is relative: it depends on all the circumstances of the case, such as the nature and context of the treatment, its duration, its physical and mental effects and, in some instances, the sex, age and state of health of the victim.

The Court recalls that the applicant, who was then nine years old, was found by the consultant paediatrician who examined him to have been beaten with a garden cane which had been applied with considerable force on more than one occasion. The Court considers that treatment of this kind reaches the level of severity prohibited by Article 3. It remains to be determined whether the State should be held responsible, under Article 3, for the beating of the applicant by his stepfather.

The Court considers that the obligation on the High Contracting Parties under Article 1 of the Convention to secure to everyone within their jurisdiction the rights and freedoms defined in the Convention, taken together with Article 3, requires States to take measures designed to ensure that individuals within their jurisdiction are not subjected to torture or inhuman or degrading treatment or punishment, including such ill-treatment administered by private individuals. Children and other vulnerable individuals, in particular, are entitled to State protection, in the form of effective deterrence, against such serious breaches of personal integrity.

The Court recalls that under English law it is a defence to a charge of assault on a child that the treatment in question amounted to "reasonable chastisement." The burden of proof is on the prosecution to establish beyond reasonable doubt that the assault went beyond the limits of lawful punishment. In the present case, despite the fact that the applicant had been subjected to treatment of sufficient severity to fall within the scope of Article 3, the jury acquitted his stepfather, who had administered the treatment.

In the Court's view, the law did not provide adequate protection to the applicant against treatment or punishment contrary to Article 3. Indeed, the Government have accepted that this law currently fails to provide adequate protection to children and should be amended. In the circumstances of the present case, the failure to provide adequate protection constitutes a violation of Article 3 of the Convention.

---

## Notes and Comments:

1. Compare the result in *Case of A.* with *DeShaney v. Winnebago County* (1989) where the U.S. Supreme Court ruled that the failure of the Department of Social Services to protect four-year-old Joshua DeShaney from physical beatings from his father, which eventually left the child in a coma, did not rise to the level of a constitutional violation, despite the fact that the DSS repeatedly sent Joshua back into his father's custody. According to the Court, the Constitution only protects against harms carried out by the state or in

some instances if an individual was in state custody, such as in prison. There is a special irony that the ruling was handed down in 1989 – the same year the *Convention on the Rights of the Child* was opened for signature.

2. As noted earlier, the *Convention on the Rights of the Child* is the most widely ratified international human rights treaty (only the United States is not a party), yet how much effect this international treaty has had on improving the lives of children the world over remains in strong doubt. For an insightful analysis of how the CRC could be vastly more effective in the context of educating the young see Katherine Covell and R. Brian Howe, *Empowering Children: Children's Rights Education as a Pathway to Citizenship* (2005).

---

**Box 12.3: International Law at the Movies: Children's Rights**

There is not a single word of dialogue in *The Inheritors* (2008) but that does not matter in this dazzling documentary showing children working endlessly – but still finding joy in the manner that perhaps only children can. In *The Devil's Miner* (2005), the viewer is taken deep into the dangerous silver mines of Bolivia with two young brothers who work there while aspiring to live normal lives outside and on the earth's surface. *Born Into Brothels* (2004) was awarded an Academy Award for Best Documentary and this captivating story of a British photographer who taught photography skills to children of Indian prostitutes is impossible to resist.

Two films from Romania could not be any different from one another. *Children Underground* (2001) is a loud and violent documentary on street children living precariously in a subway station. In contrast to this is the joyful *We'll Never Meet Childhood Again* (2007), a documentary about a group of teens in Romania who were born with AIDS and who were denied treatment by the communist government – and the hospital caretakers who intervened and offered these children a loving home.

Children are oftentimes the greatest casualties of war and increasingly children have been forced to fight. *Invisible Children* (2003) is an outstanding documentary showing the desperation of Ugandan children to avoid being abducted to serve in the Lord's Resistance Army. *War/Dance* (2006) covers much the same ground but includes a national music competition that serves as a temporary distraction. *Children in War* (2000) provides a series of stories of children from all over the globe trying to survive war and the traumas thereafter.

---

## Indigenous Populations

In countries all over the globe – including states that proudly and loudly proclaim their devotion to human rights – indigenous populations have not only faced centuries of discrimination, or worse, but they continue to be relegated to the fringes of society, with much lower standards of living, educational levels, life expectancies, and so on. The following case is from the U.N. Human Rights Committee brought by the Lubicon Lake Band tribe claiming, among other things, that the Canadian government had violated Article 27 of the *International Covenant on Civil and Political Rights*, which reads:

> In those States in which ethnic, religious or linguistic minorities exist, persons belonging to such minorities shall not be denied the right, in community with the other members of their group, to enjoy their own culture, to profess and practise their own religion, or to use their own language.

---

## *Lubicon Lake Band v. Canada,* Communication No. 167/1984 (26 March 1990), U.N. Doc. Supp. No. 40 (A/45/40) at 1 (1990)

The author of the communication is Chief Bernard Ominayak of the Lubicon Lake Band, Canada. The author alleges violations by the Government of Canada of the Lubicon Lake Band's right of self-determination and by virtue of that right to determine freely its political status and pursue its economic, social and cultural development, as well as the right to dispose freely of its natural wealth and resources and not to be deprived of its own means of subsistence.

Chief Ominayak is the leader and representative of the Lubicon Lake Band, a Cree Indian band living within the borders of Canada in the Province of Alberta. They are subject to the jurisdiction of the Federal Government of Canada, allegedly in accordance with a fiduciary relationship assumed by the Canadian Government with respect to Indian peoples and their lands located within Canada's national borders. The Lubicon Lake Band is a self-identified, relatively autonomous, socio-cultural and economic group. Its members have continuously inhabited, hunted, trapped and fished in a large area encompassing approximately 10,000 square kilometres in northern Alberta since time immemorial. Since their territory is relatively inaccessible, they have, until recently, had little contact with non-Indian society. Band members speak Cree as their primary language. Many do not speak, read or write English. The Band continues to maintain its traditional culture, religion, political structure and subsistence economy.

It is claimed that the Canadian Government, through the Indian Act of 1970 and Treaty 8 of 21 June 1899 recognized the right of the original inhabitants of that area to continue their traditional way of life. Despite these laws and agreements, the Canadian Government has allowed the provincial government of Alberta to expropriate the territory of the Lubicon Lake Band for the benefit of private corporate interests (e.g., leases for oil and gas exploration). In so doing, Canada is accused of violating the Band's right to determine freely its political status and to pursue its economic, social and cultural development, as guaranteed by article 1, paragraph 1, of the Covenant. Furthermore, energy exploration in the Band's territory allegedly entails a violation of article 1, paragraph 2, which grants all peoples the right to dispose of their natural wealth and resources. In destroying the environment and undermining the Band's economic base, the Band is allegedly being deprived of its means to subsist and of the enjoyment of the right of self-determination guaranteed in article 1.

The author further alleges that the State party, through actions affecting the Band's livelihood, has created a situation which "led, indirectly if not directly, to the deaths of 21 persons and [is] threatening the lives of virtually every other member of the Lubicon community. Moreover, the ability of the community to [survive] is in serious doubt as the number of miscarriages and stillbirths has skyrocketed and the number of abnormal births . . . has gone from near zero to near 100 per cent".

In substantiation of earlier allegations, the author explains that the Band's loss of its economic base and the breakdown of its social institutions, including the transition from a way of life marked by trapping and hunting to a sedentary existence, has led to a marked deterioration in the health of the Band members:

> the diet of the people has undergone dramatic changes with the loss of their game, their reliance on less nutritious processed foods, and the spectre of alcoholism, previously unheard of in this community and which is now overwhelming it. . . . As a result of these drastic changes in the community's physical existence, the basic health and resistance to infection of community members has deteriorated dramatically. The lack of running water and sanitary facilities in the community, needed to replace the traditional systems of water and sanitary management . . . is leading to the development of diseases associated with poverty and poor sanitary and health conditions. This situation is evidenced by the astonishing increase in the number of abnormal births and by the outbreak of tuberculosis, affecting approximately one third of the community.

From the outset, the State party has denied the allegations that the existence of the Lubicon Lake Band has been threatened and has maintained that continued resource development would not cause irreparable injury to the traditional way of life of the Band. It submitted that the Band's claim to certain lands in northern Alberta was part of a complex situation that involved a number of competing claims from several other native communications in the area, that effective redress in respect of the Band's claims was still available, both through the courts and through negotiations, that the Government had made an *ex gratia* payment to the Band of $C 1.5 million to cover legal costs and that, at any rate, article 1 of the Covenant, concerning the rights of people, could not be invoked under the Optional Protocol, which provides for the consideration of alleged violations of individual rights, but not collective rights conferred upon peoples.

Although initially couched in terms of alleged breaches of the provisions of article 1 of the Covenant, there is no doubt that many of the claims presented raise issues under article 27. The Committee recognizes that the rights protected by article 27, include the right of persons, in community with others, to engage in economic and social activities which are part of the culture of the community to which they belong. Sweeping allegations concerning extremely serious breaches of other articles of the Covenant (6, 7, 14, para. 1, and 26), made after the communication was declared admissible, have not been substantiated to the extent that they would deserve serious consideration. The allegations concerning breaches of articles 17 and 23, paragraph 1, are similarly of a sweeping nature and will not be taken into account except in so far as they may be considered subsumed under the allegations which, generally, raise issues under article 27.

### VIOLATIONS AND THE REMEDY OFFERED

Historical inequities, to which the State party refers, and certain more recent developments threaten the way of life and culture of the Lubicon Lake Band, and constitute a violation of article 27 so long as they continue.

**Note and Comments:**

1. *Mabo v. Queensland* are a series of landmark rulings from Australia where the High Court ruled that the lands in this continent were not "terra nullius" (land belonging to no one) and that the indigenous claimants were: "entitled as against the whole world to possession, occupation, use and enjoyment" of most of the lands in dispute. The decision led directly to the passage of the Native Title Act of 1993, which sought to regulate and protect the native title recognized in the *Mabo* rulings.

---

**Box 12.4: International Law at the Movies: The Treatment of Indigenous Populations**

There is a fantastic scene in *Even the Rain* (2010) where a Spanish film crew making a film in Bolivia about Columbus' landing is going through a script read-through where drinks are being served by some locals. One of the writers who is playing Columbus proclaims that he is coming in peace and as an emissary of God – until he spies the gold earrings of the bartender and demands to know where this precious metal is to be found. That, in a nutshell, explains the Old World's treatment of the New World and the people who live there.

*Once Were Warriors* (1994) is an unforgettable feature film depicting a family of Maori struggling to make a go of it in New Zealand's urban society. The title, which is only explained near the close of the film, describes the proud heritage of the country's indigenous people, but also how far they have fallen. *Rabbit Proof Fence* (2002) is an Australian film depicting the country's policy of forced assimilation, although the brave protagonists at the heart of the story will have none of this.

---

## *Sawhoyamaxa Indigenous Community v. Paraguay,* Inter-American Court of Human Rights Case of the Judgment of March 29, 2006 (Merits, Reparations and Costs)

On February 3, 2005, the Inter-American Commission on Human Rights (hereinafter "the Commission" or "the Inter-American Commission") filed an application with the Inter-American Court against the State of Paraguay (hereinafter "the State" or "Paraguay").

The Community alleged that the State has not ensured the ancestral property right of the Sawhoyamaxa Community and its members, inasmuch as their claim for territorial rights is pending since 1991 and it has not been satisfactorily resolved to date. As stated in the Commission's application, this has barred the Community and its members from title to and possession of their lands, and has implied keeping it in a state of nutritional, medical and health vulnerability, which constantly threatens their survival and integrity.

Towards the end of the 19th century vast stretches of land in the Paraguayan Chaco were acquired by British businessmen through the London Stock Exchange as a consequence of the debt owed by Paraguay after the so-called War of the Triple Alliance. The division and sale of such territories were made while their inhabitants, who, at the time, were exclusively Indians, were kept in full ignorance of the facts. That is how several missions of the Anglican Church started settling in the area. In 1901 the "South American Missionary Society" settled the first cattle estate in the Chaco with the purpose of starting the evangelization and "pacification" of the indigenous communities, and of facilitating their employment in the cattle estates. The company was known as "Chaco Indian Association", and its main seat was built in Alwátétkok. The economy of the indigenous peoples in the Chaco was mainly based on hunting, fishing, and gathering, and therefore, they had to roam their lands to make use of nature inasmuch as the season and their cultural technology allowed them to, wherefore they kept moving and occupied a very large area of territory.

Over the years, and particularly after the Chaco War between Bolivia and Paraguay (1933–1936), the non-indigenous occupation of the Northern Chaco which had started by the end of the 19th century was extended. The estates that started settling in the area used the Indians who had traditionally lived there as workers, who thus became farmhands and employees of new owners. Although the indigenous peoples continued occupying their traditional lands, the effect of the market economy activities into which they were incorporated turned out to be the restriction of their mobility, whereby they ended by becoming sedentary.

Since then, the lands of the Paraguayan Chaco have been transferred to private owners and gradually divided. This increased the restrictions for the indigenous population to access their traditional lands, thus bringing about significant changes in its subsistence activities. They increasingly depended on their salary for food and took advantage of their temporary stay in the various estates settled in the area to continue developing their subsistence activities (hunting, fishing, and gathering).

The Court considers that the land restitution right of the members of the Sawhoya-maxa Community has not lapsed. Once it has been proved that land restitution rights are still current, the State must take the necessary actions to return them to the members of the indigenous people claiming them. However, as the Court has pointed out, when a State is unable, on objective and reasoned grounds, to adopt measures aimed at returning traditional lands and communal resources to indigenous populations, it must surrender alternative lands of equal extension and quality, which will be chosen by agreement with the members of the indigenous peoples, according to their own consultation and decision procedures.

The Court has ascertained that the arguments put forth by the State to justify non-enforcement of the indigenous people's property rights have not sufficed to release it from international responsibility. The State has put forth three arguments: 1) that claimed lands have been conveyed from one owner to another "for a long time" and are duly registered; 2) that said lands are being been adequately exploited, and 3) that the owner's right "is protected under a bilateral agreement between Paraguay and Germany[,] which [. . .] has become part of the law of the land."

Regarding the first argument, the Court considers that the fact that the claimed lands are privately held by third parties is not in itself an "objective and reasoned" ground for dismissing prima facie the claims by the Indigenous people. Otherwise, restitution rights become meaningless and would not entail an actual possibility of recovering traditional lands, as it would be exclusively limited to an expectation on the will of the current holders, forcing indigenous communities to accept alternative lands or economic compensations. In this respect, the Court has pointed out that, when there be conflicting interests in indigenous claims, it must assess in each case the legality, necessity, proportionality and fulfillment of a lawful purpose in a democratic society (public purposes and public benefit), to impose restrictions on the right to property, on the one hand, or the right to traditional lands, on the other.

The same rationale is applicable to the second argument put forth by the State as regards to land productivity. This argument lodges the idea that indigenous communities are not entitled, under any circumstances, to claim traditional lands when they are exploited and fully productive, viewing the indigenous issue exclusively from the standpoint of land productivity and agrarian law, something which is insufficient for it fails to address the distinctive characteristics of such peoples.

Lastly, with regard to the third argument put forth by the State, the Court has not been furnished with the aforementioned treaty between Germany and Paraguay, but, according to the State, said convention allows for capital investments made by a contracting party to be condemned or nationalized for a "public purpose or interest", which could justify land restitution to indigenous people. Moreover, the Court considers that the enforcement of bilateral commercial treaties negates vindication of non-compliance with state obligations under the American Convention; on the contrary, their enforcement should always be compatible with the American Convention, which is a multilateral treaty on human rights that stands in a class of its own and that generates rights for individual human beings and does not depend entirely on reciprocity among States. Based on the foregoing, the Court dismisses the three arguments of the State described above and finds them insufficient to justify non-enforcement of the right to property of the Sawhoyamaxa Community.

Finally, it is worth recalling that, under Article 1(1) of the Convention, the State is under the obligation to respect the rights recognized therein and to organize public authority in such a way as to ensure to all persons under its jurisdiction the free and full exercise of human rights. Even though the right to communal property of the lands and of the natural resources of indigenous people is recognized in Paraguayan laws, such merely abstract or legal recognition becomes meaningless in practice if the lands have not been physically delimited and surrendered because the adequate domestic measures necessary to secure effective use and enjoyment of said right by the members of the Sawhoyamaxa Community are lacking. The free development and transmission of their culture and traditional rites have thus been threatened.

The reparation of the damages caused for the violation of an international obligation, requires, whenever possible, the full restitution (*restitutio in integrum*) which consists of the reinstatement of the situation prior to the violation. Were this not possible, the international court may determine a series of measures that, apart from the guaranteeing observance of the human rights that have been violated, may also remedy the consequences of the breaches and impose the payment of a compensation for the damages caused. The duty to remedy, which is governed in all its aspects (scope, nature, forms and determination of beneficiaries) by International Law, cannot be modified or not complied with by the State owing such duty, by alleging domestic law provisions.

As it has been proven, the lands claimed before the domestic jurisdiction by the members of the Community are part of their traditional habitat and are suitable for their ultimate settlement. However, restitution of such lands to the Community is barred, since these lands are currently privately owned. On that matter, pursuant to Courts precedent, the State must consider the possibility of purchasing these lands or the lawfulness, need and proportionality of condemning these lands in order to achieve a lawful purpose in a democratic society.

The State shall, within three years as from notice of the instant Judgment, formally and physically grant tenure the lands to the victims, irrespective of whether they be acquired by purchase or by condemnation, or whether alternative lands are selected. The State shall guarantee all the necessary funds for the purpose.

**Note and Comments:**

1. If you agree with the reasoning in this case, what about the United States? Should large tracts of land also be turned back over to Native American tribes?

### LGBTQ Rights

South Africa's post-apartheid constitution is often heralded for its commitment to international human rights standards. What follows is the Constitutional Court's historical ruling, striking down legislation that prohibited sodomy between two men.

---

## *The National Coalition for Gay and Lesbian Equality v. Minister of Justice and Others,* Constitutional Court of South Africa (1998)

ACKERMANN, J.

Section 20A of the Sexual Offences Act provides as follows:

*(1) A male person who commits with another male person at a party any act which is calculated to stimulate sexual passion or to give sexual gratification, shall be guilty of an offence.*

*(2) For the purposes of subsection (1) 'a party' means any occasion where more than two persons are present.*

*(3) The provisions of subsection (1) do not derogate from the common law, any other provision of this Act or a provision of any other law.*

The High Court found that these provisions manifested a twofold differentiation. First, differentiation on the grounds of "sex (gender)" because the provisions criminalised only certain conduct by men; no acts of an equivalent nature performed by women or by men and women together are criminalised under the Act. Second, on grounds of sexual orientation, because "the target of the section is plainly men with homosexual tendencies albeit that the wording is wide enough to embrace heterosexuals." Neither basis for differentiation, the judgment proceeds, bears a rational connection to any legitimate governmental purpose.

The discriminatory prohibitions on sex between men reinforces already existing societal prejudices and severely increases the negative effects of such prejudices on their lives.

The impact of discrimination on gays and lesbians is rendered more serious and their vulnerability increased by the fact that they are a political minority not able on their own to use political power to secure favourable legislation for themselves. They are accordingly almost exclusively reliant on the Bill of Rights for their protection.

The above analysis confirms that the discrimination is unfair. There is nothing which can be placed in the other balance of the scale. The inevitable conclusion is that the discrimination in question is unfair and therefore in breach of section 9 of the 1996 Constitution.

Thus far I have considered only the common-law crime of sodomy on the basis of its inconsistency with the right to equality. This was the primary basis on which the case was argued. In my view, however, the common-law crime of sodomy also constitutes an infringement of the right to dignity. As we have emphasised on several occasions, the right to dignity is a cornerstone of our Constitution.

Dignity is a difficult concept to capture in precise terms. At its least, it is clear that the constitutional protection of dignity requires us to acknowledge the value and worth of all individuals as members of our society. The common-law prohibition on sodomy criminalises all sexual intercourse per annum between men: regardless of the relationship of the couple who engage therein, of the age of such couple, of the place where it occurs, or indeed of any other circumstances whatsoever. In so doing, it punishes a form of sexual conduct which is identified by our broader society with homosexuals. Its symbolic effect is to state that in the eyes of our legal system all gay men are criminals. The stigma thus attached to a significant proportion of our population is manifest. But the harm imposed by the criminal law is far more than symbolic. As a result of the criminal offence, gay men are at risk of arrest, prosecution and conviction of the offence of sodomy simply because they seek to engage in sexual conduct which is part of their experience of being human. Just as apartheid legislation rendered the lives of couples of different racial groups perpetually at risk, the sodomy offence builds insecurity and vulnerability into the daily lives of gay men. There can be no doubt that the existence of a law which punishes a form of sexual expression for gay men degrades and devalues gay men in our broader society. As such it is a palpable invasion of their dignity and a breach of section 10 of the Constitution.

Privacy recognises that we all have a right to a sphere of private intimacy and autonomy which allows us to establish and nurture human relationships without interference from the outside community. The way in which we give expression to our sexuality is at the core of this area of private intimacy. If, in expressing our sexuality, we act consensually and without harming one another, invasion of that precinct will be a breach of our privacy. Our society has a poor record of seeking to regulate the sexual expression of South Africans. In some cases, as in this one, the reason for the regulation was discriminatory; our law, for example, outlawed sexual relationships among people of different races. The fact that a law prohibiting forms of sexual conduct is discriminatory, does not, however, prevent it at the same time being an improper invasion of the intimate sphere of human life to which protection is given by the Constitution in section 14. We should not deny the importance of a right to privacy in our new constitutional order, even while we acknowledge the importance of equality. In fact, emphasising the breach of both these rights in the present case highlights just how egregious the invasion of the constitutional rights of gay persons has been. The offence which lies at the heart of the discrimination in this case constitutes at the same time and independently a breach of the rights of privacy and dignity which, without doubt, strengthens the conclusion that the discrimination is unfair.

[*The Court then canvassed the practices of a number of Western states. With the exception of the United States at that time, all had struck down sodomy statutes.*]

I accordingly make the following order:

The common law offence of sodomy is declared to be inconsistent with the Constitution of the Republic of South Africa, 1996 and invalid.

#### Sachs J (Concurring)

Only in the most technical sense is this a case about who may penetrate whom where. At a practical and symbolic level it is about the status, moral citizenship and sense of self-worth of a significant section of the community. At a more general and conceptual level, it concerns the nature of the open, democratic and pluralistic society contemplated by the Constitution.

It is important to start the analysis by asking what is really being punished by the anti-sodomy laws. Is it an act, or is it a person? Outside of regulatory control, conduct that deviates from some publicly established norm is usually only punishable when it is violent, dishonest, treacherous or in some other way disturbing of the public peace or provocative of injury. In the case of male homosexuality however, the perceived deviance is punished simply because it is deviant. It is repressed for its perceived symbolism rather than because of its proven harm. If proof were necessary, it is established by the fact that consensual anal penetration of a female is not criminalised. Thus, it is not the act of sodomy that is denounced by the law, but the so-called sodomite who performs it; not any proven social damage, but the threat that same-sex passion in itself is seen as representing to heterosexual hegemony.

The effect is that all homosexual desire is tainted, and the whole gay and lesbian community is marked with deviance and perversity. When everything associated with homosexuality is treated as bent, queer, repugnant or comical, the equality interest is directly engaged. People are subject to extensive prejudice because of what they are or what they are perceived to be, not because of what they do. The result is that a significant group of the population is, because of its sexual non-conformity, persecuted, marginalised and turned in on itself.

Although the Constitution itself cannot destroy homophobic prejudice it can require the elimination of public institutions which are based on and perpetuate such prejudice. From today a section of the community can feel the equal concern and regard of the Constitution and enjoy lives less threatened, less lonely and more dignified. The law catches up with an evolving social reality. A love that for a number of years has dared openly to speak its name in bookshops, theatres, film festivals and public parades, and that has succeeded in becoming a rich and acknowledged part of South African cultural life, need no longer fear prosecution for intimate expression. A law which has facilitated homophobic assaults and induced self-oppression, ceases to be. The courts, the police and the prison system are enabled to devote the time and resources formerly spent on obnoxious and futile prosecutions, to catching and prosecuting criminals who prey on gays and straights alike. Homosexuals are no longer treated as failed heterosexuals but as persons in their own right.

Yet, in my view the implications of this judgment extend well beyond the gay and lesbian community. It is no exaggeration to say that the success of the whole constitutional endeavour in South Africa will depend in large measure on how successfully sameness and difference are reconciled, an issue central to the present matter.

The present case shows well that equality should not be confused with uniformity; in fact, uniformity can be the enemy of equality. Equality means equal concern and respect across difference. It does not pre-suppose the elimination or suppression of difference. Respect for human rights requires the affirmation of self, not the denial of self. Equality therefore does not imply a levelling or homogenisation of behaviour but an acknowledgment and acceptance of difference. At the very least, it affirms that difference should not be the basis for exclusion, marginalisation, stigma and punishment. At best, it celebrates the vitality that difference brings to any society.

The acknowledgment and acceptance of difference is particularly important in our country where group membership has been the basis of express advantage and disadvantage. The development of an active rather than a purely formal sense of enjoying a common citizenship depends on recognising and accepting people as they are.

The invalidation of anti-sodomy laws will mark an important moment in the maturing of an open democracy based on dignity, freedom and equality. As I have said, our future as a nation depends in large measure on how we manage difference. In the past difference has been experienced as a curse, today it can be seen as a source of interactive vitality. The Constitution acknowledges the variability of human beings (genetic and socio-cultural), affirms the right to be different, and celebrates the diversity of the nation.

A state that recognises difference does not mean a state without morality or one without a point of view. It does not banish concepts of right and wrong, nor envisage a world without good and evil. It is impartial in its dealings with people and groups, but is not neutral in its value system. The Constitution certainly does not debar the state from enforcing morality. Indeed, the Bill of Rights is nothing if not a document founded on deep political morality. What is central to the character and functioning of the state, however, is that the dictates of the morality which it enforces, and the limits to which it may go, are to be found in the text and spirit of the Constitution itself.

The fact that the state may not impose orthodoxies of belief systems on the whole of society has two consequences. The first is that gays and lesbians cannot be forced to conform to heterosexual norms; they can now break out of their invisibility and live as full and free citizens of South Africa. The second is that those persons who for reasons of religious or other belief disagree with or condemn homosexual conduct are free to hold and articulate such beliefs. Yet, while the Constitution protects the right of people to continue with such beliefs, it does not allow the state to turn these beliefs – even in moderate or gentle versions – into dogma imposed on the whole of society.

In my view, the decision of this Court should be seen as part of a growing acceptance of difference in an increasingly open and pluralistic South Africa. It leads me to hope that the emancipatory effects of the elimination of institutionalised prejudice against gays and lesbians will encourage amongst the heterosexual population a greater sensitivity to the variability of the human kind. Having made these observations, I express my full concurrence in Ackermann J's judgment and order.

---

## Note and Comments:

1. As of April 2018, sodomy remained illegal in 74 countries including large parts of Africa and virtually all of the Middle East. Should there be an international treaty that protects LBGTQ persons?

---

### Box 12.5: International Law at the Movies: LGBTQ Rights

*Paragraph 175* (2000) refers to the anti-sodomy provision in German law under which approximately 100,000 gay men were imprisoned from 1933 to 1945, while only 4,000 survived. The persecution of sexual minorities certainly continues today. *Born this Way* (2013) is a documentary that follows Gertrude and Cedric, two gays in Cameroon, and the daily danger they face. *Out in the Silence* (2009) is a documentary from the United States showing the kinds of societal discrimination – often fueled by religious hatred – that continues to exist even when gays obtain certain legal rights. *We Were There* (2011) is a beautifully crafted film about the AIDS epidemic that

*(Continued)*

**Box 12.5: Continued**

> devastated the gay population in major U.S. cities, especially San Francisco. Finally, in *Milk* (2008) Sean Penn plays Harvey Milk, the first openly gay politician in the United States, whose life was tragically cut short by assassination.

## Persons With Disabilities

The last major international human rights treaty is the Convention on the Rights of Persons with Disabilities (CRPD), which was adopted by the U.N. General Assembly on December 13, 2006 and opened for signature on March 30, 2007. There were 82 signatories to the Convention, 44 signatories to the Optional Protocol, and 1 ratification of the Convention, representing the highest number of signatories in history to a U.N. Convention on its opening day. The Convention entered into force on May 3, 2008. As of January 2018, there were 175 ratifications of the treaty and 92 states that are a state party to the Optional Protocol, which allows for complaints by individuals and groups of individuals subject to the jurisdiction of the state party.

Article 1 (Purpose) provides:

> The purpose of the present Convention is to promote, protect and ensure the full and equal enjoyment of all human rights and fundamental freedoms by all persons with disabilities, and to promote respect for their inherent dignity. Persons with disabilities include those who have long-term physical, mental, intellectual or sensory impairments which in interaction with various barriers may hinder their full and effective participation in society on an equal basis with others.

Article 3 (General principles) states:

> The principles of the present Convention shall be: (a) Respect for inherent dignity, individual autonomy including the freedom to make one's own choices, and independence of persons; (b) Non-discrimination; (c) Full and effective participation and inclusion in society; (d) Respect for difference and acceptance of persons with disabilities as part of human diversity and humanity; (e) Equality of opportunity; (f) Accessibility; (g) Equality between men and women; (h) Respect for the evolving capacities of children with disabilities and respect for the right of children with disabilities to preserve their identities.

One of the unique features of the CRPD is its mixture of all human rights – economic, social, and cultural rights as well as civil and political rights.

---

### Box 12.6: International Law at the Movies: Persons With Disabilities

There are a number of films dealing with disability. One of the classics is the story of Helen Keller told in *The Miracle Worker* (1962). More recently, Daniel Day-Lewis is the embodiment of Christy Brown in *My Left Foot* (1989). Another remarkable film is *The Diving Bell and the Butterfly* (2007), which tells the story of French journalist Jean-Dominique Bauby after he suffers a massive stroke. Although Johnny Depp is nominally the star of *What's Eating Gilbert Grape* (1993), a young Leonardo DiCaprio playing his intellectually challenged sibling steals the entire film. In terms of documentaries, I am quite partial toward *Pulled From the Rubble* (2005), a film by Margaret Loescher about her father, Gil Loescher, who was the lone survivor of the bombing of the UNHCR headquarters in Baghdad in 2003. Gil, a former college basketball player, lost both of his legs and his lack of self-pity as well as his determination are remarkable to behold.

Another category are films about disabled war veterans. There is the classic *The Best Years of Our Lives* (1946), which tells the story of three World War II veterans attempting to pick up the pieces of their lives. This film was awarded seven Oscars, including Best Picture. Oliver Stone's *Born on the Fourth of July* (1989) is simply Tom Cruise's best body of work; and perhaps the same can be said of Jon Voight in one of the first anti-Vietnam films, *Coming Home* (1978).

---

### References

*Books and Articles*

Katherine Covell and R. Brian Howe, *Empowering Children: Children's Education as a Pathway to Citizenship,* Toronto: University of Toronto Press (2005)

Mehlika Hoodbhoy, Martin S. Flaherty and Tracy E. Higgins, "Exporting Despair: The Human Rights Implications of U.S. Restrictions on Foreign Health Care Funding in Kenya," *Fordham International Law Journal* 29: 1–117 (2005)

Brian Wilson, "Human Rights and Maritime Law Enforcement," *Stanford Journal of International Law* 52: 243–319 (2016)

*Cases*

*Case of A. v. United Kingdom*, ECtHR (1997)
*DeShaney v. Winnebago County*, 489 U.S. 189 (1989)
*Hirsi Jamaa and Others v. Italy*, ECtHR, App. No. 27765/09 (2012)
*In Re Fauziya KASINGA*, Board of Immigration Appeals (1996)

*Lubicon Lake Band v. Canada*, Communication No. 167/1984 (26 March 1990), U.N. Doc. Supp. No. 40 (A/45/40) at 1 (1990)

*Mabo v. Queensland* (No. 2), 1992 HCA 23

*Matter of A-B-*, 27 I&N 316 (A.G. 2018)

*Matter of A-R-C-G et al.*, 26 I&N (BIA 2014)

*The National Coalition for Gay and Lesbian Equality v. Minister of Justice and Others*, Constitutional Court of South Africa (1998)

*Sale v. Haitian Ctrs. Council*, 509 U.S. 155 (1993)

*Sawhoyamaxa Indigenous Community v. Paraguay*, IACtHR (2006) (Merits, Reparations and Costs)


## International Agreements

Convention on the Law of the Sea, opened for signature on 10 December 1982, entry into force November 1994

Convention Relating to the Status of Refugees, signed 28 July 1951, entry into force 22 April 1954

Convention on the Rights of the Child, signed 20 November 1989, entry into force 2 September 1990

Convention on the Rights of Persons With Disabilities, adopted 13 December 2006, entry into force 3 May 2008

International Covenant on Civil and Political Rights, adopted 16 December 1966, entry into force 23 March 1976


## Domestic Law

Native Title Act of 1993 (Australia)

# Concluding Thoughts

## The Way Forward

This brief conclusion takes up two issues. The first is to ponder what the world would look like without international law. The second is to consider ways in which international law must be transformed.

As noted in the Introduction, many people hold the view that international law is not really "law" as such. We need not go into the specifics of this argument again, but it is hoped that the preceding pages have, in at least some way, helped to quell these objections. However, perhaps a better way to think about this issue is to consider some of the greatest challenges the world now faces – climate change, terrorism, corruption, transnational crime, cyberattacks, and nuclear annihilation, to name a few – and then try to imagine how these problems could ever be adequately addressed if states simply acted on their own without any kind of international cooperation – including international law.

This, of course, is not meant to suggest that international law has dealt with these crises efficiently and effectively. It has not. But the larger point is that as poorly as international law has performed, the absence of international law would decidedly make matters that much worse. I have used the term "our common future" in the title of this book, but perhaps a more accurate term would be "our *only* future," because without international law there is little prospect there can be a safe, secure, and healthy future.

This, then, leads to the second issue, which is the way in which international law needs to be transformed. It should be obvious that I am not in the camp that says that international law is not law. On the other hand, I can understand how people might draw this conclusion. A cynic might describe international law in these terms: states are generally able to determine which international standards apply to them – and yet even with that, they are seldom (if ever) held to account if and when they do not follow these standards.

The key is to make international law more "legal," and if that is too nebulous, a good starting point is to work toward making international law reflect the kinds of principles and values that mark virtually all domestic law systems. What this also means is that international law must begin to move away from its longstanding obsession with the state. This is not to ignore or even downplay the continued importance and centrality of the state. However, there is a strong tendency of minimizing or even ignoring the role and importance of private actors – individuals, corporations, and nongovernmental organizations – while at the same time making virtually every effort to protect the principle of state sovereignty. The larger point is this: the state is not the only player in the game and there are many situations when it is not even the most powerful or the most influential. International law needs to recognize this new reality – and move forward.

# Glossary

**Act of State Doctrine:** The principle that states are to respect the independence and sovereignty of all other states and therefore not pass judgment on their domestic policies.

**Advisory Opinions:** In addition to contentious litigation, the International Court of Justice, at the request of various U.N. organs, can also issue advisory opinions.

**Aid and Assist:** Under Article 16 of the Articles on State Responsibility, a state can incur responsibility by "aiding and assisting" in the commission of an internationally wrongful act.

**Airspace:** The area above a state's territorial borders over which other states are not to infringe upon without its permission.

**Alien Tort Statute (ATS):** From the 1789 Judiciary Act. Since the landmark decision in *Filartiga v. Pena-Irala* (1980) the ATS has provided a forum for victims of human rights violations. However, the U.S. Supreme Court ruling in *Jesner v. Arab Bank* (2018) now calls this into question.

***Bivens*-style Remedy:** A remedy the U.S. Supreme Court established for particularly egregious constitutional violations.

***Charming Betsey* Doctrine:** A principle under U.S. law that domestic law should be interpreted so as to be consonant with international standards.

**Citizenship:** The basis upon which states exercise authority over individuals, including those outside of their own territorial borders.

**Convention:** See Treaty.

**Customary International Law:** International law that is based on the practices or customs of states. There are two components of this: 1) state practice, and

2) *opinio juris* – states feel legally obligated to follow the custom. See also, *Opinio Juris*.

**Cyberwarfare:** Foreign entities that employ malware to cripple computer systems in other lands.

**Distinction Principle:** International humanitarian law makes a basic distinction between combatants and noncombatants. See also, Proportionality Principle.

***Dolus Specialis:*** In order for a state to be responsible for genocide, there must be this specific intent to destroy a people.

**Domestic Sovereign Immunity:** The immunity that states provide to themselves.

**Double Victimization:** Human rights treaties give victims the right to an "effective remedy." However, the lack of enforcement oftentimes leads to a separate violation of this right as well. See also, Effective Remedy.

**Drones:** An example of the "new" form of warfare, the use of which in the airspace of a foreign state challenges the prohibition against the use of force.

**Dualism:** A dualist approach to international law sees domestic and international law as separate and distinct from one another. See also, Monism.

**Duty to Prevent Genocide:** Under the 1948 Genocide Convention, all state parties have an obligation to work towards preventing genocide from taking place or halting it if this does occur. In *Bosnia v. Serbia* (2007), the International Court of Justice specified what these obligations are.

**Duty to Punish Genocide:** An obligation set forth in Article 1 of the Genocide Convention that states must cooperate in bringing to justice those who have engaged in acts of genocide.

**"Effective Control" Standard:** Standard set forth by the International Court of Justice in *Nicaragua v. United States* (1986) for establishing state responsibility.

**Effective Remedy:** The promise of international human rights treaties that victims will be able to pursue their perpetrators. See also, Double Victimization.

**Enemy Combatants:** The term used by the George W. Bush administration for suspected terrorists held at the U.S. military base at Guantanamo Bay, Cuba.

***Erga Omnes:*** The term in international law which means that a state has an obligation "towards all" other states.

**European Court of Human Rights (ECtHR):** The human rights adjudicatory body located in Strasbourg, France that hears cases alleging violations of the European Convention.

***Ex Gratia:*** Payment to a claimant without the state acknowledging fault.

**Executive Agreements:** In the United States, executive agreements made by the president have in large part replaced international treaties.

**Extradition:** Treaties that govern the exchange of prisoners between states.

**Extraordinary Rendition:** The term used for the kidnapping and torturing of suspected terrorists in foreign states.

**Extraterritorial Obligations (ETO):** Activities of a state outside its own territorial borders and the human rights consequences of doing so. See also, Maastricht ETO Principles.

**Foreign Embassies:** States are represented in other countries by means of their embassy staff. However, such embassies do not actually sit on the territory of this other state.

**Foreign Sovereign Immunity:** The sovereign protection one state affords another. Until the 19th century, states enjoyed absolute immunity, although since then such protection has been eroded.

*Forum Non Conveniens:* Cases brought in one country that are dismissed on the basis that the cause of action would be better pursued in another state.

**Geneva Conventions:** The laws of war have in large part been codified by the 1949 Geneva Conventions and the 1977 Additional Protocols. See also, Humanitarian Law; *Jus in Bello.*

**Genocide:** The most serious of all international crimes directed at those who attempt to destroy, in whole or in part, any national, ethnical, racial, or religious group.

**Guantanamo Bay, Cuba:** The U.S. military base that since 2003 has housed suspected terrorists.

*Habeas Corpus:* The literal translation is "show the body." In *Rasul v. United States* (2004), the U.S. Supreme Court held that "enemy combatants" at Guantanamo Bay, Cuba could file a habeas corpus petition in federal (U.S.) court.

**Head of State Immunity:** Immunity enjoyed by national leaders in one country from prosecution in other states, although the immunity does not apply to international tribunals, nor does it protect former heads of state.

**Home State:** Used in the context of the regulation of multinational corporations, the question is whether the state of incorporation has a legal responsibility to regulate the extraterritorial activities of one of its own MNCs. See also, Host State.

**Host State:** The host state is where a multinational corporation carries out operations outside its "home" country. See also, Home State.

**Human Rights:** The rights all people have by virtue of their humanity as set forth in a number of international and regional treaties.

**Humanitarian Law:** The laws of war which are now codified in the four Geneva Conventions (1949) and Additional Protocols (1977). See also, Geneva Conventions; *Jus in Bello.*

**International Criminal Court (ICC):** An intergovernmental organization founded in 2002 that sits in the Hague, the Netherlands. The ICC has jurisdiction over four international crimes: genocide, crimes against humanity, war crimes, and aggression.

**International Court of Justice (ICJ):** The successor to the Permanent Court of International Justice. Located in the Hague, the ICJ only takes up legal disputes between states.

**International Law Commission (ILC):** A U.N. body dedicated to the "promotion of the progressive development of international law and its codification." See also, State Responsibility.

**Jurisdiction:** The exercise of a certain degree of control over individuals, including foreign nationals living in other states.

**Jus ad Bellum:** The laws of war pertaining to the legality of the war itself.

**Jus Cogens:** In the hierarchy of international law, *jus cogens* norms are those from which no derogation is allowed. See also, Peremptory Norm.

**Jus in Bello:** The laws of war pertaining to the legality of the conduct of war. See also, Geneva Conventions; Humanitarian Law.

**Law of the Sea:** A U.N. treaty that was signed on December 10, 1982 and entered into force on November 16, 1994 that regulates the use of the seas.

**Lex Specialis:** The principle that a more specialized area of international law should govern rather than that which is more general. This question has arisen in the context of the relationship between international humanitarian law and international human rights law.

**Lotus Principle:** From the case of this name, this stands for the proposition that states are free to act, even outside their territorial borders, so long as they are not violating international law standards.

**Maastricht ETO Principles:** Document signed in 2011 by a group of leading international lawyers that recognizes that under international law states have human rights obligations outside their own territorial borders.

**Material Support:** In the context of engaging in the "war on terror," U.S. foreign sovereign immunity law allows suits to be brought against states that provide "material support" to terrorist organizations.

**Millennium Development Goals (MDGs):** The eight development goals for 2015 that were established at the 2000 Millennium Summit. See also, Sustainable Development Goals (SDGs).

**Monism:** A monist approach to international law sees a unity between domestic and international law rather than seeing them as two separate and distinct legal systems. See also, Dualism.

**Montivedo Convention on Rights and Duties of States:** The Convention sets forth the rights and obligations of statehood.

**Mutual Legal Assistance Treaties (MLATs):** An agreement between two or more states to cooperate in fighting transnational crime.

**Nationality Principle:** A principle under international law that allows a state to regulate the activities of its own citizens, even when those actions take place outside that state's territorial borders.

*Nonrefoulement*: Key component of international refugee law that prohibits a state from sending an individual to a state where this person's life or freedom might be threatened.

**Non–Self-Executing Treaty:** An international treaty that without implementation legislation has no judicially enforceable effect domestically. See also, Self-Executing Treaty.

**Nuremberg Proceedings:** Trials held by the Allied forces following World War II against political, military, and corporate supporters of the Nazi regime.

**Object and Purpose:** The two key elements of treaty interpretation. See also, Vienna Convention on the Law of Treaties.

*Opinio Juris*: In order to be part of customary international law, there must be state practice but this must be accompanied by the belief that the state was under a legal obligation to act this way. See also, Customary Law.

**"Overall Control" Standard:** Standard for establishing state responsibility set forth by the International Criminal Tribunal for the Former Yugoslavia, which rejected the ICJ's "effective control" test.

*Pacta Sunt Servanda*: The principle that the provisions outlined in treaties should be followed by state parties.

**Paris Climate Agreement:** International agreement aimed at reducing greenhouse gas emissions.

**Passive Personality Principle:** The jurisdictional basis allowing states to bring criminal charges against foreign nationals on the basis that these actions are causing harm to its citizens.

**Peacekeeping Operations:** Security force from member states acting under the authority and control of the United Nations serving to keep warring factions apart.

**Peremptory norm:** See *Jus Cogens*.

**Pinochet Principle:** Named after the international effort to extradite and criminally prosecute in Spain former Chilean dictator Augusto Pinochet.

**Piracy:** The fight against this scourge on the high seas led to the development of the principle of universal jurisdiction.

**Prohibition on the Use of Force:** Under the U.N. Charter, military force against another state is only permissible under two circumstances: 1) self defense, or 2) the action has been approved by the Security Council.

**Proportionality Principle:** International humanitarian law prohibits the targeting of civilians; however, an exception can be made if there is an important military objective involved and the loss of civilian life would be minimal.

**Protective Principle:** A state is able to exercise criminal jurisdiction over a person whose conduct outside its territorial boundaries threatens that state's security or governmental functions.

**Recognition of Governments:** The decision by states to recognize certain political actors in another country as exercising lawful governmental authority.

**Recognition of States:** Newly created states gain recognition when they exhibit the attributes of statehood. See also, Statehood.

**Reservations, Understandings, and Declarations (RUDs):** When ratifying an international treaty, states use RUDs to offer their own interpretation of various provisions.

**Responsibility to Protect (R2P):** A global commitment endorsed by all states at the 2005 World Summit to prevent mass atrocities.

**Rome Statute:** International treaty that established the International Criminal Court.

**Ruggie Principles:** U.N. Special Representative John Ruggie presented a "Respect, Protect, and Remedy" framework as a means of regulating multinational corporations operating in other lands. See also, U.N. Guiding Principles on Business and Human Rights.

**Self Defense:** A doctrine that allows states to use force against another state.

**Self-Executing Treaty:** The provisions of such a treaty become immediately judicially enforceable without domestic legislation upon ratification of an international agreement. See also, Non-Self-Executing Treaty.

**State Responsibility:** The term used when states have committed an internationally wrongful act.

**State Sovereignty:** One of the foundational principles of international law that prohibits states from interfering in the domestic affairs of other states.

**Statehood:** There are three essential elements for achieving statehood: 1) territory, 2) people, and 3) public authority. See also, Recognition of States.

**Sustainable Development Goals (SDGs):** These are a set of global goals established by the U.N. General Assembly in 2015 for the international community to achieve by the year 2030. See also, Millennium Development Goals.

*Terra Nullius:* A doctrine under international law that allows states to claim uninhabited land as their own.

**Territorial Principle:** Criminal jurisdiction based on the fact that the crime occurred within that state's territorial borders.

**Territory:** Under international law, it is always lawful for a state to act within its own territory, while legality is less clear when a state acts outside its borders.

**Terrorism:** Although there is no agreed upon definition under international law, the term is generally used to describe the use of force by non-state actors against state officials in order to achieve certain political ends.

**Treaty:** The term that is commonly used to denote an international agreement, either between two states (bilateral) or between a number of states (multilateral).

**Treaty of Westphalia:** Treaty of 1648 that brought an end to the Thirty Years' War and established the system of sovereign nation-states that still exists today.

**U.N. Guiding Principles on Business and Human Rights:** U.N. Initiative setting forth a "Respect, Protect, Remedy" framework to address human rights responsibilities of multinational corporations. See also, Ruggie Principles.

**United Nations:** This intergovernmental organization was established in 1945 as a way of achieving international peace and security.

**Universality Principle:** There are certain international crimes, such as piracy and torture, over which any state can exercise criminal jurisdiction against the offender.

**Use of Force:** International law prohibits using force against another state unless it is acting in self defense or the military action is approved by the U.N. Security Council.

**Vienna Convention on Consular Relations:** International treaty that provides the framework for consular relations between states.

**Vienna Convention on Diplomatic Relations:** International treaty that provides the framework for diplomatic relations between states.

**Vienna Convention on the Law of Treaties:** International treaty that provides guidance of how international treaties are to be interpreted.

# Table of Cases

## (Principal Cases in Bold)

### International Tribunals

#### Permanent Court of International Justice

*Lotus Case (France v. Turkey)*, PICJ (1927)
www.worldcourts.com/pcij/eng/decisions/1927.09.07_lotus.htm

*Mavrommatis Palestine Concessions (Jurisdiction)*, PICJ (1924)
www.worldcourts.com/pcij/eng/decisions/1924.08.30_mavrommatis.htm

### International Court of Justice

*Barcelona Traction, Light and Power Company Limited (Belgium v. Spain)*, ICJ
(1970)
www.icj-cij.org/en/case/50/judgments

**Belgium v. Senegal**, ICJ (2012)
www.icj-cij.org/en/case/144/judgments

**Bosnia v. Serbia**, ICJ (2007)
www.icj-cij.org/files/case-related/91/091-20070226-JUD-01-00-EN.pdf

# International Criminal Tribunal for Rwanda

# International Criminal Tribunal for (Former) Yugoslavia

*Prosecutor v. Tadic ´*, ICTY, Appeals Chamber (15 July 1999) (Case no. IT-94–1-A)
www.icty.org/x/cases/tadic/acjug/en/tad-aj990715e.pdf

# International Arbitration Panels

*Rainbow Warrior (New Zealand v. France)*, France-New Zealand Arbitration Tribunal (30 April 1990)
http://legal.un.org/riaa/cases/vol_XX/215-284.pdf

*Trail Smelter Arbitration (U.S. v. Canada)* (1941)
http://legal.un.org/riaa/cases/vol_III/1905-1982.pdf

# United Nations Treaty Bodies

*Lopez Burgos v. Uruguay*, Communication No. R.12/52, U.N. Doc. Supp. No. 40 (A/36/40) at 176 (1981), Human Rights Committee
http://hrlibrary.umn.edu/undocs/session36/12-52.htm

# Regional Courts

## Africa

*SERAP v. Nigeria*, ECOWAS Community Court of Justice No. ECW/CCJ/JUD/07/10 (2010)
www.worldcourts.com/ecowasccj/eng/decisions/2010.11.30_SERAP_v_Nigeria.htm

*Social and Economic Rights Action Centre and the Centre for Economic and Social Rights v. Nigeria*, African Commission on Human and Peoples' Rights, 155/96 (2001)
www.achpr.org/files/sessions/30th/comunications/155.96/achpr30_155_96_eng.pdf

# European Court of Human Rights

*A (and Others) v. United Kingdom*, ECtHR, App. No. 3455/05 (2009)
www.refworld.org/pdfid/499d4a1b2.pdf

*Al-Adsani v. United Kingdom*, ECtHR, App. No. 35763/97 (2001)
https://hudoc.echr.coe.int/eng#{%22itemid%22:[%22001-59885%22]}

*Al-Skeini v. United Kingdom*, ECtHR, App. No. 55721/07 (2011)
www.refworld.org/pdfid/4e2545502.pdf

*Bankovic et al. v. Belgium et al.*, ECtHR, App. No. 52207/99 (2001)
https://hudoc.echr.coe.int/eng#{%22itemid%22:[%22001-22099%22]}

*Case of A. v. United Kingdom*, ECtHR (1997)
www.cirp.org/library/legal/A_v_UK1998/

*Case of Open Door and Dublin Well Woman v. Ireland*, ECtHR (1992)
www.refworld.org/cases,ECHR,3ae6b7020.html

*Chahal v. United Kingdom*, ECtHR, App. No. 22414/93 (1996)
www.refworld.org/pdfid/3ae6b69920.pdf

*El-Masri v. Macedonia*, ECtHR, App. No. 39630/09 (2012)
https://hudoc.echr.coe.int/eng#{%22itemid%22:[%22001-115621%22]}

*Hirsi Jamaa and Others v. Italy*, ECtHR, App. No. 27765/09 (2012)
https://hudoc.echr.coe.int/eng#{%22itemid%22:[%22001-109231%22]}

*Ilascu v. Russia and Moldova*, ECtHR, App. No. 48787/99 (2004)
https://hudoc.echr.coe.int/eng#{%22itemid%22:[%22001-61886%22]}

*Ireland v. United Kingdom*, ECtHR (1978)
https://hudoc.echr.coe.int/eng#{%22itemid%22:[%22001-181585%22]}

*Issa v. Turkey*, ECtHR, App. No. 31821/96 (2005)
https://hudoc.echr.coe.int/eng#{%22itemid%22:[%22001-67460%22]}

*McCann v. United Kingdom*, ECtHR, App. No. 18984/91 (1995)
https://hudoc.echr.coe.int/eng#{%22itemid%22:[%22001-57943%22]}

*Nasr and Ghali v. Italy*, ECtHR, App. No. 44883/09 (2016)
https://hudoc.echr.coe.int/eng#{%22itemid%22:[%22001-113123%22]}

*Ocalan v. Turkey*, ECtHR, App. No. 46221/99 (2000) (dec. on admiss.)
https://hudoc.echr.coe.int/eng#{%22itemid%22:[%22001-69022%22]}

*Rantsev v. Cyprus and Russia*, ECtHR, App. No. 25965/04 (2010)
https://hudoc.echr.coe.int/eng#{%22itemid%22:[%22001-96549%22]}

*Soering v. United Kingdom*, ECtHR (1989)
https://hudoc.echr.coe.int/eng#{%22itemid%22:[%22001-57619%22]}

*Zubydah v. Poland*, ECtHR, App. No. 7511/13 (2014)
https://hudoc.echr.coe.int/eng#{%22itemid%22:[%22001-146047%22]}

# European Court of Justice

*Google Spain SL v. Agencia Española de Protección de Datos*, European Court
of Justice (2014)
https://eur-lex.europa.eu/legal-content/EN/TXT/?uri=CELEX%3A62012CJ0131

*Maximillian Schrems v. Data Protection Commissioner*, European Court of
Justice (2015)
https://eur-lex.europa.eu/legal-content/EN/TXT/?uri=CELEX%3A62014
CJ0362

# Inter-American Court of Human Rights

*Advisory Opinion on The Environment and Human Rights*, IACtHR
(7 February 2018)
www.corteidh.or.cr/docs/opiniones/seriea_23_esp.pdf (Spanish)

*Sawhoyamaxa Indigenous Community v. Paraguay*, IACtHR (2006) (Merits,
Reparations and Costs)
www.worldcourts.com/iacthr/eng/decisions/2006.03.29_Sawhoyamaxa_v_
Paraguay.pdf

*Velasquez Rodriguez*, IACtHR (1988)
http://hrlibrary.umn.edu/iachr/b_11_12d.htm

# Domestic Courts

## Australia

*Mabo v. Queensland* (No. 2), 1992 HCA 23
www.7genfund.org/sites/default/files/helpful-resources/Mabo%20
v%20Queensland%20%28No%202%29%20%28%2522Mabo%20
case%2522%29%20%5B1992%5D%20HCA%2023.pdf

# Canada

*Khadr v. Canada*, 2010 SCC 3, [2010] 1 S.C.R. 44
https://scc-csc.lexum.com/scc-csc/scc-csc/en/item/7842/index.do

*Choc. v. Hudbay Minerals Inc.*, Superior Court of Justice- – Ontario, 2013
ONSC 1414
www.canlii.org/en/on/onsc/doc/2013/2013onsc1414/2013onsc1414.html?auto
completeStr=choc&autocompletePos=2#document

*Lubicon Lake Band v. Canada*, Communication No. 167/1984 (26 March
1990), U.N. Doc. Supp. No. 40 (A/45/40) at 1 (1990)
http://hrlibrary.umn.edu/undocs/session45/167-1984.htm

# Israel

*Attorney General of Israel v. Eichmann*, The District Court of Jerusalem
(11 December 1961)
www.concernedhistorians.org/content_files/file/LE/521.pdf

*Beit Sourik Village Council*, HCJ 2056/04 (2004)
www.refworld.org/cases,ISR_SC,4374ac594.html

*Judgment on the Interrogation Methods Applied by the General Security Services
(Shin Bet)*, Israeli H.C. (1999)
http://versa.cardozo.yu.edu/sites/default/files/upload/opinions/Public%20
Committee%20Against%20Torture%20in%20Israel%20v.%20Government%
20of%20Israel%281%29_0.pdf

# The Netherlands

*Mothers of Srebrenica v. Netherlands and the United Nations*, Supreme
Court of the Netherlands (2014)
https://uitspraken.rechtspraak.nl/inziendocument?id=ECLI:NL:RB
DHA:2014:8748

*Urgenda Foundation v. the Netherlands*, The Hague District Court (2015)
http://uitspraken.rechtspraak.nl/inziendocument?id=ECLI:NL:RB
DHA:2015:7196

## South Africa

*Government of South Africa and Others v. Grootboom and Others*, Constitutional Court of South Africa (2000)
www.saflii.org/za/cases/ZACC/2000/19.html

*Mazibuko and Others v. Johannesburg and Others*, Constitutional Court of South Africa (2009)
www.saflii.org/za/cases/ZACC/2009/28.html

*Minister of Health and Others v. Treatment Action Campaign and Others*, Constitutional Court of South Africa (2002)
www.saflii.org/za/cases/ZACC/2002/15.html

*Soobramoney v. Minister of Health (Kwazulu-Natal)*, Constitutional Court of South Africa (1997)
www.saflii.org/za/cases/ZACC/1997/17.html

*The National Coalition for Gay and Lesbian Equality v. Minister of Justice and Others*, Constitutional Court of South Africa (1998)
www.saflii.org/za/cases/ZACC/1998/15.html

## United Kingdom

*A (FC) v. Secretary of State for Home Department*, [2005] UKHL 71
https://publications.parliament.uk/pa/ld200506/ldjudgmt/jd051208/aand.pdf

*Belhaj v. United Kingdom*, UKSC 3 [2017]
www.supremecourt.uk/cases/docs/uksc-2014-0264-judgment.pdf

*Campaign Against Arms Trade v. Secretary of State*, [2017] EWHC 1726 (QB)
www.judiciary.uk/wp-content/uploads/2017/07/r-oao-campaign-against-arms-trade-v-ssfit-and-others1.pdf

*Ex Parte Pinochet*, [1999] UKHL
www.bailii.org/uk/cases/UKHL/1999/17.html

*Lubbe and Others*, UK House of Lords [2000]
www.bailii.org/uk/cases/UKHL/2000/41.html

## Appellate and District Courts

*Klinghoffer v. S.N.C. Achille Lauro*, 739 F. Supp. 854 (S.D.N.Y. 1990), vacated
   by 937 F. 2d 44 (2d. Cir. 1991)
   https://casetext.com/case/klinghoffer-v-snc-achille-lauro-2

**Koohi v. United States**, 976 F. 3d 1328 (9th Cir. 1992)
   https://casetext.com/case/koohi-v-us

**Latif v. Obama**, 677 F. 3d 1175 (D.D.C. 2012)
   https://casetext.com/case/latif-v-obama-4

*Letelier v. Chile*, 488 F. Supp. 665 (D.D.C. 1980)
   https://casetext.com/case/letelier-v-republic-of-chile

**Ramirez de Arellano v. Weinberger**, 724 F. 2d 143 (D.C. Cir. 1983)
   https://casetext.com/case/ramirez-de-arellano-v-weinberger-2

**Sanchez-Espinoza v. Reagan**, 770 F. 2d 202 (D.C. Cir. 1985)
   https://casetext.com/case/sanchez-espinoza-v-reagan-2

**Tel-Oren v. Libyan Arab Republic**, 726 F. 2d 774 (D.C. Cir. 1984)
   https://casetext.com/case/tel-oren-v-libyan-arab-republic

**U.S. v. Ali Mohamed Ali**, 718 F. 3d 929 (D.C. Cir. 2013)
   https://casetext.com/case/united-states-v-ali-10

**U.S. v. Noriega**, 746 F. Supp. 1506 (S.D. FLA. 1990)
   https://casetext.com/case/us-v-noriega-6

**U.S. v. Perez-Oviendo**, 281 F. 3d 400 (3d. Cir. 2002)
   https://casetext.com/case/us-v-perez-oviedo

## Immigration Rulings

*Matter of A-B-*, 27 I&N 316 (A.G. 2018)
   www.justice.gov/eoir/page/file/1070866/download

*Matter of A-R-C-G et al.*, 26 I&N (BIA 2014)
   www.justice.gov/sites/default/files/eoir/legacy/2014/08/26/3811.pdf

**In re Fauziya KASINGA**, Board of Immigration Appeals (1996)
   www.justice.gov/sites/default/files/eoir/legacy/2014/07/25/3278.pdf

# Filmography

*4.1 Miles* (Daphne Matziaraki, 2016)

*5 Broken Cameras* (Emad Burnat, Guy Davidi, 2011)

*500 Years* (Pamela Yates, 2017)

*A Cambodian Spring* (Christopher Kelly, 2016)

*A Dry White Season* (Euzhan Palcy, 1989)

*A Film Unfinished* (Yael Hersonski, 2010)

*Amandla! A Revolution in Four Part Harmony* (Lee Hirsch, 2002)

*American Made* (Doug Liman, 2017)

*American Sniper* (Clint Eastwood, 2014)

*An Inconvenient Sequel* (Bonni Cohen, Jon Shenk, 2017)

*An Inconvenient Truth* (Davis Guggenheim, 2006)

*Armadillo* (Janus Metz Pedersen, 2010)

*Arna's Children* (Juliano Mer-Khamis, Danniel Danniel, 2004)

*Atomic Café* (Kevin Rafferty, Jayne Loader, Pierce Rafferty, 1982)

*Au Revoir, Les Enfants* (Louis Malle, 1987)

*Beasts of No Nation* (Cary Joji Fukunaga, 2015)

*Big Men* (Rachel Boynton, 2013)

*Black Hawk Down* (Ridley Scott, 2001)

*Blood Diamonds* (Edward Zwick, 2006)

*Bloody Sunday* (Paul Greengrass, 2002)

*Blow* (Ted Demme, 2001)

*Born Into Brothels* (Zana Briski, Ross Kauffman, 2004)

*Born on the Fourth of July* (Oliver Stone, 1989)

*Born This Way* (Shaun Kadlec, Deb Tullmann, 2013)

*Breaker Morant* (Bruce Beresford, 1980)

*Brother Number One* (Annie Goldson, Peter Gilbert, 2011)

*Budrus* (Julia Bacha, 2009)

*Burma VJ* (Anders Østergaard, 2008)

*Captain Phillips* (Paul Greengrass, 2013)

*Carla's List* (Marcel Schüpbach, 2006)

*Children in War* (Alan Raymond, Susan Raymond, 2000)

*Children Underground* (Edet Belzberg, 2001)

*Chile, Obstinate Memory* (Patricio Guzmán, 1997)

*Citizenfour* (Laura Poitras, 2014)

*Coming Home* (Hal Ashby, 1978)

*Contagion* (Steven Soderbergh, 2011)

*Control Room* (Jehane Noujaim, 2004)

*Crude* (Joe Berlinger, 2009)

*Cry Freedom* (Richard Attenborough, 1987)

*Darfur Now* (Ted Braun, 2007)

*Darwin's Nightmare* (Hubert Sauper, 2004)

*Dead Donkeys Fear No Hyenas* (Joakim Demmer, 2017)

*Dear Mandela* (Dara Kell, Christopher Nizza, 2012)

*Dr. Strangelove: Or How I Learned to Stop Worrying and Learned to Love the Bomb* (Stanley Kubrick, 1964)

*El Norte* (Gregory Nava, 1983)

*Enemies of the People* (Thet Sambath, Rob Lemkin, 2009)

*Enemy of the State* (Tony Scott, 1998)

*Even the Rain* (Icíar Bollaín, 2010)

*Extraordinary Rendition* (Jim Threapleton, 2007)

*Eye in the Sky* (Gavin Hood, 2015)

*Fire at Sea* (Gianfranco Rosi, 2016)

*First They Killed My Father* (Angelina Jolie, 2017)

*Fog of War* (Errol Morris, 2003)

*Granito: How to Nail a Dictator* (Pamela Yates, 2011)

*Gunner Palace* (Michael Tucker, 2004)

*Hissene Habre: A Chadian Tragedy* (Mahamat-Saleh Haroun, 2016)

*Hotel Rwanda* (Terry George, 2004)

*Hunger* (Steve McQueen, 2008)

*In the Name of the Father* (Jim Sheridan, 1993)

*In this World* (Michael Winterbottom, 2002)

*Invisible Children* (Jason Russell, Laren Poole, 2003)

*Journey of Hope* (Xavier Koller, 1990)

*Judgment at Nuremberg* (Stanley Kramer, 1961)

*Lilya 4-Ever* (Lukas Moodysson, 2002)

*Long Night's Journey Into Day* (Frances Reid, Deborah Hoffmann, 2000)

*Lord of War* (Andrew Niccol, 2004)

*Manufactured Landscapes* (Jennifer Baichwal, 2006)

*Milk* (Gus Van Sant, 2008)

*Milosevic on Trial* (Michael Christoffersen, 2007)

*Minority Report* (Steven Spielberg, 2002)

*Missing* (Costa-Gavras, 1982)

*Munich* (Steven Spielberg, 2005)

*My Country, My Country* (Laura Poitras, 2006)

*My Left Foot* (Jim Sheridan, 1989)

*My Neighbor, My Killer* (Anne Aghion, 2009)

*National Bird* (Sonia Kennebeck, 2016)

*Nero's Guests* (Deepa Bhatia, 2009)

*Never Sorry* (Alison Klayman, 2010)

*Night and Fog* (Alain Resnais, 1956)

*No End in Sight* (Charles Ferguson, 2007)

*No Man's Land* (Danis Tanović, 2001)

*Nostalgia for the Light* (Patricio Guzmán, 2010)

*Omagh* (Pete Travis, 2004)

*On the Bride's Side* (Gabriele Del Grande, Antonio Augugliaro, Khaled Soliman Al Nassiry, 2014)

*Once Were Warriors* (Lee Tamahori, 1994)

*One Day in September* (Kevin Macdonald, 1999)

*Out in the Silence* (Joe Wilson, Dean Hamer, 2009)

*Paradise Now* (Hany Abu-Assad, 2005)

*Paragraph 175* (Rob Epstein, Jeffrey Friedman, 2000)

*Persepolis* (Marjane Satrapi, Vincent Paronnaud, 2007)

*Pulled from the Rubble* (Oliver Stone, 2005)

*Rabbit Proof Fence* (Phillip Noyce, 2002)

*Rendition* (Gavin Hood, 2007)

*Restrepo* (Sebastian Junger, Tim Hetherington, 2010)

*Schindler's List* (Steven Spielberg, 1993)

*Sentenced Home* (Nicole Newnham, 2006)

*Shake Hands With the Devil* (Roger Spottiswoode, 2007)

*Shoah* (Claude Lanzmann, 1985)

*Sierra Leone Refugee All Stars* (Zach Niles, Banker White, 2005)

*Snowden* (Oliver Stone, 2016)

*Sometimes in April* (Raoul Peck, 2005)

*Sophie's Choice* (Alan J. Pakula, 1982)

*Spectre* (Sam Mendes, 2015)

*Standard Operating Procedure* (Errol Morris, 2008)

*State of Fear: The Truth About Terrorism* (Pamela Yates, 2015)

*Taxi to the Dark Side* (Alex Gibney, 2007)

*The Act of Killing* (Joshua Oppenheimer, 2012)

*The Age of Stupid* (Franny Armstrong, 2009)

*The Agronomist* (Jonathan Demme, 2003)

*The Ambassador* (Mads Brügger, 2011)

*The Baader-Meinhof Complex* (Uli Edel, 2008)

*The Battle of Algiers* (Gillo Pontecorvo, 1966)

*The Best Years of Our Lives* (William Wyler, 1946)

*The Circle* (James Ponsoldt, 2000)

*The Constant Gardener* (Fernando Meirelles, 2009)

*The Day After* (Nicholas Meyer, 1983)

*The Devil Came on Horseback* (Annie Sundberg, Ricki Stern, 2007)

*The Devil's Miner* (Kief Davidson, Richard Ladkani, 2005)

*The Dictator Hunter* (Klaartje Quirijns, 2007)

*The Diving Bell and the Butterfly* (Julian Schnabel, 2007)

*The French Connection* (William Friedkin, 1971)

*The Gatekeepers* (Dror Moreh, 2012)

*The Ghosts of Abu Ghraib* (Rory Kennedy, 2007)

*The Hurt Locker* (Kathryn Bigelow, 2008)

*The Inheritors* (Walter Bannert, 2008)

*The Killing Fields* (Roland Joffé, 1984)

*The Law in These Parts* (Ra'anan Alexandrowicz, 2011)

*The Lives of Others* (Florian Henckel von Donnersmarck, 2006)

*The Look of Silence* (Joshua Oppenheimer, 2014)

*The Miracle Worker* (Arthur Penn, 1962)

*The Missing Picture* (Rithy Panh, 2014)

*The Official Story* (Luis Puenzo, 1985)

*The Pianist* (Roman Polanski, 2002)

*The Pinochet Case* (Patricio Guzmán, 2001)

*The Price of Sex* (Mimi Chakarova, 2011)

*The Prisoner or: How I Planned to Kill Tony Blair* (Petra Epperlein, Michael Tucker, 2006)

*The Reckoning: The Battle for the International Criminal Court* (Pamela Yates, 2008)

*The Road to Guantanamo* (Michael Winterbottom, Mat Whitecross, 2006)

*The War Game* (Peter Watkins, 1962)

*The Whistleblower* (Larysa Kondracki, 2010)

*This Is Not a Film* (Jafar Panahi, Mojtaba Mirtahmasb, 2011)

*Timbuktu* (Abderrahmane Sissako, 2014)

*To See if I'm Smiling* (Tamar Yarom, 2007)

*Trapped* (Vikramaditya Motwane, 2007)

*Unmanned: America's Drone Wars* (Robert Greenwald, 2013)

*USA v. Al-Arian* (Line Halvorsen, 2007)

*V for Vendetta* (James McTeigue, 2005)

*Waltz With Bashir* (Ari Folman, 2008)

*War Don Don* (War Is Over) (Rebecca Richman Cohen, 2010)

*War/Dance* (Sean Fine, Andrea Nix Fine, 2006)

*We Were There* (Takahiro Miki, 2011)

*We'll Never Meet Childhood Again* (Sam Lawlor, Lindsay Pollock, 2007)

*Well-Founded Fear* (Michael Camerini, Shari Robertson, 2000)

*What's Eating Gilbert Grape* (Lasse Hallström, 1993)

*When the Mountains Tremble* (Pamela Yates, 1983)

*White Light, Black Rain: The Destruction of Hiroshima and Nagasaki* (Steven Okazaki, 2007)

*Why We Fight* (Eugene Jarecki, 2005)

*You Don't Like the Truth: Four Days Inside of Guantanamo* (Patricio Henriquez, Luc Côté, 2010)

*Zero Dark Thirty* (Kathryn Bigelow, 2012)

# Index